AF770789

Interdisciplinary Models and Tools for Serious Games:
Emerging Concepts and Future Directions

Richard Van Eck
University of North Dakota, USA

Information Science REFERENCE

INFORMATION SCIENCE REFERENCE

Hershey · New York

Director of Editorial Content: Kristin Klinger
Director of Book Publications: Julia Mosemann
Acquisitions Editor: Lindsay Johnston
Development Editor: Elizabeth Ardner
Publishing Assistant: Sean Woznicki
Typesetter: Devvin Earnest
Production Editor: Jamie Snavely
Cover Design: Lisa Tosheff
Printed at: Yurchak Printing Inc.

Published in the United States of America by
Information Science Reference (an imprint of IGI Global)
701 E. Chocolate Avenue
Hershey PA 17033
Tel: 717-533-8845
Fax: 717-533-8661
E-mail: cust@igi-global.com
Web site: http://www.igi-global.com/reference

Copyright © 2010 by IGI Global. All rights reserved. No part of this publication may be reproduced, stored or distributed in any form or by any means, electronic or mechanical, including photocopying, without written permission from the publisher.

Product or company names used in this set are for identification purposes only. Inclusion of the names of the products or companies does not indicate a claim of ownership by IGI Global of the trademark or registered trademark.

Library of Congress Cataloging-in-Publication Data

Interdisciplinary models and tools for serious games : emerging concepts and future directions / Richard Van Eck, editor.
p. cm.

Includes bibliographical references and index.
Summary: "This book discusses the need for interdisciplinary awareness in the study of games and learning"--Provided by publisher.

ISBN 978-1-61520-719-0 (hardcover) -- ISBN 978-1-61520-720-6 (ebook) 1. Educational games. I. Van Eck, Richard, 1964-
LB1029.G3.I68 2010
371.39'7--dc22

2009044470

British Cataloguing in Publication Data
A Cataloguing in Publication record for this book is available from the British Library.

All work contributed to this book is new, previously-unpublished material. The views expressed in this book are those of the authors, but not necessarily of the publisher.

Editorial Advisory Board

Katrin Becker, *Simon Fraser University, Canada*
Clint Bowers, *University of Central Florida, USA*
Jo Bryce, *University of Central Lancashire, UK*
Jillianne R. Code, *Simon Fraser University, Canada*
Richard Ferdig, *University of Florida, USA*
Brenda Laurel, *Consultant, USA*
Kurt Squire, *University of Wisconsin – Madison, USA*
Kaveri Subrahmanyam, *California State University – Los Angeles, USA*
David Williamson Shaffer, *University of Wisconsin – Madison, USA*

List of Reviewers

Amy B. Adcock, *Old Dominion University, USA*
Julian Alvarez, *University of Toulouse, France*
Bodi Anderson, *Northern Arizona University, USA*
Sanna-Mari Äyrämö, *University of Jyväskylä, Finland*
Wolmet Barendregt, *University of Gothenburg, Sweden*
Kerrin Ann Barrett, *University of New Mexico, USA*
Katrin Becker, *Simon Fraser University, Canada*
Bryan G. Behrenshausen, *Millersville University, USA*
Otto Borchert, *North Dakota State University, USA*
Johannes Breuer, *University of Cologne, Germany*
Tom Caswell, *Utah State University, USA*
Dennis Charsky, *Ithaca College, USA*
Jillianne R. Code, *Simon Fraser University, Canada*
Pierre Corbeil, *Journal of Simulation & Gaming, Canada*
Menno Deen, *Fontys University of Applied Sciences, The Netherlands*
Damien Djaouti, *University of Toulouse, France*
Lesley Farmer, *California State University - Long Beach, USA*
Jeremy N. Friedberg, *Spongelab Interactive, Canada*
Hanan Gazit, *Holon Institute of Technology and MetaverSense Ltd, Israel*
James Gentry, *Tarleton State University, USA*
Ingrid S. Graves, *Tarleton State University, USA*

Susanna Hapgood, *University of Toledo, USA*
Carrie Heeter, *Michigan State University, USA*
Kyle Heyne, *University of Central Florida, USA*
Leo A. Holly, *The George Washington University, USA*
Wen-Hao David Huang, *University of Illinois at Urbana – Champaign, USA*
Erkki Huhtamo, *University of California – Los Angeles, USA*
Putai Jin, *The University of New South Wales, Australia*
W. Lewis Johnson, *Alelo TLT, LLC, USA*
Jasmina Kallay, *University College Dublin, Ireland*
Fengfeng Ke, *University of New Mexico, USA*
Robert F. Kenny, *University of Central Florida, USA*
Jeff Kupperman, *The University of Michigan – Flint, USA*
Carrie Lavis, *Independent Learning Architect, Canada*
Renae Low, *The University of New South Wales, Australia*
Francis Maietta, *The Real Thinking Company, Ltd., UK*
Steven Malliet, *University of Antwerp; Catholic University College of Limburg, Belgium*
Tim Marsh, *National University of Singapore, Singapore*
Hans Martens, *University of Antwerp, Belgium*
Cheng-Chang (Sam) Pan, *University of Texas at Brownsville, USA*
Davin Pavlas, *University of Central Florida, USA*
Genaro Rebolledo-Mendez, *Universidad Veracruzana, México*
Debbie Denise Reese, *Wheeling Jesuit University, USA*
Tom Satwicz, *University of Washington, USA*
Matthew J. Sharritt, *Situated Research, LLC, USA*
Brett E. Shelton, *Utah State University, USA*
Lee Sherlock, *Michigan State University, USA*
Brian M. Slator, *North Dakota State University, USA*
Richard H. Swan, *Brigham Young University, USA*
Sharon Tettegah, *University of Illinois, Urbana – Champaign, USA*
Debbe Thompson, *USDA/ARS Children's Nutrition Research Center, Baylor, USA*
Zach Tomaszewski, *University of Hawaii at Manoa, USA*
Bradley Vender, *North Dakota State University, USA*
Mirjam Vosmeer, *University of Amsterdam, The Netherlands*
Ginger Watson, *Old Dominion University, USA*
Will Weaver, *Hive Media, Inc., USA*
Scott Wilson, *University of Oklahoma, USA*
Catharine Wyman, *Xavier College Preparatory, USA*
Kliment Yanev, *University of Cologne, Germany*
Thomas J. Yannuzzi, *Penn State University, USA*

Copy Editor

Sandra L. Van Eck, *University of North Dakota, USA*

Table of Contents

Section 5
Future Directions

Detailed Table of Contents

The notion of genre in serious games is problematic. This chapter highlights some of the significant drawbacks of classifying games that confound narrative and gameplay style and result in cross-genre hybrids like action–adventure. Rather than seeing narrative and gameplay as separate elements, the author argues that we should look for a common denominator that unites these two elements. Kallay argues that common cognitive–emotional constructs can be used to develop a classification system that can guide analysis and design of serious games and that the field of narrative psychology provides the key to doing so. She presents an overview of research in genre classification, a summary of the ludology–narratology debate as it relates to genre, and key concepts from narrative psychology and media studies. Kallay then proposes a model for the analysis of games and applies it to two modern games as case studies.

In this chapter, Sherlock argues for yet another perspective on resolving the problematic issue of game genre classification systems. Borrowing from rhetorical theory and Ian Bogost's argument for persuasive games, Sherlock presents a unifying framework for understanding the "social action and persuasive possibility spaces" of serious games. Sherlock presents an in-depth, well-reasoned analysis of the field of rhetoric and its application to serious games in order to propose a new notion of genre for classifying serious games.

The authors of this chapter rely on existing theory from the fields of communication and education (critical pedagogy) to describe the need for games to support the learning outcome of critical self-reflection. They argue that the modern, information-driven world tends to promote the "binarisation" of life, whereby notions of "self" and "other" are constrained by digital technologies, and critical self-reflection is de-emphasized. The authors first distinguish between two schools of thought in communication theory: information transfer, which they argue is too often the focus of serious games, and social construction of meaning, which they argue should be the focus of more serious games. They then argue for the application of the latter school of thought to understand and design serious games that support the critical self-reflection that 21st-century education requires.

Motivation is a commonly cited benefit of serious games, but Low argues that conflicting definitions and perspectives regarding motivation in serious game study hampers current research and design. Low analyzes motivation as an educational outcome and academic competency; discusses its relation to past and present educational theory; presents key research findings regarding motivation, learning, and educational technology; and outlines the relationship of this body of knowledge to serious game research and design.

This chapter identifies an overlooked narrative resource that could be used for the design of serious games. Arguing that existing storylines in games are often too simplistic and limited to capture the full range of human expression and interests, Friedlander points to sacred narratives as a way to enrich the narrative backdrop and ludic structure of serious games. Because sacred narratives tap deep social, cultural, and religious archetypes for understanding humankind's relation to the universe and to the sacred, the story structures are relevant across all cultures and religious backgrounds. And, because they are also well-structured narratives, they can be used to design serious games in ways that tap algorithmic rather than linear possibilities, thus paving the way for a new kind of serious game.

Few would disagree that the field of serious games is entering a critical period of time where theories, models, and research are needed to substantiate claims about the educational benefits of games and to validate approaches to designing games to support existing learning strategies. But with so many people coming from so many different disciplines, there are similarly few who understand the full range of educational research theory and practice well enough to evaluate existing research or to design research that optimally tests our hypotheses and models. This chapter surveys existing educational research with technology in general, and games specifically, to provide an overview of some of the key methodologies for advancing research in the field of serious games. By presenting specific descriptions of actual studies and the methods they employ and the rationale for how those methods support the research under study, Jin provides a valuable primer for understanding how to conduct the kind of rigorous, empirical research needed in serious game studies.

Interaction may be the defining characteristic of games as a medium, technology, and social experience. It follows that one of our primary areas of research in serious games lies in representing interaction and developing theory-driven tools for both describing and studying games and gameplay in situ. Sharrit argues for a blended approach of ethnomethodology and grounded theory, informed by Activity Theory and related tools for analysis (the mediational triangle). Such an approach has the advantage of capturing games as lived experiences while simultaneously allowing for analysis of natural and manipulated interventions in the learning process via serious games. He outlines this model and documents its effectiveness through a case study of how different interface elements impact gameplay and concludes with recommendations for further testing and implementation.

Theoretical perspectives from psychology are used in this chapter to explain the persuasive power of games. The authors argue that information processing theory can explain both how games can change attitudes and how to design better persuasive games. The Elaboration Likelihood Model (ELM) is used to develop a model of how individual player characteristics influence both cognitive and affective learning outcomes. The authors argue that changes in these outcomes occur as the result of intervening variables such as player motivations, implying that research that assumes direct causal relationships between interventions and outcomes will be less effective. After outlining the theoretical basis upon which their approach is based, the authors then use existing research data from 538 participants to preliminarily validate the model. Future research directions are discussed for further refinement and validation of their approach.

Section 4
Theory Into Practice

The authors argue that one of the most promising and frequently cited benefits of video games is the ability to promote problem solving. Like games, however, problems and problem solving are far more complex than they at first appear. Research in problem solving over the last 75 years has produced a rich set of theory, experimental evidence, and instructional approaches for addressing problem solving as a learning outcome. The authors detail this history, outline the cognitive skills involved in solving problems, and describe 11 different types of problems in terms of their structuredness, cognitive requirements, and other unique characteristics and requirements. This sets the stage for a discussion of how games can support problem solving and specific problem types. In order to do this, the authors concep-

In our eagerness to reform education through the use of serious games, we often forget about the practical issues involved with integrating games into the curriculum. While some discuss issues of adoption and diffusion at administrative levels and problems of infrastructure at the environmental level, few take a systemic view of integrating serious games in the curriculum. Farmer and Murphy address this in their discussion of the implications of serious games in schools for a fundamental component of educational infrastructure: the school library. If games are to become an accepted medium of learning in schools, school libraries will have to support them as they now do books, AV media, and the research process. What will this mean for libraries and teacher librarians? What policies will have to change? How will libraries work with teachers who are using games or are interested in doing so? Such questions, so obvious in hindsight, are in fact just one of their foci in this chapter. They also argue that issues of gender equity require specific responses on the part of school libraries and teacher librarians and that libraries are uniquely positioned to provide not just access to games but also to the social spaces and support systems needed to ensure that girls will benefit equally from games in the curriculum.

Chris Crawford is known for his visionary work as a game designer and the many design books and articles he has written over the course of his career. In this chapter, he argues that game designers have ignored the "sin qua non" of games: interactivity. After defining interactivity and delineating its role in games, he contends that interactivity in serious games will only be successful to the extent that we focus on processes, rather than on things. Facts and data are inert and are not good candidates for interaction. Processes, on the other hand, require interaction. Serious games, he argues, should be used to teach process-oriented learning, and process-oriented interaction can only be represented in game design by the use of algorithmic programming rather than the traditional Boolean logic most game designers rely on. Drawing on his experience as a game designer, Crawford uses specific examples to explain in lay terms how algorithmic programming can be used to create games that approximate the richness of human interaction with little more effort than traditional Boolean approaches.

Foreword

Serious games and simulations offer the opportunity to realize the full range of current theories of learning. Over the past half century, formal education has gradually broadened its span of instructional strategies. The behaviorist psychological theories from the first part of the 20th century promoted presentational/assimilative teaching coupled with drill-and-practice exercises. In successive waves, cognitivist, constructivist, and situated pedagogies based on alternative psychosocial theories of learning have expanded the types of teaching that students experience (Dede, 2008). In their modern form, all of these approaches emphasize learning as an active process in rich contexts that promote collaboration, engagement, and transfer and that provide sophisticated feedback based on formative, diagnostic assessment (National Research Council, 2000).

However, these powerful forms of teaching/learning typically have not altered conventional classroom practices, even though their practicality and effectiveness in academic settings is proven (National Research Council, 2005). At every level, education lags behind other sectors of the economy in its speed of innovation and its use of information technology. Experts in business have speculated that a *disruptive* technology may soon overcome the forces in schooling that resist change (Christensen, Horn, & Johnson, 2008). Disruptive technologies initially develop outside their context of application but eventually become so powerful that they transform practices in that context. An example is microcomputers, which in the mid-1970s were purchased primarily by hobbyists, but which by the 1980s had displaced the minicomputers entrenched in corporations.

In education, serious games and simulations may serve as a disruptive technology. As the chapters in this book document, this educational strategy has developed outside of formal education environments, synthesizing insights from other sectors such as simulation in the military, motivation in the entertainment industry, visualization in the sciences, thinking from cognitive science, and collaboration from the field of communications. As the authors in this volume delineate, the ability of serious games and simulations to enhance learning, motivation, and transfer lies not in their usage of technology (which serves as a catalyst and enabler) but instead in their ability to encompass—when well designed—powerful theories of engagement and learning (Dede, 2009). Serious games and simulations also provide powerful ways of building on the learning styles and strengths of many digital-age students, developed outside of academic settings through their activities in entertainment, communication, creative expression, and knowledge sharing (Dieterle, 2009).

Further, the potential of serious games and simulations for disruptive transformation of education goes beyond improving the process of teaching and learning. Numerous recent reports have documented the urgency of shifting the objectives and content of schooling to meet the emerging challenges of the 21st century worldwide, knowledge-based economy (e.g., Business-Higher Education Form, 2005; Levy

& Murnane, 2004; National Academy of Sciences, 2006; Organization for Economic Co-operation and Development, 2004). All of these calls to action agree that recentering schooling on 21st-century skills is vital to ensure a desirable global future. Serious simulations and games offer a powerful platform for the inculcation and development of sophisticated 21st-century skills in academic settings. Parallel to 21st-century work, these interactive media provide a context for teaching in which knowledge is situated and tacit, problem finding is central to problem solving, and formative assessment is sophisticated and unobtrusive (Dede, in press).

This book is at the nexus of important innovations in the process and content of education that may transform current models of schooling to better prepare students for the challenges and opportunities of the 21st century. However, as the authors describe, realizing the full potential of serious games and simulations will require overcoming difficult issues in design, implementation, and research. It is truly an exciting time to be part of this (r)evolution…

Chris Dede
Harvard University

REFERENCES

Business-Higher Education Forum. (2005). *A commitment to America's future: Responding to the crisis in mathematics & science education.* Washington, DC: Author.

Christensen, C. M., Horn, M. B., & Johnson, C. W. (2008). *Disrupting class: How disruptive innovation will change the way the world learns.* New York: McGraw-Hill.

Dede, C. (2008). Theoretical perspectives influencing the use of information technology in teaching and learning. In J. Voogt and G. Knezek, Eds., *International handbook of information technology in primary and secondary education* (pp. 43–62). New York: Springer.

Dede, C. (2009). Immersive interfaces for engagement and learning. *Science, 323*(5910), 66–69.

Dede, C. (in press). Technological supports for acquiring 21st-century skills. In E. Baker, B. McGaaw, & P. Peterson (Eds.), *International encyclopedia of education* (3rd Ed.). Oxford, UK: Elsevier.

Dieterle, E. (2009). Neomillennial learning styles and river city. *Children, youth and environments, 19* (1), 246–279.

Levy, F., & Murnane, R. J. (2004). *The new division of labor: How computers are creating the next job market*. Princeton, NJ: Princeton University Press.

National Academy of Sciences. (2006). *Rising above the gathering storm: Energizing and employing America for a brighter economic future*. Washington, DC: National Academy Press.

National Research Council. (2000). *How people learn: Brain, mind, experience, and school.* Committee on Developments in the Science of Learning and Committee on Learning Research and Educational Practice, J. D. Bransford, A. Brown, & R. Cocking (Eds.). Division of Behavioral and Social Sciences and Education. Washington, DC: The National Academies Press.

National Research Council. (2005). *How students learn: History, mathematics, and science in the classroom*. Committee on How People Learn, A Targeted Report for Teachers, M. S. Donovan & J. D. Bransford (Eds.). Division of Behavioral and Social Sciences and Education. Washington, DC: The National Academies Press.

Organization for Economic Co-operation and Development (OECD). (2004). *Innovation in the knowledge economy: Implications for education and learning*. Paris: Author.

***Chris Dede** is the Timothy E. Wirth Professor in Learning Technologies at Harvard's Graduate School of Education. His fields of scholarship include emerging technologies, policy, and leadership. His funded research includes four grants from NSF and the US Department of Education to explore immersive and semi-immersive simulations as a means of student engagement, learning, and assessment. His coedited book,* Scaling Up Success: Lessons Learned from Technology-based Educational Improvement, *was published by Jossey-Bass in 2005. A second volume he edited,* Online Professional Development for Teachers: Emerging Models and Methods, *was published by the Harvard Education Press in 2006. In 2007, he was honored by Harvard University as an outstanding teacher.*

Preface

ORIGINS

As I write this, my personal and professional experiences appear to have led logically to this point in time. Yet the path to this point was not so clear to me as I lived it. Like many in this emerging field, I have come to games and learning via a circuitous route. My background is in psychology (undergraduate), creative writing (undergraduate and graduate), and instructional design and technology (Ph.D.). To start with, I was never much interested in technology (perhaps because my father was a systems analyst in the 70s, and nothing your parents do is "cool"); nor did school engage me, for that matter. I preferred reading science fiction to doing homework. When I was in middle school, however, my father brought home *Cave/Adventure* (http://www.rickadams.org/adventure), and my brothers and I played it nonstop on our Heathkit H-8 computer. Technology became relevant for me because of this game, although I learned just enough about the computer to run the game. The time and effort I put into winning (including mapping that infernal maze) far exceeded my school experience in both work and reward. For the first time, I recognized something I enjoyed as much as reading but which also seemed to me to be even more relevant to learning. It was reading that convinced me that learning could be engaging and games that showed me that hard work could be engaging.

This realization was not an epiphany so much as the germination of my general belief that school should be more interesting *and* challenging. In 1976, however, it certainly did not feed into my career plans; games were played (for the most part) in arcades, and while I spent a good share of my teenage years in Flipper McGee's and Mickey Rat's pinball arcades in Ann Arbor, the idea that my interests could somehow lead to any kind of career choice not only did not cross my mind but would have been greeted with ridicule had anyone suggested it. By the time I went to college, I was interested in understanding how humans think and behave; creative writing was something I did because of my love of reading. In retrospect, of course, both of these areas have a lot to do with games and with making education more relevant and engaging.

At the end of my master's program in English, I took on the editing of a publication of student work from composition classes. The process that had been used (literally typing up stories on camera-ready blue sheets) seemed antiquated and inefficient even to a technology neophyte like me in 1991. I asked my dad what he thought, and he suggested I look into *Adobe PageMaker* (4.0) instead. For the second time in my life, technology became relevant to a problem I had to solve, and once again I taught myself just enough to solve it. I graduated the next year and began applying for English teaching positions. As it turns out, a college in the Southwest was looking for a Media Arts and Communication Program Coordinator to advise the student newspaper and student magazine and teach both English and desktop publishing. I was hired primarily because I was the only candidate able to successfully complete a desktop publishing task using (you guessed it) *Adobe PageMaker*.

Technology became a major part of my professional focus, and I learned a lot about technology in the following years there, which culminated in the creation of a multimedia authoring lab for faculty to develop multimedia. My interest in making learning more engaging and challenging now had a place in the work I did, and I wanted to show faculty how to build multimedia. But I felt I was missing something significant; how do you know if what you've developed is effective? What theories and principles exist to guide the development of multimedia? I started looking for graduate programs in multimedia and computer-based training and eventually found my way via educational or instructional technology to the field of instructional design. In contemplating returning to school, I knew I would have to do research (which I was not excited about) and began thinking about what I could study. I had continued playing games all through graduate school, and I realized that the gap between multimedia and games was small: if I could reasonably study the one, the other was also a viable research area.

I had one question of the programs to which I applied: Would I be able to do dissertation research on the educational potential of digital games? In 1995, only one program I approached—at the University of South Alabama—thought that was a potentially productive line of research, so that is where I went.

My initial search for graduate programs was my first indication that technology and pedagogy were not the same thing and that what I needed was not technology but learning theory. You can learn a given technology and know nothing about how to use it for learning, but if you know how people learn, you can teach yourself a technology and be well on your way to designing effective learning. Applying this lesson to games was another matter, however. I spent much of my time in graduate school struggling to identify "the" theory behind games. Because instructional design is itself interdisciplinary (education, psychology, communication, and technology), many of theories I found were applicable to learning in games and formed the basis of my dissertation: situated learning and cognition, anchored instruction, context, pedagogical advisement, transfer of learning, problem solving, and motivation. No single discipline had all the answers, and while a few researchers were doing direct measurement of video games and learning (Cognition and Technology Group and Vanderbilt; Patricia Greenfield at UCLA; Mark Lepper at Stanford; and Thomas Malone at Xerox Palo Alto Research Center), most of my work required synthesizing what was being done in multiple fields of learning research to formulate a conceptual framework for the design of my own game to promote transfer of mathematics skills.

The research I did during this time was instrumental in formulating my beliefs that the answers to complex questions can best be found at the intersection of disciplines rather than within them, a concept one of my mentors and colleagues, Art Graesser, later would refer to as a "fish scale model," based, I believe, on Don Campbell's chapter "Ethnocentrism of Disciplines and the Fish-Scale Model of Omniscience."[1] The lesson I learned in the process about the need for interdisciplinary awareness in the study of games and learning has never left me, and remains as critically relevant to game studies today as it was to the design of my own educational game in 1999.

WHY INTERDISCIPLINARY?

As I write this now, I am struck not only by how much progress we have made in this field but also by how far we still have to go. And that is why this book exists. Over the last decade, no one can deny that this field has made significant strides in public opinion, theory, and practice. It is now commonly accepted that games have SOME benefits, whether or not one believes games have a place in formal education or that the benefits outweigh the risks. This is a far cry from the shock Patricia Greenfield's assertions were met with in 1984 and from the reaction to Marc Prensky's assertions even 16 years later. That games can educate is no longer the radical notion it once was, and the growing canon of research in this field is no longer possible to capture in the space I have here.[2]

Yet as much progress as we've made, there are significant gaps in our praxis. This is partly due to the youth of our field and the need to establish new theoretical models and concepts. But it is also because too many have approached this field as if it were a completely new area of study with no theoretical antecedents in other disciplines. This is perhaps a natural progression for any new field, but it nonetheless presents one of our most significant challenges. It is time we stop and take notice of the work that different disciplines are conducting, to explore new ideas and approaches that perhaps have been overlooked and to attempt to synthesize multiple theoretical approaches relevant to the field. Some of the work that is going on in this field is unknowingly duplicative because of different terminology, publication venues, and readerships; integrating these different studies will allow us to see patterns instead of discrete findings. It will also allow us to identify areas that need further study and perhaps new theories that are attributable to the medium and amalgamation of different theoretical approaches.

Perhaps most importantly, we have to make sure that those entering this field understand that video games are still a somewhat new technology, not (necessarily) a new pedagogy. To be sure, we have uncovered new learning strategies, outcomes, and principles, and we will continue to do so. But we cannot tell the difference between what is new and what is existing theory wearing a new face if we don't understand how existing theories are instantiated in games. While the serious games field itself is interdisciplinary, that does not mean we take full advantage of each disciplinary perspective where and when we address it. Whether because of a lack of expertise or awareness, we at best use theory and practice from other disciplines to support minor points and perspectives.

My hope is that by making interdisciplinarity the focus of a work on games, we may find important distinctions and profit from prolonged critical analysis and application. If nothing else, we perhaps become more consciously aware of the breadth and depth of interdisciplinary practice within the growing field of games.

ABOUT THE BOOK

The chapters you are about to read are unique, in some cases because authors who don't always write about games have brought their specific disciplinary focus to bear on the topic and in others because authors who do write about games have made a specific effort to bridge disciplines. The result in all cases, I believe, is both unique and valuable. The chapters represent 13 different disciplines (digital culture, digital media, rhetoric, communication, educational psychology, literature, theater, sociopsychology, instructional design, instructional leadership, educational administration, library science, and game design), not counting various flavors of psychology and media studies, by authors from five countries (Australia, Belgium, Finland, Ireland, and the United States of America).

Many of the ideas that are dispersed across multiple disciplines are easily missed when viewed across different venues. But contracted together within a concentrated space, they become visible and are thus able to inform us in important ways, much like gas molecules in space produce nebulas when concentrated. It is of course challenging to capture different disciplinary perspectives: cast too wide a net, and you'll capture too many disparate ideas—too narrow, and you'll get too much of the same thing.

Much of what you will read in these chapters will be familiar in focus but will differ widely in language and perspective. I urge you to read closely because what at first glance seems familiar to you may in fact differ in important ways because of the disciplinary perspective it comes from. Interdisciplinarity is highly challenging, and even confrontational—much of what we do when we read is assimilation, but accommodation is the heart of human development, and no field can grow without it. It is my hope that you will find much that you like and recognize here but more that is unfamiliar and difficult; if it is not challenging for you to read, one or both us may have failed.

Each chapter is the result of an original proposal, each of which was reviewed by three peers in a double-blind review process. In doing so, I assigned reviewers chapters based on interest, expertise and, in the case of reviewers who were also authors, on the potential of the authors to benefit from a different disciplinary perspective on work similar to their own. Based on these proposal reviews, some authors were invited to submit full chapters, which were again reviewed using the same process.

Based on my readings and those of the reviewers, I have organized these chapters into five sections: Genre, Classification, and Definitions; Theoretical Perspectives; Research; Theory Into Practice; and Future Directions. These sections loosely reflect my beliefs about disciplinary process, in that each relies on its predecessor and informs its descendant. The first section in this book focuses on language and terminology for what we mean by games and related concepts. The second section discusses theories from different disciplines that can inform research and design for educational games. The third section presents research that both adds to our understanding of games and serves as a model for future research on theoretical constructs and models. The fourth section comprises chapters on how theory and models inform practice in the design of games for learning purposes, and the fifth section identifies two promising future directions for the field. Each author was also asked to generate a list of "must-reads" on their chapter topic for those who want to understand more about the theory and approach behind each chapter. In addition, they were also asked to identify what they would consider to be the most important texts for interdisciplinary studies of serious games. The "must reads" and top interdisciplinary text lists can be found at the end of each chapter, immediately after the references. I have also collated all of the authors' top interdisciplinary texts across this book and a companion volume that collected the same information.[3] I present this composite list sorted by rank and author at the end of the book. You will find both a short and long version of the table of contents, the latter of which provides my own summary of what each chapter is about, so I will confine my comments here in the preface to a discussion of each section of the book and how I think each chapter contributes to that section.

Genre, Classification, and Definitions

That this is a young field could be gleaned from nothing more than the inclusion of three different chapters in the first section, each attempting to define what games are from a different disciplinary perspective. Äyrämö and Koskimaa describe the results of their analysis of game designers' implicit and explicit definitions of narrative in nine respective game design books, while Kallay and Sherlock each attempt to propose new game classification systems based on, respectively, narrative psychology and rhetoric. Game classification is perhaps one of the most generative research areas in games right now, as we struggle to reduce the overlap and illogicality in competing definitions and systems. Language allows us to think differently about our subjects and is arguably foundational to our ability to develop theory, models, research, and practice in any discipline, so this is far more important than a tomato/tomahto argument. While many researchers are naturally attracted to the design of new games or the study of existing games, without a precise language to describe our practice, theory, and results, our research and design will proceed in a fragmented and duplicative fashion that leaves little potential for synthesis.

Theoretical Perspectives

The three chapters that make up this second section are divergent in topic and approach, and illustrate the power of looking to different disciplines to refine our explanations of phenomenon. Yanuzzi and Behrenhausen reconceptualize one aspect of what we often refer to in 21st-century learning as critical self-reflection. They illustrate the critical reasoning and theory-driven approach necessary to quantify and define our often nebulous descriptions of the benefits of game-based learning. At the same time, they point the way toward the design of future educational games. Low provides a similar treatment of the often used and misused concept of motivation in games. Her chapter pulls together some of the most significant research findings and definitions of motivation and learning from educational research, which should guide future research on motivation and games. Friedlander concludes the section with a fascinating amalgamation of theater, literature, and comparative religion that is in many ways reminiscent of Huizinga's discussion of play and culture. He identifies a promising approach to the design of engaging, cross-cultural games that rely on sacred scenarios and in doing so illustrates why it is so important to seek out and synthesize divergent perspectives from different disciplines.

Research

Few would argue that there is a pressing need for research in this field, but this need exceeds our capacity for conducting it at uniformly high-quality levels. The authors in this section provide good examples of how research methodology and implementation must flow from sound theory, models, and practice. The findings themselves are of interest and importance to the field, but the chapters are perhaps at least as significant for promoting high-quality future research. Jin describes a variety of strong research methodologies, the questions they are best at answering, and examples of research on games that reflect these methodological considerations. Sharritt, in his chapter, and Mailliet and Martens in theirs, propose two different models from different disciplines that they then validate through research. In addition to making important contributions to the field now, their chapters also serve as case studies for the generation and validation of models for the study of human interaction with games.

Theory Into Practice

Theory by itself is of little value outside of academic circles; it must also lead to practice and real change. It is only through the *application* of our theories that we are able to test, validate, and refine them as we move toward becoming a discipline rather than a collection of ideas. What is sometimes lost even in this, is that practice *itself* gives rise to theory, thus perpetuating knowledge through a cyclical process. The chapters in this section illustrate this. In the first chapter, my coauthor and I describe current theory and research on the design of instruction to promote problem-solving skills, which are often cited as a primary benefit of game-based learning. We pull equally from games research and theory and instructional design to illustrate the variety of different problems that make up problem solving, the cognitive structure and thinking skills these different problems require, and the kinds of gameplay that may best support them. Wilson and Williams provide a rare, detailed case study of the application of existing game design models and processes to the design of an educational game in an academic environment. Gaydos and Squire illustrate the design processes associated with building an educational game that instantiates current thinking in science literacy and 21st-century learning. Together, these chapters illustrate how theory informs practice and how practice in turn informs theory.

Future Directions

While it could be argued that each of the preceding chapters suggests future directions for research and design, the chapters in this section have the potential to make a significant impact in our future practice. In their chapter on girls, games, and the role of libraries in digital game-based learning in schools, Farmer and Murphy highlight the need for systemic thinking when it comes to truly reforming educational practice. As scholars and practitioners of librarianship, the importance of this chapter further highlights how critical it is that our field looks to other disciplines for new approaches and ideas. In the final chapter in this volume, Chris Crawford brings more than 30 years of experience as a pioneering game designer and author to his analysis of interactivity as both a learning process and game design principle. The result has the potential to change game design in fundamental ways and could help educational game designers get over one of the most significant hurdles they face: how to build engaging games that support learning outcomes seamlessly.

A FINAL NOTE

I struggled to decide how to refer to this field in the title of the book, my discussion here in the preface, and in my coauthored chapter. Serious games is a powerful term because of its wide acceptance and its inherent ability to address one of the primary misconceptions about games: that they are frivolous entertainment and therefore have no place in education. The term is also valuable for its ability to encompass the wide diversity of games, including those intended to promote health, to persuade, and to achieve educational outcomes. On the other hand, it is less useful in a volume like this where the focus is exclusively on games and learning. I am also troubled by the use of the word "serious," which implies that there are games that are frivolous. Terms like this are more the reflection of the intent of the game designer or the player during gameplay than of the game itself. Commercial games are quite serious in their cognitive and emotional outcomes, and serious games as a term relies on what Sherlock refers to in his chapter as "definition-through-negation." This creates a challenge for our field in terms of classification, genre, and definition.

My preference is for the term digital game-based learning in reference to the kinds of learning discussed in this book, as the term captures both the medium (digital game as opposed to other kinds of games) and the full range of implementation of games as designed instructional experiences, as environments that can support learning outcomes, and as a continuum of integration within existing formal and informal school settings. But the purpose of this book is to solicit multidisciplinary perspectives that inform our field, not to discuss what the field itself should be called. There is no question that the label "serious games" has caught on equally with practitioners, researchers, and the public, and its value in bridging audience perhaps outweighs its drawbacks. It did so to the extent of titling this volume, in any case.

My hope is that you will find the different perspectives represented here as fascinating as I do both for the ideas they present and as evidence that theoreticians, researchers, and practitioners must make a conscious effort to look to other disciplines as we strive to advance our field, no matter what we call it.

Richard Van Eck
Editor

ENDNOTES

[1] Originally published in Sherif and Sherif's 1969 book *Interdisciplinary Relationships in the Social Sciences*, published by Aldine.

[2] See Bernard Perron and Mark Wolf's *The Video Game Theory Reader 2*, 2008 (Routledge) for what may be the best and last reasonable attempt at identifying the field's most important works and which is now out of date less than a year after publication.

[3] Van Eck, R. (Ed.). (2010). *Gaming and cognition: Theories and practice from the learning sciences.* Hershey, PA: IGI Global

Acknowledgment

Anyone who has ever watched the Academy Awards show knows there is never enough time to acknowledge everyone who has contributed to a body of work. It is also painfully clear during those acceptance speeches that the more the winner tries to be inclusive, the more inevitable it is that they leave someone out or shortchange those they list at the end. To that end, I want to first thank everyone who had a hand in making this volume a reality.

In particular, I want to thank the authors and contributors to this volume for trusting me with stewardship of their work and ideas. An edited book is only as good as its contributors, and the combined intellect, creativity, and scholarship of all the submissions made the reading and editing process both rewarding and humbling. I would also like to thank my editorial assistant at IGI Global, Beth Ardner, for her support in developing the book and responding to all my questions and requests as the book evolved from proposal to publication. I would also like to acknowledge the work of the editorial board and reviewers, who dedicated many hours to reviewing the submissions to help ensure that authors got the best feedback and that I benefited from the collective intelligence of the community in my selection of chapters.

I would also like to acknowledge a few people whose contributions extend beyond the book itself. I owe my mother a debt of gratitude for convincing my elementary school teachers that my performance was the result of boredom in the days before anyone really knew what ADHD was. My mother also instilled a love of reading from an early age by reading classics to us like *The Hobbit*, *Wind in the Willows*, and *The Dark Is Rising*. Reading has been fundamental to my beliefs about the power of narrative for learning, instruction, and games. I also have my grandmother, Ann, to thank for instilling that love of reading in my mother. Ann was a children's librarian for many years, and some of my best memories are of the children's books (*The Three Billy Goats Gruff*, for one) that she "read" to us by heart every time we visited.

My father is responsible for my interest in technology in general, whether from the many times I accompanied him to work as a systems analyst at the Institute for Social Research or his patient support in showing me how to using *DocuMat*, the word processing program he wrote for the CPM operating system. The day he brought home *Cave Adventure* on an 8.5-inch floppy disk may be the single most important event in terms of leading to my scholarship in games and to the book you hold in your hands now.

I want to thank two mentors in my professional life whom I am also privileged to call friends. Jack Dempsey was my committee chair during my doctoral studies at the University of South Alabama, but this does not begin to convey the influence he had and continues to have on my life. From responding to an unknown doctoral program applicant's question about games as an area of study to involving me in research well before I could be much help to him in doing so, to treating me as much as a colleague and friend as a student, his mentorship has been key to any success I have had. His is a hard example to follow in this regard, but it has served as a guide to me in my own experience as a professor in higher education.

Likewise, I have Art Graesser to thank for showing me the true value of interdisciplinary research and productivity. My experience working with him at the Institute for Intelligent Systems at the University of Memphis convinced me that the biggest questions and the best research can only be tackled with the will and perspective of a diverse group of researchers from multiple disciplines. It takes a special person to keep a group like that focused and productive while also allowing everyone to feel like an equal partner in the process.

Finally, I would like to thank my wife, Sandy, for everything she has done for me and meant to me. What a daunting sentence—there is no way I could thank her adequately even if I were to fill the rest of the pages in this book. As a collaborator in my professional life, she is an equal partner. As my partner in life, she is the reason any of it makes sense.

Richard Van Eck
University of North Dakota, USA

Section 1
Genre, Classification, and Definitions

Chapter 1
Narrative Definitions for Game Design:
A Concept-Oriented Study of Nine Computer Game Design Guidebooks

Sanna-Mari Äyrämö
University of Jyväskylä, Finland

Raine Koskimaa
University of Jyväskylä, Finland

ABSTRACT

Enhancing the benefits of learning games by utilizing narratives or narrative elements is not a new idea. Many existing learning games utilize more or less story structures, virtual worlds, and various characters as a part of a story. Computer game genres, such as adventure games and role-playing games, have received a lot of attention in the field of serious games by researchers and game developers. Hence, the potential of narratives for learning support is already clearly recognized. However, narratives have not yet offered unambiguous solutions to the design of learning games. For example, more often than not the use of embedded stories does not lead to a desired outcome that is an entertaining and pedagogically effective game. Moreover, it is not theoretically clear what is the best way to utilize narratives in order to ease, support, and heighten the player's learning process through computer game playing. This is a multidisciplinary design task and research problem that calls for interdisciplinary concepts and models. Existing narrative computer game design guidebooks and serious game design guidebooks outline the computer game designers' current opinions on the potential of narrative game design. In this chapter, the authors focus on the concept of narrative and the definitions game designers form of the concept. The purpose is to fathom game designers' conceptions of narrative in the analysis discussed in the chapter, reveal the theoretical background that dominates the designers' thinking, and adduce the consequences of current narrative concept usage. Additionally, the chapter determines three levels of narrative phenomenon, in which narrative should be named and consistently defined within the computer game design discussion. Moreover, the chapter uncovers blind spots in the use of narrative-

DOI: 10.4018/978-1-61520-719-0.ch001

Copyright © 2010, IGI Global. Copying or distributing in print or electronic forms without written permission of IGI Global is prohibited.

related concepts, whilst further, if possible, providing suggestions for improvements. Furthermore, the chapter proposes a composite model of narrative definition that should be extensive enough for game narrative design purposes. Additionally, a new concept (co-storyliner) for the discussion related to the player's role in narrative computer game is proposed. Finally, the analysis results and conclusions, especially the proposed model of narrative definition, will be discussed from the viewpoint of the needs of narrative serious game design.

INTRODUCTION

There is growing discussion related to narrative in serious game design. This discussion concentrates on at least two larger subjects: the benefits that narrative can entail for learning purposes and the narrative possibilities of computer games. Two paths of discussion exist as independent research fields touching both academic participants as well as representatives from various practical fields. Thus, the question of narrative serious games design is highly multidisciplinary, and the topic includes both theoretical and practical aspects.

In the research and development of narrative learning game design, one extremely challenging point is the concept of narrative itself. Since various disciplines and theoretical lines use the concept in substantially different ways, there is a strong possibility that researchers and game designers do not understand each other. Subsequently, it remains unclear as to which concepts of the research field and wider discussion may be connectable or at least comparable to one another. In addition, this confusion advances futile controversies. Thus, arguably, there is a need for coherent concepts for narrative game design including narrative, story, and other concepts related to the definitions of these basic constructs. But before these concepts and definitions can be formed, it is important to understand the conceptual and theoretical roots upon which the contemporary discussion is based.

In this chapter, the definitions of narrative and story in nine game design guidebooks will be examined. The aim is to fathom game designers' conceptions of narrative: the basis that necessarily has an effect on game designers' narrative design work and opinions related to it. By using guidebooks, it was presupposed that the researchers would attain the various views of designers better than, for example, by interview. The definitions will be compared against the basic lines of existing narrative theory. In this way, the possible theoretical roots of these practical definitions may be revealed. Thus, the higher goal of analysis is to reveal the extent to which similarities can be drawn between individual game designers' conceptions and narrative. This is in addition to gauging the points at which they substantially differ. Behind the presupposition of designers' differing conceptions is the situation of the field of narrative theory: separate narrative theory lines answer the question of "*what is narrative?*" differently. In addition, it is assumed that the analysis of designers' narrative definitions will reveal the needs of game narrative design discussion in relation to several levels or aspects of the narrative phenomenon. Thus, one aim of this analysis is to determine these levels and to uncover blind spots in the use of narrative-related concepts, whilst further, if possible, providing suggestions for improvements. In the guidebooks, the definition may be conveyed explicitly or implicitly, or it may be consistent or inconsistent, but there must be some kind of definition, at least as a background assumption. This does not mean that designers would be held hostage by predetermined rules. In fact, true creativity requires some basic rules within or against which to play.

The kind of research discussed in this chapter could be characterized as concept-oriented interdisciplinary research. Phrasing of a question quite similar to the one presented in this chapter can be found in Cavazza and Pizzi (2006). In Cavazza and Pizzi's article, a considerable number of central narrative theorists are considered through observing how the works of the theorists have been applied to the field of interactive storytelling (IS) design, focusing on the field of IS design research. However, in the spirit of multidisciplinarity, narrative theories will aspire to play a greater role in the research discussed in this chapter. These kinds of concept-oriented interdisciplinary research topics are quite uncommon. Yet, we argue that they are necessary if we hope to see the interrelation of computer game design theory and multidisciplinary concepts such as narrative and to further advance related interdisciplinary research.

Other recent articles related to narrative serious game design principles can be found, for example, in Dickey (2006) and Egenfeldt-Nielsen (2004). Dickey (2006) considers how computer game narratives can support problem solving, focusing especially on the adventure game genre. As a result of the analysis, Dickey formed design heuristics by which it is possible to create narratives for learning purposes in game-based environments or other interactive environments. Egenfeldt-Nielsen (2004) proposes a new perspective on narrative utilization in the design and use of computer games for learning purposes. In his approach, he exploits Marie-Laure Ryan's theory of narrative and narrativity as well as Jerome Bruner's theory of the role of narrative in human thinking. Egenfeldt-Nielsen emphasizes that one cannot guarantee that the learning subject will emerge in the central role of the play experience simply by including the learning subject in a game story. While characterizing the potentials of narrative utilization in learning game purposes, Egenfeldt-Nielsen stresses players' own narratives in a game experience. From this viewpoint, narrative can serve as a tool for ordering events and experiences. Dickey's and Egenfeldt-Nielsen's opinions are interesting and noteworthy, for as we will comment later in relation to the results discussed in this chapter, these kinds of facets of research discussion could be further reviewed regarding underlying narrative definitions and their consequences.

In the next part of this chapter, the theoretical background of the analysis will be framed. The relevant elements of narrative theory will be introduced, and there will be an attempt to form a generalized classification of three main narrative theory lines. The chapter's empirical section begins with a description of the research material and method. In the following section, the findings of the analysis of game design guidebooks will be presented. The classification of narrative theory formed in the previous part of the text will act as a starting point for the classification of definitions under consideration. Next, the results of the analysis will be discussed more specifically concerning the use of selected subconcepts or other narrative-related concepts that emerge as problematic cases during the analysis. Further, in this section, we propose a new concept for game narrative discussion. In addition, based on the research results and applicable narrative theory, we strive to form a holistic, yet functional, narrative definition for the needs of game design. Lastly, the research results will be discussed in the design contexts of serious games.

THE FRAMEWORK: THREE CATEGORIES OF NARRATIVE THEORIES

In this section, the purpose is to consider a relatively extensive topic, the multidisciplinary narrative theory. It is clear that discussion cannot be extensive and detailed within the limitations of a chapter. Therefore, the object of this section is to make clear the general picture concerning different theoretical approaches in relation to the concepts of narrative and/or story in the field of narrative research. Thus, our focus regarding narrative theory reflection is to examine *the prime differences* of approaches. This survey is limited mainly to the *research of narratives* in which narratives are situated in the role of the research object as distinct from *narrative research*, whereby narratives are utilized in the methodological sense (like in some psychological research efforts that utilize the interview method and read the data as narratives). Further, narrative theories considered here are mainly limited to the subset of narrative theory that addresses narrative as expressed in some forms of media.

We propose that the discussed theories could be crudely grouped into three main areas. The theories in the first and second groups will be familiar to those who know at least the basics of narrative theory, as they have been introduced many times in textbooks. Thus, these will be discussed in less detail than the theories included in the third group, which are perhaps less familiar to the general reader.

Traditional Theories

The first group covers theories ranging from Aristotle's theory of drama to Vladimir Propp's study of story functions, in addition to the literature research applications of Carl Gustav Jung's archetype theory. Roughly, it includes the early trends of literature research to the advent of French structuralistic narrative theory, also known as narratology. However, this division is not airtight, as already the formalists' approach to literary theory contained characteristics of classical theories that are discussed in the next section. Commonality of traditional theories lies in their way of approaching narrative through some specific elements, for example characters or plots, which means in this context, events and their progression. Typically, in traditional theories, the given element is presented in the form of classification that determines, via generalization, the possible forms in which the element can manifest. It is essential that the element considered in traditional theories is tied to the level of story content that is presented through narrative expression. In these theories, the concept of narrative covers the forms of expression, where the manifestations of the examined element take place. Nevertheless, narrative is discussed only by implication because, at the time, an independent research topic such as narrative did not exist (Ryan, 2005a).

In the category of traditional theories, Aristotle's theory of drama is noticeably the most well-known and largely influential example. In *Poetics*, Aristotle says that art is an imitative activity by nature (Aristotle, 1967). According to this view, the expression comes closer to the narrative content and referent on the level of form, and thus the division of content and its expression exists only by implication and is not the overall focus of discussion. In *Poetics*, the plot is said to be the most important component of tragedy. Aristotle refers to the concept of plotting as the composition of the events. This includes the artist's tasks of selecting and organizing suitable events. From an Aristotelian viewpoint, through the plot, the artist attempts to imitate certain events, and more generally, activities or life itself. According to Aristotle, life *is* activity. In simpler terms, the main thesis of Aristotle is that in a story there is a beginning, middle, and end. In drama especially, the ending should include an element of *catharsis*, a kind of purification. Moreover, fitting with our description of traditional theories, characters are highly stereotyped, and there are only a limited number of possible character types (according to Aristotle, all characters of a story must be noble, seemingly true to life, and consistent). Furthermore, the selected mood (tragedy, comedy) dictates which sorts of events and characters can be presented.

Classical Theories

The second group encompasses the field usually referred to as narratology. However, some of the earliest narratologists can be situated within the first group, as also they foreground some specific elements of narrative (for example, Todorov foregrounds the events of the level of story content in his theorization). The roots of this approach rest firmly on Ferdinand de Saussure's theories related to sign and language use and Claude Lévi-Strauss's way of using the structuralist paradigm in myth research in the field of anthropology.

De Saussure states that language is a system of signs that connects certain speech sounds with meanings or ideas, thereby leaving all other kinds of sounds outside of the system (Culler, 1994). While constructing this type of system, de Saussure uses two main divisions, the first one considering the essence of signs and the second illustrating the difference between a single conversational situation and the system by which the communicating parties are operating. In de Saussure's (1983) theory, a sign consists of two parts: the representative element and the concept, *a signifier* and *a signified*, respectively. The term signifier refers to an appointed and observable side of a sign, for example a certain series of letters (Culler, 1994). Signified then, refers to a particular meaning, an idea or a concept, which is evoked by the signifier in the particular system of the language at hand (Culler, 1994).

As was said before, de Saussure additionally distinguishes between a language system that exists in communal use and conversational situations, that is, individual language uses (de Saussure, 1983). The former is named *langue* (system), and the latter is named *parole* (speech act) (Culler, 1994). In this division, the field of langue, "the nature of signs and the laws governing them" (de Saussure, 1983, p. 15), is the focus of the discipline Saussure was establishing. This later became the focus of narratologists as well. Structural narratologists consider individual narrative works as partial instances of a universal narrative structure. The main interest is on this narrative structure, and analyses of individual works mainly serve for a better understanding and specification of it.

As David Herman (2004) notes, one distinct characteristic of classical narratology is the attempt to separate the form of expression from the content of expression. This attempt is based on the Saussurean construct of sign. In the context of narratological research, the division of what a story is and the means of telling the story is further developed as the concept pair of *story* and *discourse*. This is where a story embodies the contents of narrative (i.e., events and existents that are communicated via narrative), whereas discourse refers to the form of expression in narrative (i.e., in literary text technical choices related to tense, mood, and narrator's voice). Furthermore, both of the levels are further divided into substance and formal aspects (Chatman, 1980). *Fabula* and *sjuzet*, the concepts based on Russian formalism (see, for example, Boris Tomashevsky 1925 *Teorija literatury. Poètika*), were acquired in structuralism and narratology. Through these concepts, the division is made between the chronological series of story events (fabula) and the presentation order of the events (sjuzet). In the context of classical theories, the concept of plot refers to the second option. These concepts, and several other alternatives proposed for the dividing purpose of narratology to consider narratives in detail, are only partly overlapping. The confusion is yet worsened by reducing translations: in narratological texts translated to English, fabula is often translated as "story," whereas sjuzet has been referred to as "narrative" (Rimmon-Kenan, 2006).

The technique by which the events are revealed and arranged is a question regarding the level of discourse. Furthermore, questions related to (the character of) a narrator can be separated from a path, "shaping principle or dynamic" (Abbott, 2008, p. 18), which takes form in the presented logical and causal continuum that connects the events of a story:

The events in a story are turned into a plot by its discourse, the modus of presentation. The discourse can be manifested in various media, but it has an internal structure qualitatively dif-

Table 1. The three levels of narratives according to structuralist narratology

Concept	Levels
Story/Fabula	Events in chronological order
Plot/Sjuzet	Events in the order they are recounted
Discourse	The way in which the plot is presented

ferent from any one of its possible manifestations. (Chatman, 1980, p. 43)

Thus a different composition of events of a story produces new plots, and it is possible to tell the same series of events by using various plots.

Both Lévi-Strauss's structuralism and Saussurean semiotics are meant to be applicable to multifaceted areas of human culture. In addition, the stories conveyed through different media should not be beyond the scope of such approaches. According to Claude Bremond (Chatman, 1980) and Roland Barthes (1977), narratives can be translated from one medium to another and remain unchanged. In addition, according to Barthes (1977), narratives can be mediated by spoken or written language and additionally through images, animations, and gestures. This view was particularized later by the concepts of structural narratology, story, and fabula or was more generally signified as something that can be transferred from one medium to another, whereas discourse, sjuzet, or the signifier, is more dependent on the characteristics of the given medium (Herman, 2004; Rimmon-Kenan, 2006).

However, throughout the research of narratives in new media forms, it is obvious that classical narratology has problems regarding its application outside the research of literature or conventional narratives. The problem is that the theories of narratology tend to foreground verbal language and especially the level of narrative discourse. Thus researchers of new multimodal media forms have not found these theories sufficient. Further, in some cases, the application of the narratological narrative approach has even evoked irritation and accusations for subordinating new media forms to the logic of traditional verbal language-based media forms.

New Theories

The theories constituting the third group are to some extent reactions to the limitations of the previous approaches. Additionally, the growth of cognitive theories in psychology since the 1960s has had a strong influence on some new narrative theories, which will be discussed soon. Furthermore, behind new theories lies the larger humanities phenomenon, generally called the Narrative Turn, in which narrative was adopted not only as a research object but also as a methodological tool for several disciplines. The new period of narrative research did not mean total reversal, since in many cases theorists have utilized the structuralist starting point, or Aristotelian plot concept. As a result, new definitions of narrative have emerged.

The highly influential narratologist Shlomith Rimmon-Kenan (2006) proposes a new definition for narrative that should be suitable for the new circumstances. She imposes two principal features that must play a central role. The features are *double temporality* and *transmitting* (or *mediating*) *agency*. The first feature refers to the separation between story events that inevitably include a temporal aspect (also called story time), and the presentation of events in a text (the term text is used in a general way covering all types of signifying systems) that takes place on its own time level (also called narrating time or discourse time). The second feature, transmitting agency, refers to a significantly larger meaning than just (the character of) the narrator. Thus the definition additionally yields to media such as films and other forms that do not necessarily utilize narrators in the same sense as conventional verbal language-based media. The structuralistic spirit is clear in Rimmon-Kenan's definition, as it highlights the story–discourse separation and grounds the approach for examining meaning-making mechanisms in media other than those which are verbal language-based.

Humans' *narrative competence* has been studied in the field of cognitive psychology along with other forms of gaining, organizing, and using knowledge (Polkinghorne, 1988). Jean Matter Mandler (1984) states that "story grammar is a rule system devised for the purpose of describing the regularities found in one kind of text. The rules describe the units of which stories are composed" (p. 18), whereas "[a] story schema … is a mental structure consisting of sets of expectations about the way in which stories proceed" (p. 18). That is to say, these two constructions represent two sides of narrative communications: mental and concrete. In Mandler's story grammar, stories comprise a start-up section, called "setting" in Mandler's terms, in addition to one or more episodes. The setting section presents the characters and describes the time and place of a story. In episodes, the protagonist encounters an event or events that cause him/her to set up some particular goal that he/she aspires to reach. The episode includes this action and its consequences: success or failure. Episodes constitute the plot of a story (Mandler, 1984). Probably the most influential scholar in applying this sort of approach has been Monika Fludernik whose "natural narratology" is based on everyday language use, mainly oral stories, instead of complex and lengthy literary narratives (Fludernik, 1996).

Marie-Laure Ryan has utilized the cognitive approach in her narrative definition, which aspires to cater to the new media context. Ryan (2004) makes the distinction between two potential situations: *to be narrative* and *to include narrativity*. In the first case, the semiotic object has been created for the purpose of producing a narrative script in the minds of the audience. In the latter case, an object has the capacity for producing a narrative script irrespective of its purposefulness. Partially, the distinction highlights that the content, which is aimed at being narrative, does not necessarily realize this target. By this distinction, the contemporary habit of referring to narratives in wildly different contexts can be understood. The division offers concepts by which to explain why some objects, such as history or human life, have been considered as narratives even though they *are not* truly narratives (the object is *narrativized*); they are not narratives as such, but they contain narrativity and are thus able to evoke narrative scripts in the receiver's mind.

Ryan (2004, 2005a, 2005b) participates in the discussion related to the transferability of the narrative, saying that if narrative is a "medium-independent phenomenon," then it has to be a cognitive construction by nature. This mental image is a type of meaning produced by a recipient, as a response to certain stimuli. Ryan further expands the elaboration to specify her definition for the concepts of narrative and story. She starts from the conception of H. Porter Abbott (2008), according to whom narrative is a combination of story and discourse, where story means an event or a series of events, and (narrative) discourse is the entity where the events are presented. In Ryan's media-free description, story has to be further specified because a bare series of events cannot constitute a story: only its raw material.

Ryan defines story by three necessary characteristics. First, story has to have a construction of a world including characters and objects. Second, some surprising "changes of state that are caused by non-habitual physical events" (Ryan, 2005a, p. 347) must occur. Third, the events have to be connected by causal relations, and there has to be a psychological aspect aroused by the connection of physical events as well as mental states and events. According to Ryan (2005a), the features of the third item then constitute the plot of a story. Thereby, it seems as though Ryan's plot definition would be closer to the Aristotelian definition than the definition of narratology. When the three mentioned items are in force, a text can produce an effect that is by Ryan's concepts *a narrative script* (Ryan, 2004).

Herman (2003), another spokesman of the new narrative theory group, proposes that narrative theories could be considered a subdomain of cognitive science. Thereby, narratives could serve as research material for studying the models by which people understand the world. For this purpose, Herman (2003) defines narratives as cognitive artifacts, which are materials or objects enabling cognition, or at least making cognition more effective. Therefore, Herman's definition subordinates narrative under cognitive artifact. His goal is to find out the characteristics of narrative regarding its vitality and ability to serve as a mental tool and instrument in a variety of situations and domains. Herman (2003), states that narratives can offer tools for thinking, especially in problem-solving situations. According to Herman (2004), it can be said that *the form of the signified* is what especially matters when defining narrative, particularly when considering the use of a narratological chart, in which the story content and its expression, in addition to aspects of substance and form, are both distinguished.

In comparison to classical narratologists, new narratologists such as Fludernik, Ryan, and Herman seem to be more concerned with the *phenomenon* of narrativity than with the complex *forms* of a narrative. As a consequence, there is a tendency to disregard many of the nuanced narrative structures in favour of structurally simpler modes of human narrative usage. If we accept the so-called ludologist position in which games are not narratives, it makes sense to adopt this narrativity perspective: games and gaming experiences may be narrativized in various ways.

The newest narrative theories have arisen at a time when the concept of narrative has become popular in numerous disciplines (which can be said to be a manifestation and consequence of the Narrative Turn). The popularity and progress of the concept has caused some theorists to note that the concept of narrative is at risk of losing its meaning. This is especially true when it is connected to so many various research concerns and its meaning is expanded to include loose meanings such as assumption or hypothesis, as is the case in the contexts of psychoanalysis (Rimmon-Kenan, 2006; Ryan, 2005a). In sum, psychoanalysis-based meanings for the concept of narrative can be generalized to refer to mental tools for reflecting human self and experience of reality (Polkinghorne, 1988; Rimmon-Kenan, 2006).

Although the description of proposed narrative theory categories demonstrates how the categories have partially developed as research trends at certain time periods, the chronological consecution was not the reason for this order of information. As Table 2 presents, the differing concerns of the theories and their unequal approaches to the concept of narrative and various central subconcepts such as plot were used as assessment principles.

LOOKING FOR NARRATIVE DEFINITIONS FROM COMPUTER GAME DESIGN GUIDEBOOKS

The main goal of the following analysis was to find out how concepts of narrative and/or story are defined in contemporary computer game design guidebooks. Both explicit and implicit definitions were analyzed. The hypothesis was that definitions reveal the theoretical backgrounds that shape the writers' overall approach to the relationships and potentials of narratives in computer games. Hence, the definitions of narrative would also have an effect on the advice of the guidebooks. One presupposition was that at least some applications

Table 2. The main differences of the three groups of narrative theories

Group	Where is the focus?	What forms the concept of narrative?	What is meant by the concept of plot?
Traditional Theories	Some element of story content, e.g., events or characters	Pinpoints narrative in some particular element of content	Series of events
Classical Theories	(General) narrative structure that becomes concrete in the text on hand	Divides narrative into levels of content and expression (and discourse)	"Path" of expression, whereby the story's events are revealed
New Theories	The phenomenon of narrativity	Considers narrative, e.g., as operations where narrative stimuli cause mental narrative pictures in the receiver's mind	Varies according to the influence of the preceding narrative theory (Traditional or Classical)

of the definition of narrative based on traditional theories would be found. This is due to baselines of these theories being common in, for example, prose- or screenplay-writing guidebooks.

Research Material and Method

The research material consisted of nine computer game design guidebooks (see Table 3). The research material we have considered in this survey includes books that: 1) discuss computer game design, 2) are targeted to people who need practical information about computer game design, and 3) are written by people who can be viewed as practical and/or theoretical experts of computer game design. Thus, the theoretically centered material (i.e., handbooks consisting of research articles, etc.) related to narrative computer game design was excluded from the analysis. The guidebook authors' approaches to narrative creation and serious game design were stressed in the analysis. Thus computer game design guidebooks that do not mention narrative creation or narrative utilization were excluded from the material. Moreover, the aim of analyzing *present-day* guidebooks meant that the guidebooks must have been published within the last 10 years. The nine books selected for the research material do not constitute all existing present-day computer game guidebooks. However, the number of them seem to present an adequate sample for our purposes.

Guidebooks focusing on interactive storytelling were borderline cases. Further, the topic of these books additionally implied that other kinds of products, rather than just computer games, were included in the scope of the subject. Yet, these guidebooks also discussed computer games. Therefore, two interactive storytelling guidebooks were included in the research material.

The analysis is principally qualitative, but it includes general quantitative notices as well. The analysis was conducted in two steps. In the first step of the analysis, the main goal, viewpoint, and focus areas of the guidebooks were recognized. The first step of the analysis was realized by the data-driven analysis method. This means that the general approach selected by the guidebook author(s) was recognized from the book itself. The key words used in the analysis included "narrative," "story," and "storytelling." Further, several other derived and synonymous words (on the level of standard language) were included if they were suitable for the framework (for example, "back story" and "storyteller" but not "storyboard"). One borderline case was the term "tale." This was included in the descriptions when found in the survey.

At the end of the first analysis step, the research material was classified into subgroups according to the main goal of the guidebooks, presented explicitly by the writers. In this analysis step, the classification was structured primarily according

Table 3. Classification of guidebooks by specified purpose

Guidebooks which focus on guiding in general with game design work (3)
McCarthy, Curran, & Byron (2005) The Complete Guide to Game Development, Art & Design
Rollings & Morris (2003) Game Architecture and Design
Vuorela (2007) Pelintekijän käsikirja [Game-Maker's Handbook]
Guidebooks which focus on guiding especially with game narrative or game story creation (5)
Bateman (Ed.)(2007) Game Writing: Narrative Skills for Videogames
Chandler (2007) Game Writing Handbook
Crawford (2005) Chris Crawford on Interactive Storytelling
Glassner (2004) Interactive Storytelling. Techniques for 21st Century Fiction
Krawczyk & Novak (2006) Game Development Essentials: Game Story and Character Development
Guidebooks which focus on guiding with narrative learning game design (1)
Iuppa & Borst (2007) Story and Simulations for Serious Games

to the guidebook authors' approach to narrative creation (i.e., Is narrative design featured according to the focus of the book, or not?) and secondarily according to the guidebook authors' approach to serious game design (i.e., If the book focuses on narrative design, is it focusing on serious game design too?). Narrative focus was emphasized in this way in the analysis. As a result we defined three subgroups of guidebooks:

1. guidebooks which focus on guidance in general with game design work
2. guidebooks which focus on guidance, especially with game narrative or game story creation
3. guidebooks which focus on guidance with narrative learning game design

The second analysis step was conducted by using both the theory-based analysis method and data-driven analysis method. This means that the research material was observed through certain theoretical frameworks, but, if possible, the findings were specified further. The classification of three frameworks formulated from the basis of narrative theory was used as a theoretical starting point in the analysis. The frameworks were named Traditional, Classical, and New theories. In the second analysis step, the research material was read through for the relevant parts in order to recognize what kinds of definitions of the key concepts ("narrative," "story," "storytelling," "tale," and relevant derivatives) were formed and utilized in the guidebooks to teach and describe how to create game narratives or game stories. The definition can be outspoken (explicit), read between the lines (implicit), or both (if there was conflict between the outspoken definition and the other discussion related to narrative). In particular, the central characteristics of the three narrative theory categories were utilized as criteria in the categorizing process (see Table 2). Questions posed included the following:

1. Does the definition in question include the division between separate levels of content and expression?
2. Is narrative approached only from the story content point of view?
3. What does the concept of plot mean in this guidebook?

Table 4. The distribution of theory-based occurrences

Categories	**Traditional**	**Classical**	**New Theories**			**Psycho-analysis**
Subcategories			Cognitive theory	Media-specifism	Series of events	(Story = experi-ence)
A) Guidebooks which focus on guiding in general with game design work						
McCarthy et al.	**X**					**X**
Rollings & Morris	**X**					**X**
Vuorela						**X**
B) Guidebooks which focus on guiding with game narrative or game story creation						
Bateman (Ed.)	**X**	**X**	x		**X**	**X**
Chandler	**X**	x	x	**X**	**X**	
Crawford	**X**		**X**	**X**		
Glassner	**X**	**X**			x	
Krawczyk & Novak	**X**	x		**X**	**X**	**X**
C) Guidebooks which focus on guiding with narrative learning game design						
Iuppa & Borst	**X**		**X**			

The frequency of the appearance of some specific definitions was not the main criterion, and thus the analysis is more qualitative than quantitative in nature. The main goal was to reveal the theoretical basis that the authors used when concepts of narrative and story were considered and the consequences of doing so.

Results of Definition Analysis Reviewed

Division into Subgroups

In the first step, the nine guidebooks were divided into subgroups according to their agenda. In the first subgroup, the main purpose of the authors was to provide a general guide for computer game design tasks. In the second subgroup, the main purpose of the authors was to provide a guide especially for narrative computer game design. The third subgroup of the research material consists of the group of guidebooks that consider narrative creation in the context of the learning game development. Thus, the agenda of the books in the third subgroup was clearly much more specified than in the case of the first subgroup. The distribution between the subgroups can be seen in Table 3.

Occurrences of Narrative Theory Categories in the Data

In the second analysis step, the analysis of narrative and/or story definitions revealed the diversity of viewpoints, theoretical backgrounds, and other influences. There were several different definitions of narrative, employing various elements of the theories in different combinations, in some cases even in mutually contradictory ways. In this section, we gain an overall glance of the occurrences of narrative definitions based on the three narrative theory categories (see Table 4). A more detailed review of the guidebook material will be conducted in the next section.

The majority of the narrative definitions utilize some ideas based on the traditional theory group. From the first theory category, the Aristotelian view of plot and the need for conflict were often adapted in the definitions. The Aristotelian plot explication—the plot as a series of events—was applied even to cases in which the structuralistic division of story content and its expression was also taken into account. Other characteristics of the Traditional theory group were also widely favored. In practice, this meant the utilization of several classifications, such as Jungian archetypes and various plot structure or conflict-type divisions. One often-mentioned source book was Joseph Campbell's *The Hero with a Thousand Faces* (1949), which does not focus on narrative theory but utilizes the theory of Jungian archetypes and considers a number of event series in stories collected from various cultures on different sides of the world. Furthermore, the guidebooks of computer game design often referred to other writing and scriptwriting guidebooks, and the theories adopted from these books were based on the traditional theories.

The structuralistic classical theories were found in three of the books. In Bateman (2007), the definition began with a separation of "narrative" and "story." The former was at first defined as consisting of methods by which a story is mediated to the audience. "Story" meant "the set of events driven by or affecting a certain set of characters (or character archetypes), which combine to provide a coherent narrative framework" (Bateman, 2007, p. 299). However, this clear division was soon obscured when game narrative was discussed in particular. It was said that the meaning of "narrative" should not be understood as simply a "story," since story functions only as a starting point for narrative. In this context, it is said that narrative is not the same as the methods by which it is produced. Instead, narrative is created along with the player's actions. It seems that in this statement, narrative is some kind of object of activity. The statement may refer to the player's experience, but it is apparent that narrative no longer refers purely to the level of expression. Later, it is stated that characters and events, which in fact were previously defined to be elements functioning on the level of story, drive narrative forward. Thus, in this guidebook, story and narrative seem to be interchangeable at different times. In the present definition, "story" and "narrative" constitute a combination that operates in particular circles. Yet, there seems to be problems in the description of how these operations take place.

In Glassner (2004), various divisions are outlined when narrative is defined explicitly. There is discussion of the external and internal structures as well as of the seen and unseen structures. However, these divisions are related to the manifestation of the final work and the writer's unrevealed plans and background knowledge about the story during the production process. Later, Glassner (2004) presents a division between plot sequence and view sequence. Here, the Aristotelian conception of plot is applied, so that it refers to a series of story events. View sequence refers to the order in which the events are presented to the audience. It is said that all the events of plot sequence do not exist in view sequence. The division is said to be the consequence of an author's selection and ordering of the material. Thus, in this narrative definition there seems to be a touch of recognition of the structuralistic division; however, the application of Aristotelian theory is still highlighted. Even the concept of plot is defined mainly by Aristotelian arguments regardless of the implicit recognition of the division between content and expression, although the structuralistic idea of plot is tentatively recognized in the definition of view sequence. Nevertheless, neither one of these two guidebooks made further use of the structuralistic approach.

Furthermore, Chandler (2007) makes a distinction between the concepts of story and narrative, even if more implicitly and only through the choice of words, in addition to other, more dominant, approaches. Thus, the case of Chandler will be discussed in the next section.

The third group, new narrative theories, is the second most utilized category. The group of new theories consists of so many different approaches to narrative that it was decided to further divide the category into subcategories according to the findings encountered during the analysis. The subcategories are based on the cognitive theory-based approach, media specifism-based approach, and the definition of narrative as a series of events. The narrative theories based on the cognitive viewpoint include extensive "narrative as a mental construct" approaches as well as ideas based on the "aim-structure" (like Mandler's story grammar) of narrative or story. The third subcategory of the new theory category, the series-of-events definition, is extremely wide and as such also problematic, as we will illustrate later.

The narrative definition based on the psychoanalytical approach is so often mentioned in the guidebooks that it was decided to add it to the classification as an extra category. In these definitions, narrative is defined as the player's experience (or mental reflection) of a single play session. That is to say, narrative is defined as an individual and unique experience attained through one session of playing a certain game. The guidebooks vary in relation to whether or not the definition also includes external events such as interruptions to the narrative experience.

In some guidebooks there are, explicitly or implicitly, attempts to construct a definition of story or narrative (or both), as well as a separate definition of game narrative or game story (see for example Bateman, 2007; Krawczyk and Novak, 2006). All of these will be elaborated on in the next section.

Table 4 represents the occurrences of various approaches. The bolded X means that there is some explicit or clear application of the viewpoint, the smaller x means that there are more implied references to the theories or ideas utilized in the discussion.

Data Description: Designers Constructing Narrative Definitions

Group A: Guidebooks Focusing on Game Design Work

Table 4 shows that in Group A of the guidebooks, which focused in general on game design work, the narrative definitions are (in two cases of three) constructed by drawing on the traditional theory basis. They also always utilize the psychoanalytical-based definition of narrative as the form of one's own unique experience. In the case of Vuorela (2007), the definition rests completely on the psychoanalytical model. In this definition, a plot is said to be a plan related to what a player is going to experience during a game. Story, then, is the true experience that a player gets by playing a game and can include, for example, the situations where a player is having difficulties whilst playing the game. Therefore, according to Vuorela (2007), in all games there is a story and all happenings during game playing are included in that story.

Rollings and Morris (2003) build the definition of story on the classical, especially Aristotelian, theory of plot, as well as on the psychoanalytical-based viewpoint of narrative as experience. Here it is said that all games include a plot, yet the plot is mainly constructed by players. The guidebook drafts two possible cases. In the "bad" case, a game designer has determined one linear path (a plot) through the game and the player must follow the path to complete the game successfully. In the "better" case, a game designer has situated the plot elements (events) so that a player can find them through his/her actions. The difference seems to lie in how the player can receive and experience the story events. Are the story events imposed on the player, or does the player have to find them? In the context of character design, the game designer's opportunity to shape the playing experience and story content through allowing certain potential for the character is also discussed. Moreover, a conceptual extension occurs once again. This time, it is the concept of setting: according to Rollings and Morris (2003), all games have a setting. Thus any kind of space, even an abstract one, is enough. A particular world is not required for the definition of the setting. In this definition, the story is the experience that a player receives through playing the game, and which he/she can relate to others after the playing session.

McCarthy et al. (2005) rely heavily on the Aristotelian definition when they state that a game takes a narrative route when it "offers the player a prescribed beginning, middle, and end" (p. 58) as a linear experience. Furthermore, the psychoanalytical definition is employed through claiming that other kinds of games such as *Tetris* (Pajitnov, 1984) can be seen as abstract games or as games that enable players to create their own stories. According to McCarthy et al. (2005), then, all games include a story, at least in the psychoanalytical sense.

Group B: Guidebooks Focusing on Game Narrative or Game Story Creation

The guidebooks in Group B, which focused especially on game narrative or story creation, are distributed quite evenly into the given categories (see Table 4). Each guidebook falls into three or five separate subcategories, which illustrates the diversity of the aspects included in the narrative definitions. Traditional theories and series of events, which is a subcategory of the new theories, are the most used concepts or ideas in this group of guidebooks.

The case of Bateman (2007) was already discussed in the context of the utilization of classical theories or, more precisely, the utilization of the structuralistic division between signifier and signified. In this case, the definition of game narrative turned to take form as a combination, whereby the story and narrative operated in circles. In the definition of story, the meaning of characters as an inevitable element of the story is stressed. In this narrative definition, characters' desires determine all the central story events, and thus, without the character, there would be no story.

Bateman (2007) represents four basic forms of video game storytelling, which include implicit narrative, formal narrative, interactive narrative, and interactive story. In implicit narrative, or *emergent narrative*, the single events are predetermined but not connected through formal design. It is expected that story could take form from the interactions between different game elements. In the opposite way, the formal narrative includes formally designed story elements. In the case of interactive narrative, the two forms of storytelling are combined so that the player's selection causes the player to follow a particular prewritten story path. In an interactive story, the player's choices have an effect not only on the level of narrative, but also on the level of story, which comprises characters, settings, and events.

In Chandler (2007), the medium-specific viewpoint of a story and narrative is advanced. Within the basic elements of a game story, there are namely cinematics, pacing, dialogs, text, and the arts of the game (such as graphics). Via these tools, it is possible to realize two kinds of narrative design modes: *logocentric* and *mythocentric*. Chandler borrows these concepts from Plato.1 According to Chandler, Plato defines two ways of reaching the truth: the rigorous logocentric way, which uses science and intelligence, and the spiritual mythocentric way, which operates through dreams and myths. In the logocentric case, Chandler argues that a game and its story include particular predetermined moments or situations, and the progression of the story is linear and controlled by the designer (cf., implicit, formal, and interactive narrative in the guidebook edited by Bateman). In a game designed in the mythocentric way, a player has the freedom to create the situations in an open game world (cf., the interactive story in the guidebook edited by Bateman). In this case, the player is named as author of the game events, because he/she selects the goals of the action and the tools needed for them, whereas the designer has to limit the larger framework of the events. Narrative, which seems to refer to the stage of the narration, is considered to be a spectrum. It includes the different possibilities of the logocentric and mythocentric approaches. Thus, it is somewhat discordant to say that in a mythocentric game, the "narrative context will not be as robust as that of a logocentric game, because the tools are simply not available" (Chandler, 2007, p.

112). However, this is possibly partly a consequence of the medium-specific viewpoint. After all, the medium-specific approach often ends up speculating about the question as to what extent a story, or more generally content, is bound to its expression forms and tools.

Crawford (2005) is a guidebook of IS design, one of the two borderline cases. When compared to the other IS guidebook, Glassner (2004), this book situates computer games in the margin of the application area. Whereas Glassner mainly considers the possibilities of computer game application, Crawford's story/narrative definition is quite different. The Aristotelian approach is used, but only as a starting point. Crawford says that the story, as such, is composed of a linear series of events and that all stories include some kind of conflict combined with the protagonist's key selection. In addition, Crawford sets one more content modifier for story: stories always boil down to human beings. But this is not Crawford's entire definition.

What makes Crawford's definition especially interesting is that it is based on both cognitive and medium-specific approaches. The cognitive viewpoint is particularly stressed. Story is said to be an entity and its content can be understood only by going through it in its entirety. Hence a story holds a particular capability of carrying and conveying knowledge, not in the form of a list but in the form of a complex system of facts and ideas. The medium-specific part of the definition stresses the idea that story is data, while storytelling is a process. In the case of IS, the (Aristotelian) plot has to be replaced by a network of possibilities. According to Crawford, in this kind of story space there is a metaplot, which is not determined by events, but by rules. This means that for a designer, the meaning of the theme is pronounced. A designer has to work on a "higher" or more abstract level of a story, and his role is to influence the larger curves of a story and only mediate the final manifestation of the story, which is an end result of the user's selections. Thus, the designer's work with narrative is characterized as potential-based design. However, Crawford specifically distinguishes his view on interactive story and its design from the idea of emergent story. He connects the idea of the emergent phenomena with confidence in serendipity by saying that it is "the hopeful fantasy that somehow, if programmers diddle around with complicated systems long enough, they'll eventually get a story to emerge" (Crawford, 2005, p. 137). In this way, Crawford stresses the designer's role and responsibility in interactive storytelling, even if it is true that it may enable new freedom also for the audience.

The other IS guidebook, Glassner (2004), was already discussed in the context of structuralistic applications. In this case, various divisions sketched in the book were considered. This was especially true in the division of plot sequence and view sequence, which was dissolved by the observation of plot and character work as a combined mechanism. Glassner explicitly asserts: "A story follows an interesting protagonist seeking a clear goal by addressing an ever-escalating set of difficulties" (2004, p. 36). The three basic elements in this definition are a protagonist, a goal, and a challenge. Later, the relationship of plot and character is further defined as "*character is action under pressure of plot*," and "*plot is what happens when characters act*" (Glassner's emphasis) (Glassner, 2004, p. 69). This is to say, the level of expression or narration has an influence on the level of story content. In this kind of definition, the story world would not exist as an independent entity. However, the division recognized in the book is stressed again by saying that story creation requires a narrator. On the other hand, the book pays much attention to the psychological depth of character creation. For example, Maslow's hierarchy of needs is proposed as support or a mental tool for character design. The object is to observe the character as a real person, who has a real person's mental depth. The story works as a process, which leads to the exposure of a character's inner self. Thus, the character's psychological progression dominates the approach. This definition generalizes and foregrounds some psychological aspects of the character in the story content and, in that way, seems to lean towards the approach of traditional theories in its narrative definition.

Krawczyk and Novak (2006) offer the first part of their definition to the concept of story when various means of expression in different media forms are discussed. The emerging definition could be formulated, for example, in the following form: *a story is a human experience, or series of experiences, that becomes concrete as an event or series of events*. The writers also list the necessary elements of storytelling, which include theme, character, conflict, resolution, and message. Afterwards, story and plot as its components acquire additional definitions, such as "story is a causal path in its entirety" (p. 74) or "A plot is not a story. It only serves to help reveal a story" (p. 73). The revealing role of a plot is compared to how a hanger helps to show a coat, without the need for the viewer to interfere with it. Moreover, there seems to be a definition of plot that refers to the structuralistic plot concept, connected to the level of narration. This is surprising, as earlier the writers presented the idea differently, even in reverse to the basic idea of structuralism: "It wasn't until Aristotle that we started to see actual thought and structure emerge as a cohesive form" (p. 9). In addition, Aristotle's basic concepts (including plot) are explicitly and unconditionally approved. Furthermore, when writers discussed the player's ability to interact with story events, the Aristotelian plot definition is brought into play. The writers refer to the ideal situation as "story play," where a player can affect both the level of story content and the level on which the story is told.

In the introduction it is said that "the challenge for the game developer becomes how to guide players through the game space while allowing them to have their own personal story experience and even story 'co-authorship'" (Krawczyk and Novak, 2006, p. xiii). Later, in a general sense, it is said that "when we sit down to play a game, we may not always realize it, but we are engaging in a story—a story of our own design" (p. 181). Hence in the psychoanalytical narrative definition, the form that a player's unique experience takes is taken into account even though it is not discussed in depth in the guidebook. It can be said that in this case the two parallel definitions are accepted or conflated.

One obvious contradiction occurs when the writers—despite explicitly listing the character as one of the necessary elements of storytelling—say that there are also games without characters. They further say that in these cases, the role of setting becomes essentially important for storytelling. In this way, the writers implicitly argue that characters would not be fundamental elements of stories after all. This kind of viewpoint is deeply in conflict with, for example, Crawford (2005) and Bateman (2007).

Group C: Guidebooks Focusing on Narrative Learning Game Design

One book features in Group C of the guidebooks, and it is focused on narrative learning game design. Iuppa and Borst (2007) received two strong markings on Table 4 for the categories of traditional theories and for cognitive theory, which is a subcategory of new theories. In the book, it is explicitly said that a story should have a hero, a goal, and a challenge between them. Moreover, stories have a structure that can be determined in various ways. The writers note that, in this case, they have focused on the Hollywood structure, which refers to the Aristotelian notion of a story. Later in the book, the writers added a note to the previous list of story elements, which said that a hero should have some kind of fault that makes him especially vulnerable to the challenge of the story. By sketching the definition of narrative in the form of a situation, the writers present the story basically as a learning situation, whereby a hero is a learner who finally has to overcome his faults.

Iuppa and Borst (2007) stated that if one tries to ask an expert about issues usually mediated as tacit knowledge, one will probably get a vague answer. Yet, if one asks the expert to tell a story related to the subject, one may get much more knowledge. The writers explain the phenomenon using Roger Schank's explication, according to which people understand the world by forming mental models of it. Hence, in the writers' definition, the story seems to be first of all a mental tool by which it is possible to convey contents that otherwise are not able to be verbalized (cf., Crawford's definition of story as a system of facts). Thus, the definition of the concept of story seems to rely mainly on the cognitive approach.

Complete Results: The Variety of Narrative Definitions

To summarize, in the material, the concepts of narrative and story were used in the following ways:

1. Constant predetermined linear story (and its narration). (McCarthy et al.; Bateman; Chandler)
2. The player's own unique story and narrative that arises as a consequence of playing a computer game. This pertains to all kinds of computer games. (Rollings and Morris; McCarthy et al.; Krawczyk and Novak)
3. The player's own unique story and narrative that arises as a consequence of all of the happenings that are confronted during game play. This pertains to all kinds of computer games. (Vuorela)
4. Partially preformed and partially potential-based story content set by the designer and presented through narrative which arises from potentiality determined by the designer (i.e, player controls narrative; Bateman (ed.); Rollings and Morris)
5. Story and narrative that can have both preformed and potential-based manifestations. (Bateman; Chandler; Crawford; Krawczyk and Novak)
6. Non-preformed story that can be produced through potential-based narrative (story emergence; Bateman)
7. Story as a complex system of facts. (Crawford)
8. Story as a mental model. (Iuppa and Borst)
9. Story as a situation, which includes a hero, a goal, and a challenge between them. (Iuppa and Borst)
10. Story as human experience, or series of experiences, which becomes concrete as an event or a series of events. (Krawczyk and Novak)
11. Story as following the main character and events, while the character seeks a clear goal by addressing a set of difficulties. (Glassner)

The narrative and story definitions discovered in the analysis are diverse and operate on different levels. Definitions 1–6 relate to how the experience of story and narrative is created and how preordained this experience is. The first definition is completely conventional, and it can be found from the traditional and classical theory categories. Both Definitions 2 and 3 are based on the psychoanalytical approach. In Definition 2, the experience involves only game-related issues, whereas in Definition 3, there is not this limitation. Further, interruptions and other events extraneous to the game world may be involved in the narrative and story experiences. Definitions 4–6 focus more on the predictability or stability of narrative and story. In these definitions, the structuralist division between the content and the expression is recognized. Definition 5 seems to also include Definitions 1 and 4. In fact, it seems to be so extensive that it additionally includes an intrinsic contradiction: the combination of a potential-based story and formally designed narrative. However, none of the guidebooks present this kind of vision. In Definition 5, narrative and story are presented as two-level spectrums of manifestations. Definition 6 differs radically from definitions 4–5, because it includes the idea that a player could be led to construct narration, which in turn creates the story content. This is to say that narrative could ontologically precede story content.

If Definitions 1–6 approach the key concepts by answering the question of how narratives and stories arise or are produced (both passive and active definitions included), Definitions 7–11 approach the concept of story by answering the questions of what story consists of, or what story is. Definitions 7 and 8 are based on the cognitive approach. The origins of Definitions 9 and 10 are more difficult to trace. The effect of the psychoanalytical-based approach can be seen in these definitions, but they are more refined compared to Definitions 2 and 3. Definitions 9 and 10 appear to be incomplete, possibly because there do not seem to be any implicit references to the recognition of the division of content and expression. In Definition 11, however, there seems to be a small attempt to recognize the level of expression ("following"), but it is not sufficiently distinguished from the level of content, and thus the definition appears to be unfinished.

According to the analysis results, in the field of game design there seems to be a need for various narrative concepts. Narrative/story should be named and consistently defined on three different levels. The three levels that came up are:

- the level of constant predesigned narrative/story,
- the level of narrative/story achieved by predetermined potential, and
- the level of narrative/story that is experienced during a single play-through.

BLIND SPOTS IN GAME NARRATIVE DISCUSSION

In the computer game design guidebooks, narrative theorists of the traditional class are often mentioned in the context of narrative definitions, whereas the influences of the classical or new narrative theories are adopted inconspicuously, without explicit notices. Especially in the case of the new theories, this is probably the consequence of writers' practical take on the subject.

During the analysis, a series of inconsistent concepts related to narrative arose in the context of narrative definitions. Often these concepts played an important role in the definitions of narrative or story. In other cases, the terms were used to describe possibilities of game narrativity or narratives. Inconsistent concepts include the following:

- plot
- setting
- coauthorship
- plot points
- metastory or metaplot
- emergence
- linearity

Plot

In the guidebooks, the concept of *plot* is defined in the following ways: the events of a story told in chronological order from beginning to end (McCarthy et al., 2005); the events that constitute a story (Bateman, 2007; Krawczyk and Novak, 2006); a series of events (Glassner, 2004); the one particular linear path through a story and/or game (Rollings and Morris, 2004); the plan concerning events or experiences that will be materialized during a game, at least in the starting situation of a game (Vuorela, 2007); the predestined plan for the outcome of a story, which is analogical for determinism (Crawford, 2005); the form of expression, for example non-linear or three-act-based

(Chandler, 2007); and the plot as a tool that helps reveal a story (Krawczyk & Novak, 2006).

In Iuppa and Borst, a particular plot definition was not found. Furthermore, McCarthy et al. (2005) as well as Rollings and Morris (2004) stated that games always have a plot (Aristotelian). However, according to Rollings and Morris (2004) plot can be mainly created by the player. Contrary to this, Vuorela (2007) stated that all games have a story, even if there would not be a plot.

In sum of these plot definitions, the general confusion between the concepts of plot, story and narrative illustrates reflections of different narrative theory categories. In particular, the definition examples highlight the difference of traditional and classical theory bases, as they offer different plot definitions; the majority of designers connect the plot to the level of story events, whereas only Chandler and Krawczyk and Novak in their second-mentioned plot definition illustrate the classical theory-based view of plot while connecting the concept to the level of expression. This result was surprising, as in the data there were other guidebooks that for some other reasons were more strongly influenced by classical theory in their narrative definition (see Table 4). Thus, the result illustrates how designers combine various influences inconsistently in their narrative definitions, based on different narrative theory bases.

In the context of plot, designers also revealed their conceptions related to the story and its potential to provide freedom for the player. In some plot definitions, the fixed nature of plot is especially emphasized so that it is presented as "the fault of plot," if a player cannot enjoy the free mode of playing in a narrative game. This conception may be the consequence of applying event-centered traditional theories like Aristotle's model for the dramatic arc.

The case of Vuorela (2007) illustrates the odd consequences from applying mere psychoanalytical-based narrative definition. What kind of story or narrative is without plot? Is it a story anymore?

Constitutives of Story

In the material, there was variation related to the basic elements that are seen as necessary subconcepts for constituting narrative or story. Glassner (2004), in addition to Iuppa and Borst (2007), leaned towards the definition that all stories include *a main character*, *a goal*, and *a challenge*. The combination of goal and challenge can be interpreted as a conflict. Also, Crawford (2005) agreed that all the stories include a conflict. Furthermore, Bateman, in agreement with Glassner (2004), as well as Iuppa and Borst (2007), maintains that all stories need to include a character. Crawford's view considering the inevitability of a character is presented implicitly; he discusses the content of a story by saying that in all stories the case is about humans, even if the characters are not human beings.

On the contrary, Krawczyk and Novak (2006) contend that story could be constructed without characters. "In games, where sometimes characters do not exist, setting becomes an essential part of the storytelling process" (Krawczyk and Novak, 2006, p. 46). Also, Rollings and Morris (2004) stated that setting, which is at the least "formalized universe governed by a few logical rules: the landscape of the reasoning mind" (p. 14), is featured also in the most abstract games such as *Tetris* (Pajitnov, 1984).

These differing notions related to the overall definitions of narrative and story may cause significant confusion to designers working with game narratives. Obviously, a computer game does not always need to have characters. But, whether the narrative definition is based on the traditional, classical, or new theories, characters are inevitable elements for story content. Equally, it is a matter for some speculation as to whether or not the space in a computer game without story content is always the same kind of setting as it is in a story that requires the depth of a fictional world. If not, then should the abstract game space be separated from a story-related setting, or story world, by its own concept, such as the *virtual environment* proposed by Aarseth (2004)? According to Aarseth, this concept refers to "a simulation of a physical world, not necessarily our own and usually much less complex" (Aarseth, 2004, p. 364).

In summary, it can be said that story content needs to include a world, character(s), events, goal (the motive force), and challenges (the opposite force). We will utilize this list later in the section discussing a composite model of narrative definition.

Plot Points

The often-mentioned subconcept related to plot was the concept of *plot points*. Glassner (2004) defined plot points as basic units of storytelling, during which something happens in a story. Crawford (2005) used the term "substory" in quite a similar sense. According to Krawczyk and Novak (2006), "each point in time that causes further action is a plot point" (p. 74), and additionally, each plot point reveals more of the story. Rollings and Morris's (2004) definition is a bit different. Plot points were defined to be situations or events in which the player's expectations do not match with what happens in the story. Mainly however, these differences of definitions are matters of different viewpoints or emphasis and do not constitute remarkable confusions for game narrative discussion.

Metalevels

In the guidebooks, there are discussions related to the possible *meta*levels of story and, especially, possible metalevels of game story. Chandler (2007) used the term "metastory" to refer to events that take place around the player and in the background. According to him, especially in fixed story design (in Chandler's terms, logocentric story design), the design of metastory is stressed. But is this level of story really a metalevel? Usually metalevel is understood as presenting a higher abstraction level, and perhaps it would be clearer to reserve the metaconcepts for this kind of use. Crawford (2005) states that in a potential-based story design, the designer has to operate on a more abstract level of the story. This level does not consist of the story events which define the (Aristotelian) plot but instead consists of the rules, which define a sort of metaplot of the story. This metaplot includes all the potentials from which the actual plot can grow during each separate playing session. This kind of use of metaconcept seems to be more justifiable because it shifts the discussion to a higher level and explains the mechanism which makes the more concrete embodiment (the story plot) possible.

Emergence

Emergence is a concept often applied in the context of computer game narratives. In the material, the term is used in at least two different cases. In the guidebook edited by Bateman (2007), emergent narrative is the other name for the game storytelling type that in the presented classification is primarily named "implicit narrative." This emergent narrative "involves the interaction of elements within the game system to develop events that may be interpreted by the players as story—narrative results that are implicit to the game system" (Boon, 2007, p. 45). Seen from another viewpoint, the citation says that actually there is no narrative content in a game but that the player constitutes it by his conceptualization. Crawford described this kind of idea of emergent storytelling as a fantasy, where a sufficiently complicated system produces surprises that no one could expect beforehand. McCarthy et al. (2005) described a sample game stating that the emergent game play is utilized to enhance a narrative-driven adventure. In this view, the phenomenon of emergence is tied to the creative game-playing mode and to the design style that enables that kind of playing. In the first and second cases of guidebooks, the concept of emergence is used essentially in the same way amongst them. In the last case, emergence is used in a strong way (emergence as something wholly unpredictable), whereas in the former case, it is a weaker emergence limited by predetermined rules and thus at least partially predictable. As it seems that these two types of emergence do not share the same problems, it is important to be specific when applying them.

Linearity

The concept that causes the greatest unclarity and confusion is obviously *linearity*. In the research material, descriptions such as linear-level design, nonlinear narrative or (game) story, nonlinear game world, linear objectives, nonlinear story missions, nonlinear game, nonlinear narrative content, player's nonlinear experience of story, nonlinear plot, nonlinear game play, the moment of nonlinearity, and nonlinear path are all present. Almost always, "linear" was not solely used in the descriptive sense but instead implied that in other kinds of cases, the opposite (nonlinear) alternative could be possible as well. Extensive use of the concept of linear meant that the ideas of the separate guidebooks were not comparable with each other. Also, every now and then it seemed that the concept had lost any exact meaning. Thus, linearity seems to have ended up as a kind of empty buzzword. The question of how this concept should be used in a uniform way in the context of game narrativity is challenging, and, as it would require deeper discussion concerning the game narrative expression, the question cannot be resolved in the limits of this chapter.

About the Nature of Narrative and Story

In Glassner (2004), the specific characteristic of narrative is illustrated through a comparison of story and game. It was said that on the level of content, "games are primarily about results, while stories are primarily about process" (Glassner, 2004, p. 214). In turn, Crawford (2005) characterized story on a more technical design-level by suggesting that story itself should be viewed as data, whereas storytelling is a process by nature. In many guidebooks, characteristics of narrative or story were described as alternatives and in some cases (especially in Chandler, 2007), as a continuum, whereby the poles are fixed narrative and freer form. Narrative is constructed in some kind of space of possibilities. According to the three levels related to the game narrative design that we mentioned at the end of the summary of definition findings, we could further add to the spectrum of narrative the psychoanalytical definition of story as a reflection of experience (then the continuum would include fixed narrative–potential narrative–the entire experience). It seems however, that this kind of narrative definition for game design purposes would be overextended. Thus, it might render meaningless the concept of narrative. This implies that all three levels should not be defined under the same concept of narrative, but the psychoanalytical aspect of narrative should be discussed with distinguishable concepts.

From Co-Authority to Co-Storyliner?

The last confusing concept was *co-authority*. The case is related to the often repeated declarative sentence that generally features in the form: "In a computer game, a player becomes an author of the game narrative/story"; or "In a computer game, a player can become an author of his own story." These kinds of statements are inevitably inaccurate if the psychoanalytical definition of narrative is dismissed as too vague. Besides, it does not help game designers in their work when it is stated that in games stories should not be (entirely) preformed and that a player will have the responsibility of storytelling. It is clear that there has to be *something* preformed in regards to the story, and it is the designer's work to organize it. But maybe it is easier to start by asking: What exactly is the role that a player may fill in the computer game in terms of narrative?

In the guidebook edited by Bateman (2007), it is said that as a result of interactivity, a player receives control of narrative elements of the game, but mainly these elements are related to *how* the story is told (for example, the control of the camera) and not *what* the story is about. Krawczyk and Novak (2006) stated that players can further influence the causal relationships of story contents and, in this way, the plot (used here in the Aristotelian sense). The writers argue that thus, a player can be seen as a coauthor of the playing experience and plot. Moreover, the writers add that a player can also have an effect on characters if a game enables players to customize their own characters. However, Glassner (2004) presented two central spheres of a story author's responsibility, which are the design of the protagonist's psychological completeness and the ordering and timing of the most important plot events.

We propose that whether the game narrative is based on fixed story design or on potential-based design (as we previously argued, pure emergent-based design was considered as being founded on a problematic narrative definition from the viewpoint of game narrative design), the player's role could be defined and delimited as a "co-storyliner." In this case, the structuralist plot definition is brought into play. This means that in a fixed game story, the player can have an influence on the way that the story is being told. During this process, he/she carries out selection and ordering processes by which he/she forms the narration of the story for him/herself. In a narrative computer game, the interpretation of events and objects is inevitable for progression purposes (Eskelinen, 2001). The concept has roots in both "co-narrator" as defined by Koskimaa (2000), with reference to the role of the reader of hypertext fiction (although as there is no clear narrator–agent in games, the term cannot be adopted as such), and in Aarseth's concept of "intriguee" (Aarseth, 1997). Aarseth inserts the level of negotiation between the levels of events and progression and especially discusses the case of text–adventure games, where the negotiation takes the form of intrigue; the voice both describing the narrative situation and posing challenges or riddles for the player is intriguing. Thus the player adopts the role of intriguee, forced to solve the puzzles in order to proceed in the game. In nontextual games there is no such intrigant, and typically in action games, many of the challenges are not riddles but rather require dexterity and reaction speed.

With the co-storyliner concept it is possible to, first, employ the intuitively appealing notions of traditional narratology (co-storyliner is partaking in the formation of the sequence of events and driving them from the beginning to the end) and, second, to raise the abstraction level to encompass at least some of the structural relations of classical narratologists. Thus it may prove of important heuristic value for game development to recognize the role of co-storyliner in manipulating such dimensions in games, which relate to the Genettian notions of mood, voice, and tense (Genette 1980). With this approach, we may recognize aspects such as "gaming style," the fact that it is not only about playing through a game or winning the game but about playing the game in an individual style by, for instance, repeating certain episodes for the pure pleasure of it, slowing down or speeding the action at will, assuming a role as protagonist or as bystander. Thus, such juxtaposition as Glassner (2004) posited between the natures of game and story ("games are primarily about results, while stories are primarily about process" [p. 214]) will not become critical for narrative game design.

Composite Model of Narrative Definition for the Purposes of Game Narrative Design

Returning back to the definitions of narrative and story found in the material, we noticed that three of the samples deserve further scrutiny. In Definitions 7 and 8, the cognitive approach emphasizes *the form of signified.* As Herman (2004) claimed, these kinds of definitions may provide us with key information about the nature of story but are not enough in the instances of game narrative design. The last remaining definition, Definition 11, is as follows: a story follows a main character and events, while the character seeks a clear goal by addressing a set of difficulties. To construct a more complete narrative definition, we propose that Ryan's (2005a)*stimuli* could be taken into account, as well as the concept of story world (this element can also be found in Ryan's narrative definition). When these elements are combined with a structuralistic chart that recognizes the division between content and expression, we get the composite model of narrative definition presented in Table 5.

According to the composite model of the narrative concept for the needs of game design, the designer should create narrative stimuli that refer to some particular world, character(s), events, goal, and challenges. On the level of content, story is a complex system, whereby meaning is understood only through its entirety. In the composite model, "story" and "narrative" constitute a combination that operates in circles, as it appeared in the definition outlined in Bateman's (2007) guidebook. Here, our intention was to describe the relationships between the two ontologically divergent stages of content (signified) and expression (signifier) so that the mechanisms between them can be described in a reasonable way.

The three levels that proved to be needed for the game narrative design discussion were the level of constant predesigned narrative/story, the level of narrative/story achieved by predetermined potential, and the level of narrative/story that is experienced during a single play-through. The narrative definition presented in Table 5 aspires to be comprehensive enough so that at least the two first-mentioned levels can be considered under the concept of narrative as defined in this way. As was previously proposed, the psychoanalytical aspect of narrative, as the form of a player's experience, should be discussed with some concept other than narrative for the sake of clarity.

Furthermore, this analysis does not answer all relevant questions. In the future, aspirant game narrative designers will need more detailed theoretical knowledge about *the form of narrative expression* in the context of multimodality of computer games. Currently, this further detail can neither be found from scrutiny of the guidebooks, nor from the narrative theories discussed before. There is a need for transmedial narratology, which should focus on the possible forms of the narra-

Table 5. The composite model of narrative definition

	SIGNIFIED	SIGNIFIER
SUBSTANCE	• world • main character • events • goal challenges on the level of content, i.e., in the fictional reality	• narrative stimuli that result in the mental image or cognitive construction of story • witnessing
FORM	• story as a complex system of facts • story as a mental model containing its requirements, i.e., constructions of the substance components of story	the multimodal discourse of a game, requiring both interpretative and constructive participation from the player

tive stimuli (e.g., Ryan, 2003). The multimodal qualities of computer games should be more effectively emphasized. Additionally, existing theory related to narrative structures should be further developed with the aid of cognitive science, so that the language-based approach would not dominate to such an extent. Although Ryan (2004) states that language seems to be the best semantic system for narrative because of its ability to present propositions, in our approach, the verbalization of narrative relations can happen on the level of the co-storyliner. Theories related to game mechanics, player's selecting possibilities, and progression in game, could also inform game design.

FUTURE RESEARCH DIRECTIONS: A PROPOSED NARRATIVE DEFINITION AND THE NEEDS OF NARRATIVE SERIOUS GAMES DESIGN

In this section, the consequences of the analysis results are discussed from the viewpoint of serious games design. If the purpose is to build an enchanting game narrative so that it supports learning and related operations, some psychological theories (with psychoanalytical or cognitive-based narrative definitions) addressing narrative may prove helpful. But this alone is not enough, as there are several simultaneous requirements of a successful serious game. A combination of requirements includes the needs of narrative design, game design and learning tool design.

From the viewpoint of narrative definition utilized in game design, the question remains; is the proposed cognitive–narratological definition (the composite model, see Table 5) for the purposes of game narrative design compatible with the narrative definition evoked by the psychological theory selected for enhancing learning purposes? Two potentially applicable psychological viewpoints may come from David Herman and Jerome Bruner. Previously, Herman's viewpoint of narrative as an artifact which may enhance cognition was discussed. According to Herman (2003), narrative can serve as a tool for problem solving. One special characteristic of narrative is its ability to "establish spatiotemporal links between regions of experience and between objects contained in those regions" (p. 169). This approach to narrative is strongly rooted in cognitive psychology, and it also seems to be compatible with the proposed narrative definition. While Herman discusses the nature of cognitive artifacts and their use, he quotes Don Norman:

The powers of cognition come from abstraction and representation: the ability to represent perceptions, experiences, and thoughts in some medium other than that in which they have occurred, abstracted away from irrelevant details... . we can make marks or symbols that represent something else and then do our reasoning by using those marks. (Herman, 2003, p. 167)

This does not conflict with de Saussure's conception of sign, which represents something that is absent. Thus, the approach of cognitive artifacts could be compatible also with the structuralist viewpoint. At least, their connection would be worth closer observation.

Bruner (1986) argues that in human beings' cognitive functioning, there are two modes of thinking that produce different constructions of reality and experience. The modes are *paradigmatic* and *narrative* thinking. The paradigmatic, also named logico-scientific, mode of thinking uses mathematical devices in describing or explaining contents. The narrative mode approaches content in a different way. In several books, Bruner discusses human beings' universal ability to use narrative to construct a conception of reality, ourselves, and our powers. Bruner (1996) states that culture shapes minds. It provides a narrative mode by which its members can receive their identity and agency.

Bruner's (1996) conception of knowledge is networklike. He says that "[w]hen we understand something, we understand it as an exemplar of a broader conceptual principle or theory" (Bruner, 1996, XII). Thus, according to Bruner (1996), for the learner it is better that knowledge is gained through his/her own cognitive efforts, as it will thereby be internalized and utilized together with the learner's previous knowledge.

Bruner's conception of knowledge seems to be compatible with the cognitive view of narrative as a system of facts, or more generally, as a mental model or tool. His view of narrative however, is not only cognitive, but also psycho-cultural as he describes it (Bruner, 1996). Bruner mentions Freud as one of the influential persons in the growth of the psychological approach to narrative that he himself also represents. "We live in a sea of stories, like the fish who [.. .] will be the last to discover water, we have our own difficulties grasping what it is like to swim in stories" (p. 147). Here, Bruner refers to the automaticity of the use of narrative mode in cognition.

In many places Bruner's ideas relate to issues which in Ryan's division would be described as *including narrativity* but not necessary *being narratives*. This may limit straight application of his theory in narrative learning tool design. At least in the first place, the concepts related to a player's (narrative) expression should be clearly defined and separated from game narrative definition.

In serious game design, one should not overlook the communicative potential of fully adopted narrative structure, despite its apparent complexity. Character-to-character communication, narrator-to-narratee communication, and author-to-audience communication levels, with the additional rhetorical twists of short-circuiting these levels (e.g., a character addressing the narrator) offer vast heuristic value for serious game design. The same can be said of the numerous other features of narratological theories, such as the filtering of information mediated (focalization), which are not even hinted at in the current game design books. Not all games need to be narrative in nature, but for many serious gaming purposes, the narrative form offers invaluable features that cannot be fully employed without some level of narratological knowledge. Those game design books that explicitly discuss narrative game design would serve their audience better by incorporating such concepts and their applications in the design process. But, of course, this may require additional advances in the field of game narrative research, especially related to the form of game narrative expression.

CONCLUSION

In this chapter, we have considered different narrative definitions discovered in the analysis of nine present-day computer game design guidebooks. In the research material, three different narrative theory bases were utilized. Moreover, a psychoanalytical definition arose from the analysis. Throughout the discussion, significant consequences of different and varied theoretical bases of definitions have appeared. The consequences include disruptive factors and unclarity for design-related discussion, as well as misleading assumptions of the possibilities of game narratives. One regrettable consequence is that, because of the very different definitions of narrative and its related concepts, various ideas of separate designers remain noncomparable, and thus further development of the ideas becomes difficult.

Therefore, to help the progress of the game narrative discussion, we have proposed three necessary levels of game narrative that should be distinguished and clearly named. Based on the research results (the functional narrative definitions) and the needs set by the three above-mentioned levels, we have built a composite model of narrative definition that should be extensive enough for game narrative design purposes. As one new concept, we have proposed the concept of the co-storyliner, referring to the player's role in the computer game from the narrative viewpoint.

For further study, we propose various needs that rise from the research results. First, concerning the three aforesaid levels of narrative, especially the level of playing experience that when viewed from the psychoanalytical-based perspective can take the form of narrative in the player's mind, should be separated by distinct concepts from narrative that designers are pursuing by fixed or potential-based narrative design style. Furthermore, we highlighted the directions where the theorization related to game narrative design should be elaborated in the future. The propositions included, above all, the need for transmedial narratology, which should focus on the possible forms of narrative stimuli, and further development of existing theory related to narrative structures with the aid of cognitive science. In this context, the use of the concept of linearity (when related to game narrative) should additionally be clarified.

The notions of this chapter are not only noteworthy for game designers, but also for game design researchers. Narrative definitions and their consequences could be further analyzed in the future in the context of research papers. In this kind of analysis, the papers discussing narrative serious games design would constitute highly interesting research material. For example, the approaches of Dickey (2006) and Egenfeldt-Nielsen (2006) utilize different narrative definitions and thus yield highly different comments on the possibility of game narratives in educational game design. This goes to show the importance of rigorous definitions of concepts, especially in multidisciplinary contexts, as is often the case with narratives.

REFERENCES

Aarseth, E. (1997). *Cybertext: Perspectives on ergodic literature*. Baltimore, MD: The Johns Hopkins University Press.

Aarseth, E. (1997). *Cybertext: Perspectives on ergodic literature*. Baltimore: The Johns Hopkins University Press.

Aarseth, E. (2004). Quest games as post-narrative discourse. In Ryan, M.-L. (Ed.), *Narrative across media: The languages of storytelling* (pp. 361–376). Lincoln, NE: University of Nebraska Press.

Abbott, P. (2008). *The Cambridge introduction to narrative* (2nd ed.). New York: Cambridge University Press.

Abt, C. (2002). *Serious games*. Lanham, MD: University Press of America.

Aristoteles. (1967). *Runousoppi* [*Poetics*]. Helsinki: Otava.

Arnseth, H. C. (2006). Learning to play or playing to learn—A critical account of the models of communication informing educational research on computer gameplay. *Game Studies—The International Journal of Game Studies, 6*(1). Retrieved August 20, 2009, from http://gamestudies.org/0601/articles/arnseth

Barthes, R. (1977). *Image—Music—Text*. New York: Hill and Wang.

Bateman, C. (Ed.). (2007). *Game writing: Narrative skills for videogames*. Boston, MA: Charles River Media.

Bogost, I. (2007). *Persuasive games: The expressive power of videogames. Cambridge, MA*. London: The MIT Press.

Boon, R. (2007). Writing for games. In Bateman, C. (Ed.), *Game writing: narrative skills for videogames* (pp. 43–70). Boston, MA: Charles River Media.

Bruner, J. (1986). *Actual minds, possible worlds*. Cambridge, MA: Harvard University Press.

Bruner, J. (1996). *The culture of education*. Cambridge, MA & London: Harvard University Press.

Campbell, J. (1949). *The hero with a thousand faces*. Princeton, NJ: Princeton University Press.

Cavazza, M., & Pizzi, P. (2006). Narratology for interactive storytelling: A critical introduction. In S. Göbel, R. Malkewitz, & I. Iurgel (Eds.), *TIDSE 2006, LNCS 4326* (pp. 72-83). Berlin Heidelberg: Springer-Verlag. Retrieved April 2, 2009, from http://www-scm.tees.ac.uk/users/f.charles/publications/conferences/2006/Cavazza_Pizzi_TIDSE06.pdf

Chandler, R. (2007). *Game writing handbook*. Boston, MA: Charles River Media.

Chatman, S. (1980). *Story and discourse*. Ithaca, NY: Cornell University Press.

Chatman, S. (1980). *Story and discourse*. Ithaca, NY: Cornell University Press.

Crawford, C. (2005). *Chris Crawford on interactive storytelling*. Berkeley, CA: New Riders.

Culler, J. (1994). *Ferdinand de Saussure* [*Saussure*]. Helsinki: Tutkijaliitto.

Dickey, M. D. (2006). Game design narrative for learning: Appropriating adventure game design narrative devices and techniques for the design of interactive learning environments. *Educational Technology Research & Development, 54*(3), 245–263. Retrieved April 2, 2009, from http://www.springerlink.com/content/h3gn553h68002q47/fulltext.pdf

Egenfeldt-Nielsen, S. (2004). Understanding the educational potential of commercial computer games through activity and narratives. *Game Research*. Retrieved September 2, 2008, from http://game-research.com/index.php/articles/understanding-the-educational-potential-of-commercial-computer-games-through-activity-and-narratives/

Eskelinen, M. (2001). The gaming situation. *Game Studies—The International Journal of Game Studies, 1*(1). Retrieved March 26, 2009, from http://www.gamestudies.org/0101/eskelinen/

Eskelinen, M. (2009). *Travels in cybertextuality: The challenge of ergodic literature and ludology to literary theory.* Doctoral dissertation thesis, University of Jyväskylä, Jyväskylä, Finland.

Fludernik, M. (1996). *Towards a "natural" narratology*. London: Routledge.

Frasca, G. (2001) Ephemeral games: Is it barbaric to design videogames after Auschwitz? In M. Eskelinen & R. Koskimaa (Eds.), *Cybertext yearbook 2000* (pp. 172–182). Jyväskylä, Finland: University of Jyväskylä. Retrieved August 20, 2009, from http://cybertext.hum.jyu.fi

Gee, J. P. (2003). *What video games have to teach us about learning and literacy*. London, New York: Palgrave Macmillan.

Genette, G. (1980). *Narrative discourse. An essay in method.* Ithaca, NY: Cornell University Press.

Glassner, A. (2004). *Interactive storytelling: Techniques for 21st century fiction*. Natick, MA: A.K. Perers.

Herman, D. (2003). Stories as a toll for thinking. In Herman, D. (Ed.), *Narrative theory and the cognitive sciences*. Stanford, CA: CSLI Publications.

Herman, D. (2004). Toward a transmedial narratology. In Ryan, M.-L. (Ed.), *Narrative across media: The languages of storytelling* (pp. 47–75). Lincoln: University of Nebraska Press.

Iuppa, N., & Borst, T. (2007). *Story and simulations for serious games: Tales from the trenches*. Oxford, UK: Elsevier.

Kankaanranta, M., & Neittaanmäki, P. (Eds.). (2008). *Design and use of serious games*. Dordrecht: Springer.

Koskimaa, R. (2000). *Digital literature: From text to hypertext and beyond*. Jyväskylä, Finland: University of Jyväskylä.

Krawczyk, M., & Novak, J. (2006). *Game development essentials: Game story and character development.* Albany, NY: Thomson Delmar Learning.

Mandler, J. M. (1984). *Stories, scripts, and scenes: Aspects of schema theory.* Hillsdale, NJ: Lawrence Erlbaum Associates.

McCarthy, D., Curran, S., & Byron, S. (2005). *The complete guide to game development, art & design.* Cambridge, UK: Alastair Campbell.

Moulthrop, S. (2005). After the last generation: Rethinking scholarship in the days of serious play. *Proceedings of the 6th Digital Arts & Culture Conference.* Copenhagen: IT University of Copenhagen.

Nousiainen, T. (2008). *Children's involvement in the design of game-based learning environments. Jyväskylä Studies in Computing, 95.* Jyväskylä, Finland: University of Jyväskylä.

Pajitnov, A. (1984) *Tetris* [computer game]. Published by Spectrum HoloByte in 1986.

Polkinghorne, D. E. (1988). *Narrative knowing and human sciences.* Albany, NY: State University of New York Press.

Rimmon-Kenan, S. (1991). *Narrative fiction: Contemporary poetics.* London, New York: Routledge.

Rimmon-Kenan, S. (2006). Concepts of narrative. In M. Hyvärinen, A. Korhonen, & J. Mykkänen (Eds.), *The travelling concept of narrative: Studies across disciplines in the humanities and social sciences 1.* Helsinki: Helsinki Collegium for Advanced Studies. 10–19. Retrieved April 2, 2009, from http://www.helsinki.fi/collegium/e-series/volumes/volume_1/001_03_rimmon_kenan.pdf

Rodriguez, H. (2006). The playful and the serious: An approximation to Huizinga's *homo ludens. Game Studies—The International Journal of Game Studies, 6*(1). Retrieved August 20, 2009, from http://gamestudies.org/0601/articles/rodriges

Rollings, A., & Morris, D. (2003). *Game architecture and design.* Indianapolis, IN: New Riders.

Ryan, M.-L. (2003). Transmedial narratology and concepts of narrative. In *2nd International Colloquium on Narratology beyond Literary Criticism,* University of Hamburg, 20–22 November 2003. Retrieved April 2, 2009, from http://www.narport.uni-hamburg.de/index2.php?option=com_content&do_pdf=1&id=110

Ryan, M.-L. (2004). Introduction. In Ryan, M.-L. (Ed.), *Narrative across media: the languages of storytelling* (pp. 1–40). Lincoln, NE: University of Nebraska Press.

Ryan, M.-L. (Ed.). (2004). *Narrative across media: The languages of storytelling.* Lincoln, NE: University of Nebraska Press.

Ryan, M.-L. (2005a). Narrative. In Herman, D., Jahn, M., & Ryan, M.-L. (Eds.), *Routledge encyclopedia of narrative theory* (pp. 344–348). London, NY: Routledge.

Ryan, M.-L. (2005b). Media and narrative. In Herman, D., Jahn, M., & Ryan, M.-L. (Eds.), *Routledge encyclopedia of narrative theory* (pp. 288–292). London, NY: Routledge.

Saussure, F. d. (1983). *Course in general linguistics.* London: Duckworth.

Top texts for interdisciplinary studies of serious games

Vuorela, V. (2007). Pelintekijän käsikirja. [Game-Maker's Handbook.] Helsinki: BTJ Finland Oy.

"MUST-READS" FOR THIS TOPIC

Wardrip-Fruin, N., & Harrigan, P. (Eds.). (2004). *First person: New media as story, performance, and game. Cambridge, MA*. London, UK: The MIT Press.

Woods, S. (2004). Loading the dice: The challenge of serious videogames. *Game Studies—The International Journal of Game Studies, 4*(1). Retrieved August 20, 2009, from http://www.gamestudies.org/0401/woods/

TOP TEN TEXTS FOR INTERDISCIPLINARY STUDY OF SERIOUS GAMES

Abt, C. (2002[1970]). *Serious games*. Lanham, MD: University Press of America.

Arnseth, H. C. (2006). Learning to play or playing to learn—A critical account of the models of communication informing educational research on computer gameplay. *Game Studies—The International Journal of Game Studies, 6* (1). Retrieved August 20, 2009, from http://gamestudies.org/0601/articles/arnseth

Bogost, I. (2007) *Persuasive games: The expressive power of videogames*. Cambridge, MA, & London, England: The MIT Press.

Frasca, G. (2001) Ephemeral games: Is it barbaric to design videogames after Auschwitz? *In M. Eskelinen & R. Koskimaa (Eds.), Cybertext yearbook 2000* (pp. 172–182). Jyväskylä, Finland: University of Jyväskylä. Retrieved August 20, 2009, from http://cybertext.hum.jyu.fi

Gee, J. P. (2003). *What video games have to teach us about learning and literacy*. London & New York: Palgrave Macmillan.

Kankaanranta, M., & Neittaanmäki, P. (Eds.). *Design and use of serious games*. Dordrecht: Springer.

Moulthrop, S. (2005). After the last generation: Rethinking scholarship in the days of serious play. *Proceedings of the 6th Digital Arts & Culture Conference*. Copenhagen: IT University of Copenhagen.

Nousiainen, T. (2008). *Children's involvement in the design of game-based learning environments*. Jyväskylä Studies in Computing, No. 95. Jyväskylä, Finland: University of Jyväskylä.

Rodriguez, H. (2006). The playful and the serious: An approximation to Huizinga's homo ludens. *Game Studies—The International Journal of Game Studies, 6* (1). Retrieved August 20, 2009, from http://gamestudies.org/0601/articles/rodriges

Woods, S. (2004). Loading the dice: The challenge of serious videogames. *Game Studies—The International Journal of Game Studies, 4* (1). Retrieved August 20, 2009, from http://www.gamestudies.org/0401/woods/

ENDNOTE

1 The choice of concept is confusing, as in the context of narrative theories, Aristotle's use of mythos ("plot") is better-known.

Chapter 2
Rethinking Genre in Computer Games:
How Narrative Psychology Connects Game and Story

Jasmina Kallay
University College Dublin, Ireland

ABSTRACT

"Rethinking Genre in Computer Games" is an attempt to find a new way of categorising game genre. Instead of dividing gameplay and game story as two separate entities, and regarding them by different genre standards, what if there were a way of distinguishing shared psychological qualities of a game's narrative and gameplay components? If the gameplay and the game narrative can be seen to conform to the same psychological underpinnings (as in the same cognitive–emotional responses), then such a common denominator may open up this particular area of game studies to a new perspective on game genre. By analysing two games as case studies, the intention is to provide a widely applicable theoretical model for game analysis, with suggestions provided on possible future directions. The proposed model should challenge preexisting ideas on genre organisation and emphasise the value of employing psychology to better understand computer games.

INTRODUCTION

When it comes to computer game genre classifications, we are still forced to navigate a terminology jungle, having to simultaneously consider the game platform, the narrative, the game world milieu and, last but not least, the mode of gameplay. With multiple terms in each of these subcategories the norm, the plethora of descriptive words makes the taxonomy all but impenetrable. And yet a clear taxonomy system is important in order to make further progress in game studies, as well as enabling the new denizens of the gaming workforce—the "non-techie" screenwriters—access to the theoretical underpinnings of writing for games.

By way of making sense of the genre profusion and rendering it wieldy, it is prudent to first address one of the sources of this current genre state—the gameplay–story schism. While this debate has already begun losing steam in recent years with

DOI: 10.4018/978-1-61520-719-0.ch002

Copyright © 2010, IGI Global. Copying or distributing in print or electronic forms without written permission of IGI Global is prohibited.

the opposing camps more willing to bridge the theoretical gap, it nonetheless epitomises the fundamental split in the conception of a computer game. Is a game primarily about gameplay or story? Regardless of how one answers this question, it is beyond doubt that our understanding of game genre hinges on this problematic issue, which is why the most salient aspects of the gameplay–story debate will be discussed here, although without delving into an unnecessarily detailed charting of all the different views.

The aim of this chapter is to put forward a theory for genre classification that unites gameplay and story by applying narrative psychology and cognitive behavioural psychology to the gaming experience. The crucial question explored here concerns the psychological appeal and motivation in gaming—if the psychological impact of the narrative mirrors the psychological impact of the ludic aspect, then this could be a potential new model for a more integrated gaming genre system. Following on from the school of thought that stories have long served our psychological needs, narrative psychology allows us to probe the potentially psychotherapeutic role of gaming narratives. Concomitant with this exploration, cognitive behavioural psychology provides revealing insights vis-à-vis the gameplay, or rather the gamer's behavioural patterns. By bringing these two strains of psychology together in the analysis of games, we may be able to marry the narrative and gameplay aspects more cohesively as well as finding a new way of classifying game genre.

In addressing this question, I will refer to Bruno Bettelheim and Clarissa Pinkola Estés' analyses of myths, folk tales, and fairy tales as guidelines to dealing with stages of psychological development. I will also delve into the writings of narrative psychologists Paul Ricœur and Jerome Bruner. George Kelly's cognitive behavioural model of fixed-role therapy will complete the psychological theoretical framework of this chapter.

To support the proposed ideas, two games will be used as case studies to demonstrate the validity of the new theoretical model: *Bully* (Rockstar, 2006) and *American McGee's Alice* (Rogue Entertainment, 2000). Apart from the fact that both games feature strong narratives, there are two reasons for selecting these particular games. Firstly, both share a similar narrative and gameplay type: within the wider coming-of-age narrative context, the games foster a gameplay attitude that I have termed as "rebel." By exploring and comparing the story and gameplay through the psychological theories mentioned above, I endeavour to see whether the rebel category holds up as an actual genre tag. Choosing two rather than one game of a specific type is intended to show whether the methods and terms can be applied more widely. Additionally, *American McGee's Alice* provides a female point of view, thus presenting an interesting variation. The second reason relates to *Bully* rather than *Alice* and has to do with the media furore the game sparked because of its controversial subject matter of bullying. While the case study will neither defend nor denigrate the game based on its treatment of bullying or violence, the topic of bullying, especially when presented in a relatively realistic environment (as opposed to a more fictionally removed fantasy landscape) offers intriguing and rich material for psychological study. It has to be also noted that while these games do not qualify as serious games, what emerges as a potential developmental and psychological tool from the analysis of these games places them within the nonentertainment clause of serious gaming.

Following the analytical appraisals of the two games, I will conclude by suggesting ways of applying the new genre theoretical model to other game categories, with a view of ushering in a more creative way of thinking about game classification. The emotional–cognitive ideas explored in the chapter will challenge the assumptions that certain dramatic forms are not suited to gaming (i.e., tragedy).

GENRE AND THE LUDOLOGY-NARRATOLOGY ARGUMENT

A cursory glance at any gaming site, such as *GameSpot,* reveals a veritable genre profusion. One single game may straddle as many as six or seven categories, or the reverse situation sees games as different as *The Legend of Zelda, Max Payne, Grand Theft Auto,* and *Bully* all grouped under the same heading of 3rd-person action adventure. There have been attempts at game genre lists that exclude the platform and gameplay mode, but this simplification can still result in an overwhelming 42 categories (Wolf, 2002) that are, ironically, too limited in their reductive broad organisation. Even when gaming Web sites and associations stick to a certain "palette" of terms, there can be "little indication of what criteria are used to place a given title in a given genre" (Smith, 2006, p. 48). Part of this confusing plethora of classifications stems from the marketing drive to cover all bases, but part of it comes down to the still adolescent-aged territory of game theory, which has either gotten stuck in debates such as the ludology vs. narratology series of academic repartees[1] or has been hijacked by theorists from other fields, sometimes pejoratively labelled as "academic refugees," who are keen to transpose the terminology from their fields onto game studies (film and literature genre categories being a case in point).

If we look at genre in a wider context, the plurality of terms used and the hybrid nature of games are actually in keeping with the postmodernist view of genre. One of the defining characteristics of the postmodern, according to Ihab Hassan (1992), is "hybridisation, or the mutant replication of genres" which ultimately leads to the "deformation of cultural genres" (pp.196–197). Hassan (1992) goes on to state that "traditionally, genre assumed recognizable features within a context of both persistence and change; it was a useful assumption of identity ...(b)ut that assumption... seems ever harder to maintain. Even genre theorists invite us, nowadays, to go beyond genre..." (pp. 196–197). So this call to go beyond genre—does it mean inventing new generic coordinates, or giving up altogether on attempting to classify? The destructuralist Derrida calls for "undoing genre" (in Hassan, 1992, p. 200). In that case, is perhaps the most prudent course of action to continue to analyse game narrative and gameplay and suggest different approaches but without attempting to impose a prescriptive set of categories?

In gaming genre, we currently have, on the one hand, the importing of film and literary genres, manifest in categories such as action, adventure, or fantasy, coexisting simultaneously with gameplay, deriving from agency types (strategy, 1st-person shooter). Lee Sheldon (2004) settles for a similarly dualistic distinction between game genre (as in the classification inherited from film and literature) and game type (i.e., action, adventure, role-playing, simulation, etc.), except that in his conception of genre and type, he runs into contradictory usage of terminology: apart from the imprecise quality of the word "type" in this context, the terms "action" and "adventure" are narrative rather than ludic categories and should not be equated with gameplay categories such as role-playing or multiplayer. Even if the categories stopped at this binary level, the symbiosis is an uneasy one. For instance, Jenkins (2004) is quick to recognise how a game's spatial characteristics won't necessarily conform to the film genre ascribed to it. A film noir triggers expectations of shadowy, nocturnal urban scenes, and a Western denotes the arid desert traversed by the lone hero. A game might feature these visuals, but the story type might differ from the cinematic narrative that would normally accompany the "look," which is why milieu, or the setting, gains its own category, distinct from both the narrative and gameplay genre. According to King and Krzywinska (2002), a comprehensive game classification system comprises four dimensions: platform, genre, milieu, mode. And by genre, they mean the narrative/film genre category such as horror or action–adventure.

According to King and Krzywinska's four-partite organisation, a game like *BioShock* (2K Games, 2008) can be described as PC and Xbox, survival horror, sci-fi mystery, dystopian Atlantis-type world, third-person shooter, or role-playing. From this long list of game characteristics, it's clear that the complexity of game classification goes even beyond the gameplay–story division.[2] And so, when genre classification consists of a Web of overlapping as well as disparate terms, as is the case with games, then how can we build a system that will reconcile the genre disparities and remain organic to the field? Before the search for a potential new genre paradigm can begin, the ludology-narratology debate needs to be briefly touched upon, in order to explain the tension between two concepts that still don't coexist in a theoretically reconciled relationship—gameplay and story.

Gameplay vs. Story

The ludology–narratology argument in game studies began as a crude opposition: on the one hand, the ludologists declared that the main point of a game was gameplay, with narrative as an arbitrary addition, whereas the narratologists claimed story's supremacy as being the main draw to play. This was, to an extent, an artificially created yet nonetheless impacting division between the advocates of the superiority of the gaming experience and the proponents of the story's importance. It is also, in some respects, an unfortunate by-product of the academic system. A new field of studies is, to some, ripe territory for plunder, and as such needs defending by the pioneers who have brought it into being. Espen Aarseth (2004), the prominent ludologist (even though he has personally never proclaimed himself as such; his theories have led others to place him in that camp), calls it the "land rush" (p. 45). This metaphoric staking of new terrain sees academics from other fields approaching game studies as a way of providing them with new comparative study material with which to make their names. The other facet of the academic system that has, in part, allowed for this type of schism is the issue of funding. If the interdisciplinary scholars had their way, the ludologists would have had slimmer chances at establishing Game Studies as a department in its own right that isn't to be confused with Cultural Studies or Digital Media Studies (Jones, 2008). Viewed from this angle, it's easier to comprehend why ludologists have felt so fiercely protective of their "creation," so to speak, and have refuted attempts at attributing a greater role to narrative.

From the stark antagonism of the initial debates, there have been rapprochements. For instance, applying the most literal interpretation of narrative, the cutscene seems to be the one area where ludologists concede ground to the narratologists—it is the most cinematic component of a game, providing either backstory or narrative motivation for the subsequent level, and it is (in most cases) devoid of interactivity. Following on the back of the cutscene, the game as a postgaming narrated experience appears to be the other concession (Juul, 2001), although this is a somewhat hypothetical aspect, as the gamers' verbalising of their gaming experience may or may not take place. However, this aspect will be expanded upon later on, as it is concordant with the narrative psychologist's view of life being interpreted in a narrative context (McLeod, 1997).

Any more comprehensive attempts at attributing greater meaning to the story's relevance within a game meet with objections from the ludology camp. "Story fetishism" is the accusation Espen Aarseth (2004) levels at all the attempts to apply narratology to the "gaming situation" (Eskelinen, 2001), and some of his concerns are valid. For instance, the commercial drive to endow games with more marketable appeal might have contributed to the emphasis on story: "games need narratives to become better products" (Aarseth, 2004, p. 49). Stories have universal appeal; therefore, games can only benefit from relying more heavily on narrative. Aarseth's claim of academic colonialism is a reasonable concern, but where he loses ground is in his assertion that games are self-contained and neither textual nor intertextual. To bolster this statement, Aarseth (2004) suggests that one doesn't need to know anything about the snakes and ladders board game in order to play chess, and that chess itself can be played with any arbitrary pieces. Furthermore, a piece of text within the game doesn't make the game itself a text. However, if one looks at a game like *American McGee's Alice*, the intertextuality immediately becomes apparent. Alice is based on Lewis Carroll's *Alice in Wonderland* series of children's books and operates by purposely twisting the familiar narrative elements. If we take Jenkins' (2006) transmedia storytelling theory as an indicator of the direction forward, whereby the cross-pollination of entertainment media content across different platforms and formats will mean no entertainment product will be a stand-alone entity, the intertextuality factor is only going to increase. When defining what makes a game, Aarseth (2004) isolates three essential aspects: rules, game world (material/semiotic system), and gameplay. Of these three, the game world is "the most coincidental" (Aarseth, 2004, p. 48). But surely the lure of the game world, the narrative that explains its existence and its characters' roles within it, is what mainly attracts the gamer in the first instance? It is to this aspect of games, the game world, that Henry Jenkins (2004) brings a compelling construct, that of "narrative architecture" (p. 121). By striving towards a middle-ground position in the gameplay–story conflict, Jenkins (2004) proposes to look at games "less as stories than as spaces ripe with narrative possibility" (p. 119). The game's navigable environment becomes the narrative site, its objects, artefacts, and spaces carrying narrative "affordances."

Naturally, not all games have a narrative underpinning, and it is counterproductive to attempt to reveal narrative meaning in games such as *Tetris*, as Murray (1997) does, reading into the simple block-building a metaphor for overcoming and managing our over-stressed, pressurised modern lives. But even excluding such explicitly nonnarrative games, the crux of many a gameplay–story discussion involving the narrative-oriented games—"are games narratives"—feels too simplistic and precludes from anything other than a yes/no answer. A more useful definition could read: games are narrative experiences being played into existence. Jenkins (2004) points out that the gameplay–story debate misses the point by focussing on whether or not a game tells a story and thereby omits to take a closer look at the narrative elements at a more localized level, or so-called "micronarratives" (p. 125). Jenkins' reading of the possibilities of spatial storytelling not only provides an interesting way to link gameplay and narrative, but the micronarrative approach of reading games also proves useful when applying psychology to games. When juxtaposed with narrative psychology, the isolated actions of the micronarrative (which can be anything from a game level to a sublevel scene) allow for a much more in-depth analysis of the common factors in narrative and the gameplay, as will be demonstrated in the case studies. These smaller game increments reveal the always unique (or transformative, as Murray describes it) experience that happens between the gamer and the game through interaction, the result of which could be termed a "macronarrative." The macronarrative is the story created by the gamer based on his gameplay, but it is also based on his perception of the game's fictional universe/story/gameplay, which is where narrative psychology comes in.

Applying Psychology to Game Narrative and Gameplay

If we observe the paths games and psychology have crossed thus far, the most interesting development in the last number of years has been the scattered acknowledgment from different game theorists that psychology has been an underused tool in gaining deeper understanding of games and needs to be engaged more profoundly (Järvinen, 2009; Klug & Schell, 2006). Overall, the most common psychological studies of games have been oriented toward gamer behaviour and attitude, quite frequently with a negative slant, emphasising the violent nature of games and questioning their merit (Walkerdine, 1997), especially in relation to children. Social interactions (especially in the context of massive multiplayer online role-playing games) and the psychological impact of such activities, while receiving wider academic coverage, are not within the scope of this chapter. Among the less biased psychological readings, we have identification of gamer types, slotted by personality factors: aggressive, competitive, challenging, fantasist/escapist (Hartman & Klimmt, 2006). This is a very broad categorisation that ultimately doesn't prove very revealing, staying on the perimeters of analysis. For instance, an aggressive gamer plays to vent aggression, but then does this mean any game with violent aspects will satisfy them? Or someone seeking escapism: will any fantasy world do? There needs to be more fine tuning in establishing what draws a gamer to a game.

Similarly, motivational categories can be seen to be equally lacking in the kind of complexity that is necessary: motivation classifications such as competition, living vicariously (through avatar), conducting electronically "safe" relationships, or being in control of the game world (Klug & Schell, 2006) are just as vague and don't facilitate more probing questioning. Järvinen (2009) proposes a more innovative approach through his emotional experience categorisation: prospect-based emotions, fortunes-of-others emotions, attribution emotions, attraction emotions, and well-being emotions (as well as a subcategory covering variables affecting intensity of emotions, which spans any modalities not included in the main categories). This accent on emotions is a clear step forward from the basic assumption that games primarily entice gamers for their competitive or challenging qualities. Emotions are also a category that is recognised by narrative psychology as eliciting self-narrative constructs, whereby a person creates a story around a certain emotion so that either the pleasant or negative effect of the emotion can be incorporated into the larger life narrative (Bruner, 1990; McLeod, 1997). Thus far, neither narrative psychology nor cognitive behaviouralism have made inroads in relation to game studies, and it is the author's hope that this chapter proves persuasive in eliciting more study in these areas. At the same time, one caveat needs mentioning: other schools of thought in psychology might prove equally fruitful; there is no attempt here to suggest that narrative psychology or cognitive behavioural psychology are the only or even the best two psychology directions to pursue when it comes to gaming.

The most promising contribution in discovering the potential for psychological change in games was made by Janet Murray (1997). She identifies the power of transformation alongside agency and immersion as one of the three components of interactivity. The term has a three-fold meaning: it can mean transformation as variation (in the sense that no interactive text repeats itself verbatim), transformation as role-playing (taking on an avatar's identity) and, most relevantly, transformation as a tool for psychological change. If a gamer assumes an avatar's identity and plays "as if" they are in the game world under a new persona, then the gamer's behaviour will reflect these new circumstances and will differ from his or her real-life persona. Murray doesn't elaborate further on this aspect, but what we can ascertain is that this behaviour shift is precisely the assumption upon which George Kelly built his theory of cognitive behaviourism and fixed-role therapy (Fransella, 1995). By getting patients to behave as if they were something other than their usual self (i.e., extroverted instead of introverted), playing a new role, new behavioural patterns emerged, and these could be used to break the emotional or psychological blockage that the patients suffered (Fransella, 1995). Naturally, a personality experiment conducted in real life carries more weight than a similar personality change in a virtual world. However, these findings in cognitive behavioural psychology clearly point to the still underexplored area of psychological study of the gaming experience.

The significant link in the cognitive behavioural psychology and gaming is agency. A cognitive behaviouralist will not recommend that the patient change his or her behaviour based on reading or watching films that feature the desired new behavioural pattern; it can only be through active engagement that real psychological change can occur. So, from this premise, it follows that a game, by engaging the gamer actively through agency, has a greater transformative power than noninteractive media and, therefore, more potential to be harnessed in this vein. As the case studies will show, the game guides the gamer to actively participate in certain psychological behavioural patterns as well as to sublimate psycho-emotional states. The aim here is to discern whether a game's narrative and gameplay psychological dimensions fall under the same category, which would point to a new way of identifying genre.

If we now take a look at storytelling in isolation from gameplay, we can already discern clear psychological foundations to the way stories are built. From Aristotle's *Poetics*, which explains dramatic techniques in a psycho-emotional context, to Jung's view of the collective unconscious as spawning narratives that are the same in their essence right across centuries and continents, because of our shared set of fears and concerns, the art of storytelling has played a psychological role in every culture. We need stories to better understand the world. Through stories, we can exorcise existential, social, and cultural anxieties and deal with reality. The cathartic moment of Greek tragedy, after all, is not just the release of the emotional buildup of the story but the accompanying release of all of the other emotions from daily life: the purging of stress and sadness in order to invigorate one's mind and spirit. In this light, stories come very close to fulfilling the role of psychotherapy.

The preexistent narratives that games have most predominantly turned to have been adventure tales (Atkins, 2003), and the simplistic rendition of the adventure story (which in itself doesn't rank highly in the literary canon), has contributed to the underestimation of the game's narrative value. Yet to dismiss the quest story as rudimentary and clichéd and a mere device to get the game going is to ignore the enduring power of this category of tale. Joseph Campbell's seminal *The Hero With a Thousand Faces* (1993) has shone light on the psychological significance of each step undertaken by the hero along the "monomyth." His findings were based on Jung's link between myths and their fulfillment of psychological needs as well as serving as teaching tools in life (Campbell, 1993). The monomyth has since become appropriated by Hollywood through the adapted version of it by Christopher Vogler (*The Writer's Journey*, 1999) that has influenced metaphoric interpretations of this formula by screenwriters writing in a variety of genres, demonstrating the versatility and universality of the dramatic formula. The dissection of the narrative arc of the overall hero's goal into its smaller increments (the stages of the hero's journey) and Campbell's (1993) explanations of the purpose of these smaller portions are actually not that far removed from Jenkins' micronarrative approach.

Apart from the obvious correlative between Campbell's monomyth and gaming narratives, a direct psychological application of the monomyth can also be found in gameplay, namely in Juul's (2009) assessment of failing and the gamer's almost ambivalent relationship with failing. On the one hand, to not be able to win is deeply frustrating, but to win too easily is just as unsatisfying. The perfect balance is achieved when the gamer is able to win but not without considerable difficulty (even including reconsidering strategy after a few initial fails) (Juul, 2009). This finding ties in with the adventure hero's need to come face to face with several difficult situations in order to fully mature, grow, and deserve the ultimate reward. Without the struggle, there is no psychological learning and no satisfaction. This mantra, as evidenced in myths and folk tales, is as psychologically valid for gaming as it is for narrative.

Pinkola Estés (1992) uses a similar method to Campbell in breaking down folk tales along their psychological fault lines and discerning their subtextual psychological meaning. Her focus remains on tales with female protagonists, so her analysis brings a valuable new dimension to the male-centric studies of myths, fairy tales, and folk tales. Estés (1992) also brings a microscopic eye to the smallest of actions within the stories, finding deeper significance to what might seem, at first glance, a mundane act (i.e., the act of washing linen), yet is revealed to be a potent symbol (i.e., for cleansing or starting afresh). Bettelheim (1991) also dismantles folk and fairy tales to reveal their psychological import, although he turns his attention on children and their psychological relation to stories. Despite this emphasis on children, his findings have wider psychological implications and can equally be applied to adults (especially adults who have scars dating back to their childhood). What makes Bettelheim's (1991) study especially relevant to gaming is his groundbreaking defence of the violent and dark elements in children's stories, arguing that such ingredients are vital in both introducing the reality of the world in a controlled manner as well as offering insight that destructive feelings and thoughts are normal and should not be repressed. It's the self-doubt and self-disgust, stemming from being taught that negative thoughts are bad, which lead to psychological imbalances. In view of this, games that allow for violent expression can be seen as allowing the gamer to relieve him- or herself of negative thoughts and feelings, revealing a cathartic function. Bettelheim's work also suggests that psychology can go a long way in dispersing the negative perception of games.

To further bolster the narrative and psychological links in gaming, let's invert the way of looking at their relationship. So far, we have noted how narrative serves an important psychological function. However, in a reversal of the above-outlined correlative between storytelling and psychology, the point that narrative psychology makes is that we all create stories out of everyday moments in order to process them and incorporate them into the greater narrative that is each person's life story (Bruner, 2004). This tendency to narrativise even situations that don't, at first glance, demonstrate what we might consider classical narrative structure, becomes highly significant when transposed to a gaming scenario. Following the same logic, an encounter with an enemy, or a conversation with an NPC, while not a narrative in its "texton" form (meaning as the "text" is written/devised), may become narrativised in the "scripton" form (meaning as the "text" is read/interpreted) through the gamer's experience of it (Aarseth, 1997). This relates to the macronarrative concept: the story, or rather narrative experience, is the unique result of the gamer interacting with the game. Such an individualised experience of a text inevitably calls to mind reader-response criticism, albeit in a more literal rendering than the concept ever allowed in literary theory. Apart from the genuine interaction taking place, there is also the tangible traces left by each unique gameplay session compared to the amorphous individualised interpretation of a literary text.

As was previously mentioned, further proof for this narrativising of game content during play can be gleaned from the postgame narrativised discussion of the game (Juul, 2001), which points to the absorption of the gaming moments as a narrativised construct. To briefly sum up: if a person builds stories around everyday events (in order to better process them) and if a gamer describes the game they've played in narrative form, then from these two premises it follows that the gameplay moments themselves, in the time frame of the game, can be experienced within a narrative context. Moreover, if we apply narrative psychology to the gaming experience and recognise that each level and each challenge may be understood by the gamer in a more narrativised context than its texton form suggests, then we can see the value of analysing the micronarrative at the expense of the overarching storyline. What has to be remembered, though, is that these micronarratives do not necessarily conform to traditional narrative structures and rules. They may not abide by a tightly plotted structure, but there are sufficient narrative elements both at the texton and scripton level to distinguish these segments as micronarratives/macronarratives and not just ludic segments.

Juxtaposing narrative and gameplay and viewing the results through a psychological lens establishes the greater value of the micronarrative for both narrative and gameplay purposes. The overarching storyline and gameplay description of any game, when summarised in a sentence or two, would yield little in terms of narrative or ludic complexity and potential and would indicate none of the psychological impact. Yet by taking the focus away from the overarching structure of the story and isolating the smaller game increments, both the narrative and the gameplay of these segments become more revelatory of the psychological processes they relay and prompt.

CASE STUDIES

Before proceeding on to the case studies, I want to briefly explain my approach to the analysis of the two games with regard to the psychological theories introduced in the chapter. The questions I have posed while observing the games are:

- Does the game narrative reveal psychological meaning?
- Does the gameplay prompt the gamer into psychologically revealing behavioural patterns?

These two questions, naturally, open up an array of further probes, however, by premising the analysis with these simple queries, we have a quick and efficient way of recognising whether a game can be analysed in this manner. Once the narrative psychology and cognitive behavioural questions have been answered, the next task is to see whether the findings correlate—is there a mirroring; are there significant parallels? If there is a clear common denominator, this result could be tentatively regarded as a new genre category.

Bettelheim's work is key to the case studies, mainly because he argued for re-interpretation of texts that were seen as violent (he was arguing against the cleaned-up version of the original Brothers Grimm tales) as instead serving important moral and psychological needs. It therefore follows that one of the easier ways to see how this applies to games is to select those games that contain violent themes and which might otherwise be rejected outright (as the original Grimm fairy tales were) and attempt a similar reinterpretation of these games from a psychological perspective. By selecting two games that each feature a male and female protagonist, I hope to establish cross-gender applicability.

Case Study: *Bully*

Even before *Bully* hit the retail shelves, it had garnered a great deal of negative media attention, with various parents' associations calling for it to be banned, based on the title and a few game stills released in advance. The topic alone—bullying—is such a highly sensitive social issue that one would imagine a game tackling this subject head on would be a welcome development for airing all of the problems associated with school bullying. In the politically correct climate of the West, with liberal democracies defining social norms, the idea of resolving bullying behaviour through counterbullying, as in by employing violence, is anathema. Social workers and counselling are the methods applied, but they often prove ineffectual and the adults appear to the children as though they're failing them. Yet the game proved popular, and if we take into account that the gamers were not just school kids (which is the age of *Bully's* avatar/characters) but young adults as well, this could be read as a sign that the game answered a deeper need to vent repressed actions and emotions that were deemed as taboo and unacceptable in the person's childhood/youth. In this sense, the game can be seen as a revisiting and reenactment of a developmental teenage coming-of-age stage that has left some trauma. More specifically, in both the storyline and the gameplay, *Bully* addresses the teen rebellion phase of going against adults and the establishment, with the gaming experience sublimating such emotions.

For this reason, the term I propose to describe this gaming–narrative experience is "rebel" game. By allowing the acting out of the rebellious behavioural patterns and recreating a relatively realistic narrative landscape, the game provides a safe arena to exorcise the suppressed negative, violent impulses. Bettelheim (1991) warns that unless the scars of any suppressed stages in a person's life are addressed, there will inevitably be severe consequences on the person's adult behaviour. In this respect, Bettelheim's theories discussed here, while primarily explaining children's/teens' responses, bear relevance to all adults whose growing up was marred in some respect. Equally, Bettelheim's remarks may be based on fairy tales, but it could be argued that the ideas still apply in a game context with older gamers. Fairy tales are intended for children who are not consciously aware of the narrative and psychological mechanics involved and absorb the material at a more subconscious level. But if we look at gaming, the full attention of the gamer is never on the story, it is split between narrative developments and the gameplay, meaning that there is less of a conscious preoccupation with how the story may be influencing the gameplay at a deeper psychological level.

To begin the game analysis, I will first look at the game narrative in search of psychologically significant elements, after which the gamer's prompted actions will be examined for psycho-emotional clues.

The game follows Jimmy Hopkins (the gamer's only choice of avatar), freshly enrolled at the aptly named Bullworth Academy boarding school. All the backstory we need to know about him is that his mother has just married for the fifth time and has offloaded him while en route to her yearlong honeymoon. This detail places us straight away in the fairy-tale sphere of abandoned/orphaned children, with the first anti-adult seed sown. As soon as Jimmy arrives on campus, he is the target of the Bullies clique, and he fights back. In this respect, Jimmy can be seen as a reluctant hero of the Campbellian mould. He has set off on an adventure into a new, unknown world against his will, to begin with (he has no other options), but as the challenges mount, he is able to overcome them by facing them head on. The set of missions slowly builds to a positivism, as they prove Jimmy is capable of surviving what is a tough year at Bullworth. Bettelheim (1991) has this to say on the subject: "a struggle against severe difficulties in life is unavoidable … but if one does not shy away, but steadfastly meets unexpected and often unjust hardships, one masters all obstacles and at the end emerges victorious" (p. 120). This positive assessment of overcoming obstacles and its benefit in character building tallies with Campbell's monomyth—hardship is to be embraced for its ultimate psychological reward. In terms of relating to the avatar, Jimmy falls into that perennial character prototype—the outsider. This chimes strongly with the teen emotional mindset but is also an easily relatable role for any age.

Jimmy's fighting back against the Bullies is what caused controversy. However, if this game had been set in a mythical, fantasy world, and the protagonist were a young, brave hero attacked by "bullying" orcs, goblins, or aliens, his retaliation would be seen as normal and expected, and would not have elicited any commentary. This same double standard is also evident in action films; Barry Atkins (2003) provides a perfect example: "The 'realistic' violence of the opening Normandy landing sequence of the film *Saving Private Ryan* (1998) was critically praised: the "'realism' of first-person shooting games is often subject to condemnation and potential censorship" (p. 22). So what this tells us is that violence is accepted at a comforting fictional remove,or within a certain genre and medium, but not when tackling a very real and thorny issue through the medium of computer games in a more realistic setting.

By placing the narrative in a realistic school and not in a fantastical realm, the darker undercurrents of human nature—the cruelty, power games, selfishness, betrayal—confront the gamer with greater immediacy. As Bettelheim (1991) explains:

There is a widespread refusal to let children know that the source of much that goes wrong in life is due to our very own natures—the propensity of all men for acting aggressively, asocially, selfishly, out of anger and anxiety. Instead, we want our children to believe that, inherently, all men are good. But children know that they are not always good; and often, even when they are, they would prefer not to be. This contradicts what they are told by their parents, and therefore makes the child a monster in his own eyes. (p. 7)

If such states are denied or repressed in a youth, then that person will be ill-equipped to deal with reality and will develop a habit of laying blame on others. Essentially, by exposing the dark side of human behaviour as inherent to all of us, the game propagates a positive message that we shouldn't look elsewhere for scapegoats but should take full responsibility for our actions.

However, if we dig deeper, a greater taboo lies at the heart of the game. The real taboo isn't Jimmy fighting back against the Bullies clique; if observed closely, the game isn't constructed as a series of gratuitous bullying tactics. Rather, the mission for Jimmy is winning the respect of all the cliques (Jocks, Preppies, Nerds, Greasers, and Townies). So the real taboo lies in Jimmy's relationship with the adults of the game and their negative portrayal.

From the outset, it's clear that all the adult characters in the game, with the exception of the sexy art teacher Ms. Phillips, are seen in a pejorative light, whether as sleazy pervs sniffing pupils' underwear, as alcoholics, as teachers who sell test papers to students or as workers who spit into the cafeteria food. Add to that the less than nurturing mother figure (Ms. Phillips), and you have an environment in which a young gamer can vent his or her frustrations with the adult world. This is where the source of the taboo lies, as Bettelheim (1991) demonstrated—in the unacceptability of children/youths exhibiting destructive behaviour and hatred towards adults/parents. What's important to note here is that this enjoyment of a gaming world in which adults are so maligned is not something that is limited to a child or adolescent—this enjoyment is equally applicable to adults harbouring unresolved issues with authority figures that can occur at any time in one's life.

A child's psychological issues are not just limited to his or her parents; they can stretch to adulthood in general, and Bettelheim (1991) warns us that "all children are jealous, if not of their parents, then of the privileges the parents enjoy as adults" (p. 204). Children frequently feel "unjustly treated by adults and the world in general, and it seems that nothing is done about it" (Bettelheim, 1991, p. 141). So, as a consequence, the child who has been treated unjustly wishes to see those who have mistreated him punished—severely. If and when they are not punished, "the child thinks that nobody is serious about protecting him" (Bettelheim, 1991, p. 141). So here is where fantasy and fiction take their cue by allowing the child to fantasise, without feeling guilt, of great vengeance. Bettelheim (1991) warns: "children, not having their ids in conscious control, need stories which permit at least fantasy satisfaction of these 'bad' tendencies, and specific models of their sublimation" (p. 52). A game like *Bully* can become such a model of sublimation for a bullied child when the adult world fails him in his attempt to resolve his problem. This means the gamer's pent-up anger and frustration can find a harmless, guilt-free, yet constructive release.

Given this insight, we can view all the hopeless and inadequate adults at Bullworth as firstly allowing the gamer to feel free to view figures of authority as hypocritical. Moreover, these are figures that are allowed to be hated; there is valid reason to withhold respect without feeling guilty. This allows for sublimation. It also frees up Jimmy to behave with adult impunity, without having to account to any adult. As the game gets going, Jimmy will eventually be in the position to help the alcoholic Galloway and his girlfriend, Ms Phillips, so even the adults in this world need help from the pupils. This reversal of roles translates into behaving "as if" you have the perceived perks of adult freedom, removing the envy aspect. For a short while you can forget that you are powerless, which leads to a feeling of empowerment.

One example of empowerment that is also especially relevant to Campbell's steps in the hero's quest is the case of the Korean hobo. Here we have an instance reminiscent of the fairy-tale dragon lair, in which the hero is warned of false guises and cautioned to not be fooled by appearances. But before the hero can learn this lesson, he has to first confront the ferocious dragon and enter the lair, which in this case happens to be the scary Korean hobo. Firstly, Jimmy is keen to pelt the hobo with eggs and generally insult him, but when the hobo frightens off his cohorts, Jimmy stands his ground, showing courage. This is rewarded by the Korean revealing he has valuable lessons to impart to young Jimmy, as long as Jimmy brings him any transistor he comes across. Through this exchange, Jimmy learns fighting skills and has, on one level, symbolically learnt that what he initially perceived as a type of monster can become an ally. This incident matches with the way the alcoholic Galloway is revealed to have become a drunk because of his disillusionment with the system (adult world) when he witnessed the head teacher selling tests to the pupils. This reveal makes him a good guy, and Jimmy helps get him out of the sinister rehab facility. What is of note about the rehab facility is that while it *is* a bad place, this does not mean the game is implying seeking treatment for alcoholism is bad or that players will automatically transfer such beliefs to the real world. This might seem like a digressive comment, but in actual fact, it relates to one of the key issues in interpreting stories and games, which is the misperception that the surface details will automatically lead to concrete judgments and knowledge about their counterparts in the real world. Bettelheim points out that the violence employed in the story/game is not taken literally by the child nor applied as a solution strategy in the real world. This is because the context of the world, characters, and stories creates its own unique space that is recognized by the child as "not the real world."

In psychological terms, these two instances move away from the initial sublimating of the anger and hatred felt towards adults/authority and pave a way to seeing that things can be very different than initially perceived—some adults can, after all, be trusted. The complexity revealed through this shift in perspective demonstrates how the game provides the gamer with sublimation and venting tools but doesn't leave it at that—following this stage, there is the restorative part of the game arc, whereby the anger, frustration, and disappointment are mended and transformed into positive emotions.

The gamer's progress, via Jimmy, can be interpreted by using Erikson's model of the human life cycle, according to which "the ideal human being develops through … 'phase-specific psychosocial crises'" (Bettelheim, 1991, p. 275), which are basic trust, autonomy, initiative, industry, and identity. This cycle is particularly pertinent to the coming-of-age stage in life, but in a more condensed form, it is also manifest when encountering crises throughout adult life. The bond of basic trust with the most important adults in a child's life is broken right from the outset: Jimmy has been let down by his parents, and the adults at Bullworth don't do anything to restore this lost trust in adults (things change towards the end, which will be discussed below). With no one to trust, Jimmy has to carve his path on his own and show autonomy. His independence is foisted on him whether he wants it or not, and the newfound autonomy is a frightening, uncharted territory. Jimmy's enforced autonomy ripples through to the gamer, as there is, as of yet, no mentor figure and no significant, helpful nonplayer character (NPC). Campbell's formula usually introduces some form of mentor, helper, or trickster early on to assuage the anxiety caused by this thrust-upon autonomy, but here the self-reliance is geared to increase the gamer's involvement in the game.

In terms of Jimmy's characterisation and arc, the narrative understandably caters to missions through which Jimmy gains in experience, money, and weapons (but note, this is no Columbine scenario; there are no real weapons, simply the boyish slingshot, spud gun, etc.). However, the main goal for Jimmy is to earn all of the cliques' respect and to survive the year at school. Although Jimmy never fully aligns himself with any one clique, which continues the autonomous/outsider strand, the game is structured in such a way as to psychologically place the gamer into wanting and preferring social acceptance rather than staying on the social fringes and shying away from social contact, which is a positive measure.

While the first two crises form the very opening segment of the game, it is initiative that manifests throughout most of the game, with the gamer having to demonstrate it aplenty on the missions. To successfully progress through the game, industry accompanies initiative hand in hand. Both in terms of class attendance and odd jobs, the gamer is encouraged by the game to be industrious (i.e., cleaning snow, doing homework, etc.). In a way, the opposite of industry would result in several options being blocked to proceed with gameplay, so that's not a viable alternative. While accomplishing missions is mostly done by fighting, it has to be pointed out that all sides are willing to fight. There are also times when apologies work or mischievous pranks do the trick, in much the same vein as Dennis the Menace or Beryl the Peril. Frequently, as Jimmy's skills and power grow, he is asked to protect the weaker groups against the more intimidating cliques, which is a huge step toward creating a strong identity if we compare that to the initial start-off point of being the bullied new kid on the block. Apart from the testosterone-fuelled fights or spud gun attacks, there is nothing in the game encouraging you to indulge in antisocial behaviour such as skipping classes (in fact, attendance is a boon and will unlock various useful tools) and in addition, you're given a chance to earn money by doing chores. In brief, positive rather than destructive behaviour is promoted.

Identity is the real goal of the game, albeit the unspoken one. And Jimmy gains his own identity by the end by fighting first for his own survival, then on behalf of those weaker than him, as well as some of the adults on campus. He gains respect and self-worth. So this brief outline of the Erikson model demonstrates how the gamer can, on a certain level, be working through a psychological developmental process. The phases have a literal manifestation in the game but can be metaphorically interpreted as overcoming situations that have parallels in the real world.

This analysis of *Bully* shows that the game is built around psychologically logical constructs, allowing the gamer to behave "as if" he or she is in a rebel phase and enabling him or her to sublimate hate and anger for parents/adults/authority figures. The game's positive input is revealed in its viewpoint shift of some of the adults as well as granting release from the frustrating situation by allowing the gamer, through his or her efforts, to feel like he or she has come out of the rebel phase, overcome all the obstacles, and become socially integrated. The term rebel fits both the game narrative and the gamer's psychological involvement with the game, thus bridging both the narrative and ludic categories, so it follows that we could qualify *Bully* as a "rebel" game.

Case Study: American McGee's Alice

In many respects the 3rd-person shooter game engine driving *American McGee's Alice* makes for a less sophisticated story and less subtle character interactions than *Bully*. However, there are still valuable elements hidden under the flurry of attacks and killings that deserve psychological interpretation, and as mentioned earlier, there are pertinent points to be made that enhance the "rebel" category as seen through a female prism.

The game story is based on the *Alice in Wonderland* novel; however, the game universe is more sinister, and the dreamlike, surreal elements of the book are heightened by a sense of ominous danger hanging over the main character, Alice (just like with *Bully*, the gamer's only choice of avatar). The opening cutscene signals the game's ambitions to put some distance between it and the literary source material. Alice is residing in an asylum, catatonic, following the death of both her parents. In this respect, Alice starts off in a similar psychological place as Jimmy, albeit more exaggerated—she is deeply traumatised and literally abandoned by the most important adults in her life, her parents.

The catatonic state has greater symbolism than just communicating Alice's grief. Pinkola Estés (1992) identifies the apathetic state as symbolic of a woman's spirit that is crushed (usually by the oppressive, restrictive patriarchal social norms). The placement of a girl/woman who is emotionally upset into an asylum is also significant, as it's historically known that this was a frequent measure undertaken when women showed signs of behaving hysterically (and, of course, the term hysteria is so negatively associated with the possession of the womb: gr. *huster*). Markedly, such measures were not applied to men. In an echo of the monomyth, it takes a woman to reach her lowest ebb in order to reawaken and fight back to restore her soul. Alice is in a much more desperate situation than Jimmy at the outset; however, because of the cushioning of the fantasy setting, the starkness is not felt as acutely. But this starting position signals that it will also take much more spunk and rebellion to break from the strictures of Alice's predicament than the *Bully* situation.

Once again, we have reverberations of Campbell's dramatic structure in the game's unfolding. The White Rabbit delivers the requisite "call to adventure" (Campbell, 1993), which sets Alice off on an autonomous journey with the Cheshire cat serving as an ambiguously helpful NPC. Because the Cheshire cat is not a reliable ally, the issue of trust is continuously at the fore, which also means the gamer will feel more alone than aided by an ally. The world of Wonderland has been suffering under the tyrannical Queen of Hearts, so the overall mission for the gamer/Alice is to destroy her. It is no accident that the goal is destroying Wonderland's ultimate authority figure as well as an adult figure. Lewis Carroll's creation lends itself well to the ludic context, as in its book form it already contained numerous references to games (chess and card games) as well as puzzles and word games, and this aspect is maximised in the game.

Like the hero's quest progress, the path through the game is beset with obstacles and characters that need to be eliminated, and the means and frequency of these actions don't differ greatly from the standard 3rd-person shooter. The one factor that needs recognising in the killing acts is that none of the adversaries are of Alice's age—they are either adults or animal creatures, so there is a case for arguing that there is a process of acting out against those in power and in control, which befits the rebel category. The anger and frustration of a child/teen towards the adult world is much more accentuated in the game's storyline than in Lewis Carroll's version, which is in keeping with Bettelheim's theory of a need for such a domain in which one can express socially unacceptable and taboo feelings.

What deserves closer attention, though, are the female figures in the game, notably the Duchess, the White Queen, and the Red Queen. Folk and fairy tales traditionally abound with good fairy and wicked witch character types, but rather than seeing them as a representation of the duality of good and evil in the world, there is a more psychologically grounded explanation to be found. Estés (1992) perceives such contrasting forces as outward manifestations of the psyche. To put it crudely, one has to fight the bad part of oneself in order to grow and overcome vicissitudes. Near the final confrontation with the Red Queen, Alice sees the good White Queen beheaded at the guillotine. This doesn't mean, however, that evil has momentarily prevailed. Instead, it is a necessary death of the old self, which is requisite in order for the new Phoenix-like self to emerge. Once again, Campbell's monomyth parallels this narrative necessity in the death/rebirth stage, where the hero appears to die, only to be then resuscitated. For Alice there is additional significance in watching the White Queen perish. She is the only visible maternal figure, so her death signals the need to move on. Alice needs to get over her grief and rejoin the world. The mother figure is the comfort zone from which the child needs to step away and become autonomous from in order to mature and forge his or her own identity (as demonstrated by the Erikson model, see above). By killing her old self, moving on from the mother figure and killing the dark shadow aspect of the psyche, Alice establishes her own identity and can leave Wonderland and the asylum. And the gamer, through the gameplay, acts out the anti-authority rebellious streak, establishing his or her control over the game universe that was to begin with incomprehensible, overwhelming, and sinister.

This case study does not provide as detailed of a map for rebel-type behaviour or rebel-type story as *Bully* does, as the game is in many respects less sophisticated (and older, predating some of the narrative and game engine developments). However, it is valuable in showing the rebel variation from the female point of view, which is socially an even less accepted mode of behaviour than for males. If the situations were inversed, it would be very interesting to see how a female Jimmy would have been received in his stead in handling bullies. Alice being female doesn't mean, however, that the game is aimed at female gamers. For instance, while the Red Queen can serve to reflect Alice's dark side, for the gamer she can also be the site of transference, whereby negative emotions against one's own mother, socially inadmissible, can be played out and released. This also brings us to the mythical ur-rebellion against one's parent, which in the male version is the more talked about Oedipal complex but in this case reflects the Electra complex, although Bettelheim (1991) equates the child's ambiguous longing for his or her parent (of the opposite sex) as Oedipal in both male and female cases. Extricating oneself from the "oedipal predicament" (Bettelheim, 1991, p. 39) is something that many battle with even after puberty, and so on a metaphoric level, removing the desired-after parent from the equation may be a sign that this has been accomplished. In the case of *Alice,* a male gamer destroying the mother figure is committing the ultimate rebellious act against the parent after patricide and is reconciling with the Oedipal complex.

Where *Alice* is more evocative of the psyche than *Bully* is in the game world design and choice of settings. The number of underground tunnels and doors and impenetrable woods are all recognisable metaphors for the slippery, hard-to-pin-down psyche, and it takes skill and trickery to penetrate this landscape. An interesting parallel can also be drawn with *The Wizard of Oz,* in that some of the Wonderland characters mirror the real-life asylum characters. This underscores the need to retreat into a dream world or fantasy world when reality becomes too harsh, so that the problems can be worked out under the protective cloak of a make-believe world. The world's distortions are reflections of the person's damaged psyche, so any bizarre or disturbing sights Alice encounters are essentially her interior thoughts and feelings being exteriorised, which from an aesthetic point of view makes *American McGee's Alice* an expressionist work. This untrammelled visual expression of the darkest impulses and visions creates a nonjudgmental sphere within which all the forbidden, taboo emotions of the gamer can be sublimated.

It is clear that the term rebel has a different application in this game than in *Bully*, not merely because of the emphasis on the female point of view, but because of the oedipal rebellion that doesn't feature in *Bully*. More importantly, though, the psychological interpretation of the game demonstrates that again the gamer's actions, motivations, and emotional responses match the narrative universe of the game (maturing/rebelling), and the psychological value of the game raises it far above the 3rd-person shooter category it belongs to in most gaming classifications.

FUTURE RESEARCH DIRECTIONS

While it is not within the scope of this chapter to analyse other games in similar detail, it would be useful to see whether this model of analysis can be applied to a wider range of games. As this is a new idea, it has yet to be tested extensively. There is also a likelihood that even if a game demonstrates psychological aspects in the narrative and gamer's behavioural prompts, these two may not necessarily fall under the same aegis.

A topic that may, in particular, gain from this approach is that of tragedy and the possibility of a tragic game. Murray (1997) has questioned whether tragedy in gaming is viable "in a medium that resists closure" (p. 175) and wonders about the effect of a tragic process in the stead of the tragic ending. For a tragedy to fulfill its dramatic goal, it needs to provide catharsis, and this is where a psychological interpretation can help determine a slightly different brand of catharsis, one that has been adapted to interactive narrative formats, which would align the tragic in the narrative with the tragic in the gameplay. Even in the context of drama, catharsis has spawned a lengthy polemic, with the precise definition of what exactly Aristotle meant by that term missing. In this theoretical opening, some scholars have put forward ideas that catharsis not only encompasses the emotional or spiritual aspect, but that it also includes the intellectual (Belfiore, 1991, p. 1). The intellectual in the dramatic context is considered the viewer's ability to understand what has happened, to unlock the puzzle that the story presented; however, in a gaming context, the intellectual can be associated with the literal puzzle solving and the cognitive processes that take place throughout the game. Coupled with Kelly's theory that the cognitive and the emotional cannot be considered as separate entities and coexist in a much more complicated, intertwined manner (Fransella, 1993), we can begin to see how a case can be made in defining catharsis along the cognitive–intellectual lines. Additionally, catharsis could be explored through the cathartic moments in psychotherapeutic treatment and by applying the micronarrative analytical approach, there could be several microcathartic moments within one single game.

Inversely, the ideas presented in this chapter may serve as an impetus to write new games or come up with new genres based on psychological study—by working "backwards" and taking a behavioural model or process-of-development stages like the Erikson model, a game writer may find inspiration to create a psychologically meaningful game. To name one example, what if the five stages of grieving were incorporated into a game's narrative and gameplay, so that the gamer could act out the five emotional states as a response to the narrative scenario? This brings to mind Chris Crawford's (2005) exhortation to start thinking more about people than things in gaming scenarios or else they will remain emotionally (and I would add, psychologically) impoverished.

CONCLUSION

This study shows that games can indeed satisfy deeper psychological needs than mere entertainment and can be situated within a more complex classification framework. The intention behind this chapter has not been to insist on a prescriptive set of new genre categories that would start with the "freshly" discovered "rebel"-type game. Rather than focussing on the term used to describe the meeting point of narrative and gameplay through psychology as the common denominator, the author hopes it is the approach itself that will prove useful to other theorists in making sense of both the genre issue in gaming and the game–story paradigm. Or, at the very least, it might reinforce the untenable nature of the current unmanageable set of genre descriptors and prompt a different path to solution seeking.

The psychology-based approach might also be the only way to build solid, intractable arguments against the hysterical and mostly unfounded accusations made against games and the gamers' ability to differentiate between reality and the game world. Equally, the argument put forward here should counter the negative view that Atkins (2003) warns against, typified by the attitude that "the playing of games 'wastes time' that might have been put to better use" (p. 5). And who knows, maybe games will someday come to replace the therapist's couch!

REFERENCES

Aarseth, E. (1997). *Cybertext: Perspectives on ergodic literature*. Baltimore: John Hopkins University Press.

Aarseth, E. (2004). Genre trouble: Narrativism and the art of simulation. In Wardrip-Fruin, N., & Harrigan, P. (Eds.), *First person: New media as story, performance and game* (pp. 45–55). Cambridge, MA: The MIT Press.

Atkins, B. (2003). *More than a game: The computer game as fictional form*. Manchester, UK: Manchester University Press.

Bettelheim, B. (1991). *The uses of enchantment: The meaning and importance of fairy tales*. London: Penguin Books.

Bruner, J. (1990). *Acts of meaning*. Cambridge, MA: Harvard University Press.

Bruner, J. (2004). Life as narrative. *Journal of Social Research, 3*(71), 691–710. Retrieved January 2009, from http://www.plataforma.uchile.cl/fb/cursos_area/cognit/unidad2/tema2/doc/bruner_2004_lifeasnarrative.pdf

Campbell, J. (1993). *The hero with a thousand faces*. London: Fontanta Press.

Crawford, C. (2005). *Chris Crawford on interactive storytelling*. Berkeley, CA: New Riders Games. Belfiore, E. (1992). Aristotle on tragic and comic mimesis. *Bryn Mawr Classical Review, 4*(01). Retrieved January 2009, from http://hegel.lib.ncsu.edu/stacks/serials/bmcr/bmcr-v4n01-belfiore-aristotle

Entertainment Arts Games. (2000). *American McGee's Alice* [PC Game]. Redwood City, California: EA Games.

Eskelinen, M. (2001). The gaming situation. *Game Studies, The International Journal of Computer Game Research, 1*(1). Retrieved March 2007 from http://www.gamestudies.org/0101/eskelinen/

Fransella, F. (1995). *George Kelly*. London: SAGE Publications.

Hartmann, T., & Klimmt, C. (2006). The influence of personality factors on computer game choice. In Vorderer, P., & Bryant, J. (Eds.), *Playing video games: Motives, responses, and consequences* (pp. 115–132). New York: Routledge.

Hassan, I. (1992). Pluralism in postmodern perspective. In Jencks, C. (Ed.), *The post-modern reader*. London: Academy Editions.

Järvinen, A. (2009). Understanding video games as emotional experiences. In Perron, B., & Wolf, M. J. P. (Eds.), *The video game theory reader 2* (pp. 85–108). New York: Routledge.

Jenkins, H. (2004). Game design as narrative architecture. In Wardrip-Fruin, N., & Harrigan, P. (Eds.), *First person: New media as story, performance and game* (pp. 118–130). Cambridge, MA: The MIT Press.

Jenkins, H. (2006). *Convergence culture: Where old and new media collide*. New York: University of New York Press.

Jones, S. E. (2008). *The meaning of video games*. New York: Routledge.

Juul, J. (2001). Games telling stories? A brief note on games and narratives. *Game Studies, The International Journal of Computer Game Research, 1*(1). Retrieved June 2007, from http://www.gamestudies.org/0101/juul-gts/

Juul, J. (2009). The fear of failing? The many meanings of difficulty in video games. In Perron, B., & Wolf, M. J. P. (Eds.), *The video game theory reader 2* (pp. 237–252). New York: Routledge.

King, G., & Krzywinska, T. (2002). Introduction: Cinema/videogames/interfaces. In King, G., & Krzywinska, T. (Eds.), *ScreenPlay: Cinema/videogames/interfaces* (pp. 1–32). London: Wallflower Press.

Klug, G. C., & Schell, J. (2006). Why people play: An industry perspective. In Vorderer, P., & Bryant, J. (Eds.), *Playing video games: Motives, responses, and consequences* (pp. 91–100). New York: Routledge.

McLeod, J. (1997). *Narrative and psychotherapy*. London: SAGE Publications.

Murray, J. H. (1997). *Hamlet on the holodeck: The future of narrative in cyberspace*. Cambridge, MA: The MIT Press.

Pinkola Estés, C. (1992). *Women who run with the wolves*. London: Rider.

Ricœur, P. (1991). Life in quest of narrative. In Wood, D. (Ed.), *On Paul Ricœur, narrative and interpretation*. London: Routledge.

Rockstar Games. (2006). *Bully* [Console game]. New York, NY: Rockstar Games.

Sengers, P. (2004). Schizophrenia and narrative in artificial agents. In Wardrip-Fruin, N., & Harrigan, P. (Eds.), *First person: New media as story, performance and game* (pp. 95–116). Cambridge, MA: The MIT Press.

Sheldon, L. (2004). *Character development and storytelling for games*. Boston, MA: Thomson Course Technology.

Smith, B. (2006). The (computer) games people play: An overview of popular game content. In Vorderer, P., & Bryant, J. (Eds.), *Playing video games: Motives, responses, and consequences* (pp. 43–56). New York: Routledge.

Vogler, C. (1999). *The writer's journey: Mythic structure for storytellers and screenwriters*. London: Pan Books.

Walkerdine, V. (1997). *Children, gender, video games*. New York: Palgrave, MacMillan.

Wolf, M. J. P. (2002). *The medium of the video game*. Austin, TX: University of Texas Press.

"MUST-READS" FOR THIS TOPIC

Aarseth, E. (1997). *Cybertext: Perspectives on ergodic literature*. Baltimore: John Hopkins University Press.

Bateman, C. (Ed.). (2007). *Game writing: Narrative skills for videogames*. Boston, MA: Charles River Media.

Crawford, C. (1996–97). *The art of computer game design*. http://www.vancouver.wsu.edu/fac/peabody/game-book/Coverpage.html

Egenfeldt-Nielsen, S., Heide Smith, J., & Pajares Tosca, S. (Eds.). (2008). *Understanding video games: The essential introduction*. New York: Routledge.

Laurel, B. (1993). *Computers as theatre*. Reading, MA: Addison-Wesley.

Manovich, L. (2001). *The language of new media*. Cambridge, MA: The MIT Press.

Murray, J. H. (1997). *Hamlet on the holodeck: The future of narrative in cyberspace*. Cambridge, MA: The MIT Press.

Turkle, S. (1995). *Life on the screen*. New York: Simon & Schuster.

Wardrip-Fruin, N., & Harrigan, P. (Eds.). (2004). *First person: New media as story, performance and game*. Cambridge, MA: The MIT Press.

Wardrip-Fruin, N., & Montfort, N. (Eds.). (2003). *The new media reader*. Cambridge, MA: The MIT Press.

TOP TEXTS FOR INTERDISCIPLINARY STUDY OF SERIOUS GAMES

Bettelheim, B. (1991). *The uses of enchantment: The meaning and importance of fairy tales*. London: Penguin Books.

Bruner, J. (1990). *Acts of meaning*. Cambridge, MA: Harvard University Press.

Campbell, J. (1993). *The hero with a thousand faces*. London: Fontana Press.

Genette, G. (1997). *Paratexts: Thresholds of interpretation*. Cambridge, UK: Cambridge University Press.

Propp, V. (1977). *Morphology of the folk tale. (L. Scott, Trans* (Wagner, L. A., Ed.). 1st ed.). Austin, TX: University of Texas.

Ryan, M. L. (2001). *Narrative as virtual reality*. Baltimore: The Johns Hopkins University Press.

Thomas, M., & Penz, F. (Eds.). (2003). *Architectures of illusion: From motion pictures to navigable interactive environments*. Bristol, UK: Intellect Books.

Vogler, C. (1999). *The writer's journey: Mythic structure for storytellers and screenwriters*. London: Pan Books.

Vorderer, P., & Bryant, J. (Eds.). (2006). *Playing video games: Motives, responses, and consequences*. New York: Routledge.

Wood, D. (Ed.). (1991). *On Paul Ricœur, narrative and interpretation*. London: Routledge.

ENDNOTES

1 While there is no one text that covers the entirety of this debate, given that it has been ongoing for several years and across several platforms, from articles, books, and conferences to blogs, the reader looking for more information on these discussions may want to look up some of the main proponents of the two camps. Espen Aarseth, Gonzalo Frasca and Jesper Juul have been at the fore of the ludology side, whereas Janet Murray

and Marie-Laure Ryan are the more outspoken narratology defenders, with the likes of Henry Jenkins advocating a more median position. The online version of *First Person: New Media as Story, Performance, and Game* features all of the above-mentioned theorists and includes online posts typical of the repartee mentioned.

2 The milieu adds extra layers of complexity to the genre issue; however, the generic hierarchy of milieu falls beyond the remit of this chapter.

Chapter 3
Toward a Rhetoric of Serious Game Genres

Lee Sherlock
Michigan State University, USA

ABSTRACT

This chapter examines the construction of serious game genre frameworks from a rhetorical perspective. The author argues that to understand the forms of persuasion, learning, and social action that serious games facilitate, perspectives on genre must be developed and applied that situate serious gaming activity within larger systems of discourse, meaning-making, and text circulation. The current disconnect between popular understandings of serious game genres and those expressed by serious game developers represents one instance where rhetorical genre studies can be applied to generate knowledge about the "genre work" that serious games perform. Advocating a notion of genre that seeks to identify forms of social action and the persuasive possibility spaces of gaming, the author concludes by synthesizing digital game-based formulations of genre with perspectives from rhetorical theory to suggest implications for serious game research and design.

INTRODUCTION

Given the purpose of this collection—to examine trends related to serious games/gaming from a variety of disciplines and place them in dialogue with each other—I begin with the question of what affordances might be gained from using rhetoric to study serious games. At a general level, rhetoric seems like a perfectly suitable set of ideas to bring in for the study of serious games, especially for the kinds of serious games that are specifically designed for persuasive purposes. I use "rhetoric" here to foreground the persuasive and symbolic potentials of discourse, design, and human expression, carried out not only through language but through the construction of material objects and even computational processes, as argued by Bogost (2007). A common working definition of a serious game, as presented by Michael and Chen (2006), for instance, is a game that does *not* have entertainment as the

DOI: 10.4018/978-1-61520-719-0.ch003

Copyright © 2010, IGI Global. Copying or distributing in print or electronic forms without written permission of IGI Global is prohibited.

primary purpose. This distinction in purpose, which is recognized by both designers and players in a conscious way, is the exact kind of situation that rhetoric is concerned with examining, as it involves a specific communicative "move" that intersects with issues of audience and genre. As a discipline, rhetoric is often itself conceived as interdisciplinary or metadisciplinary space (e.g., Vitanza, 1987), making it a productive starting place to construct a cross-disciplinary dialogue about the persuasive potential of serious games.

It should also be noted that rhetorical studies approaches have the potential to be applied to any kind of digital game (as a multimodal text that communicates meaning) and not just games that are explicitly "persuasive." These approaches are particularly valuable in unpacking the assumptions and values underlying representation in digital games, whether that representation is self-constructed (which remains a function of the game's rule-based affordances and limitations) or more explicitly imposed by the designers. For example, rhetorical readings of gender and sexuality in *The Sims* (Consalvo, 2003; Flanagan, 2003) or race and ethnicity in the *Grand Theft Auto* series (Blackmon, 2007; Garrelts, 2006) address the persuasive, political, and ideological impact of digital games as a cultural form, even though these kinds of games are classified as designed for "entertainment."

Of course, rhetoric can also be brought in as a way of assessing how serious games that claim to be designed for persuasion actually carry out that purpose. Serious games falling under this category would include games designed for political or social change, environmental awareness, advertising, and so on. Although approaching these games using a rhetorical framework would not attempt to *measure* the persuasive outcome in terms of audience effects, as in particular forms of communications and social psychology research, it would be useful in assessing what strategies of language, representation, and meaning-making are at work in persuasive games. Additionally, subsets of rhetoric such as visual and digital rhetoric are especially relevant to the study of serious games because games as artifacts rely on visual and digital aspects of composition as an essential component of meaning-making. In this sense, rhetoric can be used to critically examine how serious game elements like interface design are themselves persuasive texts and cannot automatically be read as "neutral" or only in instrumental terms. Reading serious games rhetorically would also mean that games are placed within a larger system of texts, references, and circulation. Rather than existing as standalone persuasive artifacts, a rhetorical approach to serious games calls for a contextualization of serious games as existing within a broader system of discourse.

In this chapter, I begin with a brief literature review that examines how digital games, and serious games more specifically where applicable, have been taken up in the literature on rhetoric. I employ the term "rhetorical studies" for this review to emphasize that it is critical to push beyond the boundaries of the *field* of rhetoric and composition to look for literature exercising rhetorical *approaches* to gaming, even if the conventional venues within rhetoric and composition serve as the logical starting points. I then shift to the main topic of analysis in this chapter, which is a critique of serious game genres from a rhetorical perspective.

DIGITAL GAMES LITERATURE IN RHETORICAL STUDIES

There have been few major works that attempt to connect serious games with rhetorical studies, but one of the scholars actively working to bridge the two areas is Bogost (2007). Although "serious games" has become the de facto term for games that deal with educational content areas, politics, social issues, and so forth, Bogost questions the value of this term and proposes "persuasive games" as an alternative. Part of the reason he proposes this change in terminology is because calling such games "serious" confines the rhetorical impact of games in general while marking "entertainment" titles as frivolous or incapable of achieving legitimate meaning. As Bogost (2007) argues:

> *The concept of serious games as a counter movement apart from and against the commercial videogame industry eliminates a wide variety of games from persuasive speech. It is a foolish gesture that wrongly undermines the expressive power of videogames in general, and highly crafted, widely appealing commercial games in particular. (p. 59)*

Bogost also notes that the term "serious" does not capture the full potential of games to challenge existing conditions and ideologies. He argues that serious games should not be defined as "in the service of governments, corporations, educational institutions, and their kindred but games that challenge such institutions, creating opportunities to question, change, or eliminate them" (p. 58). Even if one questions the proposal to adopt Bogost's term over the existing "serious games," he presents an important reminder about the rhetorical status of video games, especially in their potential to critique institutions and enact social or cultural criticism.

Bogost's main argument centers on the idea of procedural rhetoric, which he defines as "the art of persuasion through rule-based representations and interactions rather than the spoken word, writing, images, or moving pictures" (p. ix). Bogost suggests that this form of persuasion is unique to video games in that they are multimedia artifacts that rely on computational architecture to carry out their meaning (p. ix). To some extent, this argument is presented in opposition to visual or digital rhetorical frameworks that might otherwise be applied to the study of games, as Bogost emphasizes that a new rhetorical perspective is needed to account for the unique persuasive function of digital games. For example, Bogost argues that digital rhetoric (for many scholars) focuses on "culturally modified versions of existing oral and written discourse" and "abstracts the computer as a consideration, focusing on the text and image content a machine might host and the communities of practice in which that content is created and used" (p. 25). For Bogost, understanding the persuasive capacities of digital gaming requires a full consideration of the procedural functions of computer-based artifacts and not simply a grafting of nondigital genres onto digital spaces.

Bogost also provides his own review of rhetoric history, dating back to the ancient Greek tradition but also covering recent arguments in visual and digital rhetoric. This review sets up a discussion of various rhetorical devices that are relevant to Bogost's construction of procedural rhetoric, including the Aristotelian enthymeme and Kenneth Burke's discussion of "human symbolic production" that extends beyond the study of verbal and written texts (pp. 19–21). Although Bogost's purpose is to lay the groundwork for his procedural rhetoric argument, thus influencing the selectivity and treatment of his review, this section of Bogost's book serves as a valuable lens to read serious game studies *through* rhetoric.

Other works in rhetorical studies have argued for a "grammar" or "rhetoric" of digital gaming while not specifically focusing on serious games. McAllister's (2004)*Game Work: Language, Power, and Computer Game Culture* is one of the major efforts to outline such a framework. McAllister puts forth five "general propositions" that emphasize the role of computer games as dialectical artifacts (p. 31). What McAllister calls "rhetorico-dialectical inquiry" would look at the relationship between "a particular computer game's rhetoric and the broader social antagonisms that rhetoric feeds and is fed by" (p. 33). Given this larger rhetorical framework, what might rhetorical events in computer games actually look like? McAllister argues that such events are *constructed primarily out of: (a) developers' and marketers' idiosyncratic, homological, and inclusive ideologies, and (b) players' (or more generally, "experiencers'") interactions with the systems put in place by the developers, which are influenced by their own idiosyncratic, homological, and inclusive ideologies. (pp. 31–32)*

Additionally, McAllister notes that, taken as dialectics, these events are "always connected to other rhetorical events and struggles that are not game-related" (p. 32). Thus, while Bogost shifts his rhetorical focus to account for the computational nature of digital games, McAllister foregrounds digital games within a broader system of cultural argumentation and meaning-making.

A similar construction of a "grammar" and "rhetoric" of digital gaming has been proposed by Garrelts (2003). Garrelts's version of a video game rhetoric consists of "regulating configurations, embedded narratives, and social systems," which he refers to collectively as "orienting systems" (p. 116). Garrelts goes on to argue that "if present in a video game, these orienting systems are pervasive and require gamers to define their player-controlled agents within the world of the video game in relationship to these systems" (p. 116). Garrelts's focus on rhetorical address, identification (via Burke), and agency emphasizes a third axis, the *player's* co-construction and negotiation of rhetorical meaning, which can be placed in relation to games as a computational, expressive artifact and the larger rhetorical and dialectical systems in which games are situated.

Beyond the specific efforts to establish rhetorical models for digital gaming, Bakhtin's (1986) discussion of the dialogics of speech genres and other theories of reading, more broadly, can be mobilized to examine how meaning is generated from the interaction between game players and the rhetoric constructed by game design (or as McAllister points out, rhetorical systems linked to or invoked by the game as an artifact). Rosenblatt's (1978) "transactional theory" of literary reading focuses on the interactions and exchanges between reader and text in meaning-making, and Rosenblatt uses the musical performance as an analogy to unpack the notion of reading as an "event" or "reenactment." Multimedia texts in general and game design in particular have the potential to challenge and push forward these theories of text-based reading as dialogical, event-based, and/or interactive.

Perspectives on digital and visual rhetoric can also be applied to the study of games as multimodal texts. As Bogost's framing of digital rhetoric illustrates, however, the role of digital rhetoric theory, or what digital rhetoric theory "should be," is not easily definable. Losh claims that in the "standard model of digital rhetoric, literary theory is applied to technological phenomena without considering how technological theories could conversely elucidate new media texts" (as cited in Bogost, 2007, p. 28). However, Manovich is skeptical about the value of pursuing a "new rhetoric of hypermedia," a claim that stands in opposition to scholars such as Losh and Landow. Manovich argues that "the sheer existence and popularity of hyperlinking exemplifies the continuing decline of the field of rhetoric in the modern era" (as cited in Bogost, 2007, p. 26).

There are also interpretations between these two ends, such as Zappen's (2005) claim that the affordances and constraints of new media "support and enable the transformation of the old rhetoric of persuasion into a new digital rhetoric that encourages self-expression, participation, and creative collaboration" (p. 321). While Zappen views this rhetoric as simultaneously remediated ("transformed") off the old rhetoric and defined as "new," Bogost suggests that this definition uplifts the old rhetoric while giving only a cursory consideration to what "digital" actually means in terms of computation (Bogost, 2007, p. 25). With these tensions in play, the question becomes whether to apply existing digital rhetoric theory to games, craft new iterations of digital rhetoric theory to account for games, or move in a different direction (such as Bogost's procedural rhetoric, which is founded on but presented as an alternative to digital rhetoric as it is traditionally defined). The question gets trickier when we consider the literature on digital visual rhetorics, such as Wysocki's (2003) work, which suggests a range of questions for considering how visual materials and forms of representation establish relationships across texts or within multiple "screens" of the same text. The interplay between these elements (images, symbols, icons, texts, and other modes of expression) also inform how genres are constructed and understood; for example, in the context of game design, both aesthetic themes and gameplay mechanics are argued as characterizing particular genres, a phenomenon I take up in more detail in the next section.

FROM RHETORIC TO GENRE

With an overview of the literature from rhetorical studies, as it intersects with serious games and with theoretical efforts to define a "rhetoric" or "grammar" of gaming, now in place, the problem becomes how to use the various questions and themes brought up by these scholars to construct ways of looking at serious games rhetorically. With this goal in mind, the larger question I would like to pose here is: how can we revise (or alternately, renegotiate or reinterpret) existing ideas and frameworks in rhetoric to accommodate serious games as a site of rhetorical production?

As the literature review suggests, there are many possible ways of approaching this question and many strategies for generating research ideas out of the juxtaposition of serious game work across various scholarly treatments. The area that I intend to examine in response to the question above is that of genre. Genre is only one domain of work within rhetorical studies, but I have selected it to assess how the above question can be narrowed down for a particular case study that attempts to interrogate one branch of rhetorical theory in relation to serious games.

I begin addressing the relationship between genre and serious games by first outlining my rationale for selecting genre theory as the basis for this more focused inquiry into rhetorical theory and serious games. I then thematically survey existing theories or models of genre that have been developed for digital games, with particular attention given to serious games. Following this thematic overview, I discuss the "gaps" in the collection of game genre models reviewed; here, I evaluate particular areas of emphasis (or lack of emphasis) and suggest further questions, possibilities, and problems that arise when we look at game genre discussions in a comparative sense. I then apply the same process of thematic overview and a critique of the "gaps" to genre treatments that have been developed within rhetorical studies. I conclude with a move toward synthesis, suggesting what happens (or what *can* happen) when we put digital gaming discussions of genre together with what rhetorical theory has to say about genre. More specifically, I argue that commonly applied serious game genre labels, while useful as shorthand in particular contexts, do not adequately account for the genre work that serious games perform, and that we need to pursue alternative models of genre to fully account for the ways in which serious games operate through genre work and play.

WHY GENRE THEORY?

Looking at genre in relation to serious games opens up an opportunity to consider how existing rhetorical theory is set up to handle, for example, the design and "content" of serious games, the player's gameplay experience, and the systems of texts that surround serious games. More specifically, though, I would like to discuss three reasons for bringing in genre as the main focus for this inquiry into rhetoric and serious games.

First, genre is used as a mode of classification to distinguish "serious" games from their nonserious counterparts, which usually refers to games for entertainment. At one level, this distinction is marked by an assumption of purpose, namely that the designers of serious games must be trying to *do* something serious, such as educate, improve health, raise awareness of social issues, and so on. At the same time, because of the definition-through-negation, this distinction implies that mass-market, commercial games are incapable of achieving "serious" outcomes. Beyond this attribution of purpose, though, serious games are defined as their own genre within the digital game universe, and the term "serious game" is sometimes treated as having multiple subgenres. For example, the Wikipedia entry on digital game genres contains a section on video games classified "by purpose," which includes adult, advergame, art, casual, Christian, educational, electronic sports, exergame, and serious games ("Video Game Genres"). This genre classification is again set up as a binary, treating serious games as different in purpose rather than through their structural gameplay features, which is how entertainment games are typically classified. Interrogating how this genre distinction is made can achieve a critical understanding of how serious games are distinguished in terms of audience and purpose, as well as how their "content" or typified features are made meaningful in terms of gaming as a rhetorical situation. As hinted at above, genre is also an important issue because it intersects with how digital games are valued and even influences where and how digital games are used institutionally. More broadly, this discussion points to the use of genre for interrogating modes and criteria of *classification*, the implications of which can be connected to questions of purpose, audience, and the construction of value.

The second reason for using genre as a focal point is that genre theory is already an established concept within rhetorical studies. Of course, genre theory is not something that exists as a "finalized" idea, but it is nonetheless well developed in the domain of rhetorical studies and is applied as a common framework for the rhetorical critique of texts and their concomitant activities. The implications of this are that serious games can be included in genre-based critiques that include other textual forms and other practices of reading and writing; in other words, this approach situates serious games within a tradition of genre studies and is intended to extend that tradition. Because genre theory is used as the lens for giving "attention" to serious games, the result is an examination of and a series of possible revisions for existing rhetorical theory rather than a "new" approach that is presented as an oppositional alternative.

Finally, working with genre suggests some ways in which this study can serve a practical or functional purpose for looking at serious games; the intent is to produce a heuristic or a possible set of tools that can be applied to serious games in scholarly work. For example, developing a genre-based approach to serious games can generate a strategy for the analysis and critique of individual serious games. Such an approach could be used in scholarly work on digital games, or it could be incorporated as a pedagogical tool for examining serious games as a rhetorical artifact in the classroom. Since genre is a major theme in university first-year composition courses in the U.S., for instance, serious games could be more readily integrated in such courses with a genre framework in place. Serious games could also be used in courses on multimedia writing and digital rhetoric and across a variety of disciplinary teaching contexts.

DIGITAL GAMES AND GENRE

Overview

The first part of this section surveys genre systems that have been developed specifically for digital games, including both mass-market entertainment games and serious games. While these treatments of genre are not necessarily referred to or labeled as "theories," I will be considering how they line up with other ways of thinking about genre from a theoretical perspective.

Multiple systems for game genres have been developed, and how these systems have been constructed varies in terms of audience and purpose. One way of looking at game genres is to consider "popular" genre systems used to label mass-market entertainment games. This genre system is popular in the sense that it is used by game publishers and the mainstream gaming press (e.g., Gamespot and IGN) to describe games, and players use this language to interpret the characteristics of individual games and understand what "kind" of game they will be playing. Other ways of thinking about game genres come from game designers who propose an extension or revision of the popular genre set (e.g., Bateman & Boon, 2005). Academics in various disciplines have also taken up the question of digital game genres (e.g., Apperley, 2006; Wolf, 2001). Although all of these game genre approaches share the objective of characterizing digital games and making meaningful distinctions among the many digital games that exist, they differ somewhat in purpose. For game developers, publishers, and marketers, genre can be used as a buzzword to attract gamers to their product. For academics, however, one objective might be to consider how the issue of genre fits into digital games as extended from a tradition of print-based writing (including literature), film, and other forms of cultural production.

Wikipedia's entry on video game genres provides one window into how the popular view of game genres has been constructed by game players at large. I have selected this particular text for inclusion because it represents a public space where understandings of genre can be openly discussed, critiqued, and revised. In this sense, the article is consensus-based, but as a genre it is only "relatively stable," as Bakhtin (1986) describes. I should also note that I am not necessarily arguing for the Wikipedia video game genre article as reflecting a "better" or "worse" understanding of genre than other frameworks, only that it involves different assumptions about genre and modes of production and revision in how it is collaboratively composed.

The introduction to the Wikipedia article states that video games are "categorized into genres based on their gameplay interaction" ("Video Game Genres"). In other words, this genre system attempts to identify a set of *formal features* that characterize different games, which depend upon the player's engagement to realize a particular type of interaction. However, games cannot be entirely made distinct in this way, as "it is important to think of each individual game as belonging to several genres at once" ("Video Game Genres").

With this philosophy in mind, the Wikipedia article attempts to employ gameplay interaction as a framework for genre categorization. For example, platform video games are described as follows:

These games involve traveling between platforms by jumping (very occasionally other means are substituted for jumping, like swinging or bouncing, but these are considered variations on the same mechanic). Other traditional elements include running and climbing ladders and ledges. Platformers frequently borrow elements from other genres like fighting and shooting (such as the Castlevania series, which incorporates role-playing). ("Video Game Genres")

Action–adventure games are defined by their focus on "exploration" and "usually involve item gathering, simple puzzle solving, and combat" ("Video Game Genres"). Gameplay, in the sense of how these genres have been determined, refers to the mechanics or structure that the player encounters within a particular designed environment. These definitions recognize a significant amount of slippage in how strongly the genre boundaries should hold; for example, the platform genre definition cites the borrowing of mechanics from other genres. The action–adventure genre is itself a hybrid of "action" and "adventure," which also exist as their own independent genres. However, the separation of these categories implies that there are still gameplay differences or patterns significant enough to maintain a genre system.

SERIOUS GAME GENRES

In addition to the genre systems for mass-market entertainment games, more specific frameworks establish genre categories for *serious* games. The Wikipedia game genre article also includes a discussion of serious game genres, which it identifies as a list of "video game genres by purpose" ("Video Game Genres"). On the face of it, this seems like a curious move to make; why would these games be treated "by purpose" and not according to their gameplay structures or how they engage the player in "procedural" forms of interaction? For entertainment games, this might be the equivalent of calling survival horror games "games for grotesque abjection" and real-time strategy games "games for world domination." However, the attempt here is to match up games with a "real-world" purpose that they are designed to carry out. For example, advergames are video games designed to "advertise a product, organization, or viewpoint" ("Advergaming"). Educational games "attempt to teach the user using the game as a vehicle," and subgenres of educational games include games for specific areas of academic instruction, such as geometry or biology ("Video Game Genres"). The genre of casual games is included under the discussion of genres "by purpose," which are defined as having "very simple rules or play techniques and a very low degree of strategy. .. making them easy to learn and play as a pastime" ("Video Game Genres").

Another way of thinking about serious game genres has been developed by Bergeron (2006). Bergeron's audience, however, is not primarily a "popular" one that would engage the average gamer, as his book is geared toward instructing game developers and related professionals about the serious game world. Most of the book's chapters address serious game development issues such as technology platforms, standards and programming practices, and business management strategies. As a result, Bergeron's way of thinking about serious game genres emphasizes the values and practices of a game designer rather than those of players.

Bergeron (2006) divides serious games into "five primary categories and two secondary categories" (p. 26). The primary categories include "games with an agenda; news games; political games; realistic games; and core competency games," while the secondary categories include "repurposed COTS [commercial off-the-shelf] games and modifications (mods)" (p. 26). Bergeron notes that the secondary categories are forms of game technology rather than typifications of serious game content, but they are included because they hold special potential "as a means of acquiring and developing serious games" (p. 26). In response to "educational" games, Bergeron avoids this label as a major category, claiming that

> *Because games in the five primary categories can be considered a variation of educational games, that term isn't used as a separate category. Another reason to avoid the label educational game or edutainment is that the genre has a bad reputation among educators. (pp. 26–27)*

By making this move, Bergeron suggests that game genres have particular values associated with them that need to be taken into consideration, especially for serious games attempting to achieve a specific rhetorical objective. Rather than try to reclaim the credibility of "educational" games, though, Bergeron advocates dismissing the term altogether.

Bergeron (2006) does qualify his genre framework by claiming that, within his "games with an agenda" category, there are "no hard and fast rules on the subdivisions" (p. 27). However, he notes that he would consider the main subdivisions to be "activism, advergames, business games, exergaming, health and medicine games, news games, and political games" (p. 27). Bergeron relies on the interpretation of the game designer's intent to make distinctions *between* serious game subgenres as well. For example, Bergeron distinguishes political games from other subgenres by claiming that, "as defined here, political games are different from news games or ordinary military games in that the developer's intent to generate controversy seems to override other considerations" (p. 49). The mode of genre classification used here is almost entirely outside both the structural features of gameplay and meanings generated as a player interacts with a rhetoric or grammar of gaming; for political games, Bergeron argues that it is necessary to "read" to what extent the game developers considered it to be controversial. In fact, he suggests that players could read some of these games as "propaganda," depending on the "perspective of the player" (pp. 48-49). Although this genre system makes references to the player's subjective position of "reading" or interpreting the genre, the main criteria for classification still remains what the game developers *intended* the game to mean and do.

IDENTIFYING THE GAPS

The major genre "divide" noted above is the distinction between classifying games via gameplay structures (as is primarily applied to mass-market entertainment games) and classifying games via purpose (as is primarily applied to serious games). However, even though gameplay has been claimed as the main criteria for developing entertainment game genres, game studies scholars such as Apperley (2006) have been troubled by the idea that gameplay is the only consideration at work. In the Wikipedia article on game genres, which sets out to identify distinct gameplay structures that can be used to classify games, the genre definitions also rely on what Apperley calls "representational" characteristics, which refer to the "visual aesthetics" of games (p. 7). For example, games in the survival horror genre "focus on fear and attempt to scare the player via traditional horror fiction elements such as atmospherics, death, the undead, blood and gore" ("Video Game Genres"). Part of the genre definition here relies not on *how* players interact with a survival horror game—i.e., the game mechanics—but the appearance of representational themes brought over from a particular literary/filmic genre. For survival horror, the (visual) content or theme of the game is what "counts" over its structure and gameplay, even though there are also characteristic gameplay elements such as the "low quantity of ammunition or number of breakable melee weapons" ("Video Game Genres"). Thus, the gameplay criterion appears to not be the only consideration at work in genre building, despite the statement leading off the Wikipedia article, as these genre classifications also rely on visual representation to make distinctions between games. For serious games, then, a parallel claim can be drawn that visual rhetorics and strategies of representation are critical to consider for the construction of serious game genres. Such a consideration would encourage increased attention, for example, to forms of critique and parody that rely on visual representation, such as the egomaniacal McDonald's executives in Molleindustria's *The McDonald's Video Game* or the Kinko's employees bored witless in Persuasive Games' *Disaffected!*

Likewise, there are some ways of problematizing the other half of the genre "divide" mentioned above, namely that of serious games being classified according to purpose. Even though a primary purpose "other than entertainment" seems to be the favored method for distinguishing entertainment games from serious games, this binary classification contradicts itself and falls apart in the serious games section of the Wikipedia article on game genres. This article classifies *casual* games under the list of games "by purpose," even though casual games share the objectives of other mass-market entertainment games ("Video Game Genres"). In other words, casual games are made for entertainment, but the difference is that they are designed for easy access and short play sessions.

As a related problem in the Wikipedia game genre article, serious games are not used as an umbrella term for all games classified "by purpose," but rather as a separate genre distinguished from advergames, educational games, and so on. Serious games, in the Wikipedia game genre entry, are defined as games "intended to educate or train the player" ("Video Game Genres"). Thus, the distinction between serious games and *educational* games has been blurred, in that serious games include educational objectives but somehow extend beyond the mode of strictly "educational" academic instruction and are not as strongly associated with school-based learning. Because the basis for this classification has not been made clear, the genre treatment of serious games as an identification of purpose remains problematic.

Another critique that can be raised with respect to serious game genres is that the identification of purpose used as a basis of classification is that of the *designers'* purpose and not the player's purpose; in this sense the possible rhetorical action of serious games is delimited to the game developers' intentions. As an example of this theme, Bergeron's (2006) "primary categories" of serious game genres are defined mostly through the intentionality of the game developers and not through gameplay features or "representational" content. Bergeron leads off his serious game genre discussion by defining games with an agenda, which refers to games "developed to influence opinion, share knowledge, or simply to make a point" (p. 27). He also claims that this agenda is one that is primarily "owned" by the developer, arguing that "as in a well-crafted novel or movie, the agenda of the developer behind this type of serious game might not be obvious to the untrained observer" (p. 27). Although this claim gives credit to the subtlety and complexity with which serious games can be crafted, it places emphasis on the uncovering of an agenda (or not) with a player adequately trained to locate it. It also delimits the *agency* of the player to searching for a singular and predetermined agenda; nowhere in this definition do we come across the "procedural" rhetoric described by Bogost that allows players to experiment with cause-and-effect systems and learn from the interplay with computational, rule-based frameworks. Or to use McAllister's (2004) rhetorico-dialectical focus, Bergeron does not present an account of how a *player's* agenda can dialectically engage with the developer's agenda.

After setting up his framework for serious game categories, Bergeron (2006) works through a number of serious games as individual examples. However, his discussion of these examples, for the most part, does not extend beyond his interpretation of the designer's purpose and a summary of the basic concept of the game. For instance, Bergeron cites the game *Steer Madness* as an example of an activism game. Activism games, Bergeron argues, "actively promote an opinion and attempt to increase public awareness in areas from vegetarianism to global warming" (p. 27). In his discussion of *Steer Madness*, Bergeron presents a description of how the genre aligns with mass-market entertainment game genres ("3D action-adventure game"), information related to the game developer ("developed by Vancouver-based Veggie Games"), and the basic game narrative ("Bryce the Steer. .. narrowly escapes the slaughterhouse and goes on a mission to save his animal friends") (p. 27). Bergeron then describes the purpose of *Steer Madness* as follows: "The game supports vegetarianism and environmentalism while vilifying slaughterhouses and those involved in the meat trade" (p. 27). Bergeron's discussion of *Steer Madness* does not engage in a description of how the player engages with the game's mechanics or rule systems, nor does it attempt to analyze how the player might be persuaded about the respective values associated with vegetarianism and the meat trade. Instead, the game's purpose and its resulting genre classification are determined by an interpretation of what the designers intended as their "agenda" for the game. Additionally, how this purpose is carried out is not articulated in detail; Bergeron claims that the game "supports" certain practices while "vilifying" others, but there is no clear strategy that he presents to examine how those persuasive outcomes happen when the player encounters the game. I should be clear that I am not trying to discredit these kinds of genre accounts, as they are no doubt crucial to understanding the range of purposes and forms of social action that serious games can address. My claim is that we need alternative frameworks to *supplement* this conception of genre, especially in terms of accounting for how players interact with games to carry out forms of social action, whether that action aligns ideologically with the developer's intent or resists and undermines it. As suggested in the main approach to entertainment game genres, identifying the structures of gameplay at work in serious games and applying the "procedural" rhetoric developed by Bogost (2007) represent a couple of ways in which serious game genres can be complicated beyond a description of the designers' purpose.

GENRE APPROACHES FROM RHETORICAL THEORY

Overview

This section transitions from digital game genres to cover approaches to genre that have been developed within rhetorical theory. Although I will discuss multiple approaches to genre in this section, I do not intend to provide a comprehensive review of genre theory. Rather, the purpose of this section is to discuss a selection of existing genre approaches that might be productively applied, drawn upon, or critiqued in response to the question of serious games and genre.

One branch of the literature that might be informative for interrogating serious game genres is the work that examines the broader relationship between *digital texts* and genre. In their article "IText: Future Directions for Research on the Relationship Between Information Technology and Writing," Geisler et al. (2001) outline a project that researches "information technologies with texts at their core—the blend of IT and texts that we call ITexts," a form that they describe as "a relatively recent development" (p. 270). Their collective goals in the project are to "explore fundamental theoretical issues of text in new ways" and "participate with other information researchers in shaping the evolution of future IText technologies in directions consistent with social values, human needs and capacities, and our best knowledge" (p. 270).

Having established this definition that locates the development of ITexts and the objectives of their IText project, Geisler et al. address the issue of genre in relation to ITexts. In their review of genre theory, the authors cite Miller's (1984) definition of genre as a foundation; they claim that "in rhetorical terms, genres are typified responses to typified situations, providing typified motives and forms of realization" (Geisler et al., 2001, p. 277). They also articulate how genres structure the ways in which audiences respond to and interpret texts, arguing that "genres help give shape to situations and people's actions, helping orient writers to their communicative needs and opportunities and providing audiences with means of making sense of the texts they receive" (p. 277). In terms of the relationship between genre theory and digital texts, Geisler et al. claim that "understanding of genre is crucial to moving activities and social networks into electronic environments. The use of prior forms for early recognizability needs to be balanced with innovation that restructures communicative forms, social relations, and activity" (p. 277). In considering this claim for serious games, one of the major questions is what "communicative form" digital gaming represents.

Geisler et al. (2001) also discuss the relationship between genre and social norms, claiming that digital genres "reflect both the capabilities of the technology and the evolving norms for communicative purposes and forms" (p. 293). However, this is not an easy relationship to pin down and research, as "genre norms are a moving target, requiring ongoing study as the changes triggered by evolving new technology continue" (p. 293). Some of the questions that are raised by foregrounding and studying this relationship include: "Who participates in such new IText-mediated communities? How do communication norms affect participation (gender and other dimensions of diversity may play a role here)? How do newly formed communities without previous norms develop norms?" (p. 294).

Continuing along the line of genre, activity, and social norms, Freedman (1996) argues that "the notion of genre has in fact been reinterpreted and redefined" in the last ten to fifteen years (pp. 1–2). Considering that her statement was made in 1996 and that the IText group research outline was published in 2001, we have an even more complex genre landscape to consider now in the context of genre theory's historical development. Freedman claims that this reinterpretation has been framed

so that rather than focusing on formal and textual regularities, (genres as text-types), genre scholars focus on the ACT, the action or the activity that is undertaken through the genre. The textual regularities are seen to be correlates or traces of the social action that takes place. (p. 2)

Interestingly, the same tension between genre interpretations appears in the discussion of game genres above; game genres are described, along one axis, according to "textual regularities" (the structure of gameplay), but Bergeron (2006) and others who have defined serious game genres point to various forms of social action (such as creating political controversy) as the main criterion.

Freedman (1996) also describes genre as engaging in "interplay and interaction," which suggests that serious games might be especially worthwhile to engage at the level of genre (p. 4). In her discussion of Miller's (1984) article, "Genre as Social Action," Freedman notes that "one of the important notions highlighted in this work is that genres not only respond to specific contexts but also reshape those contexts in the process of responding to them" (p. 4).

In synthesizing the arguments of Freedman (1996) and Geisler et al. (2001), a position emerges that genres should not be treated as discrete, separate texts but as a component within a larger system of texts and interactions. In an attempt to articulate what this "larger system" represents and does, Spinuzzi and Zachry (2000; see also Spinuzzi, 2003) have developed the "genre ecology" framework to negotiate the relationships between genres and how people use them. They claim that a genre ecology

includes an interrelated group of genres (artifact types and the interpretive habits that have developed around them) used jointly to mediate the activities that allow people to accomplish complex objectives. In genre ecologies, multiple genres and constituent subtasks co-exist in a lively interplay as people grapple with information technologies. (p. 172)

Although Spinuzzi and Zachry have developed the genre ecology framework for thinking about computer documentation as an open rather than closed system, this way of thinking about genre can also be considered for the "activity" of serious gaming.

Additionally, Spinuzzi and Zachry's (2000) review of genre studies points to the same reinterpretation of genre theory that Freedman argues for.

In citing four works on genre published between 1988 and 1995, Spinuzzi and Zachry note that "genres are stable only within temporal limits and that the exact form and function of future instantiations of a genre cannot be accurately predicted. Genres are not static forms; they are dynamic, organic, and messy" (pp. 172–173). To account for the "messiness" of genres, Spinuzzi and Zachry argue that the genre ecology framework must "account for how official and unofficial documentation genres are animated by and connected through contingency; how the documentation's functionality is consequently decentralized, distributed across the ecology; and how ecologies of genres achieve relative stability despite their contingent, decentralized nature" (p. 173). In previous work on the "activity system" of online gaming in *World of Warcraft* (Sherlock, 2007, 2009), I have traced how players use (and themselves compose) distributed genre ecologies to mediate the activity of grouping, which I argue is a "localized form of social networking" (p. 16). This genre ecology is one example of the decentralization that Spinuzzi and Zachry refer to, which they define as "the distribution of usability, design, and intention across the ecology of genres" (p. 174). For players who have the objective of finding the "right" group to play in, they draw not only upon the game's user interface but also decentralized genres such as written FAQs and message board threads.

Extending the genre ecology framework presented by Spinuzzi and Zachry (2000), Christensen, Cootey, and Moeller (2007) establish a connection between play theory and the conceptualization of genre. They argue that

play theory provides a powerful heuristic for conceptualizing social structures, as well as the role genres play within them. We posit that play theory provides a dimensional perspective, granting further understanding into social structures that explain which genres play a mediational influence within specific contexts and scenarios. (p. 1)

Building on this relationship, the authors present the concept of a genre field, which functions as a "transformative locale" (p. 2). More specifically, a particular genre within a genre field not only "adapts to varying social structures" but also "can be seen as an agent, mediating some degree of transformation, activity, or change within itself as well as human agents within that transformative locale" (p. 2). The framework developed by Christensen, Cootey, and Moeller contains three elements that comprise the "grammar" of genre fields: player–agents and genre–agents, genre field, and play scenarios (p. 2). Regarding the first term, the authors claim that "focusing on human agents as much as the genres within a genre field, identifying the players in a field, and understanding the "stakes" of participation allows us to better understand the nature of transactions within various genres" (p. 2). The second grammatical element, genre field, "denotes the entire spectrum of space surrounding a genre artifact or artifacts" and "includes the agents, influences, social structures, and constraints that are productive of genres and the relationships influenced by genre" (p. 2). Finally, play scenarios are situations that "employ some or all of the genres normally present within the genre field" (p. 3). As an example of how genres adapt and transform within particular play scenarios, Christensen, Cootey, and Moeller point to "the shifting roles of the referee with the invention of the nearly instantaneous video replay in football or the photo finish in track and racing" (p. 3).

Identifying the Gaps

With the assumption that my objective is to search for the intersection of serious games and work on genre, the most immediately apparent gap in the rhetorical theory discussion of genre is the lack of reference to digital games, and serious games in particular, *as genres*. The closest that genre theory gets to this inclusion is Geisler et al.'s (2001) formulation of "ITexts" and Christensen, Cootey, and Moeller's (2007) case studies on game design documents, which are closely tied to the game but cannot functionally be equated with the game itself. One objection to raise in response might be that genre theory's role isn't to account for and document examples of all text-types; genre theory functions as a theoretical frame for understanding the activities of texts and agents.

However, I argue that the omission of digital games represents more than a lack of visibility of games as "example" genres. If genre theory is to account for all of the functional and agentive features that it suggests—Freedman's (1996) "interplay and interaction," for instance—then the interactive, computational play spaces of digital games (and related forms such as virtual worlds) need to be considered alongside other digital and non-digital genres. This development would be especially valuable for serious games, as genre theory could foreground the relationship between procedural forms of game interactivity and the social action carried out in the process of gameplay.

Bringing in digital games and other interactive media as subjects within the scope of genre theory would also allow for an interrogation of concepts such as "relative stability" and "contingency" in Spinuzzi and Zachry's (2000) discussion of genre ecologies. Contingency, for example, would not only depend on the gaming situation (such as when and how players draw upon outside genres such as written FAQs) but would also be influenced by individual gameplay styles and learning styles. Because the style of gameplay changes the "experience" of the genre every time players interact with a digital game, the idea of contingency could be articulated as something that reshapes and restructures individual genre artifacts through each instance of use. The notion of relative stability could also be examined using digital games as a foundation. For example, what does "relative stability" mean when individual gameplay decisions alter the sequence and content of the text at every moment? What forms of the genre remain stable during this process?

Another gap in this discussion of genre theory is the "when" of genre use. Genre theory does not provide a method of tracing, for instance, when players draw upon distributed genres outside the game to mediate gameplay activity. Some of this may be reflected in what players self-report in the textual content of these genres (for example, if players post a request to a message board claiming that they've been frustrated for hours about something), but genre theory itself does not offer a heuristic for assessing this temporal aspect.

SYNTHESIZING GAME GENRES AND GENRE THEORY

Overview

The following section is intended to bring together the discussions of digital game and serious game genres with the genre theory literature discussed from rhetorical studies. Looking thematically at the intersections between these two areas, I identify some of the possibilities and implications of this work for thinking about serious games in terms of genre. Thus, my goal here is not to prescribe a particular way of approaching serious game genres but to outline how that discussion might be framed and applied in various rhetorical contexts.

OPENINGS AND POSSIBILITIES

One way to think about serious game genres is to return to Geisler et al.'s (2001) discussion of ITexts and genre. Although serious games are not explicitly discussed as an IText, analyzing serious games using the same kind of framework would allow researchers to pay more consistent attention to the "cultural, cognitive, and material arrangements" that comprise serious game design, gameplay, and reception (p. 270). Applying the IText article to serious gaming would also raise the question of to what extent, and how, serious games function as a "text." Additionally, the IText research project calls for artifacts such as serious games to be located within a *constellation* of texts and interactions, such that the game itself is not the only "text" that carries out the purpose(s) associated with the game. This claim is suggestive of similar approaches to studying literacy in online gaming spaces (and more generally, studying digital literacy practices), such as Steinkuehler's (2007) analysis of the constellation of literacy practices at work in the massively multiplayer online game *Lineage*.

Geisler et al. (2001) also point to the "use of prior forms" in ITexts, which help direct the process of orientation and genre reception. In other words, readers encounter a tension between familiar genre characteristics and the innovation of digital genres. Because of the interactive nature of digital gameplay, the issue of reception becomes complicated; players do "receive" a system with particular affordances and constraints, but they also co-construct the text through their choices during gameplay, thus resulting in a different "text" every time the game is played. However, the "use of prior forms" also figures into the construction of serious game genres. For example, some educational games (such as *Dimension M*, a serious game for algebra and geometry instruction) rely upon assessment forms such as the multiple-choice quiz for "testing" what players have learned from earlier gameplay. How these other genres are embedded in and how they influence the activity of serious gaming, then, also presents itself as an important question to consider.

Likewise, the discussion of genre norms from the IText article raises questions for serious gaming as well. Player communities can be defined in the context of multiplayer online gaming over distributed networks; groups of players who gather in collaborative online writing spaces such as message boards, blogs, or wikis; and/or players who share the same physical space (e.g., a classroom). In turn, these definitions of "player community" shape what genre norms will be in play, what genre forms get valued/devalued, and by whom. The same questions about genre and social norms could also be applied to serious game *designers* as a means of assessing how community norms influence what genre expectations are made explicit as serious games are developed.

Freedman's (1996) discussion of interplay and interaction, as well as her review of Miller's (1984) work on genre as (transformative) social action, bring up a few interesting problems in the context of serious games. For serious games, this "interplay" statement raises the question of genre interplay at two levels: the level of the player's agency and interactivity *in response to* the genre and the level of the genre's response (to a situation) beyond the scope of a single player. Regarding the latter level of genre interplay, Freedman also argues that "by learning the genres of a particular community we understand then what in fact are the social interpretations of reality of that community" (p. 6). The "social interpretation of reality" here seems especially crucial for understanding persuasive games that respond to, raise awareness of, or critique a particular social problem. For example, one issue would be how genre conventions are employed in serious games to frame and make reference to a specific representational notion of "reality."

The genre ecology framework, as presented by Spinuzzi and Zachry (2000), suggests that researchers should more actively look to related genres that contribute to the activity of serious gaming. One place to start might be the online spaces where serious games are rhetorically framed before the player even starts playing. For example, in Molleindustria's *The McDonald's Video Game*, the Web site hosting the game visually mimics the official McDonald's U.S. Web site. In addition to acting as a space for documentation and information *about* the game, the Web-site co-constructs the persuasive message (through visual and textual strategies of parody and critique) that is developed more deeply during gameplay.

Furthermore, we might ask how Christensen, Cootey, and Moeller's (2007) discussion of *genre fields* can be connected to digital gaming, and serious games in particular. In their article, Christensen, Cootey, and Moeller discuss a case study of serious game design (in particular, the construction of a design document for a serious game concept) using this framework, but it has not yet been shifted over to look at the activity of serious game players. For example, the interplay among the three genre field elements (player–agents/genre–agents, the genre field, and play scenarios) could be applied as a framework to supplement analyses of player or playing "styles." This discussion could then be placed in the context of how genres influence or transform play styles and, working in the other direction, how play styles change the ways in which genres work procedurally.

CONCLUSION: ACCOUNTING FOR SERIOUS GAME GENRE WORK

In the last section, I have suggested a number of "openings and possibilities" in response to the synthesis of game genre frameworks (dealing with both "entertainment" games and serious games) and work from rhetorical studies that deals with genre. Among other things, this particular juxtaposition of work opens up ways of thinking about serious gaming that extend beyond the game itself and situate the game within a larger rhetorical framework. What exactly to call this framework is not a task that I have undertaken here, but this idea has come up consistently in the notions of, for example, a "constellation" of gaming texts and literacy practices, a genre ecology, and a genre field. One of the implications here is not just that serious games are rhetorically situated, but that processes of learning and persuasion have already been engaged before the player even begins gameplay. In the case of the *McDonald's Video Game*, for instance, the player's reading of the rhetorical features of the game's Web site influences how he or she interprets the game's persuasive "message" and engages the game's procedural rhetorics. Serious games also raise interesting questions and problems for the idea of "genre interplay," much like the formal features of games call for a revision of how multimodality is conceived in rhetoric and composition. Serious gaming calls for alternative genre heuristics, ones that account for multiplicity, procedural rhetoric, notions of resistant play, and social action in the public arena. Perhaps this is best achieved through a *visual* representation: for instance, mapping how players draw upon genres to mediate their serious gaming activity, as outlined in Spinuzzi's (2003) genre tracing methodology and genre ecology diagrams or using the play theory and genre model from Christensen, Cootey, and Moeller (2007) to map out mediations between genre-agents and player-agents within particular serious gaming contexts.

FUTURE DIRECTIONS: RESEARCH SCENARIOS AND POSSIBILITIES

Although I have not attempted to build a "new" serious game genre framework out of the various threads addressed in this chapter, I would like to suggest some research moves that might lead in that general direction. Some of the research questions that can be constructed to explore the relationship between serious games and genre include:

- How and why have the current genre models for serious games been developed, and by whom? Whose interests, values, and understandings are represented in these models?
- How does the interactivity of serious games figure into our discussion of serious game genres? What about the idea of play?

- What is the role of related texts/genres/actions that players draw upon in playing serious games? How do these forms of activity that mediate gameplay influence how we talk about and construct serious game genres?

In addition to this set of questions, there are broader questions that can be asked to investigate the relationship between serious gaming and rhetoric and composition as a field:

- In what ways can serious games be analytically described as a multimodal text? What does "multimodality" mean in this case?
- Assuming that rhetorical meaning is *not* located only in game designers' intentions behind the game, how does rhetorical meaning get constructed through the process of play? What implications does this have for existing discussions on "producer" and "consumer" roles related to new media?
- How should serious games be located in relation to other genres and forms of media production that engage with similar "serious" purposes, such as political blogging?

Of course, these questions are only examples, and there are many other productive angles to be taken up in response to these themes. In the following paragraphs, I outline a few specific applications and investigations that could be developed out of the literature on serious games and genre and the above research questions.

One possibility for thinking about serious game genres is to adapt Bogost's (2007) discussion of procedural rhetoric and procedural literacy to the construction of game genres. By considering the various forms of procedural rhetoric involved in serious games and how these forms of procedural rhetoric are structurally aligned and disaligned, Bogost's work can help elaborate a genre framework that accounts for the player's co-construction of rhetorical meaning.

In considering the implications of Bogost's work for game genres, I argue that one of the first questions to consider is the function of play styles and learning styles (Heeter, 2008) in the configuration of procedural rhetorics. While Bogost discusses the role of general player participation, he does not attempt to outline how different types of play styles might lead to different patterns of social action or persuasion. A player's strategy for engaging a serious game might range from complacent and casual to resistant and radical. I suggest turning to play styles and learning styles as a next move because a recognition of these player contingencies reveals the contingent and dynamic nature of game genres. Such a research move would also shift from a taxonomic, top-down approach to serious game genres toward a decentralized theory that recognizes the "relatively stable" (Bakhtin, 1986, p. 78) and "stable-for-now" (Schryer, 1994, p. 108) qualities of genre. Another implication of this research direction is that it could produce more richly descriptive ideas of genre as a range of social outcomes or as a collection of "possibility spaces" (Sawyer & Smith, 2008) rather than a single label that stands in for the entire experience of playing a serious game. Gee's (2007) work on "affinity groups" is also relevant here, as the possibility spaces opened up by serious gaming experiences involve particular ways of "thinking, acting, interacting, valuing and believing, as well as the typical sorts of social practices associated with a given semiotic domain" (pp. 27–28).

The perspective on genre and play theory provided by Christensen, Cootey, and Moeller (2007) could also be developed into a genre framework for serious games that helps to address genre's shifting role in carrying out the social action of serious gaming. Christensen, Cootey, and Moeller note that "the meaning-making activities within genre fields are formed by the interplay between genres and their human agents. Consequently, genres function as agents, leading to the creation, reification, and transformation of the social structures that initially called them into being" (p. 8). In response to this claim of genres as agents, one of the research questions to pull out for serious games would be how to locate the issue of agency within the activity of serious gaming. For instance, in Selfe and Hawisher's (2007) collection of case studies on digital gaming literacies, the theme of agency comes up as one of the primary motivating factors in gaming. For example, Fleischer, Wright, and Barnes (2007) discuss one player who cites "his desire for a sense of effective agency—the ability to have control over some aspect of the world" as one of his major reasons for playing games (p. 147). As "agency" and "control" are often paired with the interactivity of digital games as affordances of the medium, an investigation into how serious game players experience agency can contribute to our understanding of the role of the "player–agent." Likewise, we can explore how serious game *genres* might be involved the performing of "agency," which is suggested by Freedman's (1996) description of genre "interplay and interaction" (p. 4).

To address the intersection between serious gaming and agency, one move I suggest here is expanding the kind of agency discussion that Fleischer, Wright, and Barnes (2007) focus on to include the forms of "real-world" social action at stake in serious gaming. Fleischer, Wright, and Barnes analyze how agency is a function of having control over the game world, of feeling that in-game actions will result in some meaningful and efficacious outcome. In this sense, agency is a kind of psychological or emotional pleasure that a system of gameplay affords an individual player, but agency is not represented as socially transformative in the way that Christensen, Cootey, and Moeller (2007) describe. As one example of how gaming agency might be reconfigured to account for these social actions, *Darfur is Dying* (mtvU, 2006) foregrounds agency in a way that connects the player's participation in the game world with several rhetorical exigencies for "taking action" to intervene in the Darfur crisis. For instance, the main interface of the refugee camp area in the game features a "Take Action" button that, in effect, temporarily removes the player from the game and directly links him or her to options for exercising agency in response to the real-world problems the game is responding to. Options include "Send a Message to President Obama," "Ask Your Representative to Support the People of Darfur," and "Start a Divestment Movement on Your Campus," among others.. To fully account for agency in serious gaming experiences, then, we must extend the concept of agency as control over a game world and link it to the performance and perception of agency in other environments.

Another possible research frame to look at would be Spinuzzi and Zachry's (2000) formulation of the "genre ecology." Taking a genre ecology approach suggests that researchers look beyond the player's interaction with the game itself to frame the larger activity of serious gaming and examine how players draw upon distributed genres to mediate that activity. For a serious game, a sample genre ecology might include official game documentation, related online tutorials, wiki articles, blog entries and comments, FAQs or walkthroughs, and other genres. I also argue that more work in methodology is needed to account for how players use "outside" genres to mediate gaming activity, especially for serious games. A few places to start surveying existing methodologies for this purpose include usability studies approaches such as cognitive walkthrough, "cognitive ethnography" approaches that have been applied to online gaming (Steinkuehler, 2007), "genre tracing" in studies of professional writing (Spinuzzi, 2003, 2008), and iterative models of playtesting and prototyping used in game design (Winn, 2008). Testing out these various methodologies and methods will generate knowledge about how players negotiate gameplay in serious games and how they understand the persuasive/learning functions of games as they intersect with the typical goals of completing game objectives. Extending work on methodology in these directions has potential for both understanding the various rhetorical configurations that players participate in and informing the design of assessment for serious games.

In discussing the implications of the genre ecology framework, Spinuzzi and Zachry (2000) also present a set of three "heuristic tools" that could be applied toward further research in serious gaming, which are "exploratory questions, genre ecology diagrams, and organic engineering" (p. 176). The latter two techniques would be valuable not only for understanding how players draw upon genres as they play but also as a way to inform serious game design processes such as prototyping, playtesting, and user interface design. For instance, Spinuzzi and Zachry note that "genre ecology diagrams can help designers to lay out relationships, analyze the interplay among genres, and identify which genres are central or peripheral to the use of the technology. The diagrams thus can be a resource for replanning the ecology" (pp. 177–178). In terms of user interface design, genre ecologies can be employed to facilitate "user interfaces that include space (or spaces) that users can fill with their own ideas" (p. 179). Although individualized feedback and the logging/journaling of game information are common elements of user experience design, letting players document their own "ad hoc" information might help players synthesize and apply meaningful information as they advance through the game.

One implication I have been hinting at throughout my discussion of serious gaming and genre is the notion of gameplay *as composition* or *as authorship*. Winn (2008) discusses the "player's story" as the resulting narrative that is constructed by individual sequences of gameplay choices, which differ from player to player and even differ for the same player across multiple sessions. In thinking about this from the perspective of rhetoric and composition, the player's story represents not just a design consideration but could also serve as a reflective commentary on what the player has "composed" during gameplay and how that material has been composed. The notion of gameplay as composition introduces some intriguing new angles to consider in what "counts" as writing or what "counts" as a literacy practice.

Likewise, considering gameplay in serious games *as authorship* introduces new angles and problems to consider for the work on authorship in digital environments. For studies of authorship in digital environments such as wikis, the traces of collaborative writing are often more transparent: version histories are archived so that earlier versions of a particular text can be comparatively viewed, and collaborative, decentralized groups of authors deliberate publicly on what revisions to make in "Talk" or "Discuss" pages. Although this is "messier" than the tradition of single-authored print texts, the notion of serious gameplay as authorship is messier still. Because digital games depend on player participation, is it always the case that the player is a coauthor in some sense? Is a game "authored" if players cannot advance in the game because of the difficulty level or other barriers? How do player-authored genres such as FAQs and message board threads participate in the authorship of a gaming experience? These are just a few of the related questions that might be undertaken in response to this study of serious games and genre.

In taking a broader perspective on rhetorical studies and serious games, then, another problem becomes how to locate the digital/visual/procedural rhetorics of serious games within larger systems of social and political discourse. For instance, "political" or "news" games that deal with global terrorism, such as Frasca's *September 12th* (Newsgaming.com, 2003), not only *respond to* political discourse (e.g., major news media coverage, political blogging, representations in popular culture) but shape, participate in, and advance that discourse. *September 12th* is a game that the Wall Street Journal has described as "one interesting example. .. of games' growing influence on contemporary art, politics, and culture" (Newsgaming.com, n.d.).

In the pursuit of these questions and the attempt to account for the persuasive work done by serious gaming, it makes sense to use rhetoric as just one branch of inquiry among many; for instance, it is important to also draw on theories of persuasion that have been developed in communication and advertising. The benefits of doing so lie not just in applying these theories "outside" of their original disciplinary contexts but in interrogating their value and relevance in response to new situations. For the issue of authority as a persuasion technique, for instance, there are a whole host of questions raised about the rhetorical construction of authority in serious gaming experiences as compared to other media platforms and modes of communication. Another example would be using theories of interactivity from communication to interrogate Bogost's (2007) formulation of procedural rhetoric. Although Bogost does some of this work himself, his theory depends heavily on the idea of interactivity, which suggests that an expanded review of the literature on interactivity might help define an even richer idea of procedural rhetoric. All of us, as scholars and designers interested in the persuasive and educational impacts of games, can thus benefit by reaching across disciplines to interrogate our own work and by critically *synthesizing* work across multiple disciplinary spaces as we explore new research questions related to serious games.

REFERENCES

Advergaming. (2009, August 23). Wikipedia, The Free Encyclopedia. Retrieved August 23, 2009, from http://en.wikipedia.org/w/index.php?title=Advergaming&oldid=309656941

Apperley, T. H. (2006). Genre and game studies: Toward a critical approach to video game genres. *Simulation & Gaming*, *37*(1), 6–23. doi:10.1177/1046878105282278

Bakhtin, M. M. (1986). *Speech genres and other late essays* (Emerson, C., & Holquist, M., Trans.). Austin, TX: University of Texas Press.

Bateman, C., & Boon, R. (2005). *21st century game design*. Hingham, MA: Charles River Media.

Bergeron, B. (2006). *Developing serious games*. Hingham, MA: Charles River Media.

Blackmon, S. (2007). Racing toward representation: An understanding of racial representation in video games. In Selfe, C. L., & Hawisher, G. E. (Eds.), *Gaming lives in the twenty-first century* (pp. 203–215). New York: Palgrave Macmillan.

Bogost, I. (2007). *Persuasive games: The expressive power of videogames*. Cambridge, MA: MIT Press.

Christensen, D. M., Cootey, J. L., & Moeller, R. M. (2007). Playing in genre fields: A play theory perspective on genre. In *SIGDOC'07: Proceedings of the 25th ACM International Conference on Design of Communication* (pp. 1–8). New York: Association for Computing Machinery.

Consalvo, M. (2003, February). *It's a queer world after all: Studying The Sims and sexuality*. Gay & Lesbian Alliance Against Defamation. Retrieved March 29, 2009, from http://www.glaad.org/documents/csms/The_Sims.pdf

Flanagan, M. (2003). *SIMple & personal: Domestic space & the Sims*. Paper presented at the 2003 Melbourne Digital Arts & Culture Conference. Retrieved March 29, 2009, from http://hypertext.rmit.edu.au/dac/papers/Flanagan.pdf

Fleischer, S. O., Wright, S. A., & Barnes, M. L. (2007). Dungeons, dragons, and discretion: A gateway to gaming, technology, and literacy. In Selfe, C. L., & Hawisher, G. E. (Eds.), *Gaming lives in the twenty-first century* (pp. 143–160). New York: Palgrave Macmillan.

Freedman, A. (1996). *ReACTivating genre: Re-GENERating discourse theory, research and pedagogy*. Keynote address presented at the European Writing Conferences, Barcelona, Spain.

Garrelts, N. (Ed.). (2006). *The meaning and culture of Grand Theft Auto*. Jefferson, NC: McFarland.

Garrelts, N. C. (2003). *The official strategy guide for video game studies: A grammar and rhetoric of video games*. Unpublished doctoral dissertation, Michigan State University, East Lansing, MI.

Gee, J. P. (2007). *What video games have to teach us about learning and literacy* (2nd ed.). New York: Palgrave Macmillan.

Geisler, C., Bazerman, C., Doheny-Farina, S., Gurak, L., Haas, C., & Johnson-Eilola, J. (2001). IText: Future directions for research on the relationship between information technology and writing. *Journal of Business and Technical Communication*, *15*(3), 269–308. doi:10.1177/105065190101500302

Heeter, C. (2008). Play styles and learning. In Ferding, R. (Ed.), *Handbook of research on effective electronic gaming in education* (pp. 826–846). Hershey, PA: IGI Global.

McAllister, K. S. (2004). *Game work: Language, power, and computer game culture*. Tuscaloosa, AL: University of Alabama Press.

Michael, D., & Chen, S. (2006). *Serious games: Games that educate, train, and inform*. Boston: Thomson Course Technology.

Miller, C. R. (1984). Genre as social action. *The Quarterly Journal of Speech*, *70*, 151–167. doi:10.1080/00335638409383686

mtvU. (2006). *Darfur Is Dying* [Online game]. Retrieved March 29, 2009, from http://www.darfurisdying.com

Newsgaming.com. (2003). *September 12th* [Online game]. Montevideo, Uruguay: Newsgaming.com. Retrieved March 29, 2009, from http://newsgaming.com/newsgames.htm

Newsgaming.com. (n.d.). *Homepage*. Uruguay: Newsgaming.com. Retrieved March 29, 2009, from http://newsgaming.com

Rosenblatt, L. M. (1978). *The reader, the text, the poem: The transactional theory of the literary work*. Carbondale, IL: Southern Illinois University Press.

Sawyer, B., & Smith, P. (2008). *Serious games taxonomy*. Retrieved from the Serious Games Initiative Web site: http://www.dmill.com/presentations/serious-games-taxonomy-2008.pdf

Schryer, C. F. (1994). The lab vs. the clinic: Sites of competing genres. In Freedman, A., & Medway, P. (Eds.), *Genre and the new rhetoric* (pp. 105–124). London: Taylor & Francis.

Selfe, C. L., & Hawisher, G. E. (Eds.). (2007). *Gaming lives in the twenty-first century: Literate connections*. New York: Palgrave Macmillan. doi:10.1057/9780230601765

Sherlock, L. M. (2007). When social networking meets online games: The activity system of grouping in World of Warcraft. In *SIGDOC'07: Proceedings of the 25th ACM International Conference on Design of Communication* (pp. 14-20). New York: Association for Computing Machinery.

Sherlock, L. M. (2009). Genre, activity, and collaborative work and play in World of Warcraft: Places and problems of open systems in online gaming. *Journal of Business and Technical Communication*, *23*(3), 263–293. doi:10.1177/1050651909333150

Spinuzzi, C. (2003). *Tracing genres through organizations: A sociocultural approach to information design*. Cambridge, MA: MIT Press.

Spinuzzi, C. (2008). *Network: Theorizing knowledge work in telecommunications*. New York: Cambridge University Press. doi:10.1017/CBO9780511509605

Spinuzzi, C., & Zachry, M. (2000). Genre ecologies: An open-system approach to understanding and constructing documentation. *Journal of Computer Documentation, 24*, 169–181. doi:10.1145/344599.344646

Steinkuehler, C. (2007). Massively multiplayer online gaming as a constellation of literacy practices. *E-learning, 4*, 297–318. doi:10.2304/elea.2007.4.3.297

Video game genres. (2009, August 26). Wikipedia, The Free Encyclopedia. Retrieved August 26, 2009, from http://en.wikipedia.org/w/index.php?title=Video_game_genres&oldid=310139217

Vitanza, V. J. (1987). Critical sub/versions of the history of philosophical rhetoric. *Rhetoric Review, 6*(1), 41–66.

Winn, B. (2008). The design, play, and experience framework. In Ferding, R. (Ed.), *Handbook of Research on Effective Electronic Gaming in Education* (pp. 1010–1024). Hershey, PA: IGI Global.

Wolf, M. J. P. (2001). Genre and the video game. In Wolf, M. J. P. (Ed.), *The medium of the video game* (pp. 113–134). Austin, TX: University of Texas Press.

Wysocki, A. F. (2003). The multiple media of texts: How onscreen and paper texts incorporate words, images, and other media. In Bazerman, C., & Prior, P. (Eds.), *What writing does and how it does it: An introduction to analysis of text and textual practices* (pp. 123–163). Mahwah, NJ: Lawrence Erlbaum and Associates.

Zappen, J. P. (2005). Digital rhetoric: Toward an integrated theory. *Technical Communication Quarterly, 14*(3), 319–325. doi:10.1207/s15427625tcq1403_10

"MUST-READS" FOR SERIOUS GAMES AND GENRE

Apperley, T. H. (2006). Genre and game studies: Toward a critical approach to video game genres. *Simulation & Gaming, 37*(1), 6–23. doi:10.1177/1046878105282278

Artemeva, N. (2008). Toward a unified social theory of genre learning. *Journal of Business and Technical Communication, 22*, 160–185. doi:10.1177/1050651907311925

Artemeva, N., & Freedman, A. (Eds.). (2006). *Rhetorical genre studies and beyond*. Winnipeg: Inkshed.

Bakhtin, M. M. (1986). *Speech genres and other late essays* (Emerson, C., & Holquist, M., Trans.). Austin, TX: University of Texas Press.

Bergeron, B. (2006). *Developing serious games*. Hingham, MA: Charles River Media.

Bogost, I. (2007). *Persuasive games: The expressive power of videogames*. Cambridge, MA: MIT Press.

Christensen, D. M., Cootey, J. L., & Moeller, R. M. (2007). Playing in genre fields: A play theory perspective on genre. In *SIGDOC '07: Proceedings of the 25th ACM International Conference on Design of Communication* (pp. 1–8). New York: Association for Computing Machinery.

Gee, J. P. (2007). *What video games have to teach us about learning and literacy* (2nd ed.). New York: Palgrave Macmillan.

McAllister, K. S. (2004). *Game work: Language, power, and computer game culture*. Tuscaloosa, AL: University of Alabama Press.

Miller, C. R. (1984). Genre as social action. *The Quarterly Journal of Speech*, *70*, 151–167. doi:10.1080/00335638409383686

Sawyer, B., & Smith, P. (2008). *Serious games taxonomy*. Retrieved from the Serious Games Initiative: http://www.dmill.com/presentations/serious-games-taxonomy-2008.pdf

Schryer, C. F. (1994). The lab vs. the clinic: Sites of competing genres. In Freedman, A., & Medway, P. (Eds.), *Genre and the new rhetoric* (pp. 105–124). London: Taylor & Francis.

Spinuzzi, C. (2003). *Tracing genres through organizations: A sociocultural approach to information design*. Cambridge, MA: MIT Press.

Spinuzzi, C., & Zachry, M. (2000). Genre ecologies: An open-system approach to understanding and constructing documentation. *Journal of Computer Documentation*, *24*, 169–181. doi:10.1145/344599.344646

Steinkuehler, C. (2007). Massively multiplayer online gaming as a constellation of literacy practices. *E-learning*, *4*, 297–318. doi:10.2304/elea.2007.4.3.297

Wolf, M. J. P. (2001). Genre and the video game. In Wolf, M. J. P. (Ed.), *The medium of the video game* (pp. 113–134). Austin, TX: University of Texas Press.

TOP TEXTS FOR INTERDISCIPLINARY STUDY OF SERIOUS GAMES

Apostel, S. (2008). Thinking through persuasive play: Encouraging a reflective gaming experience. *Computers and Composition Online*, Fall 2008. Retrieved from http://www.bgsu.edu/cconline/gaming_issue_2008/Apostel_Thinking_through/apostel.html

Bogost, I. (2007). *Persuasive games: The expressive power of videogames*. Cambridge, MA: MIT Press.

Bono, J. J. (2008). Alternate reality games: Composition, collaboration, and real community play. *Computers and Composition Online*, Fall 2008. Retrieved from http://www.bgsu.edu/cconline/gaming_issue_2008/Bono_ARG/index.html

King, M. (2008). Remapping Rhetorical Peaks: A video game for first-year writing. *Computers and Composition Online*, Fall 2008. Retrieved from http://www.bgsu.edu/cconline/gaming_issue_2008/King_Rhetorical_peaks/index.html

McAllister, K. S. (2004). *Game work: Language, power, and computer game culture*. Tuscaloosa, AL: University of Alabama Press.

Moeller, R. M., & White, K. (2008). Enter the game factor: Putting theory into practice in the design of Peer Factor. *Computers and Composition Online*, Fall 2008. Retrieved from http://www.bgsu.edu/cconline/gaming_issue_2008/Moeller_White_Enter_the_game/index.html

Robison, A. J. (2008). The design is the game: Writing games, teaching writing. *Computers and Composition*, *25*(3), 359–370. doi:10.1016/j.compcom.2008.04.006

Selfe, C. L., & Hawisher, G. E. (Eds.). (2007). *Gaming lives in the twenty-first century: Literate connections*. New York: Palgrave Macmillan. doi:10.1057/9780230601765

Sheridan, D. M., & Hart-Davidson, W. (2008). Just for fun: Writing and literacy learning as forms of play. *Computers and Composition*, *25*(3), 323–340. doi:10.1016/j.compcom.2008.04.008

Wardrip-Fruin, N., & Harrigan, P. (Eds.). (2004). *First person: New media as story, performance, and game*. Cambridge, MA: MIT Press.

Section 2
Theoretical Perspectives

Chapter 4
Serious Games for Transformative Learning:
A Communication Perspective on the Radical Binarisation of Everyday Life

Thomas J. Yannuzzi
Penn State University, USA

Bryan G. Behrenshausen
Millersville University, USA

ABSTRACT

This chapter discusses the ways in which an understanding of key concepts from both communication studies and critical pedagogy can improve the use of serious games in learning environments. By exploring a history of educational theory that champions the ontological work of critical pedagogy, the authors note how critical self-reflection can be facilitated by serious games. This chapter then distinguishes between models of human communication as information transfer (on which some educational gaming situations are implicitly based) and models of human communication as social construction, or a process of co-constructing social realities and identities (on which new and future gaming situations might be based) as a way of demonstrating to both designers and educators the benefits of viewing games communicatively. Because video games are symptom and emblem of life in informatic control societies, their role in education is exceedingly important for cultivating students' critical reflection on the binarisation of everyday life (which is increasingly structured by algorithmic logics that polarize lived experience). Serious games often provide opportunities for gamers to become "experts" of scientific or informational knowledge and often more skilled technique—or skilled, technical know-how. However, they often fail to provide opportunities for critically reflective practice or the development of praxis. Incredibly rapid technological/scientific advancements in societies focused on production leave little room for mindful activity. Although we continue to "advance," we often fail to unite two fundamental aspects of critical learning: the moral and political (praxis) with the technical and productive (techne). Serious games can assist in doing this.

DOI: 10.4018/978-1-61520-719-0.ch004

Copyright © 2010, IGI Global. Copying or distributing in print or electronic forms without written permission of IGI Global is prohibited.

INTRODUCTION

Experiential methods, including case studies, simulations, role-plays, and group work have become commonplace in most K-12 and undergraduate- and graduate-level classrooms. One of the newest and perhaps most potentially influential experiential tools is the video game. Gee (2008) notes that "during the past several years, many people have become interested in video games as a site to study human thinking, problem solving, and learning" (p. 253). Bousquet (2008) suggests that "the use of such simulations, models and games is [also] widespread in bureaucratic, professional, service, and manufacturing training environments" (p. 72). He further states:

The serious gaming trend has seen the emergence of games designed to promote environmental awareness, armed forces recruitment, white supremacy, religious tolerance, better eating habits, approaches to living with chronic diseases, and so on. Wherever there is real-world rhetorical and practical purpose, institutions and activist organizations have commissioned games to propagandize, train, inform, and recruit. (p. 72)

There is no question that the games commissioned and developed to educate aim to provide much more than the information and skills necessary to participate in required roles or perform specific functions. These games, like all aspects of experience, help instill the cultural norms or structural resources used to guide desired behavior. Such an increased use of video games specifically and technology in general, therefore, has spawned growing interest in the potential ability for using these experiential tools to impact higher-order learning and enhance critical pedagogy (Arnseth, 2006). This chapter is one more piece of the growing puzzle surrounding issues of experiential learning and critical pedagogy, especially as they relate to the use of video games and gaming. Indeed, the body of existing scholarly work on experiential learning theory is vast, and this corpus has contributed fruitfully to theorizing the role of games in metacognitive education (see Kolb & Kolb, 2009, for an extensive review of past research and key concepts within the field of education). In this chapter, we specifically discuss ways in which video gaming might act as a pedagogical tool to help transcend critical reflection and facilitate more critical self-reflection, enhancing the ontological goals of contemporary education. We situate our exploration in the field of communication studies, and suggest that approaching games from within our field provides tools to mindfully construct and deconstruct the gaming experience.

Furthermore, we suggest that only through becoming mindful of the discursive *praxis* encasing the gaming experience—pulling game and gamer together in an uncertain, co-constituted experience of gaming—can critical self-reflection occur. We must caution against the use of serious games, or any experiential tool for that matter, that enhances or teaches connections between scientific/technical knowledge (*episteme*) and skillful technique (*techne*) without a solid grounding in practical wisdom (*phronesis*) and reflective action (*praxis*). In short, we suggest that a communication model housed in social constructionism and geared toward grounded practical theory (Craig & Tracy, 1995) provides the best opportunity for serious games to reach their ontological objectives. Craig and Tracy (1995) argue that such grounded practical theory can enhance our understanding of the relationships between practice and technique. They further note that a basic problem in the communication discipline (and of many who attempt to incorporate communication processes as links between self and society) is one of uniting these two aspects of communication—the moral and political (*praxis*) with the technical and productive (*techne*) (p. 252). In many respects, we suggest that research on and design of serious educational gaming has focused too heavily on learning of *techne* in the absence of *praxis*. It is our hope that by describing how this alternative approach can be used to better develop and use games for learning, we can begin to close the *praxis/techne* gap and better address the ontological call of education.[1].

To demonstrate such an approach, we distinguish between models of human communication as information transfer (on which some educational games are implicitly based) and models of human communication as social construction, or a process of co-constructing and organizing social relationships and personal identities (on which new and future games might be based). Because video games are symptom and emblem of life in informatic control societies (Deleuze, 1992), their role in education is exceedingly important for cultivating students' critical self-reflection on the process by which selves and others are individuated in social and cultural contexts structured by digital technologies: a process we refer to as the radical binarisation of complex, everyday life events. Because everyday life is increasingly pervaded by algorithmic systems that structure lived experience according to digital logics, utilizing video games in educational settings is a way of interrogating these logics and helping players explore their consequences for agency, identity, and embodiment.

The chapter begins with a brief review of the "ontological" call of education and the importance of incorporating *praxis* into the design and implementation of serious games. We then provide a brief overview of a communication perspective and suggest it provides a fresh way of thinking and talking about gaming. Next, we suggest that integrating a communication perspective with critical pedagogy, pragmatism, constructivism, experiential learning, and contemporary video game theory enhances the potential for using games to facilitate critical self-reflection. This view is particularly advantageous for addressing the embodiment of binarisation, of which, not incidentally, video games are a prime example. It also helps designers and teachers think differently about what we conceive of as an educational game and the boundaries we place on the educational experience.

BACKGROUND

Transformative Learning

Much of the renewed interest in experiential methods focuses on what Packer and Greco-Brookes (1999) refer to as the "ontological work of school," which specifically demands that schools "change the kinds of person their students become" (p. 134). In other words, teachers have been granted the privilege and the challenge to educate and develop the person, not just the student, in learning environments. Accordingly, students are encouraged to engage in case studies, small-group activities, role-plays, simulations, and other experiential methods that claim to promote deeper levels of self-reflection and increase critical thinking. Presumably, this mindful consideration of tacit knowledge allows interlocutors to enact more sensitive judgment and more appropriate discursive choices in everyday interactions.

Such ontological goals of education draw from a variety of educational roots, including those of critical pedagogy aligned primarily with educational scholars such as Paulo Freire (1994, 2000) and Jack Mezirow (1990, 1991, 1997, 1998; Mezirow & Associates, 2000). While Mezirow's thoughts on transformative learning (and the subsequent work that comes from them) hint at a grand theory of education (Brookfield, 2000), According to Cranton and King (2003), Mezirow's core assumption remains somewhat basic:

We make meaning of the world through our experiences. What happens once, we expect to happen again. Through this process, we develop habits of mind or a frame of reference for understanding the world, much of which is uncritically assimilated. In the process of daily living, we absorb values, assumptions and beliefs about how things are without much thought. (p. 32)

Transformative learning, then, takes place when students' "habits of mind" are challenged and reflected upon. The idea that experience forms "mental models" (Senge, 1994) or default assumptions from which we can operate with "logical force" (Pearce, 2007) is not necessarily new. The question for critical pedagogy, however, is how to change the course of "minding." Mezirow, like Dewey, seems to conceive of a mind that is "largely unconscious and essentially social and historical in its constitution" (Craig, 2001. It is a mind that "appears in individuals" but is not an "individual mind." Rather, it is a field of symbolic forms "instituted under the influence of custom and tradition" (Dewey, 1929, p. 180; see also Craig, 2001 p. 136). Cunliff (2004) suggests that from this constructionist perspective, learning becomes an embodied (whole body), responsive understanding in which we become more aware of, and skilled in, constituting and maintaining our realities and identities. In practical terms, we can equate learning with moments in which we are "struck. .. and moved to change our ways of talking and acting" (p. 410).

This process seems supported by numerous scholars. Piaget notes that learning involves "a series of active constructions and adjustments on the part of the child in response to external perturbances" (Dimitriadis & Kamberelis, 2006, p. 171). Children adapt to these perturbances through the processes of assimilation and accommodation, where assimilation attempts to make new experiences fit into existing mental models, and accommodation attempts to make existing models consistent with new experiences. Piaget suggests a symbiotic learning process driven by a dynamic equilibrium in which children are consistently attempting to bridge that which they know with that which they are experiencing. The sense of equivocality (see Weick, 1995) or uncertainty between known and experienced is mitigated through assimilating and accommodating. "Together," therefore, "assimilation and accommodation account for children's continual adaptation to the world around them, which most people call learning" (p. 171).

The primary objective of the transformational approach to ontological learning, therefore, is to "jolt" students into recognizing and critically challenging their "habits of mind" with the hope of cultivating new ways of thinking and talking about their experiences in social worlds they help construct. Obviously, to sustain this new way of thinking and talking, one must gain an ability to enact critical *self*-reflective practices (Mezirow, 1998; Brookfield, 2000), and this is where critical pedagogical practice becomes a little messy. Before addressing the messiness, however, we first discuss critical pedagogy as it relates to transformative learning and serious games.

Critical Pedagogy

Critical pedagogy pulls on a basic, powerful, synergistic element of most contemporary learning theories: that human thought about self is constructed in the self's interaction with her/his world and, in turn, serves to form a world into which self can fit more easily. This view is very consistent with those expressed above; learning, especially self-learning, is driven through social experience. The learner must first interact with someone or something in his/her environment and then attempt to make sense of what is already learned with what is novel, so that s/he may act again. Running through the works of Dewey (1938), Mead (1934), Vygotsky (1978), Friere (1994) and others is the notion that human sense of self and self-learning is formed through social/individual interaction. "[A] central message in Vygotsky's work is that an essential condition for understanding the psychological development of an individual is to understand the system of social relations within which the individuals live" (Lainema, 2009, p. 53). Vygotsky's (1978) zone of proximal development (ZPD) or, as he describes it, "*the distance between the actual developmental level as determined by independent problem solving and the level of potential development as determined through problem solving under adult guidance or in collaboration with more capable peers*" (p. 86; italics in original; also cited in Dimitriadis & Kamberelis, 2006, p. 196) emphasizes the inherent social process of learning. The theoretical importance of the ZPD, Dimitriadis and Kamberelis (2006) argue, is that it is "situated within the context of the specific social and cultural environments with which the child or learner is involved" (p. 197). Cultural environments are inherently communicative and "constructed in a web of social interactions and relations, and so learning in the ZPD leads not only to the development of concepts and knowledge but also to the development of culturally appropriate practices" (Dimitriadis & Kamberelis, 2006, 197). Dimitriadis and Kamberelis note that for Vygotsky,, "it is through others that we develop into ourselves.. .. Development does not proceed toward socialization but toward the conversion of social relations into mental functions" (p. 192). Vygotsky refers to this as a process of internalization, or the process whereby cultural ways of thinking and structural resources enacted within social interactions becomes part of participants' intrapersonal mental models. Vygotsky specifically points out that "internalization transforms the process itself and changes its structures and functions.... [The] process of internalization is not the transfer of an external activity to a preexisting, internal 'plane of consciousness': it is the process by which the plane is formed" (in Dimitriadis & Kamberelis, 2006, p. 193). According to Kisiel (1985), Gadamer is consistent with Vygotsky, noting that "long before we understand ourselves in retrospect we understand ourselves as a matter of course in the family, society and state in which we live.. .. Hence the individual's prejudgments much more than his judgments are the historical reality of his 'Being'" (p. 7).[2]Borofsky (1994) also argues that among "the most prominent factors structuring knowing are the experiences of everyday life" (p. 338), and Piaget, notes, "the shaping of cognitive constructions is not passive information adaptation through senses (empiricism, behaviorism) or information selection to channels of limited capacity (information processing) but active functioning in the real world and a coordination of these actions as consistent constructions" (Lainema, 2009, pp. 52–53). Finally, Dewey (1938) suggests a similar drive toward "coordination" and "consistency" when he describes inquiry as "the directed or controlled transformation of an indeterminate situation into a determinately unified one" (p. 117).

As noted above, coordination and consistency between the known and that being experienced, including self-experienced, is not conceived as a reachable static goal but as an interactive accomplishment in a constant state of dynamic equilibrium. Cognitive development, and therefore self development, is an ongoing process of sense-making as we work through and dialogue about problematic events—those episodes in which routine actions may have undesirable or unpredictable impact—in everyday situations. Human interaction, then, is the process through which we construct and organize our worlds, including the our part of that world. Every moment of interaction positions a self with an other in some context. "[T]he referential process is one in which subjects, objects, and social relations are simultaneously produced in the course of even the most mundane utterances" (Hanks, 1996, p. 237). Language, in all the symbolic forms through which we mold it, allows us to "realize ourselves; effect changes in our worlds; connect with other people; experience beauty, rage, and tenderness; exercise authority; refuse; and pursue our interests" (Hanks, 1996, p. 236; see also Packer & Greco-Brooks, 1999, p. 136). Giddens (1991) suggests that individuals are constantly remaking their selves through reflexively constructing autobiographical narratives that connect their personal histories with social histories that are rapidly and continually changing (Cameron, 2000). Gergen (1991) also points out that persons "exist in a state of continuous construction and reconstruction; it is a world where anything goes that can be negotiated. Each reality of self gives way to reflexive questionings, irony, and ultimately the playful probing of yet another reality. The center fails to hold" (pp. 5–6). Therefore, although coordination and consistency suggest a dynamic interplay between two separate entities, the mind/self and environment exist as one, co-constituting each other into wholeness of structure (Giddens, 1984). Organisms, then (i.e., humans), only exist in and because of environments in which the "processes of living are enacted by the environment as truly as by the organism; for they are an integration" (Dewey, 1938, p. 25). Obviously, this seamless, co-constitutive nature of "Being" needs to be recognized and highlighted in any pedagogy using games as tools for critical self-reflection. Bateson (1972) notes "the essential stock-in-trade of educators, can be seen as various habits of punctuating the stream of experience so that it takes on one or another sort of coherence and sense" (p. 163). However, it also needs to be recognized and utilized by designers of serious games as well; not only to help better design games but to reexamine what they include in the educational gaming experience.

Perhaps the most prominent shift in this perspective is that critical reflection becomes very different from critical self reflection. While critical reflection or thinking can exist in a dichotomized self–other world, critical self-reflection cannot. Critical self-reflection requires one to see one's self as part and parcel of the problem being experienced. The very construction of the problem is in part the construction of the self constructing it. All reflection, then, in and of itself, is not necessarily critical. Critical self-reflection on assumptions, Mezirow (1998) argues, "emphasizes critical analysis of the psychological or cultural assumptions that are the specific reason for one's conceptual and psychological limitations, the constitutive processes or conditions of formation of one's experience and beliefs" (p. 6).

Critical self-reflection, then, allows us to acknowledge our prejudices (what is already learned) and work with them to better understand novel situations. As Gadamer notes, "Prejudices are not necessarily unjustified and erroneous [but] are simply the conditions whereby we experience something—whereby what we encounter says something to us" (in Bernstein, 1985, pp. 274–275)

"The trick," Kisiel notes, "is to begin appropriately in knowledge where we have already been begun in 'Being.' The epistemological problem for finite understanding is therefore not a matter of discarding prejudices in order to begin absolutely, but to determine what distinguishes the legitimate prejudices from the prejudices which obstruct understanding" (1985, p. 7).

Steedman (1991), therefore, is seemingly right in noting that critical self-reflection involves a stereoscopic account of the construction of meaning: "one lens is on the individual context of interpretations [and actions], the other is on the social context which creates the individual" (p. 55). However, the underlying structure this statement suggests is why critical pedagogical practice, especially in how it relates to experiential learning and gaming in particular, can become so messy.

"Messiness" Between Critical Pedagogical Theory and Practice

Lainema (2009), in reviewing Duffy and Cunningham's (1996) work on constructivism, suggests

technology should be seen as an integral component of cognitive activity. The focus is not on the individual but on the activity in the environment. The task of the learner is no longer seen as static—the computer applied to the task—but rather it is dynamic. The computer opens new opportunities and makes available new learning activities. (p. 60)

Lainema (2009) further notes "the strategy that Duffy and Cunningham are calling for is called 'the problem as a stimulus for authentic activity.' The focus should be on developing the skills to solve the problem and other problems like it" (p. 60). Furthermore, problems should be approached using breadth and not just depth of information. Duffy and Cunningham (1996) themselves note "success will increasingly depend on exploring interrelationships in an information-rich environment rather than accept the point of view of one author who pursued one set of relationships and presents conclusions reflecting his or her implicit biases" (p. 188). At one level, we would agree with these statements by Lainema or Duffy and Cunningham. However, at a transformational level, we suggest they inherently, although perhaps unintentionally, limit our thinking about gaming and transformational learning in at least two ways. First, they imply an inherent duality between self and society. Secondly, they emphasize skills based on knowledge, while assuming students have the wisdom to use the skills they develop. We address both of these issues below.

Transcending the Self/ Other Antimony

The statements by Lainema (2009) and Duffy and Cunningham (1996) are perfectly legitimate statements that, unfortunately, imply a fundamental duality is often overlooked in practice. Failing to acknowledge and address the implied duality between self and society focuses critical analysis outward. This self–society antinomy (Gergen, 1999) in our own talk about learning continues to reify a dichotomy in practice:

The critical problem in moving toward a fully relational formulation again inheres in the discursive resources with which we approach the issue. In particular, our traditional account of "relationship" presumes the independent preexistence of the elements to be related. Thus, when attempting to create the sense of unity, we are inevitably forced to speak of that which enters into the unity—thus essentializing the very elements we wish to transcend. (p. 177)

Therefore, although we espouse theories of serious games that are consistent with critical pedagogy, we often practice theory in ways that limit our framing of the process, thereby limiting our understanding of the pedagogical challenges and possibilities in teaching critical self-reflection. In critical pedagogical practice, often the activities to which Duffy and Cunningham refer and upon which learning should be focused become "informatic. Gaming becomes a process of expertly gathering and deploying information as opposed to defining and being defined by the gaming process itself. We believe a communication perspective helps teachers and designers reframe and rethink the gaming experience and, accordingly, the potential learning that comes from it. We will expand this point below; for now, let us look closer at the inherent antimony in critical pedagogical practice.

According to Dimitriadis & Kamberelis (2006), De Saussure, asserted that language can be understood only in terms of relationships. "Because signs are arbitrary, the meaning of any particular sign is determined in terms of similarity and difference in relation to other signs. Thus, meaning is founded on *binary oppositions*. .. . Meaning, then, is predicated on difference. Sacred means 'not profane,' inside means 'not outside,' and so on" (, p. 40; emphasis in original). Therefore, in our thinking about self, we often see and speak of it as separate from society, and in our thinking about society (the other, the context, the problem, the information, the game, etc.) we see it separate from self. Consequently, we fail to provide the necessary component to Steedman's (1991) stereoscopic view—depth. This unavoidable process of linguistic binarisation is indeed a foundational problem in communication studies (see Bateson, 1968). Early systems theorists who laid the groundwork for communication as a distinct field of inquiry typically distinguish between "analog" and "digital" communication. The former operates according to an inclusive "both/and" logic (Lanigan, 1988), which "operates within all behavior, all action, all haptic spatio-temporal arrangement of material conditions, and as an ineradicable emotive underbelly to the spoken word" (Anton, 2003, p. 132). Analog communication is concretely connected to the lived conditions of persons and things; or, as Anton stresses, "*there are no differing levels of abstraction* [with regard to analog communication], *and so, there are neither classes nor different logical types* (p. 132, emphasis in original; see also Bateson (1972) for description of logical types). Analog communication—exemplified in human speech by nonverbal qualities such as vocal volume, intonation, and gesture, or in nonhuman behavior by similar nonverbal, kinesic maneuvers that regulate relations between organism and environment—is fundamentally relational (Watzlawick, Bavelas, & Jackson, 1967). The "both/and" logic by which it operates keeps organisms tethered to both other organisms and environments in a continually ebbing and flowing, ongoing, relational state of flux. Because it is "not denotative and is void of propositions," we can say that "it is the regard and management of *differences within* relation-states" (Anton, 2003, p. 133, emphasis in original). Bateson (1972), in his original thinking about logical types, recognized the challenge of understanding analogue communication. He notes "[t]he theory in its original form deals only with rigorously digital communication, and it is doubtful how far it may be applied to analogue or iconic systems" (p. 291).

Digital communication parses analogic flux as the means by which organisms mark distinctions in their perpetually ongoing relational comportments (i.e., sounds are parsed into recognizable syllables, syllables into words, words into sentences, and sentences into larger statements, which consequently allow for distinguishing classes and types, objects and environments, figure and ground). Digital communication—exemplified by spoken, linguistic speech, writing, and other propositional forms of expression and perception—is fundamentally denotative. The "either/or" logic by which it operates "cuts" relation–states into discrete and discussable objects; it parses relational flux and abstracts experience when attempting to mark distinctions between otherwise contiguous relation–states. It allows humans to "frame" and make sense of ongoing "strips" of experience (Goffman, 1974). "Taking the infinity of prepositional possibilities, speech introduces boundaries; it punctuates relation–states.... We digitally codify concrete contexts and therein disclose categorical apprehensions" (Anton, 2003, p. 136). Bateson (1972) notes, however:

In the punctuation of human interaction. .. the adjectives. .. which purport to describe individual character are really not strictly applicable to the individual but rather describe transactions between the individual and his material and human environment. No man is "resourceful" or "dependent" or "fatalistic" in a vacuum.. .. . In such a system, words like "dominant" and "submissive," "succoring" and "dependent" will take on definable meaning as descriptions of segments of interchange. (p. 298)

Pertinent to the present context of serious games and learning, then, is the notion that talk of analog experience introduces digital distinctions that erect, reify, or reconfigure semantic boundaries which are arbitrary and contingent. Talking about, or digitizing, learning as a set of "activities" in an "information-rich environment" involving multiple perspectives seems to separate the learner from the activity itself, and the process seems to become a matter of integrating and using more breadth and depth of information to better manage self in social worlds.

In practice, therefore, the problem is often located *in* the learner (agent), the game (social structure), and/or the process (the relationship between them). Our goal becomes acquiring information to 1) develop greater self-awareness or more information about self (understanding our personality type, conflict style, etc.), 2) develop a greater awareness of the social context or more information about different social contexts (understanding cultural factors, group dynamics, an so forth), and/or 3) develop a greater awareness of the process between 1 and 2 or more information about social interaction (social influence, management, empathy, listening, etc.). Such a view assumes that awareness and understanding of these items as pieces of information will allow students to become more critically self-reflective and perhaps even initiate forethought in moment-to-moment enactments of their social worlds.[3] If the process is problematic, the solution is to merely obtain more information and change the necessary parts of the process. For example, one classic approach to conflict resolution under this paradigm insists that, instead of blaming in a conflict situation, one should describe behavior and tell the other how it makes one feel. Another is for managers to provide criticism by first pointing out positive features, then identifying the features you want to change, and ending with positive features. The process itself becomes inherently informatic and isolated from the immediacy, historicity, and futuricity of "Being."

Praxis: The Forgotten Learning

A second and even more sinister shift that occurs in comments like those from Duffy and Cunningham (1996) is the lost connection between informed, morally reflective action (*praxis*) and the skilled techniques we promote (*techne*). To better understand this argument, we must first consider the three types of knowledge about which Aristotle spoke—episteme, *praxis*, and *techne*. Aristotle made a clear distinction among scientific knowledge (episteme) and the practical wisdom one must have when applying that knowledge to everyday life experiences:

Scientific knowledge, is knowledge of what is universal, of what exists "of necessity" and takes the form of scientific demonstration. The subject matter, the form, the telos, the way in which episteme is learned and taught, differ from phronesis, the form of reasoning appropriate to **praxis**, *where there is always a mediation between the universal and the particular which involves a deliberation and choice. (in Bernstein, 1985, p. 277)*

Today, serious games, in specific, and education, in general, tend to emphasize an acquisition of knowledge (information) to better perform some type of skill. However, we often fail to recognize the gap we leave between the teaching for knowledge and skills and the teaching for critically self-reflective practice (*praxis*) when we enact the knowledge and skills we possess. It is in the *praxis*, not the knowledge or the skill that ontological learning must occur. *Praxis*, unlike episteme and *techne* involves phronesis, "a form of reasoning, yielding a type of 'ethical know-how' in which both what is universal and what is particular are co-determined" (Bernstein, 1985, p. 276). Bernstein, citing Gadamer, goes on to note that "phronesis involves a 'peculiar interlacing of being and knowledge, determination through one's own becoming.' It is not to be identified with or confused with the type of 'objective knowledge' that is detached from one's own being and becoming. .. authentic learning. .. is not detached from the interpreter, but constitutive of his or her *praxis*" (p. 276).

According to Bernstein (1985), Gadamer highlights the gap between *praxis* (ethical, moral, and political know-how) and *techne* (skilled or technical know-how). First, technique as a skill can be learned and forgotten. "By contrast, the subject of ethical reason, of phronesis, man always finds himself in an 'acting situation' and he is always obliged to use ethical knowledge and apply it according to the exigencies of his concrete situation" (Gadamer, 1979, p. 140). A second distinction highlights the inherent difference in the relationship between the means and ends of *techne* and *praxis* (phronesis). Unlike *techne*, whose ends aim to produce a particular product, phronesis looks toward a "complete ethical rectitude of a lifetime" (Gadamer, 1979, p. 142)). More importantly, technical know-how has an end that can be directly measured against standards of action, while phronesis, or ethical know-how can only produce ends that must be measured through the deliberation about the means appropriate to the particular situation. Finally, unlike technical know-how, ethical know-how is directly connected to the "knower." In other words, the person who understands technique can do so as an unaffected participant. However, the person with ethical, moral, and political understanding cannot know and act as one who is separate from or unaffected by the very act being performed. Nor can these acts take place outside of the interdependence between self with other (Bernstein, 1985, p. 277).

Today's learning environment tends to place greater emphasis on scientific and technical thinking. Unfortunately, as Craig (1989) notes:

Technological thought. .. attempts to reduce action to a series of repeatable motions (operationalizations) the consequences of which can be predicted according to scientific theory. Questions of evaluation... are removed to the background and even exiled from the realm of rational inquiry by technological thought, but they become the central questions for inquiry when action is regarded from the standpoint of praxis. (p. 108)

Turning our educational attention, including the design and implementation of serious games, toward greater emphasis on *praxis* seems particularly important at this time. As Gadamer notes "in a scientific culture such as ours the fields of techne and art are much more expended... many forms of our daily life are technologically organized so that they no longer require personal decision (Gadamer, 1981 in Bernstein, 1985, pp. 279–280)

The purpose of this chapter, therefore, is not to critique or criticize critical pedagogical practice or gaming but an attempt to add perspective to the practice of teaching critical self-reflection. More specifically, we suggest that a communication perspective on serious gaming allows designers and educators to better realize the ontological goals of experiential learning. In the following section, we present a brief interpretation of this perspective.

TAKING A COMMUNICATION PERSPECTIVE

While Gergen (1999) rightly points out the inherent antinomy in how we speak about self/society, the field of communication must take some of the blame for perpetuating this mindset. While our scholarship crosses many interests, our discipline is often known for its rhetorical grounding, which defines communication primarily as a skills oriented approach to practice—a practice which is often meant to help clarify and represent information more effectively, often in the hopes of influencing others. Penman (2000) captures this approach to communication when she states:

In the everyday world of organizations in which I usually work, the imaginings about communication are taken very much for granted. Members of these organizations usually present their concerns to me as centered on the need to improve communication, or to resolve some problem of communication. They expect that this can be done in a straightforward, technical manner. What they want to do is 'get their message across better,' 'improve the information flow from the top down,' or make sure that others 'comply with their instructions.' These requests reflect a certain imagining of communication that is predominant in our society and that by its very imagining precludes other possibilities from being. In this common imagining, communication is a relatively straightforward activity that we use to achieve effects—sending messages or controlling others. In this imagining, communication is merely an instrumental activity. (p. 3)

While many scholars might suggest we have moved beyond the information transfer model of communication, it is actually quite amazing and perhaps a little confusing that we continue to "dismiss the complexities and messiness of communication and treat it as a straight-forward, success-without-effort process" (Penman, 2000, p. 3).

Much of this emphasis on the explicit behavioral causes and effects of communication stems from an emphasis on the cybernetic tradition of communication studies. Craig (1999) points out that although it is the youngest trend in communication theory, it has certainly had the most impact on the current shape of the field.

The cybernetic tradition is perhaps best known from the works of Claude Shannon and Warren Weaver. Working at Bell Telephone Laboratories in 1948, Shannon famously developed an information theory that addressed "the limiting relationship between system capacity, signal, transmission speed, and signal degradation or 'noise'" (Ritchie, 1986, p. 278). When his work was published in the 1949 volume *The Mathematical Theory of Communication*, Shannon's essay was bundled alongside a paper by physicist Warren Weaver, who extrapolated Shannon's mathematical theory of communication beyond its original context—telephony—and attempted to apply Shannon's model of information transfer to the social sciences.[4] This historic maneuver set quite an unproductive course for a discipline that would soon become communication studies—one whose ramifications are still deeply felt to this day.

The most pervasive of these ramifications might be the deeply troubling presumption that human communication involves principally the linear transmission of content (messages) from one point to another with varying degrees of success. Indeed, as Penman (2000) notes above, this perhaps describes the pedestrian, commonsense understanding of "what" communication, as both product and process, "is" and "does" for humans. But when reading Shannon's (1949) assertion that "the fundamental problem of communication is that of reproducing at one point either exactly or approximately a message selected at another point" (p. 3), it is important to remember that the engineer was describing the purposes of mechanical systems of information exchange—not the more complex process of human interaction. Yet, from this common point of view, communication is thus identified as any overt, observable behavior (typically called a "message") whose goal is the replication of information in another with little alteration or resultant confusion. In short, the purpose of communication (and communicating) is reducing uncertainty and increasing the accuracy of message transmission to better align shared meanings (Lanigan, 1988).

Consequently, under the paradigm outlined by Weaver (1949), the study of communication is concerned primarily with problems of accuracy, precision, and effectiveness (which the physicist calls "the technical problem," "the semantic problem," and "the effectiveness problem," respectively [p. 96]). The question for a communication theorist thus becomes: How can one achieve a desired effect by transmitting information with the least possible resistance and ambiguity? The cybernetic model of communication, while hugely popular and useful in its own right, unfortunately reifies what many contemporary communication scholars from social constructionist, symbolic interactionist and constitutive theoretical approaches see as a severe limitation. As a result, much of communication scholarship, especially with the advent of postmodernism, has engendered profound shifts in the foci of communication studies. These shifts are numerous and nuanced (see Craig, 1999, for a fuller understanding of these traditions and shifts in focus). Elaborating on them all is beyond the scope of the current paper; however, for our purposes here, suffice it to say that these trends in communication scholarship directly challenged the presumptions and perceived limitations of Weaver's conjecture.

If communication is not merely an act of clearly and accurately transmitting information in the hopes of replicating meaning and influencing others, then what else is it? And how does this alternative definition help us better conceive of experiential learning, especially gaming, in a way that better promotes and facilitates critical self-reflection? Before discussing how a communication perspective can help gaming and learning, we wish to first discuss the perspective itself.

To break from the transmission model, we must first break from the concept of communication as something that exist in the world between people. For our purposes, it is better to think of communication as inherent to being together. It is constitutive and constructs who we become together. Communication, then, is the act of being in moments of time, in which "Being" persists both individually and socially. Craig (1999) notes that "communication, from a communication perspective, is not a secondary phenomenon that can be explained by antecedent psychological, sociological, cultural, or economic factors; rather, communication itself is the primary, constitutive social process that explains all these other factors" (p. 68). Deetz (1994) describes a communication perspective as "how the inner world, outer world, social relations, and means of expression are reciprocally constituted with the interactional process as its own best explanation" (p. 577). In other words, a constitutive communication perspective acknowledges that we are only individual in a social context, only social as individuals. Furthermore, the process that encapsulates individual/social is not only one of sharing information (although that is certainly one aspect of it), but rather one of human creation.

In order for humans to exist, we must construct and organize our lives together. For communication scholars, this means that communicators are often attempting to accomplish several goals at any one moment in attempts to coordinate and cohere persons and actions. One goal communicators consistently attempt to manage is task goals. In other words, in order to organize our "being together" we must somehow attempt to accomplish certain tasks with each other by performing acts such as complimenting, criticizing, questioning, consoling, joking, explaining, challenging, commanding, requesting, informing, correcting, and so forth. Individual/social life would be impossible without performing these tasks. Tracy (2002) relates these goals to speech acts (Austin, 1962; Searle, 1969) and notes that they attempt to answer "what act is being performed by uttering a particular set of words?" (p. 12). In other words, what was this person trying to do to me when he/she said/did something? Although Tracy highlights the use of words to accomplish these acts, other symbolic forms are intertwined with words to ultimately perform any specific act. Bateson (1972) concludes that in "the natural world, communication is rarely either purely digital or purely analogic. Often discrete digital pips are combined together to make analogic pictures as in the printer's halftone block; and sometime, as in the matter of context markers, there is a continuous gradation from the ostensive through the iconic to the purely digital" (p. 291). Tracy also acknowledges that acts are not always performed directly and, in fact, are oftentimes accomplished through indirect acts or strategic ambiguity (Eisenberg, 1984).

Four Levels of Identity

If communication were simply a matter of transferring information, there would be no reason for being strategically ambiguous or indirect in order to accomplish our task goals. In fact, according to Shannon and Weaver, humans would go out of their way to avoid ambiguity and enhance both the clarity and accuracy of messages. However, in the performing of acts together in hopes of accomplishing task goals, we must also manage relational and identity goals. Tracy (2002) identifies four levels of Identity operating in any one moment of "inter-acting." The first level can be considered master identity, or the more stable characteristics an individual brings to the act. For example, the authors of this piece could be seen as average height Caucasian males. There would also be additional nuances in our master identities, such as height, age, skin tone, weight, physical appearance, etc. Any of these more stable characteristics can change; however, accomplishing such change is difficult.

In addition to master identities, individuals also bring into being their interactional identities, personal identities, and relational identities. interactional identity is the role we take (or are given) in reference to another. For example, we are children in reference to our parents; they are parents in reference to us. We are teachers in reference to our students; they are students in reference to us, their teachers. Again, these interactional identities, or what they "mean," shift as we move through moments of time and space. For example, although our students may be seen as students in reference to us, the teachers, they may also become the "teachers" in reference to other students or, in certain moments, even to us. Even more subtle, we may be one type of "teacher" in one moment in time and another type of "teacher" in another moment in time.

In addition to being some one in reference to another, we also judge what we think about that some one, which refers to our personal identity. Personal identity, Tracy (2002) notes, is "what in ordinary life we talk about as personality, attitudes, and character" (p. 18) and refers directly to the attributions we ascribe to the "personhood" of self and others. In other words, given who we are and who we are not with each other, we make judgments about dispositions—are self and other aggressive, passive, genuine, inauthentic, overbearing, caring, etc.? Again, these identities shift in moments of time as we consistently attempt to organize our selves together. Also, as mentioned earlier, the language we use to talk about them is transactional. A person's "characteristic, whatever it be, is not his but is rather a characteristic of what goes on between him and something (or somebody) else" (Bateson, 1972, p. 298).

Finally, relational identities are those specific face concerns (Brown & Levinson, 1987; Goffman, 1974) we attempt to negotiate in specific contexts. In other words, while master, interactional, and personal identities are always present, in each moment of time with others we attempt to manage what these identities mean and how they impact who we are consistently becoming together. Although it is easy to see the player as having these identity concerns (the player being some "one" with agency in relation to the game), it is more difficult to imagine the game with identity (the game being some "one" with agency in relation to the player). However, it is precisely this shift that we recommend later in the chapter.

Finally, in the accomplishment of tasks, identities, and relationships, we must manage conversational or process goals. All human "Being" must take place through actions with others (whether others are physically copresent or not). Contexts and relationships assume understanding of and cooperation in processes of establishing, maintaining, or challenging such contexts and relationships. We manage these "cooperative principles" (Grice, 1975) in a manner that allows us to achieve tasks (or speech acts) while maintaining who self/others need to be in particular contexts during specific moments in time.

Task, relational/identity, and conversational goals are the primary goals that must be attended to in order to construct social meaning, and therefore have implications for serious game design. In this respect, communication becomes a process of organizing together. It is a process in which we construct the roles, rules, privileges, responsibilities, and other structural resources (Giddens, 1979,

1984) that constitute our social worlds, including our "self" within those worlds. Therefore, from a communication perspective, it may be better to think of communication concepts as verbs as opposed to nouns. Relationships, therefore, become seen as "relationshipping" and communication is better seen as communicating or, better yet, "commorganizing." From this perspective, humans are in a constant process of reducing equivocality (Weick, 1979, 1995) and making sense together, not simply through information exchange but through being human together. Furthermore, the sense we continue to make together is the structure into which we live (Giddens, 1979, 1984). Finally, these structures are established, maintained, and challenged through how we narrate individually and socially (Giddens, 1991). In other words, humans are in a constant state of constituting their "Being" together. Although we recognize that it may be difficult to envision games and gaming through this perspective—after all, objects like games are often ignored in theories of human communication—we propose that that is exactly what they could become if we allow them to be. In fact, they are others bringing specific identities to the gaming situation, attempting to accomplish particular tasks within perceived "structural" constraints. Therefore, video games provide the ideal environment to replicate the increasing social fluidity and negotiability of these dynamic layers of identity in increasingly global, heterogeneous social worlds.

Video games, if we can get beyond the learning-as-knowing model, provide great potential for a learning-as-learning model of education and allow more critical reflection upon the self one chooses to become and the social worlds he/she participates in constructing. Next, we demonstrate the affinity between video gaming and critical reflection on contemporary lived contexts of personal/social becoming. This affinity exists, we argue, because the all-too-common binarisation of everyday life is exacerbated by digital technologies—which, in turn, can become powerful mechanisms for making this logic and its consequences explicit.

Video Games and Critical Self-Reflection

In spaces structured to foster critical self-reflection, the video game acts as a point of entry, a prism refracting social and cultural issues through a mechanism that is both emblem and consequence of these conditions. An algorithmic medium executed on computational platforms—one that foregrounds the act of materially reconfiguring a technological object by way of discrete, finite sets of codified instructions—the video game is one of many informatic technological systems that co-constitute and modulate control in postindustrial societies (Deleuze, 1992).

Wark (2007) argues, in fact, that gaming characterizes the predominant logic of contemporary thinking, doing, and living. And this logic is a curiously binary one. "All games are digital. Without exception. They all come down to a strict decision: out or in, foul or fair, goal or no goal. Anything else is just 'play'" (Wark, 2007, par. 79). To further understand not only the implications of this logic but also the role experiential learning can play in exploring it, we join with Wark (2007) in asking "the final question for a gamer theory": How to "move beyond the phenomena of gaming as experienced by the gamer to conceive of gaming from the point of view of the game?" (par. 223).[5] Such a move forces both theorists and educators to engage video games as more than merely texts to be "read" or media with "effects." Instead, it prompts recognition of the ways in which subjects incorporate space–times structured by bodily participation in algorithmic systems. Perhaps this sounds too serious, too dreary. "But a video game is not simply a fun toy," Galloway (2006) reminds us. "It is an algorithmic machine and like all machines functions through specific, codified rules of operation. .. In our day and age, this is the site of fun" (p. 5). To be sure, these rules are semiotic, governed and negotiated interpersonally, socially, culturally, and politically. They are also material, instantiated at the level of code, individuating bodies, making cuts.

For some educators, having fun with video games might mean helping students understand what happens when they're having fun with video games—or even how video gaming gets marked as a "site of fun" from the outset. How are agency and identity constrained, enabled, fostered and foreclosed in these finite, bounded, digital systems? After all, while gaming, algorithmic logic is everywhere inscribed; its protocols—its rules for standard behavior, its regulatory apparatus for defining possibilities in closed systems—perpetuate the modulation of control Deleuze describes (Galloway, 2004). Video games arise from these circumstances and are complicit in them; yet as "sites of fun," video games present an opportunity for the playful negotiation of their logics. Here exists exploration, reiteration, arbitration, and deprecation as players probe rules, test boundaries. To play video games is to toy with codes, to structurate (Giddens, 1979, 1984).

How might this activity be reflexively brought to bear on students' lives? Our first task is demonstrating the conditions under which students construct their worlds. And this means (as we've already noted) adopting a slightly different perspective on their lived conditions. From the "point of view of the game"—and here we use the term "game" to indicate both an artifact executed on a computational platform as well as a social and cultural structure engendered by increasingly pervasive systems of control—the world appears radically bifurcated. This radical binarisation of everyday life often occurs in ways that go unnoticed, as informatic systems become more pervasive and diffuse into personal, social, and political spaces, thereby reworking them. Subjects emerging from the gaming situation are always already coded, sorted, and structured in discrete and specific ways according to the algorithmic logic of the informatic systems with which they be-come "selves." Healthy bodies, wealthy bodies, valuable bodies, winners, losers—all such identities and relationships are brutally and relentlessly individuated, categorized, arranged and ranked (occasionally explicitly, often inconspicuously) as they modulate through systems of control that continue to define the contours of their everyday practices. Practitioners of critical pedagogy might therefore ask how to foster recognition of the ways in which subjects are both constituted and positioned in spaces governed by the digital logics of contemporary informatic systems. Asked another way—and here again Wark (2007) is prescient—"When gamespace chooses you as its avatar, which character does it select for you to play?" (par. 218): What identities are thrust upon players? What tasks does it assume appropriate and necessary to participate in the game? And by what rules and processes does it expect players to abide?

Video gaming can aid the process of critical self-reflection because "the form of the digital game is an allegory for the form of being. Games are our contemporaries, the form in which the present can be felt, and, in being felt, thought through" (Wark, 2007, par. 225). As such, any pedagogical attempt to cultivate critical self-reflection must help a body feel the process of brutal binarisation (including its own complicity in it) so this embodied, lived experience can be re-*collected* and examined in a way that may prompt reorientation (and it is in the process of re-*collection* that the role of the instructor is tantamount). The ontological work of critical self-refection is accomplished not in an activity whereby game-as-text is read in a selective way that reifies a preformed subjectivity coming to bear on a text, but rather an activity whereby the subject re-*cognizes*[6] the very process(es) by which its capacities as a subject are constituted in the first place. It is the type of work critical pedagogy continually attempts to accomplish through critical self-reflection. To demonstrate how a communication perspective on serious gaming might accomplish this work, we turn to two examples of serious educational games—one built on an implicit model of communication as information transfer and one more suited to fostering critical self-reflection through constitutive, communicative experience.

Math Munchers: Educational Gaming as Information Transfer

One early example of a video game designed in the 1980s to foster learning is *Number Munchers* by the Minnesota Educational Computing Consortium (MECC). This simple video game sought to teach grade school and junior high school students mathematic skills by coupling basic arithmetic functions with rudimentary ludic elements. Players control the "muncher," a frog-like creature with an oversized mouth and voracious appetite for correct answers. Using the computer's arrow keys, players move the muncher across a two-dimensional grid filled with numbers or equations. The grid is labeled with a specific criterion (such as "multiples of 2" or "equals 8") and players must use the computer's space bar to "munch" data that fulfills the criterion. For instance, if the grid is labeled "multiples of two," players attempt to move into grid squares containing, say, the numbers 8, 12, 14, 2, and 16 and then "munch" those numbers. Munching numbers like 3, 15, 19, and 5 would conversely cause the player to lose a muncher (players begin the game with four munchers). Movement around the board is complicated by various "troggles," alien enemies who can munch the muncher (resulting in a loss of life) and can change the information arranged on the grid. As the game progresses, grid data and criteria become more complex and troggles' movement speeds up. Players score points for every correct bit of data they consume, and the game is over when the player is out of munchers. When *The Learning Company* purchased MECC in the mid-1990s, it acquired the rights to *Number Munchers*, rebranding it as *Math Munchers*. While the game has undergone cosmetic revisions (the board is now rendered in three dimensions, a soundtrack has been added, voice actors have provided more depth to the munchers' universe) basic gameplay remains nearly unchanged throughout the video game's various permutations (it can still be purchased on CD-ROM for a variety of platforms).

Understanding the game's presuppositions is key to understanding our broader argument about the potential for video games to prompt a certain type of learning (namely, experiential learning). *Math Munchers* is designed with serious intentions—an educational game, a tool designed to "make learning fun"—predicated fundamentally on the notion that communication is the transmission of information. The educational "content" of the game—the math problems—is relayed from designer to player, who processes the data and makes decisions in a closed, cybernetic loop. The pedagogical aim of a game like *Math Munchers* is the transmission of information through a channel thought enticing to students—the computer—and "learning" occurs when a user's skills have been honed and refined by it. "Gameplay" becomes the panacea for other (perhaps more mundane) methods of dissemination. Thus, the video game barely conceals its strategy of rapidly drilling students on their rote memorization and quick recollection of mathematical equations. It demands increasingly speedy reactions to its on-screen messages, which are abstracted from any lived context. It rewards unreflective manipulation and punishes the unsuccessful retention of data; the gamer becomes a "loser" and is seen as "incompetent" in relation to both the game and apparently other "idealized" players the game has in mind. The learner is made over in the machine's own image; rarely is she helped to understand or critically reflect upon the "makeover."

We might call this the "add games and stir" method of appropriating games for pedagogical purposes. This approach assumes that because video games resonate with students (especially grade schoolers), using them as content delivery mechanisms is a surefire way to "enhance" a learning environment. It might be, but the "add games and stir" approach to educational gaming fails to completely appreciate serious games' complete potential. In fact, this approach often regards the medium of the video game uncritically, viewing it as a pregiven, inert channel for transmitting valuable information.

Certainly, we are not arguing that the cultivation of mathematical acuity is a wasteful or ignoble endeavor. Nor are we arguing that *Math Munchers* is representative of all content-oriented serious games (indeed, virtually any serious game requires the retention of content for successful play, and not all games with content-oriented goals rely on models of information transfer to achieve their respective aims). We do, however, wish to challenge educators and serious game designers to think about video games as more than mere static channels for the distribution of information. Instead, a focus on the video game as a medium—a particular cultural, constitutive form indissociable from the "content" it supposedly "carries"—would help enhance the pedagogical potential of serious games for both teaching *praxis* and for pursuing the ontological goals of experiential learning. A communication-oriented point of view helps realize this potential and critically evaluate the role video games and other informatic systems play in everyday life. Another example can elaborate this view.

September 12th: Educational Gaming as Embodied Reorientation

The subtitle of Newsgaming's *September 12th: A Toy World* is shrewdly ironic.[7] Drawing attention to critics' tendency to offhandedly dismiss video games as ineffectual, disconnected from reality, or mere "play," the title insists that video games do not exist in "other worlds" apart from quotidian experience. Rather, they exist right "here," among other modes of media and cultural criticism, tethered permanently to a social milieu, directly (and powerfully) influencing the world that has heretofore marginalized them. In this case, *September 12th* functions, according to its splash screen, as "a simple model you can use to explore some aspects of the war on terror." The instructions are succinct:

> This is not a game.
> You can't win and you can't lose.
> This is a simulation.
> It has no ending. It has already begun.
> The rules are deadly simple. You can shoot. Or not.
> This is a simple model you can use to explore some aspects of the war on terror. (Newsgaming, 2003)

Thus, the video game immediately situates a player–subject by way of a dualist logic structuring spaces of potentiality. Its first statement ("this is not a game") underscores the irony of the video game's subtitle, jettisoning the baggage of "play." It effaces one recognizable characteristic of the gaming situation by openly admitting that there is no win condition, exploding a "win/lose" dichotomy and instead highlighting the situation's function as a "simulation" of (presumably "real-world") conditions.[8] It negotiates assumptions about identity, tasks and process that "normal" players may bring to the gaming situation. Temporality is twisted from the comfortable confines of linear progression; here is a gamic moment with "no ending" that has "already begun." In it, players have but one capacity: "You can shoot. Or not." Game/not game, win/lose, simulation/game, open/closed, start/end, shoot/not: Binarisation constitutes and structures possibilities.

Left of these instructions are two images. The first, labeled "terrorist," whose master identity is projected as a human figure wearing a flowing Middle Eastern headpiece, has its face covered and clutches a rifle. Second is a group of "civilians," a collective consisting of one man, one woman, and one child. The game configures two types of bodies.

Clicking a mouse to clear the instructions, the player is now granted a bird's-eye view of a town situated in a sandy dessert. Terrorists and civilians bustle throughout the streets of markets and housing districts. Gamic action unfolds as "pure process," what Galloway (2006) calls an "ambience act" (p. 10): the game is running (executing code), bodies are in motion, yet no "gameplay" is apparently occurring. Left to itself, the city and its inhabitants pursue their individual courses, seemingly oblivious to the player in the sky.

The player who chooses to move the mouse, however, immediately takes control of a crosshairs that can be positioned over any portion of the game. Indeed, the mere presence of crosshairs constitutes expectations for a player's relational and interactional identities, what she is expected to do. Clicking, moreover, exercises the player's capacity as outlined in the game's instructions: the capacity to shoot. Clicking the mouse button launches a missile into the town, directly beneath the player's crosshairs. Buildings smolder in the wake of the blast as the sound of an explosion trails off. Corpses line the streets among the wreckage. And there are mourners. Players who extinguish either terrorists or civilians will instantly notice other civilian townsfolk gather around blast sites and weep for the dead. The player immediately begins reconciling her actions with the personal identities they imply. Then, in a flash, the *master* identity of civilians morph into terrorists; the associated *personal identities* that accompany them shift in turn. Their *interactional* identity in relation to the player changes. They become enemies. Players who spend enough time trying to vanquish every terrorist from the city will eventually become irked by their inability to do so. Each death produces more terrorists; each missile strike destroys more locations for civilian refuge; continuing to define the player and game in moments of time. The player must eventually begin to wonder how seriously the game will uphold its promise that the simulation "has no ending." The player must eventually wonder, too, just exactly why she started firing in the first place. How to (re)define the identities, structures, and realities she herself has helped constitute? Deciding on a course of action may now be a struggle; "playing" seems necessary to progress, perhaps even to atone. After all, games demand movement forward—progression, accumulation, assertion.

But there is one more aspect to this video (non) game that deserves attention. The player can, of course, choose to relinquish the mouse and allow the game to return to its ambient state. The player, in other words, has an ability to change the process goals, changing what is considered appropriate and inappropriate action in the gaming situation. Only now, the game must work to return to stasis—and it is indeed working, despite the player's new role as engaged onlooker. This "toy world" reconfigures itself as the player slowly realizes that her best course of action is strategic nonaction. Buildings slowly repair; terrorists silently return to their civilian clothes. Life continues.

And so the player–subject is left shunted—left to contemplate, perhaps, her singular role in this mess, the rules (both implicit and explicit) compelling and structuring her action, and the modes of becoming through which game, player and world are constituted via the radical binarisation of everyday life. *September 12th* doesn't ask players to adopt new skills, "process" new information, or learn through a model of consumption. It presupposes many skills—English literacy, basic computer operation and manipulation, spatial reasoning, strong hand-eye coordination—but it is not built to "enhance" these skills (though, collaterally, this might occur, too). It also presupposes certain tacit knowledges—knowledge of historical events, knowledge of contemporary forms of terrorism, knowledge of stereotypical embodiments—but it tends to call these knowledges into question rather than reifying them. In fact, helping players challenge these knowledges becomes the responsibility of the educator, whose debriefing of the gaming situating can guide players through the implications of their "playful" embodiments, help them re-collect lived experience streaming through a flow state (Csikszentmihalyi, 1990), and highlight the ways in which their experience was always already structured by the binary logics embedded in the material platforms on which play occurred.

This isn't to say *September 12th* isn't educational; no, its intentions are quite serious. The kind of learning that occurs when players interact with *September 12th*, however, is slightly more nuanced than that which occurs in conjunction with, say, a game like *Math Munchers*. While the latter clearly attempts to achieve its pedagogical (and, naturally, ideological) goal based on a model of content transmission, the former operates from the perspective we adumbrated above—a communication perspective. It uses the form of the video game—its computational, binary, procedural logic[9]—to force players into tightly controlled, stratified subject positions and asks them to construct a world through (in)action, to make and to do from a particular point of view. The game achieves an experiential end, one that doesn't merely reward the habituation of a skill but rather foregrounds the player's subjectivity, her realiziation of her own inextricable complicity in the game's events, her being-in-relation to the digital bodies of gamespace. *September 12th*'s mode of visuality helps this goal, of course; it operates from a first-person perspective. But, moreover, the video game is able to model a complex social situation with an algorithmic simplicity that is as compelling as it is curious.

It is curious because, to a skeptical onlooker, it might not appear as though it's teaching anything—or, more specifically, anything of value. Because the game is not explicitly branded as educational—because its content isn't the content of a more traditional (i.e., informational) transaction between teacher and learner—it might suffer from what Gee (2007) calls "the problem of content" (p. 22). Gee acknowledges the popular tendency to disregard seemingly "playful" activities as ineffectual or wasteful, simply because their contents aren't something a reasonable person would consider "educational." But in *September 12th's* carefully pruned algorithms are mechanisms purposefully designed to teach a player—even if the object with which students are engaged does not contain familiar educational content. Players here are not interactively having content merely impressed upon them; they're manipulating a complex system of constraints designed to frame their lived experience in a way that prompts a blunt recognition of their own social embodiments.[10]

The game is compelling, too, because it opens a space for discussion about both the power of algorithmic systems to structure everyday life—and the consequences of their binarisations.[11] The video game's inescapable digital logic—which is inscribed at both the material level (a consequence of its procedural platform) and at the symbolic level (a consequence of the ludic constructs arbitrarily yet strategically constraining the conduct of persons in discourse)—reduces the rich complexity of lived experience to a simulation of "real" conditions. Radical polarization of otherwise overlapping, intertwining entities occurs. This is to say that video games prescribe what Lanigan (1994, 2000) calls "a context of choice," wherein the either/or (i.e., digital) logic of information theory insists that players choose a subject position from an array of pre-given, discrete options. From this point of view (for Wark, "the point of view of the game"; 2007), reality exists independently of human activity as an option to be selected and incorporated. The video game presents a problem to be managed efficiently, much as players of *Math Munchers* are concerned primarily with selecting and processing data according to prescriptive criteria (or even as players of *September 12th* may begin firing at terrorists, which are "not civilians," after an uncritical interpretation of the game's instructions). Conversely, critical reflection on the gaming situation might assist players in making what Lanigan (1994, 2000) calls a "choice of context," wherein players perceive the consequences of the game's digital logic in conjunction with their lived experience of these rigidly codified, stratified conditions. When the player negotiates the ambiguity this reflection may produce ("Do I shoot, or not?"), the both/and (i.e., analog) logic she brings to this experience can be explained with the logic of communication theory. Unable now to see herself as an agent apart from the conditions in which she is constituted, the player synthesizes the digital and analog "abductively" (Lanigan, 2000) and is able to construct her own reality. This reality is not static or pre-constituted apart from human interaction. Instead, this inter-play of elements (literally, the conjunction of this "interactive" digital medium with the ambiguously and playfully generative human analog) dialectically constructs realty in a continually-negotiated space between player and game. Mitgutsch (2009) has described this process as a "passionate" one, wherein the player's loss of subjectivity produces an embodied (re)orientation toward both the video game and social structures beyond the scope of the video game. The video game creates a space of mutual becoming in which educators can help students choose a context and recognize the ways in which digital structures continually circumscribe their lives, relations, and selves. While other media—novels and films, for instance—may offer opportunities for critical reflection, video games' very materiality (its digital platform, its procedural nature) and emphasis on embodied, interactive choice situate them ideally for ontological pedagogies.

We do not wish to deny the important role of digital communication—without which, say Watzlawick, Bavelas, & Jackson (1967), humans' "civilized achievements would be unthinkable" (p. 63)—but do wish to note the limits of relying on this type of communication to achieve the goals of educational serious games. Digital communication "is particularly important for the sharing of information about *objects* and the the time-binding function of the transmission of knowledge" (Watzlawick, Bavelas, & Jackson, p. 63, emphasis in original), and is "eminently suited for communication on the *content level*" (p. 102, emphasis added). However, these very dependencies on transmission metaphors for describing the linear, instrumental deployment of skill-content to discrete, disembodied learners who receive this skill-content sit at the core of the current paradigm structuring serious game development and enactment in pedagogical spaces. Rather, as we have argued thus far, decisions to privilege discrete entities at the expense of relations, objects at the expense of processes,[12] content at the the expense of medium, and transmission at the expense of being have had serious ramifications for serious games that must be recognized if the field can hope to mature.

Accomplishing critical self-reflective learning through the use of video games will, however, require more than simply incorporating a communication perspective into the design and use of video games for education. As mentioned above, learning doesn't stem from the playing of the game itself, but from the *praxis* of gaming. In other words, educators must be willing and able to create dialogue around the gaming experience that allows such learning to occur. Unfortunately, very little research has been conducted to help us understand what such a dialogue would look like. For this, we look to the future directions such a perspective should take.

FUTURE DIRECTIONS

The perspective offered in this chapter is meant to challenge and extend the current use of video games as pedagogical tools to facilitate critical self-reflection. However, we must address several questions before we can realize our perspective in action.

Perhaps one of the primary questions is: What specific "games" allow us to best achieve "self" learning and "discursive consciousness" (Giddens, 1984), which enables one to critically reflect on practical conduct? While a game like *Math Munchers* could be used for the same purposes as *September 12th*, we must question whether they both possess the same degree of potential for "teaching" *praxis*. If they do not, as we may suspect, then what types of games do we use?

A second and related question is: To what extent do students have the motivation to engage in such learning? Although learning through gameplay has primarily focused on the teaching of *techne*, which is inherently beneficial and useful to students, it lacks an emphasis on ***praxis***. One reason why such an emphasis is lacking, we suspect, is the sheer effort and demands in getting students to engage in such learning. Therefore, how do we bring *praxis* to the same level of relevance as *techne*?

Another question from this perspective concerns how to focus learning. While it is a tenet of experiential learning that learning is accomplished better through experience than it is through traditional "instruction," "self" learning through experience becomes somewhat ambiquous and hard to measure. We do not dispute that learning occurs through all experience; however, we must ask if such learning is always the learning we espouse. Craig (1989) posits that the purpose of a communication approach is "to cultivate communicative *praxis*, or practical art, through critical study" (p. 98). To cultivate *praxis* suggests an "ideal" toward which we cultivate. When attempting to teach and facilitate "ontological" learning, what *praxis* do we foreground and promote and what do we challenge and discourage—if any at all. Furthermore, how do we promote and encourage particular "ontological" learning over others? In other words, if much of the learning occurs from reflection on practice, and reflection comes from debriefing the gaming experience and facilitating discussion, what discussions best facilitate the type of reflections necessary? Muller (2002) points out that while most educational researchers agree that experiential and critical reflective activities are a very important educational practice, "they have been seriously neglected in research" (p. 12).

More research and educational practice could focus on methods of assessing learning outcomes that result from the use of games as tools in experiential learning. Favoring problem-based methods over more traditional "linear" methods naturally calls for new mechanisms and standards for evaluating student growth. How will educators do this with a focus on the process of learning, in addition to its products?

In addition to assessment, we must ask: To what extent must those who intend to use games for pedagogical purposes work with those who design games for pedagogical purposes? For ontological learning, it seems clear that the gaming experience must incorporate how we ultimately make sense of the "game" and the "gamer's" roles in participating.

A final and more daunting question is: Who among us is capable of cultivating such deeply-rooted, reflective learning. Dewey (1938) correctly notes that "just because traditional education was a matter of routine in which plans and programs were handed down from the past, it does not follow that progressive education is a matter of planless improvisation" (p. 38). Greenfield and Lave (1982) concur, stating "for teachers to follow an implicit rule of doing the minimum required for learners to be successful, they must exercise careful attention and thoughtful effort in judging when to step in and when to refrain from interfering. Maintaining a constant level of difficulty for the learner is clearly a technique that places responsibility on the teacher" (p. 204). Too often, however, proponents of new curricula in professional education ignore the possibility that not all teachers are prepared to handle the added responsibilities that accompany experiential and critical self-reflective pedagogy. We do not mean to imply that educators are not committed to their vocational efforts. However, as Brookfield (2005) points out, although a vocational calling to education (becoming "selfless servants," as he puts it) is a sign of commitment and passion, it can also become a way to "justify workers taking on responsibilities and duties that far exceed their energy or capacities" (p. 100). Experiential methods aimed at increasing critical self-reflection require more than simply implementing, with good intent, games in which students participate and to which they relate. Educators must be skilled in critically and appropriately challenging the construction of meanings that arise during these activities. For our purposes, this means being skilled not only in pedagogical practice, but also in the practice of the games being used. Unfortunately, many teachers have not had the opportunity to develop the teaching competencies required to participate in the less formal, highly interactive, ontologically focused models promoted here. In fact, too little research exists to fully understand what competencies are actually beneficial. In addition, many teachers are not "gamers" themselves. Therefore, the question arises as to who should teach in the new curricula. And, if these curricula are to include everyone, then how do we develop those of us who are not prepared?

CONCLUSION

We have argued that the binarisation of everyday life by systems of control indicates the need for pedagogies that cultivate awareness of ways in which self and other are constituted, managed, and negotiated in technological and social systems whose logic is becoming increasingly more gamic. This logic—an inherently dichotomous one—likewise demands such pedagogies to employ heuristic mechanisms capable of highlighting and articulating the core problematics of contemporary life in post-Fordist systems of production and exchange, wherein students' sense of self is constantly modulating through informatic systems and structures. Video games—so stunningly emblematic of these systems—are such mechanisms. Introduced to spaces structured to foster the ontological, self-reflective goals to which critical pedagogy aspires, gaming promises to speak directly to students' personal, social, cultural and political situation(s). Moreover, communication studies can enhance our understanding of this educational process by providing a rich model of sense-making not couched in traditional models of information transmission whose binary logic treats potential ambiguities as problems to be managed and eliminated (and, consequently, treats education as the transmission and reification of a skill). Rather, contemporary conceptualizations of communication as both a product and a process of continual identity formation treat the gaming situation[13] as a rich site for critical reflection on the subject's ambiguous, indeterminate negotiation of video games' algorithmic (and, hence, binary) structures. Designers can benefit from understanding this approach by building serious video games purposefully constructed to prompt critical self-reflection; educators can benefit from this approach by realizing their role as facilitator of reflection on systems that may otherwise slip beneath players' conscious awareness.

One further point of caution is this: Gaming is not necessarily an inherently "liberating" practice. This is to say we disagree with studies championing the use of "games for games' sake." Just as scholars of critical pedagogy recognize that not all self-reflection is necessarily self-critical, those interested in the pedagogical potential of video games must remember that the mere introduction of games in learning environments does not guarantee the kind of ontological learning we have detailed will occur. Approaching ontological education with the aforementioned "add games and stir" approach could be more disadvantageous than helpful. After all, we have already discussed the ways in which gamic systems operate at the level of everyday experience to reify binary logics that brutally (re)configure personal, social, and cultural systems according to their particular algorithmic protocols. If the goal of experiential pedagogy using video games is the cultivation of critical self-reflection on the logics that produce and sort bodies and subjects, educators should be thoughtful in their application of games that purport to have heuristic value. As Galloway and Thacker (2007) explain about the video game *State of Emergency*:

The game has no aim except to incite riot, and it's unclear whether the titular "state of emergency" refers to the oppressive corporate State or the apparent chaos that ensues. [...] One can imagine the game played from the other side—that of the riot police. Here the goal would be crowd control, surveillance, and military blockading. The computer skills necessary for playing either scenario amount to network management skills. [...] The lesson of State of Emergency is not that it promotes an anarchic ideology but that, in the guise of an anarchic ideology, it promotes computer and network management skills. (pp. 114–115)

This is not to say that computer and network management are inherently inconsequential or even detrimental. We applaud the use of video games in education, but we challenge educators to be exceedingly critical of their games' lessons, the skills they teach, and the value systems they perpetuate. Communication studies can contribute to game studies an understanding of the ways in which bodies and subjectivities are constituted, sorted, and negotiated in contemporary contexts, can offer new registers for thinking and talking about video gaming as a productive activity, and can continue to cultivate a critical orientation toward the radical binarisation of everyday life.

REFERENCES

Anton, C. (2003). Playing with Bateson: Denotation, logical types, and analog and digital communication. *American Journal of Semiotics, 19*(1–4), 127–152.

Arnseth, H. C. (2006). Learning to play or playing to learn: A critical account of the models of communication informing educational research on computer gameplay. *Game Studies, 6*(1), n.p.

Austin, J. L. (1962). *How to do things with words*. Oxford, UK: Oxford University Press.

Bateson, G. (1968). Information and codification. In Ruesch, J., & Bateson, G. (Eds.), *Communication: The social matrix of psychiatry*. New York: W. W. Norton & Company.

Bateson, G. (1972). *Steps to an ecology of mind*. New York: Ballentine Books.

Bernstein, R. J. (1985). From hermeneutics to praxis. In Hollinger, R. (Ed.), *Hermeneutics and praxis* (pp. 272–296). Notre Dame, Indiana: University of Notre Dame Press.

Bogost, I. (2007). *Persuasive games: The expressive power of videogames*. Cambridge, MA: MIT Press.

Borofsky, R. (1994). *Assessing cultural anthropology*. New York: McGraw-Hill.

Bousquet, M. (2008). *How the university works: Higher education and the low-wage nation*. New York: New York University Press.

Brookfield, S. D. (2000). The concept of critically reflective practice. In Wilson, A. L., & Hayes, E. R. (Eds.), *Handbook of adult and continuing education* (pp. 33–50). San Francisco: Jossey-Bass.

Brookfield, S. D. (2005). *The power of critical theory for adult learning and teaching*. New York: McGraw-Hill.

Brown, P., & Levinson, S. C. (1987). *Universals in language usage: Politeness phenomena*. Cambridge, UK: Cambridge University Press.

Cameron, D. (2000). *Good to talk? Living and working in a communication culture*. London, UK: Sage.

Craig, R. T. (1989). Communication as a practical discipline. In B. Dervin, L. Grosberg, B. J. O'Keefe, & E. Wartella (Eds.), Rethinking communication: Vol. 1 paradigm issues (pp. 97–122). Newberry Park, CA: Sage.

Craig, R. T. (1999). Communication theory as a field. *Communication Theory*, *9*, 119–161.

Craig, R. T. (2001). Dewey and Gadamer on practical reflection: Toward a methodology for the practical disciplines. In Perry, D. K. (Ed.), *American pragmatism and communication research* (pp. 131–148). Mahwah, NJ: Lawrence Erlbaum Associates.

Craig, R. T., & Tracy, K. (1995). Grounded practical theory: The case of the intellectual discussion. *Communication Theory*, *5*(3), 248–272. doi:10.1111/j.1468-2885.1995.tb00108.x

Cranton, P., & King, K. (2003). Transformative learning as a professional development goal. *New Directions for Adult and Continuing Education*, *98*, 31–38. doi:10.1002/ace.97

Crawford, C. (in press). Interactivity, process, algorithm. In Van Eck, R. (Ed.), *Interdisciplinary models and tools for serious games: Emerging concepts and future directions*. Hershey, PA: IGI Global.

Csikszentmihalyi, M. (1990). *Flow: The psychology of optimal experience*. New York: Harper and Row.

Cunliffe, A. L. (2004). On becoming a critically reflexive practitioner. *Journal of Management Education*, *28*(4), 407–426. doi:10.1177/1052562904264440

Deetz, S. A. (1994). Future of the discipline: The challenges, the research, and the social contribution. In Deetz, S. A. (Ed.), *Communication yearbook, 17* (pp. 565–600). Thousand Oaks, CA: Sage.

Deleuze, G. (1992). Postscript on the societies of control. *October, 59*, 3–7.

Dewey, J. (1929). *Experience and nature* (2nd ed.). LaSalle, IL: Open Court.

Dewey, J. (1938). *Experience & education*. New York: Collier Macmillan.

Dimitriadis, G., & Kamberelis, G. (2006). *Theory for education*. New York: Taylor & Francis.

Duffy, T. M., & Cunningham, D. J. (1996). Constructivism: Implications for the design and delivery of instruction. In Jonassen, D. H. (Ed.), *Handbook of research for educational communications and technology* (pp. 170–198). New York: Macmillan.

Eisenberg, E. M. (1984). Ambiguity as strategy in organizational communication. *Communication Monographs*, *51*, 227–242. doi:10.1080/03637758409390197

Entertainment, V. I. S. (2002). *State of Emergency* [PlayStation 2]. London: Rockstar Games.

Fairhurst, G. T., & Sarr, R. A. (1996). *The art of framing: Managing the language of leadership*. San Francisco, CA: Jossey-Bass.

Freire, P. (1994). *Pedagogy of hope*. New York: Continuum.

Freire, P. (2000). *Pedagogy of the oppressed*. New York: Continuum.

Gadamer, H. G. (1979). The problem of historical consciousness. In Rabinow, P., & Sullivan, W. M. (Eds.), *Interpretive social science: A reader* (pp. 103–162). Berkeley, CA: University of California Press.

Galloway, A. R. (2004). *Protocol: How control exists after decentralization*. Cambridge, MA: MIT Press.

Galloway, A. R. (2006). *Gaming: Essays on algorithmic culture*. Minneapolis, MN: University of Minnesota Press.

Galloway, A. R., & Thacker, E. (2007). *The exploit: A theory of networks*. Minneapolis: University of Minnesota Press.

Gee, J. P. (2007). *What video games have to teach us about learning and literacy*. New York: Palgrave Macmillan.

Gee, J. P. (2008). Video games and embodiment. *Games and Culture*, *3*(3–4), 253–263. doi:10.1177/1555412008317309

Gergen, K. (1991). *The saturated self*. New York: Basic Books.

Gergen, K. (1999). Beyond the self-society antimony. *Journal of Constructivist Psychology*, *12*, 173–178. doi:10.1080/107205399266172

Giddens, A. (1979). *Central problems in social theory: Action, structure and contradiction in social analysis*. London, UK: Macmillan.

Giddens, A. (1984). *The constitution of society: Outline of the theory of structuration*. Cambridge, MA: Polity Press.

Giddens, A. (1991). *Modernity and self identity: Self & society in the late modern age*. Stanford, CA: Stanford University Press.

Goffman, E. (1974). *Frame analysis: An essay on the organization of experience*. Cambridge, MA: Harvard University Press.

Greenfield, P., & Lave, J. (1982). Cognitive aspects of informal education. In D.A. Wagner and H. W. Stevenson (Eds.) Cultural perspectives on child development (pp. 181-207). San Franscisco: W.H. Freemen and Company.

Gregersen, A., & Grodal, T. (2009). Embodiment and interface. In Perron, B., & Wolf, M. J. P. (Eds.), *The video game theory reader* (pp. 65–83). New York: Routledge.

Grice, H. P. (1975). Logic in conversation. In P. Cole & J. Morgan (Eds.), Syntax and semantics: Vol. 3 speech acts (pp. 41–58). New York: Academic Press.

Hanks, W. F. (1996). *Language and communicative practices*. Boulder, CO: Westview Press.

Juul, J. (2005). *Half-real: Video games between real rules and fictional worlds*. Cambridge, MA: MIT Press.

Kisiel, T. (1985). The happening of tradition: The hermeneutics of Gadamer and Heidegger. In Hollinger, R. (Ed.), *Hermeneutics and praxis* (pp. 3–31). Notre Dame, IN: University of Notre Dame Press.

Kolb, A. Y., & Kolb, D. A. (2009). The learning way: Meta-cognitive aspects of experiential learning. *Simulation & Gaming*, *40*(3), 297–327. doi:10.1177/1046878108325713

Lainema, T. (2009). Perspective making: Constructivism as a meaning making structure for simulation gaming. *Simulation & Gaming*, *40*, 48–67. doi:10.1177/1046878107308074

Lanigan, R. L. (1988). *Phenomenology of communication: Merleau-Ponty's thematics in communicology and semiology*. Pittsburgh: Duquesne University Press.

Lanigan, R. L. (1994). Capta versus data: Method and evidence in communicology. *Human Studies*, *17*, 109–130. doi:10.1007/BF01322769

Lanigan, R. L. (2000). The self in semiotic phenomenology: Consciousness as the conjunction of perception and expression in the science of communicology. *American Journal of Semiotics*, *15–16*, 91–111.

Mead, G. H. (1934). *Mind, self, and society*. Chicago: Chicago University Press.

MECC. (2004). *Math munchers* [PC CD-ROM]. San Francisco: The Learning Company.

Mezirow, J. (1990). Fostering critical reflection in adulthood. San Fancisco: Jossey-Bass.

Mezirow, J. (1991). *Transformative dimensions of adult learning*. San Francisco: Jossey-Bass.

Mezirow, J. (1997). Transformative learning: Theory to practice. In Cranton, P. (Ed.), *New directions for adult and continuing education: No. 74* (pp. 5–12). San Francisco: Jossey-Bass.

Mezirow, J. (1998). On critical reflection. *Adult Education Quarterly*, *48*(3), 185–198. doi:10.1177/074171369804800305

Mezirow, J. (2000). *Learning as transformation: Critical perspectives on a theory in progress*. San Francisco: Jossey-Bass.

Mitgutsch, K. (2009). Passionate digital play-based learning: (Re)learning in computer games like *Shadow of the Colossus*. *Eludamos*, *3*(1), 9–22.

Muller, H. (2002). *Navigating the dilemmas of collegiate classroom discussion*. (Doctoral dissertation, University of Colorado at Boulder, 2002). Retrieved May 3, 2009, from Dissertations & Theses: A & I database. (Publication No. AAT 3057795).

Newsgaming. (2003). *September 12th*. [Macromedia Shockwave]. Available online at http://www.newsgaming.com/games/index12.htm.

Packer, M., & Greco-Brooks, D. (1999). School as a site for the production of persons. *Journal of Constructivist Psychology*, *12*, 133–151. doi:10.1080/107205399266154

Pearce, W. B. (2007). *Making social worlds: A communication perspective*. Malden, MA: Blackwell.

Penman, R. (2000). *Reconstructing communicating: Looking to a future*. Mahwah, NJ: Lawrence Erlbaum Associates.

Ritchie, D. (1986). Shannon and Weaver: Unravelling the paradox of information. *Communication Research*, *13*(2), 278–298. doi:10.1177/009365086013002007

Searle, J. R. (1969). *Speech acts: An essay in the philosophy of language*. London: Cambridge University Press.

Senge, P. (1994). *The fifth discipline: The art and practice of the learning organization*. New York: Doubleday.

Shannon, C. (1949). *The mathematical theory of communication*. Urbana: The University of Illinois Press.

Steedman, P. (1991). On the relations between seeing, interpreting and knowing. In Steirer, F. (Ed.), *Research and reflexivity* (pp. 53–63). London, UK: Sage.

Tracy, K. (2002). *Everyday talk: Building and reflecting identities*. New York: Guilford Press.

Vygotsky, L. S. (1978). *Mind in society: The development of higher psychological processes*. Cambridge, MA: Harvard University Press.

Wark, M. (2007). *Gamer theory*. Cambridge, MA: Harvard University Press.

Watzlawick, P., Bavelas, J. B., & Jackson, D. D. (1967). *Pragmatics of human communication: A study of interactional patterns, pathologies, and paradoxes*. New York: W. W. Norton & Company.

Weaver, W. (1949). Recent contributions to the mathematical theory of communication. In C. Shannon and W. Weaver, The mathematical theory of communication (pp. 95–117). Urbana, IL: The University of Illinois Press.

Weick, K. (1979). *The social psychology of organizing*. Reading, MA: Addison-Wesley.

Weick, K. (1995). *Sensemaking in organizations*. Thousand Oaks, CA: Sage.

"MUST-READS" FOR THIS TOPIC

Bateson, G. (1972). *Steps to an ecology of mind.* New York: Ballentine Books.

Chen, M. G. (2009). Communication, coordination, and camaraderie in *World of Warcraft*. *Games and Culture*, *4*(1), 47–73. doi:10.1177/1555412008325478

Consalvo, M. (2009). Communication theory. In Perron, B., & Wolf, M. J. P. (Eds.), *The video game theory reader 2* (pp. 336–338). New York: Routledge.

Craig, R. T. (1989). Communication as a practical discipline. In B. Dervin, L. Grossberg, B. J. O'Keefe, & E. Wartella (Eds.), Rethinking communication: Volume 1: Paradigm issues (pp. 97–122). Newbury Park, CA: Sage.

Craig, R. T. (2001). Dewey and Gadamer on practical reflection: Toward a methodology for the practical disciplines. In Perry, D. K. (Ed.), *American pragmatism and communication research* (pp. 131–148). Mahwah, NJ: Lawrence Erlbaum Associates.

Craig, R. T., & Tracy, K. (1995). Grounded practical theory: The case of intellectual discussion. *Communication Theory*, *5*, 248–272. doi:10.1111/j.1468-2885.1995.tb00108.x

Crookall, D., & Thorngate, W. (2009). Acting, knowing, learning, simulating, gaming. *Simulation & Gaming*, *40*(1), 8–26. doi:10.1177/1046878108330364

Gillispie, P. H. (1973). *Learning through simulation games*. New York: Paulist Press.

Lanigan, R. L. (2007). Communicology: The French tradition in human science. In Arneson, P. (Ed.), *Perspectives on philosophy of communication* (pp. 168–184). West Lafayette, IN: Purdue University Press.

Zagal, J. P., & Bruckman, A. (2008). Novices, experts, and scholars: Exploring the challenges of teaching about games. *Game Studies, 8*(2).

TOP TEXTS FOR INTERDISCIPLINARY STUDIES OF SERIOUS GAMES

Craig, R. T. (1999). Communication theory as a field. *Communication Theory*, *9*(2), 119–161.

Galloway, A. R. (2006). *Gaming: Essays on algorithmic culture*. Minneapolis, MN: University of Minnesota Press.

Gee, J. P. (2007). *What video games have to teach us about learning and literacy*. New York: Palgrave Macmillan.

Giddens, A. (1984). *The constitution of society: Outline of the theory of structuration.* Berkley, CA: University of California Press.

Lanigan, R. L. (1988). *Phenomenology of communication: Merleau-Ponty's thematics in communicology and semiology*. Pittsburgh: Duquesne University Press.

Mead, G. H. (1934). *Mind, self, and society.* Chicago: Chicago University Press.

Mezirow, J. (1991). *Transformative dimensions of adult learning*. San Francisco: Jossey-Bass.

Ruesch, J., & Bateson, G. (1951). *Communication: The social matrix of psychiatry*. New York: W. W. Norton & Co., Inc.

Wark, M. (2007). *Gamer theory*. Cambridge, MA: Harvard University Press.

Wilden, A. (1987). *The rules are no game: The strategy of communication.* New York: Routledge.

ENDNOTES

1 As noted earlier in the paper, episteme, or theoretical/scientific knowledge is also an integral part of learning, and the consistency among all three, we suggest, is important for authentic understanding.

2 Kisiel references the 2nd edition of Hans-Georg Gadamer's *Wahrheit und Methode: Grundzuge einer philosophischen Hermeneutik,* published in 1965.

3 Fairhurst and Sarr (1996) refer to "fore-thought" as an active or mindful attempt to monitor discursive choices.

4 Specifically, Weaver (1949) says the theory is applicable not only to "written and oral speech, but also music, the pictorial arts, the theatre, the ballet, and in fact all human behavior" (p. 95).

5 It is important to note here Wark's specific use of the term "gamespace." For Wark (2007), gamespace is the space of the everyday—a space that is increasingly ludic, governed by logics heretofore exclusive to games (themselves merely idealized versions of gamespace). "You are a gamer whether you like it or not, now that we all live in a gamespace that is everywhere and nowhere" (par. 001).

6 We use the prefix "re" here to convey the complexity of terms. For example, "re-called" is used to emphasize the dual meaning of "recalled" and "collected again," drawing attention to the way in which this process is not simply passive and mental but also active and iterative. Likewise, we use "re-cognize" instead of recognize to stress the cyclical, repetitive, iterative nature of this process, which is not merely a process of "identification" but a continuous process of "thinking again" about a specific moment of embodiment, a process/event of reorientation, the goal of critical self-reflective practice(s).

7 To play this serious game, visit http://www.newsgaming.com/games/index12.htm

8 Thus, we realize some readers may question *September 12th*'s status as a game (let alone a serious game) and might therefore object to its juxtaposition with *Math Muncher*'s on the grounds that the two examples are not similar enough to warrant a comparison. For instance, ludologist Jesper Juul (2005) might insist that *September 12th* is not a "game" in the proper sense because it lacks a quantifiable outcome, and because no specific outcome is overtly valorized. While we admit that *September 12th* does eschew several design conventions that would seem like necessary conditions for its being a "game," we maintain that these very exclusions are precisely what create the ambiguity necessary for achieving the game's ontological goals. It's technical status as "game" or "toy" is less important, we feel, than its material form and potential. Surely, other serious games may achieve their ontological goals differently, even while taking the more traditional form of a "game."

9 We invoke the term "procedural" as a way of echoing video game critic Ian Bogost's (2007) use of the term to designate a representational process that is not descriptive but rather sequential and processual. Bogost notes that computational media "are particularly adept at representing real or imagined systems that themselves function in some particular way—that is, that operate according to a set of processes" (p. 5).

10 Gregersen and Grodal (2009) likewise emphasize embodiment as a key component of video gaming that is possible because of the ways in which the medium intersects with players' body images and corporeal schemas. As players vacillate through various ludic moments of creativity and constraint, their personal and social embodiments (re) structure.

11 For this reason, Bogost (2007) would not consider September 12th a serious game, but rather a "persuasive game." The former, he writes, "are often deployed in the service of institutions," (p. 57) while the latter can additionally challenge these institutions, can "deal with the exposition of the fundamental structure of existing situations" and can "support, doubt, or debate about their validity or desirability, or universality" in order to "question, change, or eliminate them" (p. 58).

12 See Crawford (this volume) for more on serious games' role in highlighting process over object.

13 We use the phrase "gaming situation" in sympathy with Eskelinin (2001), who regards video gaming not as a traditional linear process of narrative construction and reception but as a constellation of dynamic, configurative, nonlinear moments.

Chapter 5
Examining Motivational Factors in Serious Educational Games

Renae Low
University of New South Wales, Australia

ABSTRACT

One of the assumptions in promoting serious educational games is that such engagements are playable and enjoyable. The social cognitive research has already generated and tested a number of motivational theories and models. To advance both theoretical developments and empirical research into serious educational games, it is beneficial to examine the relevant motivational factors from existing social cognitive perspectives. Although there have been some studies in the field of simulations and games reporting elevated self-efficacy and reduced learner anxiety under certain circumstances, it is important to conduct systematic research to examine learner motivation in the context of educational games and select appropriate tools for checking motivational elements in instructional design.

INTRODUCTION

It is widely accepted that meaningful learning is associated with motivation. It is also widely assumed that learning will eventuate if the process is fun. The English philosopher John Locke (1968) once said, more than 300 years ago, that it would be desirable to make learning a play or recreational activity rather than an assigned task or a have-to-do business. In other cultural settings, this educational "fancy" was also favored and regarded as one of the learning principles. For instance, in the Analects of ancient Oriental educationist Confucius (Leys, 1997), it was proclaimed that students should immensely enjoy their learning by pursuing, reviewing, and applying knowledge. What Confucius and Locke proposed is perhaps the ultimate goal of all dedicated educators and learners. In an era that is characterized by the advancement of information technology and proliferation of educational software, are we getting nearer to that goal? More specifically, can serious educational games, often presented as digital multimedia environments, contribute to fostering users' enjoyment as well as achievement?

DOI: 10.4018/978-1-61520-719-0.ch005

Copyright © 2010, IGI Global. Copying or distributing in print or electronic forms without written permission of IGI Global is prohibited.

As Mayer (2005) points out, there are two perspectives on the relation between new technology and education. The technology-centered approach focuses on how to use all the capabilities of a cutting-edge technology in classroom learning, homework, and self-study. For example, it was thought in the 1920s that the then emerging technology—motion pictures—would be widely used in schools (which was done) and thus would eventually replace a considerably large proportion of textbooks (which did not eventuate). Likewise, television was later considered an advanced means to provide distant or convenient education. Mayer (2005) suggests that we should learn a lesson from the modern history of introducing new technology to education and adopt a different perspective: the learner-centered approach. Such an approach, according to Mayer (2005), focuses "on using multimedia technology as an aid to human cognition" (p. 9). During the recent decade, researchers have conducted a number of experiments and field studies in the cognitive processes associated with the usage of educational technology. Consequently, this line of research has offered a number of evidence-based cognitive principles for instructional design.

However, as Martens (2006) comments, it appears that another important aspect of the learner-centered approach—motivational research in the use of educational technology—deserves more attention. For example, in *The Cambridge Handbook of Multimedia Learning* edited by Mayer (2005), there are at least two chapters about gaming, simulation, microworlds, and virtual reality (Cobb & Fraser, 2005; Rieber, 2005), but none of them discuss motivational aspects. There are also three other chapters in this comprehensive handbook that deal with learning in advanced computer-based contexts, such as using animation, hypermedia, and other techniques in e-courses (Clark, 2005; Dillon & Jobst, 2005; Moreno, 2005), but only one of them has touched on a motivation-related phenomenon (Moreno, 2005). In her chapter, she describes an agent-based environmental science game where students using an animated agent with a personalized style (i.e., game information being presented in the first and second person) exhibited better learning outcomes than their counterparts who received content explanations in a neutral style (i.e., in the third person). Martens (2006) suggests that researchers consider intrinsic motivation as an indispensable aspect in effective learning. The motivational variables involved in digital learning programs, such as computer games designed for a particular course, need to be addressed.

Although public opinions regarding educational games are divided and systematic research in motivational aspects of educational games is still sparse, there are at least six well-founded indicators of the potential for educational games to promote motivation (e.g., Garris, Ahlers, & Driskell, 2002; Malone, 1981; Thomas & Macredie, 1994). First, instructional games are usually interactive and thus engage players in the processes of rapid reaction and timely feedback. Second, games that match players' levels are often challenging enough to grab their attention, yet the playing process does not raise too much learning anxiety (except in pathological cases) because players know there will be no real severely negative consequences (i.e., real-world punishment) if they "lose." Third, the nonthreatening aspect of games enhances players' (especially young children's) fantasy in gaming, which can result in curiosity, enjoyment, and satisfaction. Fourth, the sensory stimuli (visual, auditory, kinetic, etc.) and manual involvement can send strong signals to the central nervous system and thus strengthen learners' mental activities and persistence. Fifth, most educational games permit players to have a certain degree of control over their processes so that they can set up achievable goals according to their own judgment and the rules of games. Sixth, some types of educational games allow students to design their own games or choose a character to be personally and temporarily attached to, providing learners with a sense of "ownership" and thus leading to elevated interest in learning material and internalized responsibility to learning outcomes. As vividly shown in a factor analysis of character attachment in role-playing video games, for players, the self-selected character in a video game is not only pixels but *their* pixels (Lewis, Weber, & Bowman, 2008). This suggests that the power of such motivational involvement in the entire learning processes cannot be underestimated.

The aim of this chapter is to address motivation issues in the application of educational technology, especially in the use of educational games. The following sections will discuss the nature of academic competencies supposed to be attained in modern schooling, the composition of motivation in educational settings, motivational factors from a social cognitive perspective, motivational issues in serious educational games, evidence-based applications, and future directions of motivation research in the usage of educational games.

THE NATURE OF ACADEMIC COMPETENCIES

From the perspective of evolutionary educational psychology, Geary (2002, 2008a, 2008b) proposes two types of knowledge that human beings possess: biologically primary knowledge and biologically secondary knowledge. Over numerous generations, natural selection leads to the survival of human beings and enables normal individuals in the society to naturally learn primary knowledge without too much effort. By just living in a community and interacting with other folks, one can acquire biologically primary knowledge for survival in a relatively easy way. This bulk of basic knowledge can be classified as (a) folk psychology, such as verbal language, interpretation of other individuals' facial expressions and body language (welcoming, disproving, or threatening), comprehension of social relations, and theory of mind; (b) folk biology, such as available food, plants, and animals in the ecological environment; and (c) folk physics, such as counting with fingers up to a certain natural number, use of simple tools, distance, space, and dimensions in the physical territory. Knowledge in those folk domains is essential for human survival and is thus biologically primary. Individuals, especially children, are able to learn such biologically primary knowledge easily and unconsciously in various social contexts.

Biologically secondary knowledge in various domains, on the other hand, has been developed and accumulated much later in human history. It is built on biologically primary knowledge but also requires learners' extra effort to overcome some biases from folk psychology, folk biology, and folk physics. Rapidly changing modern societies demand that children (as well as adults) learn specific knowledge and skills so that one day they can function as effective members in society. According to Geary (2002), there are basically three categories of biologically secondary knowledge that modern life imposes on individuals, namely, (a) psychology, reading, writing, social sciences and humanities; (b) biological sciences; and (c) physical sciences. These domains are mainly taught in schools, and it is much harder for children and adults to acquire such knowledge and skills than to acquire biologically primary knowledge. For instance, on the one hand, normal children learning to speak their own native language find it such a smooth and natural process that the learning of language occurs almost without any need of formal instruction or educational resources. This is simply because the long period of evolution has equipped generations with the survival ability to acquire oral or body language for essential communication in a spontaneous way. On the other hand, a formal and well-structured education system (either institutional or home-learning units) is needed to help children learn how to read and write. This is a much more difficult task than the learning of a native language, because the relative short period of civilization associated with the invention of written language systems has not prepared our current generations to learn reading and writing effortlessly. In other words, whereas biologically primary knowledge has enabled numerous human generations to deal with their environment effectively, it is the demand of modern society that almost every member should attain academic competence, which is mainly characterized by various domains of biologically secondary knowledge. This type of learning often requires extra effort and specific assistance.

In additional to the differences in the ease of acquisition biologically primary vs. secondary knowledge, there are also attitudinal and motivational discrepancies between the two types of learning. According to Geary (2002, 2008a, 2008b), children's initial motivational dispositions are in line with play, interpersonal or group activities, social interactions, and exploration of the ecological environments and objects that are essential for obtaining basic folk knowledge (i.e., biologically primary knowledge). These child-initiated activities are important for achieving a certain degree of control over social relations and critical resources that are crucial in human evolution and do not necessarily lead to the activities employed in the promotion of academic learning. Such motivational "biases" must be taken into account for programs designed to facilitate academic competence. It is not realistic to assume that students will have as strong a motivation and spontaneity to learn academic knowledge (which is mainly biologically secondary) as they do to learn biologically primary knowledge.

Serious educational games may provide an optional means to bridge biologically primary knowledge and biologically secondary knowledge. There are at least three reasons for this. First, most educational games use plain language in instruction and part of the instruction can be delivered via auditory channel in a conversational manner. This type of delivery utilizes biologically primary knowledge (understanding plain language together with simple psychomotor movements for the game operation) to direct learners' attention to academic material. Second, educational games, especially computer games, are akin to child-initiated activities. For instance, in a format of exploring jungles and rescuing a trapped pet, children would have elevated motivation to accomplish this mission by engaging in associated academic tasks like crosswords. Third, although educational games are "serious" in terms of their ultimate aims (academic learning rather than pure entertainment), the instant consequences of losing at any point in the game is not so serious—the loss is not "real" and one can always try again (Anderson & Moore, 1960). Therefore, such a nonserious form of activities may provide a relatively anxiety-free and friendly learning environment (Rakoczy, 2008). Since the effectiveness of learning is always dependent upon the positive emotional and motivational climate in the learning place (Ellis, 2008), educational games, if properly designed and used, may be helpful in the transition from primary to secondary learning.

SELF-DETERMINATION AND INTRINSIC MOTIVATION

As discussed above, academic learning, focusing on biologically secondary knowledge, is a hard job (or mission) that requires both instructional and motivational supports. One of the common assumptions for those who endorse the use of educational games is that the interesting features of games could enhance learners' intrinsic motivation. Motivation is generally regarded as a complex psychological and physiological process that imbues a particular behavior with direction, energy, and perseverance (Bergin, Ford, & Hess, 1993; Murphy & Alexander, 2000; Pintrich, 2000). According to Ryan and Deci (2000), there are two types of motivation: (a) intrinsic motivation (i.e., one undertakes a task simply because the task is interesting and enjoyable) and (b) extrinsic motivation (i.e., one performs a task in order to attain a reward that is outside the task activity itself).

Ryan and Deci have proposed self-determination theory in an attempt to identify factors that foster self-motivated behavior, examine innate psychological needs in a social context, and address the relationship between intrinsic motivation and extrinsic incentives.

In general, research guided by self-determination theory, with cultural constraints, confirms that it is human nature to achieve competence, obtain autonomy, and seek relatedness of actions (Ryan & Deci, 2000; Schwartz, 2000). Inherent intrinsic tendencies can strengthen self-regulation and related productive activities. Self-determination theory further proposes that researchers and practitioners should focus on the maintenance and enhancement of intrinsic motivation, because this valuable propensity can be easily disrupted and hindered under nonsupportive conditions. Such phenomena are evident in educational environments. For example, a new Year 7 student may have a genuine interest in taking a high school subject that has not been offered in previous study at a primary school. This fresh, hopeful start could be totally disrupted if the course is found to be mechanically delivered, ill-structured, and not challenging enough. Personal choice, acknowledgement of learners' feelings and intentions, and the availability of self-directed activities are some factors found to enhance intrinsic motivation (Ryan & Deci, 2000). Research has been further carried out on the relations between intrinsic motivation and external rewards. An over-emphasized external reward could lead to an exaggerated external locus of control, diminished perceived autonomy, and thus lowered intrinsic motivation (Deci, Koestner, & Ryan, 1999; Eisenberger & Cameron, 1996). However, extrinsic motivation does not necessarily always have negative correlation with intrinsic motivation. Carefully guided and well-internalized forms of extrinsic motivation can promote learners' feelings of autonomy and thus facilitate self-motivated behavior (Luyten & Lens, 1981; Vansteenkiste, Lens, & Deci, 2006).

If both educational games and their academic content can be embedded in the entire learning procedure, the attractive features of gaming may enhance learners' engagement in learning activities. The consequences of utilizing such game features could be that (a) the completion of certain phases of a game leads to a sense of competence, (b) the self-directed game operation strengthens learners' feelings of autonomy, and (c) the close link between the game storyline (e.g., the emergency unit in a hospital) and the course content (e.g., medical analysis and diagnosis) highlights relatedness of the learning program to the reality and importance of the target academic knowledge. In cases where the learners may have strong extrinsic motivation to play electronic games but have very limited information (and thus enthusiasm) about a new course, a well-integrated educational game may initially just attract learners to be involved in the course and later on gradually cultivate learners' interest in the subject matter. In this way, educational games may facilitate the transition from extrinsic motivation to intrinsic motivation (see Van Eck, 2006a).

Research using educational games has provided some evidence of the efficacy of gaming in motivational enhancement. For instance, based on Vygotsky's (1978) assertion that play should be regarded as a scaffolding activity for the children to develop their potential in deep learning, a multimedia learning game *Quest Atlantis* (*QA*, Barab, Thomas, Dodge, Carteaux, & Tuzun, 2005) was used for Year 5 pupils in Singapore to learn mathematics, English and science curricula by assuming the role of responsible global citizens (Lim, 2008). In this *QA*-mediated game-like environment, a pre- and postacademic motivation questionnaire was administered with a sample size of 80 pupils. The within-subjects test indicated that the pupils had significantly higher intrinsic motivation and extrinsic motivation after the *QA*-mediated learning than the baseline. Students reported: "I think learning English is important," "What I learn in mathematics is useful," and "I find science interesting." Although this own-control design cannot rule out some confounding factors (e.g., history and maturation), the reported positive motivational effects are typical (e.g., Coleman, 2002).

It is not uncommon for educational researchers and practitioners to use motivational embellishments in instruction. From socioconstructivist instructional perspectives (Hickey, 1997) and Vygotskian contextualized development theory (Vygotsky, 1978), motivational embellishments can be broadly defined as pedagogical interventions to enhance learning motivation and enrich learning activities. Such pedagogical interventions are usually embedded in the learning context and may take the form of an agent, a story line, an intrinsic or extrinsic incentive, an expected or unexpected reward, or a form of personalization (a self-selected role).The efficacy of adequately developed educational games in the enhancement of academic motivation and the promotion of effective academic learning has been to some extent confirmed in experimental studies. For instance, in a series of controlled experiments (Lepper & Cordova, 1992), hypothesized motivational and cognitive benefits of appropriately designed motivational embellishments (computer games) for educational activities are scrutinized. Although computer-based educational programs that turn instructional drills into educational games have been introduced to schools and families, educators (teachers and parents) and educational researchers still have legitimate concerns about the side-effect that children may focus on winning the game rather than learning the material. Therefore, Lepper and Hodell (1989) adopted games in which educational indicators and motivational goals were mutually congruent. In other words, the games are designed "appropriately" in the sense that winning with enjoyment was dependent upon the positive learning outcomes from the subject material. When learning Cartesian coordinates, both boys and girls in primary schools showed strong preferences for the motivational embellished game version (i.e., finding hidden treasures buried on a deserted island) over the conventional version (i.e., hunting for hidden dots), and both groups spent more time for the motivational embellished game version than they did for the conventional version. Overall, the fantasy context tended to heighten intrinsic motivation.

The subsequent two experiments (Lepper & Hodell, 1992, as cited in Lepper & Cordova, 1992); Parker & Lepper, 1992) employed different versions of a motivational embellished game: using the "masculine" fantasy version, *Armed Hunting*, for boys and the "feminine" fantasy version, *Save Baby Mouse*, for girls or providing options of learning context for students to choose for themselves (e.g., assuming the role of a pirate in search of buried treasure, a detective chasing criminals, or an astronaut in the mission to explore other planets). The results showed that students, regardless of their gender, had higher motivation for motivational embellished game versions than for the control version. Moreover, boys and girls using motivational embellished learning games that provided a fantasy context produced better learning outcomes and after a period still showed greater interest in the subject matter than under the motivational unembellished condition. Pedagogically, it is worthwhile to notice that those students' subsequent interest in and attitude toward the target subject remained positive even when the motivational embellished "incentives" were no longer available. This is important because initial experience obtained from educational games in a fantasy context triggered learners' prolonged intrinsic motivation of academic learning. On some occasions, personalized context instead of generic context can be adopted. Research suggests that the personalization of instructional material may enhance the sense of relevancy and improve initial learning and the subsequent transfer of learning to new tasks (Anand & Ross, 1987; Cordova & Lepper, 1996; Lepper & Cordova, 1992).

In educational game settings, researchers (e.g., Lepper & Cordova, 1992) have attempted to examine the impact of both intrinsic enhancers and extrinsic rewards on the learning process and outcomes. For instance, using a 2 (intrinsic enhancer vs. no intrinsic enhancer) X 2 (extrinsic reward vs. no extrinsic reward) factorial design, experimental sessions were conducted for Years 4 and 5 primary school students to learn hypothesis generation. The task for students was to establish hypothetical links between "facts" and corresponding "crimes," and they were given feedback for each "hypothesis" generated. Such concept-learning activities allowed the researchers to record the learning processes step by step and examine the quantity and quality of the learning outcomes (i.e., the working hypotheses produced by the learners). While the intrinsic enhancer was in the form of a fantasy context designed for children to take the roles of "detectives," the extrinsic reward was a toy from the teacher's (in fact, experimenter's) gift box. It was found that a fantasy context, compared with the context without motivational embellishments, led to significantly higher utility of effective problem-solving strategies, elevated confidence at the task, better quality of solutions, and more willingness to choose difficult problems at a later time. After a period, many of those positive effects obtained in the experiment session persisted and generalized to new learning tasks. In contrast, the offer of an extrinsic reward (i.e., a toy rather than the excitement generated from problem-solving activities) for finding correct answers appeared to have negative impact on learning outcomes. Students anticipating an extrinsic reward generated their hypothetical proposals in a much less systematic way, evaluated themselves as less capable at the task, and took many more trials to reach an acceptable solution. In order to get a tangible extrinsic reward (a toy in the gift box), students generated many illogical hypotheses, almost ten times more than in the condition that no extrinsic rewards were provided. Interestingly, when those students were also exposed to motivational embellishments, the anticipation of an extrinsic reward still made them less involved in serious problem-solving activities and thus less productive. In general, although internalized extrinsic motivation can be helpful for learners' engagement, the provision of tangible extrinsic rewards, particularly in serious educational games, may have a detrimental effect on the quality as well as quantity of academic learning.

It is evident that some characteristics of game can be used for motivational embellishments. Malone (1981) initially proposed four main features of computer games that have motivational appeal: challenge, fantasy, complexity, and control. Later, based on evidence gathered from empirical studies, Malone and Lepper (1987) identified four aspects to be targeted for the enhancement of intrinsic motivation, namely, challenge, fantasy, curiosity, and control. More recently, in order to form a common vocabulary for researchers and practitioners to depict and manipulate the core elements of educational games, Garris and associates (2002) provide a useful six-category taxonomy: fantasy, rules/goals, sensory stimuli, challenge, mystery, and control. A variety of games can be developed by the combination of those variations.

However, care must be taken not to lavishly apply motivational embellishment strategies in the design and delivery of educational games. If motivational goals are irrelevant to learning goals, motivational activities require time and attention that could otherwise be distributed to knowledge/skill learning. In some cases, providing "seductive" information in an educational game may raise players' interest and attract their attention, but such manipulation will not result in any concrete learning outcomes of the targeted academic knowledge (Garner, Alexander, Gillingham, Kulikowich, & Brown, 1991; Garner, Gillingham, & White, 1989; Hidi, 1990). For instance, in a study intended to examine the effects of "seductive details" on the learning of differences among insects, both adults and children were given an expository text in one of two conditions: a) essential information plus seductive details (i.e., interesting information not important to the gist of the text, such as clicking *beetles' flipping, flies' buzzing*, and *snakes' consuming live animals*) presented or b) no seductive details but just essential information presented (Garner et al., 1989). Subjects exposed to provocative but unimportant details recalled an average of 43% of the main ideas in the text; by contrast, those not provided with such interesting but unnecessary details recalled an average of 93% of the key concepts in the text. Hence, in the design or selection of educational games, we need to be aware of the possibility that "seductive" details included in instructional procedures, perhaps appealing from marketing perspectives, can be pointless and even harmful to the planned academic learning. On the other hand, when the actions required for winning a game and the actions required for academic learning are congruent and mutually reinforcing, significant educational gains in terms of heightened intrinsic motivation and deep learning can occur.

Although some researchers (e.g., Habgood, Ainsworth, & Benford, 2005; Malone, 1981, 1983) are still divided on the issue of whether motivational elements such as fantasy and seductive details should be considered endogenous or exogenous representations, most would agree that fantasy is a prominent motivating feature of gaming and that relatedness of learning to reality is an important instructional strategy. A question of interest is: if the game procedure combines the fun components and the learning content, will this practice ensure effective acquisition of intended knowledge? One tentative approach to this issue is to examine whether the memory requirements for the fun activities will leave sufficient working memory for cognitive processing of information essential to desired learning outcomes (see Low, Jin, & Sweller, in press).

OTHER SELECTED MOTIVATIONAL CONSTRUCTS

Apart from the issue of intrinsic vs. extrinsic motivation discussed above, there are a number of other motivational constructs elaborated on in a comprehensive review on motivation literature associated with the research of academic achievement or academic development (Murphy & Alexander, 2000; Pintrich, 2000). Based on physical inspection of 17 journals nominated as main outlets of academic learning research and extensive on-line search, Murphy & Alexander (2000) have listed four major categories: goal, intrinsic vs. extrinsic motivation, interest, and self-schema, which in total consist of 20 motivation terms relevant to academic achievement and motivation. The next section, not intended to discuss those terms in detail, will highlight some motivational constructs (except the construct of intrinsic vs. extrinsic motivation already discussed in the previous section) that are closely associated with serious educational games. Obviously, those constructs can be interrelated at conceptual and operational levels from wider social cognitive perspectives.

Multiple Goals

According to a review by Locke & Latham (2002), research on goal-setting theory has overall confirmed a positive relationship between the level of goals and performance. Higher goals are conducive to higher levels of effort and thus performance. Furthermore, the action of setting specific, difficult goals is probably a more feasible and effective strategy than the do-your-best strategy (in which vague or no goals are specified) This is because the former strategy can reduce ambiguity in operations, whereas the latter strategy often lacks a clear external framework of reference. Research also shows that the effectiveness of goal-setting can be enhanced when timely feedback is provided and individuals have the opportunity to participate in decision making (Locke & Latham, 2002). An educational game with its unique features, if used properly, may facilitate effective goal-setting learning. For example, the game procedure can define different achievement levels according to the difficulty level of a specific learning task (a player's grade, points earned, "health" status, "resources" accumulated or further required, "weapons/gems" obtained or needed, etc.) and the learners can be encouraged to choose more challenging tasks. The indicators of the current performance level and progress records are often instantly available in computer games, so learners in an educational game can obtain immediate feedback. More importantly, an educational game player is usually one of the decision makers (sometimes the sole decision maker) for the learning process, and thus a sense of personal control as well as responsibility can be fostered.

The goal-setting perspective has been further developed in the area of academic achievement (e.g., Boekaerts, de Koning, & Vedder, 2006; Murphy & Alexander, 2000; Pintrich, 2000; Vansteenkiste et al., 2006). According to Pintrich (2000), three different levels of goal construct exist in achievement contexts. The first level is related to the target goals, which are an individual's goals for a specific task or problem (e.g., aiming to get 80 of 100 correct in a forthcoming statistics test). Secondly, individuals have general goals, which are a range of potential goals that function as a generic means for motivated behavior (e.g., resource acquisition, safety, and belongingness). Finally, achievement goals serve as an intermediate level between target goals and general goals, which consist of various orientations.

In recent years, researchers have attempted to identify different types of goal orientations towards academic achievement (DeShon & Gillespie, 2005; Elliot & McGregor, 2001; Lee, Sheldon, & Turban, 2003; Midgley, Kaplan, & Middleton, 2001; Zweig & Webster, 2004). Pintrich (2000) proposed a 2 (mastery orientation vs. performance orientation) X 2 (approach state vs. avoidance state) matrix to depict goal orientations: mastery orientation, learning avoidance orientation, performance orientation, and performance avoidance (learned helplessness) orientation. Among them, mastery orientation, which is characterized by a desire to fully utilize one's potential, can lead to positive outcomes and self-regulated learning. Performance orientation, which refers to a desire to merely demonstrate one's competence, has a less positive impact on learning. Both learning avoidance orientation and performance avoidance orientation have a negative impact on achievement (Bruning, Schraw, Norby, & Ronning, 2004; Dembo, 2004; Kolic-Vehovec, Roncevic, & Bajsanski, 2008; Pintrich, 2000). The implications for educational practice guidelines are (a) relevance—that instruction should highlight the relevance of the learning material and associated activities, (b) intrinsic goal orientation—that instruction should emphasize intrinsic goal framing, (c) promoting self-regulation—that instruction should adopt an autonomy-supportive format, and (d) learner-centered orientation—that instruction should be designed and delivered from the students' perspective (Vansteenkiste et al., 2006). Educational games can be appropriately designed to incorporate such guidelines. For example, students can be engaged in the gaming activities to learn relevant academic knowledge (relevance); the game instruction can urge users to maximize their potentiality and achieve higher levels of competence (intrinsic goal orientation); the game procedures can allow learners to have a certain degree of supported autonomy—to decide their own pace and short-term as well as long-term goals (promoting self-regulation); the game can be designed to accommodate learners' preferences by providing a repertoire of storylines to follow, special roles to act, virtual worlds to play, and favored goals to pursue (learner-centered orientation). As summarized by Lepper & Cordova (1992) in the Congruent and Mutually Reinforcing Principle, if the game goals match the academic goals, the educational benefits are significant.

Study of the relationship between students' goals and self-regulated learning has revealed a noteworthy phenomenon concerning the validity of self-report in the context of classrooms (Lemos, 1999). When students were asked to list the goals that they normally pursue in the classroom environment, perhaps because of social desirability and situational constraints, they mentioned a number of study-related goals but few goals related to entertainment, interpersonal relations, and social interactions. Boekaerts and colleagues (2006) argue that an innovative learning environment should recognize and accommodate students' multiple content goals, such as "I want to do well on the task," "I want to be entertained," "I want to belong," "I want to feel safe," and "I want to be valued for who I am." They urge researchers and practitioners to adopt a multiple-goal approach in order to ascertain the real driving forces behind students' goal-directed behavior. In reality, a proportion of students may be strongly interested in electronic games but not so interested in subject matter (e.g., elementary math). An educational game based on the Congruent and Mutually Reinforcing Principle, which combines appropriate learning material and entertainment, may be able to accommodate a pupil's spontaneous goal ("I want to be entertained") while providing a vehicle toward mathematical proficiency via a "kingdom" of arithmetic by allowing the manipulation of "weapons" like abacus and pebbles. In this way, the educational game may be able to guide the pupil, after obtaining an initial successful experience, to set up another goal—a subject-related goal (this time, "I want to do well on the task").

Self-Efficacy

Another factor that contributes to motivation to learn is self-efficacy. The construct of self-efficacy, developed from social learning theory, designates a person's judgments of his or her own capabilities in performing a designated task to achieve desired outcomes (Bandura, 1977, 1986, 1993, 1997). Self-efficacy is task-specific and thus related to a concrete working or learning environment (e.g., a student sitting a quiz related to the sine rule). More specifically, self-efficacy is about the self-judgment of one's capability of performing a specific task regardless of the value attached to the given task (a student feels capable of completing a quiz related to the sine rule but may not consider the quiz truly valuable).

Self-efficacy has been demonstrated as one of the best predictors of performance in work, sports, and learning (e.g., Bandura, 1993; Burke & Jin, 1996; Klassen, 2007; Schunk, 1989, 1991; Shores & Shannon, 2007; Souvignier & Mokhlesgerami, 2006). Individuals with high self-efficacy for an achievement task tend to put forth great effort when facing difficulties in the task activities. On the other hand, those with low self-efficacy tend to avoid attempting the task. This is also evident in research using educational games. For instance, in Lim's (2008) quasi-experiment in which a computer learning game for key learning areas was adopted, the post-hoc test shows that students increased their self-efficacy (e.g., "I can do the hardest work in my class if I try," "I am sure I can do difficult work in my class," etc.) and attained positive learning outcomes.

Derived from social cognitive perspectives, self-efficacy has a unique characteristic—psychological modeling. Individuals can form and change their beliefs through their interaction and comparison with their everyday associates. This process is fairly effective when individuals perceive themselves as similar to their peer models, especially in a situation that is relatively novel or uncertain in which they are required to make judgments about their own capabilities. As Bandura (1993) points out, when one is unsure about one's own capabilities for a specific task, one tends to rely heavily on modeled indicators. This principle applies to learning tasks with educational technology. A typical example is reported in a study of pedagogical agents as learning companions (Kim, Baylor, and PALS Group, 2006). In a Web-based learning environment, undergraduate students were required to develop a lesson plan (including teaching strategies and class activities) to assist a 13-year-old girl in learning basic economic concepts. A virtual pedagogical agent (learning companion) with the appearance of a man in his early 20s was provided in two versions: high-competency pedagogical agent (i.e., an advanced peer) and low-competency pedagogical agent (i.e., a novice peer). The results indicated that students in the low-competency condition had significantly higher self-efficacy about the assigned task than their counterparts in the high-competency condition, with an effect size in the medium range (Cohen's $d = .49$). This is likely due to the cognitive appraisal of the discrepancy between the individuals and their peers. Judgments of individuals' own capabilities can be strengthened when individuals compare themselves to similar but slightly underperforming peers. This study clearly demonstrates the advantages of properly designed educational games in terms of their flexibility of changing delivery versions (e.g., the competency levels of a pedagogical agent) with relatively low costs.

Self-efficacy, as part of self-schema, is naturally linked with other parts of self-schema, such as attribution and self-competence (Murphy & Alexander, 2000). Geary (2002) suggests that one of the priorities of schooling is to build children's academic self-efficacy and other beliefs related to their self-awareness that will help them to maintain long-term effort and motivation in school learning. Positive self-referenced appraisal processes may lead to benign attributional changes in the direction that perceived causes of progress are associated with individual or group effort. Scientifically tested, evidence-based educational games can play a constructive role in facilitating positive self-schema formation for children. For instance, quite a number of children may assume that the learning of mathematics requires special talent ("He is genius—I am not good in math, so I won't do it") and thus become anxious when dealing with difficult learning material (problem solving). An experiment with random assignment and proper controls was conducted in middle schools where a computer-based math game was introduced (Van Eck, 2006b). The game for mathematics curriculum included contextual pedagogical advisement ("aunt and uncle" dressed in jeans and work shirts to give advice in video) and a virtual "competitor" (with a face icon). It was found that students in the contextual pedagogical advisement group had decreased their anxiety level toward mathematics, especially under competitive conditions provided in the game context. Likewise, Wang (2008) reported that students participated more actively in the Web-based quiz-game-like test than the normal Web-based test when the content of assessment was kept identical, indicating heightened learning motivation for the game-like assessment format. In addition, the feeling of control and enjoyment in the Web-based quiz-game-like test enabled students to perform better than those in the normal Web-based test and the paper-and-pencil test. In another study, an educational video game was provided to young hockey players for the purposes of reducing aggressive and negligent behaviors that could cause concussions and other injuries (Ciavarro, Dobson, & Goodman, 2008). As a result of the implicit learning features embedded in the sport–action game, teenagers in the experimental group increased safe play behaviors. Overall, the findings demonstrate that a properly designed educational game can be used as an effective tool for social learning and motivational enhancement, thus leading to positive attitudes towards learning, improved performance, and desirable changes in behavior.

THE ARCS MODEL AND DEVELOPMENT: TOWARD A PRACTICAL FRAMEWORK OF INSTRUCTIONAL MOTIVATIONAL STRATEGIES

Facing a growing body of diversified research information in the area of academic motivation and achievement, practitioners as well as researchers are often in need of a working model that is characterized by its congruity and simplicity. In instructional design using multimedia technology, the attention, relevance, confidence, and satisfaction (ARCS) model is an innovative approach incorporating motivational strategies with learning material (Keller, 1987; Keller & Suzuki, 2004; Song & Keller, 2001). In this working model, four critical aspects have been proposed in accordance with established motivational principles: (1) the instruction must attract and sustain the learner's *attention*, which is endorsed by the research on curiosity and arousal; (2) the course material must build *relevance*, which is consistent with the research on intrinsic motivation and competence; (3) the lesson delivery must enhance learners' *confidence*, which is supported by the research of self-efficacy and attribution; and (4) the entire learning program must lead to learners' *satisfaction*, which is in line with research on goal attainment, reinforcement, and equity.

In short, the ARCS model is a practical framework that includes essential motivational components in instructional design and delivery. The model and its simplified versions have been validated in various learning contexts and cultural settings (e.g., Astleitner & Hufnagl, 2003; Gao & Lehman, 2003; Keller & Suzuki, 2004; Means, Jonassen & Dwyer, 1997; Small & Gluck, 1994; Song & Keller, 2001; Visser & Keller, 1990). For instance, the ARCS model was employed to construct motivationally adaptive computer-assisted instruction (Song & Keller, 2001) and proactive WebCT learning (Gao & Lehman, 2003).

Efforts have also been made to introduce the ARCS approach to research on games with potential educational values. On the basis of Keller's (1987) Instructional Materials Motivational Scale (IMMS), Dempsey and Johnson (1998) developed the ARCS Gaming Scale, consisting of three subcategories for each of the four categories in relation to the use of games with potential educational usage: (a) attention, including perceptual arousal, inquiry arousal, and variability; (b) relevance, including goal orientation, motive matching, and familiarity; (c) confidence, including learning requirements, success opportunities, and personal control; and (d) satisfaction, including natural consequences, positive consequences, and equity. The exploratory factor analysis yields limited yet reasonable support to the latent variable structure in Keller's framework. More recently, Kebritchi (2008) adapted the ARCS Model in a mathematics motivation questionnaire to examine the effects of a series of mathematics computer games on high school students' mathematics achievement and motivation. It was found that the students who played the mathematics computer games in their school lab and classrooms had higher motivational enhancement than those who only played the games in the school lab. The study also demonstrates that the use of mathematics computer games was effective for the improvement of students' mathematics skills. Overall, the ARCS model has been endorsed as a solid and practical protocol for both educators in their routine professional activities and researchers in their investigation of the effectiveness of motivational elements embedded in instructions.

FUTURE RESEARCH DIRECTIONS

As discussed above, motivation is an indispensable variable in the equation of academic achievement via serious educational games. Research in this area can be backed up by well-established motivational theories and models. Some suggestions for future research are offered below:

Develop Suitable Motivation Instruments Related to Educational Games for Practitioners and Researchers

For the purpose of effective design and research in educational games, reliable and valid instruments are needed. There are two trends of using proper motivation instruments for teaching and investigation. One way is to adapt well-established instruments that have been used in similar or broader fields, For instance, to examine the effectiveness of a multimedia educational game known as *Quest Atlantis* in learning main subjects (English, mathematics, and science), Lim (2008) used a questionnaire adapted from the Motivation Strategies for Learning Questionnaire, known as MSLQ (Pintrich, Smith, Garcia, & McKeachie, 1993), and the Patterns of Adaptive Learning Survey, known as PALS (Midgley et al., 1997). Another way is to develop specific instruments for motivational research of educational games. For example, Dempsey and Johnson (1998) developed the ARCS Gaming Scale to pinpoint motivational factors that are associated with games having identifiable potential for educational use. Furthermore, Adcock & Van Eck (2005) designed and validated the Attitude Toward Tutoring Agent Scale (ATTAS) in response to the increasing use of tutoring agents as a tool for evaluating users' performance in digital environments. Another example is the construction of a metric of Character Attachment (CA) to examine the personal connections felt by video game players toward a certain video game character (Lewis et al., 2008). Using this validated instrument, Lewis and associates found that a video game player's character attachment was significantly correlated with self-esteem, game enjoyment, addiction to gaming, and time spent in playing games, revealing a deeper psychological mechanism associated with role-play video games. Whereas adapting generic motivation instruments has the advantage of using other researchers' existing data banks with broader frameworks of reference, the development of specific motivational instruments for educational games, although costly and time-consuming, is needed for this rapidly growing field.

Use Special Game Features to Provide Timely and Informative Feedback

The information technology embedded in most modern educational games enables the system to record operational movements, monitor progress, and provide quick feedback to engaged learners. The timely and personalized feedback, in turn, can further raise players' learning motivation and enhance their involvement in the learning process. This game feature can be used to introduce adaptive testing/modules (Kelly, 2008; Moreno-Ger, Burgos, Martínez-Ortiz, Sierra, & Fernández-Manjón, 2008; Roy, 2008) and foster self-regulated learning (Lodewyk, Winne, & Jamieson-Noel, 2009; Zimmerman, 2001, 2008).

Construct a Repertoire of Game Versions to Accommodate Individual and Cultural Differences

Research indicates that learners generate different types of fantasy and prefer certain roles in games (Cordova & Lepper, 1996; Lewis et al., 2008). When the role in a particular educational game matches the player's fantasy well, learning motivation can be heightened and more effort will be exerted to learn the material contained in the program. For instance, school children in the United States have diversified self-identified preferences, such as a hunter to defeat an aggressive gigantic beast, a rescuer to save and protect little animals, and a sky-walker to explore unknown planets (Cordova & Lepper, 1996). In a different cultural environment, for example Turkey, two recent large-scale investigations revealed that, while overall the most preferred type of computer game was the violent version, female high school students, despite considering that computer games might help them learn mathematics and history, strongly disliked computer games having stories of aggressive behavior and worried that playing some computer games could lead to laziness

(Karakus, Inal, & Cagiltay, 2008; Tahiroglu, Celik, Uzel, Ozcan, & Avci, 2008). When designing educational games, it is important to take into account individual, group, and cultural differences. The unprecedented technological advancement provides great opportunities for educational game developers to design a variety of personalized versions at considerably low costs.

Examine Pathological Aspects of Gaming

Broadly speaking, the proliferation of computer games for entertainment purposes has attracted the attention of many educators, psychologists, and health professionals across the world (e.g., Dill, Brown, & Collins, 2008; Hill & Peters, 1998; Olson, 2004; Peters & Malesky, 2008; Sun, Ma, Bao, Chen, & Zhang, 2008; Tahiroglu et al., 2008). Some concerns have been raised in terms of the negative consequences on players' mental and physical health as a result of excessive and improper use of computer games. Educational game developers should be mindful of such issues related to pathological motivation (e.g., obsession). Taking a lesson from the entertainment game industry, we need to prevent gaming addiction in at least three aspects. First, in the design of an educational game, any improper sensational content and procedures (e.g., extremely violent or obscene) must be excluded. Second, in the educational game design, the gaming process and the gradient of learning material must be tightly combined together so that there is no way for a gaming-motivation-only player just playing around without any concrete academic learning (e.g., a "Game Over" mechanism can be activated immediately after a few trials of random playing). Third, wherever appropriate, an educational game can include a brief orientation session and an in-game pedagogical agent (i.e., a talking head adviser with friendly, responsive, and encouraging characteristics) as a motivational enhancer.

Implement Motivational Training

Educational games, by and large, have been used as a motivational "trigger," because some features of games (e.g., sensory stimulation, requirements of psychomotor reactions, and storylines associated with fantasy) can raise learners' interest. Notwithstanding the fact that the initial motivational enhancement is beneficial, we may further consider how to use educational games as a motivational "trainer" in a digital environment. Motivational training is a process for cognitive restructuring and priority repositioning (de Jong-Meyer, 2004). In an educational context, motivational training procedures are usually derived from evidence-based motivational theories and models. Although it is informative to analyse and identify relationships among motivational variables, academic motivation, especially learner's motivation in the classroom, can be examined in a transitional/developmental context, for example, the shift from situational interest to personal endurance (Hidi & Renninger, 2006; Krapp, 2002; Turner & Patrick, 2008). The effectiveness of motivational training can be examined by using valid motivation instruments in a "pretraining vs. posttraining" design. Educational games can include periodical motivation analysis and motivation maintenance procedures. The ARCS model provides a systematic protocol for constructing motivational components in instruction (Keller & Suzuki, 2004). If the games are online, log data such as the time spent on learning material and the depth and scope of learning activities can be used as objective indicators of learners' academic motivation. Further research in this direction is warranted.

CONCLUSION

In an era of unprecedented advancement of information technology and the proliferation of educational games, both practitioners and researchers adopting learner-centered approaches need to pay more attention to motivational factors involved in academic learning when using educational technology. The learning of academic knowledge in various domains, which is mainly biologically secondary knowledge, requires an effective motivation supporting system embedded in instruction. Serious educational games possess motivating features such as fantasy, rules/goals, sensory stimuli, challenge, mystery, and self-control. If the games are properly designed and used, they may be conducive to elevated intrinsic motivation, positive goal orientation, reduced learning anxiety, and enhanced self-efficacy, which, in turn, can facilitate the transition from biologically primary knowledge to biologically secondary knowledge and result in desirable learning outcomes. According to the Congruence and Mutually Reinforcing Principle, the goal of motivational embellishments must match the goal of academic learning, and any "seductive" details and redundant procedures included in educational games may be counterproductive. The educational game design should also take into account individual, group, and cultural differences. The ARCS model and other well-established motivation instruments are recommended for motivation analysis (e.g., finding out learners' specific interests), motivation maintenance (e.g., keeping instruction relatively short with step-by-step disclosure, and motivation enhancement (e.g., using sounds, flashes, or animations to attract would-be-bored learners).

REFERENCES

Adcock, A. B., & Van Eck, R. (2005). Reliability and factor structure of the Attitude Toward Tutoring Agent Scale (ATTAS). *Journal of Interactive Learning Research, 16*(2), 195–212.

Anand, S. M., & Ross, P. G. (1987). A computer-based strategy for personalizing verbal problems in teaching mathematics. *Educational Communication and Technology Journal, 35*, 151–162.

Anderson, A. R., & Moore, O. K. (1960). Autotelic folk-models. *The Sociological Quarterly, 1*, 203–216. doi:10.1111/j.1533-8525.1960.tb01474.x

Astleitner, H., & Hufnagl, M. (2003). The effects of situation-outcome-expectancies and of ARCS-strategies on self-regulated learning with web-lectures. *Journal of Educational Multimedia and Hypermedia, 12*(4), 361–376.

Bandura, A. (1977). Self-efficacy: Toward a unifying theory of behavioural change. *Psychological Review, 84*, 191–215. doi:10.1037/0033-295X.84.2.191

Bandura, A. (1986). *Social foundations of thought and action: A social cognitive theory*. Englewood Cliffs, NJ: Prentice Hall.

Bandura, A. (1993). Perceived self-efficacy in cognitive development and functioning. *Educational Psychologist, 28*, 117–148. doi:10.1207/s15326985ep2802_3

Bandura, A. (1997). *Self-efficacy: The exercise of control*. New York: Plenum.

Barab, S. A., Thomas, M., Dodge, T., Carteaux, R., & Tuzun, H. (2005). Making learning fun: Quest Atlantis, a game without guns. *Educational Technology Research and Development, 53*(1), 86–107. doi:10.1007/BF02504859

Bergin, D. A., Ford, M. E., & Hess, R. D. (1993). Patterns of motivation and social behaviour associated with microcomputer use of young children. *Journal of Educational Psychology, 85*, 437–445. doi:10.1037/0022-0663.85.3.437

Boekaerts, M., de Koning, E., & Vedder, P. (2006). Goal-directed behaviour and contextual factors in the classroom: An innovative approach to the study of multiple goals. *Educational Psychologist, 41*(1), 33–51. doi:10.1207/s15326985ep4101_5

Bruning, R. H., Schraw, G. J., Norby, M. M., & Ronning, R. R. (2004). *Cognitive Psychology and Instruction* (4th ed.). Upper Saddle River, NJ: Merrill.

Burke, S., & Jin, P. (1996). Predicting performance from a triathlon event. *Journal of Sport Behavior, 19*, 272–287.

Ciavarro, C., Dobson, M., & Goodman, D. (2008). Implicit learning as a design strategy for learning games: *Alert Hockey. Computers in Human Behavior, 24*, 2862–2872. doi:10.1016/j.chb.2008.04.011

Clark, R. C. (2005). Multimedia learning in e-courses. In Mayer, R. E. (Ed.), *The Cambridge Handbook of Multimedia Learning* (pp. 589–616). New York: Cambridge University Press.

Cobb, S., & Fraser, D. S. (2005). Multimedia learning in virtual reality. In Mayer, R. E. (Ed.), *The Cambridge Handbook of Multimedia Learning* (pp. 525–547). New York: Cambridge University Press.

Coleman, D. W. (2002). On foot in SIM City: Using SIM COPTER as the basis for an ESL writing assignment. *Simulation & Gaming, 33*, 217–230. doi:10.1177/1046878102332010

Cordova, D. L., & Lepper, M, R. (1996). Intrinsic motivation and the process of learning: Beneficial effects of contextualization, personalization, and choice. *Journal of Educational Psychology, 88*(4), 715–730. doi:10.1037/0022-0663.88.4.715

de Jong-Meyer, R. (2004). Systematic motivational analysis as part of a self-help technique aimed at personal goal attainment. In Cox, W. M., & Klinger, E. (Eds.), *Handbook of motivational counseling: Concepts, approaches, and assessment* (pp. 259–281). New York: Wiley.

Deci, E. L., Koestner, R., & Ryan, R. M. (1999). A meta-analytic review of experiments examining the effects of extrinsic rewards on intrinsic motivation. *Psychological Bulletin, 25*, 627–668. doi:10.1037/0033-2909.125.6.627

Dembo, M. H. (2004). Don't lose sight of the students. *Principal Leadership, 4*, 37–42.

Dempsey, J. V., & Johnson, R. B. (1998). The development of an ARCS Gaming Scale. *Journal of Instructional Psychology, 25*(4), 215–221.

DeShon, R. P., & Gillespie, J. Z. (2005). A motivated action theory account of goal orientation. *The Journal of Applied Psychology, 90*(6), 1096–1127. doi:10.1037/0021-9010.90.6.1096

Dill, K. E., Brown, B. P., & Collins, M. A. (2008). Effects of exposure to sex-stereotyped video game characters on tolerance of sexual harassment. *Journal of Experimental Social Psychology, 44*, 1402–1408. doi:10.1016/j.jesp.2008.06.002

Dillon, A., & Jobst, J. (2005). Multimedia learning with hypermedia. In Mayer, R. E. (Ed.), *The Cambridge Handbook of Multimedia Learning* (pp. 569–588). New York: Cambridge University Press.

Eisenberger, R., & Cameron, J. (1996). Detrimental effects of reward: Reality or myth? *The American Psychologist, 51*, 1153–1166. doi:10.1037/0003-066X.51.11.1153

Elliot, A. J., & McGregor, H. (2001). A 2 x 2 achievement goal framework. *Journal of Personality and Social Psychology, 80*, 501–519. doi:10.1037/0022-3514.80.3.501

Ellis, G. (2008). Commentary on an evolutionarily informed education science by David C. Geary. *Educational Psychologist, 43*, 206–213. doi:10.1080/00461520802392216

Gao, T., & Lehman, J. D. (2003). The effects of different levels of interaction on the achievement and motivation perceptions of college students in a web-based learning environment. *Journal of Interactive Learning Research, 14*(4), 367–386.

Garner, R., Alexander, P. A., Gillingham, M. G., Kulikowich, J. M., & Brown, R. (1991). Interest and learning form text. *American Educational Research Journal, 28*, 643–659.

Garner, R., Gillingham, M. G., & White, C. S. (1989). Effects of seductive details on macroprocessing and microprocessing in adults and children. *Cognition and Instruction, 6*(1), 41–57. doi:10.1207/s1532690xci0601_2

Garris, R., Ahlers, R., & Driskell, J. E. (2002). Games, motivation, and learning: A research and practice model. *Simulation & Gaming, 33*, 441–467. doi:10.1177/1046878102238607

Geary, D. (2002). Principles of evolutionary educational psychology. *Learning and Individual Differences, 12*, 317–345. doi:10.1016/S1041-6080(02)00046-8

Geary, D. (2008a). An evolutionarily informed education science. *Educational Psychologist, 43*, 179–195. doi:10.1080/00461520802392133

Geary, D. (2008b). Whither evolutionary educational psychology? *Educational Psychologist, 43*, 217–226. doi:10.1080/00461520802392240

Habgood, M. P. J., Ainsworth, S. E., & Benford, S. (2005). Endogenous fantasy and learning in digital games. *Simulation & Gaming, 36*(4), 483–498. doi:10.1177/1046878105282276

Hickey, D. T. (1997). Motivation and contemporary socio-constructivist instructional perspectives. *Educational Psychologist, 32*(3), 175–193. doi:10.1207/s15326985ep3203_3

Hidi, S. (1990). Interest and its contribution as a mental resource for learning. *Review of Educational Research, 60*, 549–571.

Hidi, S., & Renninger, K. N. (2006). The four model of interest development. *Educational Psychologist, 41*(2), 111–127. doi:10.1207/s15326985ep4102_4

Hill, J. O., & Peters, J. C. (1998). Environmental contributions to the obesity epidemic. *Science, 280*, 1371–1374. doi:10.1126/science.280.5368.1371

Karakus, T., Inal, Y., & Cagiltay, K. (2008). A descriptive study of Turkish high school students' game-playing characteristics and their considerations concerning the effects of games. *Computers in Human Behavior, 24*, 2520–2529. doi:10.1016/j.chb.2008.03.011

Kebritchi, M. (2008). Effects of a computer game on mathematics achievement and class motivation: An experimental study. *Humanities and Social Sciences: Dissertation Abstracts International Section A, 69*(6-A), 2121.

Keller, J. M. (1987). Motivational design and multimedia: Beyond the novelty effect. *Strategic Human Resource Development Review, 1*(1), 188–203.

Keller, J. M., & Suzuki, K. (2004). Learner motivation and e-learning design: A multinationally validated process. *Journal of Educational Media, 29*(3), 229–239.

Kelly, D. (2008). Adaptive versus learner control in a multiple intelligence learning environment. *Journal of Educational Multimedia and Hypermedia, 17*(3), 307–336.

Kim, Y., & Baylor, A., & PALS Group. (2006). Pedagogical agents as learning companions: The role of agent competency and type of interaction. *Educational Technology Research and Development, 54*(3), 223–243. doi:10.1007/s11423-006-8805-z

Klassen, R. M. (2007). Using predictions to learn about the self-efficacy of early adolescents. *Contemporary Educational Psychology*, *32*, 173–187. doi:10.1016/j.cedpsych.2006.10.001

Kolic-Vehovec, S., Roncevic, B., & Bajsanski, I. (2008). Motivational components of self-regulated learning and reading strategy use in university students: The role of goal orientation patterns. *Learning and Individual Differences*, *18*, 108–113. doi:10.1016/j.lindif.2007.07.005

Krapp, A. (2002). Structural and dynamic aspects of interest development: Theoretical considerations from an ontogenetic perspective. *Learning and Instruction*, *12*, 383–409. doi:10.1016/S0959-4752(01)00011-1

Lee, F. K., Sheldon, K. M., & Turban, D. B. (2003). Personality and the goal-striving process: The influence of achievement foal patterns, goal level, and mental focus on performance and enjoyment. *The Journal of Applied Psychology*, *88*(2), 256–265. doi:10.1037/0021-9010.88.2.256

Lemos, M. S. (1999). Students' goals and self-regulation in the classroom. *International Journal of Educational Research*, *31*, 471–485. doi:10.1016/S0883-0355(99)00016-6

Lepper, M. R., & Cordova, D. (1992). A desire to be taught: Instructional consequences of intrinsic motivation. *Motivation and Emotion*, *16*(3), 187–208. doi:10.1007/BF00991651

Lepper, M. R., & Hodell, M. (1989). Intrinsic motivation in the classroom. In Ames, C., & Ames, R. (Eds.), *Research on motivation in education* (*Vol. 3*, pp. 73–105). New York: Academic Press.

Lewis, M., Weber, R., & Bowman, N. D. (2008). They may be pixels, but they're my pixels: Developing a metric of character attachment in role-playing video games. *Cyberpsychology & Behavior*, *11*(4), 515–518. doi:10.1089/cpb.2007.0137

Leys, S. (1997). *The analects of Confucius*. New York: W. W. Norton.

Lim, C. P. (2008). Global citizenship education, school curriculum and games: Learning Mathematics, English and Science as a global citizen. *Computers & Education*, *51*, 1073–1093. doi:10.1016/j.compedu.2007.10.005

Locke, E. A., & Latham, G. P. (2002). Building a practically useful theory of goal setting and task motivation: A 35-year odyssey. *The American Psychologist*, *57*(9), 705–717. doi:10.1037/0003-066X.57.9.705

Locke, J. (1968). The educational writings of John Locke: A critical Ed. with introduction and notes by James L. Axtell. London: Cambridge University Press.

Lodewyk, K. R., Winne, P. H., & Jamieson-Noel, D. L. (2009). Implications of task structure on self-regulating learning and achievement. *Educational Psychology*, *29*(1), 1–25. doi:10.1080/01443410802447023

Low, R., Jin, P., & Sweller, J. (in press). Learners' cognitive load when using educational technology. In Van Eck, R. (Ed.), *Gaming & cognition: Theories and practice from the learning sciences*. Hershey, PA: IGI Global.

Luyten, H., & Lens, W. (1981). The effect of earlier experience and reward contingencies on intrinsic motivation. *Motivation and Emotion*, *5*, 25–36. doi:10.1007/BF00993659

Malone, T. W. (1981). What makes computer games fun? *Byte*, *6*(12), 258–277.

Malone, T. W. (1983). Guidelines for designing educational computer games. *Childhood Education*, *59*(4), 241–247.

Malone, T. W., & Lepper, M. R. (1987). Making learning fun: A taxonomy of intrinsic motivations for learning. In Snow, R. E., & Farr, M. J. (Eds.), *Aptitude, learning and instruction: III. Conative and affective process analyses* (pp. 255–286). Hillsdale, NJ: Erlbaum.

Martens, R. (2006). What about motivation? *PsycCRITIQUES, 51*(52), 11. doi:10.1037/a0005828

Mayer, R. E. (2005). Cognitive theory of multimedia learning. In Mayer, R. E. (Ed.), *The Cambridge Handbook of Multimedia Learning* (pp. 31–48). New York: Cambridge University Press.

Means, T. B., Jonassen, D. H., & Dwyer, R. M. (1997). Enhancing relevance: embedded ARCS strategies vs. purpose. *Educational Technology Research and Development, 45*(1), 5–18. doi:10.1007/BF02299610

Midgley, C., Kaplan, A., & Middleton, M. (2001). Performance-approach goals: Good for what, for whom, under what circumstances, and at what cost? *Journal of Educational Psychology, 93*(1), 77–86. doi:10.1037/0022-0663.93.1.77

Moreno, R. (2005). Multimedia learning with animated pedagogical agents. In Mayer, R. E. (Ed.), *The Cambridge Handbook of Multimedia Learning* (pp. 507–523). New York: Cambridge University Press.

Moreno-Ger, P., & Burgos, D., Martinez-Ortiz, Sierra, J. S., & Fernández-Manjón, B. (2008). Educational game design for online education. *Computers in Human Behavior, 24*, 2530–2540. doi:10.1016/j.chb.2008.03.012

Murphy, P. K., & Alexander, P. A. (2000). A motivated exploration of motivation terminology. *Contemporary Educational Psychology, 25*, 3–53. doi:10.1006/ceps.1999.1019

Olson, C. K. (2004). Media violence research and youth violence data: Why do they conflict? *Academic Psychiatry, 28*(2), 144–149. doi:10.1176/appi.ap.28.2.144

Parker, L. E., & Lepper, M. R. (1992). The effects fantasy contexts on children's learning and motivation: Making learning more fun. *Journal of Personality and Social Psychology, 62*, 625–633. doi:10.1037/0022-3514.62.4.625

Peters, C. S., & Malesky, L. A. (2008). Problematic usage among highly-engaged players of massively multiplayer online role playing games. *Cyberpsychology & Behavior, 11*(4), 481–484. doi:10.1089/cpb.2007.0140

Pintrich, P. (2000). The role of goal orientation in self-regulated learning. In Boekaerts, M., Pintrich, P. R., & Zeidner, M. (Eds.), *Handbook of self-regulation* (pp. 451–502). Mawah, NJ: Lawrence Erlbaum. doi:10.1016/B978-012109890-2/50043-3

Pintrich, P. R., Smith, D., Garcia, T., & McKeachie, W. (1993). Predictive validity and reliability of the Motivated Strategies for Learning Questionnaire (MSLQ). *Educational and Psychological Measurement, 53*, 801–813. doi:10.1177/0013164493053003024

Rakoczy, H. (2008). Pretence as individual and collective intentionality. *Mind & Language, 23*(5), 499–517. doi:10.1111/j.1468-0017.2008.00357.x

Rieber, L. P. (2005). Multimedia learning in games, simulations, and microworlds. In Mayer, R. E. (Ed.), *The Cambridge Handbook of Multimedia Learning* (pp. 549–567). New York: Cambridge University Press.

Roy, D. D. (2008). Assessing validity of web-based computer adaptive training modules. *Journal of the Indian Academy of Applied Psychology, 34*(1), 127–136.

Ryan, R. M., & Deci, E. L. (2000). Intrinsic and extrinsic motivations: Classic definitions and new directions. *Contemporary Educational Psychology, 25*, 54–67. doi:10.1006/ceps.1999.1020

Schunk, D. H. (1989). Self-efficacy and cognitive skill learning. In C. Ames & R. Ames (Eds.), Research in motivation in education. Vol. 3: Goals and cognitions (pp. 13-44). San Diego, CA: Academic Press.

Schunk, D. H. (1991). Self-efficacy and academic motivation. *Educational Psychologist, 26*, 207–231. doi:10.1207/s15326985ep2603&4_2

Schwartz, B. (2000). Self-determination: The tyranny of freedom. *The American Psychologist, 55*, 79–88. doi:10.1037/0003-066X.55.1.79

Shores, M. L., & Shannon, D. M. (2007). The effects of self-regulation, motivation, anxiety, and attributions on mathematics achievement for fifth and sixth grade students. *School Science and Mathematics, 107*, 225.

Small, R. V., & Gluck, M. (1994). The relationship of motivational conditions to effective instructional attributes: A magnitude scaling approach. *Educational Technology, 34*(8), 33–40.

Song, S. H., & Keller, J. M. (2001). Effectiveness of motivationally adaptive computer-assisted instruction on the dynamic aspects of motivation. *Educational Technology Research and Development, 49*, 5–22. doi:10.1007/BF02504925

Souvignier, E., & Mokhlesgerami, J. (2006). Using self-regulation as a framework for implementing strategy instruction to foster reading comprehension. *Learning and Instruction, 16*, 57–71. doi:10.1016/j.learninstruc.2005.12.006

Sun, D., Ma, N., Bao, M., Chen, X., & Zhang, D. (2008). Computer games: A double-edged sword? *Cyberpsychology & Behavior, 11*(5), 545–548. doi:10.1089/cpb.2007.0145

Tahiroglu, A. Y., Celik, G., Uzel, M., Ozcan, N., & Avci, A. (2008). Internet use among Turkish adolescents. *Cyberpsychology & Behavior, 11*(5), 537–543. doi:10.1089/cpb.2007.0165

Thomas, P., & Macredie, R. (1994). Games and the design of human-computer interfaces. *Educational and Training Technology International, 31*(2), 134–142.

Turner, J. C., & Patrick, H. (2008). How does motivation develop and why does it change? Reframing motivation research. *Educational Psychologist, 43*(3), 119–131. doi:10.1080/00461520802178441

Van Eck, R. (2006a). Using games to promote girls' positive attitudes toward technology. *Innovate, 2*(3).

Van Eck, R. (2006b). The effect of contextual pedagogical advisement and competition on middle-school students' attitude toward mathematics and mathematics instruction using a computer-based simulation game. *Journal of Mathematics and Science Teaching, 25*(2), 165–195.

Vansteenkiste, M., Lens, W., & Deci, E. L. (2006). Intrinsic versus extrinsic goal contents in self-determination theory: Another look at the quality of academic motivation. *Educational Psychologist, 41*(1), 19–31. doi:10.1207/s15326985ep4101_4

Visser, J., & Keller, J. M. (1990). The clinical use of motivational messages: An inquiry into the validity of the Arcs model of motivational design. *Instructional Science, 19*(6), 467–500. doi:10.1007/BF00119391

Vygotsy, L. (1978). *Mind in society: The development of higher psychological processes*. Cambridge, MA: Harvard University Press.

Wang, T. (2008). Web-based quiz-game-like formative assessment: Development and evaluation. *Computers & Education, 51*, 1247–1263. doi:10.1016/j.compedu.2007.11.011

Zimmerman, B. (2001). Theories of self-regulated learning and academic achievement: An overview and analysis. In Zimmerman, B. J., & Schunk, D. H. (Eds.), *Self-regulated learning and academic achievement: Theoretical perspectives* (2nd ed., pp. 1–37). Mahwah, NJ: Lawrence Erlbaum.

Zimmerman, B. J. (2008). Investigating self-regulation and motivation: Historical background, methodological development, and future prospects. *American Educational Research Journal*, *45*, 166–183. doi:10.3102/0002831207312909

Zweig, D., & Webster, J. (2004). Validation of multidimensional measure of goal orientation. *Canadian Journal of Behavioural Science*, *36*(3), 232–243. doi:10.1037/h0087233

"MUST-READS" FOR THIS TOPIC

Astleitner, H., & Hufnagl, M. (2003). The effects of situation-outcome-expectancies and of ARCS-strategies on self-regulated learning with web-lectures. *Journal of Educational Multimedia and Hypermedia*, *12*(4), 361–376.

Boekaerts, M., de Koning, E., & Vedder, P. (2006). Goal-directed behaviour and contextual factors in the classroom: An innovative approach to the study of multiple goals. *Educational Psychologist*, *41*(1), 33–51. doi:10.1207/s15326985ep4101_5

Cordova, D. L., & Lepper, M, R. (1996). Intrinsic motivation and the process of learning: Beneficial effects of contextualization, personalization, and choice. *Journal of Educational Psychology*, *88*(4), 715–730. doi:10.1037/0022-0663.88.4.715

Dempsey, J. V., & Johnson, R. B. (1998). The development of an ARCS Gaming Scale. *Journal of Instructional Psychology*, *25*(4), 215–221.

DeShon, R. P., & Gillespie, J. Z. (2005). A motivated action theory account of goal orientation. *The Journal of Applied Psychology*, *90*(6), 1096–1127. doi:10.1037/0021-9010.90.6.1096

Geary, D. (2002). Principles of evolutionary educational psychology. *Learning and Individual Differences*, *12*, 317–345. doi:10.1016/S1041-6080(02)00046-8

Geary, D. (2008). An evolutionarily informed education science. *Educational Psychologist*, *43*, 179–195. doi:10.1080/00461520802392133

Geary, D. (2008). Whither evolutionary educational psychology? *Educational Psychologist*, *43*, 217–226. doi:10.1080/00461520802392240

Kim, Y., & Baylor, A., & PALS Group. (2006). Pedagogical agents as learning companions: The role of agent competency and type of interaction. *Educational Technology Research and Development*, *54*(3), 223–243. doi:10.1007/s11423-006-8805-z

Locke, E. A., & Latham, G. P. (2002). Building a practically useful theory of goal setting and task motivation: A 35-year odyssey. *The American Psychologist*, *57*(9), 705–717. doi:10.1037/0003-066X.57.9.705

Moreno, R. (2005). Multimedia learning with animated pedagogical agents. In Mayer, R. E. (Ed.), *The Cambridge Handbook of Multimedia Learning* (pp. 507–523). New York: Cambridge University Press.

Moreno-Ger, P., & Burgos, D., Martinez-Ortiz, Sierra, J. S., & Fernández-Manjón, B. (2008). Educational game design for online education. *Computers in Human Behavior*, *24*, 2530–2540. doi:10.1016/j.chb.2008.03.012

Ryan, R. M., & Deci, E. L. (2000). Intrinsic and extrinsic motivations: Classic definitions and new directions. *Contemporary Educational Psychology*, *25*, 54–67. doi:10.1006/ceps.1999.1020

Song, S. H., & Keller, J. M. (2001). Effectiveness of motivationally adaptive computer-assisted instruction on the dynamic aspects of motivation. *Educational Technology Research and Development*, *49*(2), 5–22. doi:10.1007/BF02504925

TOP TEXTS FOR INTERDISCIPLINARY STUDIES OF SERIOUS GAMES

Dempsey, J. V., & Johnson, R. B. (1998). The development of an ARCS Gaming Scale. *Journal of Instructional Psychology*, *25*(4), 215–221.

Geary, D. (2008). An evolutionarily informed education science. *Educational Psychologist*, *43*, 179–195. doi:10.1080/00461520802392133

Keller, J. M. (1987). Motivational design and multimedia: Beyond the novelty effect. *Strategic Human Resource Development Review*, *1*(1), 188–203.

Lepper, M. R., & Cordova, D. (1992). A desire to be taught: Instructional consequences of intrinsic motivation. *Motivation and Emotion*, *16*(3), 187–208. doi:10.1007/BF00991651

Mayer, R. E. (2005). Cognitive theory of multimedia learning. In Mayer, R. E. (Ed.), *The Cambridge Handbook of Multimedia Learning* (pp. 31–48). New York: Cambridge University Press.

Murphy, P. K., & Alexander, P. A. (2000). A motivated exploration of motivation terminology. *Contemporary Educational Psychology*, *25*, 3–53. doi:10.1006/ceps.1999.1019

Pintrich, P. R., Smith, D., Garcia, T., & McKeachie, W. (1993). Predictive validity and reliability of the Motivated Strategies for Learning Questionnaire (MSLQ). *Educational and Psychological Measurement*, *53*, 801–813. doi:10.1177/0013164493053003024

Van Eck, R. (2006). The effect of contextual pedagogical advisement and competition on middle-school students' attitude toward mathematics and mathematics instruction using a computer-based simulation game. *Journal of Mathematics and Science Teaching*, *25*(2), 165–195.

Vansteenkiste, M., Lens, W., & Deci, E. L. (2006). Intrinsic versus extrinsic goal contents in self-determination theory: Another look at the quality of academic motivation. *Educational Psychologist*, *41*(1), 19–31. doi:10.1207/s15326985ep4101_4

Zimmerman, B. J. (2008). Investigating self-regulation and motivation: Historical background, methodological development, and future prospects. *American Educational Research Journal*, *45*, 166–183. doi:10.3102/0002831207312909

Chapter 6
Sacred Geographies:
Myth and Ritual in Serious Games

Larry Friedlander
Stanford University, USA

ABSTRACT

In this paper, the author suggests that designers create serious games by turning to an interesting class of stories called sacred scenarios. Such sacred stories are found in many, if not all, cultures. These are richly promising sources for game narratives: They are serious yet entertaining; they combine fantasy with deeply held and emotionally charged visions of life; they offer situations that express basic human experiences; and they bring together the basic elements of story—plot, action, and spatial setting—in rich and surprising ways. They are also easy to program and can be used to create complex narrative experiences from simple elements. The author describes different modes of these sacred scenarios and sketch some possible games to be drawn from this source.

INTRODUCTION

In churches, temples, and caves and on remote mountaintops, cultures celebrate their origins and make contact with the divine forces surrounding them in intricate rituals full of movement, choreographed action, words, and music. Though these ceremonies sometimes look like spontaneous outpourings of religious fervor, they typically closely follow age-old scripts that prescribe every detail of the event. These scripts guide the group as it integrates its myths with its traditional rituals. I term this pairing of myth and ritual a sacred scenario for, like a theatrical scenario, it provides the outline for the ritual performance. The rites may differ from place to place, but they have one thing in common: They all are attempts by a community to maintain and extend contact with the great divine forces that surround its world. Groups may supplicate, praise, and even threaten those powers, but the ritual always affirms the absolute importance of the community's relationships with the sacred as a source of safety, power, and knowledge. Typically the scenarios concern an encounter between human and nonhuman realms

DOI: 10.4018/978-1-61520-719-0.ch006

Copyright © 2010, IGI Global. Copying or distributing in print or electronic forms without written permission of IGI Global is prohibited.

and involve some transference of power from one realm to the other. As such, the scenarios implicitly connect their particular view of human–divine relationships with a sacred geography. Where do the gods live? How do humans make contact with them? Where do demonic forces lurk? Where do the dead go when they depart this world? The answers to these questions reveal in dramatic fashion how a society conceives the structure of the cosmos and the place humans occupy within that structure.

Ceremonies invoke myths to tell the story of the community and its gods, and ritual action enacts certain features of the story and actualizes it in the present. An example familiar to us from Western European culture is the Christian Mass. The Mass has both a text and a rite: The text recounts the story of Christ's passion and his redemptive sacrifice; the accompanying rite recreates that story through the actions of priest and communicants. The story assumes a sacred geography that situates God up in heaven and humans below on the earth. Given that geographical disposition, the ritual of the Mass functions as a kind of spiritual tool for drawing the deity down to the human plane where He can be encountered, ingested, and made potent in the lives of the communicants. The story explains what the priest is doing, and the rite makes the story active in the life of the community. The entire event—text, ritual, music and so on—serves to transport participants into a kind of sacred time where they become actors in the original event and are spiritually renewed by their intimate contact with the divine.

Games that draw on such sacred scenarios would be serious in two ways. First, they can be used to program complex, thematically intricate stories. Because these sacred stories are set in universes made of intersecting yet geographically separate worlds, we can use them to create a long complex narrative that at the same time is easily divided into discrete segments or chunks,[1] each chunk being one of the realms through which the character travels. By combining these chunks into larger wholes, we could produce surprisingly sophisticated "macro" narratives. A program could exercise firm control over each individual segment and then combine them all into a long and complex narrative. And second, these scenarios could provide players with serious learning experiences, for these scenarios express in a concrete, embodied form a culture's deepest intuition about how the world functions and how humans can connect to the divine. As gamers navigate through these sacred geographies, they can gain a deep feel for the nature and function of religious systems and for the intricacy of cultural difference.

There has been much debate over whether or not computer games are, or can be, narrative. I will not enter into the ludology–narratology controversy, which has been "chewed over" by too many for too long. Wardrip-Fruin and Harrigan (2004) provide a detailed overview of the debate, devoting two entire sections to the problem without coming to any firm conclusions (pp. 1–60). Kallay (this volume) gives a trenchant account of the debates and explains her own reservations about how the problem has been framed.

Jenkins (2004) points out that the gameplay-story debate misses the point by focussing on whether or not a game tells a story, and thereby omits to take a closer look at the narrative elements at a more localized level, or so-called "micronarratives" (p.125). Jenkins's reading of the possibilities of spatial storytelling not only provides an interesting way to link gameplay and narrative, but the micronarrative approach of reading games also proves useful when applying psychology to games. When juxtaposed with narrative psychology, the isolated actions of the micronarrative (which can be anything from a game level to a sub-level scene) allow for a much more in-depth analysis of the common factors in narrative and the gameplay, as will be demonstrated in the case studies. (Kallay, this volume)

Suffice it to say that I personally do not believe that games are inherently incapable of producing good stories, nor do I think that we have any idea of what future artists can do with this form. It seems somewhat premature to define or prescribe the limits of a form that is still in its infancy, as though critics in 1900 would have prescribed what movies are and what they should be. Rest assured, new technological and cultural developments will profoundly impact the design of games. It seems sensible, therefore, to encourage active and radical experimentation before we rule out any possibilities. Even if at the moment there are few game narratives that all would agree are adequate "stories," there is no reason that there could not be ones in the future. My paper is an attempt to suggest some practical avenues that we might explore to that end.

THE PROBLEM

A good story, as I understand it, expresses through its artful shape a coherent view of life, one that connects action to motive, the human to the physical and cultural, the world of desire to the world of values and to an (implied) world order. Such a story reaches out to capture in its net the intricacy of a chain of causes and effects and, in doing so, reveals how life's tone emerges from choices driven by fear and desire and how human will is complicated by fate and by the limitations of mortality. As a story unfolds, we experience how thought and motive engender event, how accident and opposition disturb and dislodge thought, and how this concatenation of motive and accident lead us inexorably to some significant conclusion.[2]

Let us assume that our goal is to devise shapely, aesthetically sophisticated stories in the digital medium. What are the obstacles that prevent us from producing games with carefully unrolled plots, nuanced characters, exciting pacing, and thematic unity? Ironically enough, one obstacle to making this kind of shaped and controlled game flows directly from games' greatest strength: its interactive nature. Interactivity, the ability of the player to intervene in nontrivial ways in the unfolding of a story is a defining feature of digital media. As Crawford (this volume) states, "Interactivity—not graphics, not animation, not sound—is the essence of what computers do." Interactivity is what decisively separates digital media from earlier narrative ones. Gamers are in the unparalleled situation of coauthoring the very work they are "reading," and this coauthoring undermines some of traditional strengths of the authored work. Textual and filmic narratives succeed because someone tightly controls the delivery of the story at every minute. It is the author's sustained presence that holds together the web of meaning. While the author is active, the readers/spectators remain passive; indeed, it is precisely this passivity that permits readers to suspend disbelief and imaginatively open to the tale. Game designers, however, are under great pressure to continually increase the gamer's opportunities for interaction. But the player's intensive intervention actually interferes with the program's ability to control the story's pace and tension and its artful revelation of character and motive. Interactivity can cause narrative to become pluralized, centerless, and disrupted.

A second problem arises from the digital medium's other great feature: its immersive environment. In games, the aesthetic focus shifts from creating a well-designed "stand-alone" story to delivering an all-encompassing environment *within which* stories take place. Digital narratives aspire to the variety and plentitude of a "world" rather than to the fixed structure of a text. As Hayles notes, "Computers are not tools, they are environments" (2004, p. 291). By world, I understand an articulated space that simulates the heterogeneity, variety, and three-dimensional configurations of our world. This "world" is not structurally equivalent to a well-made story, or to any formal structure at all. It is more like a boundary around structures, a circumference that delimits an inexhaustible field of possibilities. A world is where stories happen. In this environment, space acts as a container for and an enabler of narrative meaning. Many critics have sought to characterize the unique role space plays in digital experience. As Kallay notes:

Henry Jenkins (2004) brings a compelling construct, that of "narrative architecture" (p.121). By striving towards a middle-ground position in the gameplay–story conflict, Jenkins (2004) proposes to look at games "less as stories than as spaces ripe with narrative possibility" (p. 119). The game's navigable environment becomes the narrative site, its objects, artifacts, and spaces carrying narrative "affordances." (Kallay, this volume)

Unlike the flat and unchanging spatial field of the book, the electronic screen is complex, dynamic, and open-ended, a space of quick and endless transformations, one linked invisibly to an almost infinite variety of other spaces. We grasp this world not by viewing it but by exploring it; as we move along, it spreads all about us, behind us and in front of us, and its variety is not exhausted by our passage. Though we may uncover the world by following one path through it, we are aware that we can go back and choose to explore differently. While this openness is exhilarating, it tends to diffuse the focused form of narrative, causing the story's outlines to blur. (Wark's (2007) book treats the implications of this "geographical" element under the rubric of topologies.) These environments are "synthetic worlds," to use Castranova's (2005) term where, as he states, "computing technology has erased the distinction between actor and audience, here and there, scenery and landscape, role and self" (p. 11). Our challenge as story-makers is to coordinate the tight shape of the plot with an open environment and to make the fact that we are in a world integral to the unfolding meaning of the story.

Finally there are problems on the level of content. Many games employ a formulaic repertoire of narratives that feature fantastic or pseudomedieval settings, space travel, or inner city violence. Designers like such phantasmagoric landscapes because they provide the player with multiple opportunities for trigger-quick, adrenalin-laced strategic responses. Unfortunately, not only have these settings lost much of their novelty, but their simplified either–or vision of reality also limits the games' aesthetic, social, and psychological complexity. If we wish to extend the range and depth of game narratives, we need to look to other narrative models.

In summary, telling stories in a digital medium confronts us with some basic problems:

1. How do we integrate interactivity into well-formed plots?
2. How do we mesh the global immersive experience with the unfolding meaning of the story?
3. Where do we find fresh and rich content that is suitable to highly interactive immersive environments?

A SUGGESTED SOLUTION

I would suggest a two-pronged approach: 1) create stories that are structurally designed so that a program can control the pace and feel of a narrative while allowing intensive interaction and immersion and 2) provide content that supports these programming strategies and deliver stories where the space (or environment) reflects the changing state of the plot.

If we aim for sophisticated and complex game narratives, the program ideally should maintain a firm sense of the plot structure even as the plot is being tugged in all kinds of unexpected directions by the user's interactions. The program should be able to steer the plot through the gamer's many interventions while maintaining the underlying structure of the narrative and, in so, endowing the story with a beginning, middle, and end. But a program is not a person, and it cannot understand a story nor can it, at any one point, foresee what the user will do or choose. If we compensate by reducing opportunities for interaction, we end up granting the player only trivial interventions in the story. In short, the more power the program allows the gamer, the more difficult it is for the program to create an aesthetically pleasing narrative. To avoid this formal incoherence we need to design a program that can "understand" the overarching shape of a story and then integrate the user's actions into an aesthetically satisfying story.

Chris Crawford (this volume) recognizes that part of the problem with game narratives is that programmers respond to the challenges stated above by "keeping it simple." And so, he suggests that programmers employ a mathematical model rather than a Boolean one for writing code, a change that will allow for more nuanced handling of moments of choice. My approach is somewhat differently focused, not on the code but on the kinds of narrative materials. By using plots that naturally divide into semiautonomous units, each with its own narrative rules and worldscapes, we can create manageable "micro" stories that won't tax the resources of the code. In this kind of narrative, each segment has its own prescribed "state" that dictates the total environment of each individual segment, including its physics, its social structure, its topography and visual style, its temporal flow, and the kind of actions and interactions that are possible and efficacious within it. For the player to succeed in the game, she must learn how to act in a specific realm by discovering its topology and its rules. A given realm, for example, might have laws that allow you to fly if you have a sacred fire, might allow you to become invisible if you utter certain mantras, might have only friendly or unfriendly inhabitants and so on. The program should be able to control the events within any one segment because the player does not remain in any one realm for very long and because in each realm only a limited set of interactions is permitted. With the narrative so divided, the player has interactive freedom within each segment, but the program controls the order and unrolling of the segments and thus preserves the pace and timely unfolding of the narrative. There are many advantages to this chunking of the story. As each segment has its own architecture, we can make each realm express itself in significant and surprising ways: If you are in danger, the sky turns black; if you err, the space turns two-dimensional; if you help an inhabitant, time slows down and allows you to move hyper-fast. As a player moves from one realm to another, her identity and physical form may also change—from warrior, to priest, to supplicant, to demon, to inventor and so on.

There is a danger that by chunking the story into manageable bits we end with a long chain of thinly connected parts in an episodic structure that has no thematic unity. But the unity of the story can arise from the hero's (gamer's) progress physically and morally, as she learns, deciphers, and chooses. While the story flows from episode to episode, the player's progress through these separate worlds has a cumulative force, revealing the inner qualities of the overall cosmic vision. By stringing sequences together, we should be able to build a fairly complex and varied story that still has an artful narrative shape.

Myths and Ritual

Sacred scenarios combine myth, ritual, and "world" in ways analogous to the way games combine story, action and immersive environment. We should consider these three elements not as separate but rather as "modes" of each other. Theorists of myth have understood that there is no way to separate story from action:

Myth creates the context in which ritual becomes effective. In entering the realm of mythology, it is necessary to be fully aware of the fact that it is the very landscape of the gods themselves. The division between myth and cult is an artificial one, convenient in that it helps the outsider to understand religious artforms; but it should be remembered that [myth+cult] is a unity, and it is that unity we call religion. (Maxwell 1998, p. 215)

Huizinga also emphasizes how ceremony, cult, ritual, and game are interacting parts of a machine designed to have real effects in the world:

The whole of the ancient Vedic sacrificial rites rests on the idea that the ceremony—be it sacrifice, contest, or performance—by representing a certain desired cosmic event, compels the gods to effect that event in reality. We could well say by "playing" it. (Huizinga 1953, p. 15)

So rite, story, and performance are variables within one unified experience. By bringing together these various modes, we multiply our expressive possibilities, for the meaning of the narrative changes as we change any one of these elements. When we tinker with the story, we change the meaning of the rite and vice versa. For example, Christians and Jews have similar rituals—the Mass and the Passover Seder—that involve the consumption of bread and wine. What differentiates the two is the explanatory story that accompanies the ritual actions. At the Seder feast, the participants recite the *Haggadah* (literally, the recitation) that tells of the exodus of the Jews from Egypt; at a Mass, priest and communicants chant a liturgy that describes Christ's death and resurrection—similar rites with very different interpretations. Story and action are intimately and inextricably bound together; they explain each other. That is why rites have to be expounded to the uninitiated, otherwise they will be misunderstood. In the Passover Seder, the ritual feast begins with the child questioning the father about the purpose of the strange customs of the evening. Here is the "script" for this moment from the *Haggadah*[3] The youngest child asks the father "Why is tonight different from all other nights?" to which the father duly responds:

1. On all other nights we may eat either leavened bread or matzah; tonight, only matzah, that we may recall the unleavened bread our ancestors baked in haste when they left slavery.
2. On all other nights we need not taste bitterness; tonight, we eat bitter herbs, that we may recall the suffering of slavery.
3. On all other nights we needn't dip our food in condiments even once; tonight we dip twice, in saltwater to remember our tears when we were enslaved, and in *haroset* to remember the mortar and the bricks which we made.
4. On all other nights we eat sitting up; tonight, we recline, to remind ourselves to savor our liberation.

The father and all others then respond:

We were slaves to a Pharaoh in Egypt, and the Eternal led us out from there with a mighty hand and an outstretched arm. Had not the Holy One led our ancestors out of Egypt, our children and we and our children's children would still be enslaved. Therefore, even if all of us were wise, all-discerning, scholars, sages and learned in Torah, it would still be our duty to tell the story of the Exodus. (Haggadah)

The child asks for an explanation and the answer is both the retelling of the story of the exodus and the enacting of the ritual of the Passover feast. Both together enable the participants to become one with the original Israelites, so that past and present converge in the ritual moment. Story and rite are in a dialectical relationship, and each action begets a new element of rite and vice versa.

Another variable that can contribute to enriching a story experience is the particular topology of the immersive environment. In some ways, the Christian and the Shamanistic worldviews seem alike, for they both feature worlds stacked vertically. The Western culture's mythic imagination conjures forth a sacred geography that places hell below, the earth in the middle, the lower heavens of the angelic powers above earth, and finally the upper heavens of "God" above all these. In this cosmos, rules stipulate that the inhabitants of the lower and upper worlds can travel to the middle realm (the earth) but not vice versa. In the Shamanistic traditions, the cosmos is also imagined as a tripartite structure, one that is held together by a World Tree that links the human world with heaven and the underworld. However, in this cosmos people can, and indeed must, travel to the other realms in order to sustain the human community. In the first, god must descend to earth; in the second, people must climb up (or down) to god. So geography is also rule-bound, and the rules change from one scenario to another.

How the Program Would Exploit Sacred Scenarios

A specific sacred geography engenders specific narrative themes. For the shaman, the action peculiar to this myth/ritual is the journey up and down the tree. "At the heart of shamanism lies the journey. It is this that helps to distinguish shamans from other ecstatics, healers, and mystics" (Walsh, p. 151). Shamans travel to discover or recover knowledge from the other worlds in order to benefit their community on earth. Traveling along this perpendicular path is difficult, and only certain gifted and skilled spiritual technicians can navigate its perils and penetrate into the forbidden upper and lower realms. Indeed, in their travels, shamans often are boiled alive and their bodies reconstituted, or they are menaced by terrifying demons and monsters. These spiritual technicians overcome these dangers through the community's presence at the rituals and through the sustaining belief in the efficacy of the rite that is fostered by the repeated tellings of the myth. The shaman relies not only on the rituals that accompany the event but also on traditional and well-known "silent" narratives that retell the adventures of earlier shamans and so guide him in his tasks. These traditional "backstories" teach the shaman what he must do in order to succeed; they also explain to him what he is undergoing while he is, for example, being boiled alive. They explicate and encourage the voyager and give shape to his actions. They also give the designers a rich spectrum of actions (such as being boiled alive!) to draw from.

In a game based on the World Tree, for example, the program could understand what actions are possible within this sacred scenario, what goals are acceptable, and how to dramatically enhance the story by the inclusion of obstacles and helping agents. The program could specify rules based on simple polarities and binary categories such as up–down, in–out, gate/threshold–interior, center–circumference, leave–return and so on. These simple spatial categories could be amplified and made dramatic by the addition of more emotionally charged yet still simple ones such as enemy–friend, protector and deceiver, and self–other. Using these sets of polarities and descriptors, we could devise algorithms that control an interactive experience, keeping the experience anchored to the space/time structure of the story.

Sacred scenarios are awash with persona richly endowed with goals, attitudes, and gifts: supplicants, shamans, warriors, communicants, choice-makers, and riddle-solvers. I have not space to explore how these scenarios can enlarge our repertoire of interactive "actions" but can suggest that participants in rituals engage in complex practices that can be adapted for use in games. A sample might include the following: 1) symbolic self-destruction like smashing a coconut, representing the self, on the steps of a Hindu temple) 2) *Imitatio Dei,* acting as if one were a deity in Tantric rites, 3) engaging in gruesome rites, like ingestion and reconstitution of corpses, 4) possession through ecstatic movement, like dance, and 5) purification rites, like being sprinkled with a piglet's blood in Greek rites.

By making the gamer a participant in the rite, we endow her actions and choices with purpose, variety, and challenge. The player's felt need to acquire power will lead her to acquire the technical skills needed to complete the tasks at hand. As the actions proceed, a larger meaning will emerge from the microactions and -events, one that both reveals the nature of the world and also transforms the player through that knowledge.

What I Don't Mean by Sacred Stories

I use the term "religious" in a very broad sense, as shorthand for those material and spiritual practices that express how a society organizes itself, how it understands the world, how it defines individual and communal morality, and how it distinguishes between acceptable and nonacceptable life choices. What makes these practices and concepts "religious" is that they are grounded in a sacred sphere that authorizes and guides their application to people's lives. For a game to be serious about "religion," in my meaning of the term, it should present religion as an interlocking and multicausal system and should demonstrate how different elements of that system—practices, beliefs, images—relate to each other. The gamer should be led to understand what cosmology has to do with morality and what the physical elements of culture—tools, artifacts, and narratives—have to do with values and social practices. Such serious games would teach a kind of spiritual ecology.

While games seem already replete with religious symbols, terms, and events, they generally exploit these in a trivial fashion. Often games put religious materials at the service of a rather impoverished Manichaean conception of the world, one that features a black–white battle between good and evil. At its most trivial, we have Bible games, such as those published by Wisdom Tree, in which the gamer has to exhibit knowledge of scripture and in effect learn how to quote the Bible. Other more ambitious games still rely on a black and white vision of the world. *Left Behind*, for example, places us in a world in which the final battle between God and Satan takes place. Even though there are uncertainties in the world, the way moral choices are imagined is severely limited. Or, designers may model characters drawn from esoteric and exotic sources in order to add an aura of mystery to the narrative. For example, in *Populous: The Beginning*, the player becomes a shaman who leads her tribe in a fight for dominion of the solar system. This character has no connection to an authentic shamanic tradition but is merely a kind of warlord. To really play the shaman would mean to penetrate into the life experience of a culture and to understand what it means to be a good and wise person in that world.

So called "God games" are to my mind even less conducive than Christian-themed games to a "serious" engagement with religious experience. In such games, the player is given great power over a large territory or group and can intervene and perform miracles and exercise other divine powers. It is hard to imagine a less "religious" vision than one that endows humans with god-like powers. Religion, like its dark cousin tragedy, begins with our *human existential* predicament. We are born into a huge and shadowy world that we do not fully understand nor control. The humbling fact of human limitation and error leads to a set of challenging questions: What is the world? Who governs it? How do I navigate it successfully? Moreover, religion turns its sights not only on the all-encompassing nature out there in the external world but also on the equally confounding nature within: Who am I? How do I understand my desires and fears? What can I do to be more fully functioning in the world?

By working with an expansive view of religion, we can focus the games not only on specific rites and myths but also on the deeper problems attendant on religious experience. Serious games could be designed to nudge players to examine and challenge their own assumptions and the unwritten assumptions of gaming itself. One such assumption is that it is important to win and that power is an absolute good (there are games that try to introduce third choices and complex distinctions, and they should be encouraged). But what does it mean to have power and to win? To begin with, power may be constructive or destructive. But even "good" power may mean many things: It may consist of the knowledge we can gather on a journey that will give us an answer, it may be a relationship with a powerful agent outside of ourselves who can aid us and guide us, it may consist of new skills and supernatural powers granted to the player, it may mean patience and acceptance, and it may involve a process of inner transformation, a purification of self that allows us new perspectives and opens the way to a redefinition of goals. These different meanings are often mutually contradictory: To persevere by aggressive attack is not really compatible with winning through acceptance and relinquishing control. A game should make the player take account of the fluctuating and ambivalent nature of power and in doing so stretch the player's notion of what it means to succeed in this world.

Contrary to a fundamentalist's belief in the clarity of dogma, most religions acknowledge the profound ambiguity coiled at the center of all sacred story. The divine is always, in some sense, hidden; it is apart, nonhuman, only dimly glimpsed. To understand sacred utterance, we must interpret a language we can barely grasp. Most games featuring gods do not find the nature of the divine problematic. In *Black and White* (Lionheart), the only thing problematic about the sacred is how it can successfully gain control of all the villages. Some games, such as *Deus Ex*, have sought to introduce the shadowy into their worlds by presenting the gamer with difficult choices between opposing, ambiguous forces. Who is good? Who is bad? Indeed, the seemingly different forces seem to converge as well as to move apart agonistically. The game does not feel "religious" because the gamer does not try to actualize a system of values that have their source in the holy. Instead the paranoia that pervades this game reflects contemporary cynicism and our tendency to deflate or relativize all values. But the game is to be commended for making the gamer think about choices and about the difficulty of judging between alternatives. Peter Molyneux, in an interview with *Wired* magazine's Chris Baker (2008), expresses his desire to create a more shaded, grey, morality:

The tests were too obvious in the last game. Save lives good, kill people bad. This time, we know what we're doing with the morality system. If you want to be truly good, you have to sacrifice. If I can make you stop and have to really think about what you're about to do next, I've succeeded. (Baker, 2008)

Part of graying out the black-and-white morality system includes altering the spectrum itself. It's no longer just a measurement of good and evil: "We're measuring purity versus corruption, and cruelty versus kindness. That's different from good versus evil. I tell my son to go to bed and he thinks I'm cruel, but I'm really being kind" (Baker, 2008).

Some might argue that the very notion of sacred scenarios is irrelevant, as we no longer have such stories in our secular culture. But all societies without exception create sacred narratives. Our modern scientific culture, for example, imagines the cosmos not as a series of discrete worlds arrayed in space but as a series of worlds strung out in time, starting with the Big Bang and ending somewhere in the distant future. When we gaze at the sky we do not see sacred fires of the gods, nor orbs guided by angels, nor mythological creatures in the constellations. Instead we read the sky as a bewildering, pulsing, flow of different far-flung times all coexisting in the same plenum, from earliest cosmic radiation to new stars, to black holes that bend time and space. We find order in this chaos because we interpret these conflicting temporal phenomena as the revelation of causally related processes unrolling in vast reaches of time. This roiling explosion of events provides us with our sacred scenario; we constantly refer to it to explain the puzzling and overwhelming features of our universe. Our scenario narrates the universe as a vast temporal revelation, which defines and delimits how we construct morality, how we pose and answer questions, and how we order community. The astronomer, the paleontologist, and the geneticist are modern shamans who help us make sense of phenomena. There is no reason why we could not base a game with this timescape as the matrix for its events and for its goals.

Sacred scenarios reflect the absolute interdependence of our views of god, nature, and society. They assume that personal morality or holiness arises out of a matrix of practices and beliefs—indeed out of a culture's entire life experience. For teaching purposes, these games should clarify the interdependence of cultural story, rite, and value so that the gamer understands that religious story is embedded in specific cultural practices and that myths are quite powerful ways to express this radical interdependence. By engaging with this web of relationships, the gamer would get an insight into why religion is universal and powerful, why it is another word for managing our path through life. (A game like *Civilization* [2K Games] does try to get us to engage in the multicaused evolution of cultures but focuses on the material and not on "spiritual" factors.) Imagine a game that started with the player arbitrarily set down in a part of the world (India, Central America, Sweden) and forced to play out the game in the scenarios that prevail in that region. If the gamer is then flown to another region, she will find not only a different spatial and symbolic landscape but also a different set of personal attributes that make one good and successful in that culture. In seeking to understand and master the specifics of the scenario she finds herself in, the gamer will be led to grasp how individual identity and power grow out of structures of communal activity and how community takes shape as a relationship to forces outside of itself.

Examples of Scenarios and Possible Applications to Game Design

Luckily for game designers, there are as many sacred architectures as there are cultures. Let me briefly point to some further examples of sacred architectures/scenarios, and describe how each potentially generates story. I will discuss a variety of world models and 1) identify kinds of narrative associated with each and 2) suggest some possible ways these spaces can work to form and enrich digital narratives. Each kind of sacred architecture is distinguished by a specific cosmic geography and by the types of actions possible in this space. I will further divide these sacred spaces into ones situated outside our own realm and sacred spaces that are located here on earth in countries, cities, buildings, and in our own bodies.

Journeys Up and Down

Many cultures imagine a cosmos as a layered set of worlds held together by an axial structure that penetrates through its middle, such as the World Tree found in shamanistic lore. Sometimes this axial structure is not a tree but a magic mountain—like Mount Meru—or even a phallus—like Shiva's lingam. The poet Dashakumaracharita in the 6th century meditated on the many forms the basic axial pillar could assume:

The pillar with its leg of Trivikrama [Vishnu] is the shaft of the parasol above the cosmic egg, the stem of the lotus seat of Brahma, the mast of the ship of earth, the pole supporting the banner which streams like the river of deathlessness (the Ganga), the axle-rod of the wheel of the stars, the column of victory over the three worlds. (Maxwell 1998, p. 223)

The basic tripartite division of the cosmos can be elaborated and made extraordinarily complex. Here again is the Hindu cosmology, or at least one version of it:

Space is conceived as the egg of Brahma (brahmanda), made up of seven concentric spheres. Seven successively higher heavens where the gods and immortal beings live are situated above the earth, and seven lower worlds where demons live are below. The earth, on which human beings live, is located in the middle. On earth the central location is Jambudvipa, surrounded concentrically by six other circular lands separated by seven seas: one each of salt water, milk, ghi, curds, liquor, sugar cane juice, and fresh water. Holy Mount Meru rises in the center of Jambudvipa. Four lesser mountains support Meru from the four directions. A godly city sits on Meru where Brahma, Vishnu, and Siva dwell, worshipped by mortals and lesser gods. On the sides of the great mountain in the four major and four intermediate directions lie the sites of the lesser gods. The river Ganga falls from the heavens and passes through the lands of Jambudvipa. One of these lands is Bharatavarsa, the ancient name for the land of India. (Rao, 2004, p. 100)

Would it not be interesting to have a game where travelers float down the Ganges from heaven to earth?

The Hindu scheme, marvelously rich with possibilities, echoes more culturally familiar schemes. Its underworld, for example, is divided into seven progressively wider layers, which sounds much like the nine circles of hell we find in Dante's Divine Comedy. In the poem, Dante is a kind of shaman being tutored by an elder magician, the poet Virgil, and is taken on a journey down and up through the three worlds of Hell, Purgatory and Heaven, in order to bring news of these realms back to the earth. This up and down scenario reminds one of many games in which the player must journey through hostile territory, encounter enemies, and solicit helpers. But the motifs in sacred stories are often quite novel, and the shamanistic paradigm is sometimes inverted. In Inuit stories, the shaman goes down, not up, diving to the depths of the sea to visit the house of the goddess of animals to discover why she is withholding the prey from the community (Walsh, 2007, p. 153). Here the shaman must pass by a threatening cordon of creatures and figure out how to pacify the goddess. This inversion of direction gives a different twist to the shamanistic journey and suggests how varied these stories could be as models for games.

What is particularly important about these journeys, I believe, is that they are focused on spiritual testing. The player succeeds only when she finds way to change her own self in profound ways. That is why the gamer must find a guide who will teach her how to change and grow.

Solving Problems and Paradigms of Choice: Crossroads and Labyrinths

"In a labyrinth, you do not lose yourself," the lady told me at Grace Cathedral. "In a labyrinth, you find yourself." –Kerman

Crossroads are sites that challenge us to name who we are and to decide who we want to be. We stand at the crossroads and must choose. Oedipus chooses to kill the stranger at the crossroads who, it turns out, is his long-lost father. His choice traps him in the intersection between his past, present, and future; he flees from himself only to find himself. No wonder crossroads were feared and worshipped. Bodies were buried there, and the corpses of criminals displayed for all to see. There dwelt Hecate, the dreaded Queen of the Night. She had three faces and three arms, suggesting her position at the intersection of times and worlds. Her abode was also the door to the underworld, and there she was supplicated by the sacrifice of puppies, a particularly cruel rite to the modern imagination. Yet she was also a guardian for those who could see past the terrors of the crossroads, for she guided people through the underworld to safety and protected the natural world by ensuring the return of spring after the false death of winter. Her ambiguous status as goddess and demon derives from the intuition that choice leads to the grave and that the power of decision is framed by the limitation of human choice. Eventually all our choices will only lead us to the final moment of decision, when past and future fold into a present that disappears into the maw of death.

The myth of Oedipus suggests that we all make our choices in some mixture of knowledge and ignorance, and that ignorance does not absolve us of our responsibility for the consequences of choice. Many stories turn on the agonizing choices we face at a crossroads of life. In a story very popular in the early 20th century, Frank Stockton's "The Lady or The Tiger," a princess falls in love with a commoner. Her father, infuriated by the man's presumption, has him placed in a public amphitheater with the princess in the audience. He must there choose between two doors, behind one lurks a tiger and behind the other a gorgeous woman. He waits for the princess to indicate which door to choose. She knows which door is which, but which will she choose? The story ends with the princess caught in the moment of decision.

Now, the point of the story is this: Did the tiger come out of that door, or did the lady? The more we reflect upon this question, the harder it is to answer. It involves a study of the human heart, which leads us through devious mazes of passion, out of which it is difficult to find our way. Think of it, fair reader, not as if the decision of the question depended upon you, but upon that hot-blooded, semi-barbaric princess, her soul at a white heat beneath the combined fires of despair and jealousy. She had lost him, but who should have him? (Stockton, 1886, p. 10)

Labyrinths and mazes suggest that choice involves stumbling about in the darkness of ignorance. In labyrinths we go astray until we have found a strategy for deciphering the twists and turns of life. In the Greek myth, Minos, the king of Crete, constructs a labyrinth to hide the monstrous child begot by his errant wife who had mated with a bull. The hero, Theseus, must find his way to the center, kill the beast, and reemerge safely. In Euripides' play *Hippolytus,* Minos' daughter Phaedra also must choose between dying herself and seducing her stepson. Here the gods are of no help; there is no escape from the decision at the crossroads. A human and vulnerable hero must encounter and slay the beast at the heart of the puzzle in order to find his way out of the maze. The hero acts for us all and his enemy has many names—Satan, the Leviathan, Typhon, or the raging Boar who threatens the Hindu cosmos. The pagan labyrinth myth was interestingly enough adopted and adapted by the Christians, who substituted the figures of the Warrior and the Devil for the Minotaur and Theseus, adjusting the context but preserving the sense that at the heart of the maze is the secret enemy whom the hero must confront and conquer if he is to progress spiritually.

We can imagine a game that revolves around a scientist who must decide whether he will work on a new weapon of mass destruction. In the game, the hero must follow two divergent time paths, exploring what will ensue from each of his choices. He must then live through, and perhaps try to alter, the consequences of his choice. He must also convince others to make the choice with him. So his actions need to be justified by a complex calculus of consequences and moral prohibitions. Such a story could be part of a real -life class on ethics.

The Moveable Dwelling: The Tabernacle

Then the cloud covered the tent of the meeting, and the glory of the Lord filled the tabernacle. Moses was not able to enter the tent of the meting because the cloud settled upon it, and the glory of the Lord filled the tabernacle. Whenever the cloud was taken up from the tabernacle the Israelites would set out on each stage of their journey; but if the cloud was not taken up, then they did not set out until the day it was taken up. For the cloud of the Lord was on the tabernacle by day, and fire was in the cloud by night, before the eyes of all the house of Israel at each stage of their journey. (Exodus 40:34; in Meeks, 1989, p. 150)

Scholars distinguish between fixed (locative) and moving (utopian) sacred spaces. As an example of the latter, the Tabernacle is a site of a divine presence that is constantly on the march. It is a moveable temple, in effect, created specifically for the Jews' journey through the desert of Sinai. It houses the Ark of the Covenant, a portable altar, and other ritual implements and serves as a temporary meeting place for the community. But, in addition to serving as a dwelling of the Lord on Earth, it also is acts as a kind of divine tank battalion, blitzing fire and lightening as it advances over terrain which it colonizes in the name of God. It is thus a missionary space, a traveling road show of God's wonders. Wherever it goes, it transforms ordinary space into holy space, converting alien into personal territory. Its aggressive and dynamic nature is well suited to nomadic cultures. For the Jews in their Diaspora, it becomes the model of the permanently available sanctuary, inviting the numinous presence even in the most hostile environments.

As a paradigm, the tabernacle is particularly well suited to Western imperialistic cultures, as can be seen in a contemporary incarnation: the Starship Enterprise. A massive technological tabernacle, the spaceship transports the God of technology into all corners of the galaxy and converts hostile space to friendly colony. In a game, players could move into enemy territory and "convert" it as they move through it. And more generally, we can reimagine conflict not as a battle against an alien entity but as a battle against a place.

The Earth, Country, and City as Body

The Hindu tradition often figures the earth itself and, more particularly, the land of India as a goddess. Landscapes are dotted with hidden portals to the divine, "hot spots" where the sacred can be glimpsed and propitiated, for the tradition regards certain geographical features, such as mountains, rivers, lakes, and caves, as sacred in themselves.... While these geographical hierophanies are often associated with a particular deity or saint, it is place itself that is sacred. In Hinduism there developed an elaborate system of pilgrimage to Tirthas, literally, river fords, places where one can "cross over" from the human to the divine realm. (Erndl & Sakta, 2004, p. 156)

Indeed, the world itself can be seen as the actual body of god. In Hindu myth, the world arose from the corpse of a god, the primeval cosmic being Purusha. Purusha sacrifices his body so that all its individual parts can generate our universe.

The three principal sections of purusa's body—head, navel, and feet—are correlated with the three worlds that constitute the cosmos—heaven, midregions, and earth. Specific parts of purusa's psychophysiology—mouth, breath, eye, ear, and mind—are correlated with specific components of the natural order—fire, wind sun, cardinal directions, and moon—as well as with specific deities (Mittal and Thursby, 2004, p. 217).

So if we look with the eye of the spirit, we can discern the body of god in all the objects and beings of our existence. But it is not always easy to discern the sacred hidden in the profane. In Greek myth, the sacred groves are often difficult to distinguish, placing the unwary traveler in peril. In Sophocles' Oedipus at Colonus, all fear that they are trespassing on a sacred grove and might inadvertently offend the god and be killed for it.

A place may not only be a god, it also may embody a sacred story. One myth associated with these Indian pilgrimage sites recounts how, as the Goddess flew over the country, her body was dismembered and pieces of it fell down in these holy cities. By visiting these locations, pilgrims can access the holy power that was created when the Goddess fell (Flood, 1996, p.192; Mittal & Thursby, 2004, p.157). So the pilgrim's journey retells, in effect, the story of the Goddess and also gives the pilgrim an opportunity to encounter the deity and profit from that interaction. The pilgrims' journeys intersect with the goddess' descent and a transaction occurs transferring divine substance from one to the other. A story and an action come together to create a new force or power centered on the body of the god.

Schechner (2006), in his article on the city and festival, describes an elaborate thirty-one day drama festival that takes place in Benares. Thousands of actors perform different segments from the epic Ramayana in a profusion of places around and outside the city in locales that are identified with the epic's events. As Schechner notes, "Throughout India… places have multiple meanings, layered associations and significances, one or several or many of which can be called into immediate action by the performance of a ritual" (p. 91). Closer to our culture, we find the same fusion of spatial itinerary and story in the stations of the cross visited by worshippers on Easter weekend.

We can imagine a game where an everyday landscape or cityscape is revealed to be the manifestation of a divine body, which gamers have to actualize by visiting the appropriate sites in the correct narrative order. Such a game might be very effective using mobile devices and groups of payers roaming through an actual site. Players might have to discover objects, buildings, or sites that correspond to a narrative about the city's founding, for example.

Contemporary artists and critics have explored the possibility of using the city itself as a narrative and experiential terrain. Debord's influential essay (2006) argues that we must free the city from the rigid grids of utilitarian passages and commercial throughways by stirring up a latent energy that can spontaneously manifest and reveal an alternative geography, geography of freedom. For Debord, each place had precise effects on the psychology and behavior of its inhabitants, a phenomenon he called "psychogeography." By interacting with the urban grid, he claims, we can transform the places themselves. So spontaneous actions and festivals that erupt in its streets can free it from its rigid order and inhuman machine-like layouts. If we let ourselves go, we not only release our authentic energies, we make over the very spaces that seek to define us. The idea of a game that centers on the transformation of a real environment is fascinating.

The Temple as Body: The Mandala

Many traditions construct elaborate parallels between the macrocosm and the microcosm and, in particular, between the human body, the earthly temple, and the abode of god. Hindu temples are a fine example of this coexistence of realms for they are the residence of a deity, but they are also, and simultaneously, the body of the deity and the body of the worshipper. In the temple, the icon or divine image is hidden deep in the innermost precincts in a *gharba-griha* or womb house. In this small, dark, and unadorned chamber, priests dress, bathe, and feed the statue as one would a guest or a child. Worshippers circumambulate the precincts in a clockwise direction, gradually penetrating the temple through increasingly sacred spaces until they come upon the womb chamber of the god and are privileged to have sight of the numinous statue, a *Darshana.* The innermost precincts are gateways to the divine realms, a place where journeying between realms is possible. They are also for the worshipper a journey inward to the self's spiritual center, where the image of the god lives in the heart.

Hindu and Buddhist rituals are particularly rich in techniques for turning the self over to and into the deity. In Java, for example, priests of Shiva, through a mixture of ritualized actions and meditative states, expel their own personalities and replace themselves piece by piece with the god (Maxwell p. 27). Tibetan Buddhism makes explicit the connection between god, universe, and the self in rituals in which the worshipper internalizes the temple by mentally focusing on an abstract visual representation of the temple (a mandala). A mandala is a visual or sculptural representation of the palace of a deity that the devotee uses to guide his mediations. It may in fact not be a physical object at all but merely a mental image that the meditator creates during his practice. The purpose of the mandala is not aesthetic appreciation but practical spiritual profit. By entering the mandala in guided meditation, the aspirant moves along a carefully constructed spiritual path that eventuates in the sight of the inner Buddha who presides over this realm; in advanced practice, the meditator merges with the central deity, thereby incorporating the deity's wisdom and potency. Mandala means circle, and it alludes to the shape of the mandala, a series of squares embedded in a series of circles which represents the typical shape of a Hindu temple. The point is to visualize one's journey to the center where the deity resides. Each circle has its own features and qualities, and the meditator learns to move through progressively more elevated spheres, overcoming obstacles and gaining insight, until she reaches the center. For example, the meditator must enter by one of four gates, each of which offers both a moral virtue and its opposite (such as equanimity and laziness) and she must pass by fierce demonic deities who represent the spiritual obstacles to each area. Finally, the body itself can be understood as a living mandala. "In Tantric ritual the worshiper is transformed into the deity to be worshiped, and each part of the worshiper's body and personality is transformed into the corresponding part of the cosmos" (Mittal & Thursby, 2004, p. 281). In this practice, the deity is first visualized and then drawn into the inner world of the practitioner to be then absorbed and released. The point is to train and cleanse our perceptions and to sharpen our spiritual sensitivity so that we will be like gods ourselves.

In most video games, the obstacles that the gamer encounters exist outside the self in the vast, bewildering external world. But Indian scenarios hint at another approach: the voyager is a world in herself, a bodily and spiritual environment that has its own obstacles, hurdles, powers and its own possibilities of transformation. The body itself as sacred architecture is a larger theme in many traditions, where the body is seen as a cosmology with different parts homologous to the cosmos, and energy is directed through different centers (chakras) in order to transform the self. All of these practices suggest that common gaming interaction modes (shooting, finding, exploring, and so on) can be enriched by interactions that focus the player back on herself, in a search for the development of inner vision. For example, whenever the gamer is stymied by a challenge, she may be transported back to her inner body where she has to transform certain channels of energy to move her body to a higher state. When she succeeds, she can then return to the game where she left off, newly fortified by her "inner" work, and confront whatever faces her. Finally, she can be a god who guides and counsels others.

Proust's masterwork (A La Recherche du Temps Perdu) depends on this pattern of outside and inside, center and circumference. The narrator is drawn into the center of his world (of Parisian high society) and encounters its deities: glamour, fame, social prestige, and artistic accomplishment. As he proceeds deeper and deeper into this mundane palace, he increasingly sees through the illusion of these worldly realms and substitutes a more accurate and spiritual view of the inhabitants, until finally, as at the end of work, he is granted a vision of the innermost deity, the great principle of time and decay and mortality. Then he is granted the power to go and construct his own palace, the palace of art, the very work we are reading. This progression through realms of illusion in search of a purification of vision and an encounter with innermost truth shapes many great works and introduces into sacred scenarios the factor of human consciousness and its ability to redefine our reality by changing our perceptions. Both the mandala and the Proust are stories that promote personal transformation through the acquisition of new powers of perception and insight.

NARRATIVE AS PLAY AND FESTIVAL

"Ritual is seriousness at is highest and holiest. Can it nevertheless be Play?" – Huizinga, Homo Ludens, p. 18

It may seem surprising to link, as I have done, ritual and myth with games and with playing in general. But this link is a deep one for our culture. As we move from a work-centered to a leisure-centered society, so do our narratives become play. Dovey and Kennedy (2006) distinguish between work-based and play-based economies and societies and trace a "historical development from work-based structures of social organization to play-based forms of commodity and meaning production" (p. 19). As many have noted, our culture replaces seriousness, the great bourgeois virtue, with game and play. Under the influence of Nietzsche, important modern thinkers—such as Bergson, Huizinga, and Heidegger—found in the extravagant excesses of play a means to release the human spirit from the narrow constrictions of a utilitarian society. Huizinga asserts that ritual springs from play and that it shares with play the serious task of structuring and humanizing culture. "Now in myth and ritual the great instinctive forces of civilized life have their origin: law and order, commerce and profit, craft and art, poetry, wisdom and science. All are rooted in the primaeval (sic) soil of play" (1953, p. 5).

In play, we move "outside" of ourselves, for playing involves a loss of the separate self through a rapt immersion in the game. Influential philosophers in the 20th century have seized upon the notion of play as a key to formulating modern concepts of the self. "For Gadamer, the notion of 'play' goes beyond the notion of subject or object. In playing, we have to learn to lose ourselves in order to remain true to the game" (Moran, 2000, p. 282). Taylor (1989), in discussing Derrida, also stresses the possibility that playfulness is a means of transcending human separation in a site of unconstrained freedom, "a mode of thinking that affirms free play and tries to pass beyond man and humanism" (p. 590). If we substitute game for dance or play, we get a hint of an activity that moves towards a reconciliation of opposites and a new sense of "winning."

Myth often acknowledges the primal, divine nature of play. In the Hindu tradition, Shiva is the Lord of the Dance, and in his lila, his ecstatic trance, he dances the world into being, then sustains it, and finally destroys it.

To his devotees, the Lord of the Dance symbolized not only the forces at work throughout the universe, but also the point at which all opposites are reconciled. The sound of the drum is the pulse of creation; the flame in his upper left hand is the fire of destruction. The eternal war between these two forces creates the dance, and paradoxically it is in the dance that the devotee discovers the stillness which is moksha, liberation from the wheel of time." (Maxwell, 1998, p. 24).

When we collaborate with others, as for example in massive multiplayer games, individual play transforms into the communal form of festival. Festival is the most profound exemplification of art we have, for art is a form of excess, a manifestation of superabundant (ueberschluss) and overflowing energy. (See Gadamer, 1986, for a full discussion of festival, especially pp. 22, 40, 42, and 139.) Nowhere in our experience is this overflowing more evident than in festival. For Aristotle, narratives are held together by the coherence of their internal parts. By contrast, in festival-like stories, narrative structures continually arise and dissolve through the play of interaction, as objects and events dissolve and recombine.

As a professor of theater, I have been struck by the way playwrights use rituals to advance the drama. In theater, the narrative emerges through a process of playing. Narrative is actualized by the performance in the same way a myth is actualized by ritual. Especially in Shakespeare, ritual structures narrative. In Hamlet, for example, the play starts with rituals of funeral, of wedding, and of coronation, then proceeds to court rituals such as "play within a play" and ends with a ritual of sport—a courtly duel. The rituals serve to locate and define important moments of the narrative but also they complete the story by enacting it, by making it happen. A wedding, for example, can be understood as a kind of story that tells us that two people have entered into a new personal and social "state," but it is also the action that causes that state to exist. It both narrates and effects a transformation. Passing from a single state to one of marriage changes the structures of a personal reality. Rituals transform the meaning of action because they take us out of ordinary time and make us actors in trans-temporal events. And then our actions circle back and change our ordinary, nonritual experience. What strikes me is how this same circularity reappears in computer games and how directly accessing the repertoire of myth/ritual may help us reimagine the structure of games. If ritual + myth = religion (Maxwell, 1998, p. 15), so story + interaction = digital narrative.

FUTURE RESEARCH DIRECTIONS

If used creatively, sacred scenarios can present religion not as a list of facts or beliefs but as a set of relationships. If we understand religion as a process, we can help the player to grasp herself also as process. The player is not simply watching a story; she is *making herself* as she makes the story. By including the gamer in the equation, we can make the exploration of worlds into an exploration of a self, one that is revealed to be a series of scenarios that flash by and that add up to an identity. Journeying through starkly differing worlds, the player copes by changing and transforming and by adapting new sets of powers, needs, and emotions. In other words, the player assumes multiple and flexible identities to suit the environments through which she passes. The gods themselves, in the avatara tradition, are really successive selves who incarnate as time requires. Vishnu descends to earth in many forms: the Fish, the Boar, the Dwarf, the Buddha (!), the Man-Lion, and so forth. Vishnu does not arbitrarily assume a form but chooses one precisely suited to the needs of the specific situation, such as Vishnu taking the form of a dwarf to trick a demon into giving him possession of the universe (Kloetzel & Hiltebeitel, 2004, p. 564). So, too, the gamer should change as she successively encounters the different realms of the scenario. She should muse thusly: "I am continually transformed by my encounters with the sacred. I am now in a certain world, with a certain set of physical abilities, with a certain shape and look, and a certain set of goals. If I move elsewhere, I change." Designers should make this process of change explicit for the gamer. Changes can be signaled by physical changes in the character, by altered perceptions—What can it see in this world? What can it feel? What can it do?—and by changes in the way others treat it. There have been interesting experiments, particularly in the work of Peter Molyneux, to actualize the changes that occur as we engage in games, changes that are both physical and mental/spiritual.

We should continue these experiments but with a focus on the inner changes and on the correlations between worldview, choice, and self.

CONCLUSION

"The practice of the gamer as theorist might be to reinstall what is undecidable back into the gamespace... The real violence of gamespace is its dicing of everything analog into the digital, cutting continuums into bits" (Wark, 2007, section 023).

Bogost, in his book, *Persuasive Games* (2007), stresses that algorithms are "procedures" that initiate an unfolding process of representation. "The computer magnifies the ability to create representations of processes" (p. 5). Games, he argues, are ideally suited to demonstrate how any object or event emerges from a set of evolving relationships. Crawford (this volume), as well, emphasizes that because interactivity is the defining feature of the digital medium, games have the power to make us see the world not as fact but as process. "We can view the world through either of two lenses (or a combination of both): the world as a collection of things, or the world as a system of processes." As Crawford further remarks, "To understand a complex system, the student must see those processes in operation, twiddle with them, examine how slight changes in the components of the system reflect the result—in other words the student must interact with the system" (this volume).

By having the gamer play with the different possibilities of self, testing how a modification here causes a transformation there, she will intuitively sense this codependent arising of all experience, as a Buddhist would say. She can realize that in confronting the world we confront ourselves and that we thus gain a more delicate and tentative relationship to our reality. This strategy shifts the focus of the game from winning over an enemy or influencing an environment to effecting a change within the self.

I hope that these strategies may help us to create resonant, many-layered stories that reflect our deepest intuitions about the mystery of our experience, narratives that help us glimpse the tangled relationships we have with the sacred around and within us. In the Bhagavad-Gita, when Arjuna asks Krishna to let him see the truth, Krishna opens up his third eye and reveals to Arjuna the world as a god views it, a vast and seething panorama of events endlessly dancing and transforming (Maxwell, 1998, p. 222). What would be the equivalent of giving the gamer the third eye that sees the world as the deity sees it?

REFERENCES

Baker, C. (2008). Peter Molyneux: My next game a 'significant scientific achievement. Interview with Peter Molyneux. *Wired.* Retrieved July 20, 2009, from http://www.wired.com/gamelife/2008/05/molyneux-my-nex/

Bogost, I. (2007). *Persuasive games: the expressive power of videogames.* Cambridge: MIT Press.

Castranova, E. (2005). *Synthetic worlds, the business and culture of online games.* Chicago, London: University of Chicago Press.

Civilization [computer software]. (n.d.). Novato, CA: 2K Games.

Cobley, P. (2001). *Narrative.* London, New York: Routledge.

Crawford, C. (in press). Interactivity, process, and algorithm. In Van Eck, R. (Ed.), *Interdisciplinary models and tools for serious games: Emerging concepts and future directions.* Hershey, PA: IGI Global.

Debord, G. (2006). *Report on the construction of situations. Situationist International Anthology* (Knabb, K., Trans.). Berkeley, CA: Bureau of Public Secrets.

Dovey, J., & Kennedy, H. W. (Eds.). (2006). *Game cultures*. Maidenhead, UK: Open University Press.

English Haggadah with instructional guide. (n.d.). Retrieved July 20, 2009, from http://www.chabad.org/holidays/passover/pesach_cdo/aid/1737/jewish/Maggid.htm

Erndl, K. M. (2004). Sakta. In Mittal, S., & Thursby, G. R. (Eds.), *The Hindu world* (pp. 140–161). New York: Routledge.

Flood, G. (1996). *An introduction to Hinduism*. Cambridge, UK: Cambridge University Press.

Gadamer, H.-G. (1986). *The relevance of beauty*. Cambridge, UK: Cambridge University Press.

Hayles, N. K. (2004). Metaphoric networks in lexia to perplexia. In Wardrip-Fruin, N., & Harrigan, P. (Eds.), *First person: New media as story, performance, and game*. Cambridge, London: MIT Press.

Hopkins, T. J. (1971). *The Hindu religious tradition*. Belmont: Wadsworth Publishing Company.

Huizinga, J. (1953). *Homo ludens, a study of the play-element in culture*. Boston: Beacon Press.

Kallay, J. (in press). Rethinking genre in computer games: How narrative psychology connects game and story. In Van Eck, R. (Ed.), *Interdisciplinary models and tools for serious games: emerging concepts and future directions*. Hershey, PA: IGI Global.

Kerman, J. (2004, June 24). That old labyrinth song. *The New York Review of Books*, *LI*(11).

Killingley, D. (2004). Kama. In Mittal, S., & Thursby, G. R. (Eds.), *The Hindu world* (pp. 264–287). New York: Routledge.

Kloetzel, J., & Hiltebeitel, A. (2004). Kala. In Mittal, S., & Thursby, G. R. (Eds.), *The Hindu world* (pp. 553–586). New York: Routledge.

Maxwell, T. S. (1998). *The gods of Asia*. Delhi: Oxford University Press.

Meeks, W. (Ed.). (1989). *The new revised standard version bible*. New York: HarperCollins Publishers.

Mittal, S., & Thursby, G. R. (Eds.). (2004). *The Hindu world*. New York, London: Routledge Press.

Moran, D. (2000). *Introduction to phenomenology*. London, New York: Routledge.

Rao, V. N. (2004). Purana. In Mittal, S., & Thursby, G. R. (Eds.), *The Hindu world* (pp. 97–118). New York: Routledge.

Schechner, R. (2006). Performed imaginaries. In Katyal, A. (Ed.), *Sacred to profane*. New York: Seagull Books.

Stockton, F. R. (1886). *The lady, or the tiger?*New York: Charles Scribner's Sons Publisher.

Taylor, C. (1989). *Sources of the self.* Cambridge, MA: Harvard University Press.

Walsh, R. (2007). *The world of shamanism*. Woodbury: Lewellyn Publications

Wardrip-Fruin, N., & Harrigan, P. (Eds.). (2004). *First person: New media as story, performance, and game*. Cambridge: MIT Press.

Wark, M. (2007). *Gamer theory*. Cambridge: Harvard University Press.

"MUST-READS" FOR THIS TOPIC

Aarseth, E. (1997). *Cybertext perspectives as ergodic literature*. Baltimore, MD: Johns Hopkins Press.

Barthes, R. (1977). *Image, music, text, Essays selected and translated by Stephen Heath*. New York: Hill and Wang.

Bergson, H. (1910). *Time and free will*. New York: Macmillan.

Cavarero, A. (2000). *Relating narratives: Storytelling and selfhood*. London, New York: Routledge.

Cobley, P. (2001). *Narrative*. London, New York: Routledge.

Cooper. R. (2007). *Alter ego: Avatars and their creators*. London: Chris Boot.

Coyne, R. (1999). Technoromanticism. Cambridge, MA, and London: MIT Press.

Critchely, S., & Schroeder, W. R. (Eds.). (1999). *A companion to continental philosophy*. Oxford, UK: Blackwell. doi:10.1111/b.9780631218500.1999.x

Douglas, J. Y., & Hargadon, A. (2006). Pleasures of immersion and interaction. In Wardrip-Fruin, N., & Harrigan, P. (Eds.), *First person: New media as story, performance, and game* (pp. 192–206). Cambridge, MA: MIT Press.

Eagleton, T. (2003). *After theory*. New York: Basic Books.

Gadamer, H.-G. (2004). *Truth and method*. London, New York: Continuum.

Gray, C. H. (Ed.). (1995). *The cyborg handbook*. New York: Routledge Press.

Haraway, D. (2006). Simians, cyborgs, and women. In Dovey, J., & Kennedy, H. W. (Eds.), *Game cultures*. Maidenhead, UK: Open University Press.

Jenkins, H. (2004). Game design as narrative architecture. In Wardrip-Fruin, N., & Harrigan, P. (Eds.), *First person: New media as story, performance, and game*. Cambridge, London: MIT Press.

Pease, D. E. (1995). Author. In Lentricchia, F., & McLaughlin, T. (Eds.), *Critical terms for literary study*. Chicago, London: University of Chicago Press.

Schiesel, S. (2007, May 4). Finding fellowship (hairy feet optional). *New York Times*.

Scholes, R., Phelan, J., & Kellogg, R. (2006). *The nature of narrative*. New York: New York University Press.

Sell, R. D. (2000). *Literature as communication*. Amsterdam, Philadelphia: John Benjamins Publishing.

TOP TEXTS FOR INTERDISCIPLINARY STUDIES OF SERIOUS GAMES

Campbell, J. (2008). *The hero with a thousand faces* (3rd ed.). Novato, CA: New World Library.

Cobley, P. (2001). *Narrative*. London, New York: Routledge.

Cooper. R. (2007). *Alter ego: Avatars and their creators*. London: Chris Boot.

Gray, C. H. (Ed.). (1995). *The cyborg handbook*. New York: Routledge Press.

Mookerjee, A., & Kharma, M. (1977). *The tantric way*. London: Thames and Hudson.

Pease, D. E. (1995). Author. In Lentricchia, F., & McLaughlin, T. (Eds.), *Critical terms for literary study*. Chicago, London: University of Chicago Press.

Rotman, A. (Trans.). (2008). Divine stories, Divya-vadana part 1. Boston: Wisdom Publications.

Scholes, R., Phelan, J., & Kellogg, R. (2006). *The nature of narrative*. New York: Oxford University Press.

Sell, R. D. (2000). *Literature as communication*. Amsterdam, Philadelphia: John Benjamins Publishing.

Wolf, M., & Perron, B. (2003). *The video game theory reader*. New York, London: Routledge.

ENDNOTES

1. For this term, I am indebted to Glorianna Davenport of the MIT Media Lab's interactive video group.
2. For a good overview of issues concerning narrative in general, you might consult Cobley (2001).
3. Haggadah means the retelling or the teaching.

Section 3
Research

Chapter 7
Methodological Considerations in Educational Research Using Serious Games

Putai Jin
University of New South Wales, Australia

ABSTRACT

The literature on using serious games for learning has been growing exponentially during the last decade. It is time to examine some methodological issues associated with this line of research. There is evidence that research on serious games, if designed with methodological rigor and executed properly, such as the serial studies of prisoners' dilemma, modality effect in individual interactive learning, and changes in attitude toward mathematics in a computer-based simulation game, can be fruitful and have a profound, positive impact on learning and training. Since adopting serious games as an educational technology tool is by no means cheap, we should ensure that methodological issues are carefully considered before conducting a study on educational games. Whereas there are excellent studies in the existing literature of simulations and games, it is not uncommon for some studies to adopt convenience samples or own-control designs. Studies on serious games tend to be conclusive if they have used true experimentation, well-controlled quasi-experimental design, surveys with representative samples and validated instruments, comprehensive design research, or training programs having a pretest–posttest design with group comparisons. The potential values and informative contributions of using different methodologies for serious game research should be recognized because of the ecological relevance. Future research should pay more attention to randomized sampling, controlled but feasible research design, validity of instruments, appropriate analytical methods, and interdisciplinary or cross-disciplinary research to enhance the internal/external validity of various approaches. In regard to analytical methods, both quantitative approaches and qualitative evaluations, if applied appropriately, are considered as valuable, indispensable, and complementary to each other. It is hoped that this chapter can be helpful not only for future researchers in this field to design and execute rigorous projects but also for wider readership to understand and evaluate research outcomes in the discipline of serious games.

DOI: 10.4018/978-1-61520-719-0.ch007

Copyright © 2010, IGI Global. Copying or distributing in print or electronic forms without written permission of IGI Global is prohibited.

INTRODUCTION

Although game playing has long been used for studies on conflict resolution, business training, group psychotherapy and children's experience (e.g., Charness, Fréchette, & Qin, 2007; Graetz, 1995; Kay, 1997; Kirova, 2006; Pratto, Pearson, Lee, & Saguy, 2008;Pruitt & Kimmel, 1977; Vinacke, 1969; Wiener, 1999; Zhong, Loewenstein, & Murnighan, 2007; Zizzo & Tan, 2007), educational games equipped with advanced informational technology for the learning of a wide range of academic knowledge and skills have attracted researchers' attention only during the last two decades or so. In line with the proliferation of personal computers and internet usage across nations and cultures, a number of conceptual models as well as guidelines for the design and execution of educational computer games have been proposed (e.g., Dempsey, Haynes, Lucassen, & Casey, 2002; Dipietro, Ferdig, Boyer, & Black, 2007; Garris, Ahlers, & Driskell, 2002; Jones, 2007; Karakus, Inal, & Cagiltay, 2008; Kebritchi & Hirumi, 2008; Raybourn, 2007; Reese, 2007; Spencer-Oatey, 2007; Tahiroglu, Celik, Uzel, Ozcan, & Avci, 2008). In line with Moore's Law predicting periodically remarkable increases in the number of transistors economically available on an integrated circuit, the advancement of software designed for computer games is partially due to the rapid expansion of processing capabilities of CPUs. Consequently, research activities on both games for purely entertainment purposes and serious games for educational/training purposes have been growing exponentially. While educational and technological experts are still debating the theoretical bases of gaming and its pedagogical implications, methodological concerns in this diversified field have also been raised. According to de Freitas and Jarvis (2007), many studies on digital game-based learning (DGBL) lack firm empirical evidence and thus are not conclusive. In his assessment of serious games as a field and the associated challenges in forthcoming years, Van Eck (2007) calls for more rigorous research of both a grounded-theory and empirically oriented nature. As pointed out by Dipietro and colleagues (2007) in their recent effort to promote a framework for understanding electronic educational gaming: "We need more research, but this research must be structured and rigorous" (p. 241).

In a meta-analytic review on computer gaming and interactive simulations for learning conducted by Vogel et al. (2006), 248 studies were identified from electronic databases (PsycInfo, ERIC, AMC, Google Scholars, etc.), dissertation abstracts, and the references from main articles. Of these studies, only 32 met the criteria for the meta-analysis (Vogel et al., 2006). Since educational computer gaming is a relatively new research field, both theoretical bases and methodological aspects (sampling, design, instruments, data analysis, etc.) can be further developed and improved. For instance, in a review of methodological practices in research examining effects of playing violent video games on behavior, cognition, affect, and arousal, Anderson (2004) was able to classify the studies in this area into two categories: "best methodologies practices" versus "not best methodologies practices." It was found that methodologically weaker studies yielded smaller effect sizes than methodologically stronger studies. In general, methodological weaknesses are demonstrated in the lack of adequate manipulation or inclusion of independent variables, flawed research designs, nonrepresentative sampling, formation of nonequivalent groups, improper use of difference scores in pre- and post-measurements, experimenter influence or observer bias, inaccurate selection and recording of outcomes, and problematic presentation of relationships among dependent variables. It is understandable for an emerging area to contain a variety of research design and instruments; this may lead to different findings and interpretations, as evident in some previously emerging areas, such as research on the arousal reduction effects of meditation (Holmes, 1987; Jin, 1992) and the psychological benefits of physical exercise (Biddle, Fox, Boutcher, & Faulkner, 2000; Folkins & Sime, 1981; Taylor, 2000) in the 1980s and 1990s.

There have been well-designed and effectively executed studies on the efficacy of serious games for educational purposes accumulated in the past decades, and this trend is currently quite promising. For instance, according to de Freitas and Jarvis (2007), researchers in electronic game-based learning at three of the research-oriented British Universities (University of Birmingham, University of London, and University of Sheffield), together with educational computer game developers and deliverers in the learning industry, have formed a consortium to synthesize the knowledge and strength of both game technologists and pedagogical experts for a project called Serious Games–Engaging Training Solutions (SG-ETS). The fundamental purposes of SG-ETS are (a) to produce a standardized process for the development, selection, and evaluation of learning games targeting different groups of clients and (b) to promote publications in game-based learning (de Freitas & Jarvis, 2007). More recently, the *Computers in Human Behavior* journal has devoted a special issue to electronic games and personalized learning, indicating increased quantity as well as improved quality of the research in educational computer games (Burgos, Fernández-Manjón, & Richards, 2008).

Two additional important aspects of educational gaming research need to be considered. First, we need to bear in mind that electronic gaming has its unique features, which attract millions of school children and other players in the world. For many students, playing electronic games via computers or other apparatuses is part of their normal lives (Ang, Zaphiris, & Mahmood, 2006; Dempsey et al., 2002; Dipietro et al., 2007; Kebritchi & Hirumi, 2008; Olson, 2004; Reese, 2007; Sun, Ma, Bao, Chen, & Zhang, 2008; Tahiroglu et al., 2008). If educators and parents wish to turn at least some of such spontaneous gaming activities into ubiquitous learning sessions that incorporate player enthusiasm, we must recognize the importance of situational and contextual factors. In other words, researchers must remember that learning experiences associated with educational gaming occur in students' ecological environments that include classrooms, homes, science and technology learning centers, friends' places, and other nonconventional "learning" and recreational locations. Educational game research carried out in those natural settings will be meaningful and characterized by higher external validity and generalizability.

Secondly, because neither the majority of teachers nor educational researchers have been trained as gaming software experts, they need close collaborations with information technologists to design, select, and evaluate electronic games for various learning tasks. To achieve optimized learning outcomes, for instance from a computer game associated with a school curriculum of personal development and health education, educators, researchers, and technologists ought to involve authorities in educational administration, parents, ethics specialists, community leaders and, of course, the end users. Therefore, the development of educational game software that requires the participation of main stakeholders should be regarded as an essential and fruitful part of educational gaming research. As suggested by Rieber (2005), we need to apply appropriate methodology to this line of research.

Since adopting serious games as an educational technology tool, whether self-developed or modified from commercial versions, is by no means cheap, we should ensure that methodological issues are carefully considered before conducting a study on serious educational games. A systematic review on methodological issues in serious game studies will pave the way for conclusive and cost-effective research in the future. The aim of this chapter is to examine sampling, research design, validity of instruments, and analytical methods used in previous studies on serious games and discuss issues related to internal and external validity in this research field.

It should be noted that the objective of this chapter is not to conduct an exhaustive meta-analysis of studies on serious games. Rather, it attempts to (a) review various types of methodologies that are frequently adopted in this field, (b) elaborate on some well-conducted empirical studies as exemplary enquiries for interested researchers to refer to as examples, and (c) point out areas for improvement where preliminary studies have been conducted. Empirical studies in the field of serious games published in high-impact peer-reviewed journals and academic books were searched for through electronic databases (Catalogue, Oxford Scholarship Online, PsycBOOKS, PsycInfo, ERIC, Google, etc.), International Dissertation Abstracts, and selected journals, ranging from specialized periodicals (*Simulation and Gaming, Computers and Education, Journal of Computers in Mathematics and Science Teaching, Medical Education*, etc.) to general research outlets (*Science, Nature, Journal of Educational Psychology, Journal of Personality and Social Psychology*, etc.). The chapter will focus equally on true experimentation and well-controlled quasi-experimental design. In addition, it takes into account the variety of research in serious games and recognizes the potential values and contributions of using different methodologies. In regard to analytical methods, both quantitative approaches (e.g., Dempsey & Van Eck; 2003; Green & Bavelier, 2003; Mayer, Mautone, & Prothero, 2002; Peters & Malesky, 2008) and qualitative evaluations (e.g., Ang, Zaphiris, & Mahmood, 2006; Coleman, 2002; Lim, 2008; Satwicz & Stevens, 2008), if applied appropriately, are considered equally valuable and complementary.

METHODOLOGICAL CONSIDERATIONS OF EMPIRICAL STUDIES ON SERIOUS GAMES

Experimental Studies on Gaming

Experimental studies, mainly used for hypothesis testing, are characterized by purposefully systematic manipulation of independent variables, effective control of confounding variables, the establishment of equivalent treatment and control groups, and valid measurement of well-defined dependent variables. Gaming has been employed as a conventional means for experiments in social psychology and political–economic behavior research. For instance, the longstanding experimental research using the prisoner's dilemma games and their extended *N*-person formats, although initially criticized for its lack of theory and inadequate concern with external validity, has contributed to our understanding of the basic mechanisms of negotiation and compromise. These processes in turn have been mirrored by the processes of the Cuban missile crisis in 1963 and the subsequent establishment of hotlines between superpowers (e.g., Charness, Fréchette, & Qin, 2007; Pratto, Pearson, Lee, & Saguy, 2008); Pruitt & Kimmel, 1977; Vinacke, 1969; Zhong, Loewenstein, & Murnighan, 2007; Zizzo & Tan, 2007). Likewise, experimental methodology has been chosen by a number of researchers interested in the effects of interactive video games on attention, motivation, and learning outcomes. This line of experimental approaches has revealed some noticeable causal effects under complex conditions associated with the utility of electronic gaming in educational and other settings. The following sections will review some methodological issues in gaming studies of various topics, such as changes in attention and perception as a result of playing video games, the impacts of motivational embellishments in educational games, the applications of cognitive principles to e-learning courses, and the role of pedagogical advisors in computer environments.

Experimental Studies on the Potential Consequences of Video Game Playing on Perception, Cognition, and Psychomotor Skills

As video game playing has become a prevalent activity in our society, a question of concern is: what are the potential consequences of this newly introduced activity on human perception, cognition, and psychomotor skills? *Nature* published a report based on five experiments with action video games to examine whether action video games modify players' visual selective attention (Green & Bavelier, 2003). In the first four experiments, comparisons in various aspects of visual attention were made between young male habitual video game players (VGPs) and young male nonvideo game players (NVGPs). The results indicated that VGPs possessed more enhanced attentional capacity than NVGPs in terms of performance in various difficult tasks. However, these four experiments, although well-conducted and properly analyzed, used two self-selected groups (i.e., VGPs versus NVGPs). Therefore the experiments could not rule out the confounding factor that VGPs chose to frequently play action video games because they might have already had natural psychomotor ability superior to NVGPs. The next step of this experimentation was to recruit both young male and female NVGPs and randomly assign them into two groups for a period of video game training (one hour per day for 10 consecutive days). In the experimental group, NVGPs underwent action video game training by playing *Medal of Honor* (DreamWorks Interactive, 1999) which required that attention be distributed and switched around the field; their counterparts in the control group were trained by playing *Tetris* (Pajitnov & Gerasimov, 1984), which served as a condition of visuo-motor coordination but only demanded that subjects focus on one object at a time. This fifth experiment demonstrated that (1) all participants improved their scores by the end of training (indicating the effectiveness of training sessions) and (2) novice participants showed greater improvement in their attention abilities for enumeration, useful-field-of-view and attention-blink tasks under the action game training conditions than the control condition. Thus, the two-step methodology employed in this series of study by Green and Bavelier (2003) has clearly established the role of action video games in the enhancement of players' visual selective attention. We can use this strategy in similar research on the effectiveness of educational games by firstly examining the differences between players and nonplayers and then, in order to rule out the confounding effect of self-selection, setting up a training session for confirmatory investigation.

It is not uncommon for existing self-selected groups to be used in research, especially at the initial stages to identify the size of an effect. For instance, Sun and associates (2008), on the estimation that in China alone there are 40 million people engaged in daily online games, decided to investigate the impact of excessive computer game playing, or ECGP, on cognitive functioning. The experimental procedures were to (1) recruit 65 male students in a Chinese university; (2) administer an ECGP inventory; (3) divide the participants into a currently engaged ECGP group, a previously engaged ECGP group, and a control group (with low ECGP scores); and (4) run a multiple-object tracking (MOT) test on those three groups. Analysis of variance (ANOVA) yielded complex and somewhat confusing outcomes: the previous ECGP group had higher MOT scores than both the current ECGP and the control group. Because of the self-selection problem, caution should exercised in interpreting the data obtained.

Another trend in this field is to adopt random assignment to test a short-term effect of video games. For instance, to examine effects of exposure to sex-stereotyped video game characters on tolerance of sexual harassment, Dill, Brown, and Collins (2008) used male and female college students in an introductory psychology course and randomly assigned them into an experimental group and a control group. The former group viewed a *PowerPoint* presentation of images of sex-stereotyped video game characters; the latter viewed press photos of current U. S. senators and congresspersons (half male and half female). The participants were later requested to fill out attitudinal questionnaires such as sexual harassment judgments and routine violent video game exposure. This design revealed that men exposed to sex-stereotyped video games were more tolerant of sexual harassment in real-life instances than were controls. A similar research design was employed to investigate the impact of violent and nonviolent computer games on cognitive performance (Barlett, Vowels, Shanteau, Crow, & Miller, 2009). Both male and female college students (Caucasian majority) in a general psychology course were randomly assigned to the violent video game experimental group (playing *Red Alert 2* [Westwood Studios, 2008], for 18 minutes), the nonviolent video game experimental group (playing *Tile* [Barlett et al., 2009] game and marked numbers for 18 minutes), and the control group (using the Internet to search for information about air traffic controllers for 18 minutes). All participants had a cognitive performance test *SynWin* (Elsmore, 1994) to measure their working memory, auditory perception, visual attention, and mental attention: three trials before and two trials after the corresponding interventions. This design was able to demonstrate that playing either a violent or nonviolent video game elevated participants' cognitive performance, whereas no changes in cognitive performance happened for participants not playing video games. This type of experimental approach that employs randomization and proper controls appears to be conclusive.

Experimental Studies on Functioning of Motivational Embellishments in Educational Computer Games

While more and more "interesting" educational computer games are available in the software market, educators' and parents' major concern is how the motivational embellishments in the games work for educational rather than entertainment purposes. Motivational embellishments are parts of the theme or procedure in an educational game that enhances players' interest in learning or behavioral involvement (see Low, this volume). This widely accepted usage was derived from a series of earlier experiments conducted by some educational psychologists (Cordova & Lepper, 1996; Garner, Gillingham, & White, 1989; Lepper & Cordova, 1992). Initially, a simple experimental design was used: primary school students learning mathematics were tested under three different conditions - the motivationally appealing condition (helping a graphic character in the computer game seek hidden treasures on a deserted island), the unembellished activity condition, and the control condition (Lepper & Cordova, 1992). According to data analysis, students preferred the computer program with motivational embellishments. The methodological strategy used in the subsequent two experiments was to further manipulate the independent variable by introducing various fantasy contexts to computer learning, such as the learner assuming the roles of armed hunters to chase a vicious lion, an adult mouse to look after an excited baby, a pirate in a search for buried gems, a detective to catch criminals, or an astronaut on a mission to a remote planet (Parker & Lepper, 1992). Those controlled experiments confirmed that both boys and girls expressed strong preference for the motivationally embellished versions over the motivationally unembellished versions.

Cordova and Lepper (1996) extended this line of motivational research by comparing the effect of intrinsic stimulation (e.g., a storyline of fantasy in the game) with the impact of extrinsic reward (e.g., a token toy for correct responses) on learning outcomes in educational computer games. The sources of motivational manipulations were converted to two independent variables (intrinsic and extrinsic), and a 2 (presence versus absence of intrinsic stimulation) × 2 (presence versus absence of extrinsic reward) factorial design experiment was conducted in the classroom setting for problem solving. It was found that intrinsic motivational embellishments had positive effects on correct hypothesis generation whereas providing extrinsic rewards had detrimental effects on learning.

The next enquiry was how to effectively and economically enhance intrinsic motivation in educational computer games. In addition to the strategy of contextualization (e.g., fantasy) that had been used in previous studies, Cordova and Lepper (1996) examined two other strategies: (a) the personalization of learning activities to be associated with characters and objects of inherent interest to students and (b) the provision of choice over some aspects of learning activities in order to increase students' sense of self-determination. Their experiment comprised a 2 (personalized fantasy versus generic fantasy) × 2 (choice versus no choice) factorial design with pre- and post-repeated measures plus a no-treatment control condition for learning arithmetical and problem-solving material content in computer games. ANOVA and analysis of covariance (ANCOVA) using a pretest score as a covariate demonstrated that all three motivational embellishment strategies, (contextualization, personalization, and choice) as independent variables had a statistically significant positive impact on students' motivation and aspiration, their perceived competence, their depth of engagement in learning, and the efficiency of learning.

A further question of interest is this: Can we extrapolate that the application of motivational embellishment strategies in educational computer games are always beneficial to the learning of academic knowledge? Lepper and Malone (1987) proposed that the goals of the motivational embellishments in a computer-aided course must be congruent with the goals of learning specified in the course. Garner, Gillingham, and White (1989) examined the effects of "seductive details" on macroprocessing and microprocessing in adults and children in two experiments using randomization. In the first experiment, graduate students in the treatment group read an expository text about insects with seductive (i.e., interesting but unimportant) details whereas those in the control group read the text with no seductive details. In the second experiment, seventh graders were randomly assigned to one of the three conditions: (a) minimal signaling of the main theme and seductive details; (b) minimal signaling of the main theme and no seductive details; or (c) semantic, lexical, and graphic signaling of the main theme and no seductive details. In general, subjects in the "no seductive details" conditions recalled more key ideas than did their counterparts in the "seductive details" condition. The findings obtained from controlled experiments support the proposition that motivational embellishments must be carefully designed and tested to ensure that they enhance rather than diminish the learning of academic content. Researchers interested in the efficacy of DGBL may conduct these types of experiments in natural settings (e.g., classrooms) by using different versions of games, each having a specific component with others serving as controls.

Experimental Studies on Applications of Cognitive Principles to Computer-Aided Learning

Multimedia presentations are often used in computer-aided learning. Research on multimedia instruction has developed and tested a series of cognitive principles (e.g., the modality principle) for proper design of instruction and effective delivery (see Clark & Mayer, 2008; Low & Sweller, 2005; Mayer, 2005). Many experiments have been conducted to examine instructional issues such as the efficacy of multimodal input, effective use of text and graphic presentations, and optimal utility of animation. For example, Mayer, Mautone, and Prothero (2002) conducted a series of experiments by using the *Profile Game* that was developed for geology courses. College students were randomly assigned to the treatment group or the control group. The treatments included strategic scaffolding (verbal statements about strategies for drawing lines and points) and pictorial scaffolding (pictorial representations of each of the surface features). Pictorial aids were found to be an effective component in cognitive apprenticeship for geological problem solving in the randomized experiments.

In the Education Forum of *Science*, de Jong (2006) reported that cognitive tools (e.g., exercise designating an appropriate state, background knowledge, explanations, on-screen monitoring system, hypothesis scratchpads, predefined hypotheses, experimentalist hints, and process coordinators) can be used in e-learning programs like *SimQuest* (cf. van Joolingen & de Jong, 2003), *Co-Lab* (cf. de Jong et al, 2003), *GenScope* (cf. Horwitz & Christie, 2000), and *Inquiry Island* (cf. White et al., 2002). Experimental evaluations have revealed positive effects of integrating cognitive tools with computerized simulation games on the acquisition of conceptual framework, procedural knowledge, and inquiry skills in various learning areas. A more recent example is an experiment conducted in a realistic e-course setting to examine the applicability of selected cognitive principles to the design of instructional materials (Thompson & McGill, 2008). The independent variable was the application of cognitive design principles, such as the contiguity principle, modality principle, split-attention principle, and redundancy principle (Mayer, 2005; Sweller, 1988; Sweller & Chandler, 1994). The dependent variables were (a) knowledge retention and (b) knowledge transfer. In the e-course, the Web site link was set up to randomly direct the participants (staff and students in an Australian university) to either the experimental group or the control group. Data analysis indicated that the instruction designed with cognitive principles was both practical and feasible to facilitate academic learning, although the magnitude of the effect associated with each cognitive principle was not reported. Thus a factorial design is needed to test the main effects and interactions of selected cognitive design principles in educational games, in which two or more independent variables, such as the interactivity of learning material contained in educational games and the learners' experience in computer games, are involved and manipulated.

Experimental Studies on the Role of Pedagogical Advisors in Computer Environments

In multimedia environments involving animation, research has shown that learners who receive personalized explanations, whether verbal elaboration or on-screen text, perform better than those who are given a neutral monologue (e.g., Moreno & Mayer, 2000; Moreno, Mayer, Spires, & Lester, 2001). In the computer game *Design-A-Plant*, college students imagined themselves to travel to alien planets to design plants suitable for the environmental conditions there. Moreno and Mayer (2000) introduced an animated pedagogical agent called "Herman the Bug" to the educational computer game. The function of "Herman the Bug" was to verbally explain and visually describe the relationships between certain plant features (such as leaves, stem, and roots) and environmental factors (such as rainfall, sunlight, and atmosphere) on new planets. Subjects were randomly assigned to either a personalized condition or a neutral condition. Data gathered from the randomized controlled study indicated that the use of an animated pedagogical agent in a personalized condition to be an effective cognitive tool.

To test the utility of contextualized advisement (using a video of Uncle Bob and Aunt Ann to explain mathematical questions and concepts at grade 7 and 8 levels) and its interaction with competition in a computer-based simulation game, Van Eck and Dempsey (2002) employed a 2 (the presence or absence of a contextualized advisement) × 2 (with or without competition) factorial design plus an outside control group with a phase factor of repeated measures (pretest, intervention, and posttest). The transfer score was considered as the indicator of learning outcomes. ANOVA yielded a significant interaction of contextualized advisement and competition. Subsequent simple main effect analysis revealed that participants who were exposed to contextualized advisement but not under competitive conditions learned better than those with no access to contextualized advisement. Analysis of experimental data also indicated that the students who used contextualized advisement tended to have reduced anxiety toward mathematics, even under the pressure of competition (Van Eck, 2006).

To examine the functioning of modality and placement of a pedagogical adviser in individual interactive e-learning, a 2 (modality: a video of a human adviser versus a text-based adviser) × 2 (placement of a pedagogical adviser: pull-down menu versus on-screen access) factorial design experiment with random assignment was conducted in a graduate course of statistics by Dempsey and Van Eck (2003). The dependent variables included the number of times the adviser was used by participants, participant performance scores, and motivation indices. They found that the on-screen presentation of a video-based adviser resulted in higher frequency of the adviser use than the pull-down presentation of a text-based or video-based adviser. In addition, performance scores during instruction were significantly correlated with the utility of a pedagogical adviser.

A further exploration of the role of pedagogical agents examined the effects of a pedagogical agent's competency level and interaction type on learners' self-efficacy with task, attitudes toward pedagogical agents as learning companions, and performance (Kim, Baylor, & PALS Group, 2006). A 2 (competency of a pedagogical agent: low versus high) × 2 (interaction type between the learners and pedagogical agents: proactive versus responsive) factorial design experiment with random assignment was conducted among undergraduate students in a computer-literacy course. Results indicated a significant main effect for the pedagogical agent's competency level on students' learning, attitude, and self-efficacy score. Students with a high-competency agent performed better in the recall test and showed more positive attitude toward a pedagogical agent-based environment than those with a low-competency agent, whereas students in the low-competency agent condition reported higher self-efficacy beliefs. The study was thus able to provide guidance for the design of and research on adaptive computer-based learning systems with "intelligent" pedagogical agents. For instance, at the initial stage, a low-competency agent may be used to lift up students' self-efficacy (in particular for those with relatively low self-efficacy beliefs); at a later stage when performance becomes the main focus of the course, the learning system should be flexible enough to introduce a high-competency agent.

Repeated Measures Used in Experimental Studies on Educational Games

The previous discussions of research demonstrate that true experimental approaches are very effective for testing hypotheses that are developed from educational practice (by using learning games) and for generating new research questions after systematic analysis of the data obtained. In experiments on serious games, repeated measures (e.g., a within-subjects factor of phase) have also been used as a useful way to reduce variability. This is possible because the measures that are made in several episodes on the same person tend to be more reliable (i.e., with less random errors) than measurement data obtained from different players. However, some assumptions must be met before conducting ANOVA with repeated measures (Bird,

1975; Jennings, 1987; Jin, 1992; Vasey & Thayer, 1987). For example, the researcher needs to check whether there is a carryover effect among several game episodes (i.e., a hidden learning effect). If so, either a counter-balanced procedure should be employed or a control group should be set up.

In addition, when using a mixed design with between-subjects and within-subjects cells in research on learning games, outliers (i.e., extremely unusual and unlikely cases) should be identified and excluded in further analysis. For instance, in a randomized experiment to examine the effect of implicit learning in a video game on the safe play behavior of youth hockey players, the participants whose scores showed them to be disinterested in or who had tampered with the *Alert Hockey* game created by Ciavarro, Dobson, & Goodman (2008), were identified and excluded from the conventional analysis and ANOVA. Some experimental reports on computer games (e.g., Sun et al., 2008) include repeated-measures analysis justifications, such as multivariate analysis of variance or Greenhouse-Geiser adjustment of the degrees of freedom in univariate analysis. This approach is rigorous and thus, wherever feasible, should be implemented.

Moreover, if the analysis uses pretest scores or a confounding factor as a covariate (e.g., Wang, 2008), assumptions for covariance analysis should be tested (Huitema, 1980; Lord, 1967, 1969; 1975). When using such "adjusting" methods, we need to be mindful of two potential problems in the interpretation of results: (a) the adjusted scores are sample-dependent and (b) some outliers can dramatically affect statistical analysis (Jin, 1992; Rubin, 1977).

Quasi-Experimental Design and Other Approaches

Researchers on gaming have employed a number of research approaches. Apart from randomized experimentation, many studies on learning games report using own-control, quasi-experimental, design research, survey, instrument establishment, natural observation, and case analysis designs. Data obtained from such methodologies have also enriched our understanding of the complexity and potentiality of educational games.

Own-Control Design

Own-control design is often used by practitioners and researchers in natural settings where random assignment to experimental and control conditions may be cumbersome (e.g., the size of a class is too small), there is a lack of feasibility (e.g., the school curriculum does not allow extra time for setting up a control group), and even where the study might be conducive to the Hawthorn effect (e.g., the members in the control group regard their exclusion from the experimental activities as an opportunity for competition, and thus put forth excessive effort in a an attempt to "beat" their counterparts in the experimental group). In this type of design, the discrepancy between the pre- and post-intervention scores is examined for its magnitude. For instance, an educational multiuser virtual environment, *Quest Atlantis* (Barab, Thomas, Dodge, Carteaux, & Tuzun, 2005) was introduced to pupils of two fifth-grade classes in Singapore to help them learn English, mathematics, and science by having them play the role of global citizens (Lim, 2008). The study adopted a bottom-up approach that involved four teachers in the school's ecological system, thus creating a sense of relevancy to the local curriculum while having the advantage of connection with a globally distributed community of participants. In the game-like environment, pupils were required to engage in intensive self-regulated learning activities (e.g., building a secret garden in a *Quest Atlantis*-mediated science lesson). Multiple methods of data collection and analysis were used, including the administration of a pre–post academic motivation questionnaire (intrinsic versus extrinsic motivation, self-efficacy, task values, personal goal orientation, etc.), a pre–post commitment questionnaire, observations by keeping a record of events, and interviews with students and teachers. The results supported the utility of educational multiuser virtual environments in a meaningful context for motivated academic learning and highlighted the importance of developing a research culture in schooling. However, caution must be exercised in interpreting the data because the own-control design cannot rule out the influence of history, maturation, and experimenter bias (Cook & Campbell, 1979; Shadish, Cook, & Campbell, 2002).

In the field of gaming research, own-control design applied in natural settings can be extended from classroom to home, where both qualitative and quantitative data collection and analysis can be used. This type of design may allow researchers to keep in contact with a small group of participants and observe them for a relatively long period without too much logistic workload in administering the data-gathering procedure. An exemplary study using this approach has been recently reported by Satwicz and Stevens (2008). Based on Vygotskian grounded theory of children's cognitive development in the social context (Vygotsky, 1962) and some evidence about the positive impact of digital or nondigital game play on STEM (i.e., science, technology, engineering, and mathematics) derived from previous studies by Greenfield (1994), Guberman & Saxe (2000), Lowrie, (2005), and Squire (2006), Satwicz and Stevens (2008) selected and gender-balanced a group of eight children ranging from 9 to 15 years of age and visited them weekly at their homes for a 6-month period. In an attempt to understand children's video game-playing processes from those players' own viewpoints, Satwicz and Stevens (2008) employed an ethnographic methodological strategy for data collection and analysis. The research team video-recorded over 100 hours of both in-room activities and on-screen images, integrated both sources of data into a synchronized file, applied interactive and comparative analysis of the content logs, and conducted exit interviews with participants. Based on the data reflecting multifaceted aspects of participants' video game playing and relevant occurrences in their daily lives, the qualitative analysis indicated that children applied quantitative measures in games (e.g, the number of lives, time limits, and scores) to make predictions which were in turn used for organizing subsequent actions in gaming, thus providing firm evidence for supporting the hypothesis of the positive impact of quantitative practice in video gaming on STEM thinking. We can learn from this type of research that a) uses representative sampling techniques in own-control design and b) employs well-structured qualitative as well as quantitative analytical methods.

Own-control design has also been used in serious game design research, which is aimed at seeking software improvement and testing the feasibility of an educational game (Rieber, 2005). For example, Carbonaro and associates (2008) attempted to focus on the issue that learners were not simply computer game players but also builders and constructors of educational games. They conducted a pilot and two subsequent own-control studies by using a game story construction tool, *Aurora Toolset* (BioWare) and an associated interactive tool, *ScriptEase* (Carbonaro et al., 2008), in two English classes at the tenth-grade level. In the pilot study, feedback about the usage of *Aurora Toolset* and *ScriptEase* was used for revising instructional materials. In the subsequent studies conducted in two English classes, the interaction stories were compared with the traditional short stories in terms of common criteria, such as characters, sitting, plot, conflict, theme, and style. Effect size was used as an indicator of the magnitude of changes in performance. Both quantitative and qualitative results showed that students benefited from the construction of sophisticated interactive stories. Similarly, own-control methodology has been used for software development studies on an adaptive training system using serious games in the classroom (Raybourn, 2007) and on the use of *PowerPoint* presentations in a virtual computer game engine world for teaching contemporary physics (Price, 2008). Such a type of research is useful for improving gaming design, checking the effect size of an intervention, and establishing a framework for further research.

Design Research Using Quasi-Experimental Methodology

Quasi-experiments use a research design that does not meet all requirements necessary for controlling the influences of confounding variables (Cook & Campbell, 1979; Shadish, Cook, & Campbell, 2002). In particular, when random assignment of participants, which is essential for true experimentation, is not feasible, researchers may alternatively conduct a quasi-experiment. For example, in the situation where only two schools are available for a study on the effectiveness of a new math game, but the curriculum does not allow different treatments within a class, the researcher may decide to use one school for game-mediated learning (i.e., the experimental group) and another school for conventional learning (i.e., the control group). Because the two schools are nonequivalent in terms of location, teachers, and many other conditions, at best the study can be regarded as a quasi-experiment. In real-life situations, especially in classroom or home settings where often only nonequivalent groups are available for observation or intervention, quasi-experimental design is a feasible and sensible option.

Harel and Papert (1990) conducted a quasi-experiment in a Boston inner-city public school where a fourth-grade class was available for the design and development of a Logo-based computer environment for learning fractions. Two other classes were used as controls during the same 1-semester period. Pupils in the experimental and control groups were tested before and after the trial/intervention. Based on quantitative and qualitative analyses, Harel and Papert (1990) reported that simultaneously learning both Logo programming and other content areas resulted in better performance than did isolated conditions.

A more recent example of design research is Hämäläinen, Oksanen, and Häkkinen's (2008) study on the development of a pedagogically reasonable game environment to enrich the understanding of work safety in a vocational context. In this design experiment, 64 young vocational students were evenly divided into 16 groups to play a work safety game and sat for a knowledge test immediately after the learning session; however, only three quarters of the groups completed the learning game. Data were collected by means of an online survey, videotaping, observation, chat room discussion, and other logging activities. According to the descriptive and correlational analyses, the scripted game environment not only promoted the learning activities that could not be carried out in traditional classroom settings but also facilitated players' collaborative interactions as well as transitions from initial to final learning phases.

Unlike much of experimental research engaging participants for a relatively short duration (ranging from brief sessions to several weeks), design research often requires investigators and developers to work together or take the dual role for a fairly long period. Both investigators and developers tend to gain significant insightful knowledge about the advantages and pitfalls of a specific educational game because they have had direct contact with end users and received timely feedback from them. As Rieber (2005) points out, although design studies have been criticized as being anecdotal and lacking scientific rigor, this line of research, if based on sophisticated data collection methods and well-established theories/principles, can offer great promise in the aspects of computer-based educational games' cost-effective production and pedagogically sound operation.

Surveys on Gaming

As games have continued to grow in popularity, researchers have also been working to understand their associated mechanisms, consequences, and utilities (e.g., Anderson, 2004; Hill & Peters, 1998; Peters & Malesky, 2008). A survey with reasonably large and representative samples, whether conducted online, verbally (e.g., telephoning), or by mail, is an efficient way to gather information from large numbers of people on a wide variety of topics. For instance, in 2008, two studies on Turkish teenagers' behaviors and their computer usage were published, all using survey methodology (Karakus et al, 2008; Tahiroglu et al., 2008). In one survey, Karakus and colleagues conducted a learner analysis to identify Turkish high school students' preferences, playing habits, expectations, and opinions concerning computer games. A total of 1550 questionnaires were distributed with a return rate of 79%. The analysis was mainly descriptive and suggested that computer games might be employed as vehicles for learning mathematics and history. Although males had more positive views of computer games than females, the effect size (as indicated by the eta square value here, .006) was less than 1% of the total variation investigated. In other words, the strength of the relationship between the independent variable (males versus females) and dependent variable (attitudes to computer games), is trivial. Since survey data are usually collected from relatively large samples, the large numbers are likely to give "significant" results in statistical reports. Such results can be misleading: the reported relationship might be *statistically* "significant" but not of great impact because of a small effect size. Therefore, data analysis, especially in large-scale surveys, should examine the significance level as well as effect size and highlight whether the effect being examined is of any noticeable strength that deserves further attention.

In another large-scale survey, Tahiroglu and associates (2008) investigated Turkish adolescents' Internet use habits. They found that (a) the most common purpose for using the Internet was playing games and (b) violent games were chosen as the most preferred type of gaming. Although the sample size was impressive (n = 3975), no return rates were reported. It is essential for the survey reporter to include corresponding return rates so that other researchers or survey data consumers (game developers, policy makers, etc.) can judge whether the results are based on representative samples. Nevertheless, the patterns reported in the above-mentioned study appear to be similar to the findings in Taiwan, Korea, the United States, Germany, and mainland China (Chou & Tsai, 2007; Lemmens & Bushman, 2006; Lucas & Sherry, 2004; Quaisser-Pohl, Geiser, & Lehmann, 2006; Wei, 2007).

As noted earlier, a survey with proper sampling procedures can be a useful method to identify the patterns, types, relationships, determinants, and trends in the area of serious games. Investigations using small, nonrandom, or nonrepresentative samples are likely to yield biased or conflicting results. For example, there are conflicting or inconclusive data reported on the link between exposure to violent interactive video games and violent or criminal behaviors (e.g., school shootings) in real life (Olson, 2004). This is partly due to (a) vague definitions of *aggressive* and *violent* themes, thoughts, and actions (i.e., poor operational definitions of those themes resulting in biased sampling), (b) special contextual factors of a particular study, and (c) sampling problems (e.g., using undergraduate students in psychology courses as convenience samples or other samples narrow in age range or geographic region).

At the current stage, descriptive presentations (i.e., providing statistics such as proportions, frequencies, and means) seem to be the focus of survey studies in the area of computer gaming. Methodologically, finer-grained analysis can be employed to squeeze more information from the survey data. For instance, regression models can be used to check relationships and determinants in cyber behavior, as done by Chou and Tsai (2007). This type of analysis was able to indicate that for Taiwanese male high school students, the most powerful predictor of their enjoyment experience of computer game playing was the motivational factor for entertainment followed by the motivational factor of seeking information. It further showed that for Taiwanese female high school students, the most powerful predictor of their enjoyment experience of computer game playing was also the motivational factor for entertainment, followed by the motivational factor of filling time, which was somewhat in contrast to the orientation of male students.

To examine different types of computer game players, latent class analysis can be also conducted, as done by Quaisser-Pohl, Geiser, and Lehmann (2006). This type of analytical method applied to the data of a computer-game preference scale was useful in identifying three types of players among German secondary school students: non-players, action and simulation game players, and logic and skill training game players. Moreover, since the effectiveness of educational games is largely determined by cognitive and motivational factors, structural equation modeling can also be used to empirically test the fit of a comprehensive framework for effective educational gaming. For instance, Astleitner and Wiesner (2004) have proposed a model that depicts the impact of both cognitive and motivational variables on multimedia learning. Researchers who intend to adopt this model for research in DGBL (often in the multimedia format) may employ structural equation modeling techniques to verify the effects of both cognitive and motivational aspects on self-regulated learning behavior and outcomes (Arbuckle, 2005; Conrad & Munro, 2008; Jöreskog & Sörbom, 1993).

Case Studies on Serious Games

In contrast to survey methodology that usually requires large and sometimes cross-sectional samples, a case study is an in-depth investigation of a relatively constrained and often self-contained system by means of extensive collection of qualitative and sometimes quantitative data (Creswell, 2007, 2008). In a case analysis of serious games, the object under investigation can be individuals (e.g., educational game players), groups (e.g., a class at a certain level), organizations (e.g., a school to which game-like assessment is introduced), events (e.g., a new business course with computer-based simulation games), or processes (e.g., a science education program embedded with games in a revision phase). The information used for case study is very detailed, and thus, the analysis is relevant to concrete activities. For instance, the case analysis carried out by Coleman (2002) described a computer-assisted simulation game package *SimCopter* (which was based largely on the popular software *SimCity*) and its usage for English as a second language (ESL) writing practice. In two scenarios, ESL students took the role of a pilot and a visitor consecutively to find destinations and write up their journeys. The findings showed that the activities stimulated by the writing game *SimCopter* made the concept of audience more accessible by concretizing it than did the conventional ESL texts.

Case study can be used to depict how an educational game is developed and thus may enrich our understanding of the underlying processes of edutainment software design. For instance, the case study by Jones (2007) documented and discussed the development of the *Resource Allocation Game*, a strategy game for enterprise education. Students were assigned in pairs to the business game, required to deal with a puzzling scenario, and urged to make optimal decisions for the industry. Based on the feedback from students and the researcher's reflections, the qualitative analysis not only demonstrated the success of this educational game development as evident by students satisfaction, acceptance and overall learning, but it also revealed some of the mechanisms underlying the use of games in experiential learning, such as essential challenge, mystery (i.e., cryptic content), and a balance between the freedom of exploration and disciplined assessment processes. In other words, it was necessary for the innovative business education program to initially create a cryptic situation that made students struggle with the game's rules and strategies, because this process enhanced their curiosity and persistence in handling ambiguity.

Case study has also been used to examine cognitive load in massively multiplayer online role-playing games (MMORPGs) and to develop a pretrial model for game designers (Ang et al., 2006). The focus was solely on the cognitive activities involved in gaming. Qualitative analysis was conducted on the transcription of 20 hours of logging data obtained from one female expert (13 years of age), one female novice (16 years of age), and one male novice (18 years of age) in playing *Maple Story*, a typical MMORPG. There were five categories of cognitive overload identified during the game, including multiple game interaction overloads, user interface overloads, identity construction overloads, parallel game and social interaction overloads, and multiple social interaction overloads. Cognitive overloads led to misidentification of signals, frequent mistakes, and frustration. The study suggested a guideline that games should be easy to learn or play but should also be challenging enough. The implication is that combining game playing with academic learning will require more cognitive capacities, and thus caution should be taken to ensure that unnecessary cognitive loads are eliminated when designing an educational game. This type of research shows that qualitative analytical techniques are very helpful for both researchers and game developers to gain insightful understanding of game players' mental processes, emotional reactions, and other game-related behaviors.

Training Using Computerized Simulation Games

Business sectors and business schools have a history of using game play for training personnel or graduate students (e.g., Starbuck & Kobrow, 1966; Perotti & Pray, 2002). The digital environment provides numerous opportunities to apply computer-based simulation games to training individuals and teams in business dynamics such as proactive management, effective marketing, organizational change, strategic planning, contingent leadership, and professional development. On the one hand, digital game-based training programs have employed cognitive and motivational principles derived from the controlled experiments and other rigorous research on the efficacy of educational games. On the other hand, the first-hand experience gained by trainers and feedback/comments from trainees have enriched our understanding of the underlying mechanisms of DGBL, facilitated the development of curriculum-related hypotheses (not just wishful speculation or profit-oriented propaganda), and improved the selection and implementation of commercial off-the-shelf (COTS) DGBL in the training room and classroom.

Pannese and Carlesi (2007) experimented with blended experiential training sessions by introducing digital technology to the classroom and tracking learners' perceptions and responses. They conducted a series of studies in Italy on digital simulation game training that was designed on the basis of simulation algorithms and branching or nonbranching storylines. The external validity of game-based training was strengthened by a wide range of scenarios: (a) training of staff in charge of sales in the pharmaceutical sector by a simulation game of conducting an interview with a specialist doctor, (b) training of product managers in the pharmaceutical sector by defining effective communication strategies in a simulated interaction with a medical practitioner; (c) training of operators in a specialized outbound call center by learning how to manage customers' objections; and (d) training on health care for children with chronic pathologies by playing serious games involving a social support system. Statistical analysis of user perceptions and responses of serious games was based on the data obtained from the questionnaire answered by two different groups of participants, namely, the business employees' group and the university students' group. The training study design enabled the researchers to compare the users from companies with those from universities in their ratings on effectiveness, pleasure, involvement, freedom of behavior, and usability of the serious games played. According to Pannese and Carlesi (2007), the findings were used for trainers to redevelop or revise DGBL programs for different client groups. In a methodological sense, this spiral exploratory process resembles Lewin's (1946) action research.

Serious game-based adaptive training systems have been developed by using simulation experience design methods (Raybourn, 2007). The purpose is to provide personal and leadership training on adaptive (critical and reflective) thinking and effective communication skills, which are much needed when industry, nongovernmental organizations, government organizations, and emergency relief organizations are confronted with uncertain times and limited resources. In this study, trainees played single or multiplayer games to learn about their strengths and weaknesses, deal with multicultural issues, receive in-game feedback with statistical analysis, and conduct after-action reviews. Methodologically, ongoing multipoint measurement was used in this own-control design. According to Raybourn, preliminary evaluations were positive, but the training program should further track the players' skill development and the long-term transfer effects in cross-sectional and follow-up designs. Computer-based simulation games have been intensively used for modern military training. For instance, directed by the U. S. Army Office of Economic Manpower Analysis, a multiplayer game called *America's Army* (U.S. Army, 2002) has been developed by using the simulation experience design method and introduced to the U. S. Department of the Army John F. Kennedy School for adaptive thinking and leadership training (Raybourn, 2007). The above-mentioned adaptive thinking and leadership training method has also been employed for enhancing multinational task forces' cultural awareness and communication competencies (Raybourn, 2007).

Principles for effective serious games have also been widely applied to military training at the operational level. An example is *Bottom Gun* (The Naval Air Systems Command of USA, 2003), a game-based submarine periscope trainer developed for the U. S. Navy, to enhance naval service students' submarine technical skills and learning motivation (Garris et al., 2002). This training study nicely adopted controlled experimental methodology and proper evaluation procedures. The *Bottom Gun* version, which was designed as the experimental version, incorporated most of the game features, such as fantasy, rules/goals, sensory stimuli, challenge, mystery, and control. In particular, this experimental version was characterized by simulated contacts, high interactivity, scoring, visual and sound effects, and other virtual reality components, which formed an array of independent variables related to this game-based training. In addition, the researchers devised a control simulation training version, which provided the same contacts within the same scenarios as the experimental version but lacked the game features that were embedded in the experimental version. After a period of training, initial between-subjects evaluation endorsed the effectiveness of the experimental version. Naval trainees perceived the *Bottom Gun* trainer to be more game-like than the control trainer in the aspects of fantasy, curiosity, competitiveness, control, and visual and sound effects. Moreover, data analysis on periscope performance indicated that naval trainees using the *Bottom Gun* game-based version had greater improvement in periscope skills and fewer operation errors than did their counterparts in the control condition. Such evaluations adopting a controlled experimental design are not only valuable for the implementation and revision of game-based virtual reality training but also informative for hypothesis generation in further studies using true experiment, quasi-experiment, and model-building survey methodologies.

Scales for Gaming and Factor Analysis

Since gaming is such a complex social phenomenon with significant educational implications, multifaceted measures have been used to depict its processes and consequences. Reliable, valid scales for games and related variables are essential in data collection and analysis. Researchers in gaming have adopted or modified instruments commonly used in psychological and educational research. For instance, in order to identify individuals having excessive computer-game playing behavior in China, Sun and colleagues used Tejeiro and Morán's (2002) Problem Videogame-Playing Questionnaire, which had been adapted from the *DSM-IV* in relation to substance abuse and pathological gambling (American Psychiatric Association, 1994). However, this study did not report the process of back-translation (English ↔ Chinese), cultural validation, and other critical psychometric parameters for the Problem Videogame-Playing Questionnaire, making the subsequent excessive computer-game playing group classifications questionable. In Lim's (2008) previously mentioned study using a pretest–posttest own-control design to investigate the effects of *Quest Atlantis* on the learning of fifth-grade English, mathematics, and science curricula in Singapore, the pre–post academic commitment and motivation questionnaire was adapted from the widely used Patterns of Adaptive Learning Survey (Midgley et al., 1997) and the Motivation Strategies for Learning Questionnaire known as MSLQ (Pintrich, Smith, Garcia, & McKeachie, 1993). Since the medium of instruction in Singaporean schools is English, the adoption of questionnaires used in English-speaking countries seems to be feasible, although psychometric details need to be presented.

To ascertain the modality effect and the placement of a virtual pedagogical advisor in individual interactive learning, Dempsey and Van Eck (2003) used a modified version of Keller's (1987) Instructional Motivational Scale to record attention, relevance, confidence, and satisfaction specifically oriented toward interactive computer-based learning. They also adopted Lee and Lehman's (1993) Passive–Active Learning Scale (Cronbach's alpha = .81) to identify learning styles. In addition, a simplified version of the Computer Anxiety Rating Scale with a Cronbach's alpha coefficient of .82 (Miller & Rainer, 1995) was used to obtain the computer anxiety score as a covariate for statistical analysis. Likewise, in Van Eck's (2006) report on middle-school students' changes in attitude to mathematics as a result of the use of a computer-based simulation game in the classroom, the Math Beliefs Survey, originally developed by Van Haneghan and Hickey (1993) with reasonable Cronbach alphas, was employed to measure task orientation, ego orientation, work avoidance, math anxiety, confidence in math ability, interest, understanding, competitiveness, effort, time consuming, challenging, and utility. The use of well-established standard instruments is advantageous to develop an appropriate conceptual framework and measure relevant latent variables.

Attempts have also been made to construct specific scales for research in computer behavior or gaming. For instance, researchers have applied factor analysis to developing the computer attitude scale for computer science freshmen (Palaigeorgiou, Siozos, Konstantakis, & Tsoukalas, 2005), the attitude toward computer-based learning (CBL) questionnaire in medical education (Hahne, Benndorf, Frey, & Herzig, 2005), and the Computer Technology Use Scale with three domains, namely, computer self-efficacy, attitudes to technology, and technology-related anxiety (Conrad & Munro, 2008).

Efforts have also been made to produce scales for studies on games with educational potential, such as the ARCS Gaming Scale based on Keller's

(1987) ARCS model containing categories of attention, relevance, confidence, and satisfaction associated with electronic games of educational prospects (Dempsey & Johnson, 1998), the Attitude Toward Tutoring Agent Scale (Adcock & Van Eck, 2005), and the motivation and enjoyment scales for computer game playing (Chou & Tsai, 2007). Researchers have also used factor analysis or other techniques to form scales to assess significant variables in video game playing, such as the Video Game Questionnaire focusing on the exposure to video game violence and the amount of time spent playing video games (Anderson & Dill, 2000; Dill, Brown, & Collins, 2008), the Problematic Usage–Engagement Questionnaire designed for highly engaged online players of *World of Warcraft* (Blizzard Entertainment, 2004; Peters & Malesky, 2008), and the Character Attachment Scale with distinct components of identification/friendship, suspension of disbelief, control, and responsibility (Lewis, Weber, & Bowman, 2008).

The majority of scale development studies have employed exploratory factor analysis. This approach is effective for the initial stage of forming conceptual frameworks and conducting item selection (DeVellis, 2003; Meredith, 1993; Thompson, 2004). While data from empirical studies in a defined area accumulate and the related theories progress, confirmatory factor analysis can be useful for testing whether there is substantial evidence to support the hypothesized relationship between observed variables and their underlying latent constructs (Byrne, 1989; Hayduk & Glaser, 2000; Thompson, 2004). For instance, in order to examine the relationship between computer self-efficacy, technology, attitudes, and anxiety, Conrad and Munro (2008) developed the Computer Technology Use Scale in their two-stage study. Firstly, based on social cognitive theory and previous empirical research in attitudes toward computer use and technology-related anxiety, the researchers compiled an initial version of the Computer Technology Use Scale, which was included in the questionnaires distributed to 600 university students. Principal component analyses were conducted on the data from 479 returned valid questionnaires to determine the factor structure, item retention and the internal consistency reliability (indexed as Cronbach's alpha). In the next step, confirmatory factor analyses were performed on the data collected from another sample of 355 volunteers to test the stability of factors generated and the overall model fit in terms of the chi square value, the root mean square error of approximation (RMSEA), adjusted goodness of fit index (AGFI), comparative fit index (CFI), and the Tucher–Lewis Index (TLI). The instrument validations confirmed an optimized five-factor solution with high factor loadings, including computer-self efficacy, complexity, negative attitudes, positive attitudes, and technology-related anxiety.

However, in Conrad and Munro's (2008) study, respondents for exploratory factor analysis were less experienced in software programming and computer systems than those for confirmatory factor analysis. This sampling variation may affect the stability of factor structure. An alternative procedure to take advantage of both exploratory and confirmatory analyses is (a) to draw a large, randomized sample out of the targeted population, (b) to obtain two randomly split subsamples, (c) to perform exploratory factor analysis on one randomly split subsample, (d) to execute confirmatory factor analysis on another randomly split subsample, and (e) to conduct post hoc modifications for the improvement of model fit.

FUTURE RESEARCH DIRECTIONS

Recommendations for Design and Analysis in Serious Game Research

Recommendation One

We need to further enhance controlled experimentation, using either randomly assigned or nonequivalent groups. Such investigations may require more resources than routine game playing, but studies with such additional costs and efforts are likely to be conclusive and conducive to the generation of warranted research questions for further enquiry. Wherever appropriate, both quantitative and qualitative data should be systematically collected. If repeated measures are employed, the design includes nonequivalent groups, or the focus of research is on individual differences, the possible impact of initial value must be taken into account and proper analytical procedures should be adopted (Cleary, 1986; Jin, 1992; Myrtek & Foerster, 1986a, 1986b). For example, as mentioned earlier, serious game researchers can take advantage of the reliability as well as cost-effectiveness of repeated-measures designs (i.e., testing the same game player several times rather than testing several game players under different conditions) for their experimentation or design studies. However, since the repeated measures, in a strict sense, are not independent, such violations in sphericity should be inspected before carrying out analysis of variance with repeated measures (Bird & Hadzi-Pavlovic, 1983; Maxwell & Bray, 1986). Software (e.g., SPSS) is available to conveniently check whether the violations of independency and normality are negligible. If the answer is yes, routine analysis can be logically carried out without specific adjustments in data analysis. If the violations are of concern, there are a number of ways to deal with this issue, such as using multivariate analysis or adjusting the degrees of freedom in analysis of variance (see Jin, 1992, for detailed advice). In observational studies, quasi-experimental, or nonequivalent control group designs, using traditional ANCOVA that include a confounding factor (or factors), as a covariate (or covariates) is likely to result in biased estimates of average causal effect (Rubin, 1974; Weisberg, 1979). As such, it is desirable to include baseline × treatment interactions and summaries of the propensity scores as additional baseline variables in ANCOVA (Schafer & Kang, 2008). Even under randomized experimental conditions, if the research question needs to be answered by covariance analysis, preassumptions for ANCOVA must be checked and should be briefly reported (Huitema, 1980; Wainer, 1991).

Recommendation Two

Both cross-sectional and longitudinal enquiries with representative sampling and valid instruments are much needed. Game-related scales need to be developed and sophisticated analysis such as exploratory and confirmatory factor analysis should be used for future surveys on serious games. Special instruments can be constructed based on findings from previous empirical studies, commonly used inventories, and theoretical development. To understand the complexity and profound impact of gaming, multivariate analysis (Tabachnick & Fidell, 2001), factor analysis and structural equation modeling techniques using software like LISREL and Amos (Arbuckle, 2005; Bollen, 1989; Conrad & Munro, 2008; Jöreskog, 1993; Jöreskog & Sörbom, 1993) can be employed to test competing hypotheses and produce optimal models that reflect the underlying mechanisms of serious games and interrelations among psychological, social, and technical variables in digital learning environments.

Recommendation Three

Systematic design research during serious game development and testing should be encouraged and recognized as a valuable, prospective, and indispensable aspect of gaming research (Rieber, 2005). This is a rare, expensive, and considerably time-intensive occasion when theme planners, experienced technologists, multimedia innovators, educational psychologists, human–machine relation experts, marketing specialists, budget controllers, field practitioners, community representatives (e.g., from parents associations, child protection groups, and ethics forums), and game testers (invited "potential" users in the pilot study) are working together to produce a masterpiece of quality work (i.e., a serious game) for learning purposes. Few academic grants would have the "luxury" in terms of human, financial, and time resources to accomplish such extensive projects for computer games. In design research, all of the stakeholders should be regarded as researchers. This is because their participation is a dynamic process similar to action research, which will not only attain a desirable goal with satisfactory educational outcomes but will also gain insightful ideas about the underlying mechanisms of gaming and learning for further theoretical development and model building.

Recommendation Four

We can turn various training courses/programs into research arenas (Garris et al., 2002; Pannese and Carlesi, 2007; Raybourn, 2007). To strengthen training studies with methodological rigor, assuming a low cost in terms of hardware supply, software usage, and allocated time involved, a pretest–posttest design with comparison groups, wherever possible, needs to be implemented. In addition, a follow-up study, when feasible, should be conducted to check whether the previous trainees in game-based courses/programs have transferred their learned knowledge and skills to their current curriculum study or professional activities.

Recommendation Five

Natural observations in classrooms or at other teaching and learning locations (homes, Internet cafés, digital game-playing centers, etc.) provide a valuable means of conducting research within the ecological environments of education, and thus the findings are useful for examining the external validity of game-based instruction. Detailed qualitative information recordings as well as quantitative data collection should be implemented in further gaming studies. For instance, to analyze videotaped classroom conversations about computer simulations and game design, standard methods in applied linguistics and cognitive anthropology can be used (Goodwin, 2000; Hutchins, 1995; Roth, 2009).

Recommendation Six

Since the playing of serious games involves cognitive, motivational, emotional, and kinetic aspects of human reactions, interdisciplinary and cross-disciplinary research should be considered in future research. For instance, to examine the working memory capacity in gaming and learning, developmental data collected from different age groups, psychophysiological measurements, and neuroimaging techniques can be employed (Cowan, 2005). To understand the computer anxiety and mood changes associated with gaming, psychosomatic indicators used in the research areas of mental and emotional stress such as cardiovascular arousal and endocrine responses (Jin, 1992) can be used for the validation of psychological scales. Also, an issue of common interest is learners' selective attention while playing games. Interdisciplinary approaches that adopt methodologies from cognitive psychology and brain topology are suitable to determine the magnitude of interference by task-irrelevant distractors (Lavie, 2005). Along with the rapid expansion and progress of gaming studies, it is time for research projects that make use of interdisciplinary and cross-disciplinary approaches to be on the agenda.

CONCLUSION

An emerging research area usually contains a variety of research designs and instruments; this may lead to different findings and interpretations, as evident in some previously emerging areas (such as the arousal reduction effects of meditation and the psychological benefits of physical exercise). The topic of this chapter was to classify and examine some of the methodological issues in serious game research. Whereas there are excellent studies in the existing literature of simulations and games, it is not uncommon for some studies to adopt convenience samples or own-control designs. Studies on serious games tend to be conclusive if they have used true experimentation, well-controlled quasi-experimental design, surveys with representative samples and validated instruments, comprehensive design research, or training programs with pretest–posttest design with group comparisons. In addition, the potential values and informative contributions of using different methodologies for research in serious games should be recognized to establish ecological relevance. Future research on serious games should pay more attention to randomized sampling, controlled but feasible research design, validity of instruments, and appropriate analytical methods. Effort should be made to enhance the internal and external validity of educational research on serious games through interdisciplinary or cross-disciplinary research. It is hoped that this chapter can be helpful not only for future researchers in this field to design and execute rigorous projects but also for a wider readership to understand and evaluate research outcomes in the discipline of serious games.

REFERENCES

Adcock, A. B., & Van Eck, R. (2005). Reliability and factor structure of the Attitude Toward Tutoring Agent Scale (ATTAS). *Journal of Interactive Learning Research, 16*(2), 195–212.

American Psychiatric Association (APA). (1994). *Diagnostic and statistical manual of mental disorders* (4th ed.). Washington, DC: APA.

Anderson, C. A. (2004). An update on the effects of playing violent video games. *Journal of Adolescence, 27*, 113–122. doi:10.1016/j.adolescence.2003.10.009

Anderson, C. A., & Dill, K. E. (2000). Video games and aggressive thoughts, feelings, and behaviour on the laboratory and in life. *Journal of Personality and Social Psychology, 78*(4), 772–790. doi:10.1037/0022-3514.78.4.772

Ang, C. S., Zaphiris, P., & Mahmood, S. (2006). A model of cognitive loads in massively multiplayer online role playing games. *Interacting with Computers, 19*, 167–179. doi:10.1016/j.intcom.2006.08.006

Arbuckle, J. L. (2005). *Amos user's guide version 6.0*. Chicago, IL: Smallwaters Corporation.

Army, U. S. (2002). America's Army. [computer game]. U.S. Army (PC). http://www.americasarmy.com/

Astleitner, H., & Wiesner, C. (2004). An integrated model of multimedia learning and motivation. *Journal of Educational Multimedia and Hypermedia, 13*, 3–21.

Barab, S. A., Thomas, M., Dodge, T., Carteaux, R., & Tuzun, H. (2005). Making learning fun: *Quest Atlantis*, a game without guns. *Educational Technology Research and Development, 53*(1), 86–107. doi:10.1007/BF02504859

Barlett, C. P., Vowels, C. L., Shanteau, J., Crow, J., & Miller, T. (2009). The effect of violent and non-violent computer games on cognitive performance. *Computers in Human Behavior, 25*, 96–102. doi:10.1016/j.chb.2008.07.008

Biddle, S. J. H., Fox, K. R., Boutcher, S. H., & Faulkner, G. (2000). The way forward for physical activity and the promotion of psychological well-being. In Biddle, S. J. H., Fox, K. R., & Boutcher, S. H. (Eds.), *Physical activity and psychological well-being* (pp. 145–168). London: Routledge.

Bird, K. D. (1975). Simultaneous contrast testing procedures for multivariate experiments. *Multivariate Behavioral Research, 10*, 343–352. doi:10.1207/s15327906mbr1003_7

Bird, K. D., & Hadzi-Pavlovic, D. (1983). Simultaneous test procedures and the choice of a test statistic in MANOVA. *Psychological Bulletin, 93*, 167–178. doi:10.1037/0033-2909.93.1.167

Blizzard Entertainment. (2004). *World of Warcraft* [computer game]. Irvine, CA: Blizzard Entertainment.

Bollen, K. A. (1989). *Structural equations with latent variables*. New York: John Wiley.

Burgos, D., Fernández-Manjón, B., & Richards, G. (2008). Special issue: Electronic games and personalised elearning processes [Editorial]. *Computers in Human Behavior, 24*, 2475–2476. doi:10.1016/j.chb.2008.03.008

Byrne, B. M. (1989). *A primer of LISREL–Basic applications and programming for confirmatrory factor analytic models*. New York: Springer-Verlag.

Carbonaro, M., Cutumisu, M., Duff, H., Gillis, S., Onuczko, C., Siegel, J., & Waugh, K. (2008). Interactive story authoring: A viable form of creative expression for the classroom. *Computers & Education, 51*, 687–707. doi:10.1016/j.compedu.2007.07.007

Charness, G., Fréchette, G. R., & Qin, C. (2007). Endogenous transfers in the Prisoner's Dilemma game: An experimental test of cooperation and coordination. *Games and Economic Behavior, 60*, 287–306. doi:10.1016/j.geb.2006.10.010

Chou, C., & Tsai, M. (2007). Gender differences in Taiwan high school students' computer game playing. *Computers in Human Behavior, 23*, 812–824. doi:10.1016/j.chb.2004.11.011

Ciavarro, C., Dobson, M., & Goodman, D. (2008). Implicit learning as a design strategy for learning games: *Alert Hockey. Computers in Human Behavior, 24*, 2862–2872. doi:10.1016/j.chb.2008.04.011

Clark, R. C., & Mayer, R. (2008). *E-learning and the science of instruction: Proven guidelines for consumers and designers of multimedia learning* (2nd ed.). San Francisco, CA: John Wiley.

Cleary, P. J. (1986). L.I.V.: R.I.P.?: Comments on Myrtek and Foerster's "The law of initial value: A rare exception.". *Biological Psychology, 22*, 279–284. doi:10.1016/0301-0511(86)90031-1

Coleman, D. W. (2002). On foot in SIM City: Using SIM COPTER as the basis for an ESL writing assignment. *Simulation & Gaming, 33*, 217–230. doi:10.1177/1046878102332010

Conrad, A. M., & Munro, D. (2008). Relationships between computer self-efficacy, technology, attitudes and anxiety: Development of the *Computer Technology Use Scale* (CTUS). *Journal of Educational Computing Research, 39*(1), 51–73. doi:10.2190/EC.39.1.d

Cook, T. D., & Campbell, D. T. (1979). *Quasi-experimentation: Design & analysis issues for field setting*. Boston: Houghton Mifflin.

Cordova, D. L., & Lepper, M, R. (1996). Intrinsic motivation and the process of learning: Beneficial effects of contextualization, personalization, and choice. *Journal of Educational Psychology, 88*(4), 715–730. doi:10.1037/0022-0663.88.4.715

Cowan, N. (2005). *Working memory capacity*. New York: Psychology Press. doi:10.4324/9780203342398

Creswell, J. W. (2007). *Quality inquiry and research design: Choosing among five approaches* (2nd ed.). Thousand Oaks, CA: Sage.

Creswell, J. W. (2008). *Educational research: Planning, conducting, and evaluating quantitative and qualitative research* (3rd ed.). Upper Saddle River, NJ: Pearson Education.

de Freitas, S., & Jarvis, S. (2007). Serious games–engaging training solutions: A research and development project for supporting training needs. *British Journal of Educational Technology, 38*(3), 523–525. doi:10.1111/j.1467-8535.2007.00716.x

de Jong, T. (2006). Computer simulations: Technological advances in inquiry learning. *Science, 312*(5773), 532–533. doi:10.1126/science.1127750

de Jong, T., van Joolingen, W. R., Ehmke, T., Savelsbergh, E. R., Lazonder, A. W., & Manlove, S. A. (2003). *Co-Lab - collaborative laboratories for Europe*. Paper presented at the Tenth Biennial Conference of the European Association for Research in Learning and Instruction, Padova, Italy.

Dempsey, J. V., Haynes, L. L., Lucassen, B. A., & Casey, M. S. (2002). Forty simple computer games and what they could mean to educators. *Simulation & Gaming, 33*, 157–168. doi:10.1177/1046878102332003

Dempsey, J. V., & Johnson, R. B. (1998). The development of an *ARCS Gaming Scale*. *Journal of Instructional Psychology, 25*(4), 215–221.

Dempsey, J. V., & Van Eck, R. (2003). Modality and placement of pedagogical adviser in individual interactive learning. *British Journal of Educational Technology, 34*(5), 585–600. doi:10.1046/j.0007-1013.2003.00352.x

DeVellis, R. F. (2003). *Scale development: Theory and applications* (2nd ed.). Thousand Oaks, CA: Sage.

Dill, K. E., Brown, B. P., & Collins, M. A. (2008). Effects of exposure to sex-stereotyped video game characters on tolerance of sexual harassment. *Journal of Experimental Social Psychology, 44*, 1402–1408. doi:10.1016/j.jesp.2008.06.002

Dipietro, M., Ferdig, R. E., Boyer, F., & Black, E. W. (2007). Towards a framework for understanding electronic educational gaming. *Journal of Educational Multimedia and Hypermedia, 16*(3), 225–248.

DreamWorks Interactive. (1999). *Medal of Honor* [Computer game]. Redwood City, CA: Electronic Arts.

Elsmore, T. (1994). Synwork1: A pc-based tool for assessment of performance in a simulated work environment. *Behavior Research Methods, Instruments, & Computers, 26*, 421–426.

Folkins, C. H., & Sime, W. E. (1981). Physical fitness training and mental health. *The American Psychologist, 36*, 373–389. doi:10.1037/0003-066X.36.4.373

Garner, R., Gillingham, M. G., & White, C. S. (1989). Effects of seductive details on macroprocessing and microprocessing in adults and children. *Cognition and Instruction, 6*(1), 41–57. doi:10.1207/s1532690xci0601_2

Garris, R., Ahlers, R., & Driskell, J. E. (2002). Games, motivation, and learning: A research and practice model. *Simulation & Gaming, 33*, 441–467. doi:10.1177/1046878102238607

Goodwin, C. (2000). Action and embodiment with situated human interaction. *Journal of Pragmatics, 32*, 1489–1522. doi:10.1016/S0378-2166(99)00096-X

Graetz, K. A. (1995). Experimental gaming made simple: A review of social dilemmas. *Contemporary Psychology: A Journal of Reviews, 40*, 309–310.

Green, C. S., & Bavelier, D. (2003). Action video game modifies visual selective attention. *Nature*, *423*, 534–537. doi:10.1038/nature01647

Greenfield, P. M. (1994). Video games as cultural artifacts. *Journal of Applied Developmental Psychology*, *15*, 3–12. doi:10.1016/0193-3973(94)90003-5

Guberman, S. R., & Saxe, G. B. (2000). Mathematical problems and goals in children's play of an educational game. *Mind, Culture, and Activity*, *7*(3), 201–216. doi:10.1207/S15327884MCA0703_08

Hahne, A. K., Benndorf, R., Frey, P., & Herzig, S. (2005). Attitude towards computer-based learning: Determinants as revealed by a controlled interventional study. *Medical Education*, *39*, 935–943. doi:10.1111/j.1365-2929.2005.02249.x

Hämäläinen, R., Oksanen, K., & Häkkinen, P. (2008). Designing and analysing collaboration in a scripted game for vocational education. *Computers in Human Behavior*, *24*, 2496–2506. doi:10.1016/j.chb.2008.03.010

Harel, I., & Papert, S. (1990). Software design as a learning environment. *Interactive Learning Environments*, *1*(1), 1–32. doi:10.1080/1049482900010102

Hayduk, L. A., & Glaser, D. N. (2000). Jiving the four-step, waltzing around factor analysis, and other serious fun. *Structural Equation Modeling*, *7*(1), 1–35. doi:10.1207/S15328007SEM0701_01

Hill, J. O., & Peters, J. C. (1998). Environmental contributions to the obesity epidemic. *Science*, *280*, 1371–1374. doi:10.1126/science.280.5368.1371

Holmes, D. S. (1987). The influence of meditation versus rest on physiological arousal: A second examination. In West, M. A. (Ed.), *The psychology of meditation* (pp. 81–103). Oxford: Clarendon Press.

Horwitz, P., & Christie, M. A. (2000). Computer-based manipulatives for teaching scientific reasoning: An example. In Jacobson, M. J., & Kozma, R. B. (Eds.), *Learning the sciences of the 21st century: Research, design, and implementing advanced technology learning environments* (pp. 163–191). Mahwah, NJ: Lawrence Erlbaum Associates.

Huitema, B. E. (1980). *The analysis of covariance and alternatives*. New York: Wiley.

Hutchins, E. (1995). *Cognition in the wild*. Cambridge, MA: MIT Press.

Jennings, J. R. (1987). Editorial policy on analyses of variance with repeated measures. *Psychophysiology*, *24*, 474–475. doi:10.1111/j.1469-8986.1987.tb00320.x

Jin, P. (1992). Toward a reconceptualization of the law of initial value. *Psychological Bulletin*, *111*(1), 176–184. doi:10.1037/0033-2909.111.1.176

Jones, C. (2007). Enterprise education: The frustration of a pure contest. *Education + Training*, *48*, 596–604. doi:10.1108/00400910710834030

Jöreskog, K. G. (1993). Testing structural equation models. In Bollen, K. A., & Long, J. S. (Eds.), *Testing structural equation models* (pp. 294–316). Newbury Park, CA: Sage.

Jöreskog, K. G., & Sörbom, D. (1993). *LISREL 8: Structural equation modeling with the SIMPLIS command language*. Chicago: Scientific Software International.

Karakus, T., Inal, Y., & Cagiltay, K. (2008). A descriptive study of Turkish high school students' game-playing characteristics and their considerations concerning the effects of games. *Computers in Human Behavior*, *24*, 2520–2529. doi:10.1016/j.chb.2008.03.011

Kay, M. (1997). On playing in the group. *Group Analysis*, *30*, 173–186. doi:10.1177/0533316497302003

Kebritchi, M., & Hirumi, A. (2008). Examining the pedagogical foundations of modern educational computer games. *Computers & Education, 51*, 1729–1743. doi:10.1016/j.compedu.2008.05.004

Keller, J. M. (1987). Strategies for stimulating the motivation to learn. *Performance and Instruction, 26*(8), 1–7. doi:10.1002/pfi.4160260802

Kim, Y., & Baylor, A., & PALS Group. (2006). Pedagogical agents as learning companions: The role of agent competency and type of interaction. *Educational Technology Research and Development, 54*(3), 223–243. doi:10.1007/s11423-006-8805-z

Kirova, A. (2006). A game-playing approach to interviewing children about loneliness: Negotiating meaning, distributing power, and establishing trust. *The Alberta Journal of Educational Research, 52*(3), 127–147.

Lavie, N. (2005). Distracted and confused?: Selective attention under load. *Trends in Cognitive Sciences, 9*(2), 75–82. doi:10.1016/j.tics.2004.12.004

Lee, Y. B., & Lehman, J. D. (1993). Instructional cueing in hypermedia: A study with active and passive learners. *Journal of Educational Multimedia and Hypermedia, 2*(10), 25–37.

Lemmens, J. S., & Bushman, B. J. (2006). The appeal of violent video games to lower education aggressive adolescent boys from two countries. *Cyberpsychology & Behavior, 9*, 639–941. doi:10.1089/cpb.2006.9.638

Lepper, M. R., & Cordova, D. (1992). A desire to be taught: Instructional consequences of intrinsic motivation. *Motivation and Emotion, 16*(3), 187–208. doi:10.1007/BF00991651

Lepper, M. R., & Malone, T. W. (1987). Intrinsic motivation and instructional effectiveness in computer-based education. In Snow, R. E., & Farr, M. J. (Eds.), *Aptitude, learning, and instruction: III. Conative and affective process analyses* (pp. 255–296). Hillsdale, NJ: Erlbaum.

Lewin, K. (1946). Action research and minority problems. *The Journal of Social Issues, 2*, 34–46.

Lewis, M., Weber, R., & Bowman, N. D. (2008). "They may be pixels, but they're my pixels:" Developing a metric of character attachment in role-playing video games. *Cyberpsychology & Behavior, 11*(4), 515–518. doi:10.1089/cpb.2007.0137

Lim, C. P. (2008). Global citizenship education, school curriculum and games: Learning mathematics, English and science as a global citizen. *Computers & Education, 51*, 1073–1093. doi:10.1016/j.compedu.2007.10.005

Lord, F. M. (1967). A paradox in the interpretation of group comparison. *Psychological Bulletin, 68*, 304–305. doi:10.1037/h0025105

Lord, F. M. (1969). Statistical adjustments when comparing preexisting groups. *Psychological Bulletin, 72*, 336–337. doi:10.1037/h0028108

Lord, F. M. (1975). Lord's paradox. In Anderson, S. B., & Murphy, R. T. (Eds.), *Encyclopaedia of educational evaluation* (pp. 232–236). San Francisco, CA: Jossey-Bass.

Low, R. (this volume). Examining motivational factors in serious educational games. In Van Eck, R. (Ed.), *Interdisciplinary models and tools for serious games: Emerging concepts and future directions*. Hershey, PA: IGI Global.

Low, R., & Sweller, J. (2005). The modality principle in multimedia learning. In Mayer, R. E. (Ed.), *The Cambridge handbook of multimedia learning* (pp. 147–158). New York: Cambridge University Press.

Lowrie, T. (2005). Problem solving in technology rich contexts: Mathematics sense making in out-of-school environments. *The Journal of Mathematical Behavior, 24*, 275–286. doi:10.1016/j.jmathb.2005.09.008

Lucas, K., & Sherry, J. L. (2004). Sex differences in video game play: A communication-based explanation. *Communication Research, 31*, 499–523. doi:10.1177/0093650204267930

Maxwell, S. E., & Bray, J. H. (1986). Robustness of the quasi *F* statistic to violations of sphericity. *Psychological Bulletin, 5*, 149–165.

Mayer, R., Mautone, P., & Prothero, W. (2002). Pictorial aids for learning by doing in a multimedia geology simulation game. *Journal of Educational Psychology, 94*(1), 171–185. doi:10.1037/0022-0663.94.1.171

Mayer, R. E. (2005). Introduction to multimedia learning. In Mayer, R. E. (Ed.), *The Cambridge handbook of multimedia learning* (pp. 1–16). New York: Cambridge University Press.

Meredith, W. (1993). Measurement invariance, factor analysis and factorial invariance. *Psychometrika, 58*(4), 525–543. doi:10.1007/BF02294825

Midgley, C., Maehr, M., Hicks, L., Roeser, R., Urdan, T., & Anderman, E. (1997). *Patterns of adaptive learning survey (PALS)*. Ann Arbor, MI: University of Michigan.

Miller, M. D., & Rainer, R. K. (1995). Assessing and improving the dimensionality of the computer anxiety scale. *Educational and Psychological Measurement, 55*(4), 652–657. doi:10.1177/0013164495055004013

Moreno, R., & Mayer, R. (2000). Engaging students in active learning: The case for personalised multimedia messages. *Journal of Educational Psychology, 92*(4), 724–733. doi:10.1037/0022-0663.92.4.724

Moreno, R., Mayer, R. E., Spires, H. A., & Lester, J. C. (2001). The case for social agency in computer-based multimedia learning: Do students learn more deeply when they interact with animated pedagogical agents? *Cognition and Instruction, 19*, 177–214. doi:10.1207/S1532690XCI1902_02

Myrtek, M., & Foerster, F. (1986a). The law of initial value: A rare exception. *Biological Psychology, 22*, 227–237. doi:10.1016/0301-0511(86)90028-1

Myrtek, M., & Foerster, F. (1986b). Rejoinder to Cleary's Comments on Myrtek and Foerster's 'The law of initial value: A rare exception.'. *Biological Psychology, 22*, 285–287. doi:10.1016/0301-0511(86)90032-3

Naval Air Systems Command of USA. (2003). Bottom Gun. [computer game]. Patuxent River, MD: The Naval Air Systems Command (NAVAIR) of USA.

Olson, C. K. (2004). Media violence research and youth violence data: Why do they conflict? *Academic Psychiatry, 28*(2), 144–149. doi:10.1176/appi.ap.28.2.144

Pajitnov, A., & Gerasimov, V. (1984). *Tetris*. Moscow: The Dorodnicyn Computing Centre of the Academy of Science of the USSR.

Palaigeorgiou, G. E., Siozos, P. D., Konstantakis, N. I., & Tsoukalas, I. A. (2005). A computer attitude scale for computer science freshmen and its educational implications. *Journal of Computer Assisted Learning, 21*, 330–342. doi:10.1111/j.1365-2729.2005.00137.x

Pannese, L., & Carlesi, M. (2007). Games and learning come together to maximise effectiveness: The challenge of bridging the gap. *British Journal of Educational Technology, 38*(3), 438–454. doi:10.1111/j.1467-8535.2007.00708.x

Parker, L. E., & Lepper, M. R. (1992). The effects fantasy contexts on children's learning and motivation: Making learning more fun. *Journal of Personality and Social Psychology, 62*, 625–633. doi:10.1037/0022-3514.62.4.625

Perotti, V. J., & Pray, T. F. (2002). Integrating visualization into the modeling of business simulations. *Simulation & Gaming, 33*(4), 409–424. doi:10.1177/1046878102238605

Peters, C. S., & Malesky, L. A. (2008). Problematic usage among highly-engaged players of massively multiplayer online role playing games. *Cyberpsychology & Behavior, 11*(4), 481–484. doi:10.1089/cpb.2007.0140

Pintrich, P. R., Smith, D., Garcia, T., & McKeachie, W. (1993). Predictive validity and reliability of the *Motivated Strategies for Learning Questionnaire* (MSLQ). *Educational and Psychological Measurement, 53*, 801–813. doi:10.1177/0013164493053003024

Pratto, F., Pearson, A. R., Lee, I., & Saguy, T. (2008). Power dynamics in an experimental game. *Social Justice Journal, 21*, 377–407. doi:10.1007/s11211-008-0075-y

Price, C. B. (2008). Unreal PowerPoint: Immersing PowerPoint presentations in a virtual computer game engine world. *Computers in Human Behavior, 24*, 2486–2495. doi:10.1016/j.chb.2008.03.009

Pruitt, D. G., & Kimmel, M. L. (1977). Twenty years of experimental gaming: Critique, synthesis, and suggestions for the future. *Annual Review of Psychology, 28*, 363–392. doi:10.1146/annurev.ps.28.020177.002051

Quaisser-Pohl, C., Geiser, C., & Lehmann, W. (2006). The relationship between computer-game preference, gender, and mental-rotation ability. *Personality and Individual Differences, 40*, 609–619. doi:10.1016/j.paid.2005.07.015

Raybourn, E. M. (2007). Applying simulation experience design methods to creating serious game-based adaptive training systems. *Interacting with Computers, 19*, 206–214. doi:10.1016/j.intcom.2006.08.001

Reese, D. D. (2007). First steps and beyond: Serious games as preparation for future learning. *Journal of Educational Multimedia and Hypermedia, 16*, 283–300.

Rieber, L. P. (2005). Multimedia learning in games, simulations, and microworlds. In Mayer, R. E. (Ed.), *The Cambridge handbook of multimedia learning* (pp. 549–567). New York: Cambridge University Press.

Roth, W. (2009). Emergence of analogies in collaboratively conducted computer simulations. In Zheng, R. (Ed.), *Cognitive effects of multimedia learning* (pp. 340–361). Hershey, PA: IGI Global.

Rubin, D. B. (1974). Estimating causal effects of treatments in randomized and nonrandomized studies. *Journal of Educational Psychology, 66*, 688–701. doi:10.1037/h0037350

Rubin, D. B. (1977). Assignment to treatment group on the basis of a covariate. *Journal of Educational Statistics, 2*, 1–26. doi:10.2307/1164933

Satwicz, T., & Stevens, R. (2008). Playing with representations: How do kids make use of quantitative representations in video games? *International Journal of Computers for Mathematical Learning, 13*, 179–206. doi:10.1007/s10758-008-9138-2

Schafer, J. L., & Kang, J. (2008). Average causal effects from nonrandomized studies: A practical guide and simulated example. *Psychological Methods, 13*(4), 279–313. doi:10.1037/a0014268

Shadish, W., Cook, T., & Campbell, D. (2002). *Experimental and quasi-experimental designs for generilized causal inference*. Boston: Houghton Mifflin.

Spencer-Oatey, H. (2007). e-learning initiatives in China: Pedagogy, policy and culture. Hong Kong: Hong Kong University Press.

Squire, K. (2006). From content to context: Videogames as designed experience. *Educational Researcher*, *35*(8), 19–29. doi:10.3102/0013189X035008019

Starbuck, W. H., & Kobrow, E. (1966). The effects of advisors on business game teams. *The American Behavioral Scientist*, *10*(3), 28–30. doi:10.1177/000276426601000305

Sun, D., Ma, N., Bao, M., Chen, X., & Zhang, D. (2008). Computer games: A double-edged sword? *Cyberpsychology & Behavior*, *11*(5), 545–548. doi:10.1089/cpb.2007.0145

Sweller, J. (1988). Cognitive load during problem solving: Effects on learning. *Cognitive Science*, *12*(1), 257–285.

Sweller, J., & Chandler, P. (1994). Why some material is difficult to learn. *Cognition and Instruction*, *12*(3), 185–233. doi:10.1207/s1532690xci1203_1

Tabachnick, B. G., & Fidell, L. S. (2001). *Using multivariate statistics* (4th ed.). Boston: Allyn & Bacon.

Tahiroglu, A. Y., Celik, G., Uzel, M., Ozcan, N., & Avci, A. (2008). Internet use among Turkish adolescents. *Cyberpsychology & Behavior*, *11*(5), 537–543. doi:10.1089/cpb.2007.0165

Taylor, A. (2000). Physical activity, anxiety, and stress. In Biddle, S. J. H., Fox, K. R., & Boutcher, S. H. (Eds.), *Physical activity and psychological well-being* (pp. 10–45). London: Routledge.

Tejeiro, S. R. A., & Morán, B. R. M. (2002). Measuring problem video game playing in adolescents. *Addiction (Abingdon, England)*, *97*, 1601–1606. doi:10.1046/j.1360-0443.2002.00218.x

Thompson, B. (2004). *Exploratory and confirmatory factor analysis: Understanding concepts and applications*. Washington, DC: American Psychological Association. doi:10.1037/10694-000

Thompson, N., & McGill, T. J. (2008). Multimedia and cognition: Examining the effect of applying cognitive principles to the design of instructional materials. *Journal of Educational Computing Research*, *39*(2), 143–159. doi:10.2190/EC.39.2.c

Van Eck, R. (2006). The effect of contextual pedagogical advisement and competition on middle-school students' attitude toward mathematics and mathematics instruction using a computer-based simulation game. *Journal of Computers in Mathematics and Science Teaching*, *25*(2), 165–195.

Van Eck, R. (2007). Six ideas in search of a discipline. In Shelton, B., & Wiley, D. (Eds.), *The educational design and use of computer simulation games*. Boston, MA: Sense.

Van Eck, R., & Dempsey, J. (2002). The effect of competition and contextualized advisement on the transfer of mathematics skills in a computer-based instructional simulation game. *Educational Technology Research and Development*, *50*(3), 23–41. doi:10.1007/BF02505023

Van Haneghan, J. P., & Hickey, D. (1993). *Higher order analyses of children's beliefs about mathematics.* Poster session presented at the biennial meeting of the Society for Research in Child Development. New Orleans, LA.

van Joolingen, W. R., & de Jong, T. (2003). *SimQuest*, authoring educational simulations. In Murray, T., Blessing, S., & Ainsworth, S. (Eds.), *Authoring tools for advanced technology learning environments: Toward cost-effective adaptive, interactive, and intelligent educational software* (pp. 1–31). Dordrecht: Kluwer.

Vasey, M. W., & Thayer, J. F. (1987). The continuing problem of false positives in repeated measures ANOVA in psychophysiology: A multivariate solution. *Psychophysiology, 34*, 479–486. doi:10.1111/j.1469-8986.1987.tb00324.x

Vinacke, W. E. (1969). Variables in experimental games: Toward a field theory. *Psychological Bulletin, 71*, 293–318. doi:10.1037/h0026972

Vogel, J. S., Vogel, D. S., Cannon-Bowers, J., Bowers, C. A., Muse, K., & Wright, M. (2006). Computer gaming and interactive simulations for learning: A meta-analysis. *Journal of Educational Computing Research, 34*(3), 229–243. doi:10.2190/FLHV-K4WA-WPVQ-H0YM

Vygotsky, L. S. (1962). *Thought and language*. Cambridge, MA: MIT Press. doi:10.1037/11193-000

Wainer, H. (1991). Adjusting for differential base rates: Lord's Paradox again. *Psychological Bulletin, 109*, 147–151. doi:10.1037/0033-2909.109.1.147

Wang, T. (2008). Web-based quiz-game-like formative assessment: Development and evaluation. *Computers & Education, 51*, 1247–1263. doi:10.1016/j.compedu.2007.11.011

Wei, R. (2007). Effects of playing violent videogames on Chinese adolescents' pro-violence attitudes, attitudes toward others, and aggressive behavior. *Cyberpsychology & Behavior, 10*, 371–382. doi:10.1089/cpb.2006.9942

Weisberg, H. I. (1979). Statistical adjustment and uncontrolled studies. *Psychological Bulletin, 86*, 1149–1164. doi:10.1037/0033-2909.86.5.1149

Westwood Studios. (2008). *Command & Conquer: Red Alert 2* [computer game]. Las Vegas: Westwood Studios.

White, B., Frederiksen, J., Frederiksen, T., Eslinger, E., Loper, S., & Collins, A. (2002). *Inquiry Island: Affordances of a multi-agent environment for scientific inquiry and reflective learning.* Paper presented at the Proceedings of the Fifth International Conference of the Learning Sciences (ICLS), Mahwah, NJ: Erlbaum.

Wiener, D. J. (1999). Rehearsal for growth: Applying improvisational theatre games to relationship therapy. In Weiner, D. J. (Ed.), *Beyond talk therapy: Using movement and expressive techniques in clinical practice* (pp. 165–180). Washington, DC: American Psychological Association. doi:10.1037/10326-008

Zhong, C., Loewenstein, J., & Murnighan, J. K. (2007). Speaking the same language: The cooperative effects of labeling in the prisoner's dilemma. *The Journal of Conflict Resolution, 51*(3), 431–456. doi:10.1177/0022002707300834

Zizzo, D. J., & Tan, J. (2007). Perceived harmony, similarity and cooperation in 2 × 2 games: An experimental study. *Journal of Economic Psychology, 28*, 365–386. doi:10.1016/j.joep.2006.06.008

"MUST-READS" FOR THIS TOPIC

Cook, T. D., & Campbell, D. T. (1979). *Quasi-experimentation: Design & analysis issues for field setting*. Boston: Houghton Mifflin.

Creswell, J. W. (2007). *Quality inquiry and research design: Choosing among five approaches* (2nd ed.). Thousand Oaks, CA: Sage.

Creswell, J. W. (2008). *Educational research: Planning, conducting, and evaluating quantitative and qualitative research* (3rd ed.). Upper Saddle River, NJ: Pearson Education.

DeVellis, R. F. (2003). *Scale development: Theory and applications* (2nd ed.). Thousand Oaks, CA: Sage.

Jöreskog, K. G. (1993). Testing structural equation models. In Bollen, K. A., & Long, J. S. (Eds.), *Testing structural equation models* (pp. 294–316). Newbury Park, CA: Sage.

Tabachnick, B. G., & Fidell, L. S. (2001). *Using multivariate statistics* (4th ed.). Boston: Allyn & Bacon.

TOP TEXTS FOR INTERDISCIPLINARY STUDIES OF SERIOUS GAMES

Adcock, A. B., & Van Eck, R. (2005). Reliability and factor structure of the Attitude Toward Tutoring Agent Scale (ATTAS). *Journal of Interactive Learning Research, 16*(2), 195–212.

Anderson, C. A., & Bushman, B. J. (2002). The effects of media violence on society. *Science, 295*, 2377–2379. doi:10.1126/science.1070765

de Freitas, S., & Jarvis, S. (2007). Serious games–engaging training solutions: A research and development project for supporting training needs. *British Journal of Educational Technology, 38*(3), 523–525. doi:10.1111/j.1467-8535.2007.00716.x

de Jong, T. (2006). Computer simulations: Technological advances in inquiry learning. *Science, 312*(5773), 532–533. doi:10.1126/science.1127750

Dempsey, J. V., Haynes, L. L., Lucassen, B. A., & Casey, M. S. (2002). Forty simple computer games and what they could mean to educators. *Simulation & Gaming, 33*, 157–168. doi:10.1177/1046878102332003

Green, C. S., & Bavelier, D. (2003). Action video game modifies visual selective attention. *Nature, 423*, 534–537. doi:10.1038/nature01647

Low, R., & Sweller, J. (2005). The modality principle in multimedia learning. In Mayer, R. E. (Ed.), *The Cambridge handbook of multimedia learning* (pp. 147–158). New York: Cambridge University Press.

Mayer, R., Mautone, P., & Prothero, W. (2002). Pictorial aids for learning by doing in a multimedia geology simulation game. *Journal of Educational Psychology, 94*(1), 171–185. doi:10.1037/0022-0663.94.1.171

Satwicz, T., & Stevens, R. (2008). Playing with representations: How do kids make use of quantitative representations in video games? *International Journal of Computers for Mathematical Learning, 13*, 179–206. doi:10.1007/s10758-008-9138-2

Van Eck, R. (2007). Six ideas in search of a discipline. In Shelton, B., & Wiley, D. (Eds.), *The educational design and use of computer simulation games*. Boston, MA: Sense.

Chapter 8
Evaluating Video Game Design and Interactivity

Matthew J. Sharritt
Situated Research, LLC, USA

ABSTRACT

An emergent, bottom-up construction of video game interaction is presented, drawing from influences in ethnomethodology (Garfinkel, 1967), grounded theory (Glaser & Strauss, 1967), and activity theory (Cole & Engeström, 1993; Kaptelinin & Nardi, 2006; Vygotsky, 1978). Following, a qualitative case study highlights the use of affordances, or potentials for action, during video game player interaction among peers and the game interface. Relationships among affordances and levels of activity are presented, which broaden the concept of affordances to include motivations. Additionally, activity theory will complement analysis by introducing the mediational triangle (Cole & Engeström, 1993), providing a guide with which to analyze game player interactions and motives. The mediational triangle sheds light on the motivated activity itself, the tools available to complete the activity, and peer relationships (such as role specialization and rules of interaction) to evaluate game designs and their ability to fulfill serious purposes with meaningful outcomes.

INTRODUCTION

Research shows that video games can provide a rich experience while providing game players the ability to navigate a virtual world, in which complex decision making and the management of complex issues might resemble the cognitive processes that they would employ in the real world (Ducheneaut, Yee, Nickell, & Moore, 2006; Federation of American Scientists, 2006; Squire, 2005; Stokes, 2005). Literature suggests that games provide a rich learning context in which gamer strategizing and the management of complex problems can foster creative thinking skills and show players how their decisions have dynamic outcomes (Squire, 2005; Stokes, 2005; Zyda, 2005). Additionally, gamers can experience social learning through group membership and leadership situations in order to

DOI: 10.4018/978-1-61520-719-0.ch008

Copyright © 2010, IGI Global. Copying or distributing in print or electronic forms without written permission of IGI Global is prohibited.

achieve goals within a game (Foreman et al., 2004; Socially Intelligent Agents at CARTE, 2006; Zyda, 2005).

Flow (Csikszentmihalyi, 1990) can be used to describe a feeling of captivation and immersion in a game. However, negative flow can be experienced by a disturbance in the environment or a disturbance to one's concentration caused by a poorly designed interface (errors, lack of feedback, etc.), in line with Norman's (1988) idea of technological affordances and good interface design. In line with the concept of representational guidance (Suthers, 2001; Suthers & Hundhausen, 2003), a game interface can serve to both constrain and promote particular game player actions. The research presented in this chapter will examine ways in which game interface designs can affect game player motivation and create the potential for discussion among peers that lead to instances of learning. By studying these interactions, patterns in game use can assist in the design and evaluation of games by providing both a method for analysis and a frame to approach game player interaction, by taking an open-ended look at what happens as games are played.

Game designers have the burden of creating valuable gaming experiences through their designs. Serious games adds additional complexity to game design, requiring that some sort of serious outcome be served by playing the game, with intended outcomes serving purposes such as learning, civics, business, military, or health rehabilitation. Focusing analysis on patterns of interaction with game representations could aid game designers by evaluating what is most effective in serving those serious goals. Serious game design involves many tradeoffs such as balancing fidelity with fun, balancing story with action, and balancing learning with motivation.

This descriptive analysis of the use of video games in educational contexts can inform both game design and sound pedagogy by improving the game content and interface, as well as by aiding in the design of instructional content and learning curricula. Kirriemuir & McFarlane (2004) discuss the need for further research that investigates collaborative learning in the use of gaming environments to support learning:

The value of collaborative learning and the role of computers in promoting such activity have been thoroughly researched.... How this collaboration translates into a multiplayer gaming environment and how these environments might be used to support learning, remain some of the most interesting areas for potential further research and development. (Kirriemuir & McFarlane, 2004, p. 27)

This chapter will present an emergent, bottom-up, descriptive methodology to the qualitative analysis of video game interaction. This approach can inform serious game design by providing a detailed description of game player interaction, which can show the effectiveness of designed in-game representations such as icons, behaviors, and activities that serve to either assist or hinder action and goal formation. First, literature relevant to the method will be described, drawing from ethnomethodology (Clayman & Maynard, 1995; Garfinkel, 1967), grounded theory (Charmaz, 2006; Glaser & Strauss, 1967), and activity theory (Kaptelinin & Nardi, 2006; Leontiev, 1978; Vygotsky, 1978). Second, an interaction analysis of game player interaction will be presented through a case study, providing a deep analysis of game player interaction among peers and the game interface. This emergent analysis will use the concept of affordances, or potentials for action, as a common abstract concept for approaching game player activity, looking at both cognitive and social interactions. Following, activity theory (Cole & Engeström, 1993; Kaptelinin & Nardi, 2006; Leontiev, 1978; Vygotsky, 1978, 1979, 1981) will be described and applied to the case study to illustrate its power in analyzing video game play and used to further compare findings (this is done following the inductive phase in order to avoid biasing the prior bottom-up, emergent analysis).

The three levels of activity (Leontiev, 1978) and affordances found on those levels will be described, and the mediational triangle of activity theory will be applied to an interaction analysis of video game play to draw attention to relationships among the game, its players, and social groups associated with the game and its play. Features of activity theory will be compared with the results of an analysis of affordances during game player interactions to describe how the concept of affordances can be broadened beyond mere actions to incorporate game player motivations. Examples from the case study included here will illustrate the application of the mediational triangle and the three activity levels, showing how they can highlight the use of specific game features while revealing other missing features. This analysis will shed light on game player motivations and intentions and also help to inform the design and evaluation of serious video games.

BACKGROUND

Several fields have played a part in the qualitative analysis of video games described in this chapter. The theory of affordances, originally from ecological psychology (Gibson, 1977, 1979), has seen much use in the field of human–computer interaction (e.g. Nielsen, 1994; Norman, 1988). Ethnomethodology (Clayman & Maynard, 1995; Garfinkel, 1967; Heritage, 1987; Koschmann, Stahl & Zemel, 2005) and grounded theory (Charmaz, 2006; Glaser & Strauss, 1967) have helped inspire the open-ended approach that will be described, giving guidelines to help us construct an unbiased interpretation of the situation being studied. Additionally, activity theory (Cole & Engeström, 1993; Kaptelinin & Nardi, 2006; Leontiev, 1978; Vygotsky, 1978, 1979, 1981) provides our open-ended analysis with additional relationships to analyze, serving to expand our concept of affordances and to expand the cognitive and social interactions being observed. While activity theory has a significantly different theoretical background and is typically not considered in an emergent methodology, its power will be illustrated through a case study in conjunction with the other methods described in this section.

Emergence and Open-Ended Constructions of Activity

There is a strong emphasis in the literature on the learning outcomes of serious games, but emergent outcomes based upon ongoing game player interactions are just as important. The running debate on narratology vs. ludology, for example, pits two sides against each other, with ludologists arguing for the playful experience that emerges from interaction with a game and narratologists focusing on the story of the game. One can see the value of both perspectives in this process regarding serious games. Product outcomes (e.g., content-based learning) can be viewed as the result of a kind of narrative, but process outcomes (e.g., problem solving, collaboration) are more akin to ludic elements of gameplay. Therefore, we need to develop methods of design and evaluation that can be applied to the formative, emergent aspects of gameplay. Research in ethnomethodology and grounded theory can provide valuable tools for this process, including the analysis of affordances and application of activity theory.

This chapter will propose a hybrid method for an open-ended, emergent construction of game player activity. Inspiration from two different qualitative, interpretive fields of study will guide the first portion of analysis. Ethnomethodological principles (Garfinkel, 1967) inspire the open-ended, emergent, bottom-up approach that guides the first portion of the case study. Ethnomethodology, not to be confused with ethnography, is a sociological discipline (many are familiar with the most common subfield of ethnomethodology called conversation analysis). Grounded theory is a qualitative, inductive method for abstracting patterns in data, or "discovery of theory from data" (Glaser & Strauss, 1967, p. 1), which is not "based on a preconceived theoretical framework" (Glaser & Strauss, 1967, p. 45). Grounded theory will be incorporated as a tool for abstracting patterns in data in order to generalize to other situations (Charmaz, 2006; Glaser & Strauss, 1967). This idea is referred to as *emergence*, as theories emerge from the data, rather than going into the study with a predefined hypothesis to test. According to Clayman and Maynard (1995), there are several key points to an ethnomethodological perspective: it is concerned with the construction of "social order," or the way in which members of a social group create meaning in their social interactions, and follows a "bottom-up" approach, where the researcher constructs events by observing the natural flow of social actions in the environment being studied while avoiding a priori definitions or expectations of what is being studied, recovering "social organization as an emergent achievement that results from the concerted efforts of societal members acting within local situations" (p. 2).

Koschmann et al. (2005) present an updated and concise application of Garfinkel's policies (Garfinkel, 1967) for the purpose of video analysis, which is summarized by Sharritt & Suthers (2009):

A priori definitions of learning were avoided in order to follow the ethnomethodological principle of relevance, which requires that explanatory constructs be relevant to (or compatible with) participants' own accounts of their activity, rather than imposed by the analyst. The policies of contingently achieved accomplishment and indexicality describe how the process of ongoing activity by group members is contextually embedded. Actions are sequential and are both context-building and context-shaped, serving to construct social order. Data analysis (of videotaped student game play) was influenced by this principle as it suggested that analysis should shed light on how group members build context and accomplish learning through their activity. (p. 7)

Ethnomethodological policies focus on the situation being studied, which limits the generalizability of our findings, as socially constructed order is contingently achieved in the situation in which it occurs. Grounded theory seeks generalizable patterns in our observations and is an emergent, bottom-up construction of activity that can be applied to game player interaction. While inspired by ethnomethodology, grounded theory is a complementary method that can help to seek generalizable findings among interactions within serious games.

Glaser & Strauss (1967) describe grounded theory as a "general method of comparative analysis" (p. 1). The researcher makes constant comparisons of ideas while studying the data, looking for themes or "theoretical categories" (Glaser & Strauss, 1967, p. 23–24) and constantly reevaluating those categories (taking advantage of replication to test those ideas). This reevaluation is accomplished through *theoretical sampling*, or "the process of data collection for generating theory whereby the analyst jointly collects, codes and analyzes his data and decides what data to collect next and where to find them, in order to develop his theory as it emerges" (Glaser & Strauss, 1967, p. 45).

Grounded theory relies on the human brain as a pattern-matching tool, placing responsibility on the researcher to recognize similar events elsewhere in gathered data. In practice, and in this case study, the researcher often needs to recursively review data until patterns begin to emerge and similarities in observant behavior can be seen among several different instances. Grounded theory follows a process of *abduction*, which is a combination of an inductive and deductive process: inductive findings (as previously described) can be deductively tested (through the process of *theoretical sampling*). "Repeated review of data reveals regularities that might not be apparent at first, including regularities that would be missed if investigation were limited to coding criteria determined in advance, an option that is also discouraged by ethnomethodology's principle of relevance" (Sharritt & Suthers, 2009, p. 8). Grounded theory provides a framework of seeking inductive generalizations, while ethnomethodology inspires our open-ended, emergent theoretical approach to studying game player interaction. When studying ongoing, in-game interactions within serious games, these methods can aid researchers in discovering patterns in game interface use that reveal the effectiveness of underlying game designs for serious purposes.

Affordances and Levels of Activity

In studying ongoing interactions among gamers, peers, and the game interface, the concept of *affordances* provides an abstract term to operationalize for this study. Affordances are simply potentials for action provided to an actor by the environment. Gibson (1977, 1979) took an ecological perspective in defining affordances and focused the term affordances at the operational level. Gibson's perspective looks at an actor (or animal) in its environment, focusing on potentials for immediate operation (actions) with things visible in the environment. Donald Norman helped to popularize the idea of affordances in his seminal work *The Design of Everyday Things,* one of the foundations of human–computer interaction (HCI) research. Alternatively, Norman (1988) describes an affordance as:

the perceived and actual properties of the thing, primarily those fundamental properties that determine just how the thing could possibly be used.... Affordances provide strong clues to the operations of things. Plates are for pushing. Knobs are for turning. Slots are for inserting things into. Balls are for throwing or bouncing. When affordances are taken advantage of, the user knows what to do just by looking: no picture, label, or instruction needed. (p.9)

The original concept of an affordance (Gibson 1977, 1979) is an ecological theory of perception, describing an affordance as something that can be directly perceived (affording action at a physical, operational level). On the other hand, Norman (1988) discusses affordances with technology in mind, considering an actor's cultural and historical background, stating that affordances are 'perceived properties' of an object. With regard to computer software, Norman suggests that well designed interfaces "provide strong clues to the operation of things" (Norman, 1988, p. 9) and "suggest the range of possibilities" (Norman, 1988, p. 82). Debate exists on whether affordances can exist independently of perception, emphasizing that affordances are properties of an object (e.g., studies by McGrenere & Ho, 2000). However, emphasis in this paper accepts the original Gibsonian viewpoint, which requires an actor's perception of the action potentials for an object. Kaptelinin & Nardi (2006) support the perceptible requirement of affordances, stating that "affordances are a property of interaction between an animal and the world," and therefore "an animal cannot engage an affordance without perception" (p. 81).

Affordances are potentials for action residing in the relationship between an actor and an object, where an object might offer different affordances for different actors. In the case study later in the chapter the use of both elements of the game interface and peers (objects) by video game players (actors) are examined. These action potentials created by the game assist in the analysis of serious games, as these ongoing interactions (and choices among game players) can help in evaluating a game, as they provide insight into a game's ability to make particular in-game actions salient to game players.

Activity Theory and Affordance Levels

As outlined in Kaptelinin and Nardi (2006), activity theory supports the idea that human ac-

Table 1. Levels of activity (Adapted from Kaptelinin & Nardi, 2006, p. 8–83.)

Activity Level	*Accounts for motivation and cultural–historical meaning to be assigned to objects, supporting the overall objectives, motives, and gratifications of the user*
Action Level	*An actor using his or her capabilities and the tools available to perform a task in the environment (satisfying goals)*
Operational Level	*Concerned with the "objects at hand," typically part of a sequence of tasks that supports an objective (at the physical level: direct manipulation, usability, etc.)*

tivity is hierarchically organized. In relation to affordances, this differs slightly from Gibson's original ecological theory of perception, as affordances can occur on different levels: on the operational level, on the action level, and on the activity level. Activity theory extends the original concept of affordances to support human activity as a whole. Table 1 includes a brief description of these levels:

The activity theory description of affordances will not limit findings; rather, it will be applied in conjunction with the open-ended approach outlined in ethnomethodology and grounded theory to expand earlier definitions of affordances (such as those by Gibson and Norman) to fully support human activity (including activity-level motivations). The three levels of affordances highlight relationships between the actor and the environment (objects with which they are interacting) that might have been overlooked otherwise and serve to expand the notion of affordances while guiding analysis.

Representational Guidance

Conversely, while examining the action potentials (affordances) provided to an actor in his or her environment, we must also recognize the constraints introduced by the environment that guide activity. The concept of *representational guidance* addresses this idea and is very useful when applied to software and video game design. Suthers (2001) outlines two major sources of influence: how an interface can help to guide interaction (salience) and how it can serve to constrain activity. Sharritt and Suthers (2009) describe representational guidance when applied to video game analysis:

First, the environment constrains the expressive acts that are possible, as the representational notation offers a (deliberately) limited set of objects and potential actions (Stenning & Oberlander, 1995). Similarly, games might guide action by providing a constrained set of action potentials. Second, representational artifacts constructed in a visual notation make particular aspects and interpretations of the represented information prominent, possibly while hiding others (Larkin & Simon, 1987). Similarly, games might aid gamers by making certain aspects of the game state salient. (p. 29–30)

Oliver and Pelletier (2005) also consider how the design of in-game representations can influence player activity and learning. Their findings suggest that by indicating to game players that "distinct objects are of the same type (obey the same game rules) so that they will be able to transfer strategies learnt for one class of object to other related instances" (Oliver & Pelletier, 2005, p. 12). This learning strategy was encountered by game players frequently during analysis.

Collaborative behavior and work can also be influenced by in-game representations. Suthers and Hundhausen (2003) identify three ways in which representations can guide collaborative activity, as summarized in Sharritt and Suthers (2009):

First, when two persons need to decide how to act jointly on an environment, the visible potentials for action (perceived affordances) may influence the options that are considered and negotiated: there are negotiation potentials. Second, representations that result from participants' negotiation and coordinated action hold meanings for those participants that may not be apparent to others not involved in their production. These meanings may be invoked by reference (e.g., by deixis or pointing) to appropriate elements of the representation: they are private referential resources. Third, the orientation of each participation towards the current environment (e.g., their physical orientation or their locus of activity) provides clues to the other participants concerning that actor's attentional and intentional state: the representations support implicit awareness. Suthers and Hundhausen (2003) compared differences in collaborative discourse between participants using software tools supporting the same task but through different notations (text, graph, and matrix-based). Their results demonstrate "that the type of representations that learners use in collaborative investigations will impact the focus of their discourse" (Suthers & Hundhausen, 2003, p. 202). Similarly, the designed visual and behavioral features of games, particularly the ways in which they make affordances and game state visible, can influence the interaction between gamers. (p. 30)

Our analyses describe how game representations can guide individual action as well as collaborative activity, serving to highlight the need for game designers to consider the affordances provided by designed in-game representations and their associated behaviors when creating serious games (examining both the usability and the functionality of the designed representations). As previously argued, these affordances can be supported at various levels of activity (Kaptelinin & Nardi, 2006; Leontiev, 1978) to support operations, actions, and motivations of game players, especially in the presence of intended outcomes such as those associated with serious games.

The Evolution of Activity Theory

Kaptelinin & Nardi (2006) introduce activity theory, citing Leontiev's (1978) concept of an activity as being concerned with the relationship between subject and object. Activity theory stems from cultural–historical psychology (Cole & Engeström, 1993; Kaptelinin & Nardi, 2006; Leontiev, 1978; Vygotsky, 1978) and Russian psychology (Leontiev's first studies were supervised by Vygotsky, who in turn had drawn the concept of activity from Basov). In activity theory, a motivated activity is the most basic unit of analysis. Leontiev claims that properties of the subject and object only appear during the activity itself and that the activity is the key source of development for both subject and object. Human activity serves to gratify needs, both biological and psychological. Leontiev describes the true motive of an activity as "the most important attribute differentiating one activity from another" and that when "a need becomes coupled with an object, an activity emerges… from that moment on, the object becomes a motive and the need not only stimulates but also directs the subject" (Kaptelinin & Nardi, 2006). Activity theory presents an interesting model with which to examine the mediational role of video games among students playing games in educational contexts.

Cultural–Historical Actviity Theory (CHAT)

Blending Vygotskian cultural–historical psychology with Leontiev's activity theory, Cultural–Historical Activity Theory (CHAT) concerns itself with the relationship of the individual mind with that of society by examining the relationship between subject, object, and mediating artifact. Cole & Engeström (1993) extend this basic mediational triangle, adding the social aspects of community,

Figure 1. The basic mediational triangle (left) and expanded mediational triangle (right), adding community, social rules, and the division of labor. (Adapted from Cole & Engeström, 1993, p. 5-8)

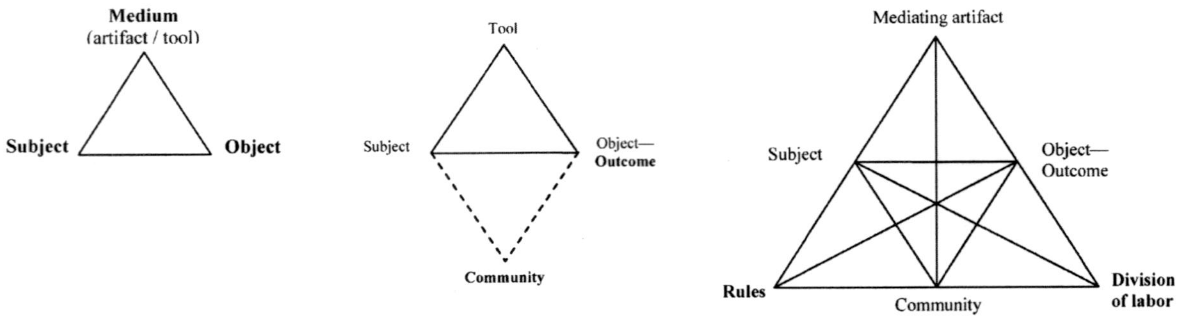

rules, and division of labor and the object–outcome link, as seen in Figure 1.

Originally, the focus of activity theory was on the link between subject and object (Leontiev, 1978). This subject-object relationship was mediated by a tool, as represented by the vertex of the first triangle in Figure 1. Later, Engeström expanded the concept of activity by adding community, linking activity between subject, object, and community, as shown in the middle of Figure 1. Additionally, a clarification of the object was made which stressed the motivational purpose of the object in reaching some outcome (thus engaging in the "motivated activity" discussed by Leontiev).

These relationships are mediated: tools (mediating artifact) mediate between subject and object (as described by Leontiev, 1978); rules mediate between subject and community; and division of labor (roles) mediates between community and object. Figure 2 shows all relationships, focusing on serious games in educational settings:

Several of the different mediational roles of tools, rules, and roles exploring relationships between subject, community, and object are useful when studying serious games. The mediational triangle can help explain patterns of interaction among game players during collaborative gameplay. These mediational relationships can help

Figure 2. Game setting using activity theory's mediational triangle. (Adapted from Cole & Engeström, 1993, p. 8)

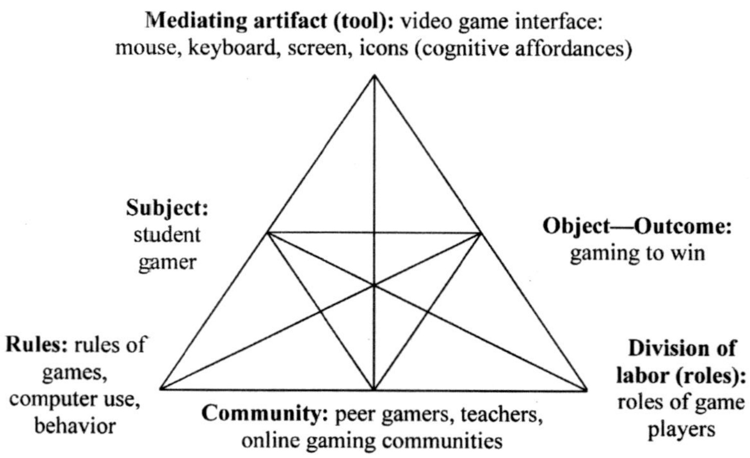

in the evaluation of serious games by examining particular interactions among game players, peers, and game interfaces. When studying collaborative play and interaction, the discussion of the expanded mediational triangle is useful (shown in Figure 2) for analyzing group behavior. Cole & Engeström (1993) provide the diagrams in Figure 1 as a means for studying their main unit of analysis: a motivated activity. This is particularly useful for studying computer-mediated activity and can be applied as a descriptive tool when analyzing collaborative video game play. Pairs of links in Figure 2 can be analyzed to examine mediational roles (of the item at the vertex of the links, i.e., how rules mediate between subject and community), providing a good conceptual diagram with which to frame activities and evaluate serious games. These internal mediational triangles will be described and applied later in the chapter.

The roles of subjects, objects, and community can be analyzed by examining the mediating artifacts, rules, and division of labor. With a focus on gaming, it is possible to analyze students, gaming to win, and the student gamer community by examining the video game interface and its cognitive affordances, the rules of computer game play and computer use, as well as the roles of game players playing the game. Cole & Engeström (1993) add an object–outcome link (see middle of Figure 1) that focuses on the outcomes expected by the object through the motivated activity: something very important for evaluating serious games, since outcomes are intentional and of high importance.

Methodology

A true ethnomethodological approach would reject the top-down, theory-driven approach required by activity theory. However, activity theory highlights relationships during game player interactions and provides a framework for game player activity. Activity theory, when applied in conjunction with an emergent approach, can both broaden our concept of affordances and remind us to look for action potentials on various activity levels and does not necessarily have to constrain findings by introducing preconceptions.

Our methodological stance initially accepts the anti-theory-driven approach of ethnomethodology, avoiding the bias of preconceptions to our analysis. Ethnomethodology, while bound to the specific situation being studied and typically not seeking of patterns in observations, can be a very useful starting point for the analysis of game player activity in order to reveal the underlying, commonly overlooked social assumptions, language, and developed context of game-player participants. Grounded theory can then help construct patterns and generalizations from our initially open-ended approach. In conjunction, ethnomethodology and grounded theory can help discover emerging patterns in serious game play that are very insightful in understanding interactions within a serious context. As a final step, activity theory can be incorporated recursively to highlight relationships and motivations that might have been initially overlooked. While this process becomes partially theory-driven in the end, it also allows us to obtain some of the benefits of initially using an open-ended ethnomethodologically inspired approach. This approach can help construct a context-relevant, open-ended, indexical representation of game player activity, which is crucial to understanding interactions within serious games and their associated outcomes.

CASE STUDY: ANALYZING VIDEO GAME PLAY IN EDUCATIONAL CONTEXTS

The design of in-game representations can create affordances that lead to certain game player behaviors, which can help maintain motivation to play. The approach drawing from ethnomethodology, grounded theory, and activity theory (outlined above) can be used to evaluate a serious game's ability to motivate and engage game players. For example, by following usability heuristics and limiting the quantity of affordances (Nielsen, 1994; Norman, 1988), game designers can assist game players in choosing an appropriate task, serving to maintain flow (Csikszentmihalyi, 1990) in the game. Activity theory provides a tool with which to study collaborative interactions in a serious game's context, which can inform game design by highlighting patterns of use in situated environments (Gee, 2003; Sharritt, 2009; Stevens, Satwicz & McCarthy, 2008). Particular game representations can support motivations by helping to guide game player objectives by giving salience to objects and constraining action (Suthers & Hundhausen, 2003) for game players. Examining affordances among interactions and using activity theory to highlight relationships can help designers create engaging games that yield serious and meaningful outcomes.

The true test of a theory's value lies in its application. Accordingly, the following section will describe a case study that examined several contemporary video games' potential for learning. An emergent, open-ended construction of activity influenced by ethnomethodology and grounded theory (the approach described above) was employed in order to describe game player interaction and collaboration. Emphasis was placed on ways in which learning occurs during collaborative game play in an educational setting, with a broad definition of learning as "any change in behavior as a result of experience."

Method

Three video games were selected for the case study (selection criteria are mentioned in the following section). Literature suggests that group phenomena require three or more participants (Wiley & Jensen, 2006). Additionally, learning may also result from between-dyad as well as within-dyad interaction (similar to what occurs in classrooms). Therefore, games were played collaboratively by dyads (pairs of two students) using a single computer. For each game, two dyads situated side by side played the game (four students playing with two per computer, similar to Figure 3). Students participated in only one of the games (four new students were obtained for each of the three games) and participation occurred over four study periods of approximately 50 minutes each.

Figure 3. Study configuration and potentials for interaction

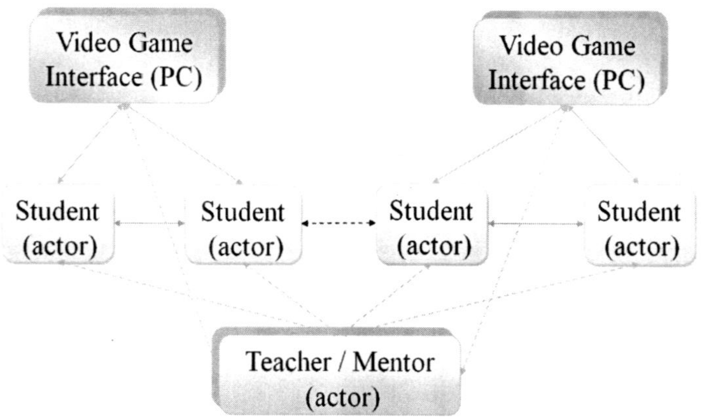

Orange = interaction with interface; blue = interaction among peers; red = interaction among peer group
solid line = most common interactions; dotted line = secondary interactions

The logic of the study is the inverse of an experiment: rather than holding all but one variable constant to see what co-varies with that variable, the study allows many variables to change (the games and the participants) to identify what stays constant (recurring patterns of behavior) that can be postulated as inductive generalizations.

Game Selection

Three games were chosen[1] for this study to compare and contrast across game subjects and game design types: *RollerCoaster Tycoon 3* (Atari, 2004), *Civilization IV* (Firaxis, 2005), and *Making History: The Calm and the Storm* (Muzzy Lane, 2007). Much was learned from the analysis of these games, and the cumulative effort and hard work of those involved in their design was evident. Preference was given to games with quality graphics, gameplay, and a well-designed interface. Additionally, games containing a blend of entertainment and educational content within subjects that correlated with formal schooling subjects were sought, which contained moderate levels of strategy development to encourage immersion and collaborative game play. Games with low levels of violence and an absence of foul language or sexually themed content were chosen (ESRB rating of "E" for everyone, age 10+).

The three games selected were strategically chosen because of their excellent presentation and potential for learning and to generalize among differing game subjects and types. Both *RollerCoaster Tycoon 3* and *Civilization IV* are *COTS* (commercial off-the-shelf games), while *Making History* was developed for educational use. *Making History* and *Civilization IV* can be applied in history classes (*Making History* focuses on World War II, while *Civilization IV* focuses on world history). In contrast, *RollerCoaster Tycoon 3* is applicable to business classes such as Economics or Marketing since it enables the creation of products and services and the managing of finances (such as balancing supply and demand). Additionally, the three games vary in complexity, with *Civilization IV* being the most complex game of the three. This allows generalizations during analysis to be made across COTS and games designed for educational use, between games of varying complexity, and between subjects (history vs. business).

Data-Gathering Procedure

Interactions were recorded on a widescreen video camera, and a complete video record of the groups was made. Each dyad was recorded with the camera angle showing the back of players' heads and the computer screen in order to observe in-game actions as well as gestures and body language. For each game, both dyads were recorded, which allowed between-dyad communication and collaboration to be observed. Additionally, clip-on microphones were wired into the left and right channels of the video camera for quality audio recording of dialogue.

While difficult to seat two students per computer, the choice was made to videotape gameplay in dyads in order to elicit both collaborative and competitive behaviors among students, and to record the increased verbosity of students who are engaged in an activity together. As described in Linn & Burbules (1991), collaborative play can result in situations where students must verbalize and discuss their beliefs, which can lead to a higher frequency of challenges by peers and teachers. This interaction can in turn lead to learning through cognitive dissonance (Festinger, 1957), socio-cognitive conflict (Doise & Mungy, 1984), or other mechanisms of collaborative learning (Dillenbourg, Baker, Blayne & O'Malley, 1996; Slavin, 1990). Collaborative play can also lead to a significant increase in physiological arousal as well as a sense of presence and identification in nonviolent games (Lim & Lee, 2007). In this study, two dyads per game were used so that interdyadic collaboration could be recorded as well (similar to what might occur when classrooms of students are involved if games are integrated into curricula).

Each game was played over four periods of approximately 50 minutes each, allowing slightly over 3 hours of gameplay per dyad to be recorded (two dyads per game; three games).

Participants

Students at two Chicago-area suburban high schools participated in the study. Teachers assisted with student selection, and students of both genders were chosen based on their willingness to participate and the authorization of their parents. In accordance with the game subjects mentioned, students from relevant, corresponding courses were chosen to participate: students enrolled in related history courses were chosen to play *Making History* and *Civilization IV*, while students enrolled in a related business course (Advanced Marketing) were chosen to play *RollerCoaster Tycoon 3*. This allowed the participating students and teachers to apply and reinforce some concepts from their coursework in the game, and vice versa.

Analysis

The Transana™ system was used to conduct the analysis of the gathered videotape. Transana supports transcription of video, labeling pieces of video with keywords, and the development of collections of related video clips to support an idea. Transcription was done using Jeffersonian transcript notation (Jefferson, 1984), as suggested and supported by the Transana software. Jeffersonian notation annotates differences in intonation, speed, pauses, and overlapping speech in the transcripts, which assists in the evaluation of participant intentions and the abstraction of patterns in the data.

Analysis followed the emergent method described previously, using an inductive, qualitative approach influenced by ethnomethodology, grounded theory and activity theory, requiring many passes over recorded video until patterns emerged. With approximately 24 hours of gathered videotape, significant data reduction was required, and the most frequently occurring patterns of learning were chosen and qualified for further analysis. These patterns were chosen by recursively reviewing the gathered video, with over 100 clips averaging a few minutes each qualifying. While this data reduction limits findings, it was required in order to conduct a deep analysis of game player interaction in the selected episodes.

Analysis was conducted in two phases: the first phase illustrated properties of the learning episodes as a whole, while the second phase described a detailed interaction analysis (Jordan & Henderson, 1995) of affordances used in those episodes discovered in the first phase. Analysis followed grounded theory's process of iteration, where focused coding helped in sorting and saturating theoretical categories to create hypotheses based on patterns in the video.

This paper focuses on the second phase of analysis. However, an overview of the first phase of analysis follows, describing properties of the episodes of learning (which are further analyzed in the second phase) discovered from the open-ended stance to learning (Sharritt, 2008). Some key findings include Sharritt, 2008:

Learning was observed at different granularities, occurring either as a short episode, a sequence of short episodes, or a trend spread over time. Trends were often observed in a moderately used game feature whose complexity and use increased over time. Short episodes and sequences of episodes often followed problematization, where pairs discovered a problem and pursued a task, followed by the problem's later resolution (when the task was successfully completed).

Learning appeared at several levels: learning the physical interface (the high school students in the study have already mastered using a computer and its physical interface); learning to use the game interface (the basic usage of the game interface, including icons, objects, etc., and their corre-

sponding functionality); and learning advanced strategies required to win the game (behavior in line with achieving goals set forth by both the game itself and game players, aimed at achieving something in the game such as winning or fulfilling other gratifications).

Learning often appeared to be triggered by social peers or by particular game features.

These factors added motivation and shifted attentional focus to another aspect of the game, which often lead to instances of learning. Failures often served to draw the attention of the students and motivated them to work on tasks related to that failure, suggesting that failure can be used as a tool in games to promote learning. However, there were examples where failures hindered interest and task pursuit when negative conditions existed, such as the lack of feedback from the game or the experience of repetitive failure. Failure can either positively or negatively impact learning, depending on the nature of the failure being experienced by students. (p. 34–35)

An expanded explanation of findings are presented in Sharritt (2008), and a detailed discussion will be avoided; however, the many discovered properties of the learning episodes serve to both frame and create opportunities for the second phase of analysis. Following will describe results of the second phase of analysis, involving a detailed interaction analysis of the affordances of gameplay interaction and collaboration, along with relationships highlighted by activity theory.

Results and Discussion of Findings

Analysis examined the use of affordances, through a sequential analysis of interaction (Jordan & Henderson, 1995). Video episodes are "chunked" into segments, as logical pieces of transcripts. These pieces are a few lines of transcript (of an episode) at a time. Transcripts are separated into chunks based on the sequence of interaction among participants while engaged in collaborative game play.

Two questions aided the discovery of interactional trajectories and the use of affordances while conducting this portion of the analysis:

1. How do teammates' individual trajectories play off each other while engaged in collaborative game play?
2. How do game representations influence the possibilities for action?

These questions assisted in revealing relevant features of the episode by focusing on what the pair was engaged in doing and achieving by examining the evolution of students' conversations, how conversational and attentional interactions flowed in collaborative game play, and what the game interface makes available for use in comparison to what was actually used by the group. This information can provide game designers with feedback on the effectiveness of their designed in-game representations based on actual game player patterns of use, helping them to creating situations that are effective in achieving serious purposes.

Additionally, convergence was examined: whether pairs appeared to be grounded (on the same page; making a concerted effort) or whether they appeared to be on their own train of thought. Ethnomethodological principles of *indexicality* and the *social construction of order* are especially relevant, as they examine ways in which context and understanding are built through the unfolding of interactions among participants. By breaking down game player interactions, serious games can be evaluated to determine the salience of affordances in the game, based on choices (actions) and behaviors (utterances and nonverbal communication) made by game players.

Overview of Findings

Findings from the second phase of analysis indicate that students used affordances provided by the game interface and learning environment in their accomplishments. Those findings specifically include the following:

- The visual representations of games afford particular actions.
- The persistent display of historical context as well as present and future potentials motivates learning.
- Specific cues can grab attention, helping to focus efforts on new or underutilized game tasks.
- Consistent and well-organized visualizations encourage learning.
- Information presented in a plurality of channels is most effective for learning.

The use of social peers in collaborative learning had several effects on the learning process: peers disclosed information to achieve shared meaning of objects' purposes and collaboratively negotiated to select game strategies. Peer teams served a cooperative role as information sources and competitively as a performance gauge.

Several examples and corresponding transcripts will be presented later in the chapter that illustrate some of the study findings described above. In the following section, the mediational triangle of activity theory is compared with findings to illustrate its use in revealing potentials for interaction in game evaluation and design.

Maintaining Motivated Gameplay

Certain game representations and peer behaviors can help maintain motivation to play. Limiting the number of affordances can assist the choice of tasks and serve to maintain flow (Csikszentmihalyi, 1990). The design of game representations can add player motivation, giving salience to objects and constraining action (Suthers & Hundhausen, 2003), thereby aiding game player objectives and outcomes. Additionally, the investment of identity in a game (Gee, 2003) of game players assists in maintaining motivation among students engaged in collaborative game play.

The original concept of activity, as outlined by Vygotsky and Leontiev, is illustrated by the darkened internal triangle in Figure 4. The focus is on motivated game play, before the addition of community by Cole and Engeström (1993): see Figure 1 for an overview.

Figure 4. Mediation between students and object by game (tool). What tools (game affordances) does the subject use to satisfy the objective?

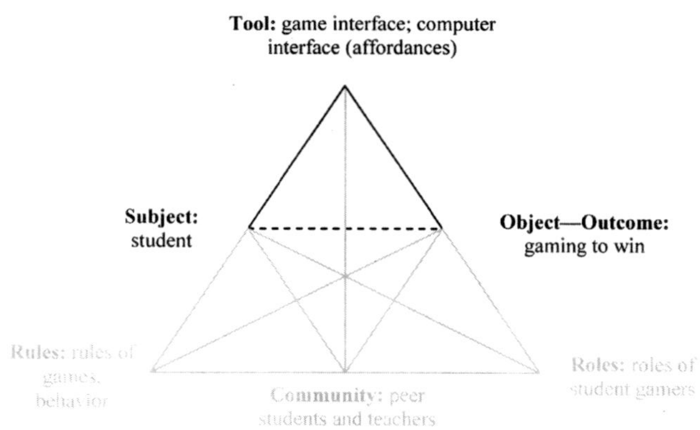

As the examples that follow describe, the game interface provides an object of reference by students in discussing their game activity, which will be discussed by illustrating other internal mediating triangles that involve community (peers, teachers, etc.). Particular game objects were used as resources (tools) in accomplishing goals in the game play. The nature of collaborative student interactions focused on the discussion about, and the subsequent use of, the tools provided by the game. By uncovering patterns of use and related discussions of in-game representations, we can evaluate the degree to which in-game affordances were understood by game players and how effectively those representations helped game players reach goals (and maintain motivated gameplay).

Maintaining Flow and Aiding Appropriation by Limiting Affordances

An example from *RollerCoaster Tycoon 3* illustrates how the design of in-game representations can maintain flow and motivation to play by limiting affordances. For those unfamiliar with the game, the player is given the opportunity to manage a virtual theme park containing rides, roller coasters, and other attractions such as food and restrooms. While building rides is entertaining, gameplay focuses both on turning a profit and customer satisfaction, as the game places much importance on both. The player can observe customers' behavior and read their thoughts as they experience the theme park and pay attention to financials (how much money to charge for rides, what to pay staff, and what profit the park is making as a whole). One must seek a delicate balance between all these factors, as customers will complain about and avoid expensive rides or leave the park if they become hungry or cannot find a bathroom.

Following, a transcript[2] of game player activity illustrates part of the process of building a ride in the theme park. The first episode includes some negotiation between students on what rides to build, how to customize them, and how to set the ride price.

L: ↑Let's just do um↑ (.5) [let's do] ((*Pulls up the ride list choices menu*))
R: [Water?]
L: ↑No. Let's do some uh↑-
R: Thrill rides, Junior Rides? ((*Reading options from 'Rides' menu*))
L: ((*Clicked on 'Junior Rides'*)) Yeah that's fine. Well there's only the one so
R: The Merry-Go-Round ((*Laughs*))
L: Yeah so we'll do that one like [here] ((*Clicks on Merry-Go-Round*))

Water rides, thrill rides, and junior rides are all different categories of rides to build in the theme park, represented by the first three icons on a ride submenu located on the left side of the screen. The first level of menus (icons) is persistent in *RollerCoaster Tycoon 3*, making them a persistent resource and potential for action, whereas the second level (submenu) of icons appears after clicking on a first-level icon.

The dyad decided to make a "Junior Ride" and then selected a "Merry-Go-Round" from a list of rides that appeared. Following ride selection, the dyad looked for an area in which to place the ride. In *RollerCoaster Tycoon 3*, the ride turns red when placement conflicts with other items on the map (or when not enough money exists) and turns blue when placement is satisfactory. When an object being placed is colored red, clicking the mouse will not result in placement, as placement is not possible. However, if the object is colored blue, clicking the mouse will place the object in the current location.

Immediately following ride placement, the game prompts for placement of ride entrances and exits, following the red and blue labeling. Each click will result in new menu visualizations popping up on the screen, creating an affordance for their exploration, discussion, and use. Selection of a ride results in the ride appearing in a blue container in the bottom left side of the screen (more ride options). After being placed, the ride appeared in the bottom-right corner of the screen (surrounded by icons for ride options), immediately followed by the appearance of a new box during entrance and exit placement (options for the ride entrance and exits). The affordance of sufficient object placement, signified by the blue and red (acceptable vs. unacceptable placement) appeared to be well understood by the students. Following, the dyad placed their ride and its entrance and exit booths:

((*Places the Merry-Go-Round in a clearing*))
R: [Yeah]
L: Is that cool?
R: Yeah that's good.
L: <And>
R: A path. (.5) What's that? Oh the booth to get in. ((*Ride entrance for the Merry-Go-Round appears*))
L: ((*Placed entrance to get into ride*)) °Yeah.°
L: ((*Placed ride exit*))
R: Exit booth and entering booth. Perfect.
L: ((*Clicked on 'Paths'*))((*Successfully connected the path from the entrance / exit to the main path*)) Cool.

At this point, the ride has been built and an entrance and exit have been placed. The dyad successfully connected the ride's entrance and exit to an adjacent footpath so customers could get to and from the ride. The process of placement appeared to be well understood. This suggests that the design of these in-game representations and behaviors created affordances that were understood by game players, serving to move them closer to achieving their goals in the game. When evaluating a serious game or other games played for a serious purpose, it is important to note that in-game activities and operations are successful and efficient at moving game players toward their overall objectives and motives for playing the game.

As mentioned, ride placement will create a ride menu in the lower-right corner of the screen. This appears as a picture of the ride, surrounded by icons that can customize the ride. The game seems to place this object on the screen in order to encourage ride customization. Selecting a ride later in the game (clicking on any ride) will result in a similar representation appearing in the lower-right corner of the screen, with options for customization appearing. This can prompt their exploration, discussion, and use (as revealed in the transcripts). With the ride selected, some of the ride options (icons) are explored in the ride menu:

R: [Is there any]
L: [Go on the Merry-Go-Round] Yeah I think people are getting on.
R: [What are] all these things mean? ((*Points to the ride options*)) Can we change them?
L: ((*Scrolls over the ride options*))
((*An explanation of each ride icon appears while scrolling over each icon*))
R: 'Test Results, open' Make sure it's open.
L: 'Not assessed yet.' ((*Reading ride status. Not yet assessed because it hasn't been tested*))
R: Go to.
L: °Vehicles.° ((*Clicked on the 'Colors' icon for the vehicles of the ride. A selection of colors popped up*))
R: All the colors of the ride. Oh that's cool. ((*Clicked on the 'Colors' icon*))
((*Changed the colors of the vehicles*))
L: °That's good.°

It is interesting to note how the game constrains activity in the process of building a ride. This appeared to assist the learning process by making salient particular features of the game. For instance, upon placing a ride, the game automatically launches the placement of entrances and exits, followed by automatically bringing up a ride customization menu. Once initiated, game play requires a sequence of related actions, one after another, in order to complete the process. This has benefits in reducing cognitive load (players are not required to memorize the sequence of building roller coasters or corresponding operations) and limiting potential actions at each step of the process. After placing a roller coaster in a theme park, the game automatically limits action by converting the mouse cursor into ride entrances and exits, with corresponding movement of the mouse serving to move the entrance or exit. This behavior affords particular action (placement) by limiting the actions possible. Limiting possible actions aids learner effectiveness by not overwhelming them with options. This is observed by less discussion and negotiation required by the dyad to proceed in the game. This helps to create flow by reducing the often-overwhelming array of affordances on the interface and focusing efforts on more specific actions.

Bringing in the affordance levels of activity theory (see Table 1), *RollerCoaster Tycoon 3* allows players to focus on goal achievement by making clearly understandable affordances at the operational level. Rather than focusing attention on the purpose of buttons or becoming lost in the individual operations required to build a ride, game players easily moved through the steps required in the process of building rides. This allowed them to focus their effort on action-level affordances, achieving specific actions and goals. Similarly, Norman's "Gulf of Execution" (Norman, 1988) addresses a similar concept: translating specific goals into meaningful action.

Supporting Activity with Relevant Action

In *Making History: The Calm and the Storm*, game players take on the role of a leader of a country during World War II. The game begins at a user-selected time (among various time points) during the war, with game players choosing from a list of countries that were historically active in World War II. Players control economic, political, and military decisions of the country they play. This is a very interesting simulation, as game players can alter the course of history by attempting different policies and decisions and seeing the outcome of those decisions. Of the dyads playing, many learned of the intricate relationships between policy, economy, and military: all dyads invoked similar initial strategies of creating military advances on many fronts, only to realize later that their economy and severed political alliances could not support their military. In other words, they spread themselves too thin, creating many battlefronts with not enough resources to win.

Before presenting an example comparing games' support of motivations by contrasting *RollerCoaster Tycoon 3* with *Making History*, a discussion of motivational-level affordances is revisited (see earlier section in the chapter titled *Activity Theory and Affordance Levels*). Previous examples illustrate both action-level and operational-level affordances: action-level affordances create a potential for interaction for game players to achieve their goals, and operational-level affordances are typically more physical in the sense that they are immediately perceptible operations that serve to assist game players in achieving a goal (such as the individual sequences mentioned in building a ride in *RollerCoaster Tycoon 3)*. However, examining motivations is an equally valuable exercise to consider, as it focuses on providing the means for achieving the broad game goals afforded by game play.

For example, in *RollerCoaster Tycoon 3*, a potential motivation to play the game (besides winning) is to become a successful theme park manager, which can be illustrated by making money. In *RollerCoaster Tycoon 3*, game objectives and motivations to play were well supported by affordances in its summary screens (the game contains several management screens that provide summaries of financials, staff, ride status, etc.). Motivations for playing the game (to manage a theme park) were well supported by action potentials available in the summary screens, each of which afforded management. Student game players made use of staff summary screens in order to manage their employees and were not required to make manual adjustments of employee properties. Alternatively, in *Making History: The Calm and the Storm*, pairs were required to micromanage their production (output) of individual cities. Manual adjustment of large quantities of information is a repetitive task that may hurt motivation to play, as demonstrated in the following transcript:

L: ((*Clicked on 'Production' of a city*))
((*Clicked 'Air Force'*))
((*Clicked on 'New Production Order'*))
((*Clicked on an Air Plane*))
((*Clicked on 'Production'*))
((*Production window popped up*))
((*Clicked on 'Air Force'*))
((*Clicked on Military*))
((*Clicked on 'New Production Order'*))
((*Clicked on 'Goods'*))
((*Clicked on 'Air Force'*))
((*Clicked on 'Fighters'*))
((*Clicked on 'New Production Order'*))
((*Clicked on three different areas of the map*))
((*Clicked on 'Production'*))
((*Clicked on 'Air Force'*))
((*Clicked on 'Bombers'*))
((*Clicked on 'New Production Order'*))

While not too much of a drain on the gameplay, the pair spent time adjusting the output of several cities to produce similar goods. The above episode highlights several things: the lack of discourse between participants, potentially highlighting boredom from the repetitive task, and the repetitive nature of changing the production orders of several cities to produce the same item. A summary screen could be beneficial, similar to what is seen in *RollerCoaster Tycoon 3*'s management screens, allowing easier management of game resources.

Providing Referential Resources for Collaboration

As previously described, winning while playing *Making History* involves making good decisions for the country the player simulates governing during World War II. The following example illustrates interdyadic communication early in game play, as one dyad overhears another dyad declaring war.

Peer 1: Declare war <on>
Peer 2: Do it (0.5) ha ha declare war.
L: ((*Scrolling through map*))
Peer 1: OK, we're declaring war on uh (0.5) on Britain here. >READY AND, GO!< We just declared war.
L: How did you [declare war?]
R: [↑How did you declare↑ war?]
Peer 2: No idea.
Peer 1: I don't know, we just clicked [International] =
L: Here you can try. ((*Mouse control traded from L to R*))
Peer 2: [Click the] middle button with like the piece of paper
L: ((*Followed the direction of the peer dyad; clicked on the Diplomacy (middle) button*))
Peer 1: = and it gave us the ability to go to war at the very bottom.

Both students appeared interested in the peer dyad's progress and were aware of what the other dyad was communicating and doing, affording the dyad an awareness of its peers. The dyad questioned its peers, used them as an information source to check its own progress, and then copied the peer dyad's strategy. Following peer direction, the dyad found the "Diplomacy" icon in the upper-right corner of the screen. Under the country name (the nation that the dyad was commanding), are five icons, which represent the game's major areas of focus and are *persistent icons* (they remain on every screen throughout the game). This property affords discussion among peers as indicated by the transcript. Next, the dyad initiates a war:

L: We don't have any °current wars°. ((*Reading from Diplomacy Screen*)) Oh, let's make some negotiations.
R: Select uh. (.5) Who should we select? ((*Clicked on 'Select Nation'*))
L: Let's get ↓uhh↓
R: Bhutan? ((*Laughs*))
L: ((*List of countries came up for the dyad to choose from*)) Let's get (.) Germany.
R: ((*The dyad selects Germany, which brings up a new menu of diplomatic options with Germany*))
((Mouse over 'Diplomatic Relations' buttons))

The representations and the terminology presented by the game create opportunities for discussion and influence strategic choices (L student reads to R student "current wars" and suggests "let's make some negotiations"). By offering lists of "current alliances" and "current wars" as well as "initiate diplomacy," the game interface affords goal selection to the game players, thereby reinforcing their motivations.

With the help of the peer dyad through the reference of a persistent resource, the dyad explores the diplomatic menu and examines options for peace treaties, alliances, and declaring war:

L: <Propose> (0.5) Should ((*Laughs*)) we declare war against them?
R: ((*Scrolls over 'Declare War' in the 'Diplomatic' menu choices*))
L: >NO NO, CHINA, CHINA< China, cuz they (.5) we need their oil.
R: Where the hell is China? ((*Clicks on 'X' button to return to previous screen*))
((*Clicks 'Select Nation', then clicks China*)) (1.0) So like, declare war against [China?] ((*Laughs*))
((*Clicked on 'Declare War' button*))
L: [Yeah I] don't know why. ((*Laughs*))
R: Cuz we need their oil. ((*Laughs*))
L: ((*Confirmed war against China*))

Negotiation occurred, changing the strategy to declare war on China. One of the students thought China was a good choice for war, justifying his choice of China because of their large supply of oil. While the game does not present information indicating China has oil, his reasoning for war seems clear: the conquest of countries with oil (coincidentally, the dyad was playing as the United States and invoked a diplomatic strategy of going to war for control of an oil-producing region).

The persistent icon in the game made it easily discussed between dyads. When the students asked the peer dyad how to declare war, the peer dyad responded with a brief description of the item's location followed by a summary of actions ("it gave us the option at the very bottom") rather than a detailed sequence of operations, allowing the peer dyad to figure out the rest of the procedure. This indicates that the brief instructions were sufficient to communicate, or the students would further question the peer dyad if needed.

Relating this example to the mediational triangle of activity theory (see Figure 5), one can see how the game interface (tool) can mediate between peers (community) and the dyad's goals (object: gaming to win), one of the internal mediating triangles with the "tool" being the triangle's vertex:

Game tools and representations (visualizations, behaviors, etc., of in-game objects) can provide a means of reference between peer dyads. Therefore, they are resources for discussion (a social affordance: they afford the social potential for discussion). This is explored in the previous transcript: students often used game-specific terminology ("click on the X button") to explain to teammates and peer teams how to accomplish actions in the game. As suggested by activity theory, the community (peer dyads or teachers)

Figure 5. Mediation between community and object by tool. How do the tools used affect the way the community meets objectives?

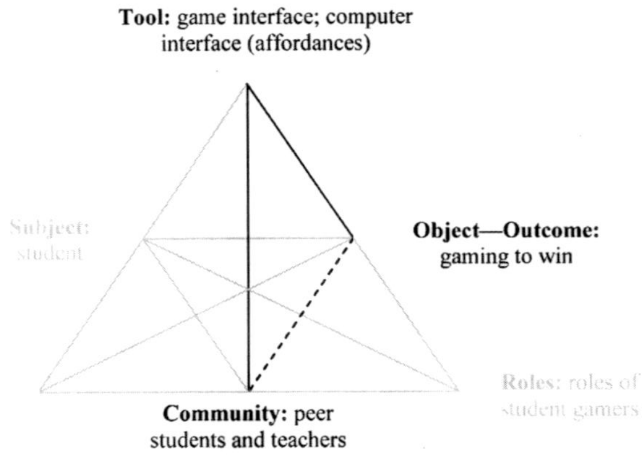

might reference persistent game items (tools: in this example, a persistent game icon) in explaining how to achieve goals or tasks. Persistent icons do not require specific operational knowledge, making them more easily discussed; however, other items are hidden (such as a game feature that only becomes available in a specific scenario),which makes their discussion and reference by community members more difficult. Generalizing away from this example, game designers may want to consider that the affordances of all game items should be relevant to the ways in which they are used. In this case, game designers made persistent the five key areas of the game, represented as five persistent icons. This persistence affords (simple) discussion by peers and promotes discovery and use of the icons.

Role Specialization in Dyadic Gameplay

So as not to bother peer teams too frequently, cooperative and competitive behaviors between the dyads occurred only several times per game. However, intradyadic discussions (with the student with whom they were playing the game) were an ongoing process. Disclosure of information was often the norm when learning how to use and control the game interface. Discussions often focused on communicating a sequence of actions to complete a task. Accordingly, most discussion of how to use something on the interface occurred frequently at the beginning of gameplay as the game interface was being learned. Pairs appeared to engage in a process of disclosure and negotiation while discovering the game interface in order to reach an agreed-upon meaning of the corresponding functionality.

The negotiation of game strategy was typical in collaborative gameplay. In forming goals and creating a game strategy, students appeared to feel the need to discuss strategy with their teammates before executing actions in the game to reach those goals. A social affordance of playing in dyads is to make use of teammates in the co-construction of goals and strategies. This behavior may be done out of politeness and respect for the teammate, as the game is being played together and should be a projection of both of their goals. The design of the study to play games collaboratively was intended to elicit this negotiation.

The following example from *Civilization IV* shows further discussion between participants in learning the game interface and the basic functionality of game objects during collaborative gameplay. In the following transcript, the left-hand person is in control of the computer (keyboard/mouse) and the right-hand person is explaining to the left-hand person his understanding of some of the game functionality, starting with the turn-based style of the game:

R: °Right click (.5) click (.5) borders expanded.° Like if you click on people and you tell them what to do, and you click Enter each time. Craig, what are you doing?
L: Zooming In. ((*Zooms in on map*))
((*Scrolling around map*))
¤<672751> (.)
R: Like, click on those people again. ((*Points to a group of workers*)) (.5) Now tell them where to go. And what to do. (.5) Why did we build a road?
L: ((*Clicked on the group of workers that R suggested*))
((*Clicked on 'Build Road' icon*)) I don't know. ((*Scrolls to bottom of map*)) So we can get through?
((*Clicks on open land*))
((*Workers move to new area*))
((*The workers start building the road*))
((*Laughs*)) See, now we can get through.
¤<695504> (.)
R: Press Enter.

Initially, the left-hand student was involved in his own train of thought and began to build a road. Following that, the right-hand student explained and questioned the left-hand student, attempting to gain shared meaning of the basic game control (turn-based style). The right-hand student properly infers the process of playing the game: giving actions to individual objects (the workers, scouts, military units, etc., on the map) and pressing "Enter" to advance the turn in the game. The left-hand student appeared somewhat distracted and he focused on the gameplay rather than his teammate. However, the right-hand student redirected the conversation back to his point by describing the turn-based style of the game.

After several attempts to explain his thoughts, it appears that his idea has been communicated. Basic game control was a major focal point of discussion, illustrated by the right-hand student repeatedly redirecting the conversation to the process of gameplay. Behavior demonstrated the desire for a higher degree of convergence (of creating shared meaning) when learning the game interface and corresponding functionality.

In *Civilization IV*, after assigning tasks to all characters, a flashing message appears at the bottom of the screen saying "Press <Enter> to end turn…" that prompts players to end their turn while informing them of the turn-based style of the game. Alongside the flashing message, there is a green circle that turns to flashing red after all moves have been completed (when it is time to end the turn), another indicator that can be clicked to successfully end the turn: an affordance that is quickly understood by game players.

Next, the pair attempts to move workers around the map and direct them to work on a road:

L: ((*Clicks on workers*))
R: Now click no, on the other guys, above them.
L: No, those are our explorers, >↑those are< our scouts.↓ ((*Points to the group of workers working on the road*))
R: No, click on the other guys. Then press Enter.
L: ((*Clicked on the workers*))
((*Clicked on open land*))
((*Workers moved to new area*))
((*Pressed Enter*))
((*Screen showed road being added after turn ended*))
↓Whoa.
¤<712088> (.)
R: See then they built their road.
L: Oh Ok I see. ((*Clicks on the workers building the road*))
¤<715747>

After clicking on the workers in the game, the dyad instructed the workers to build a road (the road icon appears in the bottom-middle of the screen: an available action for workers). After ending their turn, the left-hand student said "Whoa" after the game animated a road being added to the map. The visual changes represented by the game indicate visual progress, which serves to both inform game players and to add interest to their task.

As students played in pairs, only one person was able to control the game (typically, one person had control of both keyboard and mouse). Therefore, roles emerged in the playing of the game: for instance, the person controlling the mouse often had to verify teammate agreement in game strategy. The non-mouse-controlling student often took an information-gathering role, presenting information to his teammate (in control of the game) to aid understanding. This slight specialization of teammates showed students assuming roles to fulfill game needs. Assuming the object of the game was to win (succeed in gameplay), these roles helped fulfill that purpose.

In the above example from *Civilization IV*, intradyadic communication illustrates the need to both disclose information to peers and to negotiate strategies before executing actions. Across the many transcripts analyzed in the case study (and illustrated in the above example), the student controlling the mouse and keyboard (and therefore controlling the game) often suggested a game strategy before actually executing the strategy, as if to gain approval of his or her teammate before committing to an action. Accordingly, those without the control of the game input device often engaged in disclosure of information, suggesting their own interpretations of game elements and functionality to aid the strategies of their peer and to maintain shared meaning and a concerted effort toward winning the game. The internal mediational triangle in Figure 6 illustrates this concept.

While role specialization was limited in this case study (often simply by who had control of the mouse and keyboard, thereby executing in-game actions), it still provides a useful frame for analysis. Other games, such as massively multiplayer online games (MMOGs), frequently have high degrees of role specialization, and the above mediational triangle can be very useful when applied to that type of interaction. Game designs can involve specialization within the game (to serve roles, as in *World of Warcraft*) as well as outside the game: i.e., friends passing the game controllers to each other based on who was better at a given task.

FUTURE RESEARCH DIRECTIONS

Applying Activity Theory's Mediational Triangle to Game Design and Evaluation

Expanding on the previous example, guild formation (groups of players) in the MMOG *World of*

Figure 6. Mediation between subject and object by roles (division of labor). How does the division of labor (roles) affect the way the subject meets the objective?

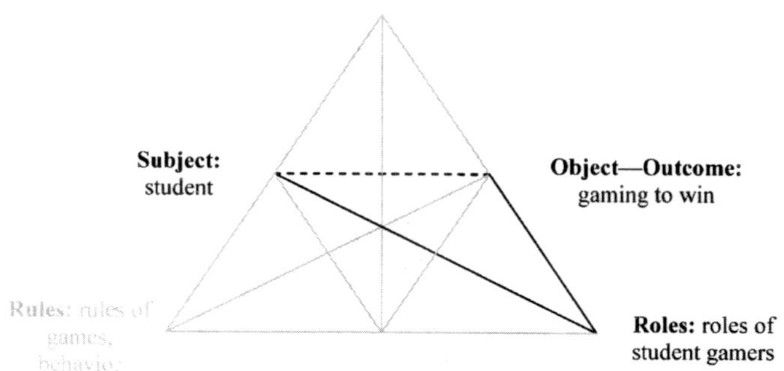

Figure 7. Mediation between community and object by roles (division of labor). How do the roles affect the way the community satisfies the objective?

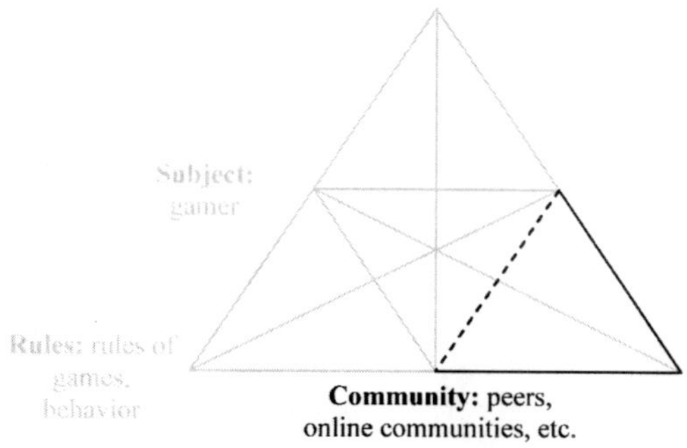

Warcraft involves groups of specialized characters. *World of Warcraft* is designed so that higher-level tasks are not achievable alone: groups (guilds) must be formed, involving characters of different abilities, in order to achieve success. For example, a *World of Warcraft* guild might make use of a "healer" to stand behind groups engaged in difficult battles to restore health of teammates, so they can fight continuously. Use of other characters for blocking, striking, and other coordinated group activities shows specialization (assuming roles) in particular games.

The previous case study illustrates the power of the mediational triangle. However, future work will examine play and interaction in MMOGs, as community aspects of play are vital to the play of the game. As seen in Figure 7, the internal mediating triangle examines how roles (specialization) can influence the ways in which the community achieves objectives. As previously described, the analysis of online guilds is very well suited for this analysis, as "community objectives" exist and are integral to success in the game.

An expansion of the concept of community to include peer teams and teachers reveals roles that they can serve in a motivated activity (the object to play and win the game). By serving as information sources, the community can aid gameplay. This was witnessed in this study: as pairs made use of each other when help was needed and when teachers stepped in briefly to assist in motivating students. Postgame interview data suggest the possible positive role of teachers in educational gaming environments: being integrated as part of the community in active gameplay, they can serve in roles to aid learning (such as figuring out the interface, etc.).

Future studies in educational environments will attempt to integrate games into a larger curriculum, using them as part of instruction. Students were pulled from class or study halls to participate in this study, thus limiting the effect of the community on their motivations and goals. While peer teams and teammates had a role in the community, it would be more interesting to observe community aspects associated with an actual classroom fully engaged in an activity together.

Additionally, literature on MMOGs suggests that role specialization creates a feeling of belonging among game players and aids in identity investment (for example, Ducheneaut et al., 2006; Gee, 2003). Many have hypothesized that this social interaction can be a huge source of motivation to play. Guilds in *World of Warcraft* often coordinate gameplay, as guilds require a variety of specialized characters in order to be successful in the game.

Additional future work could examine the effect of role specialization among gamers and MMOG communities, as illustrated in Figure 8.

Figure 8. Mediation between subject and community by roles (division of labor). How do roles affect the way the subject relates to their community?

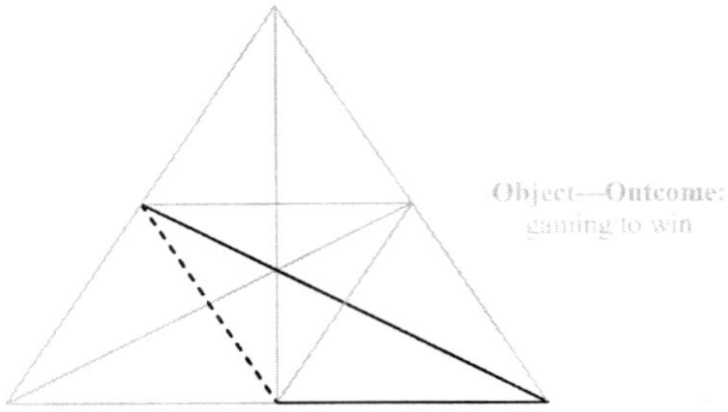

Literature on identity suggests that specialization can raise the sense of agency of one's role while playing the game (knowing that other game players are relying on you), seeming to add motivation to play and a sense of belonging to the community. Other studies are blossoming in this area, such as those by Steinkuehler (2004) that examine these roles in social (multiplayer) gameplay.

An opportunity for future work would be to develop further the concept of affordances to include motivations. This chapter takes the stance that affordances at this level are possible, although a lack of theoretical work exists on this stance. As described in Table 1 and in the case study, affordances were observed at Leontiev's "activity" level, as well as on the action and operation levels. Traditionally, affordances have been tied to directly perceptible actions and operations, and debate has ensued over whether affordances can exist without one perceiving the affordance. While the author agrees with the original stance that affordances cannot exist without an actor perceiving an action possibility, future work could theoretically extend the concept of affordances to include potentials for motivation (the activity level).

Finally, activity theory assumes that preconceived norms exist in behavior while engaging in collaborative gameplay. An ethnomethodologically informed approach helps reveal some of these rules by examining patterns in social affordances provided by peers in gameplay. However, further investigation into norms of collaborative gameplay is needed; only a few are mentioned in this study.

CONCLUSION

The mediational triangle presented by activity theory can be a useful tool for the analysis of games, showing high relevance with existing work as well as creating opportunity for future work. Particular findings showed high convergence with ideas presented in activity theory, as affordances were observed and used across the three levels of activity: at the operational level, the action level, and the activity level.

Implications for Game Design

Game designers are burdened with creating valuable gaming experiences through their designs. Many of the above considerations related to the display of game representations could be used to aid game designers; however, much more than what is presented above is required for successful game design. Game design already involves the management of many trade-offs: for example, striking a balance between learning and motivation, balancing realism with fun, and balancing narrative with in-game action.

Affordances might be examined across the three levels of activity in Leontiev's model (see Table 1), checking that all levels (activity, actions, and operations) are well supported in player interactions. Norman's "Gulf of Execution" (Norman, 1988) highlights traditional usability: verifying that goals can be translated into achievable actions. Game representations can also be tested for their ability to support the bridging between the activity and action levels, verifying that game motivations (to play) can be translated and supported by game activity.

Video game testing and user experience research can highlight problem areas where additional feedback is needed for gamers to generate meaningful strategies and actions that support game objectives. While already a balancing act, frequent inspections of game representations might help create well-understood affordances that optimally support learning. The processes described in this chapter can help to guide focus groups and play testing at formative stages of game design to gauge usability and game player motivation. When designing serious games, this is especially important to verify whether game designs are yielding serious, meaningful outcomes through play.

ACKNOWLEDGMENT

The author would like to thank his dissertation chair, Dan Suthers, for all of his hard work in guiding the research that was presented in this chapter. Additionally, the designers of the three excellent games used in this study, as well as the participating students and teachers, made this research possible. Finally, the countless hours of video transcription assisted by Michel Ann Sharritt, the author's wife, as well as family support, are recognized and received with gratitude.

REFERENCES

Charmaz, K. (2006). *Constructing grounded theory: A practical guide through qualitative analysis*. Thousand Oaks, CA: Sage Publications.

Clayman, S., & Maynard, D. (1995). Ethnomethodology and conversation analysis. In ten Have, P., & Psathas, G. (Eds.), *Situated order: Studies in the social organization of talk and embodied activities* (pp. 1–30). Washington, DC: University Press of America.

Cole, M., & Engeström, Y. (1993). A cultural-historical approach to distributed cognition. In Salomon, G. (Ed.), *Distributed cognitions: Psychological and educational considerations* (pp. 1–46). Cambridge, UK: Cambridge University Press.

Csikszentmihalyi, M. (1990). *Flow: The psychology of optimal experience*. New York: Harper and Row.

Dillenbourg, P., Baker, M., Blayne, A., & O'Malley, C. (1996). The evolution of research on collaborative learning. In Spada, H., & Reimann, P. (Eds.), *Learning in humans and machine: Towards an interdisciplinary learning science* (pp. 189–211). Oxford: Elsevier.

Doise, W., & Mugny, G. (1984). *The social development of the intellect, international series in experimental social psychology* (*Vol. 10*). Pergamon Press.

Ducheneaut, N., & Yee, N. Nickell, e., & Moore, R. J. (2006). Alone together?: Exploring the social dynamics of massively multiplayer online games. In R. Grinter, T. Rodden, P. Aoki, E. Cutrell, R. Jeffries, & G. Olson, (Eds.), *Proceedings of the SIGCHI Conference on Human Factors in Computing Systems* (pp. 407-416). New York: ACM.

Federation of American Scientists. (2006). *Harnessing the power of video games for learning.* Retrieved December 6, 2006, from http://fas.org/gamesummit/

Festinger, L. (1957). *A theory of cognitive dissonance.* Stanford: Stanford University Press.

Foreman, J., Gee, P., Herz, J., Hinrichs, R., Prensky, M., & Sawyer, B. (2004). Game based learning: How to delight and instruct in the 21st century. *EDUCAUSE Review, 39*(5), 50–66.

Garfinkel, H. (1967). *Studies in Ethnomethodology.* Malden, MA: Blackwell Publishing.

Gee, J. P. (2003). *What video games have to teach us about learning and literacy.* New York: Palgrave Macmillan.

Gibson, J. (1977). The theory of affordances. In Shaw, R., & Bransford, J. (Eds.), *Perceiving, acting, and knowing.* Hillsdale, NJ: Lawrence Erlbaum Associates.

Gibson, J. (1979). *The ecological approach to visual perception.* New Jersey, USA: Lawrence Erlbaum Associates.

Glaser, B., & Strauss, A. (1967). *Discovery of grounded theory: Strategies for qualitative research.* Piscataway, NJ: Transaction Publishers.

Heritage, J. (1987). Ethnomethodology. In Giddens, A., & Turner, J. (Eds.), *Social theory today* (pp. 224–272). Cambridge, UK: Tolety, Inc.

Jefferson, G. (1984). Transcript notation. In Heritage, J. (Ed.), *Structures of social interaction.* New York: Cambridge University Press.

Jordan, B., & Henderson, A. (1995). Interaction analysis: Foundations and practice. *Journal of the Learning Sciences, 4*(1), 39–103. doi:10.1207/s15327809jls0401_2

Kaptelinin, V., & Nardi, B. (2006). *Acting with technology: Activity theory and interaction design.* Cambridge, MA: MIT Press.

Kirriemuir, J., & McFarlane, A. (2004). Literature review in games and learning. *FutureLab.* Retrieved February 2, 2007 from http://www.futurelab.org.uk/download/pdfs/research/lit_reviews/Games_Review1.pdf

Koschmann, T., Stahl, G., & Zemel, A. (2005). The video analyst's manifesto (or the Implications of Garfinkel's policies for studying practice within design-based research. In Derry, S., & Pea, R. (Eds.), *Video research in the learning sciences.* Mahwah, NJ: Lawrence Erlbaum Associates.

Larkin, J. H., & Simon, H. A. (1987). Why a diagram is (sometimes) worth ten thousand words. *Cognitive Science, 11,* 65–99. doi:10.1016/S0364-0213(87)80026-5

Lave, J., & Wenger, E. (1991). *Situated learning: Legitimate peripheral participation.* Cambridge, UK: Cambridge University Press.

Leontiev, A. N. (1978). *Activity, consciousness, and personality.* Englewood Cliffs, NJ: Prentice-Hall.

Lim, S., & Lee, J. R. (2007). Effects of coplaying on arousal and emotional responses in videogame play. Presentation at the annual International Communication Association conference, San Francisco.

Linn, M. C., & Burbules, N. C. (1991). Construction of knowledge and group learning. In Tobin, K. G. (Ed.), *The practice of constructivism in science education* (pp. 91–119). Washington, DC: AAAS Press.

McGrenere, J., & Ho, W. (2000). Affordances: Clarifying and evolving a concept. In *Proceedings of the annual meeting of the Graphics Interface 2000 conference* (pp. 179-186). Retrieved February 12, 2008 from http://www.graphicsinterface.org/proceedings/2000/177/

Nielsen, J. (1994). Heuristic evaluation. In Nielsen, J., & Mack, R. L. (Eds.), *Usability inspection methods*. New York: John Wiley & Sons.

Norman, D. A. (1988). *The design of everyday things*. New York: Doubleday.

Oliver, M., & Pelletier, C. (2005). The things we learned on Liberty Island: designing games to help people become competent game players. In *DiGRA 2005: presentation at the Digital Games Research Association's 2nd International Conference, Changing Views: Worlds in Play*, Vancouver, British Columbia, Canada, June 16-20.

Prensky, M. (2001). *Digital game-based learning*. Saint Paul, MN: Paragon House.

Sharritt, M. J. (2008). Forms of learning in collaborative game play. *Research and Practice in Technology Enhanced Learning, 3*(2), 97–138. doi:10.1142/S1793206808000471

Sharritt, M. J., & Suthers, D. D. (2009). Video game representations as cues for collaboration and learning. *International Journal of Gaming and Computer-Mediated Simulations, 1*(3), 28–52.

Slavin, R. (1990). An introduction to cooperative learning. In *Cooperative learning: Theory research and practice* (2nd ed., pp. 1–46). Boston: Allyn and Bacon.

Squire, K. (2005). Changing the game: What happens when video games enter the classroom? *Innovate, 1*(6).

Steinkuehler, C. A. (2004). Learning in massively multiplayer online games. In Y. B. Kafai, W. A. Sandoval, N. Enyedy, A. S. Nixon, & F. Herrera (Eds.), *Proceedings of the Sixth International Conference of the Learning Sciences* (pp. 521–528). Mahwah, NJ: Erlbaum.

Stenning, K., & Oberlander, J. (1995). A cognitive theory of graphical and linguistic reasoning: Logic and implementation. *Cognitive Science, 19*(1), 97–140.

Stevens, R., Satwicz, T., & McCarthy, L. (2008). In-game, in-room, in-world: Reconnecting video game play to the rest of kids' Lives. In Salen, K. (Ed.), *The ecology of games: Connecting youth, games, and learning. The John D., & Catherine T. MacArthur Foundation Series on Digital Media and Learning*. Cambridge, MA: MIT Press.

Stokes, B. (2005). Video games have changed: Time to consider 'Serious Games'. *Developmental Education Journal*. Retrieved December 5, 2006, from http://www.netaid.org/documents/DEJ_article-Games_and_Development_Education-June05.pdf

Suthers, D. D. (2001). Towards a systematic study of representational guidance for collaborative learning discourse. *Journal of Universal Computer Science, 7*(3), 254–277.

Suthers, D. D., & Hundhausen, C. (2003). An empirical study of the effects of representational guidance on collaborative learning. *Journal of the Learning Sciences, 12*(2), 183–218. doi:10.1207/S15327809JLS1202_2

Transana. (2008). *Jefferson transcript notation*. Retrieved January 9, 2008 from http://www.transana.org/support/OnlineHelp/Team1/transcriptnotation1.html

Vygotsky, L. (1978). *Mind in society: The development of higher psychological processes*. Cambridge, MA: Harvard University Press.

Vygotsky, L. (1979). Consciousness as a problem in the psychology of behavior. *Social Psychology, 17*(4), 3–35.

Vygotsky, L. (1981). The genesis of higher mental functioning. In Wertsch, J. V. (Ed.), *The Concept of Activity in Soviet Psychology* (pp. 144–188). Armonk, NY: Sharpe.

Wiley, J., & Jensen, M. (2006). When three heads are better than two. *Proceedings of the Annual Conference of the Cognitive Science Society*. Retrieved April 18, 2007 from http://litd.psch.uic.edu/personal/jwiley/Wiley_Jensen_06.pdf

Zyda, M. (2005). From visual simulation to virtual reality to games. *IEEE Computer*, *38*(9), 25–32

"MUST-READS" FOR THIS TOPIC

Charmaz, K. (2006). *Constructing grounded theory: A practical guide through qualitative analysis*. Thousand Oaks, CA: Sage Publications.

Garfinkel, H. (1967). *Studies in ethnomethodology*. Malden, MA: Blackwell Publishing.

Gee, J. P. (2003). *What video games have to teach us about learning and literacy*. New York: Palgrave Macmillan.

Gibson, J. (1979). *The ecological approach to visual perception*. New Jersey, USA: Lawrence Erlbaum Associates.

Glaser, B., & Strauss, A. (1967). *Discovery of grounded theory: Strategies for qualitative research*. Piscataway, NJ: Transaction Publishers.

Jordan, B., & Henderson, A. (1995). Interaction analysis: Foundations and practice. *Journal of the Learning Sciences*, *4*(1), 39–103. doi:10.1207/s15327809jls0401_2

Kaptelinin, V., & Nardi, B. (2006). *Acting with technology: Activity theory and interaction design*. Cambridge, MA: MIT Press.

Koschmann, T., Stahl, G., & Zemel, A. (2005). The video analyst's manifesto (or the Implications of Garfinkel's policies for studying practice within design-based research. In Derry, S., & Pea, R. (Eds.), *Video research in the learning sciences*. Mahwah, NJ: Lawrence Erlbaum Associates.

Norman, D. A. (1988). *The design of everyday things*. New York: Doubleday.

Oliver, M., & Pelletier, C. (2005). The things we learned on Liberty Island: Designing games to help people become competent game players. In *DiGRA 2005: The Digital Games Research Association's 2nd International Conference, Changing Views: Worlds in Play*, Vancouver, British Columbia, Canada, June 16-20.

Sandford, R., Ulicsak, M., Facer, K., & Rudd, T. (2006). *Teaching with games: Using commercial off-the-shelf computer games in formal education*. Harbourside, UK: Futurelab.

Squire, K. (2005). Changing the game: What happens when video games enter the classroom? *Innovate, 1*(6).

Suthers, D. D., & Hundhausen, C. (2003). An empirical study of the effects of representational guidance on collaborative learning. *Journal of the Learning Sciences*, *12*(2), 183–218. doi:10.1207/S15327809JLS1202_2

Vygotsky, L. (1978). *Mind in society: The development of higher psychological processes*. Cambridge, MA: Harvard University Press.

TOP TEXTS FOR INTERDISCIPLINARY STUDIES OF SERIOUS GAMES

Carroll, J. M. (2003). HCI models, theories and frameworks: Toward a multidisciplinary science. San Francisco: Morgan Kaufmann publishers.

Csikszentmihalyi, M. (1990). *Flow: The psychology of optimal experience*. New York: Harper and Row.

Federation of American Scientists. (2006). *Harnessing the power of video games for learning*. Retrieved December 6, 2006, from http://fas.org/gamesummit/

Gee, J. P. (2003). *What video games have to teach us about learning and literacy*. New York: Palgrave Macmillan.

Kirriemuir, J., & McFarlane, A. (2004). Literature review in games and learning. *FutureLab*. Retrieved February 2, 2007 from http://www.futurelab.org.uk/download/pdfs/research/lit_reviews/Games_Review1.pdf

Nardi, B., & Harris, J. (2006). Strangers and friends: Collaborative play in *World of Warcraft*, 2006 20th anniversary, proceedings of the annual *Conference on Computer Supported Cooperative Work* (pp. 149-158). New York: ACM.

Sawyer, B. (2002). Serious games: Improving public policy through game-based learning and simulation. *Foresight and Governance Project, Woodrow Wilson International Center for Scholars*. Retrieved December 5, 2006, from http://wwics.si.edu/subsites/game/Serious2.pdf

Shaffer, D. (2006). Epistemic frames for epistemic games. *Computers & Education*, *46*(3), 223–234. doi:10.1016/j.compedu.2005.11.003

Shaffer, D. W., & Gee, J. P. (2006). *How computer games help children learn*. New York: Palgrave Macmillan. doi:10.1057/9780230601994

Steinkuehler, C. A. (2004). Learning in massively multiplayer online games. In Y. B. Kafai, W. A. Sandoval, N. Enyedy, A. S. Nixon, & F. Herrera (Eds.), *Proceedings of the Sixth International Conference of the Learning Sciences* (pp. 521–528). Mahwah, NJ: Erlbaum..

ENDNOTES

1 The following three video games were purchased by the researcher for use in this study: 1) Roller Coaster Tycoon 3 (http://www.atari.com/rollercoastertycoon) © 2004 Atari Interactive, Inc. All rights reserved. 2) Making History: The Calm & The Storm (http://www.making-history.com/edu) © 2007 Muzzy Lane Software. All rights reserved. 3) Sid Meier's Civilization IV (2K Games) (http://www.2kgames.com/civ4) © 2005 Take-Two Interactive Software and its subsidiaries. All rights reserved.

2 Adapted from Jefferson Transcript Notation, available at http://www.transana.org (Transana Web site, 2008). L and R refer to 'left' and 'right' group members from the camera's point of view. Text in double parentheses ((text)) refers to nonverbal behavior, and numbers in single parentheses (.5) refer to time delays, in seconds. Up and down arrows refer to voice inflections, and [text] refers to overlapping speech among individuals. For a full description of transcript notation, please visit www.transana.org.

Chapter 9
Persuasive Play:
Extending the Elaboration Likelihood Model to a Game-Based Learning Context

Steven Malliet
University of Antwerp, Belgium

Hans Martens
University of Antwerp, Belgium

ABSTRACT

Little research has examined the underlying psychological mechanisms of persuasive play. The purpose of the current study is to examine the explanatory potential of information processing approaches in a game-based learning context. Starting from the elaboration likelihood model, the authors theoretically develop a three-step model to explain how individual player characteristics (e.g., game preference) influence cognitive learning and attitude change through mediating variables like player motivations (e.g., personal involvement) and player evaluations (e.g., perceived realism). This model is empirically tested through a secondary analysis of survey data collected from Flemish adolescents (N = 538) in the 5th and 6th grade of secondary education. On the whole, the authors' results emphasize the importance of information processing variables as predictors of cognitive and attitudinal learning outcomes.

INTRODUCTION

Digital gameplay has been associated with a wide range of behavioral effects, including positive outcomes such as problem-solving capabilities (Cassell & Ryokai, 2001), spatial cognition (McClurg & Chaillé, 1987), mnemonic strategies (Oyen & Bebko, 1996), hand-eye coordination (De Aguilera & Méndiz, 2003), and social/political empowerment (Frasca, 2004), as well as negative outcomes such as aggressive script rehearsal (Anderson & Dill, 2000) or socialization of violent attitudes and behaviors (Bushman & Anderson, 2002). Although early research had a strong focus on empirically investigating these aspects, in recent years, a shift can be observed towards framing these results within a more comprehensive theoretical framework (e.g., Dipietro, Ferdig, Boyer, & Black, 2007; Van Eck, 2007).

Several models have been used to explain the learning processes that take place during digital

DOI: 10.4018/978-1-61520-719-0.ch009

Copyright © 2010, IGI Global. Copying or distributing in print or electronic forms without written permission of IGI Global is prohibited.

gameplay, including models derived from social psychology (Bandura, 2002), language acquisition theory (Johnson, Vilhjalmson, & Marsella, 2005), formal design theory (Gunter, Kenny, & Vick, 2006), or experiential learning theory (Egenfeldt-Nielsen, 2005). In this chapter, we argue that the elaboration likelihood model, or ELM (Petty & Cacioppo, 1986a, 1986b), provides a valuable additional point of view. The ELM has proven useful in explaining the effectiveness of persuasive communication in a wide range of applied research domains such as mass media (Petty, Briñol, & Priester, 2008), health communication (Braverman, 2008; Briñol & Petty, 2006; Holt, Lee, & Wright, 2008; Petty, Gleicher, & Jarvis, 1993), risk communication (Rucker & Petty, 2006), environmental communication (Mosler & Martens, 2008), computer-mediated communication (Di Blasio & Milani, 2008), and entertainment education (Slater & Rouner, 2002). As an audience-centered model focusing on message processing, the ELM can become a particularly useful tool for exploring the influence of serious games on knowledge acquisition and attitudes. This approach is in accordance with current tendencies in research on video game effects that put an emphasis on the receiver side in the communication process (e.g., Malliet, 2007). Nevertheless, the motivations and evaluations of video game players are presumably different than those of recipients of explicit persuasive messages about health, risk, or environment. For example, popular video games are able to attract audiences, not necessarily because of their educational or persuasive content, but because they are compelling as games (for a similar line of argument, see Slater & Rouner, 2002). Therefore, in order to explain how video games can elicit both unintended and intended cognitive and attitudinal effects, the main concepts of the ELM should be translated to a video game research context.

COGNITIVE RESPONSES TO PERSUASIVE MESSAGES: THE PERSPECTIVE OF THE ELM

Attitude Change According to the ELM: A Central Route and a Peripheral Route

The elaboration likelihood model is an information processing approach to attitude change. (Bohner, Erb, & Siebler, 2008). Unlike the troubling assumption that communication involves the linear transmission of messages from one point to the other (see Yannuzzi & Behrenshausen, this volume), information processing models approach persuasion as dependent on the reception of message arguments and various factors related to yielding to them (Petty, Priester, & Wegener, 1994). A common definition of an *attitude* is a general and relatively enduring evaluation of some person (including oneself), group, object, or issue. This evaluation can be based on various beliefs, emotions, and/or behaviors. *Elaboration*, in a persuasion context, denotes the extent to which a person thinks about the issue-relevant arguments contained in a message (Petty & Cacioppo, 1986a, 1986b). *Elaboration likelihood* refers to the degree to which a person is likely to engage in issue-relevant thinking. According to the ELM, there are broadly two routes through which a persuasive message is able to instigate attitude change: a *central route* and a *peripheral route* (Petty & Cacioppo, 1986a, 1986b).

The first, or central, route involves effortful cognitive activity. When the elaboration likelihood is high, the message recipient is likely to actively scrutinize all the information presented. The goal of this cognitive effort is to determine if the position advocated by the source has any merit. The end result of the effortful information processing is typically an attitude that is well articulated and bolstered by supporting information.

Attitudes can also be changed by a peripheral route, without much thinking about information central to the issue. Here, the attitude change is likely to occur as the result of a simple cue in the persuasion context (for example, an attractive audiovisual stimulus). In peripheral processing, individuals adopt a strategy by which they attempt to derive a "reasonable" attitude based on existing schemata and a superficial analysis of the veracity of the communication (Petty et al., 1994).

A Theory of Persuasive Communication

One powerful aspect of the ELM is the specification of a small number of mechanisms by which any given variable can produce attitude change (Petty & Briñol, 2008). While first generations of persuasion research emphasized the idea that persuasion variables (e.g., distraction, emotion, source credibility) could increase or decrease persuasion through a single process, in later research, persuasion was gradually tied to a dual process. Kelman & Hovland (1953) argued that the learning process that takes place in a persuasive communication context can be ascribed to two aspects that should be conceptually separated. First, there is the impact of learning the substantive arguments contained within in a persuasive message. Second, there is the observation that various simple cues (such as high- or low-credibility sources) can independently augment (or discount) the amount of influence that took place based on the message alone. Similarly, Kelman (1958) distinguished between two kinds of persuasion: internalization (acceptance of the message arguments) and identification (agreeing because one likes the message source). This suggested that attitude changes could be achieved through different routes of persuasion. Certain variables (e.g., trustworthiness) induce persuasion because a process of internalization takes place, whereas other variables (e.g., attractive sources) induce persuasion because a process of identification with the source takes place. In sum, these early dual-route theories mapped particular content onto particular processes.

Although the ELM builds upon these dual-process theories, it provides a more comprehensive set of constructs and, as such, enables us to formulate a number of specific predictions about the learning outcome associated with a persuasive message (Petty & Cacioppo, 1986a, 1986b). Four fundamental processes are identified through which any given variable (i.e., source, message, recipient, or context) can instigate an attitude change. According to the ELM, the impact of a persuasive message is expected to be stronger when it accomplishes one or more of the following aspects: (a) affecting the amount of information processing when the user is engaged in unconstrained thinking, (b) serving as a piece of substantive evidence (i.e., an argument) when processing is high, (c) biasing the ongoing thinking when processing is high, and (d) serving as a simple cue under conditions in which thinking is low (Petty & Briñol, 2008). These underlying processes have potential to explain the effects of persuasive play, especially where user-related variables such as motivation and elaboration are concerned.

Elaboration Likelihood and the Active User

Although the process of attitude change through the peripheral route does not require the receiver to take an active role, the ELM nevertheless emphasizes the importance of user involvement and user activity. From a persuasion perspective, the consequences of attitude change through the central route are highly desirable. Under the central route, an attitude schema may be accessed and rehearsed several times, strengthening the interconnections among the components and rendering the schema more internally consistent, accessible, enduring and resistant than under the peripheral route. Moreover, the greater the accessibility of the attitude itself, and the more well organized it is, the greater the likelihood that people act on it (Petty & Cacioppo, 1986a, 1986b). Given these possible benefits, it is no surprise that the ELM is scrutinized in variety of domains, such as psychology, communications, political science, advertising, and marketing.

Attitude change via the central route, however, proves difficult to achieve. First, it demands considerably more cognitive work than attitude change induced under the peripheral route. As McGuire (1985) explains, the receiver must be necessarily induced to take a number of successive response steps if the communication is to have its intended persuasive impact. For example, the intended recipient must (a) be exposed to the communication, (b) direct its attention to it, (c) become sufficiently engaged by the message, and (d) be able to comprehend its content. Second, although some information processing activities are more likely than others to produce effective knowledge acquisition, mere message reception is insufficient to elicit attitude change. Rather, a person's idiosyncratic cognitive responses (pro and counterarguments) to incoming information are responsible for persuasion. To the extent that people evaluate a persuasive message favorably, the likelihood of congruent attitude change increases (Petty et al., 1994).

Persuasion researchers have examined a variety of variables that can influence attitude change by affecting people's general motivation and ability to think (for an overview, see, e.g., Briñol & Petty, 2006; Petty et al., 2008). Existing research suggests that personal relevance is the most important determinant of motivation. If a message is perceived to be personally relevant, people will scrutinize the evidence more carefully. In case the evidence is found to be strong, a stronger attitude change will be the result. However, having the necessary motivation to process a message is not a sufficient condition for message elaboration through the central route to occur. In addition, in order to create consequential attitudes, people must also have the ability to process the message. Several factors can influence a person's ability to process a message, such as foreknowledge, the amount of distraction in the environment and the number of message repetitions. Also, features of the message itself have an impact on peoples' ability to think about it. For example, people are generally better able to process messages that appear in print media than messages that appear on radio and television (Petty et al., 2008).

As is the case with other types of messages and communications, one can expect both the central route and the peripheral route to be important in the context of electronic gaming. As for the central route, a crucial aspect will be to properly frame and conceptualize the specific types of involvement and motivation that characterize digital gameplay. As for the peripheral route, it will be an important challenge to map the audiovisual characteristics of electronic games that may serve as cues that attract the users' attention, and accordingly, exercise an influence on one's willingness to process the information contained within a game. Because a consensus exists that, where attitude change is concerned, the central route provides a stronger and more efficient base for effective persuasion, our translational move here will mainly focus on motivational aspects. In the following section, we will discuss some of the most influential theories and models that deal with motivation in a digital learning context, before moving on to the development of our empirical model.

GAME-BASED LEARNING AND MOTIVATION

Towards a Theory of Effective and Efficient Play

Most theorists and researchers who write about the educational potential of video game play have taken as their starting point the observation that we are dealing with an interactive medium, which addresses its users in a fundamentally different way than do its predecessors (of which the traditional textbook and the film are the most often cited examples). Several learning advantages have been associated with this characteristic, including adaptability and flexibility of the information that is processed (Squire, 2003), a changing dynamic in the teacher/student relationship (Rosas et al., 2003), and the possibilities for collaborative and task-based education (Squire, 2006). As such, electronic games are considered an important tool in the development of new principles for education, wherein a prominent position is reserved for elements such as life-long learning (Field, 2006), competency-based learning (Voorhees, 2001), or the development of metacognitive skills (Conati & Vanlehn, 2000).

Although the medium of the electronic game undoubtedly offers numerous possibilities for the implementation of these learning principles, there exists no consensus yet with respect to how games can be used to instigate a learning process that is both *efficient* and *effective* (e.g., Van Eck, 2006). One of the most often cited difficulties is the assertion that games should at all times be fun to play, and the resulting question is whether instructional games suffer by definition from a decrease in player enjoyment. In recent years, several theorists have attempted to overcome this apparent contradiction between fun and learning, inspired by a wide range of concepts that were translated from psychology, pedagogy, or literary theory. A central issue in most of these attempts is the concept of player motivation—a concept that has been attributed many different flavors and, accordingly, has been used to predict different types of digital learning.

Mark Prensky (2001), in one of the most influential prescient analyses of the educational potential of virtual gaming, has defined motivation in a sense that remains very closely tied to the strict notion of fun: games are fun to play, and therefore games produce a stronger sense of player involvement, which results in a stronger learning outcome. However, within this general definition of player motivation, only limited attention is paid to the specific characteristics of fun within an educational context. Gee (2003) assumes a different position, comparing the structural characteristics of electronic games to a number of new trends in the development of education theory. Although Gee also emphasizes the importance of fun in the effectiveness of game-based learning, within his theory the constructs of motivation and fun have become conceptually separated. More specifically, motivation has been defined with respect to the social and interactive characteristics of video game play, resulting in the definition of a number of motivation-specific parameters that may instigate a stronger learning effect: codesign, involvement based upon identification, and constructive learning.

Play Context and Game-Related Determinants

Although both Gee's and Prensky's theories have inspired a number of empirical investigations on the positive outcomes of digital gameplay (e.g., Bottino & Ott, 2006; Johnson et al., 2005), the aforementioned mechanisms have mainly served as a theoretical base, and provide only limited support for the development of a rigid instrument for educational or psychological research. The ideas outlined within these theories have, however, inspired the elaboration of a number of explanatory models, in which the notions of motivation, collaboration, and identification have been defined from a more specific and empirical point of view.

Egenfeldt-Nielsen (2005) identifies motivation, together with the teacher/learner relationship, as a key concept in the construction of an effective and efficient digital learning outcome. Within his model, motivation is preceded by two elements: the characteristics of the learning environment (including the teacher's skills or the contents of the games that are used) and the personal characteristics of the participants (such as the socio-demographic composition of the learning group or the interpersonal relationships between the participants). As such, motivation is not considered a mere function of either the contents of the games that are used or of the participants that are being worked with. Egenfeldt-Nielsen proposes a process-based approach, wherein motivation is considered an outcome rather than an antecedent and an element that is dependent on the educational context in which gameplay takes place.

Garris, Ahler, and Driskell (2002), following Bandura's social cognitive model, relate more closely to the notion of motivation as associated with the interactive characteristics of electronic gameplay and, accordingly, propose a content-based approach in which strong importance is attributed to the development of motivational instructional games. The main focus of their model resides in the interaction mechanisms that dictate gameplay. Motivation is considered an effect of the continuous application of a four-step process: 1) the player is provided a number of information cues, 2) the player is required to make a mental judgment on these cues, 3) the player is required to act according to the judgments made, and 4) the gaming system provides feedback with respect to the choices and judgments the player has made (theorists attribute strong importance to this last factor). The authors argue that the key to designing games that are both engaging and effective lies in the careful and detailed implementation of interactions that allow the user to engage in a flow experience, wherein information cues are judged and reacted to on a structural level. As such, this approach demonstrates resemblances to the structural semiotic point of view on game theory and game design, wherein basic patterns of interaction are considered the most essential characteristics of video game play (e.g., Myers, 2003). The interplay between, on the one hand, information and feedback provided by the gaming system and, on the other hand, cognitive evaluations performed by the users, has been studied from a similar point of view by, among others, Kiili (2005) and Paras and Bizzocchi (2005).

Psychological Determinants

Schwartz and Hartman (2007), from the perspective of developmental psychology, propose a similar approach to digital learning but focus on the role of the overall experience that is created rather than on the instructional effectiveness of the succession of programmed interactions. In this way, motivation and engagement are considered a function of the personal involvement a player has with the contents of a game. Games that instigate an effective learning experience should in the first place be successful in offering a direct experience that is perceived as both realistic and valuable. Similarly, de Freitas and Oliver (2006) suggest the subject be studied from an exploratory learning point of view. Player experience is a central aspect in their argument, which focuses on player skills and on peer support. Within this point of view, an important concern for the serious game designer should be the construction of environments wherein a player can be creative, as well as supportive, towards other users.

A last focus of attention has been provided by researchers who argue that the player and, more specifically, the learning strategies that are adopted during gameplay constitute important variables in the creation of an effective instructional learning experience. Blumberg (2000) investigates the differences in the focus of attention during instructional gameplay, and concludes that a more effective learning experience takes place with children who are able to process subject relevant information, compared to children whose attention is directed towards game elements that are less important to the central message of a game. Blumberg (1998) points out that the capability for adopting a general reasoning style can be constructive of an effective digital learning experience. De Aguilera and Méndiz (2003) have reported teamwork capabilities to be an important determinant of both the motivational involvement and the educational outcome associated with instructional gameplay. Finally, Cassell and Ryokai (2001) observe the differences in problem-solving capabilities with children and conclude that these skills constitute an important predecessor of a successful learning outcome during digital gameplay.

A THEORETICAL EXPLANATION OF PERSUASIVE PLAY

As a comprehensive theory of persuasive communication, the elaboration likelihood model departs from the specific focus on game-based learning in the theories and empirical models described above. While this might be considered a drawback, there can also be a number of advantages associated with it, which makes the model a valuable addition to the already rich domain of literature that exists on the subject of motivation in a digital learning context. First, as was argued above, this information processing approach has been extensively drawn upon to explain the effectiveness of persuasive communication in a broad variety of research domains. The key role of motivation in both persuasion research and game-based learning suggests that the ELM is particularly well suited to the study of persuasive play. Second, even though most research on the educational potential of digital gaming has focused on the use of games in an explicitly pedagogic context, a number of positive gameplay outcomes are not explicitly framed as instructional or educational. Because the ELM broadly focuses on the interplay between audiences and messages, the model provides a background for both formal and informal learning processes. Third, because the ELM offers a bird's eye view of the mechanisms underlying attitude change, it not only provides a suitable framework for experimental research but, in addition, defines a number of variables that can be used in survey research design. As such, the model can be highly useful for researchers who address the subject of serious gaming or instructional gaming from a larger and more general perspective.

In summary, although the model deals with a number of variables that connect closely to the motivation-related variables developed in the specific context of game-based learning, its focus on aspects such as cognitive processing and effectiveness of communication makes it a valuable addition to the theories described above.

As a framework for empirical research, the ELM typically proposes a three-step approach, wherein first, a number of user- and message-related parameters are studied and associated with motivational variables; second, motivational and evaluative variables are linked through the central route of persuasion to a number of cognitive outcomes; and finally, the cognitive outcomes, in combination with the motivational and evaluative parameters are associated with a change in the users' attitudes towards the central message of the information that is conveyed. Table 1 provides an overview of the most important variables that

Table 1. The ELM as a three-step model for empirical research

	Step 1	Step 2	Step 3
Independent variables	Message characteristics User characteristics	Motivation to process Ability to process	Knowledge acquisition through: - Central route - Peripheral route
Dependent Variables	Motivation to process (personal relevance, need for cognition, personal responsibility, ...) Ability to process (prior knowledge, distraction, etc.)	Knowledge acquisition through: - Central route - Peripheral route	Attitude change

Figure 1. Predicting the outcome of persuasive play following the central route

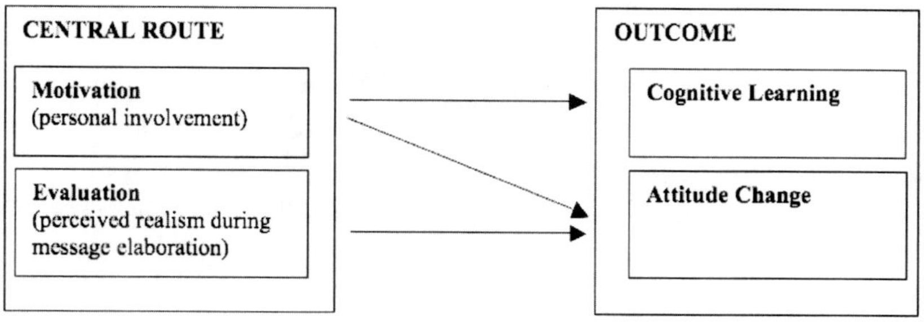

are typically accounted for within each of the aforementioned steps.

When the central route is followed, the relationship between user variables and cognitive and attitude change is mediated by two separate variables: personal motivation and evaluative judgments. Within the context of electronic gaming, motivational aspects are defined as those elements that allow the user to become engaged or immersed within the virtual digital environment that is provided—an approach that has been mirrored in other studies on the psychological processes associated with digital gameplay, including Calleja (2007), or Funk and Buchman (1996). Evaluative aspects are defined as those aspects that, under the condition of a strong player motivation, may either enforce (in the case of a positive evaluation) or diminish (in the case of a negative evaluation) the attitudinal outcome. An evaluation is considered positive where it is perceived as congruent with the game narrative's persuasive message. For example, in a game such as *Darfur Is Dying* (http://www.darfurisdying.com), the fact that one has paranoid thoughts while playing the game is considered a "positive" evaluation because it is congruent with the game's persuasive narrative that one *should* feel uncomfortable with the social situation in Sudan.

The relationship between motivational and evaluative variables on the one hand and cognitive learning and attitude change on the other is visualized in Figure 1.

In accordance with cognitive response approaches to persuasion, we postulate that strong motivation is a necessary but not sufficient condition for strong consequential attitudes. Only to the extent that a person is motivated *and* his or her thoughts during gameplay are favorable is enduring persuasion likely to occur. At this point, the ELM proposes a different approach than other learning models, as it considers user-related aspects such as metacognitive skills or user intentionality preceding constructs (which are studied in the first phase), rather than constructs that should be taken into account simultaneously (as is the case with, among others, Schwartz & Hartman, 2007 and Garris and colleagues, 2002). When the player is strongly involved during gameplay, (s) he will be more likely to make a detailed mental elaboration of the information that is provided and, as a consequence, is likely to remember more of the relevant issues in the game's narrative.

Although one might logically expect a direct association between user evaluations and any type of cognitive outcome, according to the processes outlined in the ELM, the relationship between both constructs appears more complicated. The ELM indicates that, in the case of a strong user motivation, the processing of issue-relevant information will instigate knowledge acquisition, regardless of positive or negative evaluations. In cases of a weak user motivation, a positive evaluation or negative evaluation of an information cue will not be sufficient to elicit a cognitive learning outcome.

Finally, where attitudes are concerned, the model predicts that increased player motivation can only be effective in cases where it is accompanied by a positive or congruent evaluation of the information cues. For example, in a game such as *Darfur Is Dying* (http://www.darfurisdying.com), a motivated player who responds favorably to the game narrative's main argument that one has to feel uncomfortable with the social situation in Sudan will congruently change his/her attitude towards this issue. However, with an incongruent evaluation, for example, because one does not think of the game as presenting a realistic view on the situation, the motivated player will consider the narrative cues irrelevant as issue-related evidence. As such, the game will not produce the desired attitude change.

EMPIRICALLY EXPLORING THE CENTRAL ROUTE TO ATTITUDE CHANGE

Setup of This Study

In the last part of this chapter, the predictions made within our translation of the ELM to persuasive play have been subjected to empirical testing. The data were previously collected within a larger research project (Malliet, 2007) on the impact of digital gameplay on cognitions and attitudes with adolescents. This research project did not have an explicit focus on serious gaming or digital learning. As such, this secondary analysis should be considered an exploration of the usefulness of the proposed theoretical framework, rather than a rigid formal test. Because the ELM focuses upon the mental processes underlying attitude change, rather than on the specific outcome of specific educational contexts or contents, we believe that this secondary analysis can produce a number of valuable additions to the theoretical argument made above.

The main focus of the original research project was on digital gaming in general and on a number of game genres in specific. The project aimed to link the time spent playing games to a number of cognitions and attitudes that were related to these genres. For the purpose of this chapter, we will focus on the analyses made with respect to the genre of first-person shooting games and to the resultant cognitive and attitudinal outcomes. While this may seem an unusual decision in a chapter that deals with the learning processes associated with digital gameplay, three main arguments serve to motivate this focus on first-person shooting games. The first argument deals with the observation that, within most shooting games, there exists a close congruence between the main actions a player has to perform (working alone or in a team in order to win a fight) and the narrative's promoted attitude towards violence (one has to be prepared to use violence in specific circumstances in order to win a fight). As such, the genre of shooting games corresponds closely to the ELM's assumption that a persuasive message contains one or a few favorable evaluations and that the outcome is strongly dependent of the user's willingness and ability to adopt these evaluations. In other types of games, such as role-playing games or adventure games, this congruence is not always as obvious, since the plotlines are often more complicated, and the characters are usually developed in a more subtle and multifaceted way.

The second argument deals with the fact that we are interested in the psychological processes underlying cognitive and attitude change during digital gameplay and, as such, only indirectly in the narrative or representational message conveyed within a game. As was argued above, the strength of applying the ELM to a digital learning context resides mainly in its usefulness to expose the psychological mechanisms that underlie a desired attitude change, rather than to isolate specific narrative elements that may serve to influence a certain learning outcome. Thirdly, as has been demonstrated in several analyses of the culture around shooting games, avid players of this genre tend to adopt a goal-driven and instrumental style (e.g., Grodal, 2000; Jansz, 2005). Very often this style of playing is also expected of the player of a serious game or educational game title, which would moderate the obvious narrative and contextual differences that exist between both types of games.

Method and Measures

The original study from which the data for this analysis were obtained involved examining the impact of digital gameplay on adolescents' worldviews and attitudes towards the real-life world. The study had a strong focus on the moderating role of user-related variables such as perceived realism, personal involvement, and character identification in the overall game effect model. Although the study was not framed within the context of persuasive play, its focus on knowledge acquisition and attitude change produced a significant number of variables that can be suitable for analysis within the three-step approach proposed by the ELM. As such, the measures and results that will be presented mainly serve a theoretical and descriptive purpose, providing a number of first indications as to the usefulness of the ELM in a digital-gaming context.

A questionnaire was administered to 538 Flemish adolescents (5th and 6th grade in secondary education). The questionnaires were given in class during school hours. Schools and classes were selected randomly. The ratio of boys to girls was 49% (N = 265) to 49% (N = 265)[1]. The distribution of participants between the different types of education was as follows: 45% (N = 243) of the respondents attended a general secondary school, 21% (N = 114) attended a vocational secondary school, and 33% attended a technical secondary school (N = 179)[2].

As is indicated in Table 2, the analysis was performed in three steps, which accord to the main concepts described in Table 1 and Figure 1. Within a first step, a first exploration was made of the concept of player motivation, and a correlational analysis was performed of the association between a number of user-related characteristics and player motivation. In a second step, the cognition-related part of the scheme proposed in Figure 1 was investigated. More specifically, regression analysis was performed in order to study the degree to which player motivation and player evaluation serve as predictors of the knowledge of weaponry with adolescents. Finally, in a third step, an exploration was made of the role of motivational aspects (player motivation), evaluative aspects (player evaluation), and acquired knowledge in the process of effective attitude change. The most important variables have been operationalized in the following sections.

Game Characteristics and Player Characteristics

A number of variables have been included that probed for the respondents' genre preferences, as well as for the respondents' preferences for specific types of game content (e.g., compelling narration, use of advanced tactics, competition). While the variables related to the respondents' preference for specific content elements produced a number of relevant, descriptive results, clustering these variables in order to make them suitable for correlational or regression analysis produced somewhat confusing results. For that reason, genre preference, and more specifically, preference for shooting games was used as the main measure of the "game characteristics" part of the proposed model. As for player characteristics, we included data relating to gender and education level, in addition to the amount of time spent playing digital games.

Table 2. The three-step approach adapted to the context of digital game-based learning

	Step 1	Step 2	Step 3
Independent variables	Game characteristics (fun, interactivity, etc) Player characteristics (digital game use, education level, etc.)	Motivation to process Ability to process	Knowledge acquisition through: Central route Peripheral route
Dependent Variables	Motivation to process (personal involvement, character identification,...) Ability to process (prior knowledge, perceived realism,..)	Knowledge acquisition through: Central route Peripheral route	Attitude change

Motivation

Player motivation was operationalized in terms of the personal involvement adolescents have with their favorite games. One component of this included questions relating to character identification. Another component included questions related to the presence of the self adolescents experience while playing games. In order to measure both components, a large number of items were constructed, of which the ones with the strongest intercorrelations were eventually retained. These items were based upon the insights that were obtained during a number of introductory in-depth interviews held with adolescent gamers (Malliet, 2006). Eventually seven items were kept that accounted for an alpha value of .840. For each of these items, respondents had been given five answering options, ranging from "totally agree" over "no opinion" to "totally disagree."

Evaluation

Player evaluations were operationalized in terms of the perceived realism of adolescents concerning their favorite shooting games. Once again, a large number of items were constructed, based upon Malliet (2006), and the ones with the strongest intercorrelations were eventually retained. Five items were retained that accounted for an alpha of .890.

Cognitive Learning

A series of questions was produced asking for players' knowledge of weapons. The names of 15 weapons were presented, and players were asked to render to which degree they were familiar with these weapons. Each time, three options were provided: "never heard of," "I know what it looks like," and "I know how to use it." As a control mechanism, two nonexistent weapons were included in the list. Respondents who claimed to be familiar with one of these were not included in the analysis.

Attitude Change

Finally, for the variable "attitude towards violence," the scale developed by Funk, Flores, Buchman, and Germann (1999) was used. Contrary to the standards used in most studies of the impact of video game play, this scale does not measure how violent or hostile someone feels, acts, or thinks of oneself but rather the general attitude a person has towards the use of violence in certain circumstances. Within this study, the items of the two components described in this scale did not produce sufficiently strong correlations (with alphas of .680 and .643, respectively), which made us decide to code all items in one general variable "attitude towards violence." Seven items produced an alpha value of .720.

Results

Step 1: Player Characteristics and Motivation Correlates

A first exploration of the data set (Table 3) shows a significant relationship between several player characteristics (educational level, gender, and preference for shooting games) and player motivation. Most importantly, preference for shooting games was significantly correlated with motivation, $r = .43$, $p < .001$ (two-tailed). In addition, motivation was significantly related to preference for genres such as science fiction games ($r = .49$, $p < .001$), war games ($r = .51$, $p < .001$), driving games ($r = .41$, $p < .001$), and sports games ($r = .39$, $p < .001$). In the case of educational games ($r = .07$, $p > .05$) and puzzle games ($r = -.08$, $p > .05$), no significant relation could be established with player motivation. While these results may provide additional support for the choice to focus on the genre of shooting games, they also highlight an important theoretical issue that has been raised above: today's educational game titles may serve a number of instructional purposes, but the combination of learning and player motivation remains unclear, if not problematic. The results also indicate that not all individuals are equally involved while playing digital games. This suggests that, in general, game content can be considered an important element in the assessment of the involvement of adolescent players.

As for the relationship between player characteristics and message characteristics, the analysis produced a number of results that are in line with earlier research on the uses and preferences of digital game players (e.g., Lucas & Sherry, 2004). Preference for shooting games, action–adventure games, strategy games, and fighting games was positively and significantly related to gender, indicating that these genres are more popular with boys than with girls. On the other hand, preferences for platform games and classic adventure games were significantly but negatively related to gender, indicating that these genres are more popular with girls than with boys. Educational games and puzzle games appeared to be equally popular with boys and girls. When level of education was considered, only one significant difference between the three groups involved was observed. Chi-square analysis indicated that strategy games were more popular with adolescents who attend a general secondary school.

Step 2: Motivation and Evaluation as Predictors of Knowledge

Table 4 provides support for our theoretical expectations about the relationships between player motivation and player evaluation on the one hand, and knowledge of weaponry on the other. As expected, there was a positive and significant relationship between motivation and knowledge of weaponry, $r = .38$, $p < .001$. Moreover, there was no significant relation between evaluation and knowledge of weaponry. This confirms that motivations and evaluations play different roles in eliciting learning outcomes. Only when the player is strongly involved during gameplay will (s)he make a detailed elaboration on the information that

Table 3. Player characteristics and motivation correlates †

Characteristics		Motivation correlates
Education level		.229(*)
Gender		.381(*)
Preference for shooting Games		.431(*)

† Spearman correlations were used for "Education level" and "Preference for shooting games," Pearson correlations for "Gender"
*p < .001

Table 4. Motivation and evaluation as predictors of knowledge: Regressions

	Knowledge of weaponry (st. beta)	F(df)	R^2
Motivation	.378*	29.431(2)	.141*
Evaluation	-.005		

*p < .001

is provided, and as a consequence, will learn more about relevant issues from the perspective of the game's narrative. Contrarily, evaluation was not significantly related to knowledge of weaponry. It seems that, in accordance with our theoretical framework, evaluations are not directly related to knowledge acquisition.

Step 3: Motivation, Evaluation, and Knowledge as Predictors of Attitudes.

According to our theoretical explanations, player motivation can only be effective in cases where it is accompanied by a congruent or positive evaluation of the persuasive messages substantiating the game's narrative. In other words, the perceived realism of adolescents concerning their favorite shooting games should be a better predictor of attitudes towards violence than personal involvement. Table 5 lends strength to this distinction. Evaluation is significantly related with attitudes towards violence, $r = .25, p < .001$. As expected, motivation is not. Of course, this does not mean that no knowledge is needed to form a strong attitude. As the ELM explains, persuasion following the central route is always the result of generating evaluative thoughts during message learning. It is therefore not surprising that there was also a significant relationship between knowledge of weaponry and attitudes towards violence, $r = .23, p < .001$.

FUTURE RESEARCH DIRECTIONS

In this chapter, we started from the elaboration likelihood model to explore the underlying psychological mechanisms that determine the cognitive and attitudinal outcomes of persuasive play. As mentioned before, one powerful aspect of the ELM is the specification of a small number of mechanisms by which any given variable can produce attitude change (Petty & Briñol, 2008). More precisely, the ELM has described four fundamental processes by which any given variable (i.e., whether source, message, recipient, or context) can affect attitudes depending on the elaboration likelihood (a) affecting the amount of information processing when thinking is unconstrained, (b) serving as a piece of substantive evidence (i.e., an argument) when processing is high, (c) biasing the ongoing thinking when processing is high, and (d)

Table 5. Motivation, evaluation, and knowledge as predictors of attitudes: Regressions

	Attitudes towards violence (st. beta)	F(df)	R^2
Motivation	.060	26,275(3)	.182*
Evaluation	.250*		
Knowledge of weaponry	.229*		

*p < .001

serving as a simple cue under conditions in which thinking is low. Because of our primary research interest in antecedents (i.e., mediating variables and consequences of the central route of attitude change), only the first two processes were dealt with in our theoretical and empirical analysis. More precisely, genre preferences were found to affect the amount of information processing and knowledge acquisition through motivation. Nevertheless, only when games were also evaluated to be realistic, the games' narratives served as pieces of substantive evidence.

While these findings indicate some general lessons that can be learned from information processing approaches to attitude change, further research is needed to come up with more specific and trustworthy guidelines on how to develop effective and efficient persuasive games. One key ambiguity in the existing literature remains unresolved. Is it possible to develop persuasive instructional games that are fun to play? Information processing approaches to attitude change point out the key importance of personal involvement in thoughtful persuasion. Moreover, to have an attitudinal impact, the developed games should have a persuasive narrative that is perceived to be realistic by its players. This suggests that eliciting persuasive play is not at all easily accomplished. The data we presented with respect to the relationship between genre preferences and motivation highlight the obvious, yet theoretically relevant argument that contemporary commercial games are more successful in providing the players with an engaging experience than are educational games or puzzle games. While this finding emphasises the need for research on how to develop educational games that are not only instructional but also fun, in addition it provides support for the claim that digital learning should not be exclusively studied in an educational context. As such, the approach we advocated within this chapter can become a useful tool for upcoming research to investigate both the formal and the informal learning processes associated with digital gameplay. In addition, developers could certainly benefit from reliable and valid experimental research that further explores the precise impact of specific game variables (e.g., visual style, narrative, and interactivity) on player motivations and evaluations. The numerous successful applications of the ELM in existing communication research illustrate the fruitfulness of this strategy.

While we argued that following the central route of attitude change is a necessary condition for consequential persuasive play, the ELM also holds that it might be easier to change attitudes when people have relatively little interest in the topic of the persuasive message. Given the difficulty of change via the central route, the peripheral route becomes an attractive alternative. Not coincidentally, this peripheral approach shows some resemblance to the popular idea of intuitive learning during playful activities. However, since persuasion via this route is short-lived, it will be necessary to constantly remind the targeted audience of the cues upon which attitudes are based. While a survey framework appears to be particularly useful to investigate the three-step process of attitude change through the central route, an experimental framework can prove a valuable asset in isolating specific elements of game content that are responsible for player elaborations through the peripheral route.

On a more fundamental level, while the empirical part of this chapter supports our theoretical explanations, the adapted ELM needs a more rigid formal test to *prove* its usefulness. Ideally, this dual information processing model would integrate both game and player variables to predict the cognitive and attitudinal outcomes of persuasive play.

CONCLUSION

The bottom-line message of this chapter is twofold. First, as, under the conditions described by the ELM, digital gameplay can result in both cognitive change and attitude change, it is useful to assess the subject of digital learning from the perspective of persuasive play. Simply put, the developer of an instructional game translates a core message into a persuasive game narrative. Over the past decades, a vast number of persuasion studies have examined how individual information-processing activities influence cognitive learning and attitude change. From a persuasive play perspective, the consequences of the central route are highly desirable: the stronger the attitude, the greater the likelihood that people will behave accordingly. Therefore, we developed a theoretical model that seeks to predict cognitive and attitudinal learning outcomes through information processing variables such as player motivation (personal involvement) and player evaluation (perceived realism). A secondary analysis of previously collected data illustrated how our theoretical framework succeeds in explaining both knowledge acquisition and attitude change elicited by first-person shooting games.

Second, while we applaud the growing recognition of the potential serious games hold for learning, this study illustrates that the future of persuasive play holds many challenges. More than half a century of fundamental persuasion research has produced important progress, but many practical questions about effectiveness and efficiency remain. Against this background, it seems unlikely that serious games would suddenly overcome these difficulties just because they are (sometimes) fun to play. Moreover, our data suggest that motivation to play is not a sufficient condition to elicit attitude change. In the debate on how player motivation may serve as a catalyst of a desired cognitive or attitude change, the results of this study suggest that the distinction should be made between motivation that is congruent with a game's central message and motivation that is not congruent with a game's central message. As such, motivation cannot be examined without taking into account the cognitive and emotive evaluations the player makes of the central argument the designers of a game intend to express. The empirical results of this study therefore illustrate how a comprehensive framework such as the ELM can inform both serious game researchers and developers about possible pitfalls and opportunities. Or, to quote Kurt Lewin (1951), "there is nothing so practical as a good theory."

REFERENCES

Anderson, C. A., & Dill, K. E. (2000). Video games and aggressive thoughts, feelings, and behavior in the laboratory and in life. *Journal of Personality and Social Psychology*, *78*(4), 772–790. doi:10.1037/0022-3514.78.4.772

Bandura, A. (2002). Social cognitive theory of mass communication. In Bryant, J., & Zillman, D. (Eds.), *Media effects: Advances in theory and research* (2nd ed., pp. 121–154). London: Lawrence Erlbaum.

Blumberg, F. C. (1998). Developmental differences at play: Children's selective attention and performance in video games. *Journal of Applied Developmental Psychology*, *19*(4), 615–624. doi:10.1016/S0193-3973(99)80058-6

Blumberg, F. C. (2000). The effects of children's goals for learning on video game performance. *Journal of Applied Developmental Psychology*, *21*(6), 641–653. doi:10.1016/S0193-3973(00)00058-7

Bohner, G., Erb, H. P., & Siebler, F. (2008). Information processing approaches to persuasion: Integrating assumptions from the dual- and single-processing perspectives. In Crano, W. D., & Prislin, R. (Eds.), *Attitudes and attitude change*. New York: Psychology Press.

Bottino, R. M., & Ott, M. (2006). Mind games, reasoning skills, and the primary school curriculum. *Learning, Media and Technology, 31*(4), 359–375. doi:10.1080/17439880601022981

Braverman, J. (2008). Testimonials versus informational persuasive messages: The moderating effect of delivery mode and personal involvement. *Communication Research, 35*(5), 666–694. doi:10.1177/0093650208321785

Briñol, P., & Petty, R. E. (2006). Fundamental processes leading to attitude change: Implications for cancer prevention communications. *The Journal of Communication, 56*, 81–104. doi:10.1111/j.1460-2466.2006.00284.x

Bushman, B. J., & Anderson, C. A. (2002). Violent video games and hostile expectations: A test of the general aggression model. *Personality and Social Psychology Bulletin, 28*(12), 1679–1686. doi:10.1177/014616702237649

Calleja, G. (2007). Digital game involvement: A conceptual model. *Games and Culture, 2*(3), 236–260. doi:10.1177/1555412007306206

Cassell, J., & Ryokai, K. (2001). Making space for voice: Technologies to support children's fantasy and storytelling. *Personal and Ubiquitous Computing, 5*(3), 169–190. doi:10.1007/PL00000018

Conati, C., & VanLehn, K. (2000). Toward computer-based support of meta-cognitive skills: A computational framework to coach self-explanation. *International Journal of Artificial Intelligence in Education, 11*(4), 389–415.

De Aguilera, M., & Méndiz, A. (2003). Video games and education: Education in the face of a parallel school. *ACM Computers in Entertainment, 1*(1).

de Freitas, S., & Oliver, M. (2006). How can exploratory learning with games and simulations within the curriculum be most effectively evaluated? *Computers & Education, 46*(3), 249–264. doi:10.1016/j.compedu.2005.11.007

Di Blasio, P., & Milani, L. (2008). Computer-mediated communication and persuasion: Peripheral vs. central route to opinion shift. *Computers in Human Behavior, 24*(3), 798–815. doi:10.1016/j.chb.2007.02.011

Dipietro, M., Ferdig, R. E., Boyer, F., & Black, E. W. (2007). Towards a framework for understanding electronic educational gaming. *Journal of Educational Multimedia and Hypermedia, 16*(3), 225–248.

Egenfeldt-Nielsen, S. (2005). *Beyond edutainment: Exploring the educational potential of computer games*. IT-University Copenhagen.

Field, J. (2006). *Lifelong learning and the new educational order*. London: Routledge.

Frasca, G. (2004). Video games of the oppressed: critical thinking, education, tolerance and other trivial issues. In Harrington, P., & Wardrip-Fruin, N. (Eds.), *First person: New media as story, performance, and game*. Cambridge, MA: The MIT Press.

Funk, J. B., & Buchman, D. D. (1996). Playing violent video and computer games and adolescent self-concept. *The Journal of Communication, 46*(2), 19. doi:10.1111/j.1460-2466.1996.tb01472.x

Funk, J. B., Flores, G., Buchman, D. D., & Germann, J. N. (1999). Rating electronic games: Violence is in the eye of the beholder. *Youth & Society, 30*(3), 283–312. doi:10.1177/0044118X99030003002

Garris, R., Ahlers, R., & Driskell, J. E. (2002). Games, motivation, and learning: A research and practice model. *Simulation & Gaming, 33*(4), 441–467. doi:10.1177/1046878102238607

Gee, J. P. (2003). *What video games have to teach us about learning and literacy*. New York: Palgrave/St. Martin's.

Grodal, T. (2000). Video games and the pleasure of control. In Zillman, D., & Vorderer, P. (Eds.), *Media entertainment: The psychology of its appeal* (pp. 197–213). London: Erlbaum.

Gunter, G., Kenny, R., & Vick, E. (2006). *A case for a formal design paradigm for serious games.* Paper presented at the 2006 International Digital Media Association Conference (iDMAa and IMS) Annual Conference, Oxford, OH.

Holt, C. L., Lee, C., & Wright, K. (2008). A spiritually based approach to breast cancer awareness: Cognitive response analysis of communication effectiveness. *Health Communication, 23*(1), 13–22. doi:10.1080/10410230701626919

Jansz, J. (2005). The emotional appeal of violent video games for adolescent males. *Communication Theory, 15*, 219–241. doi:10.1111/j.1468-2885.2005.tb00334.x

Johnson, W. L., Vilhjalmson, H., & Marsella, S. (2005). Serious games for language learning: How much game, how much AI? In C. K. Looi, G. McCalla, B. Bredeweg & J. Breuker (Eds.), Artificial intelligence in education (pp. 306-313). Amsterdam: IOS Press.

Kelman, H. C. (1958). Compliance, identification and internalization: Three processes of attitude change. *The Journal of Conflict Resolution, 2*, 51–60. doi:10.1177/002200275800200106

Kelman, H. C., & Hovland, C. I. (1953). Reinstatement of the communicator in delayed measurement of opinion change. *Journal of Abnormal and Social Psychology, 48*(3), 327–335. doi:10.1037/h0061861

Kiili, K. (2005). Digital game-based learning: Towards an experiential gaming model. *The Internet and Higher Education, 8*(1), 13–24. doi:10.1016/j.iheduc.2004.12.001

Lewin, K. (1951). Problems of research in social psychology. In Cartwright, D. (Ed.), *Field theory in social science: Selected theoretical papers* (pp. 155–169). New York: Harper & Brothers Publishers.

Lucas, K., & Sherry, J. (2004). Sex differences in video game play: A communication-based explanation. *Communication Research, 31*(5), 499–523. doi:10.1177/0093650204267930

Malliet, S. (2006). An exploration of adolescents' perceptions of videogame realism. *Learning, Media and Technology, 31*(4), 377–394. doi:10.1080/17439880601021983

Malliet, S. (2007). *The challenge of video games to media effect theory.* Catholic University of Leuven, Leuven.

McClurg, P., & Chaillé, C. (1987). Computer games: Environments for developing spatial cognition? *Journal of Educational Computing Research, 3*(1), 95–111.

McGuire, W. J. (1985). Attitudes and attitude change. In Gardner, L., & Aronson, E. (Eds.), *Handbook of social psychology* (*Vol. 2*). New York: Random House.

Mosler, H. J., & Martens, T. (2008). Designing environmental campaigns by using agent-based simulations: Strategies for changing environmental attitudes. *Journal of Environmental Management, 88*(4), 805–816. doi:10.1016/j.jenvman.2007.04.013

Myers, D. (2003). *The nature of computer games: Play as semiosis*. New York: Peter Lang.

Oyen, A.-S., & Bebko, J. M. (1996). The effects of computer games and lesson contexts on children's mnemonic strategies. *Journal of Experimental Child Psychology, 62*(2), 173–189. doi:10.1006/jecp.1996.0027

Paras, B., & Bizzocchi, J. (2005). *Game, motivation and effective learning: An integrated model for educational game design.* Paper presented at the DiGRA 2005 Conference: Changing Views—Worlds in Play.

Petty, R. E., & Briñol, P. (2008). Persuasion: From single to multiple to metacognitive processes. *Perspectives on Psychological Science, 3*(2), 137–147. doi:10.1111/j.1745-6916.2008.00071.x

Petty, R. E., Briñol, P., & Priester, J. R. (2008). Mass media attitude change: Implication of the elaboration likelihood model of persuasion. In *Media effects: Advances in theory and research.* New York: Taylor & Francis.

Petty, R. E., & Cacioppo, J. T. (1986a). *Communication and persuasion: Central and peripheral routes to attitude change*. New York: Springer-Verlag.

Petty, R. E., & Cacioppo, J. T. (1986b). The elaboration likelihood model of persuasion. In Berkowitz, L. (Ed.), *Advances in experimental social psychology* (*Vol. 19*, pp. 123–205). New York: Academic.

Petty, R. E., Gleicher, F., & Jarvis, W. B. (1993). Persuasion theory and AIDS prevention. In Pryor, J. B., & Reeder, G. (Eds.), *The social psychology of HIV infection* (pp. 155–182). Hillsdale, NJ: Lawrence Erlbaum Associates.

Petty, R. E., Priester, J. R., & Wegener, D. T. (1994). Cognitive processes in attitude change. In Wyer, R. S., & Srull, T. K. (Eds.), *Handbook of social cognition* (2nd ed., *Vol. 2*). Hillsdale, NJ: Lawrence Erlbaum Associates.

Prensky, M. (2001). *Digital game-based learning.* New York: McGraw-Hill.

Rosas, R., Nussbaum, M., Cumsille, P., Marianov, V., Correa, M., & Flores, P. (2003). Beyond Nintendo: Design and assessment of educational video games for first and second grade students. *Computers & Education, 40*(1), 71–94. doi:10.1016/S0360-1315(02)00099-4

Rucker, D. D., & Petty, R. E. (2006). Increasing the effectiveness of communications to consumers: Recommendations based on elaboration likelihood and attitude certainty perspectives. *Journal of Public Policy & Marketing, 25*(1), 39–52. doi:10.1509/jppm.25.1.39

Schwartz, D. L., & Hartman, K. (2007). It is not television anymore: Designing digital video for learning and assessment. In R. G. R., S. Derry, R. Pea & B. Barron (Eds.), Video research in the learning sciences. Mahwah: Erlbaum.

Slater, M. D., & Rouner, D. (2002). Entertainment-education and elaboration likelihood: Understanding the processing of narrative persuasion. *Communication Theory, 12*(2), 173–191.

Squire, K. (2003). Video games in education. *International Journal of Intelligent Simulations and Gaming, 2*(1).

Squire, K. (2006). From content to context: Video games as designed experiences. *Educational Researcher, 35*(8), 19–29. doi:10.3102/0013189X035008019

Van Eck, R. (2006). Digital game-based learning: It's not just the digital natives who are restless. *EDUCAUSE Review, 41*(2).

Van Eck, R. (2007). Six ideas in search of a discipline. In Shelton, B., & Wiley, D. (Eds.), *The educational design and use of computer simulation games*. Boston, MA: Sense.

Voorhees, R. A. (2001). Competency-based learning models: A necessary future. *New Directions for Institutional Research*, 110.

Yanuzzi, T. G., & Behrenshausen, B. G. (in press). Serious games and the ontological call of education: A communication perspective on the radical binarisation of everyday life. In Van Eck, R. (Ed.), *Interdisciplinary models and tools for serious games: Emerging concepts and future directions*. Hershey, PA: IGI Global.

"MUST-READS" FOR THIS TOPIC

Blumberg, F. C. (1998). Developmental differences at play: Children's selective attention and performance in video games. *Journal of Applied Developmental Psychology*, *19*(4), 615–624. doi:10.1016/S0193-3973(99)80058-6

Blumberg, F. C. (2000). The effects of children's goals for learning on video game performance. *Journal of Applied Developmental Psychology*, *21*(6), 641–653. doi:10.1016/S0193-3973(00)00058-7

Briñol, P., & Petty, R. E. (2006). Fundamental processes leading to attitude change: Implications for cancer prevention communications. *The Journal of Communication*, *56*, 81–104. doi:10.1111/j.1460-2466.2006.00284.x

Calleja, G. (2007). Digital game involvement: A conceptual model. *Games and Culture*, *2*(3), 236–260. doi:10.1177/1555412007306206

de Freitas, S., & Oliver, M. (2006). How can exploratory learning with games and simulations within the curriculum be most effectively evaluated? *Computers & Education*, *46*(3), 249–264. doi:10.1016/j.compedu.2005.11.007

Funk, J. B., & Buchman, D. D. (1996). Playing violent video and computer games and adolescent self-concept. *The Journal of Communication*, *46*(2), 19. doi:10.1111/j.1460-2466.1996.tb01472.x

Funk, J. B., Flores, G., Buchman, D. D., & Germann, J. N. (1999). Rating electronic games: Violence is in the eye of the beholder. *Youth & Society*, *30*(3), 283–312. doi:10.1177/0044118X99030003002

Malliet, S. (2007). *The challenge of video games to media effect theory*. Catholic University of Leuven, Leuven.

Petty, R. E., & Briñol, P. (2008). Persuasion: From single to multiple to metacognitive processes. *Perspectives on Psychological Science*, *3*(2), 137–147. doi:10.1111/j.1745-6916.2008.00071.x

Petty, R. E., Briñol, P., & Priester, J. R. (2008). Mass media attitude change: Implication of the elaboration likelihood model of persuasion. In *Media effects: Advances in theory and research*. New York: Taylor & Francis.

Petty, R. E., & Cacioppo, J. T. (1986a). *Communication and persuasion: Central and peripheral routes to attitude change*. New York: Springer-Verlag.

Petty, R. E., & Cacioppo, J. T. (1986b). The elaboration likelihood model of persuasion. In Berkowitz, L. (Ed.), *Advances in experimental social psychology* (*Vol. 19*, pp. 123–205). New York: Academic.

Slater, M. D., & Rouner, D. (2002). Entertainment-education and elaboration likelihood: Understanding the processing of narrative persuasion. *Communication Theory*, *12*(2), 173–191.

Van Eck, R. (2006). Digital game-based learning: It's not just the digital natives who are restless. *EDUCAUSE Review*, *41*(2).

TOP TEXTS FOR INTERDISCIPLINARY STUDIES OF SERIOUS GAMES

Blumberg, F. C. (2000). The effects of children's goals for learning on video game performance. *Journal of Applied Developmental Psychology*, *21*(6), 641–653. doi:10.1016/S0193-3973(00)00058-7

Calleja, G. (2007). Digital game involvement: A conceptual model. *Games and Culture*, *2*(3), 236–260. doi:10.1177/1555412007306206

De Aguilera, M., & Méndiz, A. (2003). Video games and education: Education in the face of a parallel school. *ACM Computers in Entertainment, 1*(1).

Egenfeldt-Nielsen, S. (2005). *Beyond edutainment: Exploring the educational potential of computer games*. IT-University Copenhagen.

Field, J. (2006). *Lifelong learning and the new educational order*. London: Routledge.

Frasca, G. (2004). Video games of the oppressed: Critical thinking, education, tolerance and other trivial issues. In Harrington, P., & Wardrip-Fruin, N. (Eds.), *First person: New media as story, performance, and game*. Massachusetts: The MIT Press.

Funk, J. B., & Buchman, D. D. (1996). Playing violent video and computer games and adolescent self-concept. *The Journal of Communication, 46*(2), 19. doi:10.1111/j.1460-2466.1996.tb01472.x

Gee, J. P. (2003). *What video games have to teach us about learning and literacy*. New York: Palgrave/St. Martin's.

Myers, D. (2003). *The nature of computer games: Play as semiosis*. New York: Peter Lang.

Squire, K. (2006). From content to context: Video games as designed experiences. *Educational Researcher, 35*(8), 19–29. doi:10.3102/0013189X035008019

ENDNOTES

1. Gender data were missing for six respondents.
2. Education-type data were missing for two respondents.

Section 4
Theory Into Practice

Chapter 10
Aligning Problem Solving and Gameplay:
A Model for Future Research and Design

Woei Hung
University of North Dakota, USA

Richard Van Eck
University of North Dakota, USA

ABSTRACT

Problem solving is often discussed as one of the benefits of games and game-based learning (e.g., Gee, 2007a, Van Eck 2006a), yet little empirical research exists to support this assertion. It will be critical to establish and validate models of problem solving in games (Van Eck, 2007), but this will be difficult if not impossible without a better understanding of problem solving than currently exists in the field of serious games. While games can be used to teach a variety of content across multiple domains (Van Eck, 2006b, 2008), the ability of games to promote problem solving may be more important to the field of serious games because problem-solving skills cross all domains and are among the most difficult learning outcomes to achieve. This may be particularly important in science, technology, engineering, and math (STEM), which is why serious game researchers are building games to promote problem solving in science (e.g., Gaydos & Squire, this volume; Van Eck, Hung, Bowman, & Love, 2009). Current research and design theory in serious games are insufficient to explain the relationship between problem solving and games, nor do they support the design of educational games intended to promote problem solving. Problem solving and problem-based learning (PBL) have been studied intensely in both Europe and the United States for more than 75 years. Most recently, researchers (e.g., Jonassen, 1997, 2000, & 2002; Hung, 2006a; Jonassen & Hung, 2008) have made advances in both the delineation and definition of problem types and models for designing effective problems and PBL. Any models and research on the relation of games and problem solving must build on the existing research base in problem solving and PBL rather than unwittingly covering old ground in these areas. In this chapter, we present an overview of the dimensions upon which different problems vary, including domain knowledge and structuredness and their associated learning outcomes. We then propose a classification of gameplay (as opposed to game genre) that accounts for the cognitive skills encountered during gameplay, relying in part on pre-

DOI: 10.4018/978-1-61520-719-0.ch010

Copyright © 2010, IGI Global. Copying or distributing in print or electronic forms without written permission of IGI Global is prohibited.

vious classifications systems (e.g., Apperley, 2006), Mark Wolf's (2006) concept of grids of interactivity (which we call iGrids), and our own cognitive analysis of gameplay. We then use this classification system, the iGrids, and example games to describe eleven different types of problems, the ways in which they differ, and the gameplay types most likely to support them. We conclude with a description of the ability of problems and games themselves to address specific learning outcomes independent of problem solving, including domain-specific learning, higher-order thinking, psychomotor skills, and attitude change. Implications for future research are also described. We believe that this approach can guide the design of games intended to promote problem solving and points the way toward future research in problem solving and games.

INTRODUCTION

It has been argued that games are a kind of disruptive technology (e.g., Strawn, 2007), but they can only be so to the extent that they solve a widely recognized problem that has value to sufficient numbers of people. For game-based learning to truly become a disruptive technology, it must address a critical need that is difficult to meet any other way. Many have argued that games address critical thinking and problem-solving skills (e.g, Gee, 2007a; Greenfield, in press; Van Eck, 2006a, 2007; Yanuzzi & Behrenhausen, this volume) that our current educational system is failing to provide (e.g., Broussard, La Lopa, & Ross-Davis, 2007; OECD, 2004).

Problem solving may well be the most powerful pedagogical benefit of commercial games in general and of game-based learning and serious games specifically. Whether our current educational system recognizes the need for problem solving as a learning outcome, and whether or not it can support it with existing resources and infrastructure, it seems clear that problem solving and the related research and design we do will remain an important area of study in the field of serious games.

Unfortunately, while researchers have begun to move the discussion of problem solving beyond descriptive to theoretical (e.g., Gee, 2007a & 2007b; Van Eck, 2007) and the practical (Van Eck, 2008), the majority of our discussion can be summed up as "Games are problems being solved by players; therefore, playing games will help people be better problem solvers." Our research tends to be primarily descriptive, wherein we describe the admittedly complex behavior involved in working one's way through a game like *World of Warcraft* (Blizzard, 2001) as evidence that problem solving must surely be going on during that process. This is sufficient for making the case that games most likely address problem solving and are therefore worthy of further study, but this is not sufficient to guide our development of serious games to directly address problem solving as a learning outcome. Problem solving is far more complex than many first realize, just as games are more complex than they appear at first to the general public. For example, we cannot discuss problem solving without understanding what type of problem we are referring to: creating a menu for guests who have different diet restrictions, troubleshooting a car that won't start, diagnosing a patient's back pain problem, or solving global warming. Each type of problem differs significantly in structuredness, requirements for prior knowledge, ability to embed other subproblems, cognitive structure, etc. Just as we recognize that game genres (e.g., first-person shooter, adventure, role-playing games [RPGs], massively multiplayer online games [MMOGs]) encourage different gameplay experiences, we need to recognize the different types of problem solving that exist in the world.

It is almost universally agreed in the field of instructional design (Dick, Carey, & Carey, 2005; Gagne, Wager, Golas, & Keller, 2005; Smith & Ragan, 2005) that instruction is most effective when the instructional strategies (in this case, styles of gameplay) that are employed appropriately afford the learners' development of the desired learning outcomes (in this case, types of problem solving). If we don't understand the full typology and complexity of different problem types, we cannot begin to formulate theory or practice in serious games and problem solving.

Fortunately, we are not starting from scratch in this regard. Cognitive psychology and instructional design have been studying problem solving for many years, and a rich body of research exists that can help inform our studies and design of problem solving in games. In this chapter, we will discuss problem-solving theory and research from a cognitive perspective. We begin with a brief discussion of problems and problem solving in general, then move into a discussion of the nature of different types of problems (problem typology). We will attempt to bridge theory and practice by examining the relationships between games, problems, their cognitive processes, and instructional design, including heuristic tools and examples of those problem types as they may be mapped onto different gameplay experiences typically afforded by different genres of games.

BACKGROUND

The Problem with Problem Solving

Research on problem solving goes back at least to the 1930s and Gestalt psychology.[1] Early attempts to study problem solving were hampered by assumptions that most researchers have now come to believe are flawed. Chief among these assumptions was that all problem solving was essentially the same for all individuals and, most critically, for all kinds of problems and domains.[2] Research in this tradition was focused on controlling for prior knowledge through the use of simple, novel tasks, the assumption being that this would uncover general problem-solving skills shared by all problems and all problem solvers. The tasks used to observe problem solving all had prescribed "best" solutions and were thus easy to use to compare problem solvers' moves to optimal solutions. The *Towers of Hanoi* (2002) is a well-known example. A mathematical game developed in the 1800s, this game required one to shift a pyramid-shaped stack of disks from one of three posts to another. All three posts are identical and aligned in a single row, with one of the outside (i.e., leftmost or rightmost) posts initially containing the stack of disks (often referred to as the initial state). The rules require the player to move only one ring at a time, either one or two posts distance, and to only place smaller rings on top of larger rings, until the pyramid stack of disks has been replicated on the third post (often referred to as the goal state). The solution to this task requires that the player make short-term moves which appear incorrect in order to achieve the final goal. Problems like this were thought to scale up, or generalize, to other problems in other domains.

It was not until nearly 50 years later that researchers (e.g., Bhaskar & Simon, 1977) came to believe that a general theory of problem solving was not possible, and that problem solving was very much context- and domain-dependent and that, further, problems themselves were all different according to the domain in which they were situated. For the last 30 years, problem solving has proceeded under these assumptions, although by differing methods and approaches in Europe and the United States.

Nevertheless, some elements of problem-solving research in the last century remain useful for talking about problem solving, despite their origins in abstract, well-defined problems. Early research suggested that a problem has two states: an initial state and a goal state. The initial state is the set of information and resources present at the beginning of the problem. This is the starting point for the problem, if you will. The goal state is the information and resources that will be present when the goal has been met. It is the ending point of the problem, after it has been solved. A problem, then, can be thought of as an attempt by the problem solver to do things that reduce the disparity between the initial state and the goal state. The strategies she uses and the process by which she thinks about moving toward the goal state within the constraints of the problem and prior knowledge are collectively referred to as the problem space. Problem-solving research describes the solution process with a variety of terms but most commonly as searching the problem space (Newell & Simon, 1972). We can see this in games as well, where games have an initial state and goal state (introduced by the game box, cut scenes, Web site reviews, and word-of-mouth among players), and where the playing of the game becomes the problem space.

While our conceptualization of problem solving today is domain dependent and recognizes a variety of ill-structured vs. well-structured problems (more on this later), these concepts can still be helpful in discussing problem solving. For example, while we recognize that the initial state and the goal state are complex concepts defined by the learner herself as she integrates what is known about the problem with her existing schema for the domain/problem, they remain useful labels for discussing those aspects of the problem-solving process.

Most recently, Jonassen (e.g., 2000, 2002) and Jonassen and Hung (2006, 2008) have proposed a typology of problems and associated prescriptions for the design of problem-based learning and instruction to promote problem solving in general. Given the widely held belief that games themselves are examples of problem solving, the potential for this body of research to inform research and design in serious games warrants a closer inspection of this literature to see if and how it can be mapped to the study and design of serious games.

The Heart of the Matter

The problem with problems in instructional contexts is that many are poorly formed and articulated, thus dooming from the beginning any instruction designed to promote problem solving. According to Jonassen (2002), all good problems share two characteristics. First, they have some kind of goal, which he refers to as the "unknown." By unknown, he means that the learner does not know how to reach the goal, not that the learner does not know what s/he is trying to achieve in the first place. Consequently, the goal requires the generation of new knowledge, which can be a combination of two or more elements of prior knowledge and/or the generation and combination of new knowledge with prior knowledge. The second characteristic all good problems share is a value to the learner in solving them (i.e., in generating the knowledge needed to achieve the unknown). It is not much of a stretch to see how this potentially aligns well with games and problem-solving environments; games have an overarching goal that the learner does not know how to achieve and which requires the generation of new knowledge (the unknown), and games (at least, good ones) have a value to the learner in achieving the goal (unknown).

Games as Problem-Solving Environments

Jim Gee (2007a, 2007b) has argued convincingly that all games are situated, complex problem-solving opportunities in which players are immersed in a culture and way of thinking. We've already discussed how games can be conceptualized in similar ways to problem solving from the cognitive sciences (e.g., initial state, problem space, and goal state; goal/unknown, generation of new knowledge, and of value to the learner in solving the problem). Others have made the same point, such as Kiili (2007), who contended that "a game itself is a big problem that is composed of smaller causally linked problems" (p. 396).

To be sure, games are more than just problems to be solved and will often contain not only multiple kinds of problems of varying type, structuredness, and complexity but also a variety of other learning and entertainment outcomes with their associated strategies. Nonetheless, it is difficult if not impossible to conceptualize a game that does not incorporate problems to be solved, and thus, problems can be seen as the raw materials for producing games, which can themselves be thought of as problem-solving domains.

The realization that problems are at the heart of games not only opens a new avenue for game research but also leads us to a wealth of previous research findings to draw upon. Problem solving is a long-studied cognition research area (see, for example, Frensch & Funke, 1995a; Greeno, 1980; Hayes, 1980; Jonassen, 1997; Larkin & Simon, 1987; Newell & Simon, 1972), and it behooves us as researchers in this growing field to be aware of this research as we attempt to refine our understanding about the cognitive benefits of games.

PROBLEMS, INTERACTIVITY, AND GAMES

In the next four sections, we will describe different kinds of problems and the cognitive processes they require, the learned capability outcomes they support, and their connection to gameplay styles. While the largest part of our argument will be that problems are highly differentiated by context, purpose, and domain, it is not possible to discuss this without also discussing some of the aspects by which this differentiation occurs. Therefore, in the first section we will look at structuredness, cognitive components, and domain knowledge as key dimensions along which problems vary.

Further, in order to describe how different games may or may not align with different problems, we must first establish a common set of terminology and definitions for what we mean by different types of games. While problem typologies and classification systems are well-established and accepted in the learning sciences, the same cannot be said for game classifications. Traditionally, the field has relied on genres of games to organize discussions of different types of gameplay. However, this approach has led to several challenges. There are competing genre classification systems (e.g., Apperley, 2006; Bogost, 2007), for example, that are valuable but not necessarily compatible nor widely accepted and adopted. Also, games often employ multiple gameplay strategies from different genres within the same game, leading to hybridized descriptions like action–adventure that work against meaningful classification (Kallay, this volume). This creates a significant challenge for our purpose in this chapter: how to describe what kinds of games support what kinds of problems and vice versa?

Because we believe that problem types and their associated cognitive-processing requirements will be most impacted by *gameplay* rather than game *genre* and that interactivity captures the most salient features of gameplay as it relates to problem solving, we have adopted Mark Wolf's (2006) concept of a grid of interactivity (which we refer to as an iGrid) to help quantify the interaction required by the different gameplay types. In the second section, we will describe this metric, which we believe is a better way of discussing the interaction of problem type and games than traditional genre classifications would be. Such an approach avoids the first challenge above (incompatible genre classifications that confound gameplay, platform, and marketing terminology) and solves the related second challenge (hybridized categories resulting from multiple gameplay styles within a single game).

Problems with genre classifications notwithstanding, we also recognize their value in shared understanding and familiarity. Therefore, in the third section, we have attempted to synthesize existing genre classifications with the express purpose of mapping them to the cognitive processes required by the game in a manner that takes advantage of common terminology in game studies. This is necessary in order to further map problem types, which themselves differentially support and require cognitive processes. We will rely on iGrids to help make the appropriate delineations and comparisons.

In the fourth section, we will describe the eleven different types of problems (Jonassen, 2000) and relate them to gameplay types, relying again on both iGrids and on our own gameplay classifications before closing with a discussion of the learned capability outcomes (psychomotor, attitude, etc.) in the context of games and problem types. Again, our purpose is not to perpetuate problematic genre classification systems nor to propose new ones but rather to map problem solving and problem types to appropriate kinds of gameplay design.

Problems

Structuredness

A broad definition of problem structuredness was articulated by Wood (1983) as the degree to which the information in the problem is known or knowable to the problem solver. Jonassen (1997) further refined this concept in his discussion of the continuum of well-structured and ill-structured problems, where he argued that structuredness describes the reliability of the problem space in terms of the ratio of the information about the problem known and unknown to the problem solver, the number of variables involved, number of solution paths, and the degree of ambiguity about the criteria for assessing the success of solving the problem. More specifically, he states that the factors that characterize the structuredness include known versus vaguely defined or unknown states of the problem (initial state, goal state, and operators), regular versus unconventional uses of rules and principles involved, stated constraints versus hidden constraints, predictable operators versus highly unpredictable and unprescribed operators, a preferred and prescribed solution versus multiple viable solutions, and definite versus vague criteria for evaluating the solutions.

Video games may run the gamut from highly structured (as with the need to fire weapons against hordes of zombies in *Left 4 Dead* [Valve, 2008] in order to stay alive) to poorly structured (how to win *Spore* [Entertainment Arts, 2008]). Therefore, structuredness becomes one dimension upon which we can categorize both games and problems.

Cognitive Composition of Problems

In addition to varying along the dimension of structure, solving different problems also relies on different kinds of cognition. Building a civilization over the span of 3000 years via multiple strategies such as economics, diplomacy, industry, and arts (e.g., the *Civilization* series of games) is a fundamentally different problem than trying to get from safe house to safe house without being killed by "hunters," "smokers," "boomers," "tanks," or swarming hordes of zombies (*Left 4 Dead*, Valve, 2008). Therefore, it is not logical to expect that strategies learned in one game will necessarily transfer to another. Likewise, problems in general require one or more kinds of thinking, some of which are supportive of one another and some of which are completely different. We examine here six main kinds of cognitive processes from cognitive psychology and instructional design that we will later rely on (along with structuredness and other dimensions) in our discussion of problem solving.

Logical Thinking

This cognitive process refers to the mental process that infers an expected event as a result of the occurrence of its preceding event or evaluates the validity of the conditional relations of these events. Most people are not particularly conscious of engaging in this type of thinking process; yet, in fact, it is a fundamental cognitive process that humans utilize to process and reason everyday matters (Houdé & Tzourio-Mazoyer, 2003). For example, if I see John walk into the room with a wet, dripping umbrella, I might infer that it was raining. Likewise, a jury member might notice a logical flaw in testimonial statements indicating that a suspect was seen in two locations 300 miles apart within a 1-hour period of time.

Analytic Thinking

The analytic cognitive process mainly focuses on identifying and separating an object, essay, substance, or system into its constituent components, examining their relationships as well as understanding the nature, behaviors, and specific functions of each component. This cognitive process is essential in developing a deep understanding about a subject area, a system, or a problem. An individual needs to be able to isolate individual parts in order to understand their unique nature and functions in relation to the whole. Therefore, analytic thinking can be seen as the initial cognitive process that an individual has to perform in understanding what is being studied. Analyzing bank operations in order to develop banking system software is an example of employing analytic thinking.

Strategic Thinking

Mintzberg (1994) argued that strategic thinking is an integration process of synthesizing and evaluating the analytical results of a given situation and generating a most viable plan with intuition and creativity. Liedtka (1998) further characterized strategic thinking as the cognitive processes that are intent-focused, hypothesis-driven, thinking in time, intelligent opportunism, and reasoning from a systems perspective. Thus, strategic thinking involves a goal-oriented planning process with an understanding of past and current situations, the generation and testing of hypotheses, flexible adaptation to the dynamic nature of the environment, and the taking of a systemic view during the entire thinking process. The ability to think strategically is a key to effective problem solving. Managing a multinational enterprise in a cutting-edge technology business is an example that requires effective and intensive strategic thinking skills.

Analogical Reasoning

According to Holyoak and Thagard (1997), analogical reasoning refers to the mental process in which an individual "reason[s] and learn[s] about a new situation (the *target* analog) by relating it to a more familiar situation (the *source* analog) that can be viewed as structurally parallel" (p. 35). For example, when the concept of the Internet first became known to the public, the analogy of a highway system and traffic was used to help people understand its structure and function. Moreover, analogical reasoning is the core of case-based learning (Kolodner, 1997), which is a common learning strategy employed by people in their everyday lives as well as an effective instructional approach.

Systems Thinking

Systemic thinking refers to the cognitive reasoning processes that consider complex, dynamic, contextual, and interdependent relationships among constituent parts, and the emerging properties of a system (Capra, 1996; Ossimitz, 2000). According to Sterman (2002), this cognitive skill is considered very complex and highly counterintuitive. Because of its complex nature, the cognitive load of performing systems thinking is usually beyond an individual's capacity. Therefore, cognitive tools such as modeling software are often required. One example that requires intensive systems thinking processes is constructing a weather or ecological system model.

Metacognitive Thinking

Metacognition refers to the cognitive process that an individual is consciously aware of and which he or she articulates to various aspects of his or her own thinking processes. In simpler terms, it is "cognition about cognition" (Flavell, 1985, p. 104). Metacognition and its cognitive processes and skills are the core elements for successful self-regulated, self-directed learning (Driscoll, 2005). Metacognitive thinking is a highly complex cognitive process that involves all of the cognitive thinking skills mentioned above at some point and at different levels during the thinking process.

Domain Knowledge

In addition to structuredness and cognitive composition, problems will vary by the domain knowledge they require. One cannot solve a problem if one has not mastered the prerequisite domain knowledge. We cannot expect a student to solve an algebraic equation without having mastered subordinate skills such as addition, multiplication, division, and subtraction. What has been a persistent challenge for serious games is that problem solving that is dependent on domain knowledge has sometimes resulted in edutainment that requires mastery of content delivered in a highly instructivist manner without regard to the ludic nature of video games. The focus of this chapter lies in problem solving, however, and a discussion of how to design games to incorporate the need for mastery of domain content is beyond the scope of our discussion here. We argue here only that if the designer's goal is to promote problem solving and that problem requires prerequisite knowledge, one must include prerequisite knowledge as a design goal or the problem must be reconceptualized such that it does not require that prior domain knowledge.

Domain knowledge required for problem solving can include declarative knowledge, procedural knowledge, concepts, and principles. Declarative knowledge refers to things that can be stated, also often called verbal information, and includes labels, names, and facts. Procedural knowledge is knowledge of how to conduct a process, whether it is the order of mathematical operations in solving an algebra problem or knowing how to send an e-mail. Concepts are little more slippery, both because everyone thinks they know what a concept is and because concepts can be concrete or abstract. An abstract concept (also called a defined concept) is something that cannot be pointed to but must instead be evaluated according to criteria or a definition. Patriotism is an example, in that whether something is or is not patriotic depends on its relation to a nation's laws, values, and social considerations. In contrast, concrete concepts are things that can be identified and agreed on by virtue of their nature. A ball or a chair is an example of a concrete concept, despite the fact that it can vary tremendously in appearance and surface characteristics. On the other hand, principles are defined by Sugrue (1995, p. 29) as "the rules that involve relationships among the concepts." PBL problems usually involve several concepts. The learners must conceptually interconnect the concepts based on the principles in order to apply the concepts to solve a complex problem.

It is not necessary to be an expert in applying this terminology so much as it is critical that each type of knowledge be explicitly examined during the problem design stage to ensure that all domain-specific prerequisite knowledge be identified and classified so it can be pretested and because each requires different strategies for mastery should it be determined that the strategies must be addressed within the game. It is important to note also that this is all part of the initial instructional analysis and design stages, and does not imply any kind of instructivist approach will become part of the gameplay itself!

iGrids and Gameplay Types

While serious game researchers may not agree on game genre classifications, most would agree that interactivity is one of the hallmarks of video games (Wolf, 2006). As such, interactivity is a good place to start in our attempts to classify games in ways that do not suffer from the problems current genre classifications do. Wolf argues that:

The smallest unit of interactivity is the choice.... Choices are made in time, which gives us a two-dimensional grid of interactivity that can be drawn for any game. First, in the horizontal direction, we have the number of simultaneous (parallel) options that constitute the choice that a player is confronted with at any given moment. Second, in the vertical direction, we have the number of sequential (serial) choices made by a player over time until the end of the game." (p. 80)

Wolf (2006) calls this a Grid of Interactivity, but for semantic reasons, we will refer to it as an Interactivity Grid, or iGrid. Because the frequency of choices and the number of choices make good initial measures of both pace and complexity or cognitive load, and because we believe (and evidence supports) that these constructs are likely to impact problem solving in general and problem typology differentially, iGrids make a good place to start this discussion. Of course, Wolf himself points out that it is not possible to map an entire game space on a graph. For example, in addition to the number of choices at a given time (x axis) and the frequency of opportunities for choice (or choice nexus[3]), he argues that we should further evaluate the consequences of individual choices (from trivial to game-changing). We would further argue that the amount of complexity of the information required at each nexus would be of further value in this analysis. Nonetheless, such plots remain a useful tool for conceptualizing the issue of interactivity and one which we can rely on to further define the kinds of gameplay that differentially support different problem typology.

To do this, we can imagine Aristotelian archetypes of different game genres. For example, in our descriptions of action games and simulation games, *Left 4 Dead* (Valve, 2008) and the *Civilization* series games, we might conceptualize an iGrid as seen in Figure 1.

The x-axis represents parallel interactivity, which is the number of choice options a player has at a given point in time (called a choice nexus), while the y-axis represents how often the player is presented with a choice nexus. For example, the game represented by the iGrid on the left of Figure 1 forces the player to make choices frequently over the course of the game with little time between choices but presents few options to choose from at those points. In the iGrid on the right, we see a game that presents many options to choose from but forces the player to make choices fewer times

Figure 1. iGrids for two different gameplay types

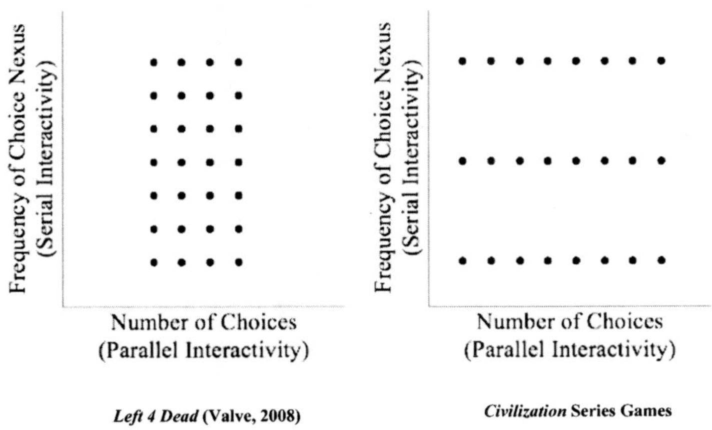

over the course of the game with long periods of time between choices.

Left 4 Dead (Valve, 2008) is a game in which players must fight their way across a city filled with zombies trying to kill them. While there are ostensibly many choices to make during gameplay, (which path to take, how long to wait between "runs," which of five or six weapons to use, or where to take cover), at any given moment (choice nexus), there are only a few choices that can be made. For example, one cannot literally choose from ANY place to take cover, as there are only a few places within immediate reach before one is likely to be attacked. Likewise, there are only a few logical weapon choices to make at any given choice nexus; the assault rifle is best for mowing down hordes of swarming zombies, while the Molotov and shotgun are best for killing large zombies called "tanks." What *Left 4 Dead* and other games with stereotypical action gameplay lack in number of choices (what Wolf calls parallel interactivity) is in this case made up for in the frequency of choice nexus over time (what Wolf calls serial interactivity). There is very little time to consider your individual choice options because gameplay in *Left 4 Dead* is predominantly characterized by repeated choice nexus with little latency. This makes a certain amount of sense from the perspective of extraneous cognitive load; high choice numbers (parallel interactivity) AND high frequency choice nexus (serial interactivity) would quickly overload the abilities of most players, and game testing reveals these limitations. As one aspect increases, the other should, in general, decrease. This can be seen in games like those in the *Civilization* series (see Figure 1).

Some might argue (and we would not disagree) that there are action games with more parallel choices (e.g., weapons, running vs. hiding, inventory, armor, etc.) and periods of gameplay with lower choice nexus frequency. However, just because a game has many *potential* choices at a given juncture, only a subset of those choices is related to that particular juncture. While any game theoretically has access to all of the game controller options—graphics levels, armor, weapons, navigation throughout the environment, etc.—serial interactivity junctures will of necessity limit those options to what is thematically relevant and chronologically possible. I may have 100 different things I *could* do, but if I am in the middle of a firefight, I am not going to check inventory, change armor, invert my game controller axis, etc. There may be other junctures in the game where I can pause and reload, equip weapons, etc., but the archetypal interaction in a first-person shooter (FPS) game is firing while under fire.

Likewise, games like those in the *Civilization* series support near-continuous serial opportunities for interaction, but they do not require it. In fact, they encourage systemic changes (high parallel interactivity) interspersed with periods of observation (serial interactivity) using time compression tools. So any games that share similar features and characteristics of games like the *Civilization* series will be characterized predominantly by an iGrid as seen in Figure 1. Of course, one can imagine any number of games that blend or bend genres, but one can also easily imagine that iGrids could be developed for different parts of those games, and that they would capture the archetypal patterns we imagine for different genres, accordingly.

Gameplay Types and Game Genres

iGrids, as measures of gameplay type, become useful tools for discussing the differences in games that are likely to impact learning. While it is possible to rely solely on these grids in our discussion of gameplay and problem solving, we recognize that mapping what for many is a new tool/concept to existing mental models of game genres will be helpful. Accordingly, we have pulled from several existing taxonomies (most notably, Apperley, 2006) to construct a basic framework of a game classification based not on genre (although we rely on many of the same names and labels as existing genre-based classification systems) but on gameplay characteristics that are commonly associated with such systems. By clarifying or redefining (for some types of games that have been defined differently by researchers) the stereotypical *characteristics* of each gameplay type, we are better able to support the analysis of the problem types and the cognitive processes in gameplay as well as the interrelationships with different types of learning.

We make no assertion that this has any value to the field beyond the ability to organize our discussion of problem solving and games. The reader is referred to any number of excellent texts on genre and game classification, including Ian Bogost's *Persuasive Games: Videogames and Procedural Rhetoric*, and the works of Lee Sherlock, Jasmina Kallay, and Sanna-Mari Äyrämö & Raine Koskimaa, all in this volume. Rather, our system is used solely as a tool for the larger analysis of problem typology and learning outcomes. By providing a description, an example, and an iGrid for each gameplay type below, our analysis can be adapted or applied to whatever classification system is desired.

With this in mind, gameplay types in the following discussion will be divided into six main categories: Action, Strategy, Simulation, Adventure, Role-Playing, and Puzzles. In the following sections, we will also discuss these categories in terms of the nature of the games, muscular–sensory coordination, muscular–cognition coordination, and reflex requirements during the gameplay for each type of game.

Action

We define action games as the type of games where the gameplay mainly consists of activities that require fast reaction time, eye–hand coordination, and reflexes, and in many cases also a familiarity with attack patterns of the game system. FPS, sports games, fighting games, and platform games are typical games under this category. We recognize that conceptually, many readers will be troubled by conflating sports and fighting games within the same category, but we remind the reader that our system is based on the alignment of gameplay with the cognitive, structural, and domain requirements of different problem types, not on narratological or fantasy characteristics of the games. FPSs refer to games where the gameplay is characterized by avoiding being killed and eliminating all enemies with the means (usually in the form of shooting) provided in the game. Sports games are electronic versions of sports that are played in the real world, such as football, tennis, or baseball. Fighting games usually feature one-on-one fighting (e.g., *Mortal Kombat*, Midway, 2004). The player wins the game by defending him/herself and also executes quick and effective attacks to defeat the opponent. Platform games generally refer to the types of games that require the player to perform a number of actions such as jumping, bouncing, running, and so forth, in order to advance through the game. The context and actions for platform games are usually fanciful or imaginary (e.g., *Super Mario Bros*, Nintendo, 1985). iGrids like the one for *Left 4 Dead* in Figure 1 are typical of the gameplay observed in what we call Action games.

Simulation Games

Simulation games are a somewhat problematic category because of the inconsistent categorization of simulation games by different researchers or game designers. For example, Frasca (2003) defined simulations as any game that simulates real-world activities. Apperley (2006) followed the same line of reasoning and included sports games and simulation of the dynamics of city growth as examples of simulations. However, we find this definition to be too broad and problematic in terms of distinguishing specific cognitive processes during gameplay. For example, by Frasca's (2003) definition, both a computer game that simulates the TV game show *Deal or No Deal* and the video game *SimCity* would be classified as simulations. Yet, the cognitive processes in which the player engages are completely different when playing these two games. Whereas *Deal or No Deal* is a game of chance and *SimCity* is a test of the ability to optimize a system by strategically balancing a variety of factors.

To better support analyzing the cognitive processes entailed in these types of gameplay, as well as the problem types associated with them, we define simulation games more narrowly as being characterized by the operations of a given system, for example, flying an airplane, driving a car, or operating machinery. We reserve the term "strategy" for games like the *SimCity* series (see below). The defined characteristics of simulation games include a requirement of specific domain knowledge about the system, specific procedural knowledge about operating the system in normal conditions as well as handling emergency situations, and coordination among cognition, sensory information processing, and muscular movement control. Simulations are also a performative oriented type of game. Successful simulation gameplay consists of accurate, effective, and efficient coordination among the player's domain knowledge, receiving and processing environmental information (situation awareness), quick response to changes in order to make optimal decisions, and performing precise muscular–motor skills in response to the desired course of action. Figure 2 presents an iGrid for a typical simulation game. Depending on the complexity of the simulation, which typically is simplified at early levels with more and more complexity of the system revealed as the player builds expertise, iGrids can vary in number of parallel choices. In general, however, they will look like the grid pictured in Figure 2.

Strategy Games

As we discussed in the simulation game section, strategy games and simulation games share a blurry boundary because of a lack of consensus on the definitions of these two categories of games. In this chapter, we define a strategy game as being characterized primarily by gameplay that involves regular episodes of careful planning, decision making, execution of actions, and adjustment of the actions in order to reach the goal of the game, which typically comprises optimizing the system the player is managing. The most prominent distinction between strategy games and simulation games, in our definition, is the degree of physical, muscular, or psychomotor manipulations involved in the reaction execution during the gameplay. Playing strategy games requires a high level of cognitive processing power in order to engage in analytic reasoning, logical thinking, strategic reasoning, and systemic reasoning. When a decision has been made, the player can execute the desired actions by giving commands. The analysis and decision-making processes in strategic games usually do not require fast reaction times as they do in simulation games. The *SimCity* series of games are examples of strategy games.

The gameplay in strategy games requires a highly sophisticated level of cognitive thinking skills and relatively advanced domain knowledge (although not prior knowledge, necessarily). In order to play and win the game, the player has to

Figure 2. iGrid for simulation games

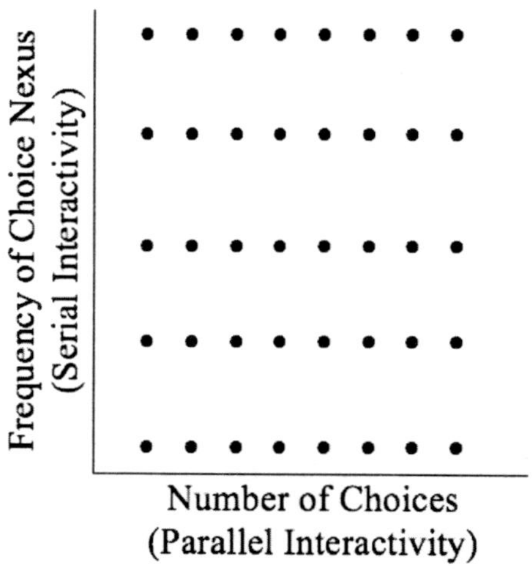

develop an understanding of the system (e.g., a city) and the nature and behaviors of all its components. Also, to maintain and ultimately optimize the system (e.g., balancing health and growth), the player has to strategically balance all components, elements, and aspects that constitute the system. Ideally, there will be multiple ways to reach the goal of the game in the game design. iGrids such as the one in Figure 1 for the *Civilization* series games are typical of strategy games.

Adventure

Although Apperley (2006) has classified adventure and role-playing games in the same category, in this chapter, we will define these two types of games as independent categories. We will discuss the reason for this decision shortly. We define adventure games as a broad category of fantasy games in which the player has to overcome a series of obstacles (usually related narratively) to reach the final goal or destination. The contexts of adventure games are usually some kind of fantasy, which allows endless possibilities for the contexts (the game world) of the games. Adventure games can place the player as a hero on a quest in a mythical land, as an artist in a dreamworld, as a detective (or wrongly accused fugitive) in a city, or as any number of characters and contexts anywhere on the continuum from realism to fantasy. In addition, the obstacles encountered can be of any type, ranging from simple puzzles to complex strategy play, depending upon the complexity and sophistication of the game. Thus, adventure games can be seen as a category that may combine a variety of other categories and gameplay characteristics. However, the most critical distinction between adventure and other categories of games seems to us to be the degree of fantasy (in the sense of narrative backdrop or context rather than the genre) in the game. The elements and degree of fantasy determine how the game player reasons through the problems encountered and solved, which Myers (2003) refers to as the "laws of physics" and "law of play" (p. 12). For the purpose of studying games from an instructional design perspective, this distinction is absolutely critical. Not only does this allow us to distinguish simulations from adventure games, but the distinction also provides us with a means of judging the relevance of subject matter or domain-specific knowledge, reasoning, and skills.

Because adventure games can combine so many different play characteristics, they are perhaps the hardest to capture with an iGrid. However, while there may certainly be periods of interaction in an adventure game that are characteristic of action games, adventure games are most *likely* to comprise opportunities for reflection and choices that require long-term planning and strategy. As a result, they might best be characterized by the grid in Figure 3.

Role-Playing

As we mentioned above, adventure and role-playing games are sometimes classified as the same type of gameplay (e.g., Apperley, 2006). One difference we see between these two gameplay types lies in the player identification with the protagonist. Players may be more likely to develop a psychological or emotional attachment

Figure 3. iGrid for typical adventure games

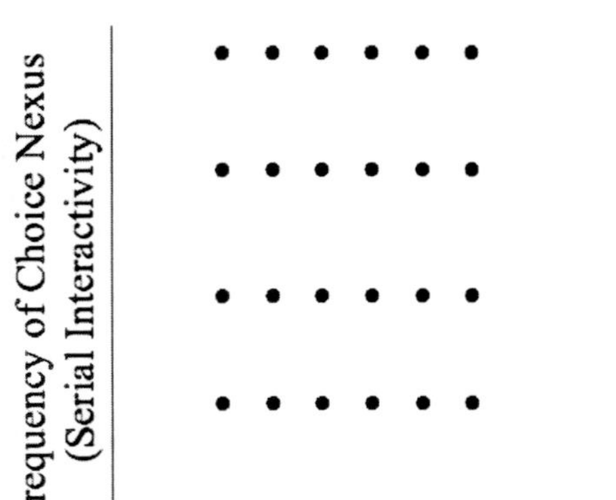

to the character they are playing in role-playing games than adventure games. This is because the characters in role-playing games may carry more salient and complex personalities than the characters do in adventure games and because the player has much more control over and investment in their character's looks and abilities in role-playing games than adventure games.

Another reason for separating these two categories is the availability and increasing popularity of massively multiplayer online role-playing games (MMORPGs). The addition of persistent worlds which continually evolve in the player's absence, and the cooperative play element inherent in MMORPGs brings a whole new dimension into gameplay that the adventure game, which we define predominantly as a single-player game, does not afford. The cooperative dimension of role-playing games enriches the complexity of psychological and social interactions in the gameplay. Similar to adventure games, role-playing games can and often are a combination of other game types, such as shooter plus war strategy. Yet, we argue that role-playing should be in its own category as it contains unique human psychological and social dimensions that could have significant instructional implications (e.g., see Yannuzzi & Behrenhausen, this volume, and Anderson, in press), especially in terms of problems and problem solving. iGrids for role-playing games are most likely to reflect the one depicted in Figure 4, where periods of fighting or action gameplay are interspersed with time for reflection and intense periods of modification of characters and resources (e.g., selling inventory, equipping items, forging new items, trading, building).

Puzzles

Puzzle games refer to any games that are relatively low- or noncontextualized, with few rules, and which can usually be solved through logical reasoning. The criteria for winning these games are often tied to the number of moves (e.g., match

Figure 4. iGrid for role-playing games

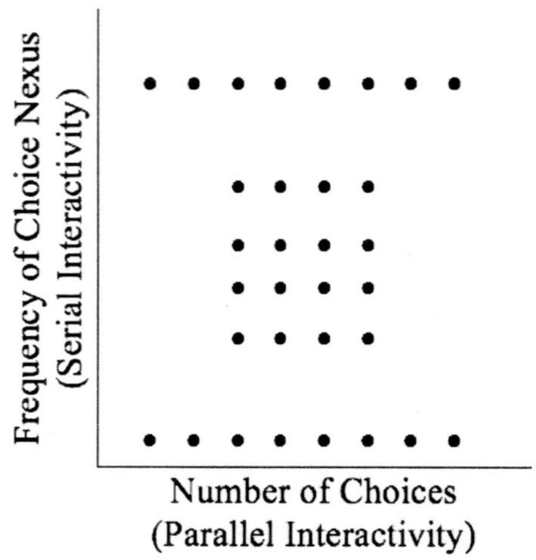

sticks game), the length of time spent, etc. There can be an indefinite number of variations developed from one basic puzzle, and puzzle games can appear as stand-alone games. Very often, however, they are embedded in other types of games, such as adventure, role-playing, or action games. Puzzles are often critical to enriching the engagement, challenge, and entertainment of gameplay in other gameplay types. Because puzzles can incorporate time constraints, the frequency of choice nexus can be varied. However, given the inverse relationship between serial and parallel interactivity described earlier, we can envision two typical forms of iGrids for puzzles that differ primarily in the number of choices presented at a given time, as seen in Figure 5. In the first example, we see a puzzle that provides a choice nexus at a fairly frequent rate over the course of the game, with only two options available at each point. In the second iGrid, we see a puzzle that presents fewer opportunities to make a choice, but requires the player to choose from more options each time.

A Typology of Problems

In the last three sections, we have discussed different types of gameplay and the cognitive skills and other dimensions upon which problems may vary.

Figure 5. iGrids for the most common forms of puzzle games

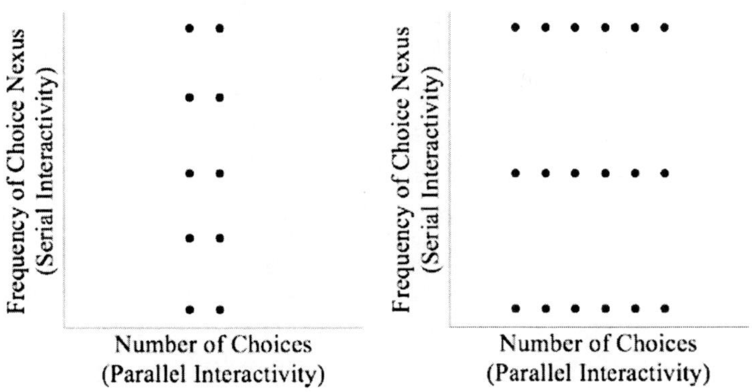

Having now outlined these four key components (structuredness, cognitive composition, prerequisite domain knowledge and iGrids/gameplay types), we now turn our attention to problem typology. In doing so, we will discuss 11 different problem types proposed by Jonassen (2000) within the context of their structuredness, cognitive composition, domain knowledge, and likely gameplay types and corresponding iGrids. We will also provide examples of both the problem types and the kinds of games we envision best supporting them and, where possible and relevant, the other problem types that may possibly be combined or related to a given problem type.

Jonassen (2000) has constructed a comprehensive typology to categorize different types of problems and their nature and characteristics. This typology consists of 11 types of problems:

- Logical problem
- Algorithm problem
- Story problem
- Rule-use problem
- Decision making problem
- Troubleshooting problem
- Diagnosis–solution problem
- Strategic performance problem
- Case analysis problem
- Design problem
- Dilemma problem

In the following sections, we will describe these types in terms of the activities the problems require to solve them, the context in which the problems usually appear, the nature of the problems, and the structuredness of the problems. These problems are, in *general*, presented in order from most to least structured, and from least to most complex. We will further map these to the gameplay types and iGrids that are best aligned with them and provide examples of some games that exemplify our classification.

Regarding these latter two mappings, however, it should be noted that the scope and complexity of any given problem plays a key role in determining which kind of gameplay would be suited for supporting the given problem type. If the problems are small in scope, they may be integrated into a wide variety of games. This is because any given game may employ multiple gameplay types. It is worth repeating that our gameplay types are NOT genres, nor are they intended to necessarily represent any single game; rather, they are descriptions of gameplay that (in some cases) share their names with game genre classifications. Accordingly, when we associate iGrids and gameplay type labels, we do so to indicate the style of gameplay that, *while occurring*, will best support the problem type and its requirements regardless of whatever other gameplay types might occur at other times in a given game. Further since all problem solving may have fluency and/or automaticity as a long-term goal, our assertions about pace of play (e.g., action vs. adventure vs. strategy) should be understood as most applicable to novices during early or intermediate stages of expertise. Players with high-expertise levels within a domain and problem type might be expected to have reduced intrinsic cognitive load and therefore be able to solve problems with gameplay types with more frequent serial interaction, parallel interaction, or both, which may open up additional gameplay types for potential use.

Logical Problems

Logical problems usually involve overcoming a small number of obstacles and a set of rules which have to be complied with in order to achieve the goal. This type of problem is at the far end of well-structured in Jonassen's (1997) structuredness continuum of problems. Solving logical problems typically involves utilizing concept and principle types of knowledge (e.g., propositional logical principles) and logical thinking and analytic thinking processes. Logical problems are often abstract and context-free. Therefore, domain-specific knowledge is not required. *Towers of Hanoi* is an example of a logical problem. There could be situations where subject matter domain knowledge may be required when logical problems are embedded in a more complex, context-specific problem, for example, writing an essay that flows logically.

iGrid and Gameplay Type

Because there are a small number of rules/constraints involved in logic puzzles, and because of the high degree of structure, we believe that puzzle gameplay (Figure 5) is most compatible with logical problems, followed closely by adventure (Figure 3). A logic problem will most commonly have rules and constraints that determine how certain resources can be arranged. This might make logic problems more appropriate for puzzle gameplay like that depicted in the second iGrid in Figure 5. On the other hand, solving a logic problem may, at least for novices, involve isolating one or two variables/constraints and making small moves to test results, which is closer to the gameplay type depicted in the first iGrid of Figure 5. Adventure gameplay also seems well suited to logic problems because of the high parallel interactivity. In both cases, the serial interactivity remains low enough to allow for processing, designing, and evaluating solutions to the problem between moves.

Example Game

Perhaps one of the best examples of gameplay that supports of the logic problem is the seminal game *7th Guest* (Trilobyte, 1992). This popular game took place in a mansion filled with puzzles that had to be solved, many of them logic problems. For example, a cake puzzle required that the cake be cut into six pieces, each having two gravestones, two skulls and one blank square, and with all the squares touching on at least one side (two rules, three characteristics).

Algorithmic Problems

These types of problems require applications of one or a series of procedures to be performed in order to solve a mathematical equation. The problem solver has to execute the steps in the procedure(s) in a certain order to reach the final goal. Algorithmic problems are well structured, abstract, and noncontextual in nature. When solving algorithmic problems, the most critical knowledge includes domain-specific (i.e., mathematics) procedural knowledge, concepts, and principles, and typically involves logical thinking processes. Problem solvers do not need subject matter domain knowledge in order to solve algorithmic problems. These types of problems are commonly seen in school settings. Similar to logical problems, algorithmic problems are often part of more complex problems, such as story problems or design problems. Examples of algorithmic problems include solving [(3+7)*6]/4, calculating the standard deviation of a set of data, or the nonmathematical example of the procedure for changing a tire.

iGrid and Gameplay Type

Their reliance on procedures and steps make these kinds of problems applicable perhaps to several gameplay types. Because they involve logical thinking and are highly structured, like logic problems, they are suited to puzzle and adventure gameplay types (see Figures 3 and 5). However, the addition of procedures also opens them up to a lesser extent for use with action gameplay. Many games provide problems that must be solved through execution of several actions in a specific sequence. When games do this with a time limit on the puzzles, the gameplay begins to resemble an action game (see Figure 1). Regardless, the key characteristic that differentiates gameplay related to algorithmic vs. logic problems is sequence. Logic problems *may* require sequential actions, but algorithmic problems *always* do.

Example Game

A good example of gameplay that supports algorithmic problem solving (albeit nonmathematical in nature) is *Phantasmagoria* (Sierra On-Line, 1995). In the final chapter of *Phantasmagoria*, the main character (Adrienne) confronts the truth about the haunted house she is living in and the disastrous effect it has had on her husband's mental health. In the culminating scene, she must execute at a minimum (depending on which items have been gathered during prior gameplay) 18 separate steps in the correct sequence (e.g, grab acid, throw it, pick up a book, hand an object to her tormentor, pull a lever, exit through a secret passage, and so on). This gameplay is characteristic of action gameplay, despite the fact that most of the gameplay in *Phantasmagoria* is closer to the adventure gameplay type.

Story Problems

Story problems, sometimes also called word problems, are context-bound, although not necessarily realistic. Solving story problems requires domain-specific declarative knowledge, procedural knowledge, concepts, and principles. In Jonassen's (1997) well- and ill-structuredness continuum of problems, story problems are one step away from the well-structured end and more complex than logical and algorithmic problems. Thus story problems can be deemed as precontextualized problems that lie between purely abstract problems (such as algorithmic problems) and fully contextualized problems (such as configuring a subway train schedule). Engaging in the process of solving these types of problems requires logical and analytic thinking, unless the problem solver merely employs formula-based methods (van Heuvelen, 1991) or direct translation strategy (Jonassen, 2003). At times, analogical reasoning could facilitate the solving of story problems (e.g., using worked-examples; Van Merriënboer, 1997). Story problems are often seen as part of the more complex types of problems that we will discuss next. A typical story problem might be "A train drives at a speed of 70 miles per hour, and there is an average of 5 miles between stops on a subway train route. Given that there are 10 stops on this route, how many hours would it take for the train to travel between the starting and the end points?"

iGrid and Gameplay Type

Depending on the nature of its incorporation into any given game, a story problem could once again be well suited to adventure and puzzle gameplay types (Figures 3 and 5). This is because story problems may have at their heart algorithm or logic problems. But because they may *also* be context-bound, be less structured than the first two types, and allow for other strategies (e.g., analogical reasoning), they are unique. This is most likely to manifest itself in the narratological/endogenous fantasy aspects of their integration within a game, more so than in different gameplay types, per se. When they are integrated within more complex problems (as outlined later), story problems may be associated with other gameplay types.

Example Game

Frankly speaking, it is difficult to identify game examples of story problems as opposed to logic or algorithmic problems that are or could be contextualized as stories within given gameplay. The format and structure of a "traditional" story problem is somewhat antithetical to gameplay conventions, in part because story problems are highly structured; many games want to allow players to discover essential elements of the problem distributed throughout the game. Accordingly, it is most relevant to consider story problems in games as types of distributed algorithmic or logic problems with short duration and that may be more implied than explicitly presented. As a hypothetical example, one might be able to integrate a story problem in a game like *Agatha Christie: And Then There Were None* (AWE Productions, 2005). If the trip by boat to the island takes 54 minutes, if we know that four people came out on three trips during one day, and if we have alibi statements from characters regarding their locations at certain times, then it might be possible to disprove one or more alibis by using math to check out their statements. This could be used as a design heuristic, perhaps, in order to integrate the problem type by requiring the player to assemble the relevant parts of the story and to recognize (transfer) story problem-solving strategies in order to solve this part of the problem. Once the player has done so, the gameplay type during that solving process best reflects adventure and puzzle gameplay.

Rule-Using Problems

Rule-using problems, in essence, are the types of problems that likely have multiple solution paths, yet the actions taken along the solution paths are constrained by a set of restrictive rules. They can be highly noncontextual, such as chess or card games, or they can be fully contextualized and fairly complex, such as filing a tax return. The structuredness of rule-using problems can range from well structured to semi-well-structured, depending upon the complexity of the problem. Domain-specific declarative knowledge is *usually* required to solve rule-using problems, while domain concepts and procedural knowledge *may* be needed in some cases. When solving rule-using problems, the problem solvers usually engage in the processes of logical and analytic thinking while complying with the rules. For example, rule-using problems can themselves be logic problems that require rules, such as arranging seating for guests in a diplomatic formal dinner where the formal dinner seating convention has to be complied with and the guests' preferences also need to be taken into account. Rule-using problems are often seen as part of more complex types of problems, for example, decision-making problems, strategic performance problems, and others that we will discuss shortly.

iGrid and Gameplay Type

All games are, to a certain extent, rule-using problems themselves, so it may come as no surprise that we believe that nearly all gameplay types are potentially useful for these types of problems. Of all gameplay types, strategy and role-playing are perhaps best suited to rule-using problems, however. Role-playing gameplay is perhaps the most open-ended of gameplay types, placing a premium on socially negotiated paths among multiple paths constrained by rules for navigation, fighting, interaction, resources at hand, etc. Figure 4 shows the iGrid associated with this gameplay type. Simulation gameplay type is not included here because it has unique requirements (based on our definition) that include psychomotor skills and decision making. Rule-using problems are primarily associated with nonphysical contexts and also do not necessarily involve decision making. Strategy gameplay is also highly open in its support of multiple strategies and paths to the end goal (see Figure 1). Regardless of the gameplay type selected, rule-using problems should have opportunities for low serial interactivity to allow for processing and thinking, although the faster pace associated with parts of role-playing gameplay (as with action gameplay) could be adapted as well for more expert learners.

Example Game

An example of a game that supports rule-using problems via the role-playing gameplay type is *Sacred 2: Fallen Angel* (Ascaron, 2009). In order to defeat many of the major monsters (bosses) in the game, the player must master different strategies, weapons, and abilities, which are in turn impacted by all the attributes of the character, as the player makes choices about where to invest resources. As a Dryad (one of five character types), you may choose to specialize in ranged weapons (e.g., bows) that do a certain amount of damage. However, because you know that some bosses are more or less susceptible to damage related to fire or ice, and because you can equip bows to do more damage by "forging" them with ice crystals or lava rocks, you need to have two bows: one for each damage type. Likewise, you have three "combat aspects," each with five combat "arts," one of which is considered a "buff," and all of which are improved by eating "runes." Combat arts each have their own respective damage type that will be better or worse for certain bosses. The more runes you eat, the more powerful you get, EXCEPT if you exceed your character-level abilities, in which case the runes slow down your regeneration time (how soon you can use them again). ALL of this has to be managed within the context of a given fight. For instance, fighting the octagolamus (a giant squid–snail thing) requires causing fire damage, but it cannot be damaged as fast as it regenerates without using something else. In the Dryad's case, this might mean getting close enough to cast a combination of three combat arts (e.g., "tangled vine" to hold the octagolamus in place, "edaphic lances" to create a series of thorns that do damage while it is held in place, and "black curse," which lowers the boss's attributes so damage is more effective) and *then* firing the fire bow to cause more damage than the boss can repair. This represents just one small part of such role-playing gameplay in which rule-using problems are routine.

Decision-Making Problems

Like rule-using problems, decision-making problems also typically involve multiple options for which the problem solver has to evaluate the advantages and disadvantages and make the most viable selection. When solving decision-making problems effectively, the problem solvers are engaging in the processes of researching as much relevant information as possible, analyzing and assessing the pros and cons of the options, making a value judgment of each option, and then ultimately deciding which option to take. Decision-making problems fall in the middle of the structuredness continuum. Domain-specific concepts and principles are the foundation for solving this type of problem, with the assistance of domain declarative knowledge. In order to perform the necessary problem-solving tasks, logical, analytic, and strategic thinking are key cognitive skills. Systemic and metacognitive thinking may or may not occur, depending upon the nature of the situation. Choosing a retirement plan or deciding which school to attend is an example of a decision-making problem. A decision-making problem can sometimes be a complex version of a combination of logical problem and rule-using problem or can be part of the following types of problems.

iGrid and Gameplay Type

Like rule-using problems, decision problems may incorporate other problem types and are also good for a wide variety of gameplay types, including action (Figure 1), role-playing (Figure 4), and adventure (Figure 3). However, unlike rule-using problems, decision-making problems are not well suited to puzzles because the complexity of decision-making problems outstrips the representational ability of most puzzle gameplay. Decision-making problems also bring the possibility of supporting simulation gameplay (Figure 2) for the first time. Decision-making problems, with their more complex and sophisticated nature, begin to get at what simulations often require. In our opinion, however, strategy gameplay (Figure 1) may hold the most potential for supporting decision-making problems, given the prevalence of decision making, the number of choices presented at a given time, and the resulting need for reflection (low serial interactivity) in this type of gameplay.

Example Game

The classic strategy game series *SimCity* is a well-known example of a game that supports decision-making problems. In this game, the player must make a series of decisions, beginning with decisions about a location to begin building on (e.g., by a river or by arable land) and progressing over time to include tax rates, amount of land or revenue to devote to industry vs. residential vs. the arts, transportation, farmland, infrastructures like fire and police, etc. All of these options require continual evaluative decisions based on tradeoffs (taxes pay for police, but high taxes lead to poverty, dissatisfaction, and riots, which all require police). If the player tries to make decisions once and never revisits those issues, the system quickly spins out of control.

Troubleshooting Problems

Troubleshooting problems are commonly seen in everyday lives. They may be as complex as scientists troubleshooting a computer glitch on the Spirit rover on Mars, or a mechanic troubleshooting an alternator problem in a car or as simple as troubleshooting a lamp with a burned-out light bulb. In terms of problem structuredness, troubleshooting problems can range from semi-well-structured to semi-ill-structured. Solving troubleshooting problems usually involves highly specific domain knowledge, including concepts and principles. Prior domain declarative knowledge is necessary but not the focus of learning how to troubleshoot. It is assumed that problem solvers already possesses a certain degree of declarative knowledge when they troubleshoot or learn how to troubleshoot problems (this assumption is also true of all of the following problem types). Hegarty (1991) suggested that domain procedural knowledge may be critically important in troubleshooting problems when a fault is identified and a procedure needs to be executed in order to restore the system to its normal state. Troubleshooting typically involves recognizing the symptoms (abnormal behaviors of system), identifying possible causes, testing the hypotheses, and then applying corrective procedures (Jonassen & Hung, 2006). Thus, analytic, strategic, and logical reasoning are the main cognitive activities during the troubleshooting process. An experienced troubleshooter also relies on analogical reasoning when encountering similar problems. Systemic and metacognitive thinking may not necessarily be performed by all troubleshooters, but when they are, troubleshooting skills are elevated.

iGrid and Gameplay Type

Whereas we have gone from problem types that are supported by a few gameplay types to those that are supported by a majority of gameplay types, with troubleshooting the picture is much clearer. Simulations (Figure 2) seem to be the only gameplay type suited to troubleshooting. While they range in complexity, the scope of troubleshooting problems remains narrow—never reaching the scale of a *SimCity*, for example. Simulation gameplay focuses on systems (as does strategy gameplay), but they are narrower systems that are tractable via hypothesis testing, for example.[4] Their emphasis on procedural knowledge also makes troubleshooting problems well suited to simulation gameplay.

Example Game

Any game that makes significant use of simulation gameplay makes a good example, and those who have played any variant of the *FlightSim* games will easily see the connection. Since the authors have not played a lot of simulation games and because we suspect this may also be true of many readers, we will focus on *The Incredible Machine* (aka *Contraptions*; Dynamix, 1993) a game that our students have considered for use in K-12 classrooms to teach science. *The Incredible Machine* requires players to design contraptions out of a variety of moving parts (e.g., conveyor belts, funnels, hard or soft surfaces, springs, tunnels) to accomplish different goals (e.g., move the ball from Point A to Point B). Once each machine has been initially designed, gameplay shifts to troubleshooting as the player begins to figure out how and why the system is breaking down. Players move parts, replace parts, change speed, etc., to test what happens and use the results to refine their model of the system and where it is breaking down.

Diagnosis–Solution Problems

These types of problems are similar to troubleshooting problems in terms of the cognitive processes involved. The most common diagnosis–solution problems are medical in nature. Doctors diagnose patients' complaints, identify possible causes of the disease or discomfort, and give a prescription to remedy the problem. Both diagnosis–solution and troubleshooting problems start with a display of symptoms or a fault state that needs to be restored back to a normal state. However, diagnosis–solution problems are usually more ill-structured and complex than troubleshooting problems because there is much more unknown with respect to human physiology than with man-made systems, which results in a higher degree of intransparency of the problem space (Frensch & Funke, 1995b; Jonassen & Hung, 2008; Spering, Wagener, & Funke, 2005). It should be noted, however, that a diagnosis–solution problem need not always be medical. To the degree that a system is open, ill-structured, complex, and intransparent (much is unknown about the system), diagnosis–solution problems may be found. Solving diagnosis–solution problems requires all types of domain knowledge and the process is cognitively engaged at a deep level. The problem solver has to analyze the symptoms, logically rule out the irrelevant or the impossible, analogically reason with similar cases, strategically test the hypotheses, and then prescribe solutions from a holistic (systemic) perspective. Moreover, metacognitive thinking is critical in this type of problem solving because it is an important mechanism for problem solvers to accumulate their knowledge repertoire, skills, and experiences. Diagnosing a patient with an irregular heartbeat rhythm and determining why a marker species is dying off in an otherwise healthy water ecosystem are examples of this type of problem.

iGrid and Gameplay Type

As might be expected, diagnosis–solution problems are supported by simulation gameplay, just as troubleshooting problems are (see Figure 2). The key to supporting diagnosis–solution problems with simulation gameplay lies in the characteristics of the system under diagnosis, as described above. Medical simulations will support medical diagnosis–solution problems, of course, but it is important to remember that much depends on the underlying conceptual model of the simulation. It would be possible to build a highly limited, well-structured, closed-system medical simulation that would in fact NOT reflect true diagnosis–solution problems. When designing such systems and games, it is necessary to at least simulate complexity through random factors and/or to rely on algorithm-based programming (see Crawford, this volume). A good way to do this is to collect real-world case data (e.g., actual medical diagnosis records), including the false leads and the data that led to them.

Because of the complexity, ill-structuredness, and intransparency of the systems underlying diagnosis–solution problems, strategy gameplay may also support these problem types (see Figure 1). We argued before that strategy gameplay does not support rule-using problems because the underlying systems in strategy gameplay tend to be too open, ill-structured, and complex. Here, this is precisely what allows this type of gamplay to support this problem type. There tend to be many factors and criteria to consider at one time (high parallel interactivity), but changes take time to occur and require significant cognitive processing to evaluate and use as inputs to generate new hypotheses and courses of action (low serial interactivity).

Example Game

There are several examples of serious games that focus on medical training (e.g., *Pulse*, by BreakAway Ltd.), but that does not mean that diagnosis–solution problems are being implemented by these games. Game artifical intelligence is not easily able to completely simulate the complexity of the human body, especially since so much is unknown. Because we can only design a game to simulate a system based on what is known, most medical games tend to focus on well-structured problems for which we can specify prescribed solutions. Best-case practices are therefore the content under study, rather than the "messy" real-world complexity of true diagnosis. The degree to which we can simulate, if not replicate, the ill-structured intransparent nature of systems is the degree to which we can support true diagnosis–solution problems.

An example of this kind of approach to supporting this problem type is a game we are currently developing to teach scientific problem solving to middle school students (also see Gaydos and Squire's description of *Citizen Science*, this volume). Based on the National Science Education Standards for science as inquiry, science as a human endeavor, and science in personal and social perspectives, this game requires students to solve a variety of environmental problems that face their hometown. In doing so, they engage in the process of problem identification through solution, implementation, and evaluation. Problems have multiple potential causes and solutions, however, and diagnosing potential causes and proposing solutions requires several rounds of testing and evaluation; information seeking from multiple, conflicting resources; and public buy-in from constituent groups with disparate and often incompatible views. In one scenario, the player hears a news story about potential neurological disabilities on the rise. In researching the story, they find that there are several potential causes (randomness, nutrition, lead poisoning), each of which has several potential sources (e.g., lead poisoning could be waterborne or soil-based from lead paint chips, agricultural runoff, or a petroleum spill), each of which must be ruled out or in. Eventually, students must conduct soil sampling at a specific site in the game to see if there is contamination there. We randomly assign a central source of contamination, using algorithms to radiate the contamination out from that point in weakening amounts, using further random generation within a range of expected contamination values. By constraining the number of tests the player can "afford," we simulate the ill-structuredness of the diagnosis process; taking a few samples at different places yields a range of values that in some cases will be high enough to indicate contamination but in more cases will indicate values within an acceptable "normal" range. The question for the player becomes whether values at the high range of normal indicate randomness or proximity to a site with even higher concentrations. This is similar also to the old board game *Battleship* (Milton Bradley, 1943), in which one "samples" on a grid of coordinates and finds they have missed, near-missed, or scored a direct hit.

Strategic Performance Problems

In Jonassen's (2000) definition of problem typology, strategic performance problems often involve psychomotor skill performance with cognitive processes and metacognitive processes operating consciously or unconsciously within the performer. Solving these types of problems requires the problem solver to fully maintain situational awareness in order to make adjustments in response to the change of the situation/environment. Typical strategic performance problems include operating an airplane, playing in a tennis match, or driving a car. Strategic performance problems are typically ill-structured in nature, since there are a number of courses of action (solution paths) that the problem solver can take. All types of knowledge are needed when solving strategic performance problems, especially procedural knowledge. The most critical cognitive activities during problem solving of this type are strategic and metacognitive thinking. A performer could well possess the domain knowledge, yet the coordination between his or her cognition and muscular control may not occur smoothly or efficiently. Some people will need more practice with muscular–cognition coordination than others. When this happens, strategic and metacognitive thinking become critical to the acceleration of learning and refinement of the performance. In addition, analytic, logical, analogical, and systemic thinking are also supportive in most strategic performance problem cases. In some cases, this type of problem may contain subproblems of troubleshooting or diagnosis–solution problems.

iGrid and Gameplay Type

Given the name of this problem, we might expect that strategy gameplay would support this problem type. That is not the case, however. The primary characteristic of gameplay for this problem type is medium to high serial interactivity, with varying degrees of parallel interactivity, making it appropriate for action, simulation, adventure, and role-playing gametypes (Figures 1–4, respectively). The key lies in the requirement for situational awareness usually coupled with psychomotor skills. When flying a plane, one has to monitor airspeed, pitch, yaw, and altitude, using them in concert to make adjustments using pedals, throttle, and other controls. There are no long periods of time in between adjustments as there are with strategy gameplay.

Example Game

Earlier we described a game with simulation gameplay (flight simulator), and simulations are perhaps the easiest type of gameplay to see in terms of strategic performance. Instead, we will describe an action game with medium-high serial and parallel interactivity because of its fit, its contemporary nature, and because it makes a good example of how problem types can be instantiated in gameplay in ways you might not immediately classify as appropriate. In the game *Left 4 Dead* (Valve, 2008), whether played cooperatively or as single-player, players must work their way from safe house to safe house through a dark, postapocalyptic urban landscape populated by zombies bent on killing humans. In the safe house and during movement through the city, players can pick up health kits and a variety of weapons with different characteristics, each of which has trade-offs and benefits (stopping to pick them up puts you at risk but not doing so puts you at risk later). If players wait in one place too long, the game AI sends more zombies after them, so the game requires consistent (though not continuous) movement through buildings, streets, subways, tunnels, and so on (continuous situational awareness). Attacks come from six different zombie types: Tanks (strong, cause high damage, and are hard to damage), Hunters (fast, unpredictable movement, and cause average damage), Smokers (attack from a distance with prehensile tongues, hold you in place for others to damage, easy to kill), Witches (stay in one place unless disturbed, very fast, high damage, very hard to kill), Boomers (projectile vomit that causes little damage but summons Hordes), and Hordes (swarms of zombies that are easy to kill individually but must be killed rapidly to avoid becoming overwhelmed). As the player moves through the landscape, auditory and visual cues signal the presence of different zombie types (situational awareness), which requires in turn the selection of and rapid switching among appropriate weapons (metacognitive thinking and selection of options, e.g., shotguns and Molotov cocktails for Tanks or automatic assault rifles for Hordes) while charting a future path through the environment (multiple solution paths). One quickly learns the value of cover and the foolishness of running into the woods or trapping oneself in a dead-end room.

Case Analysis Problems

Case analysis problems are often used to help an individual, a company, or an organization understand the individual elements and the intercausal relationships among them in a current situation from a similar situation that has happened in the past. These types of problems have long been used in law schools, business schools, and medical education. They can be seen as semi-ill-structured because there is relatively more known than unknown in the problem space because the problem occurred in the past. Because case analysis problems are highly contextualized, domain-specific knowledge is required. The problem solver's domain concepts and principles serve as the foundation of his or her ability to solve the problem. Procedural knowledge may also be required. In terms of cognitive activities, analytic thinking dominates the problem-solving process with the assistance of analogical thinking and sometimes systemic or logical thinking. This type of problem solving also involves psychological and/or emotional evolution throughout the process when attitude change is involved either consciously or unconsciously. Again, some of this type of problem may contain subproblems of troubleshooting or diagnosis–solution problems.

iGrid and Gameplay Type

Because cases are highly contextualized, rely on analogical reasoning, and often require systemic thinking, strategy gameplay is probably best suited to this problem type (see Figure 1). These problem types require significant time for reflection, making low serial interactivity a necessity. Parallel interactivity will likely be determined by the structuredness of the domain, the amount of domain knowledge required, and the complexity of the case.

Example Game

As an example game for this problem type and the next, we return to the *SimCity* series of games. One of our students developed a lesson plan around these games that required students to design a solution to rebuilding a city that had been destroyed by a variety of natural disasters. The point was not to have students learn about natural disasters in urban planning but rather to allow them to explore the various paths possible in urban planning and the differences that philosophical beliefs make in the long-term evolution of a city. Students were required to establish key goals and indicators for the redevelopment of their cities (e.g., focus on the arts, on public spaces, on industry, on entertainment) and to rebuild their cities accordingly. The resulting cities were then compared across different groups to discuss the impacts that planning decisions have on long-term success and how successful cities can be highly divergent. This in itself is more of a design problem (more on that later), but it is a short step to taking the resulting cities as cases and putting them in the hands of learners who face a different, but related problem. For example, simply using a differently configured city and cause of disaster would qualify the resulting experience as a case study. One might also present a different problem; a city with an insufficient tax base and low industry could be presented with the documented case of a city that recovered from a natural disaster by focusing on industry or a different city that focused on building a "greener" city that balanced industry and environment.

Design Problems

Design problems are highly complex and ill-structured. They usually have a vague goal state and ill-defined criteria for evaluating the success of solving the problem, and an indefinite number of solution paths (Jonassen, 2000). Therefore, on the continuum of problem structuredness, design problems are at the far end of ill-structured and complexity. Engineering design problems, instructional design problems, and interior design problems are examples of design problems. These types of problems are extremely contextualized, thus requiring a solid, domain-specific knowledge base, especially concepts and principles. Also, because of their highly ill-structured and complex nature, solving these problems is a cognitively intense process. All of the higher-order thinking skills we have discussed here are required at some point in the process of solving this type of problem.

iGrid and Gameplay Type

Once again, strategy is the best gameplay type (see Figure 1) for supporting design problems, and we have described one such approach in the prior section (*SimCity*). The key lies in placing tools in the hands of the players to design solutions, whether of a physical or abstract nature (e.g., mechanical engineering vs. human engineering). As such, gameplay requires multiple iterations interspersed with time for reflection and evaluation (medium serial interactivity) and many possible solution paths and decisions (high parallel interactivity).

Example Game

Whereas the focus in our previous example was on using a case (a city that had been redeveloped after natural disaster) to reason about a new, analogous problem, here the focus is on the prior activities we described that lead up to that use of the *SimCity* games as cases. Building a city is itself a design problem, but without constraints, the pedagogical value for novices may be limited. Imposing design constraints (e.g., building for the arts, entertainment, or industry) helps to concentrate the activity as a design problem. Another game we described earlier, *The Incredible Machine* (Dynamix, 1993), supports strategy gameplay for significant portions of the game. Because players must build machines to specifications, engineering design problems are well suited to that game. *The RollerCoaster Tycoon* and *Zoo Tycoon* series of games are also appropriate examples but only to the extent that constraints (some of which will likely need to be external to the game) are added. David Williamson Shaffer's book *How Computer Games Help Children Learn* details other examples of design problems within games such as *Sodaconstructor* (Sodaplay, 2007).

Dilemma Problems

According to Jonassen (2000), dilemma problems are often deemed to have no best solutions. Any solution to a dilemma problem often inherently incurs a similar amount of sacrifices or harm to the individuals involved or the situation when compared to other solutions. The Israeli–Palestinian conflict is a prime example of a dilemma problem.

In addition, dilemma problems usually consist of multiple interest groups or stakeholders whose interests often conflict with each other. Similar to design problems, dilemma problems are also extremely complex, highly contextualized, and very ill-structured. Excluding analogical reasoning, which may or may not be required depending on the nature of the problem, the problem solver engages in the tasks that demand exceptionally high levels of all other types of cognitive processes and thinking skills. While domain-specific knowledge is also critical to dilemma problems because of the high level of context specificity, principles are the most vital form of domain knowledge for supporting this type of problem solving. One potential unintended outcome of solving dilemma problems (it may not be true for all problem solvers) is a change of attitude. This change may be too subtle to notice. Yet, it is logical to assume that a person who goes through solving a dilemma problem has to take all sides of concerns into consideration as well as consider the problem from a systemic or holistic perspective. This person will also experience some degree of psychological or emotional realization, which could result in attitude change.

iGrid and Gameplay Type

Dilemma problems are at the heart of many games for change or persuasive games. For example, *September 12* (Newsgaming.com, 2003) presents the player with a dilemma of whether to kill terrorists (and civilians in the process, thereby creating more terrorists) or allow terrorists to have a free reign (the implication being that terrorist attacks will continue in the world). However, the dilemma in this game is highly simplified and far too well structured to be a good example of this problem type. It is, in essence, a dilemma problem that has been distilled down to the core of two choices. The gameplay types that best support dilemma problems are strategy and role-playing (see Figures 1 and 4, respectively). The more complex and ill-structured the dilemma problem is, the more likely it is that the different nuances and longer interaction times will result in attitude change. Therefore, games like *Darfur is Dying* (mtvU, 2006) have the potential to present larger, more complex dilemmas and thus impact attitude change. Games that employ role-playing will also support dilemma problems in part because of the personal investment players have in their avatars and the social aspects of this kind of gameplay type. Therefore, strategy-roleplaying hybrid games should be ideally suited to dilemma problems and attitude change. Regardless, gameplay type should reflect low-to-medium serial interactivity to allow for consideration of the different factors underlying the dilemma and to identify possible paths for resolution. The exception to this is in role-playing game types, where it is possible to have periods of high serial interactivity (e.g., fighting sequences) that are themselves interspersed throughout gameplay with lower serial interactivity. In theory, there will be higher parallel interactivity as a result of problem complexity, lack of structure, and required domain knowledge.

Example Games

The game *Bioshock* (2K, 2007) pits the player against a variety of challenges in an underwater city named "Rapture." As with *Left 4 Dead* (Valve, 2008), players must make their way through the city without being killed by Big Daddies (giant modified humans in diving suits) and demented humans while collecting weapons and resources. Among these resources are plasmids, which grant special powers by virtue of genetic modifications, and which are injected via syringes. They key to unlocking the powers of plasmids lies in the collection of ADAM, which can only be obtained in the game from Little Sisters, who appear to be preadolescent girls. Little Sisters are always accompanied by Big Daddies, who must be killed before the player can collect ADAM. The dilemma problem in the game occurs with the decision on how to harvest the ADAM. One way results in the death of the Little Sister but results in a large amount of ADAM. The other way saves the Little Sister but results in less ADAM. While this choice seems to be pretty simple (two choices) the choices have a significant impact on the difficulty of the game and the way it proceeds. Additionally, whereas the binary choice in *September 12* (Newsgaming.com, 2003) is limited to the same instances and has the same results easily seen in a short period of time, in *Bioshock* these choices are distributed over the course of up to 50 hours of gameplay with relatively high frequency (medium serial interactivity), and the effects of these choices are not fully realized until near the end of the game.

LEARNED CAPABILITY OUTCOMES, PROBLEM TYPES, AND GAME PLAYING

We have discussed Jonassen's (2000) typology of problems in light of their nature, knowledge required, and cognitive processes, as well as the degree of abstractness and contextualization. We have further matched problems and associated cognitive processes and learned capability outcomes with different gameplay types. The final results of these interrelationships can be seen in Figure 6.

We used types of problems to mediate types of learning and types of gameplay. The reasoning for this is twofold. First, gameplay is a goal-based activity that consists of a series of problem-solving events (Kiili, 2007). Therefore, the type of problems in a game determines the type of cognitive activities involved in gameplay. So identification of the type of problems in gameplay can function as an indicator of what type of learning can be supported. Second, Jonassen's (2000) typology of problems not only explains the nature of different types of problems, but also discusses the learning outcomes with which these problems are usually associated. While we have discussed these in passing in the previous section, a discussion of the specific learned capabilities that each problem type best supports is important to complete the picture of games, problems, and instructional learning outcomes. Therefore, we conclude with a discussion of the relationships between types of learning, problem solving, and gameplay.

Domain-Specific Knowledge Learning

Domain knowledge learning is sometimes referred to as verbal information learning (Gagné, Wager, Golas, & Keller, 2005). Although this type of learning is at a lower level of learning in Bloom's taxonomy of learning, it provides the fundamental building blocks for enabling the learners to engage in higher-order learning. As we can see in Figure 6, domain knowledge learning occurs in all types of problem solving except for logical problems, which can be solved without any specific domain knowledge. Although all problem-solving types involve domain knowledge, there are different subtypes of knowledge acquisition and application that occur among these problems. For example, solving the types of problems that are less complex and with lower levels of contextualization, such as story problems and rule-use problems, requires more declarative knowledge learning. On the other hand, solving more complex and contextualized problems, such as decision making, troubleshooting, diagnosis–solution, and strategic performance problems entails more conceptual and principle knowledge and relies heavily on procedural knowledge. Yet, case analysis problems, design problems, and dilemma problems mainly focus on the integration and flexible utilization of concepts and principles.

How does this information help design effective instructional games? Since all types of problems, except for logical problems, involve different degrees and types of acquisition, comprehension, and application of domain knowledge,

Figure 6. Problem types, their associated cognitive processes, and learned capability outcome, and the gameplay types that might best support them. This analysis depicts the main cognitive processes involved in the problem-solving process. For the problem types that are more complex and highly contextualized, the acquisition of domain knowledge is assumed to be required, and for purposes of readability is not marked in this figure

Knowledge and Cognitive Process															
	Domain–specific knowledge[1]				*Higher–order thinking*						*Psychomotor skills*[2]		*Attitude change*[2]	
Problem type ⇩	Declarative	Procedural	Concepts	Principles	Logical	Analytic	Analogical	Strategic	Systemic	Metacognitive	Muscular movement	Muscular–cognitive coordination	Shift of belief system	**Game type** ⇩
Logical					+	+								Adventure; Puzzle
Algorithmic		+	+	+	+									Adventure; Puzzle; .
Story	+	+	+	+	+	+	+							Adventure; Puzzle
Rule-use	+	~	~	+	+	+								Action; Strategy; Roleplaying; Adven Puzzle
Decision–making		~	+	+	+	+		+	~	~				Action; Strategy; R(playing; Simulation: Adventure
Troubleshooting		+	+	~	+	+	+	+	~	~				Simulations
Diagnosis–solution		+	+	+	+	+	+	+	+	+				Simulations; Strateg
Strategic Performance		+	+	+	+	+	+	+	+	+	+	+		Action; Roleplaying Simulations; Adven
Case Analysis			+	+	~	+	+		~	+			~	Strategy
Design			+	+	+	+	+	+	+	+				Strategy
Dilemma				+	+	+	~	+	+	+			+	Strategy; Roleplayir

[1] For Psychomotor Skills and Attitude Change: domain-specific procedural and principle knowledge and metacognitive thinking are assumed.
[2] For the learning type under Domain Knowledge, application of the knowledge is also assumed in this chart.
\+ signifies "always required."
~ signifies "sometimes required."

all types of gameplay could theoretically support basic domain-specific knowledge learning. As our problem–gameplay analysis reveals, puzzle, adventure, and action games may better support acquisition of declarative knowledge; simulations, action, and adventure could engage learners in honing their procedural knowledge; and strategy, simulation, and sometimes role-playing games may best support concept and principle knowledge application types of learning.

Higher-Order Thinking

Learning higher-order thinking skills includes a variety of cognitive reasoning skills, including logical, analytic, analogical, strategic, systemic, and metacognitive thinking. Although logical thinking could happen in a context-free condition, most higher-order thinking occurs in some type of context and involves various degrees of domain knowledge. As shown in Figure 6, diagnosis–solution, strategic performance, design, and dilemma problems require most of the higher-order thinking skills. This is consistent with our analysis that these types of problems tend to be complex, highly contextualized, and highly ill-structured. In order to deal with the level of complexity and intricacy, a sophisticated practice of integration of these cognitive reasoning skills is critical to the success of solving the problem. Thus, requiring students to solve these types of problems could providing practice opportunities for use of the associated cognitive activities, thus addressing those "critical thinking" skills we hear so much about but which are rarely operationally defined. On the other hand, case analysis, troubleshooting, and decision-making problems could engage students in various higher-order thinking activities as well. This set of problems could be considered specialized problems in terms of enhancing certain types of students' higher-order thinking skills because they tend to rely on one or two aspects of higher-order thinking. For example, case analysis problems emphasize analytic ability, troubleshooting problems focus on logical, analytic, and strategic thinking, while decision-making problems require logical, analytic, and systemic reasoning abilities to select a most viable option based on the condition given. Lastly, algorithmic, story, and rule-use problems could also be used to help students exercise higher-order thinking skills, but given their limited complexity and structuredness, the instructional effects would be less than with other types of problems.

Strategy and simulation games are perhaps the most appropriate types of games for promoting students' learning of higher-order thinking skills. Strategy games are highly cognitively oriented. They should be particularly effective in exercising students' higher-order thinking skills because the activities of these two types of gameplay involve all types of cognitive processes. Simulation games are very effective in facilitating students' development of higher order thinking skills because they require a high level and variety of cognitive reasoning in order to perform the muscular movement and to manipulate the system operation to an optimal level. However, the requirement of muscular movement control would likely take up some capacity of working memory. As a result, the exercise of cognitive processing would run at full capacity in simulation games, as opposed to strategy games where the full working memory power is devoted to cognitive processing. Therefore, simulation games may be somewhat less versatile than strategy games in enhancing the development of (pure) cognitive thinking skills. Action, role-playing, and adventure games may also provide opportunities for students to develop higher-order thinking skills, but because these games usually involve other types of gameplay activities (e.g., eye–hand coordination, quick reflex), they are less effectively used for the sole learning goal of developing higher-order thinking skills. Lastly, when the learning goal targets one or two particular types of thinking skills, then adventure and puzzle games may be an appropriate option. Puzzle games could also be embedded in more complex games, such as adventure, simulations, or strategy games. Thus they could train for one particular type of thinking skill (e.g., logical thinking) or be aggregated with several puzzle games to form an adventure game to address multiple skills.

Psychomotor Skills

Strategic performance is the main type of problem that requires the necessary cognitive processes and physical performance to support psychomotor skill learning. Psychomotor skill learning (e.g., flying an airplane, operating a crane ship, or hitting a baseball) involves perfecting both the muscular movements in a specific order and the smoothness of the transitions between each movement (Gange et al., 2005). The key to psychomotor skill learning is the coordination between cognition and muscular movements, as well as the strategic thinking that supports optimal performance. A psychomotor skill performance is usually dynamic and involves interaction between either two performers or a performer and a system.

Because of this dynamic, interactive nature of the task, cognition (i.e., strategic thinking) sometimes plays an even more important role than muscular movements. Therefore, psychomotor skill learning is an intensely muscular–cognitive process.

A number of gameplay types could afford the learning of psychomotor skills. Simulations, adventure, action, and role-playing games are appropriate but with different emphases and degrees. When the learning goal is within a specific context or profession, simulations may be the most suitable gameplay type because simulations naturally set the gameplay in a highly contextualized (or authentic) environment. Other types of gameplay, such as action, adventure, or role-playing, could be used to provide practice with eye–hand coordination or multiple modalities of inputs that are not profession-specific but could be useful in other capacities. Another advantage of these gameplay types is training for quick responses or reflexes. These are critical skills in most strategic performance problem solving and, therefore, are essential to psychomotor skill learning.

Attitude Change

Attitude change is a higher-order level of learning. It involves not only cognitive processing but also psychological, social, emotional, and affective changes of state (Gagne et al., 2005). The end result is a shift in one's belief system. The problem types that involve these internal changes of state include case analysis and dilemma problems. Both case analysis problems and dilemma problems require the problem solver to analyze all parties involved in the problem at a very deep, personal, psychological, or emotional level. However, these problems also require the problem solver to examine all parties from multiple, holistic, societal, and even global perspectives. Going through these examinations and contemplations psychologically, emotionally, scientifically, and socioculturally, it is possible that the problem solver also goes through a fundamental and philosophical retrospective journey. Therefore, solving these types of problems may bring about attitude change.

Strategy and role-playing games may be the second tier of gameplay that is likely to afford this type of learning. Strategy gameplay requires the player to manage the system (e.g., a city, a business, or a battle) to its optimal state. In order to reach that goal, the player has to have a deep understanding of each component in the system. Role-playing games have the advantage that the player is likely to develop a deep personal psychological attachment to the character that he or she plays. The features of strategy and role-playing games are capable of affording the cognitive requirements for attitude change. However, the requisite psychological, emotional, or sociocultural components in most commercial strategy and role-playing games are absent. This is understandable because commercial games are not designed to fulfill educational goals. Here, we are simply arguing that if appropriate psychological, emotional, and sociocultural components are incorporated into the game design, strategy games and role-playing games could afford attitude change learning.

FUTURE RESEARCH DIRECTIONS

The tools and processes and relationships described in this chapter suggest a variety of design research activities, some of which are summarized briefly below.

Studies of Problem Solving

If we are right about the use of iGrids and serial vs. parallel interactivity, using these grids to classify different gameplay (which will occur to varying degrees within a given game) should lead to experimental designs of specific kinds of problem-solving skills as supported by specific gameplay types. Existing research in problem solving has created a large body of potential problems that could be used as outcome measures of specific problem-solving types. Validated problem design models (e.g., 3C3R by Hung, 2006a) should be used to design analog problems that reflect the serial and parallel interactivity characteristics supported by the gameplay to increase contextual similarities.

iGrids and problem types should also be used to develop specific gameplay types, and the resulting effects on learning should be measured to validate the assumptions of our approach. Likewise, combinations of gameplay types within a given game and their ability to support corresponding problems should also be studied to see what additive or interactive effects occur, but only after validation of these types have occurred in single-mode studies.

Consequences of Choices

Wolf (2006) argues that in addition to serial and parallel interactivity, we should also examine the *consequences* of choices as another dimension of interactivity. What role does choice consequence play in learning, problem solving, and attitude change? How is choice consequence related to high and low interactivity (serial and parallel)? This is an independent variable that, like serial and parallel interactivity, can be manipulated and controlled to examine the effects on a variety of dependent variables (e.g., problem solving).

Cognitive Load of Domain Knowledge Required for Individual Choices

While cognitive load is very much influenced by individual characteristics, prior knowledge, and expertise, it is also determined by the nature of the content, the interface of the instructional medium, and the type of problem being solved. Suffice it to say that aspects of the different problem types we have addressed will require different amounts of time for processing and solving and that the demands of the interface (the game) must be designed appropriately for these processes. Further, different game ontologies often, but imperfectly, captured by notions of genre, will support this processing time differentially. For example, FPS games often have elements that require continuous attention with little time for reflection. Such elements privilege automaticity and fluency of action–reaction over planning and reflection.

Researchers and designers should look at issues of extraneous, germane, and intrinsic cognitive load (Low, Sweller, and Jin in press) at the choice nexus as a result of both the number and the complexity of choices (parallel interactivity), and at the cumulative effect of choices over time (parallel interactivity). Researchers should also examine the cognitive load that results from the interaction of gameplay type and problem elements to establish ideal frequencies for problem-solving nexuses. Researchers should further examine the role that problem complexity (germane cognitive load) plays in the amount of time needed for problem solving and metacognition. All of the different elements of problem solving may be expected to differentially impact cognitive load as well (e.g., type of cognition, the role of prior domain knowledge, structuredness of the domain) and should be studied first independently and then later for interactions.

CONCLUSION

If serious game designers hope to create games that promote problem solving, they must build on existing problem-solving research and generate new research and design heuristics on the alignment of problem solving and different gameplay types. In this chapter, we used Jonassen's typology of problem types to help analyze the cognitive processes involved in different types of gameplay and, in turn, dissected gameplay that brought the essential characteristics (for problem solving, at any rate) to light. With an understanding of the cognitive, physical, and domain knowledge requirements of each type of gameplay, instructional designers and game developers will have a better idea of what types of gameplay will most appropriately afford given learning goals and objectives. This chapter is not intended to provide a comprehensive set of guidelines for designing instructional games or selecting commercial games for instructional purposes but to promote a more cogent model for what we mean by problem solving in games and to provide a starting point for future research, design, and discussion of games to promote problem solving.

REFERENCES

2K2007). *Bioshock*. [Console game]. USA: 2K.

Anderson, B. (in press). MMOGs in support of learning: Current trends and future uses. In Van Eck, R. (Ed.), *Gaming & cognition: Theories and practice from the learning sciences*. Hershey, PA: IGI Global.

Apperley, T. H. (2006). Genre and game studies: Toward a critical approach to video game genres. *Simulation & Gaming*, *37*(1), 6–23. doi:10.1177/1046878105282278

Armstrong, S., & Warlick, D. (2004). The new literacy. *TechLearning*, *25*(2), 24–31.

Ascaron. (2009). *Sacred 2: Fallen Angel*. [Console game]. USA: Ascaraon.

Äyrämö, S.-M., & Koskimaa, R. (in press). Narrative definitions for game design: A concept-oriented study of nine computer game design books. In Van Eck, R. (Ed.), *Interdisciplinary models and tools for serious games: Emerging concepts and future directions*. Hershey, PA: IGI Global.

Bhaskar, R., & Simon, H. A. (1977). Problem solving in semantically rich domains: An example from engineering thermodynamics. *Cognitive Science*, *1*, 193–215.

Blizzard. (2001). *World of Warcraft*. [PC game]. USA: Blizzard.

Bogost, I. (2007). *Persuasive games: The expressive power of videogames*. Cambridge, MA: MIT Press.

BreakAway. (n.d.). *Pulse: Virtual Clinical Learning Lab for Health Care Training*. [Video game]. USA: BreakAway. *Ltd.*

Broussard, S. R., La Lopa, J. M., & Ross-Davis, A. (2007). Synergistic knowledge development in interdisciplinary teams. *Journal of Natural Resources and Life Sciences Education*, *36*, 129–133.

Capra, F. (1996). *The web of life: A new scientific understanding of living systems*. New York: Doubleday.

Crawford, C. (in press). Interactivity, process, and algorithm. In Van Eck, R. (Ed.), *Interdisciplinary models and tools for serious games: Emerging concepts and future directions*. Hershey, PA: IGI Global.

Dick, W., Carey, L., & Carey, J. O. (2005). *The systematic design of instruction* (6th ed.). Boston: Pearson.

Driscoll, M. P. (2005). *Psychology of learning for instruction* (3rd ed.). Boston: Pearson.

Dynamix. (1993). *The Incredible Machine*. [PC game]. USA: Dynamix.

Entertainment Arts. (2008). *Spore* [PC game]. USA: EA Games.

Flavell, J. H. (1985). *Cognitive development* (2nd ed.). Englewood Cliff, NJ: Prentice Hall.

Frasca, G. (2003). Simulation versus narrative: Introduction to ludology. In Wolf, M. J. P., & Perron, B. (Eds.), *The video game theory reader*. New York: Routledge.

Frensch, P. A., & Funke, J. (1995a). *Complex problem solving: The European perspective*. Mahwah, NJ: Lawrence Erlbaum Associates.

Frensch, P. A., & Funke, J. (1995b). Definitions, traditions, and a general framework for understanding complex problem solving. In Frensch, P. A., & Funke, J. (Eds.), *Complex problem solving: The European perspective* (pp. 3–25). Hillsdale, NJ: Erlbaum.

Gagné, R. M., Wager, W. W., Golas, K. C., & Keller, J. M. (2005). *Principles of instructional design* (5th ed.). Belmont, CA: Wadsworth/Thomson Learning.

Gaydos, M., & Squire, K. (in press). Citizen science: Designing a game for the 21st century. In Van Eck, R. (Ed.), *Interdisciplinary models and tools for serious games: Emerging concepts and future directions*. Hershey, PA: IGI Global.

Gee, J. P. (2007a). Games and learning: Issues, perils and potentials. In Gee, J. P. (Ed.), *Good video games and good learning: Collected essays on video games, learning and literacy* (pp. 129–174). New York: Palgrave/Macmillan.

Gee, J. P. (2007b). Learning and Games. In Salen, K. (Ed.), *The Ecology of games: Connecting youth, games, and learning* (pp. 21–40). Cambridge: MIT Press.

Greenfield, P. M. (in press). Video Games. In Van Eck, R. (Ed.), *Gaming & cognition: Theories and practice from the learning sciences*. Hershey, PA: IGI Global.

Hegarty, M. (1991). Knowledge and processes in mechanical problem solving. In Sternberg, R. J., & Frensch, P. A. (Eds.), *Complex problem solving: Principles and mechanisms* (pp. 253–185). Hillsdale, NJ: Erlbaum.

Holyoak, K. J., & Thagard, P. (1997). The analogical mind. *The American Psychologist*, *52*(1), 35–44. doi:10.1037/0003-066X.52.1.35

Houdé, O., & Tzourio-Mazoyer, N. (2003). Neural foundations of logical and mathematical cognition. *Nature Reviews. Neuroscience*, *4*, 507–514. doi:10.1038/nrn1117

Hung, W. (2006a). The 3C3R model: A conceptual framework for designing problems in PBL. *Interdisciplinary Journal of Problem-based Learning*, *1*(1), 55–77.

Hung, W. (2006b). *Application of 3C3R PBL problem design model: A 9-step design process*. Paper presented at the annual meeting of the American Educational Research Association, April 7–11, San Francisco.

Jonassen, D. H. (1997). Instructional design models for well-structured and ill-structured problem solving learning outcomes. *ETR&D*, *45*(1), 65–94. doi:10.1007/BF02299613

Jonassen, D. H. (2000). Toward a design theory of problem solving. *ETR&D*, *48*(4), 63–85. doi:10.1007/BF02300500

Jonassen, D. H. (2002). Integration of problem solving into instructional design. In R. A. Reiser & J. V. Dempsey (Eds.), Trends and issues in instructional design & technology 107-120). Upper Saddle River, NJ: Merrill Prentice Hall.

Jonassen, D. H. (2003). Designing research-based instruction for story problems. *Educational Psychology Review*, *15*(3), 267–296. doi:10.1023/A:1024648217919

Jonassen, D. H., & Hung, W. (2006). Learning to troubleshoot: A new theory based design architecture. *Educational Psychology Review*, *18*(1), 77–114. doi:10.1007/s10648-006-9001-8

Jonassen, D. H., & Hung, W. (2008). All problems are not equal: Implications for PBL. *Interdisciplinary Journal of Problem-Based Learning*, *2*(2), 6–28.

Kallay, J. (in press). Rethinking genre in computer games: How narrative psychology connects game and story. In Van Eck, R. (Ed.), *Interdisciplinary models and tools for serious games: emerging concepts and future directions*. Hershey, PA: IGI Global.

Kiili, K. (2007). Foundation for problem-based gaming. *British Journal of Educational Technology*, *38*(3), 394–404. doi:10.1111/j.1467-8535.2007.00704.x

Kolodner, J. L. (1997). Educational implications of analogy: A view from case-based reasoning. *The American Psychologist*, *52*(1), 57–66. doi:10.1037/0003-066X.52.1.57

Liedtka, J. M. (1998). Strategic thinking: Can it be taught. *Long Range Planning*, *31*(1), 120–129. doi:10.1016/S0024-6301(97)00098-8

Low, R., Jin, P., & Sweller, J. (in press). Learners' cognitive load when using educational technology. In Van Eck, R. (Ed.), *Gaming & cognition: Theories and practice from the learning sciences*. Hershey, PA: IGI Global.

Midway Games. (2004). *Mortal Kombat* [PC game]. USA: Midway Games.

Milton Bradley. (1943). *Battleship* [Board game]. USA: Milton Bradley.

Mintzberg, H. (1994). *The rise and fall of strategic planning*. New York: The Free Press.

mtvU. (2006). *Darfur Is Dying*. [Online game]. Retrieved March 29, 2009, from http://www.darfurisdying.com

Myers, D. (2003). *The nature of computer games: Play as semiosis*. New York: Peter Lang.

Newell, A., & Simon, H. A. (1972). *Human problem solving*. Englewood Cliffs, NJ: Prentice-Hall.

Newsgaming.com. (2003). *September 12th*. [Online game]. Montevideo, Uruguay: Newsgaming.com. Retrieved March 29, 2009, from http://newsgaming.com/newsgames.htm

Nintendo. (1985). *Super Mario Brothers*. [Console game]. Japan: Nintendo

OECD. (2004). *Problem solving for tomorrow's world: First measures of cross-curricular competencies from PISA 2003*. Organization for Economic Co-Operation and Development.

Ossimitz, G. (2000). *Teaching system dynamics and systems thinking in Austria and Germany*. A paper presented at the system dynamics 2000 conference in Bergen, Norway, August 2000. Retrieved February 27, 2004, http://www.uni-klu.ac.at/~gossimit/pap/ossimitz_teaching.pdf

Productions, A. W. E. (2005). *Agatha Christie: And Then There Were None* [Console game]. USA: AWE Productions.

Shaffer, D. W. (2006). *How computer games help children learn*. New York: Palgrave Macmillan. doi:10.1057/9780230601994

Sherlock, L. (in press). Toward a rhetoric of serious game genres. In Van Eck, R. (Ed.), *Interdisciplinary models and tools for serious games: Emerging concepts and future directions*. Hershey, PA: IGI Global.

Sierra On-Line. (1995). *Phantasmagoria* [PC game]. USA: Sierra On-Line.

Smith, P. L., & Ragan, T. J. (2005). *Instructional design* (3rd ed.). San Francisco: Jossey-Bass Education.

Sodaplay. (2007). *Sodaconstructor*. [Online game]. Retrieved from http://sodaplay.com.

Spering, M., Wagener, D., & Funke, J. (2005). Brief report: The role of emotions in complex problem-solving. *Cognition and Emotion, 19*(8), 1252–1261. doi:10.1080/02699930500304886

Sterman, J. D. (2002). All models are wrong: Reflections on becoming a systems scientist. *System Dynamics Review, 18*(4), 501–531. doi:10.1002/sdr.261

Strawn, G. (2007). *Change: the constant of modern times.* Keynote presentation for the Instructional Technology Conference, April 2 – 4, Middle Tennessee State University, Murfreesboro, TN.

Sugrue, B. (1995). A theory-based framework for assessing domain-specific problem-solving ability. *Educational Measurement: Issues and Practice, 14*(3), 32–35. doi:10.1111/j.1745-3992.1995.tb00865.x

Towers of Hanoi. (2002). In *Wikipedia, the free encyclopedia.* Retrieved July 13, 2009 from http://en.wikipedia.org/wiki/Tower_of_Hanoi

Trilobyte. (1992). *The 7th Guest.* [PC game]. USA: Trilobyte.

Valve. (2008). *Left 4 Dead.* [Console game]. USA: Valve.

Van Eck, R. (September, 2006a). Building intelligent learning games. In D. Gibson, C. Aldrich, & M. Prensky (Eds.), Games and simulations in online learning: Research & development frameworks. Hershey, PA: Idea Group.

Van Eck, R. (2006b, March/April). Digital game-based learning: It's not just the digital natives who are restless.... *EDUCAUSE Review, 41*(2).

Van Eck, R. (2007). Six ideas in search of a discipline. In Shelton, B., & Wiley, D. (Eds.), *The educational design and use of computer simulation games.* Boston, MA: Sense.

Van Eck, R. (2008). COTS in the Classroom: A teachers guide to integrating commercial off-the-shelf (COTS) games. In Ferdig, R. (Ed.), *Handbook of research on effective electronic gaming in education.* Hershey, PA: Idea Group.

Van Eck, R., Hung, W., Bowman, F., & Love, S. (2009). 21st century game design: a model and prototype for promoting scientific problem solving. In *Proceedings of the International Association of Science and Technology for Development's annual Computers and Advanced Technology in Education conference*, November 22 -24, St. Thomas, US Virgin Islands.

Van Merriënboer, J. (1997). *Training complex cognitive skills: A four-component instructional design model for technical training.* Englewood Cliffs, NJ: Educational Technology Publications.

Wolf, M. J. P. (2006, December). Emerging world of anime and manga. *Mechademia, 1*, 78–85.

Yannuzzi, T. J., & Behrenshausen, B. G. (in press). Serious games for transformative learning: A communication perspective on the radical binarisation of everyday life. In Van Eck, R. (Ed.), *Interdisciplinary models and tools for serious games: Emerging concepts and future directions.* Hershey, PA: IGI Global.

"MUST READS" FOR THIS TOPIC

Apperley, T. H. (2006). Genre and game studies: Toward a critical approach to video game genres. *Simulation & Gaming, 37*(1), 6–23. doi:10.1177/1046878105282278

Frensch, P. A., & Funke, J. (1995). Definitions, traditions, and a general framework for understanding complex problem solving. In Frensch, P. A., & Funke, J. (Eds.), *Complex problem solving: The European perspective* (pp. 3–25). Hillsdale, NJ: Erlbaum.

Hung, W. (2006). The 3C3R model: A conceptual framework for designing problems in PBL. *Interdisciplinary Journal of Problem-Based Learning, 1*(1), 55–77.

Hung, W. (2006b). *Application of 3C3R PBL problem design model: A 9-step design process.* Paper presented at the annual meeting of the American Educational Research Association, April 7–11, San Francisco.

Jonassen, D. H. (1997). Instructional design models for well-structured and ill-structured problem solving learning outcomes. *ETR&D, 45*(1), 65–94. doi:10.1007/BF02299613

Jonassen, D. H. (2000). Toward a design theory of problem solving. *ETR&D, 48*(4), 63–85. doi:10.1007/BF02300500

Jonassen, D. H., & Hung, W. (2008). All problems are not equal: Implications for PBL. *Interdisciplinary Journal of Problem-Based Learning, 2*(2), 6–28.

Kallay, J. (in press). Rethinking genre in computer games: How narrative psychology connects game and story. In Van Eck, R. (Ed.), *Interdisciplinary models and tools for serious games: Emerging concepts and future directions*. Hershey, PA: IGI Global.

Kiili, K. (2007). Foundation for problem-based gaming. *British Journal of Educational Technology, 38*(3), 394–404. doi:10.1111/j.1467-8535.2007.00704.x

Low, R., Jin, P., & Sweller, J. (in press). Learners' cognitive load when using educational technology. In Van Eck, R. (Ed.), *Gaming & cognition: Theories and practice from the learning sciences*. Hershey, PA: IGI Global.

Wolfe, M. J. P. (2006, December). Assessing interactivity in video game design. *Mechademia, 1*, 78–85.

TOP TEXTS FOR INTERDISCIPLINARY STUDIES OF SERIOUS GAMES

Cassell, J., & Jenkins, H. (Eds.). (2000). *From Barbie to Mortal Kombat: Gender and computer games*. Cambridge, MA: MIT Press.

Gee, J. P. (2003). *What video games have to teach us about learning and literacy*. New York: Palgrave MacMillan.

Koster, R. (2005). *A theory of fun for game design*. Scottsdale, AZ: Paraglyph.

Perron, B. (2009). *Video Game Theory Reader 2*. New York: Routledge.

Raessens, J., & Goldstein, J. (Eds.). (2005). *Handbook of computer game studies*. Cambridge, MA: MIT Press.

Rieber, L. P. (1996). Seriously considering play: Designing interactive learning environments based on the blending of microworlds, simulations, and games. *Educational Technology Research and Development, 44*(2), 43–58. doi:10.1007/BF02300540

Salen, K. (2007). *The ecology of games: Connecting youth, games, and learning*. Cambridge, MA: MIT Press.

Shaffer, D. W. (2006). *How computer games help children learn*. New York: Palgrave Macmillan. doi:10.1057/9780230601994

Wardrip-Fruin, N., & Harrigan, P. (2004). *First person: New media as story, performance, game*. Cambridge, MA: MIT Press.

Wolf, M. J. P., & Perron, B. (2003). *Video game theory reader*. New York: Routledge.

ENDNOTES

1 Historical data presented here are generally agreed on by researchers in the U.S. and Europe, despite different perspectives taken in the study of complex problem solving. Information presented here is based on Frensch & Funke, 1995.

2 It is ironic that the Gestaltists believed this, as their view of the importance of experience and the real world might have sooner led to the realization that problems and problem solving were likely to be differentiated by the varied nature of problem solving in different contexts.

3 Nexus is both the singular and plural form

4 It is true that one could conceptualize strategy gameplay as a series of sub-systems amenable to hypothesis testing, but larger systems like those underlying most games that employ strategy gameplay tend to be open systems that are not amenable to such approaches over time.

Chapter 11
Serious Games for the Classroom:
A Case Study of Designing and Developing a Massive Multiplayer Online Game

Scott Wilson
University of Oklahoma, USA

Leslie Williams
University of Oklahoma, USA

ABSTRACT

The University of Oklahoma's K20 Center shares the process of developing a massive multiplayer online game. This chapter identifies the process used to meet the challenge for the design, prototype, development, and beta test of a digital game-based learning environment. The project's goal was to develop a self-regulated constructivist learning environment where students work in groups to solve a series of complex, ill-structured problems. The multiuser game provides an interactive learning experience which allows students to experience authentic intellectual work in a virtual representation of a real-world context. Students are challenged through their participation in an interdisciplinary environment that leverages a real-world problem to utilize the different perspectives of the four major disciplines. The authors provide a description of the project's efforts to develop a shared learning space that creates scaffolding of social support of other students and a gaming environment that emulates successful elements of commercial video games to ensure an engaging learning experience for all students.

INTRODUCTION

The K20 Center at the University of Oklahoma entered the world of serious games through the award of a 3-year Star Schools research grant from the U.S. Department of Education (DoE). The DoE's request for proposals specified learning games on a mobile platform. The K20 Center's proposal, developed in 2004, promised to develop interactive learning applets on high-end handheld devices (e.g., Palm, Dell Axiom, etc.). After receiving the award and early in the process of working with focus groups of students and teachers, it was determined that a short-lived platform had been selected and the students in our focus group had developed higher expectations for interactive learning. These students

DOI: 10.4018/978-1-61520-719-0.ch011

Copyright © 2010, IGI Global. Copying or distributing in print or electronic forms without written permission of IGI Global is prohibited.

quickly urged us to explore the realm of a massive multiplayer online game (MMOG) as a learning environment. One option was to deliver what had been promised and risk quickly becoming irrelevant as the platform was forced into extinction by the convergence cell phone. The other option advocated by students in our focus groups was to enter a project that was fraught with unknowns—an unknown platform with unknown technical capabilities that was to be designed by a group of university students majoring in computer science, who were unaccustomed to working within a team environment on a large programming project. The K20 Center chose the latter.

In electing to take this path, the K20 Center encountered several problems that, if not mitigated, promised to derail the entire development process. These problems included (1) developing for a platform that was not currently commercially available, as opposed to developing for a platform, like the personal digital assistant (PDA), which looked as if it was to be replaced by convergence phones; (2) students' expectations of games based on their almost daily immersion in commercial off-the-shelf (COTS) games; (3) teachers' hesitation to give up direct instruction for unproven innovative learning practices; (4) developing the capacity to use university students as the development team; (5) developing a serious game, with a focus on instructional design guided by state and national standards; and (6) managing the technical challenges encountered in implementing an MMOG in schools with a diverse range of network capabilities.

Early in the development process, even before the shift from the PDA as a platform, there seemed to be a disconnect between the game design consultant, who had considerable expertise in the area of learning games, and the central philosophy of the K20 Center—engaging students with authentic learning scenarios. The Center found itself in the same dilemma that other serious game efforts have encountered: a large gulf separates game study academicians and educators who serve as gatekeepers on what type of innovation will be placed in front of the students in their classroom. So the question Holland, Jenkins, and Squire asked in 2003 still begs to be answered—"how to help these two worlds, that of gaming and that of education, to work together" (p. 29). An equally expansive separation exists between the academic area of game studies and the commercial game industry. Fernández-Vara, Grigsby, Glinert, Tan, and Jenkins (2009) cited a Microsoft researcher as challenging university scholars "to come down from the ivory tower and demonstrate the value of their theories through the building of actual games" (p. 256). The K20 Center's response to this dilemma was to develop a serious game development model that leveraged both the philosophical base of the Center and the management techniques used in the software industry for highly complex projects with a large number of factors and/or solutions unknown or unfamiliar to the development team.

In this chapter, we present a case study of the development and management of a multiplayer game engine and game: *McLarin's Adventures* (or *McLarin*). The game is cross-curricular, aligned with state standards, and designed for 8th- and 9th-grade students. It is our hope that the model that emerged from this collaborative process will help address the problems facing serious game developers today. In this chapter we will (1) highlight the theoretical framework used as a foundation for the project, (2) elaborate on the design process that maximized the end-user's voice in the development of *McLarin*, and (3) describe the project management methodology that allowed the initiative to flourish in a complex environment.

THEORETICAL FRAMEWORK FOR AUTHENTIC LEARNING

An educational game that is designed for classroom use must reflect current research-based understandings of how students learn best. Educators know that the world of work rarely asks a person to solve a predefined linear equation. Instead, a set of circumstances and a problem are encountered. Successful adults use a variety of sources of information and techniques to solve often poorly defined problems. This realization has led to a radical reconsideration of how students are best taught.

Many classes still use "the sage on the stage" model, where an expert attempts to fill the intellectual vessels of students by sharing his or her knowledge through lecture. Current research in education calls into question the effectiveness of traditional, lecture-based teaching. Having students listen while faculty present well-formed solutions to routine problems is now known to be less effective than encouraging students to directly and personally interact with the material, a learning theory called constructivism. Constructivists believe that students learn most effectively when they are actively engaged (1) with a group of students (Loyens & Gijbels, 2008; Loyens, Rikers, & Schmidt, 2007); (2) as self-regulated learners (Loyens & Gijbels, 2008; Paris & Paris, 2001); (3) in working complex, ill-structured problems resembling real-life situations (Loyens & Gijbels, 2008; Voss & Post, 1988); and (4) with multiple possible paths to a solution (Blumenfeld, 1992; Loyens & Gijbels, 2008).

Researchers find that students show an increase in knowledge gained through authentic intellectual work instead of routine use of facts and procedures (Newmann, 2007; Newmann, Bryk, & Nagaoka, 2001). To qualify as an authentic intellectual work, the task must require the student to construct his/her own knowledge through disciplined inquiry on a topic of interest to the student and show value beyond completing a school exercise. Authentic educational activities allow students to explore their current understanding of topics, to encounter contradictions, and to rework their conceptual models to include new information and theories. By connecting new information to students' existing knowledge and interests, new information becomes integrated into long-term memory instead of being erased like a blackboard at the end of the day (Bransford, Brown, & Cocking, 2000; Bransford et al., 2006).

Recent research supports the notion that interactive instruction on authentic intellectual work actually improves student scores on conventional tests (Newmann, 2007, Newmann et al., 2001), student motivation to learn (Greene, Miller, Crowson, Duke, & Akey, 2004; Roeser, Midgley, & Urdan, 1996), and is linked to student success in high school science and mathematics (Lee, Croninger, & Smith, 1997). The effectiveness of interactive methods is supported by substantiated theory on how students learn (Bransford et al., 2000; Bransford et al. 2006; Good & Brophy, 2000; Hannafin & Land, 1997; Jonassen, 1999).

As in the past, today's students should become knowledgeable in history, literature, science, mathematics, but what is urgently needed to meet the demands for a 21st-century global society are students who can also see beyond the separate academic subjects and make connections across subjects, and develop relationships and patterns that put their learning into a broader, more integrated perspective (Boyer, 1997). Interdisciplinary instruction "cuts across subject-matter lines to focus upon comprehensive life problems… that bring together the various segments of curriculum into a meaningful association" (Furner, 1995, p. 4). Gardner, Wissick, Schweder and Canter (2003) associate a technology-enhanced interdisciplinary instruction with creating "learning environments that are dynamic and generative, employing problem solving and promoting active learning" (p. 162). Knowledge becomes most powerful when students can use information across disciplines to gain deeper understanding of specific problems (Newmann et al., 2001; O'Hair, McLaughlin & Reitzug, 2000). Applebee, Adler, and Flihan (2007) correlate interdisciplinary instructional approaches with providing "real world" problems in which many disciplines and their different perspectives may be utilized. Applebee et al. (2007) associate increased student engagement, raised achievement, and the reinvigoration of stale teaching as benefits of interdisciplinary instruction.

Research demonstrates that constructivist learning, interactive instruction, and interdisciplinary approaches increase a student's level of engagement (Applebee et al., 2007; Bransford et al., 2006; Loyens & Gijbels, 2008; Newmann, 2007). The power of increasing a student's level of engagement in his or her own learning is that research has repeatedly demonstrated that student engagement is a powerful indicator of student achievement (Bryson & Hand, 2007), contributes to a student's cognitive development (Wu & Huang, 2007), correlates with higher scores on standardized tests (Wu & Huang, 2007), and is associated with higher grades (Willingham, Pollack & Lewis, 2002) and lower dropout rates (Croninger & Lee, 2001). However, developing an educational environment that today's students find engaging yet which also meet the requirements for academic rigor outlined in the No Child Left Behind (NCLB) act has been elusive for traditional publishers, schools, and teachers and is consistent with research findings of a significant decline in academic motivation from Grades 3–9 (Lepper, Sethi, Dialdin & Drake, 1996).

What is the Role of Serious Games in Student Learning?

Educational researchers are currently examining not only the design and structure of optimal educational experiences but also the role that video games can play in education. The prevalence of computers and the Internet are expected to change education just as they have changed virtually every other facet of our society. Many educators are digital immigrants who have moved into the digital world and assumed most of its customs but still speak with an accent (Prensky, 2006). The digital natives, today's students, know the customs because they know of no other. They are comfortable with instant messaging, the Internet, iPods, social networking, e-mailing, and playing video games. Barab, Ingram-Goble, and Warren (2008) explain the relationship.

Game play has the potential to immerse the player in a rich network of interactions and unfolding story lines through which she solves problems and reflects on the workings of the design of the game world, and the design of both real and imagined social relationships and identities in the game- and non-game worlds. (p. 989–990)

Squire and Jan (2007) describe game-based learning as "'post progressive pedagogy" that can engage learners with complex learning scenarios that are "driven by authentic questions, incorporate multiple tools and resources, rely on learning by doing," and require "complex performances to demonstrate mastery" (p. 8). Mayo (2009) reports learning outcome results of studies of several games as "proof" that games can improve learning:

- Supercharged! [electrostatics]—a 28% increase in learning outcomes over lecture
- Geography Explorer [geology]—a 15% to 40% increase in learning outcomes over lecture
- Virtual Cell [cell biology]—a 30% to 63% improvement in learning outcomes over lecture
- Dixenxian [algebra]—an average increase of one test grade (e.g., from B to A) for most kids, up to three grades for underachieving kids
- River City [ecology, scientific inquiry]—a 370% increase in test scores over lecture for D students; a 14% increase in test scores over lecture for B students
- NIU Torcs [numerical methods]—twice as much time spent by game-playing kids on their homework, much more highly detailed concept maps

Another interesting aspect of video games is the fact that students are "playing." Prensky (2001) highlights the work of Johan Huizenga, who characterizes play as something one chooses to do; it is "intensely and utterly absorbing," and it "promotes the formation of social groupings" (p. 6). Vygotsky (1933/1978) associates play with a student's ability to experiment with "actions and engage behavior even before he/she appreciates the meanings associated with these actions" (Barab & Jackson, 2006, p. 9). In direct opposition to the concept of play, traditional education perpetuates a cycle of failure in which students lose confidence in a subject and begin to disengage from participating in class, which in turn spawns additional failures and leads to total disengagement from the learning process (Ketelhut, 2007). Gee (2001) observes that students play games that are often complicated and difficult, even though they are not motivated to undertake a difficult task or assignment in school. He conducted a study that investigated the essential elements that the video game industry includes in their games to ensure market success. He identified 13 principles that govern the quality and success of a video game (Gee, 2001):

1. Codesign (learners as active agents/ producers)
2. Customize (learners make decisions on how they learn)
3. Identity (learners need to be invested in who they are in the game)
4. Manipulation (interaction with tools and the environment)
5. Well-ordered problems (structure and interdependence of tasks and scenarios)
6. Pleasantly frustrating (challenging, but doable)
7. Cycles of expertise (repeated cycles of skill practice and skill mastery)
8. Just-in-time and on-demand information
9. Fish tanks (training environments)
10. Sandboxes (support of experimentation and risk-taking)
11. Skills as strategies (skill integration and application)
12. System thinking (experiences need to fit into a meaningful whole)
13. Meaning as action image (experiences give meaning to knowledge)

Why a Massive Multiplayer Online Game?

Yee (2006) describes a massive multi-player online game (MMOG) as a persistent world where players, through use of an avatar, interact with "naturalistic worlds" and have opportunities for rich and collaborative social interactions with other players (p. 6). Steinkuehler and Duncan (2008) suggest that in an MMOG, "individuals collaborate to solve complex problems within the virtual world, such as figuring out what combination of individual skills, proficiencies, and equipment are necessary to" successfully complete a task/ mission (p. 531). The idea of providing a venue for the students to work with other students is especially intriguing. Vygotsky (1978) advocates the idea that social interaction plays an important role in the development of cognition. Barab and Jackson (2006) contend that through an MMOG environment, players' social interaction with others can support learning via their zone of proximal development (ZPD); "ZPD refers to the range of accomplishment that can be reached with material and social support as compared to acting alone. ZPD and this process of social and material 'scaffolding' were core tenets underlying Vygotsky's life work" (p. 8).

Equipped with the learning theories, instructional strategies, and best practices of video games, the K20 Center was prepared to begin to develop a digital game-based learning (DGBL) environment that would engage students and outfit teachers with cutting-edge instructional technology. The question to be answered was, would teachers choose to use this new tool?

What are Students' Expectations?

The Association for Supervision and Curriculum Development (ASCD) action center statistics report that an alarming number of students are not being served by traditional education. Statistics reveal (1) a national dropout rate of nearly 30% (Barton, 2009); (2) 3.5 million young people (ages 16–26) did not have a high school diploma and were not enrolled in school (Bridgeland, DiIulio, & Morison, 2006); and (3) one-third of college freshmen are enrolled in at least one remedial course (NCES, 2004). A growing number of educational researchers align this student disengagement with a shift in the fundamental learning needs of today's students. Squire and Jan (2007) propose that "inter-related technological, social, and cultural changes are changing the demands on our educational system" (p. 5). They characterize traditional schools and classrooms as based on print-based learning and not adapting to "multi-modality and the use of interactive technology" (p. 6).

If one considers that 97% of teens between the ages of 12 and 17 play video games, that 50% of all teens played a game "yesterday" (Lenhart et al., 2008), and that the average college graduate has spent 5,000 hours reading, 10,000 hours playing video games, and 20,000 hours watching television (Prensky, 2001), the students' choice for source of information becomes obvious. As of 2004, the video game industry had surpassed the Hollywood box office in gross ticket sales (Beck & Wade, 2006). Prensky advocates that since today's students are engaged with interactive media in almost every aspect of their lives that they have learned to "think and process information fundamentally differently" (p. 1). Jenkins (2006) points out that we as a society are experiencing "technological, industrial, cultural and social changes in ways that media circulates information within our culture" (p. 290). Dodge, Barab, and Stuckey (2008) connect the youth of today as both consumers and producers of media, moving between and even using multiple forms of media at once, engaging in collaborative groups without regard to geographical location. Despite students' development of these skill sets and their obvious passion for engaging in the interactive environment, "schools continue to operate with a cultural logic that fails to leverage the technological changes that increasingly influence children's lives" (Dodge et al., 2008, p. 226). This cultural logic is dominated by print-based materials that support a teacher-centered pedagogy, relegating students to the role of passive learners (Dodge et al., 2008; Squire & Jan, 2007). Wu and Huang (2006) define student engagement as a "multifaceted construct [that] implies behavioral, emotional, and cognitive participation in learning experiences" (p. 729). It could be argued that it would be a struggle for learners who are accustomed to using interactive media in every aspect of their lives to attain behavioral, emotional, and cognitive participation in a dominantly text-based classroom.

Barab and Jackson (2006) highlight the work of three critical theorists—Giroux (1983), McLaren (1997), and Lather (1998)—and suggest that the best educators in the "electronically wired contemporary era" are those who possess the financial resources to access quality instructional resources (p. 1). The availability of quality educational video games is a major concern. Mayo (2009) contends that commercial game studios refuse to develop instructional games because of the "edu-tainment bust." She commends governmental agencies and foundations that fund important research on the next generation learning environments.

This literature review suggests that the five beliefs held by educators at the K20 Center will help ensure a student learning experience marked by the following:

- A self-regulated constructivist learning environment where students work in groups to solve a series of complex, ill-structured problems based in a virtual representation of a real-life context with multiple possible paths to a final solution (Blumenfeld, 1992; Loyens et al., 2007; Paris & Paris, 2001; Voss & Post 1988)

- An interactive learning experience which allows them to experience authentic intellectual work in a virtual representation of a real-world context (Brandsford et al., 2006; Good & Brophy, 2000; Newmann, 2007)
- An interdisciplinary environment that leverages a real-world problem to utilize the different perspectives of the four disciplines (Applebee et al., 2007)
- A shared learning space through the MMOG environment with other students so that a student's ZPD is expanded to include the scaffolding of social support of other students (Barab & Jackson, 2006; Barab et al., 2008; Prensky, 2001)
- A gaming environment that emulates the 13 principles of a successful commercial video game to ensure an engaging learning experience for all students (Gee, 2001)

The project's efforts to embed these beliefs into a DGBL environment were an evolutionary process that relied upon a continuous stream of feedback from students and teachers to drive the development and improvement of their experience. This process resulted in the development of the MMOG serious game known as *McLarin's Adventures,* or *McLarin*.

What is the Nature of *McLarin's Adventures?*

McLarin, a massive multiplayer online game (MMOG), allows a group of students (5–35+) to enter into a virtual environment and challenges them with a series of cross-disciplinary (mathematics, literacy, science, and social studies) learning scenarios. To emulate the real world as much as is technically feasible, students are equipped with a series of in-game applications (journal, spreadsheet, e-mail, etc.) and instruments (pH meter, thermometer, pedometer, etc.) that allow the student to authentically collect, organize, analyze, and report data while in the game. Additionally, students are encouraged to collaborate on challenges through an in-game chat client. To enhance the reader's ability to relate the elements described in detail within the following case study, a short user story (see Figure 1) provides the context of the environment, the learning scenario, and experiences of the student and teacher, while providing an overview of the project management methodology.

Who Comprises the Development Team?

One of the first questions that the K20 Center had to answer was "who was going to write the code or develop the art assets?" If we had contracted with a game studio, we could have accessed industry-proven production results, but we would also be struggling with the communication gap that exists between educators and the game industry (Fernández-Vara et al., 2009, and Holland et al., 2003). The alternative was to recruit the brightest of university students, eager to develop their skills in an authentic large-scale game development environment. While motivated and capable, working with students was not without drawbacks. Student developers graduate and move on to their careers. While this is the ultimate goal of the students and their families, the issue with retraining and imparting the accumulated corporate knowledge to the students' replacements becomes a fairly large impediment to the development process. The project leadership quickly decided that we needed to identify a core team of developers and then recruit them to move to full-time employment after graduation to counteract this problem. As graduation occurred, original student developers from the core project team were hired as full-time employees,

Figure 1. The student experience

Heather, an 8th grade student, sits in a science room with an ultra mobile personal computer on her desk. As she boots up the machine, she reflects on the fact they are playing a game in school. Ms. O'Donnell and several of the teachers were going to use 3rd hour on Friday's as the game hour. While each teacher was going to add some specific requirements to what the students were going to be doing, they would be able to work with their friends as they attempted to be the first to find, measure, evaluate, and recommend food, water, and shelter resources for a new colony. Here UMPC finally finishes loading and she quickly enters her username and password and hits a start button. Her screen is filled with a tropic island with an avatar standing with her back turned to the screen poised for action. She sees another avatar appear in her screen, the green uniform, pony tail and *Ice Girl* label floating above her head. Heather glances up from her UMPC, across the room and sees her friend sitting at a desk, typing away. She glances down and sees that the chat button is glowing blue, clicks it and reads the message. "Ice Girl: Do you know if Katie is going to play in Ms. Jones class?" Tapping in a response, "Jester: I think so, but they had a quiz or something, she said get started and she would catch up." Ms. O'Donnell, who was roaming the room, asks for everyone's attention for a brief announcement. "I will be checking the journals tonight, so be sure to include the methodology description with each recorded measurement. Don't forget to add a journal entry once you have successfully completed the calculation of the area of the island that provides a description of how you verified the accuracy of your calculations." As Heather's attention returns to her screen she sees that a third yellow avatar, labeled "Rouge", has appeared in the screen. "Rouge: Ok, finished the quiz, so what's next?" "Ice Girl: We finished the training zone last time…" "Jester: Yep, and Fermy asked us to find the standard for our map, by determining the size of one grid." "Ice Girl: That sounds like we need to use the pedometer, like that training zone task we did." "Jester: Hmmm, we could use the mini map thing to measure the grid." "Ice Girl: Katie, we have to verify our measurements are right." "Rouge: NP, we have to describe the location we take the measurement, she is going to grade on Friday!" "Jester: didn't Ms. O say repeated measures are one way to determine accuracy?" "Ice Girl: yep." "Rouge: Sounds like we could save some time and share what measurements we get." "Ice Girl: cool! And we could go to different parts of the zone, to see if that changes at all." "Jester: Let's do it… Meet back here?" "Rouge: Deal." "Ice Girl: brb."

Heather positions her avatar so the position indicator on a small map in the upper left hand corner of her screen aligns on the cross section of the grid system. She clicks on her backpack and drags a small device, the laser pedometer, from her inventory and drops it onto a hand icon to the right. She activates the pedometer and begins to walk. Her eye darts between her avatar and the mini map. After dodging a tree or two in her path she taps her up arrow key until she is satisfied she has reached the next cross section of the grid. She clicks on her pedometer and sends her reading to her journal. Here she types a short paragraph she labels "methodology." Heather hits her chat button and types a message. "Jester: I got 52.17 meters." "Ice Girl: I got 49.23 meters." "Rouge: hold on let me finish this description…" "Rouge: Ok, I got 48.54 meters." Heather opens her journal, goes to the newest entry and adds 49.23 and 48.54 as her second and third measurements. "Rouge: Let's go see if we are right, to the comm. portal?" "Ice Girl: To the comm. portal!" A few minutes navigating her avatar through the tropical landscape and Heather moves her avatar under a tent with an input device. A quick click yields a menu, Heather clicks on the Submit Grid Measurement button, and types in 52.17 m. The screen blinks black and Dr. Fermy is back heaping on praise over her precise measurements and provides her with the next task: calculate the length of the island.

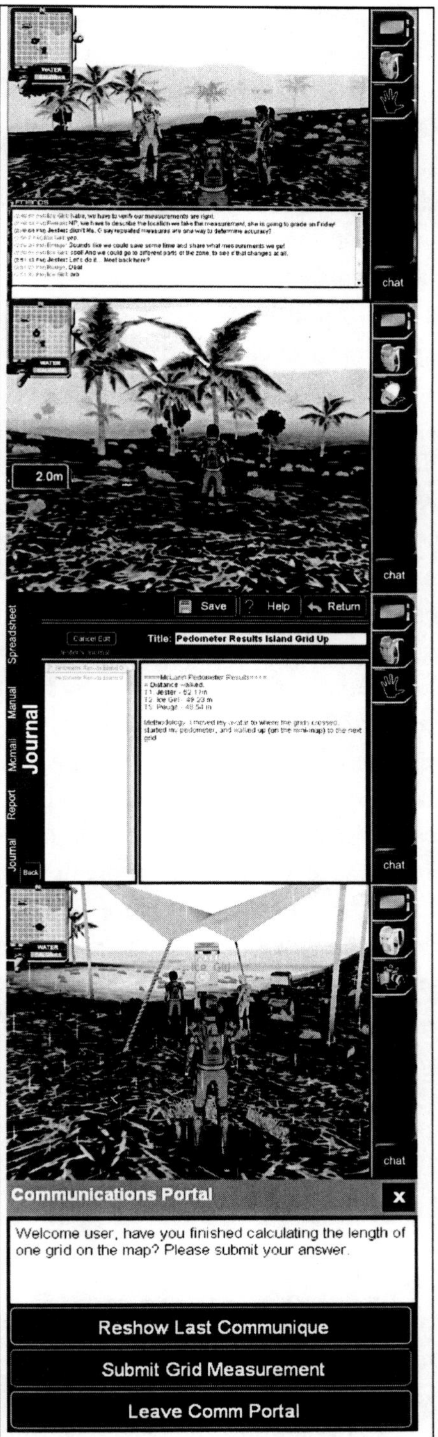

which helped to retain the intellectual capital of the development team. So, the K20 Center's core development team was originally constituted as an instructional designer/project manager, student programmers, and student 3-dimensional graphic artists (3-D artists) and was later augmented to include a full-time programmer and two full-time 3-D artists. During the project, the largest development team consisted of 10 programmers and two 3-D artists. Eight programmers were employed during the last 8 weeks of the semester so that two graduating students could do some cross-training with their replacements.

To address teachers' concerns about unproven, innovative learning practices, the project employed a rich pool of talented practitioners to provide the content expertise in the development of cross-disciplinary learning activities. The four content specialists were selected based on their (1) experience with 8th- and 9th-grade students within one of the four core content areas—literacy, mathematics, science, or social studies, (2) status as a master teacher within their discipline, and (3) regular use of authentic teaching strategies within their classrooms. While not experts in game development, they quickly were able to apply their expertise in working with the instructional designer in developing authentic learning activities embedded within the game story of *McLarin's Adventures*.

THE DEVELOPMENT OF *MCLARIN'S ADVENTURES*

In crafting the proposal, which was eventually funded, the K20 Center leadership was adamant that the game would be used as a resource within a teacher's classroom curriculum. In the No Child Left Behind era of American education, the integrity of a teacher's instructional time is a well-guarded precious resource. While eager to find more effective strategies to reach today's students, schools are also very hesitant to venture too far from the "tried and true" practices found in most of the nation's classrooms. Often this relates to the fact that in trying new programs, they often see a negative impact on learning, so it is easy for the teacher to advocate that their previous methods were more effective than the current methods. Schools are often guilty of being very reactive institutions, using a shotgun approach to school improvement. A "let's try these 10 different initiatives and see which one works" mentality has made a "this too shall pass" philosophy common to teachers within these organizations. In response to this idea, Fullan (2004) suggests that "change involves grappling with new beliefs and understandings, and with new skills, competencies and behaviors, it is inevitable that it will not go smoothly in the early stages of implementation" (p. 6). He labels this decline in performance as an *implementation dip* and shares that, without using strategies to mitigate the awkwardness of a new innovation, the implementation dip can last as much as 3 years (Fullan, 2004). Thus new innovations are faced with a produce now or perish mandate, but the more innovative they are, the higher the risk is for failure. Therefore, as we continue to describe this case study, we will pay constant attention to leveraging those components that would minimize the "awkwardness" that Fullan highlighted, thereby minimizing the implementation dip for teachers and making it more likely for the innovation to be adopted.

Selecting the Learning Standards

The development process started with the leadership team of the project, composed of several stakeholders, namely students, teachers, and subject matter experts (SMEs). These stakeholders were assigned focus groups tasked with reviewing the content of the applets describe in the original grant proposal. These focus groups generated two outcomes that proved to dramatically alter the direction of the project that was originally proposed in the grant. The students, who included several sophisticated gamers, questioned the use of the handheld computers as the platform and applets as the game environment. Meanwhile, the teachers were interested in how the game could help them in addressing those standards that their students had the most trouble in mastering in their classrooms, which they identified as relating to process skills. The teachers advocated the concept of a learning environment where students could, through a virtual representation of the world and themselves, use process skills to solve a series of authentic learning activities.

The leadership team and a group of content experts (curriculum directors, college professionals, teachers, etc.) analyzed the Oklahoma Priority Access Student Skills (PASS) process standards at the 8th- and 9th-grade levels to identify a core group of process standards from the four content areas (literacy, mathematics, science, and social studies) that would serve as the learning elements of *McLarin* and eventually would determine the game's storyline, genre, and mechanics.

The Game Development Process

The game development process (Figure 2) provides a roadmap from the development of the learning activities (scenarios) through the concept vetting by the development team, students, and content experts. If the activity is of high quality, it actually enters the technical encoding process to the final pilot/field test of the activity with stakeholders. In an effort to provide the greatest amount of detail, the process is divided into four discrete stages—design, prototype, development, and beta testing.

Figure 3 isolates the components associated with the design stage of *McLarin*. The design team consists of SMEs, practitioners, and the instructional designer. SMEs are authoritative experts of a given field. Because the goal is developing an authentic learning environment, the instructional designer needs to access real-world experts to provide data, describe processes, and/or demonstrate equipment to accurately develop a disciplined inquiry (Bransford et al., 2000; Bransford et al., 2006). Since *McLarin* targets 8th- and 9th-grade curriculum, the practitioners had a level of ex-

Figure 2. Model of the game development process

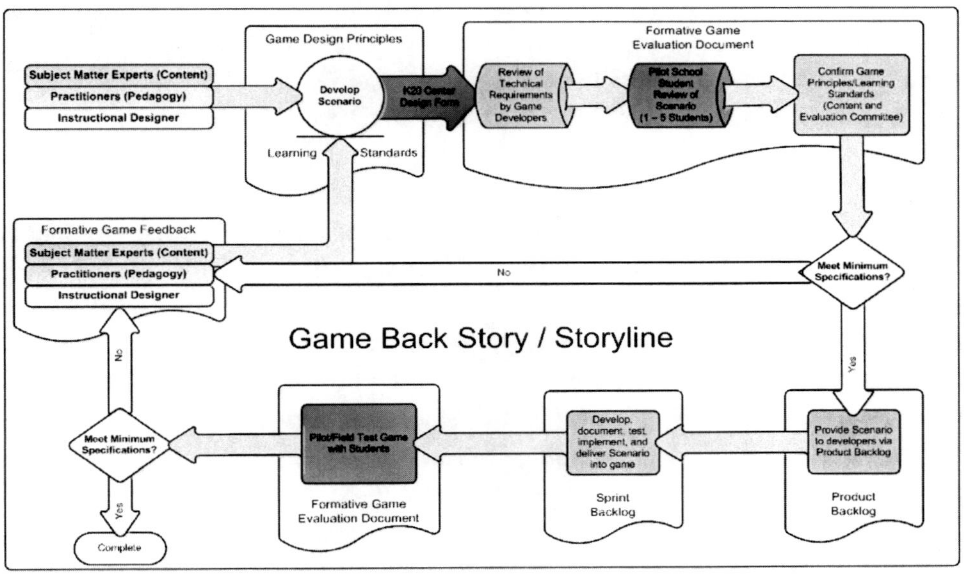

Figure 3. Design stage components

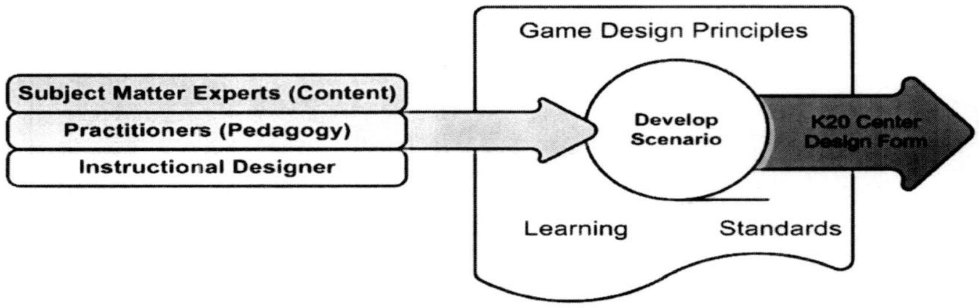

pertise with the content, and the only specialized SME utilized was that of the state water resource board. This group provided authentic data sets for a large group of water sources. These data sets were incorporated within the game.

The Design Stage

In view of the concern of teacher perceptions and eventual adoption, the project recruited a group of four practitioners who possessed a wealth of experiences with the target population of students and who were considered master teachers in a one of the targeted subject areas. The four master teachers had also demonstrated high levels of creativity in the development of engaging student learning activities while teaching. During the first design session, each teacher confessed to being a bit leery of his or her role in developing a "video game" and to feeling grossly underqualified for the task at hand. These confessions actually gave the instructional designer the opening to provide the four requirements in which the design team would be operating.

The first requirement was that the storyline was fundamental in framing the entire development process, as seen in Figure 2. A core tenet of the project was to build a virtual representation of the real world. The story became the vehicle that provided the context and purpose of each learning activity. For these activities to truly be authentic, it was essential not to ask the player to do something that could not be connected to the context of *McLarin*'s real-world environment, such as solve an algebraic equation before they could open a food container. Therefore, each and every activity of the development process, especially the design stage, had to maintain the integrity of the context of the game. A suggested activity might deliver the greatest educational gain, but if it violated the essence of the storyline, it was not incorporated into the effort.

There is consensus in the game design community that games do not require a story to be entertaining. However, there is also agreement that some genres, like that of adventure, are predisposed to develop a strong story to frame their game (Crawford, 2003; Rouse, 2005). Koster (2005) cautions against "a mismatch between the core of a game—the ludemes—and the dressing" (p. 166). He associates the "dressing" of a video game as those elements other than the game mechanics/game systems and includes graphics, back stories, plots, and sound effects. However, for *McLarin*, a core game mechanic is developing and sustaining an authentic context that occurs in gameplay.

The second requirement was that every learning scenario would be aligned to the targeted state learning standards. The alignment would be performed during the design process, confirmed during the concept stage, and reevaluated after the development stage to ensure the end product addressed the learning standard in practice. Once *McLarin* entered the release stage, the environment was incorporated into a randomized quasi-experimental matched comparison study in which one group used traditional activities to address the standards and the treatment group used *McLarin* to empirically measure the impact that the student's experience has on addressing those standards. Once analyzed, the data will be used to verify student learning.

The third requirement was implemented to resolve the issue of "game-play." At odds were the need for content mastery, rigor, and instructional experience and the understanding of the flow of a video game's experience for the player. Gee's (2001, 2003) work in investigating how commercial video games engage their audiences was a fundamental first step to bridging that gap of experience. Gee (2001) noted that these principles were most likely realized from an evolutionary process where companies that were able to engage their fan base were therefore able to make another game, strengthening that gameplay trait in a kind of digital "survival of the fittest." So, the third requirement was to have the design team evaluate each learning scenario's probability of incorporating each of Gee's (2001) 13 game principles. Gee's article provided the bridge that allowed these master teachers to reach into the world of gaming and to design a learning scenario that incorporated multiple game principles into the final scenarios. As they became comfortable with the list, they would start with learning scenarios and would begin to adjust the activity, trying to address the different components of Gee's principles.

The fourth requirement was that teachers would complete a design form that detailed the entire learning scenario that the instructional designer would use to develop concept documents and development documents for the artists and programmers. Included in this document was a formalized alignment of the identified state academic standards with gameplay principles. The ability to demonstrate this alignment was key in facilitating teacher adoption. The form also provided the design team with the ability to identify assets needed to achieve a desired outcome.

An example of some of these design considerations can be seen in the development of the Laser Pedometer. In the first learning scenario of *McLarin*, the students establish a map standard and extrapolate the island's length and surface area. The primary academic standard being addressed was the Oklahoma's PASS (2004) 8th-grade mathematics' "Standard 4: Measurement – The student will use measurement to solve problems in a variety of contexts." Within Standard 4, Skill 4.1 asks students to "[e]stimate and find the surface area and volume in real world settings" (p. 26). The initial thought was to allow students to use a flag as an end point and a laser range finder to determine the distance between two points. The contour of the land and the placement of multiple flags into the MMOG world were problematic, however. The concern was that there would be confusion, as players within the game would place their own flags intermixed with other players' flags. So the design team brainstormed a new tool. Figure 4 is the actual Game Asset Form that documented the aspects of the Super Calibrated Laser Pedometer, and it presents how the Laser Pedometer is actually used within *McLarin*. The final product deviates from the design specification as a result of some technical constraints (not allowing the pedometer to attach to the belt because it could cause some animation anomalies because of several avatar body types each student could choose from), and some additional features (see the waypoint marker—red cylinder—behind avatar) were added because of functional requirements of the pedometer in later learning scenarios. By embedding simulated real-world instruments such as pH meters or thermometers and developing or enhancing instruments such as the laser pedometer allowed the student to utilize an in-game resource that has some applicability back to his or her world, enhancing the authenticity of the learning scenario (Bransford et al., 2000; Bransford et al., 2006), and this principle has been noted by other serious game developers (e.g., Borchert, Brandt, Hokanson, Slator, & Vender, in press; Gaydos

Figure 4. Game Asset Form for laser pedometer

Resource Name	Super Calibrated Laser Pedometer
Length (meters)	0.05
Width (meters)	0.03
Height (meters)	0.01
Resource Description	Belt clip; connects to UMPC via bluetooth; supplies absolute distance from click to click in meters. (click once to start -- click again to stop measure.) Measures of angle of leg by fixture in shoe. Must have shoes on feet to utilize this tool.
Mass (kilograms)	0.1
Volume (liters)	
Link to Graphic/Drawing of Item	
Uses	determine distances and record data sets on UMPC to generate "map" of island with fringed map like screen appearance that will "scroll out" to open the map (like Blue's Clues)

& Squire, this volume). The examples showed how the design process maintained focus on the authenticity of the activity (real-world connections through the back story), the congruence to the learning standards, and the activity's suitability to the student (content and level was appropriate for targeted students). This foundation served as evidence to the adopting teachers that this innovation was grounded in theory and practice; it just used a different medium to engage the students. The products of this phase served as the roadmap to realizing the instructional environment and activities as described by the practitioners.

The Prototype Stage

Technical Review

Provided with the design documents, the instructional designer took the design team's instructional activities and incorporated them into a script that provided a narrative that detailed the environment, assets, activities, and supports required for the learning scenario. The first step of this process occurred with a rough outline that focused on the required game assets and detailed the game mechanics. This document entered the first stage of prototyping, the technical review. The instructional designer worked with the lead programmer and the lead artist to review the instructional feasibility of the scenario. Throughout this review, the technical leads were tasked with first identifying any elements of the scenario that were not feasible within the selected platform. Secondly, they were to identify the level of risk for each of the requested features of a scenario and, if possible, provide alternative or phased implementations of a feature that maintained the instructional integrity of the learning activity. The final outcome of this review was to provide the instructional designer with an estimated "cost" (in terms of development time) of each feature. The instructional designer used the level of risk and cost information for each feature and weighed that against the scope of the project, the importance of the feature to the learning activity and associated learning standards. The resulting cost–benefit analysis allowed the instructional designer to select the good, better, or best option and begin to move into the development of storyboards to vet the activity with stakeholders.

Early in the development process, the interaction between the instructional designer and the technical team was tested when the project was considering a series of design requests that were to be core mechanics of the players' experience. The first issue was how the player would interact with the game environment, whereas the second issue was how the student would collect, manage, and analyze the data while in-game. This example served to demonstrate the interplay between the design and development teams' efforts to solve technical problems while maintain the fidelity to the core values of the project and is worth further discussion.

A tropical island was to serve as the setting for *McLarin*. Early in the project, the instructional designer placed a high level of importance on creating either a single or a very limited set of environments, so that players would feel as if they were in a real-world environment and would not encounter zone perimeters and have to sit through loading screens. The technical review yielded a concern that, because of our platform limitations, we would not be able to handle the larger graphical requirements such functionality would require. An early prototype demonstrated the zone size significantly (and negatively) impacted the game's frame rate, a matrix that affects the "smoothness" of the game. A low frame rate gives the sense that the game is jumpy and limits the number of art assets the zone can hold. Since the students needed objects in the zone to interact with, the decision was made to proceed with the smaller zones.

The second example was the development of an in-game spreadsheet (see Figure 5). The students would be working on collecting data from multiple sources and would be asked to organize their data so they could present them as a work sample to show that they had successfully completed the learning scenario. When the instructional designer presented a feature that would develop an in-game spreadsheet, the technical staff was highly concerned. First, they said many times, "I never played a game with a spreadsheet in it." To the technical team, the concept itself seemed out of place in a game. Their recommended solution was to allow players to use Microsoft Excel® as the spreadsheet and import their images into the game. The instructional designer was concerned that the switching would be (1) relinquishing control of the game experience to an unknown application (what if the school didn't have a productivity suite) and (2) any time outside of *McLarin* meant that a student's activity would not be tracked. As a researcher, the idea that a database would track the amount of time and type of use a student had with each component, whether an application or a tool, used in the activity was to be a valuable source of research data. The database provided the researcher with the ability to use type of use and duration of use as variables to correlate patterns that may exist between a student's approach to solving a problem and his or her learning. These

Figure 5. In-game spreadsheet

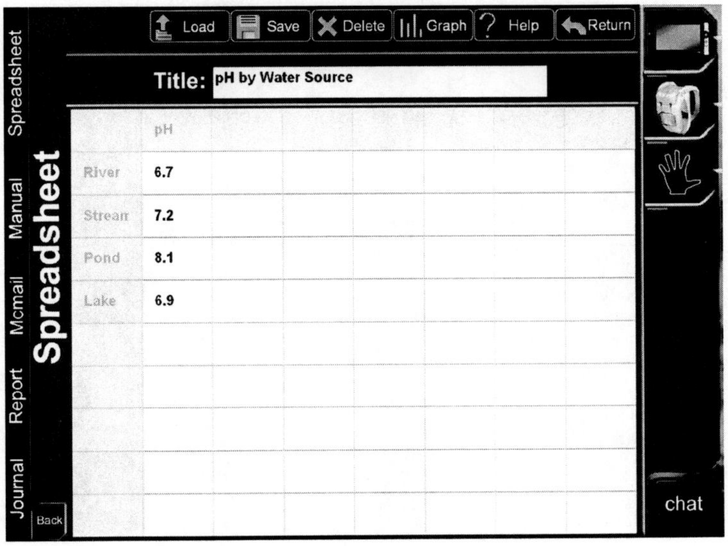

data could also serve as a valuable source of formative assessment for the teacher to help identify student interventions. The resulting spreadsheet allowed students to organize their data, while teachers and researchers were able to observe the process, including the tools that the students used to address a task.

User Review

The instructional designer expanded the outline after the technical review and began to work with an artist to produce storyboards (see Figure 6). Special attention was paid to the development of dialogue which would drive the introduction to, assistance during, and verification of success after a task. The opportunity to vet the dialogue for clarity, meaning, and style with students was an important source of feedback for the design. Each student vetting session consisted of three to five students who viewed a series of storyboard scenes. The event was videotaped, so that the instructional designer and the rest of the development team could review the event with special attention to the body language of each participant as related to the storyboard slide.

Expert Review

A final component of the prototype stage involved presenting prototypes to the Content and Evaluation Committee on a regular basis. The presentations occurred within the structure of the project management methodology, which will be discussed in more detail in the following section. The Content and Evaluation Committee consisted of a group of specialists (curriculum coordinators, college professors, content specialist, etc.) that served as the final authority on the content of the *McLarin* project by validating the design team's alignment of the activities to the academic standards. The prototype stage utilized technical, end user (student), and expert reviews to vet the feasibility and quality of the planned activities. If the instructional designer encountered suggestions that did not impact the core purpose of the learning scenario, he/she would make the suggested changes to the scenario. However, if the reviews did yield a recommendation that would affect the learning scenario's central objective, the instructional designer would bring the activity back to the design team and share the feedback, and the design team would rework the identified scenario. The scenario would then return to be processed by the three levels of reviews. Once a scenario was ready for full development, it was placed into the development queue.

The Development Stage

Accompanying the decision to move to an MMOG environment was the inevitable question of "who

Figure 6. Concepts in storyboard form

will develop this new effort?" The K20 Center is an educational center that strives to provide authentic learning opportunities to kindergarten children (usually through professional development with their teachers) though grade 20, or graduate-level, students. The Center found a computer science faculty member who agreed to join the co-principal investigator team and assist in creating a development team. The first iteration of the development team consisted of three undergraduate computer science students and one graduate computer science student. It quickly became apparent that the scope of the project required a larger team and the talents of a 3-D graphic artist. Throughout the following 28 months of the project, the development team grew to as many as eight computer science students and two art students as graphic designers. One of the first challenges in working with a student-based development team was that the students tended to be in their last two to five semesters of school. Students began to master the code-base, to truly understand the project's coding standards, and to gain, through experience, confidence in their programming skills. Soon after, they would graduate, and their replacements had to be trained. This issue caused the K20 Center to hire a few of the graduating students to stay on as full-time employees. These new employees were tasked with serving as the mentors to the next generation of student developers. A second issue was that students require flexible work schedules; this is especially true with computer science students who have team-based projects that require additional flexibility. In order to manage this complexity, the project turned to an agile project management process known as Scrum (Schwaber, 2004). This process focused on establishing a priority for each feature, which was then decomposed into discernable tasks by the development team. After the development team completed their product(s), they presented them to be reviewed by stakeholders.

As the name suggests, Scrum borrows its name from the sport of Rugby, where a scrum is a strategy for getting an out-of-play ball back in play. This structure is adaptive, quick, and self-organizing and permits few rests for the rugby players. In managing a project fraught with equal doses of complexity and unknowns, it is essential to employ a project management methodology that is adaptive and self-organizing, and generates functional software that allows for quick feedback from stakeholders. Scrum has become a favored management tool in the commercial gaming industry because of its ability to meet these requirements.

The Scrum methodology recognizes three groups of people who are essential to a software development process. They include a product owner, the Scrum team of software engineers and graphic artists, and the Scrum master who manages the process. The product owner is the individual who established the need for the development, sets the priority of the features to be developed, and can clarify any questions that could arise from the development of a feature. However, the product owner commits that he/she will not attempt to change any of the features until each development cycle/iteration ends. The scrum team is the group of five to 10 developers. The team is cross-functional by design and self-organizes so it can deliver a selection of the features identified by the product owner. The project manager in the Scrum methodology is designated the Scrum master (for the development of *McLarin's Adventures*, the instructional designer served in this role). The Scrum master's primary responsibility is to enact and maintain the Scrum process. He or she serves the Scrum team by removing impediments to productivity. For example, the Scrum master might purchase a book or hire an outside consultant to solve a particularly difficult problem. The Scrum master serves the product owner by providing daily updates on the progress of the development effort using a series of Scrum tools.

The Scrum process (see Figure 7) operates in iterations called sprints. Before the start of a sprint, the product owner identifies a set of features for development, known as a product backlog. The product owner presents the product backlog to the development team. The product backlog organizes the features by sequencing them from the most important features (which should be completed first) to the least important. The team looks for interdependencies, clarifies the identified features, and then works to decompose each feature into discrete developmental tasks. With each task, the team identifies the estimated amount of effort (in hours) it will take to complete the task. The team reviews the list (sprint backlog) and identifies the number of features they can deliver during the Sprint. Each day of the sprint, the development team conducts a 15-minute standing meeting (daily Scrum) where each member addresses three questions:

1. What have I done since the last Scrum?
2. What will I do until the next Scrum?
3. What, if any, issues are impeding development?

The Scrum master works to remove any reported impediments. Finally, the development team presents to the product owner and the project's stakeholders via a meeting titled a sprint review. The sprint review process also serves as a venue for the Content and Evaluation Committee to review the full impact, academic rigor, and quality of user experience in its ongoing evaluation and approval of the individual learning scenarios.

The Scrum process, as seen in Figure 7, is simplified and is represented as the creation and management of the product backlog and sprint backlog within the scenario development process (Figure 2). The development team, including the instructional designer/Scrum master, utilized the entire process to manage the delivery of the overall project.

The Beta Test Stage

The final element of the scenario design process is the beta test stage (see Figure 8). This stage delivers a scenario that end users can begin to engage with. Once the project enters the beta test phase, the students begin to work directly with the overall game controls (e.g., how to move characters), general game mechanics (e.g., use of resources, scoring, etc.), and the effectiveness of the learning scenarios. Early on, through carefully derived vetting sessions, the development team begins to capture these data. The instructional designer analyzes the student feedback and begins to schedule the revisions. If students' experiences with a specific learning scenario does not produce the desired results, the scenario will be returned

Figure 7. Scrum project management process (adapted from Mountain Goat Software, 1998)

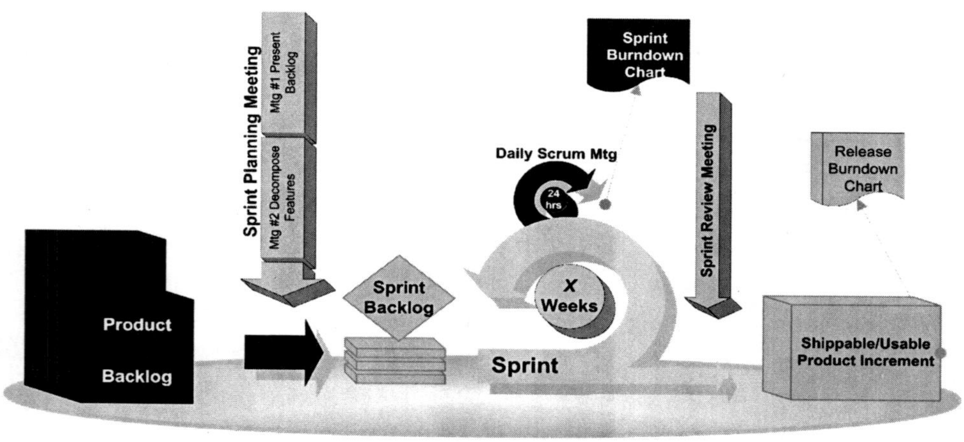

Figure 8. The beta test component

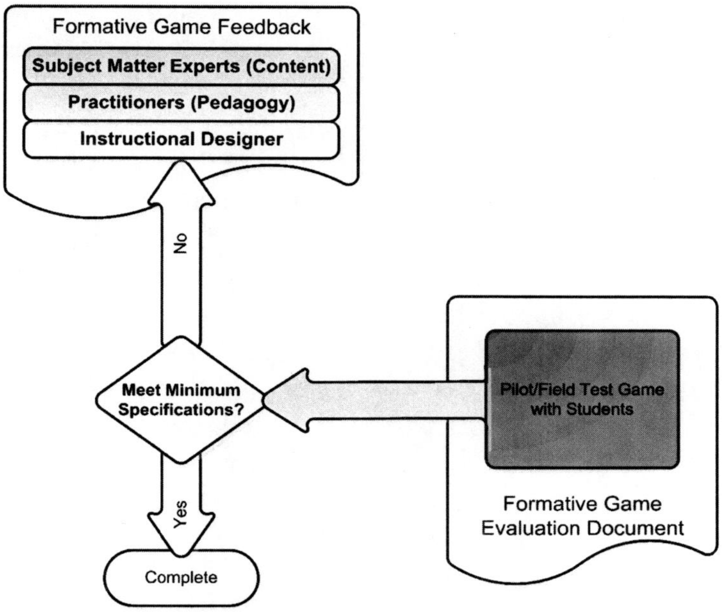

to the design team which, using the vetting data results, will rework the scenario. As the beta test phase continues, the game environment becomes more stable, the learning scenarios become much more effective, and the beta test enters the classroom for large-scale trials.

In our case, the large-scale beta test quickly highlighted an unanticipated variable that an MMOG brings to a serious game effort—a school's network infrastructure. Because of the nature of an MMOG, there is a requirement for a constant stream of packets between the server and the client (student). While the packets are fairly small, they are sent several times per second. When there are 20 students playing, there is a negligible impact on a network, but when 200 students are playing, only well-designed networks are able to support that level of constant communication. This challenge is amplified when all of this traffic is forced to travel through the school's network through its Internet service provider (ISP) to the projects centralized game servers. This challenge required the development team to rework the client–server and the server–database connections so that a local server (within the school's Intranet) could alleviate the impact on its Internet connection.

FUTURE RESEARCH DIRECTIONS

Equipped with the MMOG game engine, the technical lessons learned through the development of *McLarin*, and the K20 model that blends the roles of instructional designers, teachers, SMEs, programmers, and artists, we were able to develop a learning experience which allowed students to engage in authentic learning scenarios. While game theory influences the development process, it is the transparency and rigor of the instructional activity that the teacher must accept before serious gaming will enter the classroom. Using an agile project management philosophy (Scrum) allows the design and development team to quickly generate a testable prototype that students and teachers can interact with that provides critical feedback regarding what works and what needs to be changed in order to achieve the delicate balance of engagement and learning. Several research agendas have formed from *McLarin*, and as the K20 Center continues to generate additional serious game efforts, this research will delve deeper into the following issues: (1) the ability of the game design and resulting experience to engage students within an authentic, albeit virtual, learning experience while simultaneously assessing that experience's impact on the educational standards of the game; (2) the determination of what differences there are in playability of the scenarios from the perspective of serious gamer versus casual gamer versus nongamer (are these users in conflict with each other's requirements?) (3) the identification of necessary supports (professional development, just-in-time technical assistance, etc.) and tool sets (could teachers become designers of small, playable scenarios that directly support a specific curriculum?) and (4) the continued study of the design and development process, trying to maximize the efficiency of the process while ensuring the quality of the final product.

CONCLUSION

The University of Oklahoma's K20 Center entered the serious game arena with confidence. It had successfully developed a plan to develop applets on a proven platform. Within the window of writing the grant and starting the focus groups, the world of technology had changed. While delivering what was written in the grant was the low-risk option, the fact was that the students and teachers were asking for more, so the Center decided to attempt to take that rarely traveled path, fraught with unknowns, complexity, and risks. Through the support of the sponsor, vision from the Center's leadership, and the immeasurable patience of the administrators, teachers and, most of all, the students who endured the technical glitches and graciously provided relevant and timely feedback came a DGBL environment that is just now realizing its potential.

This chapter is not meant to be the definitive guide to serious game development but is instead an honest glimpse into how a project attempted to manage the complexity and unknowns of a significant effort. The primary reason for any success this project has enjoyed is a development management process that maximized flexibility and minimized the distance between the end user and the development team. The end user vetting and beta testing surrounding the development process ensured the voice of the teacher and student as part of the development process. It is hoped that these processes can be generalized and further validated in the design and development of other serious games.

REFERENCES

Applebee, A. N., Adler, M., & Flihan, S. (2007). Interdisciplinary curricula in middle and high school classrooms: Case studies of approaches to curriculum and instruction. *American Educational Research Journal*, *44*(4), 1002–1039. doi:10.3102/0002831207308219

Barab, S., Ingram-Goble, A., & Warren, S. (2008). Conceptual play spaces. In Ferdig, R. (Ed.), *Handbook of research on effective electronic gaming in education* (pp. 1–20). Hershey, PA: IGI Global Publications.

Barab, S., & Jackson, C. (2006). From Plato's republic to Quest Atlantis: The role of the philosopher–king. *THEN Journal*. Retrieved January 15, 2009, from http://thenjournal.org/feature/78/

Barton, P. E. (2009). *One-third of a nation: Rising dropout rates and declining opportunities.* Princeton, NJ: Educational Testing Service.

Beck, J. C., & Wade, M. (2006). *The kids are alright: How the gamer generation is changing the workplace*. Boston, MA: Harvard Business School Press.

Blumenfeld, P. C. (1992). Classroom learning and motivation: Clarifying and expanding goal theory. *Journal of Educational Psychology, 84*, 272–281. doi:10.1037/0022-0663.84.3.272

Borchert, B. L., Hokanson, G., Slator, B., & Vender, B. (in press). Principles and signatures in serious games for science education. In R. Van Eck (Ed.), *Gaming and cognition: Theories and practice from the learning sciences*. Hershey, PA: IGI Global.

Boyer, E. L. (1997). *Scholarship reconsidered: Priorities of the professoriate*. San Francisco: Jossey-Bass.

Bransford, J., Vye, N., Stevens, R., Kuhl, P., Schwartz, D., & Bell, P. (2006). Learning theories and education: Toward a decade of synergy. In Alexander, P., & Winne, P. (Eds.), *Handbook of Educational Psychology* (2nd ed., pp. 209–244). Erlbaum.

Bransford, J. D., Brown, A. L., & Cocking, R. R. (Eds.). (2000). *How people learn: Brain, mind, experience, and school committee on developments of science of learning*. Washington, DC: National Academies.

Bridgeland, J., DiIulio, J., Jr., & Morison, K. B. (2006). The Silent Epidemic. Washington, DC: Civic Enterprises, LLC.

Bryson, C., & Hand, L. (2007). The role of engagement in inspiring teaching and learning. *Innovations in Education and Teaching International, 44*(4), 349–362. doi:10.1080/14703290701602748

Crawford, C. (2003). *Chris Crawford on game design*. Boston, MA: New Riders.

Croninger, R. G., & Lee, V. E. (2001). Social capital and dropping out of high school. Benefits to at-risk student of teachers' support and guidance. *Teachers College Record, 103*(4), 548–581. doi:10.1111/0161-4681.00127

Dodge, T., Barab, S., & Stuckey, B. (2008). Children's sense of self: Learning and meaning in the digital age. *Journal of Interactive Learning Research, 19*(2), 225–249.

Fernández-Vara, C., Grigsby, N., Glinert, E., Tan, P., & Jenkins, H. (2009). Between theory and practice: The GAMBIT experience. In Perron, B., & Wolf, M. (Eds.), *Video game theory reader 2*. New York: Routledge.

Fullan, M. (2004). Core concepts. *Learning to lead change: Building system capacity.* Toronto, Canada: Change Forces. Retrieved July 16, 2009, from http://www.michaelfullan.ca/Articles_04/CoreConcepts.pdf

Furner, J. (1995). *Planning for interdisciplinary instruction: A literature review*. Paper presented at the Annual Meeting on Effective Classroom Teaching, Tuscaloosa, AL.

Gardner, J. E., Wissick, C. A., Schweder, W., & Canter, L. S. (2003). Enhancing interdisciplinary instruction in general and special education: Thematic units and technology. *Remedial and Special Education, 24*, 161–172. doi:10.1177/07419325030240030501

Gaydos, M., & Squire, K. (in press). Citizen Science: Designing a game for the 21st century. In Van Eck, R. (Ed.), *Interdisciplinary models and tools for serious games: Emerging concepts and future directions*. Hershey, PA: IGI Global.

Gee, J. P. (2001). Learning by design: Good video games as learning machines. *E-learning, 2*(1).

Gee, J. P. (2003). *What video games have to teach us about learning and literacy*. New York: Palgrave Macmillan.

Giroux, H. (1983). *Theory and resistance in education: A pedagogy for the opposition*. South Hadley, MA: Bergin and Garvey Publishers.

Good, T. L., & Brophy, J. E. (2000). *Teachers expectations: Looking in classrooms* (8th ed.). New York: Longman.

Greene, B. A., Miller, R. B., Crowson, H. M., Duke, B. L., & Akey, C. L. (2004). Relations among student perceptions of classroom structures, perceived ability, achievement goals, and cognitive engagement and achievement in high school language arts. *Contemporary Educational Psychology*, *29*, 462–482. doi:10.1016/j.cedpsych.2004.01.006

Hannafin, M. J., & Land, S. M. (1997). The foundations and assumptions of technology-enhanced, student-centered learning environments. *Instructional Science*, *25*, 167–202. doi:10.1023/A:1002997414652

Holland, W., Jenkins, H., & Squire, K. (2003). Theory by design. In Perron, B., & Wolf, M. (Eds.), *Video game theory*. New York: Routledge.

Jenkins, H. (2006). *Convergence culture: Where old and new media collide*. New York: New York University Press.

Jonassen, D. H. (1999). Designing constructivist learning environments. In C.M. Reigeluth (Ed.), Instructional design theories and model, Vol. 2: A new paradigm of instructional technology (pp. 215–239). Mahwah, NJ: Lawrence Erlbaum Associates.

Ketelhut, D. J. (2007). The impact of student self-efficacy on scientific inquiry skills: An exploratory investigation in river city, a multi-user virtual environment. *Journal of Science Education and Technology*, *16*, 99–111. doi:10.1007/s10956-006-9038-y

Koster, R. (2005). *A theory of fun for game design*. Scottsdale, AZ: Paraglyph Press.

Lather, P. (1998). Critical pedagogy and its complicities: A praxis of stuck places. *Educational Theory*, *48*(4), 487–498. doi:10.1111/j.1741-5446.1998.00487.x

Lee, V. E., Croninger, R. G., & Smith, J. B. (1997). Coursetaking, equity, and mathematics learning: Testing the constrained curriculum hypothesis in U.S. secondary schools. *Educational Evaluation and Policy Analysis*, *19*, 99–122.

Lenhart, A., Kahne, J., Middaugh, E., Macgill, A. R., Evans, C., & Vitak, J. (2008). Teens' gaming experiences are diverse and include significant social interaction and civic engagement. *Pew Internet and American Life Project*. Retrieved January 15, 2009, from http://www.pewInternet.org/pdfs/PIP_Teens_Games_and_Civics_Report_FINAL.pdf

Lepper, M. R., Sethi, A. S., Dialdin, D., & Drake, M. (1996). Intrinsic and extrinsic motivation: Developmental trends and issues. In Luthar, S., Burack, J., Cichetti, D., & Weisz, J. (Eds.), *Developmental psychopathology: Perspectives on risk and disorder* (pp. 23–50). Cambridge, UK: Cambridge University Press.

Loyens, S. M., & Gijbels, D. (2008). Understanding the effects of constructivist learning environments: Introducing a multi-directional approach. *Instructional Science*, *36*, 351–357. doi:10.1007/s11251-008-9059-4

Loyens, S. M. M., Rikers, R. M. J. P., & Schmidt, H. G. (2007). The impact of students' conceptions of constructivist assumptions on academic achievement and dropout. *Studies in Higher Education*, *32*, 581–602. doi:10.1080/03075070701573765

Mayo, M. (2009). Want to truly scale a learning program? Try gaming. *Kauffman Thoughtbook 2009*, Retrieved January 14, 2009, from http://blog.ohe-associates.com/files/0/6/3/8/4/157742148360/Mayo_Thought_Book_9.pdf

McLaren, P. (1997). *Revolutionary multiculturalism: Pedagogies of dissent for the new millennium.* Boulder, CO: Westview Press Mountain Goat Software. (1998). *A visual introduction to Scrum.* Retrieved August 14, 2009, from www.mountaingoatsoftware.com/scrum-figures

NCES. (2004). *The condition of education 2004, indicator 31: Remedial coursetaking. U.S. Department of Education.* Washington, DC: National Center for Education Statistics.

Newmann, F. M. (2007). Improving achievement for all students: The meaning of staff-shared understanding and commitment. In Hawley, W. D., & Rollie, D. L. (Eds.), *The keys to effective schools: Education reform as continuous improvement* (2nd ed., pp. 33–49). Thousand Oaks, CA: Corwin Press.

Newmann, F. M., Bryk, A. S., & Nagaoka, J. K. (2001). *Authentic intellectual work and standardized tests: Conflict or coexistence?*Chicago: Consortium on Chicago School Research.

O'Hair, M. J., McLaughlin, H. J., & Reitzug, U. C. (2000). *Foundations of democratic education.* Orlando, FL: Harcourt, Inc.

Paris, S. G., & Paris, A. H. (2001). Classroom applications of research on self-regulated learning. *Educational Psychologist, 36*, 89–101. doi:10.1207/S15326985EP3602_4

Prensky, M. (2001). *Digital natives, digital immigrants.* MCB University Press. Retrieved January 14, 2009, from %20Digital%20Natives,%20 Digital%20Immigrants%20-%20Part1.pdf

Prensky, M. (2006). *Don't bother me mom – I'm learning!*St. Paul, MN: Paragon House.

Roeser, R. W., Midgley, C., & Urdan, T. (1996). Perceptions of the school psychological environment and early adolescents' self-appraisals and academic engagement: The mediating role of goals and belonging. *Journal of Educational Psychology, 88*, 408–422. doi:10.1037/0022-0663.88.3.408

Rouse, R. (2005). *Game design theory & practice.* Plano, TX: Wordware Publishing.

Schwaber, K. (2004). *Agile project management with Scrum.* Redmond, WA: Microsoft.

Squire, K., Barnett, M., Grant, J. M., & Higginbotham, T. (2004). *Electromagnetism supercharged!: Learning physics with digital simulation games.* Paper presented at the 6th International Conference on Learning Sciences, Santa Monica, CA.

Squire, K. D., & Jan, M. (2007). *Mad City Mystery*: Developing scientific argumentation skills with a place-based augmented reality game on handheld computers. *Journal of Science Education and Technology, 16*, 5–29. doi:10.1007/s10956-006-9037-z

Steinkuehler, C., & Duncan, S. (2008). Scientific habits of mind in virtual worlds. *Journal of Science Education and Technology, 17*(6), 530–543. doi:10.1007/s10956-008-9120-8

Voss, J. F., & Post, T. A. (1988). On the solving of ill-structured problems. In Chi, M. T. H., Glaser, R., & Farr, M. J. (Eds.), *The nature of expertise.* Hillsdale, NJ: Lawrence Erlbaum.

Vygotsky, L. S. (1978). *Mind and society: The development of higher mental processes.* Cambridge, MA: Harvard University Press. (Original work published 1933)

Willingham, W. W., Pollack, J. M., & Lewis, C. (2002). Grades and test scores: Accounting for observed differences. *Journal of Educational Measurement*, *39*(1), 1–37. doi:10.1111/j.1745-3984.2002.tb01133.x

Wu, H. K., & Huang, Y. L. (2007). Ninth grade student engagement in teacher-centered and student-centered technology-enhanced learning environments. *Science Education*, *91*, 727–749. doi:10.1002/sce.20216

Yee, N. (2006). The Demographics, motivations and derived experiences of users of massively-multiuser online graphical environments. In *PRESENCE: Teleoperators and virtual environments* (pp. 309–329). Retrieved July 15, 2009, from http://www.nickyee.com/pubs/Yee%20-%20MMORPG%20Demographics%202006.pdf

"MUST-READS" FOR THIS TOPIC

Applebee, A. N., Adler, M., & Flihan, S. (2007). Interdisciplinary curricula in middle and high school classrooms: Case studies of approaches to curriculum and instruction. *American Educational Research Journal*, *44*(4), 1002–1039. doi:10.3102/0002831207308219

Barab, S., Ingram-Goble, A., & Warren, S. (2008). Conceptual play spaces. In Ferdig, R. (Ed.), *Handbook of research on effective electronic gaming in education* (pp. 1–20). Hershey, PA: IGI Global Publications.

Beck, J. C., & Wade, M. (2006). *The kids are alright: How the gamer generation is changing the workplace*. Boston, MA: Harvard Business School Press.

Bransford, J., Vye, N., Stevens, R., Kuhl, P., Schwartz, D., & Bell, P. (2006). Learning theories and education: Toward a decade of synergy. In Alexander, P., & Winne, P. (Eds.), *Handbook of Educational Psychology* (2nd ed., pp. 209–244). New York: Erlbaum.

Bryson, C., & Hand, L. (2007). The role of engagement in inspiring teaching and learning. *Innovations in Education and Teaching International*, *44*(4), 349–362. doi:10.1080/14703290701602748

Dodge, T., Barab, S., & Stuckey, B. (2008). Children's sense of self: Learning and meaning in the digital age. *Journal of Interactive Learning Research*, *19*(2), 225–249.

Gardner, J. E., Wissick, C. A., Schweder, W., & Canter, L. S. (2003). Enhancing interdisciplinary instruction in general and special education: Thematic units and technology. *Remedial and Special Education*, *24*, 161–172. doi:10.1177/07419325030240030501

Gee, J. P. (2001). Learning by design: Good video games as learning machines. *E-learning*, *2*(1).

Gee, J. P. (2003). *What video games have to teach us about learning and literacy*. New York: Palgrave Macmillan.

Hannafin, M. J., & Land, S. M. (1997). The foundations and assumptions of technology-enhanced, student-centered learning environments. *Instructional Science*, *25*, 167–202. doi:10.1023/A:1002997414652

Jenkins, H. (2006). *Convergence culture: Where old and new media collide*. New York: New York University Press.

Ketelhut, D. J. (2007). The impact of student self-efficacy on scientific inquiry skills: An exploratory investigation in river city, a multi-user virtual environment. *Journal of Science Education and Technology*, *16*, 99–111. doi:10.1007/s10956-006-9038-y

Loyens, S. M., & Gijbels, D. (2008). Understanding the effects of constructivist learning environments: Introducing a multi-directional approach. *Instructional Science*, *36*, 351–357. doi:10.1007/s11251-008-9059-4

Loyens, S. M. M., Rikers, R. M. J. P., & Schmidt, H. G. (2007). The impact of students' conceptions of constructivist assumptions on academic achievement and dropout. *Studies in Higher Education*, *32*, 581–602. doi:10.1080/03075070701573765

Newmann, F. M. (2007). Improving achievement for all students: The meaning of staff-shared understanding and commitment. In Hawley, W. D., & Rollie, D. L. (Eds.), *The keys to effective schools: Education reform as continuous improvement* (2nd ed., pp. 33–49). Thousand Oaks, CA: Corwin Press.

O'Hair, M. J., McLaughlin, H. J., & Reitzug, U. C. (2000). *Foundations of democratic education*. Orlando, FL: Harcourt, Inc.

Prensky, M. (2001). *Digital natives, digital immigrants*. MCB University Press. Retrieved January 14, 2009, from http://www.marcprensky.com/writing/Prensky%20-%20Digital%20Natives,%20Digital%20Immigrants%20-%20Part1.pdf

Prensky, M. (2006). *Don't bother me mom – I'm learning!*St. Paul, MN: Paragon House.

Schwaber, K. (2004). *Agile project management with Scrum*. Redmond, WA: Microsoft.

Shaffer, D. W. (2006). *How computer games help children learn*. New York: Palgrave Macmillan. doi:10.1057/9780230601994

Squire, K. (2006). From content to context: Video games as designed experiences. *Educational Researcher*, *35*(8), 19–29. doi:10.3102/0013189X035008019

Squire, K., Barnett, M., Grant, J. M., & Higginbotham, T. (2004). *Electromagnetism supercharged!: Learning physics with digital simulation games*. Paper presented at the 6th International Conference on Learning Sciences, Santa Monica, CA.

Squire, K. D., & Jan, M. (2007). *Mad City Mystery*: Developing scientific argumentation skills with a place-based augmented reality game on handheld computers. *Journal of Science Education and Technology*, *16*, 5–29. doi:10.1007/s10956-006-9037-z

Wu, H. K., & Huang, Y. L. (2007). Ninth grade student engagement in teacher-centered and student-centered technology-enhanced learning environments. *Science Education*, *91*, 727–749. doi:10.1002/sce.20216

TOP TEXTS FOR INTERDISCIPLINARY STUDIES OF SERIOUS GAMES

Barab, S., Ingram-Goble, A., & Warren, S. (2008). Conceptual play spaces. In Ferdig, R. (Ed.), *Handbook of research on effective electronic gaming in education* (pp. 1–20). Hershey, Pennsylvania: IGI Global Publications.

Bransford, J., Vye, N., Stevens, R., Kuhl, P., Schwartz, D., & Bell, P. (2006). Learning theories and education: Toward a decade of synergy. In Alexander, P., & Winne, P. (Eds.), *Handbook of educational psychology* (2nd ed., pp. 209–244). Erlbaum.

Dodge, T., Barab, S., & Stuckey, B. (2008). Children's sense of self: Learning and meaning in the digital age. *Journal of Interactive Learning Research*, *19*(2), 225–249.

Gardner, J. E., Wissick, C. A., Schweder, W., & Canter, L. S. (2003). Enhancing interdisciplinary instruction in general and special education: Thematic units and technology. *Remedial and Special Education*, *24*, 161–172. doi:10.1177/07419325030240030501

Gee, J. P. (2001). Learning by design: Good video games as learning machines. *E-learning*, *2*(1).

Gee, J. P. (2003). *What video games have to teach us about learning and literacy*. New York: Palgrave Macmillan.

Loyens, S. M., & Gijbels, D. (2008). Understanding the effects of constructivist learning environments: Introducing a multi-directional approach. *Instructional Science*, *36*, 351–357. doi:10.1007/s11251-008-9059-4

Newmann, F. M. (2007). Improving achievement for all students: The meaning of staff-shared understanding and commitment. In Hawley, W. D., & Rollie, D. L. (Eds.), *The keys to effective schools: Education reform as continuous improvement* (2nd ed., pp. 33–49). Thousand Oaks, CA: Corwin Press.

Schwaber, K. (2004). *Agile project management with Scrum*. Redmond, WA: Microsoft.

Squire, K. D., & Jan, M. (2007). *Mad City Mystery*: Developing scientific argumentation skills with a place-based augmented reality game on handheld computers. *Journal of Science Education and Technology*, *16*, 5–29. doi:10.1007/s10956-006-9037-z

Chapter 12
Citizen Science:
Designing a Game for the 21st Century

Matt Gaydos
University of Wisconsin – Madison, USA

Kurt Squire
University of Wisconsin – Madison, USA

ABSTRACT

In order to adapt to the educational demands of an increasingly digitized and globalized society, reformers have pointed toward games and their communities as potential models for what 21st-century educational systems might look like. As educational game research develops as a field, the need for design frameworks that leverage contemporary perspectives on education, learning, and established commercial game design techniques grows. In this chapter, the authors briefly describe current educational demands that highlight a shift away from content-focused curriculum and outline the design process used to make the game Citizen Science, a game to teach civic science literacy. By providing insight into the process of design, the authors hope to illuminate the relationship between theory and its enactment.

INTRODUCTION

Just a few short years ago, the idea of combining games and education was met with skepticism, if not scorn. This attitude has changed as educators have noted that video games are worlds capable of communicating sophisticated ideas (Jenkins, 2004; Squire, 2006), instantiate in their designs the principles of situated learning theory (Gee, 2003, 2005), are leading activities for academic or lifelong pursuits (Squire & Steinkuehler, 2005) and can, in some cases, be used for the pursuit of traditional academic goals, such as learning history, physics, or ecology (see Ferdig, 2009; Shelton & Wiley, 2007).

While investigations that design and investigate games in the pursuit of education have progressed, more specific, even pragmatic issues have started to take shape. How can these games be implemented in classrooms? Can a more precise vocabulary be developed to analyze games? *How does one actually design a game that is both educational and fun to play?* This chapter investigates the latter question by investigating one such design theory that seeks

DOI: 10.4018/978-1-61520-719-0.ch012

Copyright © 2010, IGI Global. Copying or distributing in print or electronic forms without written permission of IGI Global is prohibited.

to extend earlier notions of games as designed experiences. Before we can address this complex question, however, we need to say a little more about the current state of the educational system and the role that games may play.

Games, Education, and Civic Science Literacy

A study released by the Pew Internet & American Life project in September 2008, which showed that 99% of boys and 94% of girls play games, exposes the degree to which games have come to saturate and impact youth culture. Around the same time as the Pew study, Barack Obama called specifically for education reform that would help children "compete in a 21st-century knowledge economy." While the two events may seem disparate, we argue that these two foci—one on the impact of digital gaming (and participatory culture) on youth and the other on the importance of civic engagement—are indeed two sides of the same coin. Today's youth are raised in a media-saturated environment in which they expect to participate meaningfully in communities as media producers—perhaps even in the creation of entire virtual worlds. Yet in schools, they are trained not even for the world of today, but for that of yesterday as it was imagined to have existed.

One core theme behind the Games, Learning, and Society (Squire, 2007) initiative has been how to take seriously the mechanisms by which games (as opposed to other forms of media) engage players. The differences between the design features of video games and those of school are marked. Where games are frequently customizable, nonlinear, responsive to different play styles, transgressive, participatory and empowering to players, features of school include emphasizing standardization of curricula, uniform and linear paths through the curriculum, fixed learning objectives, uniform learning outcomes, a lack of attention to aesthetics, student passivity, and subjugation to authority (Gee, 2004; Squire, 2003). A challenge for designers then, is how to reconcile the discrepancies between video games—artifacts that are designed for consumption in player's leisure time—and the constraints of formal schooling. If there is hope for designing and developing games that honor the underlying mechanisms by which games work—and the values of gaming culture—while leading toward socially desirable learning goals like a scientifically literate citizenry, what would a design theory of such a game development process look like?

As games mature as a medium for learning, a number of educational subgenres (or models or paradigms) have emerged, including *targeted games, open-ended sandbox games, epistemic games,* and *multiuser virtual environments*, each with its own unique approaches to design. For example, one relevant design from the second author's earlier work was that of a *targeted* game, focusing on specific conceptual change with schoollike settings. The game, *Supercharged!,* was designed by a team of researchers and MIT physicists to provide players with the opportunity to adopt the perspective of a charged particle within a "world of electromagnetism,"a perspective that expert physicists frequently adopt while thinking through problems. By strategically placing charged particles around themselves, players moved through space to accomplish in-game goals. Research found that not only did students develop a more robust conceptual understanding of electromagnetic physics, but they also gained insight as to why visualizing forces was helpful. These learning gains, however, did not necessarily generalize to more advanced thinking about electromagnetism writ large, nor the development of identities among students as physicists, nor a better ability to participate in contemporary popular discourse around issues in which such understandings might be brought to bear (such as alternative energy). The shortcomings of this model drove us to look toward role-playing games, as they put players in real-world kinds of situations where they must use scientific understandings to solve problems (Shaffer, Squire, Halverson, & Gee, 2005).

Role-playing games for education aren't new (see Holland, Jenkins, & Squire, 2003). One fleshed-out theory that makes uses of role-playing is epistemic games, which are modeled on the practices of professions (Shaffer, 2006). These games have been successful in providing students with ways of thinking (knowledge, skills, values, and dispositions) that are tied to professional ways of being in the world. For example, students role-playing as science journalists develop knowledge and skills about both language and literacy practices as well as scientific content domains. Shaffer and colleagues argue that such ways of thinking can be called "epistemic frames" and are valuable because they are generative for "far transfer" sorts of tasks in which students apply skills that they have learned in-game to other contexts (e.g., analyzing newspaper articles in their local newspaper as a result of playing a game about journalism) (Shaffer, Squire, Halverson & Gee, 2005). This far transfer occurs because of the way that students learn deeper structures of the domain, which in turn can be transferred elsewhere.

Epistemic games successfully use professional practices for learning but are also somewhat limited by the real-world professions on which they are based. The design methodology for epistemic games is essentially to recreate the professional practicum in a role-playing setting, and not all practicum experiences necessarily involve socially desirable learning or make good games. Contemporary journalism practices, for example, have been criticized for the control that editors exert on the journalistic process and for stifling investigative reporting (Giordano, 1997). Further, as institutions such as journalism are being transformed to deal with the realities of the digital age, perhaps we need models that involve the cultural values of digital technologies (such as participatory structures), rather than recapitulating structures that are already outdated. As has been argued elsewhere, our educational system needs to adapt to the changing needs of students in order to prepare them for an increasingly networked and globalized world (Disessa, 2000; Gee, 2004; Shaffer, Squire, Halverson & Gee, 2005; Squire, 2008; Steinkuehler, 2006). Could there be opportunities for using the conventions of video games (e.g., power-ups, narrative conventions) to increase engagement and learning, specifically modeling socially desirable roles, such as a citizen activist?

Goal: Civic Science Literacy, a 21st-Century Education

A recurring challenge for democratic societies is the problem of how to create a scientifically literate citizenry capable of making key decisions about our global future. Today's complex scientific issues (such as climate change, gene therapy, pandemics, or personalized medicine) require an informed populace capable of understanding scientific advancements as they develop (as opposed to learning "all they need to know" in school). This sort of scientific civic literacy requires an informed individual to have the following:

- An understanding of critical scientific concepts and constructs such as ecosystems, the molecule, or DNA;
- An understanding of the nature and process of scientific inquiry;
- A pattern of regular information consumption; and
- A disposition toward taking action to make changes in one's lifestyle as necessary (adapted from Miller, 1998).

In short, civic science literacy might be described as having enough scientific literacy to make sense of contemporary issues on the front page of the newspaper and then to understand what, if any, actions one might take to resolve them. For example, a student living in an urban area with a large lake at risk of becoming hypereutrophic (and thus unusable) needs to understand core ecological concepts, be able to sift through a variety of arguments, be in the habit of seeking out and making sense of new information, and then understand how she can participate in public dialogues so that her interests are represented. This final point—connecting science education back to citizenship—is something we believe is sorely lacking in today's schools, which tend to produce inert knowledge and docile learners (cf., Miller, 1998; Sizer, 1984).

This model of expertise seeks to provide an alternative to the model that "everyone should become a professional scientist," or even a professional science journalist. Rather, it highlights the idea that there are a number of socially valued identities that citizens routinely inhabit and that, as educators, we must help students to cocreate civic-minded identities with peers, teachers, parents, community members and domain experts in order to better confront the complex problems of the 21st century. Such models of citizenship are especially important for a democratic society to function insofar as its citizens' capability to make informed decisions about multifaceted issues and construct adequate dispositions toward approaching, understanding, and contributing to public policy debates, especially in a participatory age (Kolsto, 2001; New London Group, 1996).

CITIZEN SCIENCE

The purpose of this chapter is to discuss how the theory of designed experiences was utilized in the design of an educational lake science role-playing game. Previously proposed by Squire (2006), the theory of designed experiences describes how games "privilege certain worldviews and ways of being" (p. 26) through interactions with constructed rules in ideological environments. We have leveraged this model while going through a series of design iterations for a game to teach civic science literacy and offer insight into what an educational game design process based on this theory might look like. We build on suggestions that one power of video games as a medium may be in engaging players in virtual environments and interactive communities that are already embodying 21st-century literacy practices (e.g., Gee, 2003; Shaffer et al., 2005; Squire, 2008). Specifically, we explore the idea that, rather than transmitting "content," games may be best suited for immersing players in worlds in which they gain understandings of complex systems, develop "design"-type understandings of deep problems, and leave the game mobilized to have an impact on their worlds. This chapter explores this idea through introducing Citizen Science, a game prototype currently in development by the authors in partnership with Filament Games. Although the game is not yet in the hands of users so that it may be tested, this chapter uses this game as a thought experiment (cf., Holland, Jenkins, & Squire, 2003) for exploring theory.

We describe our design study of Citizen Science in order to:

- Articulate a model for scientific citizenship role playing games that enables players to engage in socially consequential gameplay in scientific domains. This particular model is a refinement of our earlier work, as well as work done by colleagues in games, learning, and society (Barab, et al., 2005; Shaffer et al., 2005)[1];
- Provide a case study of how educational games might be developed by detailing our design efforts in relation to models of "best practice" in the field; and
- Elaborate on a theory of video games as designed experience that might be applied across domains and technological platforms more broadly.

As we believe that role-playing games can combine features of targeted games, epistemic games, and other video game conventions in order to create compelling educational gaming experiences, in this thought experiment we explore what a role-playing game specifically designed for citizenship might look like. By integrating the core principles of digital media such as simulation, participatory practices, and aesthetics of experience into a design approach for science learning, the design process described here is one attempt to build on Squire's (2006) theory of designed experience in order to generate further exploration of learning theory with games. We will propose in this chapter that the process for the design of role-playing games for civic science literacy can be conveyed by the following steps: (1) identifying complex systems that are worth understanding, (2) creating roles for students to inhabit through which they can affect that change, (3) designing game mechanics that induct students into that world and enable them to experiment by making changes on that complex system, (4) then providing multiple modes for assessing feedback, reflecting on action, (5) building bridges of understanding toward new domains, and (6) identifying and designing in-routes of participation for players to become involved in "real-life" communities extending beyond the game. Crucially this design pursuit means engaging in a conversation about goals rather than content: What kinds of roles, systems, and forms of interaction ought students *experience*?

Choosing a Content Area: Lake Ecology for Studying Complex Ecological Systems

In identifying a content area—water ecology—we asked a variety of questions:

1. Is it an area suited for a systemic approach? (Water systems are appropriate; see below.)
2. Is it important and relevant to the lives of our participants? (The majority of youth in Wisconsin and the Upper Midwest think about recreational lake activities at some point, most of which share some common issues.)
3. Can content be linked to experiences or aspects of the scientific inquiry process? (Lakes can be visited, and students can take water samples and/or water quality readings.)
4. Can this content to be taught in schools? (Water quality is a common curriculum standard.)
5. Is there the potential for youth to actually do something about this issue after playing? (Many such lakes are on the edge of eutrophication but the process could still be reversed.)

One way to think about the content selection process is to ask oneself, "Is this the sort of content that is open to becoming an ideological world? What is or could be seductive about this content area to players? Is the content area robust enough to draw in players' attention and propel them out toward doing something about it in the real world?" From an instructional design perspective, we realize that not every content area is conducive to being represented or 'taught' via a game.

Critics might argue that the last thing the world needs is another water quality unit, pointing out that few topics in schools today are taught with more frequency than water quality. We are sympathetic to this argument to a degree (and believe that it's actually a good reason to try a game in this domain in order to facilitate comparisons); however, we believe that there is also an opportunity to improve the state of the art by focusing specifically on systems concepts. Often times, these units focus on issues such as measuring water quality, managing stormwater runoff, or the movement of water in a watershed. In many cases, these proximal causes are important but nowhere near the most important in terms of water quality. We posed these questions to our subject matter experts (SMEs), Robert Bohanan and Stephen Carpenter, both of whom are science educators at our home institution and researchers conducting long-term research on urban lakes. Specifically, we asked the following questions:

- What are the "big, enduring ideas" in this domain that one would want all students to understand deeply (see Gardner, 1999)?
- What ideas are difficult for students to understand?
- Which of these lend themselves to complex simulation?

In sum, we sought concepts that could be translated into a game system that emphasizes interactivity and decision making, rather than rote memorization. We found these questions helpful, as they provided a first pass at narrowing down the available design degrees of freedom, allowing us to begin to better think about the game as providing both educational and engaging experiences for players.

Through repeated discussions via e-mail and in person, Carpenter and Bohanan suggested at least two concepts essential for understanding the lake system that this game might be able to convey: 1) events that affect the lake occur over relatively large time scales and over large distances and 2) the importance of thresholds and potential irreversibility. That is, pollution that enters the system in the present will produce measurable effects many years into the future, and chemical pollution can be carried into the lake from a variety of sources (e.g., farms) that are many miles away via runoff (Carpenter, personal communication). Additionally, passing certain thresholds of phosphorous, or undergoing a regime shift (a dominant pattern of interactions), may be extremely hard to reverse, making preventative measures to protect urban lakes all the more important.

Both agreed that water quality units, as they are currently taught, typically do not use urban lakes as instances of ecological systems; they explained how contemporary research on lakes emphasizes systemic change in the following ways that could be applied to any ecological system (Bohannon, 2008; Carpenter, 2009):

1. Multiple (not linear) causality (such as the positive feedback loops between phosphorous deposits, which lead to algae growth, which lead to increased sediments, which subsequently lead to increased algae growth);
2. Processes occur across larger spatial scales making it difficult to ascertain the effects on a local system (such as farm runoff from 100 miles away making its way into an urban lake);
3. Contemporary conditions created by events from the long past (e.g., the soil degradation that causes problems in the Madison lakes began in the 1840s and was most intensive from about 1945–1985 but has had significant impacts in 2009);
4. Small things triggering explosive effects on an ecosystem as a whole (e.g., exponential growth of small algae triggers algae blooms the size of a whole lake, beach closings, and health risks to many lake users);
5. The importance of rapid, not incremental, changes that have ecological impacts such as invasions, fishery collapses, and algae blooms; and
6. The potential for irreversibility, which is ecological systems crossing a threshold into a new state which cannot be brought back at all or without great difficulty (such as lake eutrophication).

They emphasized that these ideas are important not just because the content area (water quality) is critical for human survival, but also because it illustrates key ecological concepts that operate in larger issues from global warming to the collapse of ocean fisheries. Perhaps there are opportunities to use the relatively tangible aspects of lakes (such as water clarity, algae blooms, or beach closings) as a window into these more complex phenomena, which are illustrated in game simulation. These core attributes of ecological systems would become a core part of the rules determining how the (ideological) world is governed.

With an understanding of how to instantiate the content as a world, our next step is to turn the attention back to the player, interrogating how he or she will experience the game. Previous research suggests for example, that these processes are appropriately developmentally challenging to our target age group (middle school students). Ecological phenomena, which happen at broad spatial and temporal scales, make direct observation difficult (if not impossible), requiring highly abstract thought (Bohanan, 2009). Within our own research (Squire, in press), we also observed that students come to the area with several naïve conceptions about pollutants, namely, that all dirty water is polluted water (with little understanding of water chemistry at the chemical level). For them, once a body of water has an ounce of pollution, it is effectively "contaminated" (suggesting little sense of concentration or system thresholds). Our hope is that these phenomena, which students at this level find so tricky to understand, can create a natural sense of puzzlement—an appropriate level of challenge—within players.

Our design challenge, here, is how to create seductive identities for players to inhabit. From our previous work (see Squire & Jan, 2007), we knew that playing roles such as Department of Natural Resources officials, private investigators, or wildlife ecologists was interesting to students. However, we decided to expand on this work by exploring a new quasi-professional identity for players to inhabit, one of "citizen scientist." The player would interact with various professionals (such as limnologists) who would provide access to those various professions, but the idea was that *any* student could finish the game and see himself immediately as a citizen scientist and then choose to become a professional later if desired. This step represents an important change in our own thinking, as it pulls away from the model that "every student should learn to think like a scientist" (a model common in the learning sciences), toward one in which everyone should become an involved participant in key issues in his/her own communities. The idea is to test this previously mentioned intersection between the participatory aspects of gaming culture and grassroots organizing.

Choosing a Technological Platform

Having acquired a notion of how the game would operate acting as an "ideological world" (Squire, 2006) and the rough trajectory of student experience (from naïve novice to informed citizen), it was next time to settle on a technological platform, a critical consideration with profound design and distribution implications. Previously, we had developed similar games for both mobile and desktop computers using a variety of tools, including *Renderware*, *C#*, *Flash*, *Unreal Tournament*, and *Torque*. For this project, we committed early to working in *Flash* (eventually using a proprietary engine developed by Filament Games) because it:

1. Would enable the broadest potential technical platform;
2. Would enable us to tie into robust gaming communities (such as Kongregate) and thus build an audience beyond traditional classrooms;
3. Would enable our partner to build upon and extend its technological toolset; and
4. Would make the game technically relevant. That is, being built in *Flash*, a dominant widespread platform, the game has the least chance of obsolescence. Additionally, working with an established platform being used in another, similar title (*Our Courts*) enabled us to leverage its play tests of artwork, navigation, and mechanics and focus more heavily on creating novel interactions.

Designing Citizen Science

With the world, trajectories of experience, and technological limitations in place, we were able to shift our attention toward the design and development of the core metaphor, role, and goals for players. By answering questions like "What role should the character play?" or "What are the goals of the character?" within the context of the game, we were able to develop a framework that allowed us to begin more specific design tasks. We chose to charge the player with an overarching goal of saving a nearby lake from dying, adapting a narrative common to role-playing games (i.e., save the world from destruction). Likewise, the player experience trajectory (from nubile youngster to world-changing hero) was adapted from a standard amongst other role-playing games, allowing us to leverage pre-established genre mechanics like exploring areas, increasing skills, gathering inventory items, and using tools in the world. Further, the underlying core aesthetic experience of having a dramatic, positive impact on the world is a good one for education (and one that, curiously, we do not frequently make available to students in schools).

The resulting game narrative places participants in the role of a youth who has been transported to the future and realizes that a popular lake central to his/her community may be dying in his original time. A "Spirit of the Lake" greets the player and helps him understand key issues through cut scenes and gathering quests. The player then travels back and forth through time observing the lake and collecting physical data, talking to key constituencies to understand social factors surrounding the lake's use, and analyzing the consequences of actions made in the present. Players can not only observe and experience the consequences of their decisions as they visit different time periods and strive to create a lake that is "healthy" and responsive to human needs, but they are actively encouraged to construct and enact their own hypotheses about relationships in the system. This time travel mechanic is thus designed to do something unique and interesting that students can't easily do in the real world but is also fundamental to the domain (recall the importance of temporal causes), providing them with an up-close perspective of data and environmental effects over fairly long timescales.

With the core game metaphor/experiences of the moment-to-moment game play set (traveling across time to save a lake), we immediately faced two obvious and practical challenges: 1) maximizing player engagement while 2) maintaining the educational content within the game. Indeed, we find that for many, this is where the design gets tricky, as educators must go beyond traditional educational design processes (such as ADDIE) which are historically driven by analyses of content, skills, and/or dispositions, in favor of processes that involve cycles of interaction with a world toward having a cumulative experience. Ideally, both engagement and education are kept in mind throughout the design of any product. However, we found it beneficial to focus first on *designing experience,* which in turn provided more clues about how to design the educational aspects of the game.

The core of the design process we used involves interrogating the semiotic domain (Gee, 2003) of scientific citizenship area for tools, practices, information sources, and sources of feedback to incorporate into game play. We created mock-ups, prototypes, spreadsheets, and player narratives, iteratively going back and forth between the semiotic domain and mock-ups of game play. In the next section, we will elaborate on this process to both elucidate the structure of the game and our conception of a broader theory of designed experiences that connects research and design from commercial entertainment video games to educational ones.

Identifying Verbs

To keep the focus on game play, rather than content delivery, we sought to understand the *verbs* involved; what players could *do* rather than what they should know. This process (something we, and many other designers have borrowed from the legendary Nintendo designer, Shigeru Miyamoto – see Sheff, 1993) orients design towards what the player can *do* in the world. It is here that many educators struggle as designers, as we are often tempted to recapitulate the inquiry process without thinking as creatively about how to extend it in interesting ways, and it is here where the theory of designed experiences can specifically help guide the design process.

Working closely with Filament Games[2] and SMEs, we examined what scientists do when interacting with a lake system in order to develop a library of potential game mechanics. We looked specifically for authentic scientific activities that were complex enough to be engaging yet simple enough to be imported into the game. We first looked at how scientists collect and use data in making arguments. We looked for activities that were likely to maintain player engagement in games. For example, the notion of "swimmable days" (the number of days that a beach is open) is a powerful way to conceptualize the impact of pollution regulation on the lake to the public. Because it is a meaningful unit that people can relate to, unlike say, parts per million, it is often used and is especially helpful in conveying the impact of pollution on lakes to nonscientists. Unfortunately, "swimmable days" does not easily translate to an action that a player can perform in-game (although swimming might), but it might serve as a good source of feedback on players' actions.

On the other hand, scientists' use of a fairly simple tool, a secchi disk, translates fairly well to a game environment and so taking readings early and often became a core part of the game play (much like fighting opponents is core to certain role-playing games). A secchi disk is a small black and white disk that is lowered into water and the point at which it can no longer be seen is recorded. This depth is proportionate to the clarity of the water and an indicator of the lake's general health. Unlike swimmable days, the activity around a secchi disk is easily mappable onto in-game player actions. By using mechanics that instantiate authentic activity rather than exclusively privileging content, we create the opportunity for the player to develop an understanding of the system from the perspective of a lake scientist. By simultaneously prioritizing game play, we can choose authentic activities that are also appropriate for maintaining player engagement.

Scientific Argumentation

After many design meetings, we agreed upon argumentation as a core game mechanic and as the primary way that the player creates meaningful changes in the game environment. One way we wanted to push the field of "serious games" in general and the target area of water quality specifically was to create game mechanics in which the player could interact with a simulated system in a way that affects the outcome of the world. This had an extra benefit in that the core game mechanic (argumentation) is a process inherent and essential to the practice of science. This process also builds on our previous research developing *Mad City Mystery* (Squire & Jan, 2008) in which we found a parsimonious fit between argument construction and educational game play as well as contemporary theories of learning in games more broadly (e.g., Steinkuehler & Duncan, 2008) The idea is that players would use the construction tool to "over and over" make arguments to various non-player characters. Once arguments have been established, they become *tools* for players to manipulate (in the same way that they drag and drop data) against or with other characters. Arguments are conceptualized as objects that the player carries around with him, which are supported by data that the player collects over time, and are used to convince other actors in the system.

Basing the game on argumentation also builds on Gee's (2004) and later Squire's (2006) notion of emphasizing ways of thinking and being in the world, rather than content domains as curricular goals. This pattern, which Gee calls the "content fetish," values the world as bodies of information which then leads naturally to valuing knowledge as facts to be memorized in order to pass standardized tests. In science education, this translates to the false belief that knowledge is predominantly produced through a process of discovery, rather than constructed to explain phenomena (Sandoval & Millwood, 2005). A number of researchers have argued that argumentation, a core component of scientific practice, can help to teach students a more accurate epistemology that conveys knowledge more appropriately (Bricker & Bell, 2008; Kuhn, 2005; Steinkuehler, 2006)

Although our previous work (*Mad City Mystery*, Squire & Jan, 2008) involved argumentation as the basis of game play, the argumentation in *Mad City Mystery* occurred face-to-face and was not instantiated in software. When it came time to design an argument interface, we identified two existing games (*Resilient Planet* and *Phoenix Wright: Ace Attorney*) that could serve as models of how to instantiate argument construction in a game. In *Phoenix Wright*, the player acts as a defense attorney who navigates through a narrative of court cases, trying to prove that his clients are innocent. The game forces the player to interject at appropriate times, given evidence that runs counter to what the prosecuting attorney claims. Though the game does not have educational goals, it is proof-of-concept that argumentation can drive a game narrative.

Resilient Planet, which is designed by Filament Games to be educational, also uses an argument constructor. In *Resilient Planet*, players are scientists located off the northwestern Hawaiian Islands, in which they investigate the impact of predators, monk seals, and tiger sharks, on the local prey population. Players generate data by performing activities that scientists actually perform when investigating ocean ecosystems. Throughout the game, the player uses data as evidence to support various arguments. In one particularly unique feature of *Resilient Planet*, players drag and drop graphical representations of data into the argument constructor so that their thinking becomes visible. In doing so, the game draws on evidence that suggests that making thinking visible may be beneficial for students thinking through arguments (Bell, 1997, 2000). To better understand what the game play around arguments is like, here is a general description of the first level of play.

In the same way that commercial games provide players with support as they learn the controls and mechanics of the game, the first level of the game serves as an introduction to the argument constructor in order for the players to learn what the rest of the game is generally about. In our game world, nonplayer characters can be convinced to perform certain actions based on arguments that the player constructs. We begin with the topic of zebra mussels, an invasive species that poses a threat to Midwestern lakes. As a result of a lack of sufficient natural predators and the ease with which they can propagate (an adult female zebra mussel can produce up to 1 million eggs in a year), zebra mussels are difficult to deal with once they are introduced to a lake. In ecological terms, there is an irreversibility to the introduction of this invasive species (a common theme in ecology). They are a nuisance to humans because they attach themselves to any hard surface in water, clogging pipe drains and damaging boat engines. More significantly, zebra mussels can have devastating effects on lake ecosystems, as they act as filters, causing a decrease in lake turbidity and an increase in algal growth—some strands of which can be deadly.

Because these two effects—decreases in lake turbidity and increases in algal growth—can be misleading, and because zebra mussels are a well-known invasive specie that receives a fair amount of public media coverage, investigating their impact on the lake system provides a powerful way to get students thinking about lake ecology at an appropriate level. Rather than identifying zebra mussels as simply "bad" for a lake, we wanted to get students to think about their impact on the lake in terms of water chemistry and cultural use. In the first quest line, players must convince local boaters to clean zebra mussels from their boats. In response, and problematizing the students' conception of zebra mussels as bad for the lake, the local boaters argue that, because zebra mussels actually decrease lake turbidity (a general indicator of lake health) they should actually be introduced to the lake. To counter this argument, players must leverage this same evidence to make a more complex argument, pointing out that although decreases in lake turbidity can serve as an indicator for lake health, they can also be related to increases in algal blooms which are a major problem for a lake's recreational use.

One manner in which the argument constructor deviates from other existing software is that argumentation in *Resilient Planet* is a mechanic that players use as a ladder for advancement through a narrative trajectory (which is hopefully meaningful to players). In Citizen Science, however, players begin with very simple arguments that build and graduate in complexity through game advancement. We scale argumentation in a manner consistent with how argumentation literature describes students' advancement through using the following:

1. A single piece of supporting and relevant data as evidence in an argument is the most rudimentary;
2. Two pieces of supporting and relevant data that support an argument is more advanced; and
3. Two pieces of supporting and relevant data that support an argument and, in addition, take into consideration the potential counter arguments, is the most advanced.

Essentially, we couple the player's in-game skill progression to his/her actual argumentation ability. This is an imperfect progression, however, and through play-testing, we hope to build on the literature of how arguments might be instantiated in game play.

Content Knowledge

Although Citizen Science does not strive to "deliver content" but rather to "provide players meaningful experiences within ideological worlds," content knowledge is clearly useful, even required, for understanding systems and constructing arguments. We tend to think about content in game play as something that "comes for free" once good game play in a domain is established. If the game play experience consists of generating data in order to test hypotheses, which are to convince characters to take action, then the "content" would be whatever content is required for such actions.

After discussions with the SMEs, it became evident that perhaps the most routine practice of scientists investigating water quality is to check the water chemistry (e.g., the concentration of phosphates), so we made such tests a routine part of game play and background information about water chemistry ubiquitous. Water testing involves placing a few drops of a chemical into a collected water sample and matching the resulting color with a key in order to determine the concentration (Figure 1).

It is an action that transfers into the game well, providing players with the opportunity to endlessly test the concentration of water samples they collect in-game as they learn to use the tool as a part of the larger process of data collection in the pursuit of argumentation. That is, checking the concentration of phosphates is, in and of itself, a fairly trivial task to accomplish in real life

Figure 1. A mock-up for the water chemistry kit that player use to determine phosphate concentrations

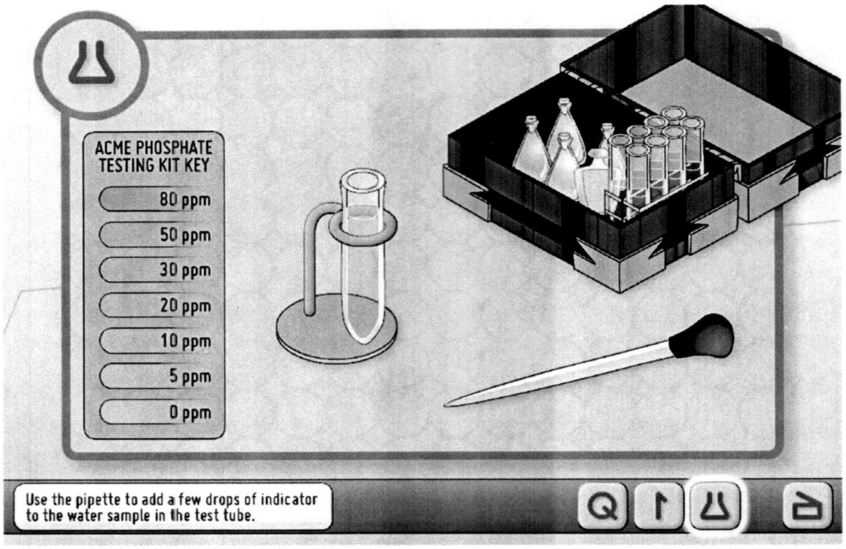

and there are likely to be many classrooms taking advantage of this. What's more important here is not its simplicity as a tool, but the meaning that it has with respect to the rest of the system - by checking the concentration of phosphates, players generate data that can be used elsewhere as evidence in arguments relating to the quality of the lake. Embedding the tool in a larger action cycle provides students with an understanding of the role of the tool rather than just its simple (and fairly mundane) nature.

Future Directions

One of the key reasons why (most) educators might use games is because of the way that games can help to create learning experiences that are more compelling than other educational materials. Indeed, commercial game designers have a host of philosophies and techniques they employ specifically to engage their audience in game play. We must be sure, however, to maintain realistic expectations of how games can be leveraged for education in order to ensure that neither educators nor designers pursue an idealized notion of games-as-educational-panacea. For example, many educators frequently critique video games based on their lack of content or pedagogy rather than on their inability to produce transformative experiences for players; many designers and game players critique educational games for their lack of usability and often thin veneer of engaging components. This mismatch of expectations can result in products that have lost the appeal that brought educators to games in the first place; the view of wrapping content in a shroud of game-like components has repeatedly had the result of creating something that looks like a game, sounds like a game, but at its core is unmistakably "edu-stuff."

How to create compelling game play for educational games is an absolutely critical but unfortunately not-well-understood aspect of design. Developing a theory that explicates this process must inevitably result in game designers and educators sharing perspectives. Leveraging the aspects of games that are most appropriate for education and understanding what educational content games are best suited for teaching will involve significant cooperation between disciplines. We think, however, that it will result in particularly powerful tools. For example, educational environments have often times attempted to scaffold students' progress based on theories of learning that emphasize the dynamic nature of the individual and need for similarly dynamic teachers that can adapt to teach just beyond the students' abilities (c.f., Vygotsky, 1980). Various methods have been used to accomplish this, ranging from helpful on-screen prompts to artificial intelligence-driven adaptive models using Bayesian statistics, each with its own shortcomings.

Game designers face a similar challenge, as they need to create an increasingly complex arc of experience so that the player develops from newcomer to more advanced status. For example, one way that they accomplish this is to "black box" functions once players become experts with them, a strategy we are also taking. After taking several successful secchi disk readings, players "level up" their field skill, enabling them to take readings more quickly and successfully. As players progress, this enables them to focus less on relatively mundane tasks (such as taking secchi disk readings), and more on systemic relationships, while at the same time, giving them a relatively simple, repetitive skill to focus on when they are stuck. Similarly, as players advance through the game, they gain access to more sophisticated tools, including vehicles (a motor scooter and a boat), water chemistry kits, and argument constructors, each of which also graduates in complexity.

Further complicating matters is the divergent number of ways in which games are played. Various play styles (Bartle, 2003) must also be anticipated and rewarded. This kind of fine tuning of games comes through rigorous and extensive play-testing, something that is frequently overlooked in educational gamesdevelopment; consider that commercial video games often spend over $1 million on testing—a number that is higher than the entire budget of most educational games—when educational games have far greater testing demands in that they need to create game experiences that are educational in addition to being engaging.

These are just some of the many issues that future educational game designers must face: They must find ways in which cycles of actions and rewards map to educative and socially valued ways of thinking and acting within specific content domains. They also highlight important questions for today's designer: How can we leverage tools from both education and commercial games to create aesthetically compelling and engaging experiences that are simultaneously educational? More importantly, how can we create modern, digitally mediated equivalents of life-enhancing, life changing kinds of experiences (or "memorable experiences," in video game parlance)? Future games research should explore how best to leverage contemporary theories of learning in conjunction with commercial design techniques in order to develop and advance theories that can specifically inform design. The approach we found to be useful here was one of design-based research, with its repeated iterations of design and implementation. Because of this feature, it may be particularly useful in developing theories that can ground more formalized theories of learning in experiences that have local impact and relevance to students and are thereby more meaningful.

CONCLUSION

In this chapter, we have presented a design narrative of Citizen Science in order to argue for a design process in educational games around designing experiences rather than designing for content mastery. We start with the observation that games enable (perhaps even create) dispositions toward understanding complex systems, seeking out leverage points within those systems, and then manipulating such systems to create change. Citizen Science seeks to build on this pattern to specifically focus on water ecology, with the hope that the ideas are generative enough to be useful for players in a variety of endeavors.

In Citizen Science, we have tried to use fantasy, time travel, and cycles of interaction with digital tools to create a compelling game experience. Rather than undermining the engaging components of game play in the pursuit of conveying content, we attempt to design activities that support educational and meaningful experiences. Through future work and implementation, we hope to develop games that can not only provide individuals with more advanced conceptual understandings of systems that exist in the world but that can convey socially desirable values that transfer to out-of-game experiences which enable and encourage civic responsibility and action.

REFERENCES

Barab, S., Thomas, M., Dodge, T., Carteaux, R., & Tuzun, H. (2005). Making learning fun: Quest Atlantis, a game without guns. *Educational Technology Research and Development, 53*(1), 86–107. .doi:10.1007/BF02504859

Bartle, R. (2003). *Designing Virtual Worlds*. New Riders Games. Retrieved from http://www.amazon.ca/exec/obidos/redirect?tag=citeulike09-20&path=ASIN/0131018167

Bell, P. (1997). *Using argument representations to make thinking visible for individuals and groups* (pp. 10–19). University of Toronto.

Bell, P. (2000). Scientific arguments as learning artifacts: designing for learning from the web with KIE. *International Journal of Science Education, 22*(8), 797–817. doi:10.1080/095006900412284

Bohannon, J. (2008). CLIMATE CHANGE: The big thaw reaches Mongolia's pristine north. *Science, 319*(5863), 567–568. doi:10.1126/science.319.5863.567

Bricker, L., & Bell, P. (2008). *Conceptualizations of argumentation from science studies and the learning sciences and their implications for the practices of science education* (Vol. 9). Retrieved from http://dx.doi.org/10.1002/sce.2027.

Disessa, A. (2000). *Changing minds: Computers, learning, and literacy*. Cambridge, MA: The MIT Press. Retrieved from http://www.amazon.ca/exec/obidos/redirect?tag=citeulike09-20&path=ASIN/0262041804

Gardner, H. (1999). *The disciplined mind: What all students should understand*. New York: Simon & Schuster.

Gee, J. (2003). *What video games have to teach us about learning and literacy*. New York: Palgrave Macmillan.

Gee, J. (2004). *Situated Language And Learning: A Critique Of Traditional Schooling*. London: Routledge.

Gee, J. (2005). *Why video games are good for your soul: Pleasure and learning*. Melbourne, Australia: Common Ground Publishing.

Giordano, A. (1997). Narco News Publishes "The medium is the middleman: For a revolution against media." Retrieved July 15, 2009, from http://www.narconews.com/themedium1.html

Jenkins, H. (2004). The cultural logic of media convergence. *International Journal of Cultural Studies, 7*(1), 33–43. doi:10.1177/1367877904040603

Kolsto, S. D. (2001). *Scientific literacy for citizenship: Tools for dealing with the science dimension of controversial socioscientific issue* (Vol. 8). Retrieved from http://dx.doi.org/10.1002/sce.101.

Kuhn, D. (2005). *Education for thinking*. Cambridge, MA: Harvard University Press.

Miller, J. D. (1998). The measurement of civic scientific literacy. *Public Understanding of Science (Bristol, England), 7*(3), 203–223. doi:10.1088/0963-6625/7/3/001

Sandoval, W. A., & Millwood, K. A. (2005). The quality of students' use of evidence in written scientific explanations. *Cognition and Instruction, 23*(1), 23–55. doi:10.1207/s1532690xci2301_2

Shaffer, D., Squire, K., Halverson, R., & Gee, J. (2005). Video games and the future of learning. *Phi Delta Kappan, 87*(2), 111, 104.

Shaffer, D. W. (2006). Epistemic frames for epistemic games. *Computers & Education, 46*(3), 223–234. doi:10.1016/j.compedu.2005.11.003

Sheff, D. (1993). *Game over: How Nintendo zapped an American industry, captured your dollars, and enslaved your children*. New York: Random House.

Shelton, B., & Wiley, D. (2007). *The design and use of simulation computer games in education*. Rotterdam: Sense Publishers.

Squire, K. (2003). Video games in education. *International Journal of Intelligent Simulations and Gaming, 2*(1), 49–62.

Squire, K. (2006). From content to context: Videogames as designed experience. *Educational Researcher, 35*(8), 19–29. doi:10.3102/0013189X035008019

Squire, K. (2007). Games, learning, and society: Building a field. *Educational Technology Magazine, 47*(5), 51–55.

Squire, K. (2008). Critical education in an interactive age. In Silberman-Keller, D., Bekerman, Z., Giroux, H., & Burbules, N. (Eds.), *Mirror images: Popular culture and education* (pp. 105–124). New York: Peter Lang Publishing.

Squire, K., & Steinkuehler, C. (2005). Meet the gamers. *Library Journal*. Retrieved June 16, 2009, from http://www.libraryjournal.com/article/CA516033.html.

Steinkuehler, C. (2006). Virtual worlds, learning, & the new pop cosmopolitanism. *Teachers College Record*. Retrieved July 12, 2009, from http://www.tcrecord.org ID Number: 12843.

Steinkuehler, C., & Duncan, S. (2008). Scientific habits of mind in virtual worlds. *Journal of Science Education and Technology, 17*(6), 530–543. .doi:10.1007/s10956-008-9120-8

Steinkuehler, C. A. (2006). Massively multiplayer online video gaming as participation in a discourse. *Mind, Culture, and Activity, 13*(1), 38–52. doi:10.1207/s15327884mca1301_4

Vygotsky, L. (1980). *Mind in society: The development of higher psychological processes*. Cambridge, MA: Harvard University Press.

"MUST-READS" FOR THIS TOPIC/TOP TEXTS FOR INTERDISCIPLINARY STUDIES OF SERIOUS GAMES

Clark, A. (2003). *Natural-Born Cyborgs: Minds, Technologies, and the Future of Human Intelligence*. Cambridge, MA: Oxford University Press.

Gee, J. (2003). *What video games have to teach us about learning and literacy*. New York: Palgrave Macmillan.

Gee, J. (2005). *Why video games are good for your soul: Pleasure and learning*. Melbourne, Australia: Common Ground Publishing.

Kirsh, D., & Maglio, P. (1994). On distinguishing epistemic from pragmatic action. *Cognitive Science, 18*, 513–549.

Malone, T. W. (1981). Toward a theory of intrinsically motivating instruction. *Cognitive Science*, (4): 333–369.

Mitchell, E. (1985). The dynamics of family interaction around home video games. Special Issue: Personal computers and the family. *Marriage and Family Review 8*(1-2), 121)-135.

Salen, K. (Ed.). Game Ecologies. The John D. and Catherine T. MacArthur Foundation series on digital media and learning. (167-198) Cambridge, MA: The MIT Press.

Squire, K. D. (2006). From content to context: Video games as designed experiences. *Educational Researcher*, *35*(8), 19–29. doi:10.3102/0013189X035008019

Steinkuehler, C. (2006). Virtual worlds, learning, & the new pop cosmopolitanism. *Teachers College Record*. Retrieved July 12, 2009, from http://www.tcrecord.org ID Number: 12843.

ENDNOTES

1 Similarly, epistemic games, games that are modeled on the professional thinking of the professions have been successful in providing students with ways of thinking (knowledge, skills, values, and dispositions) that are tied to professional ways of being in the world. For example, students role-playing as science journalists develop knowledge and skills about both language and literacy practices as well as scientific content domains. Shaffer and colleagues argue that such "epistemic frames" are valuable for students in that they not only help with target domains but also are generative for more "far transfer" sorts of tasks as they learn deeper structures in areas such as communication that can be applied to new situations. Epistemic games successfully use professions and other socially valued practices for producing engagement and facilitating learning but are also somewhat limited by the real-world professions on which they are based. There might be opportunities for using the conventions of video games (e.g., power-ups, narrative conventions) to increase engagement and learning, while also modeling socially desirable roles, such as a citizen–activist.

2 Filament Games is a Madison-based educational game company with which we have worked closely in thinking through contemporary ideas of educational game design. As advertised on their Web page (filamentgames.com/about), they are "dedicated to creating next generation learning games that combine best practices in commercial game development (high production values, engaging game mechanics) with key concepts in the learning sciences (constructivism, just-in-time learning)."

Section 5
Future Directions

Chapter 13
Egaming and Girls: Optimizing Use in School Libraries

Lesley S. J. Farmer
California State University Long Beach, USA

Nora G. Murphy
Los Angeles Academy Middle School, USA

ABSTRACT

Schools and libraries are considering the incorporation of egaming because of its attraction to youth and its potential benefit for instruction, developing information literacy skills and facilitating academic success. Although egames are played by most youth, egaming has gender-linked properties: extent of play, choice of games, social interaction in gaming (such as role-playing games), and novice gaming practice. School libraries are uniquely positioned to provide resources and services to insure gender-equitable gaming experiences: gaming periodicals, opportunities to select and review games, collaboration with classroom teachers, and single-sex activities. The emerging trends of casual gaming, mobile egaming, and gaming design offer opportunities that can attract girls, which teacher librarians can leverage in their services. Their efforts can also contribute to the larger arena of serious games.

INTRODUCTION

Gaming in school libraries? Be it board games or computer games, such activities have drawn great attention in the professional field. The American Library Association now has a gaming initiative, which incorporates a blog (http://gaming.ala.org/news/), sponsors numerous events, and offers grants for libraries to incorporate gaming into public libraries. Where K-12 settings used to ban any games on the Internet and eschewed collecting game guidebooks, teacher librarians (TL) are now reconsidering their policies, holding gaming tournaments, and locating core gaming collection lists to help them purchase viable titles and even equipment (Nicholson, 2007). Not every school library is jumping on the band wagon, but the library world is certainly talking about gaming

Just a couple of decades ago, these same school libraries were addressing the issues of cardboard games (Levine, 2006). Of particular interest now are egames: video, console, and computer games.

DOI: 10.4018/978-1-61520-719-0.ch013

Copyright © 2010, IGI Global. Copying or distributing in print or electronic forms without written permission of IGI Global is prohibited.

For this reason, the term "egaming" will be used to differentiate these electronic forms of games from their more traditional print counterparts. While egames technically predated Web 2.0, the convergence of Internet interactivity and increasingly popular MMORPGs (Massively Multiplayer Online Role-Playing Games) has led to an almost inevitable consideration by TLs. Rather than fight the technological flood, TLs are trying to figure out ways to embrace the phenomenon. A certain "cool-ness" factor has played a part in this endeavor to show that school libraries can provide recreational options as well as academic. Some TLs "translate" egaming skills into information literacy skills to help students bridge life at school and at home. Furthermore, as education is increasingly incorporating serious games (that is, games that are not developed with the sole intent of entertainment but also have educational or other communication objectives), TLs have an opportunity to collaborate with classroom teachers to locate and use serious games effectively for academic success. Egames can also serve as a vehicle to promote girls' interest in technology (AAUW, 2000; National Center for Women and Information Technology and the Girl Scouts of the USA, 2007; Van Eck, 2006).

As TLs try to attract youth to the library, they know that different library activities appeal to different segments of any population, be it calligraphy or video editing or literature circles. One of the main motivations for incorporating egaming into school libraries has been the desire to attract more boys (Nicholson, 2007). While the egaming gender gap has shrunk, egaming still has a male connotation, a fact not lost on females (Heeter, Edigio, Mishra, Winn, & Winn 2009; Krotoski, 2004). At the same time, TLs should consider factors in egaming that repel and attract girls. In that way, TLs can set up the conditions for learning via egames that can address the needs and interests of both sexes, even if those needs and interests differ. In order to do this, however, it is important to understand some of the key gender differences in game exposure, use, and preferences. We will begin with an overview of the some of the research on these differences before moving into a discussion of how libraries might best proceed in setting up egaming affinity spaces and some of the key challenges they will face in doing so.

BACKGROUND

As noted above, egaming includes a variety of digital formats: video, console, portable game devices, cell phone, and computer-based. Additionally, several genres of games exist. In its study of teen gaming, Pew Internet & American Life Project (2008) classified fourteen genres that teens play in order of preference: racing, puzzle, sports, action, adventure, rhythm, strategy, simulation, fighting, first-person shooting, role-playing, survival horror, MMOG (massively multiplayer online game), and virtual worlds.

Current Egaming Practice

At this point, egames have substantially penetrated U. S. households. For console games alone, 71% of households with boys or girls owned video consoles, and 80% of households with teenagers owned consoles (Neilsen, 2007). A 2008 Pew Internet study indicated that 93% of teens go online, and 60% of teens own two or more technological gadgets (number one being desktop computers and number two being cell phones).

Egame usage by youth has also grown in the 21st century. Back in 2001, the National Institute on Media and the Family found that practically all children either played egames or knew someone who did. By 2003, two-thirds of college students reported playing egames occasionally or regularly (Jones, 2003). A 2005 Kaiser Family Foundation study showed that 63% of boys and 40% of girls engage with video games each day (especially those between the ages of 8 and 14). By 2008, about a third of the most frequent console gamers and a quarter of the most active computer gamers were minors (Entertainment Software Association). The 2008 Pew study on video games and teens found that almost all teens play egames, that half played "yesterday." Usage by format varied as follows: 86% played on consoles, 73% played on desktop/laptop computers, 60% play on a portable gaming device, and 46% played on a cell phone or equivalent. The largest growth was seen in casual gaming and mobile use (Rainie & Anderson, 2008). The Civic Engagement Research Group study on teen gaming found that 97% played video games, about three-quarters played weekly, and a third played at least once a day. Moreover, 80% play at least five genres of games. Interestingly, most video gamers play socially, two-thirds with another person in the same room; only a quarter play strictly alone (Kahne, Middaugh, & Evans, 2008).

Gendered Egaming Practices

Gender plays a role in youth's gaming activity, although the picture has become more nuanced in the last decade. As this point, about 99% of boys and 94% of girls play video games: about two-thirds of daily gamers are male, while one-third are female; younger boys are the most likely to play and older girls the least likely, although a majority of older girls play at some point (Pew Internet & American Life Project, 2008). Boys tend to play more video games for longer periods of time, while girls prefer shorter computer or handheld games (Amory, Naicker, Vincent, & Adams, 1999; Simpson, 2005). Indeed, when the total number of hours played was calculated, only 6% of 2–11-year-old girls and 4% of teenage girls accounted for the total video game audience (that is, all ages), in contrast to 21% of 2–11-year-old boys and 20% of teenage boys (Neilsen, 2007).

Gender differences in technology attitude and behavior as a whole tend to emerge at puberty; prior to that age, children of both sexes exhibit similar play behaviors (Hackbarth, 2001). In her synthesis of gender issues in gaming behaviors, Agosto (2004) asserted that as girls enter adolescence their egaming activity drops in frequency. More specifically, Agosto found that teens are starting to explore their sexual identity, and egaming connotes masculinity, even in light of women gamers. The culture of technology remains male-dominated and mechanical (Graner Ray, 2004), so girls try to distance themselves from that stereotype, particularly since peer perception is so important to them. According to Fromme (2003), another reason that girls play egames less is because they choose to spend their time in other ways, such as reading. In addition, Fromme asserted that girls tended to have more household responsibilities than boys, and so had less time to play egames.

In their study of teen gaming behaviors, Cooper and Weaver (2003) claimed that males and females tended to master egames differently. The researchers found that boys were more likely to ask peers for help and consult cheat sheets and guides. In contrast, girls tended to work out problems independently or to ask a male for help; rather than consult a manual, girls will reset the level or start the game over. Cooper and Weaver (2003) also noted that in coed settings, boys outperformed girls in playing egames, but when physically separated, girls did equally well or better than boys, particularly if the game gave personalized textual feedback (boys, on the other hand, prefer icon-based help). Interestingly, Hargittai and Shafer (2006) found that females' online skills equaled males but that the former underestimated their expertise. Part of the issue is based on attrition theory, according to Cooper and Weaver (2003). The researchers asserted that when girls are successful with computers, they tend to attribute that success to the machine; when they are not successful, girls tend to blame themselves. In contrast, Cooper and Weaver (2003) stated that boys tended to praise their own prowess when they are technologically successful, and they blamed the computer when unsuccessful.

Wang, Wu, and Wang (2009) investigated the factors leading to the acceptance of mobile learning by Taiwanese students. The strongest predictor was performance expectancy, with males being more self-confident. Interestingly, when females thought they could self-manage their play, they were more likely to use mobile applications; males were more influenced by their peers in that if the mobile application was not considered male-appropriate, then they were less likely to use it.

In terms of the physical experience, boys enjoy mastering complex hand–eye coordination itself, while girls prefer to focus on concrete goals; if the navigation protocols are difficult to figure out or distract from achieving the goal, girls are likely to walk away from the egame (Cooper & Weaver, 2003). Beyond the issue of initial success, boys and girls sometimes play egames differently; in his study of fifth- and sixth-grade students, Van Eck (2006) found that in playing *Sim Safari* (Electronic Arts), girls tended to focus on building dwellings and interiors, and boys tended to focus on outdoor elements such as swamps and animals.

Carr (2005) claimed that gendered behaviors and attitudes about egames tend to be expressed most strongly by nonusers. Specifically, Carr (2005) found that girls would assert that egames are a waste of time. When they first see an egame, girls may confuse the look of the game (the quality of its graphics, for instance) and its playability. Because they tend to take fewer risks than boys, girls are more likely to give up on a complicated game than their male counterparts; furthermore, boys are more likely to socially value game play than girls do (Carr, 2005). On the other hand, Forssell (2008) observed that when girls find satisfaction accomplishing a gaming goal, they will continue to game, just as boys do; however, if girls have negative first experiences, they are less likely to become successful long-term gamers. Interestingly, Beavis and Charles (2007) discovered that seasoned girl gamers find that they tend to particularize their gaming behaviors as they find their place in the male-dominant culture; binary descriptions (i.e., boy–girl) do not adequately capture the variety of their experiences. As a result, a gaming minority becomes even more splintered and so loses valuable solidarity, according to Beavis and Charles (2007).

As gamers become more experienced, however, gendered differences tend to fade, according to several studies, indicating that with exposure to gaming (e.g., in structured settings like school libraries), girls and boys may benefit equally from gaming activities. MMOGs are a good case in point. Particularly in RPGs, players' first avatar tends to reflect the person's gender and age, although experienced players like to experiment with various identities and assume that little correlation exists between the avatar and the player (Kirriemuir & McFarlane, 2004; Lee & Hoadley, 2007). According to Taylor (2003), both sexes enjoy the sense of community and socialization, like to compete against themselves or to meet a goal, and like to explore virtual environments. Nevertheless, gender continues to impact behaviors in these role-playing games, as Yee (2006) found when surveying 30,000 MMORPG players. Yee revealed a five-factor model of user motivation: achievement, relationship, immersion, escapism, and manipulation. Males were significantly more motivated by achievement and manipulation factors, and females were significantly more motivated by relationships, immersion, and escapism. Males tended to work with others in order to achieve a goal while females did so to relate to other players. In examining gendered gameplay, Graner Ray (2004) asserted that females tend to spend more time polishing their avatars and feel frustrated that fewer options are available for female characters than male characters. In analyzing gender differences in digital play behavior, Bertozzi (2008) stated the need to recognize the difficulty in challenging existing gendered norms. Players tend to avoid crossing traditional gender gameplay roles, such as status of civility and sanctioned "sex talk." Lee and Hoadley

(2007) studied middle schoolers' behaviors in two MMOGs, focusing on diversity and technology design. Students were asked to assume an avatar of the opposite sex, and boys quickly experienced more courtesy and flirtation; both sexes realized how outcomes depended more on stereotypical social expectations rather than individual merit, even though the students understood the true gender of each player. Similarly, in investigating *Final Fantasy* (Square Enix) forums, Jansz, Van Zoonen, and Vosmeer (2006) reported that players based their beginning actions on everyday social contexts of gender and then gained insights about gendered performance that led to less online sexism, more equitable treatment, and more positive gendered identities in their daily lives. As modeled in Lee and Hoadley's 2007 research, educators can use RPGs as an engaging way to explore gender expectations and norms. Based on these studies, a case may be made that explicitly addressing gender issues in virtual or "artificial" environments, such as a library gendered egame space, can significantly change perceptions, stereotypes, and enjoyment of egames. Without such interventions, girls and boys may continue to use technology and games differently, with girls being more disadvantaged as a result.

As noted above, gendered egaming practices tend to disappear with successful practice. Mobile devices seem to be more inviting and less threatening for girls, and girls play egames on these smaller devices eagerly, as seen in a study by Schaumburg (2001) on gender use of mobile laptops. The researcher found that girls' ability and self-confidence increased more than boys did because girls had time to practice regularly in school with this equipment. In explaining this phenomenon, Schaumburg (2001) claimed that two features of mobile devices resonate specifically with girls: portability and communication. Girls like being able to carry these devices in their purses or pockets. Their small size seems to make the technology less threatening. Secondly, Schaumburg (2001) asserted that these communication and storage devices facilitate human interaction and connectivity; with Internet connectivity, mobile devices could be used to construct knowledge collectively. Hooper, Fitzpatrick, and Weal (2007) asserted that girls were more likely than boys to initiate discussion and sharing of information: the features of mobile devices that assist multiple perspectives and relationship-rich learning. Increasingly, mobile devices include concrete and practical applications, which resonate with females (Cassell & Jenkins, 1998). These studies point to the benefits of providing mobile devices in school settings, such as the library, in order to offer a nonthreatening way to experience egames, thus reducing girls' technology anxiety and facilitating all youngsters' opportunities for positive practice.

Choice of Egames by Girls and Boys

U. S. computer and video game software sales topped $11.7 billion in 2008; of that total, $8.9 billion bought game console software. The family entertainment genre constituted 19% of those games (Entertainment Software Association, 2008). Youth have tens of thousands of titles to choose from.

Egame genre choices have changed as games have evolved and reflect age preferences. Amory, Naicker, Vincent, & Adams, (1999) discovered that students found adventure and strategy games highly appealing, rating sound, graphics, and storyline as highly important. In Rosen and Weil's 2001 study of southern California youth ages 10 to 25, solitaire and other card games dominated computer games, and *Super Mario* (Nintendo) was the favorite video game. DeKanter (2005) found that strategy games were the most popular PC games. The 2008 Pew Internet & American Life Project study listed teens' five most frequently played video games: *Guitar Hero* (Activision), *Halo 3* (Microsoft Game Studios), *Madden NFL* (EA Sports), *Solitaire* (Microsoft), *and Dance Dance Revolution* (Konami). In terms of popularity, the top most-played genres were racing (74%), puzzles (72%), sports (68%), action (67%), and adventure (66%). When exposed to a variety of game genres, boys and girls preferred adventure games overall. Likewise, both sexes enjoy role-playing games (RPGs) and simulations such as *Final Fantasy* (Square Enix) and *Sims* (Electronic Arts). These genres actively engage students, provide both textual and visual cues, often require collaboration in order to accomplish a task, often demand clear communication, can facilitate problem-solving skills, provide immediate feedback, and foster attention to detail (Gros, 2003). Physical games such as Wii and music-related titles (e.g., Electronic Arts' *Rock Band*) also engage both sexes as they leverage kinesthetic learning style and reinforce personal improvement (McCann, 2008).

Within this larger picture, sex-linked preferences about egame choice emerged. Girls tended to play six different game genres, and boys averaged eight game genres (Pew Internet & American Life Project, 2008). Fromme's (2003) study revealed that boys' favorite egame was *Grand Theft Auto* (Rockstar Games), and they frequently chose titles that were targeted for older gamers. In terms of egame genres, Fromme (2003) noted that boys preferred action and fighting games (33%), sport games (21%), and platform games (17%), while girls preferred logic and puzzle games (20%). The 2008 Pew Internet & American Life Project study reiterated those preferences, stating that boys were more likely than girls to play violent M-rated video games. However, when youth are required to play different kinds of games, both boys and girls preferred adventure games overall, as Van Eck (2006) discovered in his study of fifth and sixth graders. Specifically, he found that both sexes liked simulations, adventure, sports, and puzzle games. Some stereotypical preference emerged: only girls liked *Rockett's New School* (Purple Moon), and only boys liked *Battlezone* (Activision). However, other games had unexpected cross-gender appeal: *Nancy Drew* (Her Interactive) and *Contraption* (Viva). This study reinforces the importance of the librarian exposing students to a wide variety of egames.

Most research about egame preferences focuses on teen and adult tastes. Joseph and Kinzie (2005) identified five gaming modes that middle schoolers enjoyed: active, explorative, problem-solving, strategic, social, and creative; the researchers contended that evaluating games using this framework was more useful than game genres. These children liked exploratory games the most; boys preferred action games, and girls preferred creative games. The children preferred characters who were the same sex as themselves.

Several studies explored the kinds of egames that girls enjoy – or shy away from. Children Now's 2001 study revealed the 90% of the top-selling titles contained violence, and two-thirds of the characters were male (one-six were female, and one-sixth were non-human); these two factors along with games that lack meaningful social interaction account for the main reasons females dislike games (Hartmann & Klimmt, 2006). Most egame motifs tend to be competitive, and many are combative, both of which stress girls (Lucas and Sherry, 2004). Boys, on the other hand, find such games to be stress relievers or helpful in managing anger (Olson et al., 2007). Nor do girls like intense problem solving or high-stake risks; they would rather explore an open-ended setting (Hayes, 2005; Schott & Horrell, 2000). On the other hand, according to Kafai (1996), girls enjoy games with nuanced characters, strong storylines, good graphical features, high collaborative interactivity, and engaging contexts. In Kafai's (1996) study, girls self-reported that ideal games have user-friendly interfaces, are challenging yet fun, encourage goals that can be quickly accomplished using logic, foster relationships, and mesh concrete characters and locales.

It should be noted that the presence of "pink software" is a mixed picture. In reviewing the literature about female-targeted game design, Hartmann and Klimmt (2006) mentioned its popularity (e.g., *Barbie Fashion Designer*, Mattel).

Fifth- and eighth-grade girls studied by Heeter, et al. (2009) expected that female-designed games would be more fun to play than male-designed games. However, many of the games targeted to girls reinforce female stereotypes: *The Clique: Diss and Make Up* (Warner Bros.); *Charm Girls Club: My Fashion Mall, My Fashion Show,* and *My Perfect Prom* (Electronic Arts); *My Boyfriend* (Eidos Interactive); and *Princess in Love* (Kiba Games; John, 2009). In addition, the concept of girl games itself raises the issue that such games are not the norm, the default option, thus marginalizing girls. The cultural messages that these games send help shape future generations, so game design is of paramount importance (Dickey, 2006).

Graner Ray (2004) asserted that one aspect of gaming that bothers females in general is the appearance of the characters or avatars; designers on the whole have not paid enough attention to this detail and its connotations. In a study of preteen boys, Harrison and Bond (2007) found that Caucasian boys were motivated by gaming magazines to aspire to the muscular images of egame characters. It should also be noted that preteen boys preferred gaming magazines over all other magazine genres, and favored them over books and newspapers. In analyzing gaming characters, Graner Ray (2004) discovered that fewer female characters are featured, even in RPGs, and the default figures represent stereotypical images that probably attract males more than females; furthermore, fewer variations among female images are available than for males. Graner Ray (2004) noted that Lara Croft was one of the first strong female gaming characters, and she has highly sexualized features. Agosto (2004) examined girls' attitudes about these characters and stated that when preteen girls play these RPGs, they may feel uncomfortable about such stereotypical avatar options and may even think that they will need to grow up having that busty figure if they are to be considered feminine. Taylor (2003) noted that women gamers tend to "bracket" their characters, distancing themselves from their online visual identity, but younger girl players are still trying to determine their real identity so may succumb to the coded societal messages. For that reason, girls tend to favor animal characters (Schott & Horrell, 2000). Although a social network rather than an RPG or egame per se, *GaiaOnline* (http://www.gaiaonline.com/) provides a happy alternative; incorporating anime and other graphic elements, the site invites girls to "make a little clone of your real-life self, or create a crazy style you could never pull off in the real world. Go ahead, express yourself."

Casual games constitute a special subdivision of egames and have attracted great attention and use by females, according to the International Game Development Association (2008). This niche industry has grown from $25 million in 2002 to $2.25 billion in 2008, particularly with advances in cell phone technology. The gaming industry has increased its focus on developing games for mobile instruments, mainly smart phones. The phone platform has dictated the egame characteristics: constrained and low-resolution graphics, minimal text, easy to learn and basic controls, little setup, and consumable in a short time period. Because of these limitations, the games themselves have to be interesting enough to foster repeat play; gameplay (repeatability of the experience) has regained dominance. In general, industry has targeted these mobile games to casual gamers, a much greater population than serious gamers and a genre in which girls make up the largest (74%) segment (Pinckard, 2007).

Casual games are used to relax, socialize, or achieve goals or challenges, and are seldom violent. The industry categorizes casual games into these genres: hidden object games (HOG), time management (e.g., Playfirst's *Diner Dash*), and adventure. Males tend to favor sports and action games while females tend to prefer casual card and word games. Because casual games are gaining so much ground, they are a good focus for inclusive game play in the library. Girls, especially, are likely to be successful with these egames and so are more apt to continue playing them than exploring other egaming options (Forssell, 2008; Schaumburg, 2001).

Because of the nature of most egames, and girls' less frequent gaming behavior, girls are likely to be disadvantaged if egames are summarily introduced into school library settings (Agosto, 2004; Hargittai & Shafer, 2006). Furthermore, according to the 2000 study of the American Association of University Women, if girls do not use computers by sixth grade, they are likely never to pursue science or technology. Therefore, TLs need to pay attention to individual students' experiences and interests if they are to insure that egaming is to benefit the school community. Van Eck (2006) discovered that, over the period of a study, boys in all-male or male-minority groups became less convinced that technology was equally appropriate for boys and girls, while girls consistently became more positive in their attitude about technology's appropriateness for both sexes. It may be that boys' negative attitudes reflected feelings of being marginalized (in girl-majority groups) or not having been exposed to girls' behaviors (in all boy groups). In any case, one important message for educators may be derived from these studies and reports; when students are exposed to a variety of games in mixed settings, they can broaden their gaming preferences and improve their attitudes toward technology as a whole. Fortunately, the gaming gender gap is closing; instead, educators can focus on gender-specific aspects of egames, either selecting games that either appeal to both sexes, or providing choices of games that speak to individual interests and needs.

Benefits of Egaming

Certainly, egames attract and engage youth, sometimes even to the detriment of academics. On the other hand, egames reflect 21st-century literacy skills: information literacy, multimedia manipulation, creative problem solving, collaboration, and effective communication (Armstrong & Warlick, 2004; Gee 2007). Even though egames may be considered a male's bastion, the learning principles behind egaming speak to females' ways of learning: interactivity, contextualized meaning, incorporation of relationships, emotional engagement, and communication (Miller, 1976).

In terms of learning theory, gaming as a learning mechanism is usually associated with activity theory. The basis of activity theory posits a relationship between a subject (person) and an object, with mediational means. Tools also mediate between the individual and the larger culture. Vygotsky and Luria (1994) focused on analyzing tasks that required the use of a goal-directed, mediated/cultural process. Leontiev (1978) viewed activity on three levels: the activity itself, the level of actions, and operations (which tended to be "automatic" or fluent). Engeström (1987) expanded this model to acknowledge the collective nature of human activity. Good game designers follow Vygotsky's zone of proximal development: providing a challenge (not just routine operations) that can feasibly be met (i.e., the outcome is doable). Designers of games that build on community set up the conditions such that the player needs to work with the community effectively in order for the outcome to be achieved. With its emphasis on persistence and community interactivity, the activity theory aspects of gaming align well with female ways of learning (Miller, 1976).

Other learning theories that apply to gaming follow:

- Social constructivist philosophy posits that environments that stimulate the senses (e.g., attractive visuals, unexpected features), encourage interaction (e.g., common spaces), and provide opportunities for practice (e.g., group raids) improve learning (Piaget, 1977).
- Situated learning theory asserts that learning occurs in a community of practice and that learning space can refer to both

physical places and the learner's mental constructs of their experiences within the social environment (Lave & Wenger, 1991).
- Kolb and Kolb's related experiential learning theory (2005) contends that learners navigate through and interact with a learning space, based on their position within the learning cycle (i.e., experiencing, reflecting, thinking, acting). Kolb and Kolb also assert that different academic fields interact with the environment differently (e.g., science labs versus philosophical discourse), which matches the learning style preferences of different individuals. Therefore, to improve learning, teachers should examine the learning space in order to optimize learners' interaction with that space: in terms of the affective, perceptual, cognitive, and behavioral aspects of learning.

Each of these theories again reinforces girls' way of knowing, so librarians and other educators would do well to leverage these principles when incorporating egaming into school settings. Particularly since girls are more likely than boys to "follow the rules" in school and be more achievement-oriented, if they are told that egaming can help them academically, they may be more receptive to taking the intellectual risk of playing egames (American Association of University Women, 2000).

In sum, games offer a rich learning environment in which to explore and achieve specific goals. (Myers, 2008). The following activity theory-based characteristics of gaming inform teaching and learning:

- Use of fixed, equitable rules
- Clear roles and expectations
- Internally consistent environment where everything is possible
- Clear goals within a rich context that gives goals personal meaning and relevance
- Opportunities to explore identities
- Cognitive and affective engagement
- (Usually) multiple ways to achieve goals through constructivist strategies
- Specific, timely feedback
- Sense of control and personal investment
- Situated learning
- Sense of reward for effort, including trial and error
- Structured interaction between players and between players and the game
- Blend of cooperation and competition (DeKanter, 2005; Deubel, 2006; Gee, 2007; Simpson, 2005; Squire, 2006; Lee & Young, 2008)

All of these elements can resonate with girls. The key to their successful incorporation is their gender-sensitive implementation.

As with other tools, egames in and of themselves will not guarantee effective learning. Egaming, specifically game simulations, incorporate gaming design into the knowledge-building process rather than simply providing a way to organize information (Halverson, 2005). This kind of structural interactivity may be intimidating to teachers, who must overcome a "certain fear factor" in order to embrace video games in the classroom (DeKanter, 2005). Squire (2006) showed that many students find games more difficult than school; contemporary pedagogical practice creates "learned helplessness" by providing students with short, solvable problems with all information laid out. Game-based learning, on the other hand, begins with failure; students must build skills and knowledge over time by accessing new information, evaluating circumstances, and through practicing (Gee, 2007; Squire, 2006). These challenges can significantly impact girls' performance because girls are less likely to take risks, are more likely than boys to avoid situations where they might fail, and sometimes exhibit learned helplessness even outside the gaming environment (Brosnan, 1998; Orenstein, 1994; Streitmatter, 1998).

However, when educators incorporate egames effectively into the curriculum, the academic results can be significant. Charsky and Mims (2008) encourage educators to integrate commercial off-the-shelf (COTS) games into teaching and learning but caution that intentional planning is required. Educators need to try a few egames in order to understand some of the underlying principles of egaming techniques, which largely embody activity theory (Engeström, 1987; Leontiev, 1998; Vygotzky & Luria, 1994). As a result, instruction can incorporate some of these principles, even without using egames themselves:

- Providing students with choices (which topic to study)
- Offering opportunities for low-pressure situations
- Emphasizing the importance of memorizing and mastering basics of a concept before applying the knowledge
- Collaborative work
- Providing extra help for struggling students
- Providing extension activities for students who excel
- Evaluate effort rather than product
- Using alternative and authentic assessments—designing demo games, tests based on mastery levels (not everyone takes the same tests), etc. (Shaffer, 2006)

What are the academic "pay offs" for incorporating egames into the curriculum and the library? Since 1982, meta-analyses of studies have demonstrated the effectiveness of games in learning, not only because of the game content but also because of the individuals' actions while playing the game (Hays, 2005; Randel, Morris, Wetzel & Whitehill, 1992; Szczurek, 1982; Van Eck, 2006). In terms of academic success, egames can introduce students to technology through motivating activities, a practice that could significantly help girls overcome their anxiety about technology (Brosnan, 1998). Foster (2008) asserted that gaming can develop individual interest in science as players experience the relevance of scientific concepts and applications More specifically, one predictor of success in computer science was computer gaming because of its relationship with programming (Wilson, 2002). In a University of Central Florida study, using immersive education video games for mathematics improved students' understanding and helped them raise their scores significantly in district mathematics benchmark exams (Kebritchi, 2008). Increased practice with video games improved girls' spatial skills, and collaborative work in computer games improved girls' mathematics problem solving (Agosto, 2004). Expert panelists at a webinar on gaming in education asserted that egames keep youth actively engaged in learning, and provide an outlet for self-expression, decision making, and experience in social interaction (Consortium for School Networking, 2008). Social gaming leads to positive identity assets: self-esteem, self-employment, personal sense of purpose, and personal positive future orientation (Helmrich & Neiburger, 2007). Such positive self-attributes are sorely needed by girls (Brosnan, 1998; Cooper & Weaver, 2003; Orenstein, 1994; Streitmatter, 1998); if egaming can be introduced in gender-inclusive ways, girls may well experience psychological and academic success. If teachers and administrators are beginning to recognize these academic benefits, it behooves libraries to be ready to do the same and to support these efforts as they do any other form of curriculum.

GAMES IN SCHOOL LIBRARIES

School library mission statements most often include supporting the school and district's curriculum initiatives, promoting a love of reading and learning, providing access to quality resources, and developing efficient and effective users of information. In some cases, school libraries diverge slightly from these goals, like Weymouth High School in Massachusetts, which strives to be the "intellectual center of the school," linking the school to "an ever wider circle of … knowledge and information" (Weymouth High School, 2008). The Sherwood School District in Missouri hopes to "help students with recreational needs" as well as "develop positive attitudes toward libraries" and "promote a lifelong use of libraries" (Sherwood Cass R-VIII School District, 2008). These variances from the most common mission of school libraries are more aligned with many public libraries, which more commonly strive to serve the personal and recreational needs of patrons, "improve quality of life of patrons" (Mid-Hudson Library System, 2005), to be "tuned in to the people" served (Seattle Public Library, 2008), and "empower" patrons (Los Angeles Public Library, 2008).

Even if the mission remains the same, TLs are increasingly reaching out to their audiences more proactively, meeting them on youth's territory. TLs are trying to encourage nontraditional reading matter, as exemplified by Easterwood and Wesson (2009). One of their first major efforts was graphic novels, elevated from their less valued comic book status. Likewise, gaming books have been successfully incorporated, and some TLs are providing egame access, hoping that youth will choose positive participatory leisure habits, including selected egames such as *Dance Dance Revolution* (Konami) and *City of Heroes* (NCsoft; Neiburger, 2007). In the process, TLs should consider the interests of girls in their game selection so that both sexes can enjoy the gaming experience.

In direct opposition to this recreational interest, almost all forms of video and computer games are restricted at many schools by classroom, school site, or school district policies. In an attempt to isolate skills needed to raise test scores, students in many schools have been given few opportunities to develop personal interests, create authentic products, or find alternative ways to express their ideas in an academic setting. Now that games are making legitimate inroads into educational settings, there is a need for more school library programs to reflect the ways in which exemplary school programs are using students' recreational interests to develop skills that will transfer to academic achievement, engage them in the school community, and encourage them to pursue information for personal gain and enrichment. Particularly since nongaming girls tend to dismiss egames, TLs should help them see the connection between personal and academic efforts, thereby legitimizing gaming as an acceptable pastime (Carr, 2005).

In a survey of 78 school libraries, Nicholson (2008) found that while 51% allowed Web-based games on library computers and 37% allowed locally installed games to be played, 33% allowed no games at all in the school library. The school libraries participating in Nicholson's study had a wide variety of goals for their gaming programs, including attracting new patrons, serving existing patrons, creating a school–community hub, recognizing the cultural significance of games, allowing users to hone skills, raising funds, addressing new literacies, and keeping patrons occupied. This may indicate a lack of specific pedagogical purpose behind some existing school library egaming programs. In addition, school library media centers may not be serving the recreational and personal interests of its patrons to the fullest extent possible (Nicholson, 2008).

Jenny Levine's 2006 case study of a Downers Grove High School gaming event (which included board games as well as video games) showed that, for students who do not value the traditional services of the school library, gaming events provided a way for them to reconsider the library as a place that offers series that are sensitive to their personal worlds. In many cases, library patrons who show up once for a gaming event return to the library later for other nongaming services (Nicholson, 2008). Neiburger and Gullett (2007) pointed out that gaming events at the library can offer players benefits that are more positive than could be experienced at home, thus making a social event out of their video game consumption, and potentially providing them with a community to which they can belong.

Currently the role of the school library includes "creating an environment that makes visitors feel welcome—and keeps them coming back" and "creating a library that serves as an alternate space—a third place—that's different than students' homes and classrooms (Kenney, 2008, p. 11). Increasingly, that environment is incorporating gaming aspects. However, little explicit attention has been paid to girls' participation in these gaming resources and services. Potentially, though, school libraries could provide a safe environment in which girls can experience egaming, particularly since a majority of TLs are female. Particularly if the TL has a positive attitude about gaming and technology, girls can identify with the same-sex model more easily than with a male TL (AAUW, 2000).

The Library as Gaming Affinity Space

Developing an egaming program to establish new or promote existing communities among students may allow the school library to attract new patrons, enhance services provided to existing patrons, and act as a model for the school community as it molds and changes with new technologies and ways of learning. Within this construct, TLs are well positioned to address gender issues relative to gaming, fostering equitable use and providing positive egaming experiences for girls as a gateway to technology.

Student gamers already belong to an affinity space, defined by Gee (2007) as a space where people interact because of a common endeavor. Student gamers interact while playing egames; by reading gaming magazines, blogs, or Web sites; by discussing games; by drawing gaming characters on their notebooks; and by making references to games in classroom discussions. While egames provide a common framework for discussion, each player experiences something different (Squire & Jenkins, 2003). In addition, gaming opens communication between teachers and students (Amory, Naicker, Vincent, & Adams, 1999; Simpson, 2005). When students are allowed access to egame-related services in the library, they are entering a portal to their egaming affinity space where they can interact, socialize, learn, and contribute to a larger information-based community (Gee, 2007).

School libraries can optimize the physical library facility as a gaming affinity space through several ways:

- Providing enough space at each computer station to allow two people to sit together
- Allowing students to play games that build on social interaction, such as RPGs
- Offering an online venue to play RPGs so that gamers of different ages and sexes can interact safely and anonymously
- Providing a venue for reviewing egames and sharing egaming experiences
- Providing a venue for designing egames

In terms of facilities, TLs can create task-specific zones, so that silent reading can be in one area, group study can be at tables in another part of the library, and production space can be located in a third corner. Within this environment, one section can be dedicated to egaming, providing comfy seating for play and reading. Mobile devices also facilitate public learning space: a common area for sharing and generating information. Because girls value the social aspect of gaming per se, setting up the library to accommodate shared gaming experiences supports girls' approach to gaming. Indeed, if boys tend to monopolize computers and egaming systems, TLs can designate girl-only and boy-only stations to optimize equitable use.

Playing egames at school can also improve student–teacher relationships. Egames allow teachers and students to get to know each other better and offer teachers new ways to relate to students, reminding them that teachers have a kid inside them. TLs, who are largely female, can mentor girls as they explore egaming. The library can serve as a curriculum-neutral, yet resource-rich, physical space where the entire school community can interact based on common interests.

Schools may be better able to tap into students' true abilities by providing more access to their recreational affinity spaces. For example, for after-school hours, school libraries could consider providing access to online games. Hosting a gaming event is a feasible beginning point for TLs to attract gamers, particularly if the TL hooks up a console game to a data projector so that the games can be viewed on a large screen. Participating in those events adds another dimension to the experience; seeing the TL wale on *Rock Band* (Electronic Arts) can raise "street cred" significantly. This cocurricular approach would appeal to those teachers who might feel uncomfortable about using school time for egaming, and it would lessen the academic pressure that some girls might feel when "forced" to deal with technology protocols that distract from the content learning. Especially for girls who have less access to technology at home, providing time and equipment to enjoy egames recreationally could help them feel more comfortable with these technologies and could bolster girls' perceived social value of games. Moreover, all youth need to balance academic and recreational activities (Alvermann et al., 2007), so making egames part of a mandatory assignment during class time could ruin them for students (Squire & Steinkuehler, 2005). Through providing a portal to existing gaming affinity spaces, school libraries may be most effective.

Choosing Games

Developing the library collection to include the recommended gaming resources offers another point of access for students to gain entry to the library's wider services. The following recommendations can help TLs develop the library's egaming collection:

- Add console-specific "official" gaming magazines to the periodical collection
- Add gaming strategy guides to the general collection
- Add student-created content, such as game reviews, to the library Web site
- Add game-related displays that include game art, game-related fiction, and information about careers in gaming (Girls can participate in this endeavor by suggesting resources, writing reviews, and creating displays.)

Nicholson (2008) notes that librarians may need guidance (and perhaps the guidance of patrons) to select games that will lead to a successful program. To make sure that no students are left out, games in other formats may need to be included at gaming events (board, trivia, card, and physical games). The Douglass Project at Rutgers (Agosto, 2008) developed the following list of criteria for selecting Web sites that attract girls and affirm their ways of knowing, which can be transferred to egames:

- Confidence: encourage and support girls' abilities
- Collaboration: facilitate working together
- Personal identification: relate to personal life
- Contextuality: present information in narrative or story form
- Flexibility/motility: offer several navigational paths

- Social connectivity: facilitate interpersonal connections
- Inclusion: portray diverse populations
- Multimedia presence: meld high-quality graphic, motion, and audio elements

Some games are for enjoyment alone, which is fine, but libraries are more likely to invest time and money in serious games, those that have other purposes than entertainment, since the library's collection needs to support the school's curriculum first and foremost. Fortunately, many COTS games satisfy that requirement. As mentioned already, how the game is incorporated into the curriculum impacts the student as much as the game itself. Nevertheless, the learning experience has to start with a high-quality and motivating game, so selection is of paramount importance. With their background in collection development, TLs are usually better positioned than anyone else at the school site to evaluate serious games. This knowledge can be used to help classroom teachers in their choice and incorporation of egames. Likewise, other teachers and technicians may well have insights into appropriate games, which give TLs another basis for collaborating with the school community.

Several good bibliographies serve as starting points for selecting games:

- http://gaming.ala.org/resources/index.php?title=Main_Page
- http://www.socialimpactgames.com
- http://www.gamesparentsteachers.com
- http://www.supersmartgames.com/
- http://www.mediafamily.org/research/2008_video_game_report_card.pdf
- http://www.clrn.org
- http://edugamesblog.wordpress.com/2007/12/15/the-top-10-free-educational-video-games/
- http://seriousgames.ning.com/

In addition, a number of game publishers focus on the K-12 market: Riverdeep's family of brands, Leapfrog, Scholastic, FableVision, and Brighter Minds Media. Unfortunately, some patently educational games bore students. Therefore, selecting COTS games is usually the best practice since those products are likely to have better gameplay, so that they will motivate students to try them.

It should be noted that most educational publishers—and selection tools—tend not to focus on the female market per se, but they do try to be gender-neutral and inclusive. As publishers increasingly provide demo versions of egames, TLs should consider asking girls to test out potential egames as part of the selection process. Not only does this practice affirm girls' perspectives, but it enables girls to get exposed to a variety of games that they might not otherwise experience.

Many egames meld educational and recreational components (Nicholson, 2008), and it is important to note that in order to be engaging to students, games should be both fun and interactive (Amory, Naicker, Vincent, & Adams, 1999). Particularly for girls, the egaming protocols need to be easy and intuitive so that the focus is on the content rather than on navigation through a virtual space. The following egames tend to be gender-neutral and gender-inclusive. Several games address science concepts, and the National Science Foundation continues to support development in this area; representative games include *Power Up* (TryScience), *Nanoquest* (Forfas), *and Logicity* (Logicom). A couple of recent educational multiuser virtual learning environments, *River City Project* (http://muve.gse.harvard.edu/riversityproject/) and *Dimension M* (http://tabuladigita.com), offer ways for students to investigate authentic problems and learn academic concepts constructively. Simulation games such as *Quest Atlantis* (Activeworlds), *Cool School* (Curriki), and *SimCity* (Electronic Arts) help students practice decision-making skills. Games that address historical content such as *Civilization*

(Take-Two), *Revolution* (Activision) and *Age of Mythology* (Microsoft Game Studios) have proven intellectually engaging and highly challenging for high schoolers (DeKanter, 2005; Gee, 2007; Squire & Jenkins, 2003). In their study of civic engagement and teen gaming, Kahne, Middaugh and Evans (2008) suggested several gaming venues that foster civic responsibility: virtual world simulations of civic processes; games with historical, civic, or economic focus; player governance; informal and formal gaming communities. These researchers found that youth with more civic gaming experience tend to engage more in civic and political life.

Educators have used serious games for decades to develop students' literacy skills; effective titles include the Leapfrog Leapster series, *Blues Reading Time* (Humongous Entertainment), and the perennial *Reader Rabbit* (The Learning Company). A recent phenomenon is the video–book connection; The 39 Clues is a series for older elementary students that links to online games. Young adult author P. J. Haarsma writes both science fiction fantasy novels and games to complement them, such as *Rings of Orbis* (Softwire) and *Vreoengard Academy* (Softwire). Publishers and librarians try to capture new readers by linking video interests to print materials, a practice that tends to favor boys but can help girls in the opposite direction: bridging existing reading success with egaming and technology (Easterwood & Wesson, 2009). Increasing effort has been made in using MMOG games as a way to improve student communication skills; as students read peers' texts and type in questions and responses, they are motivated to engage in authentic literacy experiences (Wagner, 2006). Classroom teachers and TLs can leverage girls' interests in sharing with one another as they incorporate MMOGs into the curriculum.

TLs might also consider acquiring game creation application software, which is another method that classroom teachers have been using to foster literacy. When students create their own egames, they ramp up their own skill set, drawing upon their knowledge of egaming protocols and applying them to new settings. Particularly since girls tend to like to work collaboratively on a concrete project, egame construction can be a productive and fulfilling activity. With the expansion of mobile gaming, apps for creating even more mobile games are starting to appear; TLs can provide such tools on at least one station for student use. In his article on computer game development, Brian Myers (2008) detailed the engagement and success that the public library's teens experienced when creating games using the programming tools *Scratch* and *Game Maker*.

In library literature, the term "portal" usually refers to the library's Web site, with the intent that it serves as an electronic gateway to information and resources, much like a Web directory. Gaming-related information can be integrated throughout the portal (e.g., under "new books," "reviews," "webliographies," "local resources") as well as under a separate "Games" heading for easy access. Girls can contribute to this kind of portal by writing content and helping design and maintain the Web site.

Egames and Library Instruction

Instruction can intersect with egaming in a couple of ways: 1) linking personal egaming interest and skill to academics, 2) incorporating egames in learning activities, and 3) using egaming elements in instruction.

TLs seldom teach extensively as independent teachers; they are more likely to teach one aspect of a class project, such as evaluating sources or organizing information. When serious games are incorporated into the curriculum, TLs can collaborate with the classroom teacher throughout the instructional design process:

- Evaluating, selecting, and testing appropriate games to meet specific student learning outcomes

- Addressing technical issues associated with the game (e.g., installation, licensing, networking)
- Determining and addressing prerequisite skills students need to use the game successfully
- Determining when and where (including the library) students will play the game
- Developing learning activities that link with the game (e.g., assuming roles, journaling gameplay, researching the game content context)
- Assessing student learning in consort with gaming (Van Eck, 2008)

TLs usually do not have the luxury of spending several periods over a week or more on an extensive game. However, casual games such as word games or reference-related games might be successfully incorporated into a library lesson. Moreover, the elements of gaming—such as exploratory activity, collaborating with peers, and situated learning—can make up much of library instruction. Fortunately, these same elements reinforce girls' ways of learning.

TLs can contribute to egaming at the program and curricular level, collaborating with groups of teachers to design content that lends itself to egaming resources and strategies. TLs can also conduct research for the school on serious games and curriculum integration and present the findings at curriculum development meetings and in-service development sessions. Among those research topics can be gender issues in egaming, with the intent to provide equitable gaming experiences.

Regardless of the level of instruction, current practices need to change to accommodate gaming students. To make the transfer of learning more effective requires that educators find out how students spend their time outside of school hours and how they self-identify their literacies (Alvermann et al., 2007). For example, students may be seeking information and problem solving within the community but may be bored at school, seeing no relevance in what or how they are being asked to learn (Alvermann 2007; Simpson, 2005). By "translating" egaming behaviors, such as asking expert advice or persevering until success is achieved, into academic competences, educators are acknowledging and leveraging students' personal expertise as it applies to their formal learning environments. As noted before, girls who communicate effectively in RPGs can use that skill in collaborative schoolwork; likewise, TLs can point to word games that girls like to play on mobile devices as a useful vocabulary support in school. As TLs work with students formally and informally, in groups and one-to-one, they can help students leverage their personal gaming skills in the academic arena.

Information Literacy and Gaming

Seeing the library as an access point to a gaming affinity space provides an opportunity to engage students specifically in the practice of information literacy skills. Parallel to information literacy, games establish an information goal and require the user to locate resources, evaluate those resources, and move toward the goal by using found information (Simpson, 2005). Students involved in gaming must actively participate in decoding and manipulating language as they play the game *Prospero's Island* (MIT), for instance (Squire & Jenkins, 2003), and in other highly involved games such as *Civilization* (Take-Two); the games act as a gateway to the search for further knowledge on a particular subject (Squire & Jenkins, 2003). Egaming's goal orientation melds well with girls' preference for concrete, meaningful experiences (Miller, 1976), so TLs should explain this connection between egaming and academic pursuits as a rationale for girls to get engaged in egaming activities.

Egames require the use of information tools, collaboration, and trial and error (Simpson, 2005; Squire & Jenkins, 2003; Gee, 2007) as well as promoting constructivist learning environments (DeKanter, 2005). Egames provide contexts for peer-to-peer teaching and emergence of learning communities (Squire & Jenkins, 2003); students consult peers and guides (print and nonprint) to help them be successful in their gaming efforts. Nicholson (2008) noted that games promote critical thinking skills, logic, and planning: all components of information literacy, if not traditional content-area curriculum. Students involved in gaming may access hints, tips, or codes on the Internet; post reviews or experiences; or create game-related drawings (Prensky, 2006), all of which require a variety of information literacy skills. Acting at a higher level of information literacy, Gee points out that players start to overtly realize that their choices in their gaming reflect their behaviors in real life, and they begin reflecting on and questioning those real life choices (Gee, 2007). Again, the tools used in egaming often reflect girls' methods of interacting, that is, sharing information and building meaning collaboratively. To the degree that TLs can explicitly align egame functions with information literacy, girls will see the academic "pay off" for egaming involvement.

Information literacy is in many ways aligned with gaming literacy, and the library program can offer instruction and guidance, both formally and informally, for students already involved with these literacies. To embed information literacy into gaming activities in an informal manner, the library program should provide students with regular opportunities to collaborate in order to produce shared information about games, such as Frequently Asked Questions, game reviews, and game guides published on the library Web site. Such sharing of information benefits girls in particular, because it builds on their language/communication strengths and gives them an opportunity to become experts, which can raise their self-esteem.

As noted above, several aspects of egaming potentially resonate with girls relative to information literacy. TLs need to make sure that egames include the following attributes to help girls gain information literacy skills:

- Just-in-time verbal or textual feedback when the gamer wants it
- Affirmation of effort as it leads to performance and competence
- Incorporation of the affective domain, particularly as it relates to personal priorities
- Consideration of systems and relationships as they impact information analysis and use
- Emphasis on distributed knowledge and cross-functional information seeking teams
- Acknowledgment and leveraging of multiple perspectives
- Appreciation of complex information systems (Association of College and Research Libraries, 2007)

To formally address information literacy skills and gaming, the library program could offer a short course on egaming, which could include the following girl-friendly information literacy aspects:

- Collaborative writing about egaming
- Interviews about gaming done by girls
- Creation of game-related art or game design ideas
- Research and compilation of gaming tips and tricks for shared use

Assessments should also be conducted to determine the extent that egaming impacts girls' learning. It should be noted that such a course may be difficult to schedule in the school day, even as an elective, if the TL has to supervise the library at all times. For this reason, extensive egaming programs within the library require at least one full-time TL (preferably two or more) and a full-time library assistant.

School Library Issues in Egaming

Even though egaming can benefit the school community and draw more students into the library, integrating egames in the library program can be problematic. Offering games, especially purely recreational games, in the school library program raises several issues. Technologically, most school computers are not configured for multimedia egaming (i.e., advanced video cards; high-resolution, large screens; and high-volume RAM). TLs might not have the funding to acquire the needed equipment or may be questioned about their spending priorities if they buy a Wii system instead of a laptop computer or encyclopedia. To solve this problem, TLs sometimes borrow systems from public libraries or school community members. They seek material donations and apply for grants, such as the American Library Association's gaming initiative.

Allocation of resources extends to the games themselves. In that respect, online games are more attractive for several reasons: no software is involved to be installed or maintained (or stolen), more students can access the game simultaneously, equipment is usually already present, and Internet connectivity is usually in place. With the explosion of free mobile device applications (apps), TLs might consider creating a webliography of curriculum-related apps that school community members could download. Of course, such file transfer has to comply with school technology use policies and procedures.

As with hardware, cost can be a factor in choosing games. It should be noted that TLs can start by offering one popular game that both sexes enjoy; the idea that the library is making any kind of effort can draw students in. Sometimes a teacher requests the TL to purchase a lab set of games for the library, with the intent that a class can use the facility for playing. The TL has to weigh the costs and benefits of such a purchase carefully: how many students will benefit, and what percentage of the curriculum will benefit? As egaming expands within the school, the TL should consider establishing a gaming steering committee consisting of teachers, students, and administrators to coordinate collection development and curriculum implementation. Such a committee needs to include girls.

Should the library offer games to borrow? In 2006, about 45% of libraries who responded to Nicholson's 2008 gaming survey stated that they circulated some kind of game; in 2007, about 41% circulated them. The TL has to realize from the start that games can get damaged and lost, as well as duplicated, so that the investment needs to be worth the effort. What other local entities permit borrowing or inexpensive rental? If access to other suppliers is convenient, the library might not have to worry, but if the school library is the "only game in town" and the need is great, then the service might be highly valued, particularly in low socioeconomic areas. It should be noted that the TL will also have to determine whether the equipment needed to play the game has to be made available as well. Since boys are more likely than girls to have computers or gaming systems (Pew Internet & American Life Project, 2008), providing egaming equipment might be needed in order to balance use by gender, and because of cost and that preference of girls for portable devices, devices like Play Station Portables (PSPs) and DSi or DS Lites may be good candidates. As casual gaming has expanded and more people are getting "smart" phones, the need for circulating games has probably decreased for school libraries specifically. On the other hand, the library could circulate inexpensive mobile devices preloaded with appropriate educational applications, which could address gender inequities.

Physical access can be problematic. Scheduling nightmares may arise as students compete with others for access to egames or try to upstage students who are doing library research. Normally, library computer use policy privileges curriculum-based activity over recreational use. TLs need to know which egames are being integrated into the curriculum in order to ascertain whether a student who is playing a *Sims* game is doing schoolwork or "just having fun." Sign-up sheets can at least encourage preplanning, and classes that are using games as a learning activity can be scheduled in alongside other class times. Some school libraries allow personal egaming during break periods or after school hours or designate Friday afternoons as game time. To insure gender equity, TLs may designate a boys-only station and a girls-only station. Similarly, a girls-only and boys-only egaming afternoon can insure that each sex has dedicated gaming time; this practice can be established when one sex tends to outnumber or intimidate the other (typically, the number of girls drops over time rather than the number of boys). Unfortunately, security measures need to be in place to assure physical access, since a gaming system could be tempting to steal. TLs typically store gaming systems until a gaming event occurs and then set up the room to accommodate the equipment and the students.

Physical access can also be stymied by existing educational policies. Filtering software may prohibit access to useful games. Many districts also prohibit electronic devices, including gaming equipment and cell phones. If schools are to embrace egames, they will need to review and probably revise their technology policies.

At the service level, TLs have to decide how actively involved they want to be in game consumption and creation and how proactively they want to address gender issues in egaming. Applying Loertscher's 2000 taxonomy to egaming incorporation provides a way to determine the level of instructional involvement: from no involvement to cursory planning that mentions gendered practices to curriculum development that systematically incorporates gender issues. Likewise, cocurricular involvement can take many forms:

- Permitting gaming in the library for all or by gender
- Encouraging students, especially girls, to provide input about gaming
- Hosting gaming events that are either coed or single-sex
- Training game-related skills in coed or single-sex settings
- Advising a girls-only game-related club
- Assisting or coordinating game-related cocurriculum that incorporates gender issues

In short, TLs have to weigh the different aspects of egaming as it impacts library resources and services to determine the most effective return on the library's investment. On an administrative level, TLs must determine the place of egames within the library program as a whole. How does egaming contribute to the library's mission, and how does it align with the school's charge? If the TL is the only person who thinks that egaming is a worthwhile endeavor or that girls' issues need to be addressed explicitly, then it may be difficult to get administrative support either financially or psychologically. Some TLs proceed in spite of nonsupport, convinced of the long-term benefits of egaming for both sexes; they bank on student participation and impact on the library program and student learning to make the case for future school support. In any case, TLs must comply with existing educational policies, and several may be impacted by the incorporation of egaming: technology-acceptable use, selection, use of facilities, intellectual property, security, supervision, parental permission, and gender equity. Do existing policies suffice, or do they need modification? TLs need to know the attitude of the school community relative to egaming in order to determine how to proceed. Even if just a few people like the idea, if the TL can identify those individuals and work with them, together the group can develop goals, strategies, and policies to incorporate egaming into the school, with special attention to gender equity issues.

FUTURE RESEARCH DIRECTIONS

The field of egaming continues to change significantly, particularly in two directions: platform and audience. These two developments both potentially impact girls' engagement.

Casual games, particularly those apps that can be downloaded onto cell phones and other portable devices, can bridge the academic and personal world. TLs can research micro egames that can be fun and educational (and free) and develop bibliographies to disseminate about such egames. These lists can be gender-neutral or categorized to reflect the interests of each gender. Although promising, research needs to be conducted to verify the educational claims and recommendations of casual mobile games:

- To what extent do mobile egames attract and engage females and males?
- How do mobile egaming practices of females and males differ?
- Does planning mobile egames correlate with girls' engagement in serious egaming?
- How can TLs incorporate mobile games into school library programs specifically?
- How can TLs incorporate mobile games to support student achievement and the school mission in general?
- To what extent can micro egame skills impact academic achievement?

Another issue is the production of educational gaming. In general, the gaming industry has not pursued educational egaming development for a couple of reasons: it is not cost-effective, and connections between the industry and education are difficult to establish. The U. S. Army has bucked that trend by developing egames, in collaboration with educational specialists, as a viable recruitment strategy. Another solution is to develop "templates" so students can develop their own egames. A couple of rudimentary tools have been created or adapted, such as *Virtools*, *GameBrix*, or even *PowerPoint*, but the window of opportunity is open for more robust and easy-to-navigate programs to be developed that can enable students to create their own egames. Potentially, TLs can provide production areas for students to develop egames and could archive such egames. In line with the prior discussions is the need to examine gendered issues relative to egaming production and the library's role in such learning activities.

CONCLUSION

Egaming speaks volumes about youth. It also reveals some gender-linked issues that need to be addressed explicitly in order to insure gender equity when incorporating egames and egaming elements into school library programs. It also signals a need to systematically gather data about the incorporation of egaming in school libraries to determine its impact on learning and personal growth.

It becomes clear that egaming has connoted male dominance. This social stereotype is outdated, as witnessed by the number of females engaged in RPG and casual games, in particular, but also realizing that females now constitute the majority of Internet users (Magill, 2007). TLs can help girls counter those societal messages by substituting positive attitudes and practices. TLs can encourage girls to take intellectual risks and boost their self-efficacy by offering fun, low-stress egaming environments. Specifically, TLs can provide egaming resources that resonate with girls, encourage technology use among girls, offer girls-only egaming opportunities, invite girls to talk and write about gaming, and facilitate girl egaming creation.

Egaming reveals student needs in a school setting, and girls can benefit significantly in this discussion. Youth emphasis on choice, authentic activities, mastery, and differentiation indicate a clear need to look closely at the way instruction is currently delivered and student progress is evaluated. Egaming also addresses student awareness of and affinity for information literacy skills related to collaboration, pursuit of personal interests, evaluation of information, and information sharing. Existing egaming practices provide the library program with a point of entry to engage students in leveraging their personal skills for academic success. Girl gamers can profit from this strategy because TL affirmation can validate their behaviors, which are usually not socially acceptable among their peers. Furthermore, girls who have not experienced egaming might feel more comfortable exploring this technology and develop an interest in other technologies as well. In any case, egaming principles hold promise for all students:

- With these egame opportunities at hand, probably the most pressing question remains: what role will the TL take in incorporating egaming into the library program?
- How will the collection change?
- How will facility configuration and use change?
- What services will be added or impacted?
- How will instruction and learning activities change?
- How will budgets be reallocated to insure that egaming initiatives can succeed and be sustained?
- What staffing patterns and qualifications are needed to provide professional egaming service?
- What policies need addressing?
- How does a library program that incorporates egaming fit into the school's mission and operations? How does such a program impact learning and personal growth?

These questions challenge TLs, but the payoff for their efforts can be significantly rewarding to the school community by addressing the needs of both boys and girls.

REFERENCES

Agosto, D. (2004). Girls and gaming: A summary of the research with implications for practice. *Teacher Librarian, 31*(3), 8–14.

Agosto, D. (2008). Evaluating materials. *Girls tech.* New Brunswick, NJ: Rutgers University. Retrieved from http://girlstech.douglass.rutgers.edu/gt1b.html

Alvermann, D., Hagood, M., Heron-Hruby, A., Hughes, P., Williams, K., & Yoon, J. (2007). Telling themselves who they are: What one out-of-school time study revealed about underachieving readers. *Reading Psychology, 28,* 31–50. doi:10.1080/02702710601115455

American Association of University Women. (2000). *Tech-savvy: Educating girls in the new computer age.* Washington, DC: American Association of University Women.

Amory, A., Naicker, K., Vincent, J., & Adams, C. (1999). The use of computer games as an educational tool: identification of appropriate game types and game elements. *British Journal of Educational Technology, 30,* 311–321. doi:10.1111/1467-8535.00121

Armstrong, S., & Warlick, D. (2004). The new literacy. *TechLearning, 25*(2), 24–31.

Association of College and Research Libraries. (2007, Sep.). Gaming, information literacy, and the college student. *C&RL News,* 483–483.

Beavis, C., & Charles, C. (2007). Would the "real" girl gamer please stand up? Gender, LAN cafes, and the reformulation of the "girl" gamer. *Gender and Education, 19*(6), 691–705. doi:10.1080/09540250701650615

Bertozzi, E. (2008). "You play like a girl!" Cross-gender competition and the uneven playing field. *Convergence, 14*(4), 473–487.

Brosnan, M. (1998). The impact of psychological gender, gender-related perceptions, significant others, and the introduction of technology upon computer anxiety in students. *Journal of Educational Computing Research, 18*, 63–78. doi:10.2190/LVHH-EPGB-AE7J-WEV8

Carr, D. (2005). Context, gaming pleasures, and gendered preferences. *Simulation & Gaming, 36*(4), 464–482. doi:10.1177/1046878105282160

Cassell, J., & Jenkins, H. (Eds.). (1998). *From Barbie to Mortal Kombat: Gender and computer games*. Cambridge, MA: The MIT Press.

Charsky, D., & Mims, C. (2008). Integrating commercial office-the-shelf video games into school curriculums. *TechTrends, 52*(5), 38–44. doi:10.1007/s11528-008-0195-0

Consortium for School Networking. (2008). *Measuring 21st century skills*. Washington, DC: Consortium for School Networking.

Cooper, J., & Weaver, K. (2003). *Gender and computers: Understanding the digital divide*. Mahwah, NJ: Erlbaum.

DeKanter, N. (2005). Gaming redefines interactivity for learning. *TechTrends, 49*(3), 26–31. doi:10.1007/BF02763644

Deubel, P. (2006, Jan.). Game on. *T.H.E. Journal*, 30–41.

Dickey, M. (2006). Girl gamers: The controversy of girl games and the relevance of female-oriented game design for instructional design. *British Journal of Educational Technology, 37*(5), 785–793. doi:10.1111/j.1467-8535.2006.00561.x

Easterwood, L., & Wesson, L. (2009). Gamers are readers. *School Library Journal, 55*(4), 24–25.

Engeström, Y. (1987). *Learning by expanding: An activity–theoretical approach to developmental research*. Helsinki, Finland: Orienta-Konsultit.

Entertainment Software Association. (2008). *Game player data*. Washington, DC: Entertainment Software Association. Retrieved from http://www.theesa.com/facts/gameplayer.asp

Forssell, K. (2008). Girls, games, and getting interested in technology. In K. McFerrin, et al. (Eds.), *Proceedings of Society for Information Technology and Teacher Education International Conference 2008* (pp. 991-996). Chesapeake, VA: American Association of Computer Education.

Foster, A. (2008). Games and motivation to learn science: Personal identity, applicability, relevance and meaningfulness. *Journal of Interactive Learning Research, 19*(4), 597–614.

Fromme, J. (2003). Computer games as a part of children's culture. *Game Studies, 3*(1). Retrieved from http://www.gamestudies.org/0301/fromme/

Gee, J. (2007). *What video games have to teach us about learning and literacy* (2nd ed.). Palgrave, UK: Macmillan.

Graner Ray, S. (2004). *Gender inclusive game design: Expanding the market*. Hingham, UK: Charles River Media.

Gros, B. (2003, July). The impact of digital games in education. *First Monday*. Retrieved from http://www.firstmonday.dk/issues/issue8_7/xyzgros/

Hackbarth, S. (2001). Changes in primary students' computer literacy as a function of classroom use and gender. *TechTrends, 45*(4), 19–27. doi:10.1007/BF02784821

Halverson, R. (2005). What can K-12 school leaders learn from video games and gaming? *Innovate, 1*(6). Retrieved from http://www.innovateonline.info

Hargittai, E., & Shafer, S. (2006). Differences in actual and perceived online skills: The role of gender. *Social Science Quarterly, 87*(2), 432–448. doi:10.1111/j.1540-6237.2006.00389.x

Harrison, K., & Bond, B. (2007). Gaming magazines and the drive for muscularity in preadolescent boys: a longitudinal examination. *Body Image, 4*(3), 269–277. doi:10.1016/j.bodyim.2007.03.003

Hartmann, T., & Klimmt, C. (2006). Gender and computer games: Exploring females' dislikes. *Journal of Computer-Mediated Communication, 11*(4). Retrieved from http://jcmc.indiana.edu/vol11/issue4/hartmann.html. doi:10.1111/j.1083-6101.2006.00301.x

Hayes, E. (2005). Women, video gaming & learning: Beyond stereotypes. *TechTrends, 49*(5), 23–28. doi:10.1007/BF02763686

Hays, R. T. (2005). *The effectiveness of instructional games: A literature review and discussion.* Naval Air Warfare Center Training Systems Division (No 2005-004). Retrieved from http://stnet.dtie.mil/oai/

Heeter, C., Edigio, R., Mishra, P., Winn, B., & Winn, J. (2009). Alien games: Do girls prefer games designed by girls? *Games and Culture, 4*(1), 74–100. doi:10.1177/1555412008325481

Helmrich, E., & Neiburger, E. (2007). Video games as a service: Three years later. *VOYA, 30*(2), 113–115.

Hooper, G., Fitzpatrick, G., & Weal, M. J. (2008). Does it matter who is holding the PDA in a mobile learning experience? In *JADÍS International Conference of e-Learning,* April 2008, Algarve, Portugal.

International Game Development Association. (2008). *2008–2009 casual games white paper.* Mt. Royal, NJ: International Game Development Association. Retrieved from http://www.igda.org/casual/IGDA_Casual_Games_White_Paper_2008.pdf

Jansz, J., Van Zoonen, L., & Vosmeer, M. (2006). *Videogames as technologies of gender: analyzing Final Fantasy forums.* Paper presented at the International Communications Association conference, Dresden, June.

John, T. (2009, July 13). Ridiculous life lessons from new girl games. *Wired.* Retrieved from http://www.wired.com/gamelife/2009/07/games-for-tweens/

Jones, S. (2003). *Let the games begin: Gaming technology and entertainment among college students.* Washington, DC: Pew Internet & American Life Project.

Joseph, D., & Kinzie, M. (2005, October). *Boys' and girls' game play preferences: Survey results.* Paper presented at the annual meeting of the Serious Games Summit, Washington, DC.

Kafai, Y. (1996). Video game design by girls and boys: Variability and consistency of gender differences. In Cassell, J., & Henkins, H. (Eds.), *From Barbie to Mortal Kombat: Gender and computer games* (pp. 90–114). Cambridge, MA: MIT.

Kahne, J., Middaugh, E., & Evans, C. (2008). *The civic potential of video games.* Boston: MacArthur Foundation.

Kaiser Family Foundation. (2005). *Generation M: Media in the lives of eight to eighteen year olds.* Menlo Park, CA: Kaiser Family Foundation.

Kebritchi, M. (2008). *Effects of a computer game on mathematics achievement and class motivation: An experimental study.* Doctoral dissertation, University of Central Florida, Orlando.

Kenney, B. (2008, January). The power of place. *School Library Journal, 54*(1), 11.

Kirriemuir, J., & McFarlane, A. (2004). *Literature review in games and learning: A report for NESTA Futurelab.* Bristol, UK: Futurelab.

Kolb, A., & Kolb, D. (2005). Learning styles and learning spaces. *Academy of Management Learning & Education*, *4*(2), 193–212.

Krotoski, A. (2004). *Chicks and joysticks: An exploration of women and gaming.* London: Entertainment and Leisure Software Publishers. Retrieved from http://www.futurelab.org.uk/resources/documents/lit_reviews/Games_Review.pdf

Lave, J., & Wenger, E. (1991). *Situated learning.* Cambridge, UK: Cambridge University Press.

Lee, J., & Hoadley, C. (2007). Leveraging identity to make learning fun: Possible selves and experiential learning in massively multiplayer online games (MMOGs). *Innovate, 36*(6). Retrieved from http://www.innovateonline.info/index.php?view=article&ide=348&action=article

Lee, J., & Young, C. (2008). Middle level educators and online social gaming. In K. McFerrin, et al. (Eds.), *Proceedings of Society for Information Technology and Teacher Education International Conference 2008* (pp. 1726–1732). Chesapeake, VA: American Association of Computer Education.

Leontiev, A. (1978). *Activity, consciousness, and personality* (Hall, M. J., Trans.). Englewood Cliffs, NJ: Prentice Hall.

Levine, J. (2006). Gaming and libraries. *Library Technology Reports*, *42*(5).

Loertscher, D. (2000). *Taxonomies of the school library media program.* San Jose, CA: Hi Willow.

Los Angeles Public Library. (2008). *Mission statement.* Los Angeles: Los Angeles Public Library. Retrieved from http://www.lapl.org/about/mission.html

Lucas, K., & Sherry, J. (2004). Sex differences in video game play: A communication-based explanation. *Communication Research, 31*(5), 499–523. doi:10.1177/0093650204267930

Macgill, A. (2007). *Parent and teen Internet use.* Washington, DC: Pew Internet & American Life Project.

McCann, S. (2008, November 15). Gaming basics: Not just for boys anymore. *Library Journal.*

Mid-Hudson Library System. (2005). *Sample Public Library Mission Statements.* Retrieved from http://midhudson.org/department/member_information/missions.htm

Miller, J. (1976). *Toward a new psychology of women.* Boston: Beacon Press.

Myers, B. (2008). Minds at play. *American Libraries, 39*(5), 54–57.

National Center for Women and Information Technology and the Girl Scouts of the USA. (2007). *Guide to promising practices in informal information technology education for girls.* Boulder, CO: National Center for Women and Information Technology.

National Institute on Media and the Family. (2001). *11th annual mediawise video game report card.* Minneapolis, MN: National Institute on Media and the Family. Retrieved from http://mediafamily.org/research/report_vgrc_2006.shtml

Neiburger, E. (2007). *Gamers...in the library?!* Chicago: American Library Association.

Neiburger, E., & Gullett, M. (2007, Winter). Out of the basement: The social side of gaming. *Young Adult Library Services, 5*(2), 34–38.

Neilsen Company. (2007). *The state of the console.* Chicago: Neilsen.

Nicholson, S. (2007). *The role of gaming in libraries: Taking the pulse*. Retrieved from http://boardgameswithscott.com/pulse2007.pdf

Nicholson, S. (2008). Reframing gaming. *American Libraries, 39*(7), 50–51.

Now, C. (2001). *Fair play: Violence, gender and race in video games*. Oakland, CA: Children Now.

Olson, C., Kutner, L., Warner, D., Almerigi, J., Baer, L., Nicholi, A. II, & Beresin, E. (2007). Factors correlated with violent video game use by adolescent boys and girls. *The Journal of Adolescent Health, 41*(1), 77–83. doi:10.1016/j.jadohealth.2007.01.001

Orenstein, P. (1994). *School-girls*. New York: Doubleday.

Pew Internet & American Life Project. (2008). *Teens, video games and civics.* Washington, DC: Pew Internet & American Life Project. Retrieved from http://pewinternet.org/~/media//Files/Reports/2008/PIP_Teens_Games_and_Civics_Report_FINAL.pdf.

Piaget, J. (1977). *The essential Piaget*. New York: Basic Books.

Pinckard, J. (October 31, 2007). *Casual games worth $2.25B — But where are they going?* Gigaom. Retrieved August 3, 2009, from http://gigaom.com/2007/10/31/casual-games-worth-225b-but-where-are-they-going/

Prensky, M. (2006). *Don't bother me mom – I'm learning!*St. Paul, MN: Paragon House.

Rainie, L., & Anderson, J. (2008). *The future of the Internet III.* Washington, DC: Pew Internet & American Life Project. Retrieved from http://www.pewinternet.org/~/media//Files/Reports/2008/PIP_FutureInternet3.pdf

Randel, J., Morris, B., Wetzel, C., & Whitehill, B. (1992). The effectiveness of games for educational purposes: A review of recent research. *Simulation & Gaming, 23*(3), 261–276. doi:10.1177/1046878192233001

Rosen, L., & Weil, M. (2001). *Are computer, video and arcade games affecting children's behavior? An empirical study.* Carlsbad, CA: Technostress. Retrieved from http://www.technostress.com/ADHDVideoGames3.htm

Schaumburg, H. (2001). Fostering girls' computer literacy through laptop learning: Can mobile computers help to level out the gender difference? In *Building on the Future. Proceedings of the National Educational Computer Conference,* June 25–27, 2001, Chicago.

Schott, G., & Horrell, K. (2000). Girl games and their relationship with the gaming culture. *Convergence, 6*(4), 36–53.

Seattle Public Library. (2008). *About the library: Mission statement.* Seattle: Seattle Public Library. Retrieved from http://www.spl.org/default.asp?pageID=about_mission

Shaffer, D. (2006). *How computer games help children learn.* New York: Palgrave Macmillan. doi:10.1057/9780230601994

Sherwood Cass R-VIII School District. (2008). *Library media center mission statement.* Sherwood, MO: Sherwood Cass R-VIII School District. Retrieved from http://sherwood.k12.mo.us/high%20school/libraryweb/mission_statement.htm

Simpson, E. (2005). Evolution in the classroom: what teachers need to know about the video game generation. *TechTrends, 49*(5), 17–22. doi:10.1007/BF02763685

Squire, K. (2006). From content to context: Videogames as designed experience. *Educational Researcher, 35*(8), 19–29. doi:10.3102/0013189X035008019

Squire, K., & Jenkins, H. (2003). Harnessing the power of games in education. *Insight (American Society of Ophthalmic Registered Nurses), 3*, 5–33.

Squire, K., & Steinkuehler, C. (2005, April). Meet the gamers. *Library Journal, 130*(7), 38–41.

Streitmatter, J. (1998). Single-sex classes: Female physics students state their case. *School Science and Mathematics, 98*(7), 369–375.

Szczurek, M. (1982). *Meta-analysis of simulation games effectiveness for cognitive learning*. Doctoral dissertation, Indiana University.

Taylor, T. (2003, May). Multiple pleasures: Women and online gaming. *Convergence, 9*, 21–46.

Van Eck, R. (2006). Using games to promote girls' positive attitudes toward technology. *Innovate, 2*(3). Retrieved from http://innovateonline.info/index.php?view=article&id=209&action=article.

Van Eck, R. (2008). COTS in the Classroom: A teacher's guide to integrating commercial off-the-shelf (COTS) games. In Ferdig, R. (Ed.), *Handbook of Research on Effective Electronic Gaming in Education*. Hershey, PA: Idea Group.

Vygotsky, L., & Luria, A. (1994). Tool and symbol in child development. In van der Veer, R., & Valsiner, J. (Eds.), *The Vygotsky reader* (pp. 99–174). Oxford, UK: Oxford University Press.

Wagner, M. (2006, July 29–30). *Computer games and the three dimensions of reading literacy.* Paper presented at the Sandbox Symposium, Boston.

Wang, Y., Wu, M., & Wang, H. (2009). Investigating the determinants and age and gender differences in the acceptance of mobile learning. The entity from which ERIC acquires the content, including journal, organization, and conference names, or by means of online submission from the author. *British Journal of Educational Technology, 40*(1), 92–118. doi:10.1111/j.1467-8535.2007.00809.x

Weymouth High School. (2008). *Library/media center.* Weymouth, MA: Weymouth High School. Retrieved from http://www.weymouth.ma.us/schools/commercial/library.asp?id=305.

Wilson, B. (2002). A study of factors promoting success in computer science including gender differences. *Computer Science Education, 12*, 141–164. doi:10.1076/csed.12.1.141.8211

Yee, N. (2006). The demographics, motivations, and derived experiences of users of massively multi-user online graphical environments. *Presence (Cambridge, Mass.), 15*(3), 309–329. doi:10.1162/pres.15.3.309

"MUST-READS" FOR THIS TOPIC

Agosto, D. (2004). Girls and gaming: A summary of the research with implications for practice. *Teacher Librarian, 31*(3), 8–14.

American Association of University Women. (2000). *Tech-savvy: Educating girls in the new computer age*. Washington, DC: American Association of University Women.

Cassell, J., & Jenkins, H. (Eds.). (1998). *From Barbie to Mortal Kombat: Gender and computer games*. Cambridge, MA: The MIT Press.

Cooper, J., & Weaver, K. (2003). *Gender and computers: Understanding the digital divide.* Nawah, NJ: Erlbaum.

Graner Ray, S. (2004). *Gender inclusive game design: Expanding the market.* Hingham, England: Charles River Media.

InvestiGaming. Research findings on gender and games. http://www.investigaming.com/.

Krotoski, A. (2004). *Chicks and joysticks: An exploration of women and gaming*. London: Entertainment and Leisure Software Publishers.

National Center for Women and Information Technology and the Girl Scouts of the USA. (2007). *Guide to promising practices in informal information technology education for girls*. Boulder, CO: National Center for Women and Information Technology.

TOP TEXTS FOR INTERDISCIPLINARY STUDIES OF SERIOUS GAMES

Educational games research. http://edugamesblog.wordpress.com/.

Gee, J. (2007). *What video games have to teach us about learning and literacy* (2nd ed.). Palgrave, England: Macmillan.

Hays, R. T. (2005). *The effectiveness of instructional games: A literature review and discussion.* Naval Air Warfare Center Training Systems Division (No 2005-004). http://stinet.dtic.mil/oai/.

Kirriemuir, J., & McFarlane, A. (2004). *Literature review in games and learning: A report for NESTA Futurelab*. Bristol, England: Futurelab.

Prensky, M. (2007). *Digital game-based learning*. St. Paul, MN: Paragon House.

Randel, J., Morris, B., Wetzel, C., & Whitehill, B. (1992). The effectiveness of games for educational purposes: a review of recent research. *Simulation & Gaming*, *23*(3), 261–276. doi:10.1177/1046878192233001

Shaffer, D. (2006). *How computer games help children learn*. New York: Palgrave Macmillan. doi:10.1057/9780230601994

Chapter 14
Interactivity, Process, and Algorithm

Chris Crawford
Storytron, USA

ABSTRACT

The most serious impediment to the progress of serious games is the difficulty of grasping the abstract concept of interactivity. Our brains are prejudiced in favor of thinking in terms of objects rather than processes. A firm grasp of interactivity requires a process-oriented way of thinking that does not come easily.

INTRODUCTION: SOME PERSONAL HISTORY

My first serious game was pathetic. It was an energy environment simulation, giving the player a few basic policy options and calculating results in terms of energy production and environmental consequences. The algorithms were primitive. The user interface was so bad that I had to stand next to the player, explaining what the cryptic display meant. As for graphics—they didn't exist. There were just a series of numbers and a teeny-tiny bar chart display.

I blame the hardware (a KIM-1 single board computer with support circuitry of my own design). It boasted an eight-bit processor running at 1 MHz with a grand total of 5 KB of RAM. It was mounted inside a heavy mahogany case with a huge transformer for a power supply. There was no keyboard, just a 24-button keypad. There was no video display, just a group of 6 seven-segment LEDs, the kind that you see in old calculators. The program was written in assembly language and was loaded into memory from a tape cassette (see Figure 1).

That was back in 1978. Since then, I have written quite a few serious games; indeed, almost every game I ever wrote was basically what people today

DOI: 10.4018/978-1-61520-719-0.ch014

Copyright © 2010, IGI Global. Copying or distributing in print or electronic forms without written permission of IGI Global is prohibited.

call a serious game. There was certainly nothing frivolous about my games. My war games weren't about action or violence—they were about the logic of military operations, the sad calculus of blood by which wars are won or lost. My most successful game was an "un-war" game: *Balance of Power*, a game about geopolitics during the 1980s in which the player lost by triggering a nuclear war (see Figure 2). I have also created games about environmental issues and games about interpersonal conflict.

In these years, I have made a great many mistakes and so have learned a great deal about what works and what doesn't work in designing serious games. In this chapter, I shall explain three of the fundamental principles that I have learned:

1. interactivity is the central and fundamental attribute of computing.
2. Data and process are two fundamentally different aspects of reality.
3. Process is essential to interactivity, and it requires mathematical expression.

Figure 1. The KIM-1 single-board computer

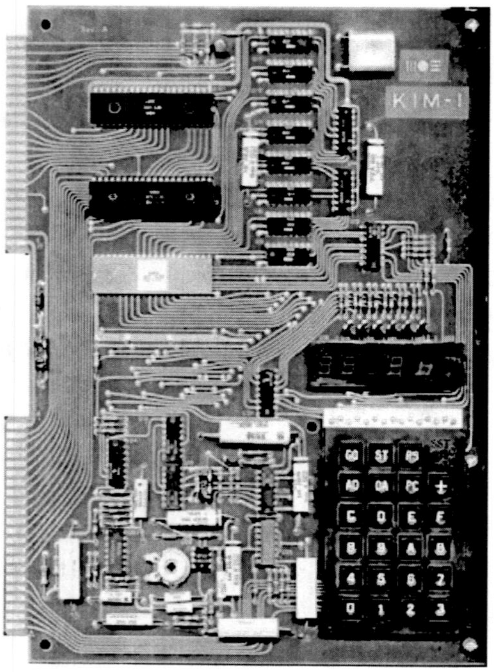

INTERACTIVITY IS THE SINE QUA NON OF COMPUTING

If the entire thrust of my career could be reduced to a bumper sticker, it would read, "It's the interactivity!" Interactivity—not graphics, not animation, not sound—is the essence of what computers do. People have difficulty realizing this because computers do graphics, animation, and sound so well. A computer is like a screwdriver. You can use a screwdriver to punch holes, to pry things apart, even as a weapon, and it does all these tasks well. But the basic task of a screwdriver is to turn screws, and in an imaginary world with a dearth of screws, people would have difficulty grasping that the essence of screwdrivers lies in the turning of screws. Graphics, animation, and sound are relatively easy to do on a computer; interaction is harder. So people naturally do what comes easily and avoid what is difficult. The problem is compounded by the dearth of good examples of interactivity; without such examples to inspire them, people continue to use the computer for familiar tasks rather than those tasks that take best advantage of the strengths of the computer.

This point is so important, and so poorly appreciated, that I'd like to spend a little space expanding upon it. Rather than concentrate on games, I propose to start at the top and work down. What is the single most common and useful application to which computers are put? I claim that word processing is that application. There are plenty of other applications that grab lots of attention, but word processing has been the single most heavily used application of computers for at least 25 years.

Word processing is now so standard that it's difficult to remember the days of typewriters. The rapidity with which the computer as word processor replaced the typewriter clearly demonstrates that word processing is much more valuable than typewriting. But what makes it so much more valuable?

Figure 2. The game Balance of Power

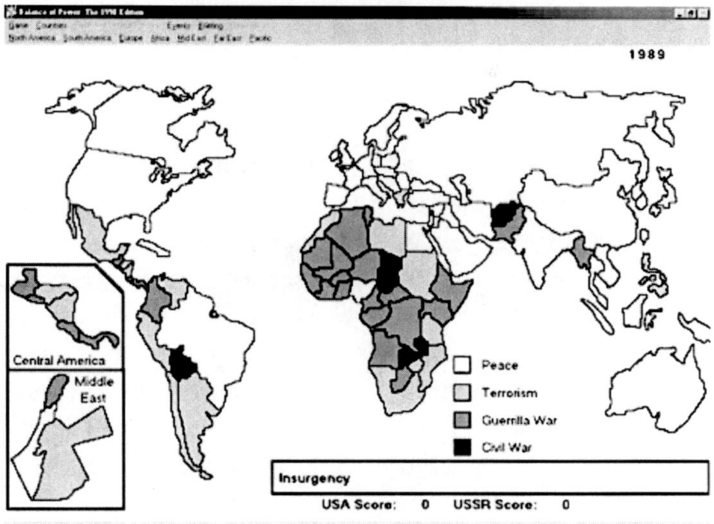

It was most definitely not the quality of the graphic output. The computer word processors that replaced typewriters in the early 1980s used dot-matrix printers, which were inferior to typewriters in terms of print quality. When laser printers arrived in 1985, they were horribly expensive: at $2,000, the typical laser printer cost more than the computer that drove it. It wasn't until the advent of inkjet printers that people had an inexpensive printer that rivaled typewriters in print quality—but typewriters were dead long before inkjet printers appeared. No, print quality didn't give word processors any advantage over typewriters. Nor was the quality of graphical display a factor in the supplanting of typewriters by computers: back then, most graphical displays presented text characters in 5 x 8 monospaced fonts that were hard to read. Here's an example of the kind of graphic display back then (Figure 3):

It was interactivity that made word processing so much more useful than typewriting. Interactivity is most easily understood by comparing it with our most common experience of interactivity: a conversation. There are three steps to each side of a conversation:

- You listen to what the other person says.
- You consider what has been said and develop your own reaction to it.
- You express your reaction to the other person.

And then the other person repeats steps 1–3. Thus, I define interactivity as a cyclic process in which two intelligent agents alternately listen, think, and speak, although in the case of the computer, the terms "listen," "think," and "speak" must be taken metaphorically to mean "accept input," "process data," and "deliver output."

So, let's apply this definition to the operation of a word processor. The user initiates the interaction by typing some portion of a thought. The computer listens to its keyboard, thinks about how to line up the words on the page, and displays the result to the user. The user listens to (well, sees) the words on the screen, thinks about how well they reflect his/her intentions, and then expresses any desired

Figure 3. Text display, 1980

changes via the keyboard. Listenthinkspeak: that's the interaction cycle, and that's what happens when you use a word processor. And the interactivity is what makes it so useful. How do we know this? Because typewriters were abandoned so quickly! Consider what happens when you compare what you see on the page with what you had intended to write and realize that you now want to change what appears on the page. The "speaking" you must do to effect your changes with a typewriter is tedious and time-consuming. For example, suppose that you make a simple typo on a typewriter; how do you correct it? First, you have to back up, move the paper up to where you can access the typo, and then erase it or use Wite-Out—a white fluid that you paint over the error. Then you move the paper back down into position, making certain that you have restored it to exactly the original position and that the Wite-Out has dried, and resume typing. The whole process could easily take a minute. With a computer, you simply back the cursor up, erasing text as you go, and retype the correct text—a process taking a few seconds.

If you want to move some text from one location in a typewritten document to another, you literally cut strips of text out of the paper, rearrange them, and literally paste them down on the paper in their new positions. Our modern usage for "cut and paste" is an echo of the realities of the past. Computer cutting and pasting is infinitely easier and more flexible than the old typewriter-style cutting and pasting.

That's the advantage of the computer: it offers easier and faster interactivity. And that's why computer word processors have completely supplanted typewriters.

This point is driven home by our experience with a simple form of word processor called a "text editor." These programs provide none of the fancy capabilities of a full-featured word processor. You work with plain text without variable fonts, paragraph styles, margins, or the other super-duper features of a program like *Microsoft Word* or *iWork*'s *Pages*. Such programs (*Notepad* in Windows or *TextEdit* on Macintosh) are widely used. Many users now do most of their initial writing in a text editor and then transfer it to a word processor only after they've done all the basic work. Why do so many people prefer text editors to full-featured word processors? Because the interactivity is faster with a text editor. On my superfast Macintosh, *TextEdit* takes less than half a second to open. *Microsoft Word* takes 8 seconds. There are similar delays upon saving, quitting, and even printing. I don't want to waste time waiting for a program; I want to interact with the text NOW. So, I prefer the text editor. This may appear to be a desire for speed, not interactivity, but if you ask the simple question, "What exactly is it that happens more speedily?" and realize that the answer is "interaction," you can see that interactivity is the sine qua non of computer use.

The deep power of interactivity lies in the way that it changes our thinking processes. With a low-interactivity technology such as a typewriter, you must figure out your intentions for your entire document and all its contents before you begin typing. Since you cannot readily make changes, you must have already decided on the final form of the text before you begin. Of course, nobody can do this except for short documents. So we prepare outlines and think it through as best we can, then hope that it all fits together properly. The end result is seldom satisfying. But with a high-interactivity technology such as a word processor, our approach changes. We can set to work with only the vaguest idea of our intentions. We can put our thoughts where we can see them, read them, and evaluate them. The development of our document becomes incremental rather than top-down.

Some might object at this stage that an incremental thought process is less reasoned than a top-down process. It is better, such people might argue, to organize all one's thoughts before attempting to write them down. Plunging in without having thought it through is lazy and yields sloppy results. This argument echoes the Druidic argument against writing: the Druids believed that memorization was the only path to true learning. The sad fact is that the human mind is not a logic machine, nor can it retain the text of a long document with perfect recall. Our minds are more efficient at evaluating a big idea in a fragmentary and incremental fashion. Computer-based interactivity greatly enhances this process. Interactivity will change the way we think in much the same way that literacy changed the way we think.

Why did spreadsheets become so popular? Because they allowed the user to interact with the numbers, trying out different values in various places to determine the effects of alternatives. Sure, you could do the same thing with pencil, calculator, and paper, but with the computer, the process is so quick and easy that you are encouraged to try out all sorts of variations. It is the interactivity of spreadsheets that makes them so useful.

I remember when I was an undergraduate student, computers were huge machines stored in air-conditioned rooms, and people like me were kept well away from the computer. You wrote up your program, submitted it to the computer center, and then came back hours later to collect your output. You pored over the output, trying to figure out what it all meant, and then made a few changes and submitted the new version of your program to the computer center. Then you waited some more.

This entire process was a blundering interaction carried out in slow motion. It could take weeks to solve a problem. You went back and forth to the computer center, trying various angles of attack. And it was truly, deeply frustrating when you made a stupid mistake that cost you an entire cycle. We got good, in those days, at writing our programs to tackle four or five problems at once. It was pretty confusing trying to keep track of multiple lines of development, but it was the only way to get the work done.

But this entire process has been short-circuited by direct programming of personal computers. The kind of analysis that would take me weeks to sort out in the old days can be finished in just a few hours with a program on a personal computer. The huge acceleration of the process has changed everything. But remember, even 40 years ago, we were still interacting with the computer—just doing so at the speed of molasses.

Browsing the Web? Same story. What makes the Web so useful is not the fact that it has a mountain of information but the fact that it makes it easy for you to find the particular bit of information you want quickly. You search for something and your first search invariably generates thousands of possibilities. But then you examine what's available and start to hone your terms, interacting with the search engine to zero in on what you want. And usually that interaction yields fruit within just a few moments. If the Web had no interactivity—if it merely dumped terabytes of data onto you—then it would be useless. The interactivity that allows you to zero in on your goal is what makes the Web so useful.

Thus, the interactive process amplifies human thought by showing the user the ramifications of different possibilities, ramifications that would be unclear without the computer. The computer and the human unite as a single mental unit, with the human providing purpose and the computer performing the mental legwork. Just as putting words down on paper forces us to think our thoughts through carefully, the interactivity of the computer permits us to explore the consequences of different avenues of thought. Just as the development of writing amplified the human ability to engage in logical reasoning, so too the development of interactivity amplifies the human ability to pursue subjunctive thinking.

The importance of interactivity is most apparent with creative programs such as photo editing programs. In these, you load in a digital photograph and then go to work on it, cropping, rotating, resizing, and modifying the image to get exactly what you want. The process is straightforward: the computer shows you the current version of the image. You compare the reality with your desires, identify the nature of any shortcomings, and express your desires with an edit that alters the image slightly. Then the computer presents you with a version of the image incorporating your change. You repeat the process over and over until the image looks the way you want it. Listen, think, speak—that's what you're doing with one of these programs.

But there's another digression I must drag you through before I can make my point about serious games: the shift in thinking from fact to process, and the concomitant need for viewing ideas in algorithmic form.

THINGS VS. PROCESSES

We can view the world through either of two lenses (or a combination of both): the world as a collection of things, or the world as a system of processes. For example, you can think of a star as a big sphere of glowing plasma (thing) or as a thermonuclear reactor generating huge amounts of energy (process). You can think of a person as a thing (limbs, bones, muscles, skin, and organs) or as a process (metabolism, blood flow, nervous system behavior, digestion, and so forth). Is a tree a collection of roots, trunk, branches, and leaves, or is it a system for photosynthesis, extraction of minerals from the soil, construction of support structures, and movement of nutrients?

This difference pervades all of our intellectual efforts: in physics, we talk about particles (things) and waves (processes). In economics, it's goods (things) and services (processes). In military science, it's assets (guns, tanks, planes) and operations (military units moving around). In linguistics, it's nouns (things) and verbs (processes). In the world of computing, it's represented by data (things) and algorithms (processes). This fundamental dichotomy underlies everything in the universe. A more poetic way of considering the difference is to think about the distinction between facts and ideas.

Although we're talking about a dichotomy, the two sides of reality are not opposed to each other; we can often view a phenomenon as one, the other, or both. In terms of economics, is a hamburger a good (a thing of value) or a service (the process of preparing the food)? Programmers know that any task can be accomplished with almost any combination of data tables or algorithms. And at the deepest levels of physics, particles and waves merge at the quantum mechanical level. Some physics experiments have shown fundamental particles to behave maddeningly like particles some of the time and like waves some of the time.

But our minds are biased towards existence; we quail from process. We prefer to see the world in terms of existence instead of process. I suspect that this prejudice arises from our heavy reliance on vision, which emphasizes instantaneous recognition of objects. Of the 1,000 most frequently used English words, about 600 are thing words (nouns, pronouns, or adjectives) and about 300 are process words (verbs or adverbs). Thing perception is phylogenetically ancient, arising with the first visual systems half a billion years ago, whereas process perception came much later. The next step was the development of sequential processing (recognition of distinctive sequences of events, such as the difference between the "boom, boom, BOOM" of the footsteps of a large approaching carnivore and the "BOOM, boom, boom" of the footsteps of a large departing carnivore), which I believe first showed up around 150 million years ago (mya) in the proto-mammals and proto-birds. But the jump from sequential processing to process processing (that is, the inference of causal factors in some sequential processes) doesn't seem to appear until much later, probably about 50 mya. The problem is that we have no direct evidence for any of this stuff—it's all my own inference from mammalian phylogeny. Indeed, I don't think that strong process thinking really developed until after language took hold maybe 50,000 years ago. And our understanding of this gigantic cognitive leap is still in its early stages.

We have an easier time remembering facts than processes. We know that Napoleon lost the Battle of Waterloo, but can we explain why he lost that battle? Most people know that we have lungs, hearts, kidneys, livers, and stomachs—but how many people can tell you how these organs function? The "what" of the world comes more easily to us than the "how" of the world.

We impress these innate preferences upon our information technologies. Our books explode with data on the world: what different birds look like, when historical events took place, how many people there are in different countries, and on and on—but they struggle to explain how these things came to be. Biologists had compiled a huge taxonomy of living creatures long before Darwin explained how that taxonomy came to be—and even today, Darwin's explanation is ill-understood by people who have spent years watching Animal Planet. Ask a librarian to find a fact, and you'll have an answer in minutes. Ask the same librarian to find an explanation, and you'll be lucky to ever get an answer.

Even our computers reveal our preference for facts over ideas. Every computer has four basic measures of computational performance: the speed of the CPU, the width of the data bus—which together determine how quickly the computer can process algorithms—and the amount of RAM and the size of nonvolatile memory (the hard disk)—which together determine how much factual information the computer can store. Those four values for the typical personal computer in 1980 were 1 MHz (1,000,000 Hz, or cycles per second), 8 bits, 48K (48,000 kilobytes), and 100K (100,000 kilobytes) for floppy disk drives.

Today, those four numbers for typical computers are 2 GHz (2,000,000,000 Hz), 64 bits, 1 GB (1,000,000,000 kilobytes), and 200 GB (200,000,000,000 kilobytes). In other words, computers today process 16,000 times faster than they did in 1980 and store 2 million times as many things (data). We've increased their ability to store data much more than we've increased their ability to process data. The most recent big leap in information technology is the Internet, another data-intensive technology. You can find a humongous amount of information on the Internet. But if you want to understand the processes that affect our lives, that information is much harder to come by, and the Internet isn't much help. The preference for facts over processes shows up everywhere you turn.

INTERACTIVITY AND (THING VERSUS PROCESS) IN EDUCATION

To recapitulate, I have now established two main points:

1. Interactivity is the sine qua non of computing.
2. We can think in terms of things or in terms of processes, or in terms of some combination of the two.

Now to my third major point: facts are best communicated noninteractively, but ideas or processes are best communicated interactively. The first part of this statement is obvious. If you have a pile of data to communicate, the most efficient way to do so is by simple exposition. Put the data in a book to be read, or rattle it off in a lecture. Dump it on the audience, and let them sort it out.

But processes—the how and why of the world—are the very devil to explain in expository terms. Any system of interconnected causal processes is impossible to explain clearly with simple exposition, because all the causal processes are taking place simultaneously (Crawford, 1984).

Let's use as an example the turning point of the Battle of Waterloo. How did Napoleon lose the battle? To answer this question, you have to explain an intricate net of causal relationships: the march of the Imperial Guard up the rise towards Maitland's Foot Guards, separating in the soggy ground into three groups; the fact that Maitland's men had lain down to use the slight rise in the ground to protect them from French cannon fire; the suddenness with which Maitland's men stood up slightly to their flank, taking the Imperial Guards by surprise; the ripple of confusion that spread through the Imperial Guard's ranks at that moment; how Maitland's volley escalated the confusion into panic; how the impact of that panic on the main body of the French Army was magnified by the Prussian assault on Placenoit; and so on through a hundred other factors. Explaining all of this in text is a cumbersome and confusing process.

I have read numerous books on the Battle of Waterloo, but the dynamics of the battle did not become clear to me until I played a war game demonstrating exactly how all this happened. The game was *Napoleon's Last Battles*, published by Simulations Publications, Inc., and it presented in board game format a recreation of the Waterloo campaign. Only after playing the game several times, trying different approaches, did I appreciate how all the different factors came together in the late afternoon of June 18th, 1815.

The fundamental superiority of interactivity for this task lies in its handling of multicausality. Suppose that we wish a student to understand that crucial moment at the Battle of Waterloo where the French Army was transformed in seconds from an army of soldiers into a mob of fugitives. In a conventional expository approach, we would explain each of the contributing factors in sequence:

- The exhaustion of the French troops saps their morale;
- The failure of Ney's charge further demoralizes the French troops;
- The soggy ground disrupts the organization of the Imperial Guard as they march;
- The Imperial Guard doesn't see Maitland's Foot Guards because of the rise in the ground;
- The suddenness of Maitland's men standing up surprises the Imperial Guard;
- The musket volley by Maitland's men causes the Imperial Guard to retreat in disorder;
- The Prussian assault on Placenoit threatens the French rear;
- All of these factors induce the main French Army to flee.

Read this way, all you have is a pile of facts. Yes, they all contributed to the collapse of French morale, but the causality is mushy; the intricacies of how these factors fed into each other over the course of that day and their relative importance are not communicated in this simple-minded list of causal factors. Even fleshing them out with more narrative doesn't really do the job, because text is a linear sequence best suited for demonstrating linear causality. Text (or any expository medium) works great when you're proceeding from A to B to C, but when you've got a whole alphabet of causal factors combining in an intricate webwork, you simply cannot explain that system in any linear medium. The only way to communicate that kind of complexity is to let an active human mind experiment with the factors, trying different arrangements and variations. What would have happened if Napoleon had earlier recalled Grouchy's corps to fight in the main battle, rather than pursuing the Prussians? What if Grouchy's pursuit had been more energetic? What if the Imperial Guard had attacked Wellington's depleted center rather than the stronger section of the line held by Maitland? All those what-ifs that did not happen are a necessary component of understanding the entire process that led to the actual historical outcome.

Explaining a complex set of simultaneous causal relationships through the sequential medium of text or lecture doesn't work. To understand a complex system, the student must see those processes in operation, twiddle with them, and examine how slight changes in the components of the system affect the results—in other words, the student must interact with the system rather than merely hear about it passively.

A second advantage of the interactive over the expository is its handling of negative lessons. For example, many beginners might assume that cavalry played a significant role in the battle. The fact is that cavalry contributed very little to the outcome. Yet this kind of negative lesson is not very convincing when stated as a bald fact. It would be far more effective to permit the student to actually use cavalry on the battlefield to learn firsthand how little staying power cavalry has against infantry. Thus, interaction is even more effective than exposition in explaining negative concepts.

An expository lesson should, in the ideal, communicate its message in a single pass. If a lecture or essay is well designed and appropriate to the needs of its audience, then the audience will learn its content in a single hearing or reading. But interactive learning expects multiple passes. Indeed, a good measure of the true value of a serious game is the number of times students play it in order to learn its lessons. Any serious game that bores students upon its second playing is a failure, because good interactivity doesn't just bear repeating, it *requires* repeating. The deeper and more powerful the content of a serious game, the more times students will play it and learn from it.

The fundamental goal of serious game design, then, must be to offer the student the clearest possible interaction with the processes at work. Presenting data—facts, figures, images, sounds—is a confusing diversion from the essence of the task. The strength of any serious game lies in the algorithms it relies upon and the clarity of the student's interaction with those algorithms.

You can't interact with a thing; you can only interact with a process. Facts are dead, static things; you can't interact with them. Ideas, however, are living, dynamic processes, and you can interact with ideas. Socrates made this point in the Phaedrus in complaining about the written word; he condemned the written word because you cannot question it, probe its strengths and weaknesses (Plato, trans.1995). In essence, Socrates was arguing that truth is revealed only through the interactive process of questioning and answering. And, indeed, the Socratic dialogue is a masterful exercise in interaction between teacher and student. A lecture is not interactive; a conversation is.

It seems to me that too many serious games are caught up in the facts and data rather than the algorithms. This is understandable, given the natural proclivity of our minds toward facts and away from algorithms. Yet the determined designer of serious games must find the discipline to approach the problem in terms of algorithms, not facts.

Let me present a hypothetical but simple example. Suppose that you wish to create a serious game about the operation of a nuclear power plant. It would be easy to present lots of pretty pictures and animations of nuclear power plants and even horrific animations of nuclear meltdowns, spreading clouds of radioactivity, and so forth. But those things can be done more easily and more cheaply in a book or DVD. If you want to create something for computer use, then you want it to be interactive, and you must therefore look to the processes at work inside a nuclear power plant. You must devise algorithms representing the generation of heat by the nuclear core, the role of the control rods in dampening this heat generation, and the all-important residual heat production of the core. You must design algorithms that calculate the transfer of heat from the fuel rods to the coolant water and the movement of that water through the core and out to the steam generators. Then you must figure out the equations describing how that heat is transferred through the steam generators to the steam and how that steam then powers the turbines that generate electricity. You must figure out how the emergency core cooling system pumps water into the core, how much heat that water can carry away, and where it goes.

These examples provide the basis for describing the matter in abstract terms. Think of the entire universe of thought as a vast three-dimensional space. Facts occupy single points in this space, but ideas connect a myriad of facts in a causal network extending over the entire space. A fact can be simply stated, but an idea can only be comprehended by experiencing its manifold nature. You can grab a fact with your fist, but to comprehend an idea, you must pull on all the threads that it comprises. You must poke, prod, test, examine, and explore an idea. In short, you must interact with it. Therein lies the essence of interactivity as an educational system: it teaches ideas, not facts.

NOW FOR THE BUGABOO

All of this requires mathematics. Here we come to the killer problem with serious game design: the necessity for the use of mathematics in the algorithms with which the player will interact. Let's face it: nobody enjoys mathematics, and most of us aren't very good at it. Poor use of mathematics is the single most important impediment to good serious game design, and effective use of mathematics is the single most important contributor to excellence in serious game design. Good interactivity requires good algorithms; algorithms are best expressed in the language of mathematics.

All interactive products use algorithms. Some designers are not even aware of the mathematics they use in their algorithms. For example, many mathematically handicapped designers rely heavily on Boolean trees to control the interaction with the player. These trees assemble collections of IF statements in grand structures that permit reactions that are predicated upon complicated sets of conditions. This is a good start for the beginner, but I urge designers to move on from there to more advanced algorithmic systems. In particular, Boolean reasoning (executed with IF statements) should be replaced with arithmetic reasoning (using numbers instead of true–false values).

Here's an example of the difference between Boolean thinking and arithmetic thinking. Suppose that Fred does something to John, something that is either nice or nasty. Will Fred's action please or displease Mary? That depends, of course, on two factors: 1) whether Mary likes or dislikes John and 2) whether Fred's action is nasty or nice. We could summarize this relationship with four simple IF statements:

- IF Fred's action is nice AND Mary likes John, THEN Mary is pleased.
- IF Fred's action is nasty AND Mary likes John, THEN Mary is displeased.
- IF Fred's action is nice AND Mary dislikes John, THEN Mary is displeased.
- IF Fred's action is nasty AND Mary dislikes John, THEN Mary is pleased.

Using Boolean logic, we can even reduce these four statements into a neater Boolean formula:

(Mary is displeased) = (Fred's action is nice)
EOR (Mary likes John)

"EOR" is the shorthand for the "exclusive OR" Boolean operator. But we can obtain better results if we shift from Boolean (yes or no, true or false) thinking to arithmetic (numerical) thinking. Instead of considering whether Fred's action is nice or nasty, let's consider *how* nice or nasty it is—in numerical terms. If it's very, very nasty then we'll use -1.0 to represent it; if it's only a little nasty then we'll use -0.2 to represent it. If it's neither nice nor nasty, then we use a 0.0, and if it's pretty nice, we'll use, say, +0.5.

In the same fashion, we can characterize how much Mary likes or dislikes John with a number between -1.0 and +1.0. Lastly, we can represent how pleased Mary is with another number between -1.0 and +1.0. If that number is, say, -0.4, then she is mildly displeased, while if it is, say, +0.7, then she is very pleased.

Having established the basic numerical guidelines, it turns out that we can use this simple formula to calculate Mary's pleasure or displeasure:

pleasure = how nice Fred's action is x how much Mary likes John

That's all it takes: a simple multiplication. Note that this approach gives us much more resolution. The Boolean approach yields black and white answers, but this numerical approach yields shades of gray. It can even handle the idea that Mary doesn't have any reaction because she doesn't care about John. My point is that the numerical approach gives us more useful results than the Boolean approach .

Moreover, the numerical approach permits greater conceptual resolution. Suppose, for example, that we wish to add another factor into the overall decision. If we were using Boolean logic, we would have to add yet more IF statements in an ever growing pile. With the numerical approach, we can simply integrate the new factor into the existing formula. It can be appended additively or multiplicatively, depending upon whether it is an augmenting factor or a controlling factor.

Let's examine a more detailed example to see how one might go about applying this process to build even more sophisticated algorithms.

HOW ALGORITHMS CAN HELP CHARACTERS GET ALONG

Let's consider the following problem: how do we decide in advance how one character in a story might assess another's personality traits? To be specific, suppose that Joe has heard a bit of gossip about Mary and he needs to form an opinion of Mary's integrity, which he will rely on in his interactions with Mary and others in her network as the game unfolds. We can't program this effectively with Boolean logic, as the web quickly exceeds our ability to capture with if-then statements. So we start by assuming that Mary has an intrinsic integrity. So let's assume a variable called Integrity (I) that numerically measures Mary's integrity on a scale from 0 to 1, with 0 meaning that Mary has no integrity whatsoever, and 1 meaning that Mary is a paragon of integrity. We want to come up with a way of calculating Joe's opinion of Mary's Integrity; we'll call it Joe's Perceived Integrity of Mary (PIM), and it will also be a number between 0 and 1. We want to calculate Joe's PIM because that will determine some decisions that Joe will be making about Mary. But since only intimate friends truly know how much integrity Mary has, and because we don't know if Joe is a friend or acquaintance (remember, his role will change throughout the game based on complex interactions of algorithms and player interaction), our design must account for Joe's perception based on his current state in regard to Mary.

So Joe's PIM will depend upon three factors:

1. Mary's true Integrity (I) value. (Obviously, Joe's perception will have something to do with reality.)
2. How well Joe "knows" Mary at any given time. We'll call this this Familiarity with Mary (FM), and again, we'll measure it from 0 to 1, with 0 meaning that Mary is a complete stranger to Joe, and 1 meaning that Joe knows Mary completely.
3. Joe's willingness to accord integrity to other people. We call this his Gullibility (G), and it is another number between 0 and 1. If Joe's Gullibility is 0, then he assumes that everyone is always lying, and if his Gullibility is 1, then he assumes that everyone is always telling the truth.

How do we put these three variables together to calculate Joe's Perceived Integrity of Mary? Let's start with the idea that Joe's Gullibility will

Table 1.

If Joe's Familiarity with Mary Is Equal to:	Then Joe's Perceived Integrity of Mary Is Equal to:
0.0	Joe's Gullibility
1.0	Mary's Integrity
0.5	Joe's Perceived Integrity of Mary = (Joe's Gullibility + Mary's Integrity) / 2

affect his perception of everyone. He simply applies Gullibility directly to complete strangers. In other words, if Joe's G = 1, then he assumes that a complete stranger has an Integrity of 1, and if his G = 0, then he assumes that a complete stranger has Integrity of 0.

So we start with this equation:

A. Joe's PIM = Joe's Gullibility

Now we have to modify this formula to take into account Joe's Familiarity with Mary AND her true Integrity. Of course, if Joe knew nothing whatsoever about Mary (that is, is Familiarity with her is 0), then we would use Equation A, because in the absence of any information to the contrary, he just applies his standard assumptions about strangers. Now, suppose that Joe were perfectly Familiar with Mary; that is, his Familiarity with Mary is equal to 1. In that case, his Perceived Integrity of her will be equal to her actual Integrity:

B. Joe's PIM = Mary's Integrity

Obviously, the greater his Familiarity value for Mary, the more he'll lean toward Equation B, and the less Familiar he is with Mary, the more he'll lean toward Equation A. Let's write down this idea in a simple table:

Joe's PIM when he has SOME, but not PERFECT, familiarity is the key, then; if he has no familiarity or perfect familiarity, we could easily capture this with Boolean logic. But characters should evolve, and while these two end points on the continuum might represent beginning and end points in the game, they do not allow us to work with points in between. Essentially, we need to know where Joe is on the continuum between these two end points as a result of progress during the game. In other words, how far has he travelled along this continuum? We can conceptualize this as his Distance from Gullibility. We want to use his Familiarity with Mary to decide his distance from Gullibility:

C. Joe's Distance = Mary's Integrity - Joe's Gullibility

And since this is in turn determined or influenced by his Familiarity with Mary, we then get:

D. Joe's Distance = Joe's FM x (Mary's I - Joe's G)

And, since we expect that as the game progresses, we move FROM Gullibility TO Integrity, the equation thus becomes:

E. Joe's Perceived Integrity of Mary = Joe's Gullibility + Joe's Familiarity with Mary x (Mary's Integrity - Joe's Gullibility)

Just to make sure, we plug in the two extreme values to check:

1. Familiarity = 0 means that Perceived Integrity = Gullibility + 0 x (Integrity - Gullibility), which is the same as Gullibility. It checks out!
2. Familiarity = 1 means that Perceived Integrity = Gullibility + 1 x (Integrity - Gullibility),

which is the same as Integrity. It checks out!

So we now have an equation for how Joe will perceive Mary's Integrity, taking into account his Familiarity with her and his Gullibility. Of course, this will work with any pair of characters; we can figure out Mary's Perceived Integrity for Joe if we use her Familiarity with Joe and her own Gullibility. And the true beauty of this is that once we have the formula, we can rely on Joe's PIM for anything else in the game, building it into additional formulas as needed.

In fact, in my Storytron technology, we take this idea one step further in abstraction: we have an equation looking like this:

Character A's Perception of Character B's Trait = A's Accordance value for that Trait + A's Familiarity with B x (B's True Value of that Trait - A's Accordance value for that Trait)

Here, we use of the idea of "Aaccordance" to refer to the willingness a character has to accord a high value of that Trait to another character. Thus, a character's accordance for Integrity would be called Gullibility, but a character's accordance for Good would be called Naivete. The same concept can be applied to all character traits, although we rarely have words that describe these accordances.

FUTURE DIRECTIONS

The point of this extended mathematical exercise is to demonstrate that complex notions such as trust can be represented in mathematical form and that algorithms calculating how trust is initially established can be built from fairly simple concepts. My point is that many aspects of reality can be handled in this way. If we can handle such intangibles as trust and integrity mathematically, why shouldn't we be able to model other, less esoteric, phenomena in like fashion?

We all appreciate the importance of graphics resolution. Back in the days of fat pixels, the images we displayed were of low resolution and fell short of our needs. As technology improved, we enjoyed higher graphics resolutions. Nowadays graphics resolutions are high enough to support most of our efforts. Contrast the concept of graphics resolution with that of "behavioral resolution." The behaviors we present to students, the behaviors that they interact with, are currently just as clunky and clumsy as the low-resolution imagery we relied upon twenty years ago. To improve the interactive potential of serious games, we need higher behavioral resolution. That behavioral resolution can only be obtained by means of more sensitive algorithms that represent behavior with higher resolution.

The development of writing had profound effects on human thought (Eisenstein, 1983; Goody, 1986; Havelock, 1986; Logan, 1986). This new medium of communication made possible more precise analysis of thought and underlay "the glory that was Greece." Later, it was largely responsible for the development of logical reasoning, mathematics, science, and technology. Writing was more than a communication system: it refined and amplified the human thinking process.

Interactivity is a medium of communication every bit as pregnant with potential as writing. When designers come to understand and exploit the full potential of serious games, human thought will be enhanced in two important ways:

First, people will become more familiar with the concept of multicausality. Our current teaching methodologies emphasize simple linear cause-and-effect relationships, because linear causality is easily taught in the linear medium of text. However, our educational methodologies do a poor job of handling multicausal phenomena. Indeed, the single greatest factor separating the hard sciences from the soft sciences is that the former can be analyzed using linear causal reasoning, while the latter require multicausal reasoning—which we can't do well with text but we can do well with interactivity. When we truly master interactive education, the soft sciences will experience an intellectual explosion akin to that experienced by physics in the early 20th century or biological sciences in the late 20th and early 21st centuries.

Second, the full-throated application of interactivity in education will stimulate the development of subjunctive reasoning. This is another form of nonlinear reasoning involving causal factors that might or might not apply to a given situation. We often deal with this kind of situation by talking about "what if" scenarios—and as yet only sophisticated thinkers handle such reasoning with aplomb. There is no reason why the average citizen could not engage in such thinking, if only it were taught at the secondary level. At the moment, we have not the means to teach such advanced material. With serious games, we can make subjunctive reasoning patent to the average high school student.

CONCLUSION

Some designers will reject mathematics because they find it unpalatable, not because they find it wrong. They will continue to build nothingburger serious games with catchy tunes and dancing walruses, and the poor state of development of the serious games medium will permit such bagatelles to survive. But there can be no question as to the fundamental forces at work and the long-term outcomes. Interactivity is the sine qua non of the computer as an expressive medium; you can interact with processes, not facts; processes are specified by algorithms; algorithms are expressed in the language of mathematics.

REFERENCES

Crawford, C. (1984). *The art of computer game design*. Berkeley, CA: McGraw-Hill.

Eisenstein, E. L. (1983). *The printing revolution in early modern Europe*. Cambridge, UK: Cambridge University Press.

Goody, J. (1986). *The logic of writing and the organization of society*. Cambridge, UK: Cambridge University Press.

Havelock, E. A. (1986). *The muse learns to write*. New Haven, CT: Yale.

Logan, R. K. (1986). *The alphabet effect*. New York: Morrow.

MUST READS FOR THIS TOPIC/TOP TEXTS FOR INTERDISCIPLINARY STUDIES OF SERIOUS GAMES

Boyd, B. (2009). *On the origin of stories*. Cambridge, MA: Belknap.

Crawford, C. (2002). *The art of interactive design*. San Francisco: No Starch.

Huizinga, J. (1950). *Homo ludens*. Boston: Beacon.

Top Texts for Interdisciplinary Studies of Serious Games

The authors of each chapter were asked to list the top texts that all researchers and practitioners interested in interdisciplinary perspectives on serious games should be aware of. Each chapter listed these individually, but I present them here as a compiled list. Texts are listed first in descending order by the number of citations, and then alphabetically by first author.

Title of Text	**Times Cited**
Gee, J. (2003 & 2007). *What video games have to teach us about learning and literacy.* New York: Palgrave Macmillan.	11
Shaffer, D. (2006). *How computer games help children learn.* New York, NY: Palgrave Macmillan.	5
Bogost, I. (2007). *Persuasive games: The expressive power of videogames.* Cambridge, MA: MIT Press.	4
Alessi, M. S., & Trollip, S. R. (2001). *Multimedia for learning: Methods and development* (3rd ed.). Boston: Allyn and Bacon.	3
Csikszentmihalyi, M. (1990). *Flow: The psychology of optimal experience.* New York: Harper and Row.	3
Huizinga, J. (1950). *Homo ludens: A study of play-element in culture* (paperback ed.). Boston: Beacon Press.	3
Kirriemuir, J., & McFarlane, A. (2004). Literature review in games and learning. *Futurelab Series, Report 8*, 35. http://www.futurelab.org.uk/research/lit_reviews.htm	3
Koster, R. (2004). *A theory of fun for game design.* Scottsdale, AZ: Paraglyph Press.	3
Prensky, M. (2001 & 2007). *Digital game-based learning.* New York: McGraw-Hill.	3

Copyright © 2010, IGI Global, distributing in print or electronic forms without written permission of IGI Global is prohibited.

Wardrip-Fruin, N., & Harrigan, P. (Eds.). (2004). *First person: New media as story, performance, and game.* Cambridge, MA: MIT Press. 3

Wolf, M. J. P., & Perron, B. (2003). *Video game theory reader.* New York: Routledge 3

Campbell, J. (1993). *The hero with a thousand faces.* London: Fontana Press. 2

de Jong, T. (2006). Computer simulations: Technological advances in inquiry learning. *Science, 312*(5773), 532-533. 2

Dempsey, J. V., Haynes, L. L., Lucassen, B. A., & Casey, M. (2002). Forty simple computer games and what they could mean to educators. *Simulation and Gaming, 33*, 157–168. 2

Geary, D. (2008). An evolutionarily informed education science. *Educational Psychologist, 43*, 179-195. 2

Gee, J. P. (2007). *Good video games and good learning: Collected essays on video games, learning and literacy.* New York: Palgrave/Macmillan. 2

Lave, J., & Wenger, E. (1991). *Situated learning: Legitimate peripheral participation.* Cambridge, UK: Cambridge University Press. 2

Michael, D., & Chen, S. (2005) *Serious Games: Games that educate, train & inform.* Washington, DC: Thomson Course Technology PTR. 2

Raessens (2005). *Handbook of computer game studies.* Cambridge, MA: MIT Press. 2

Salen, K. (2007). *The ecology of games: Connecting youth, games, and learning.* Cambridge, MA: MIT Press. 2

Salen, K., & Zimmerman, E. (2004). *Rules of play: Game design fundamentals.* Cambridge, MA: MIT Press. 2

Squire, K. (2006). From content to context: Video games as designed experiences. *Educational Researcher, 35*(8), 19-29. 2

Van Eck, R. (2007). Six ideas in search of a discipline. In B. E. Shelton & D. A. Wiley (Eds.), *The design and use of simulation computer games in education* (pp. 31–60). Rotterdam, Netherlands: Sense Publishing. 2

Vorderer, P., & Bryant, J. (Eds.) .(2006). *Playing video games: Motives, responses, and consequences.* New York: Routledge. 2

Vygotsky, L. S. (1978). *Mind in society: The development of higher psychological processes.* (M. Cole, Trans.), Cambridge, MA: Harvard University Press. 2

Aldrich, C. (2005). *Learning by doing.* San Francisco: Pfeiffer. 1

Aldrich, C. (2009). *The complete guide to simulations and serious games: How the most valuable content will be created in the age beyond Gutenberg to Google.* San Francisco: Pfeiffer. 1

Baddeley, A.D. (2003). Working memory: Looking back and looking forward. *Nature Reviews Neuroscience, 4,* 829–839. 1

Barab, S., Ingram-Goble, A., Warren, S. (2008). Conceptual play spaces. In R. Ferdig (Ed.), *Handbook of research on effective electronic gaming in education* (pp. 1-20). Hershey, PA: IGI Global publications. 1

Beck, J. C., & Wade, M. (2006). *The Kids are alright: How the gamer generation is changing the workplace* (Paperback). Boston: Harvard Business School. 1

Bettelheim, B. (1991). *The uses of enchantment: The meaning and importance of fairy tales.* London: Penguin Books. 1

Blumberg, F. C. (2000). The effects of children's goals for learning on video game performance. *Journal of Applied Developmental Psychology, 21*(6), 641-653. 1

Bransford, J., Vye, N., Stevens, R., Kuhl, P., Schwartz, D., Bell, P., Meltzoff, A., Barron, B., Pea, R., Reeves, J., Roschelle, J., & Sabelli, N. (2006). Learning theories and education: Toward a decade of synergy. In P. Alexander & P. Winne (Eds.), *Handbook of educational psychology* (2nd ed., pp. 209-244). Mahwah, NJ: Lawrence Erlbaum Associates. 1

Brown, J. S., Collins, A., & Duguid, P. (1989). Situated cognition and the culture of learning. *Educational Researcher, 18*(1), 32-42. 1

Bruce, B., Peyton, J., & Batson, T. (1993). Introduction. In P. Bruce and T. Batson (Eds.), *Network-based classrooms: Promises and realities* (pp. 1-6). Cambridge, UK: Cambridge University Press. 1

Bruner, J. (1990). *Acts of meaning.* Cambridge, MA: Harvard University Press. 1

Calleja, G. (2007). Digital game involvement: A conceptual model. *Games and Culture, 2*(3), 236-260. 1

Carroll, J. M. (2003). *HCI models, theories and frameworks: Toward a multidisciplinary science.* San Francisco: Morgan Kaufmann Publishers. 1

Cassell, J., & Jenkins, H. (Eds.). (2000). *From Barbie to Mortal Kombat: Gender and computer games.* Cambridge, MA: MIT Press. 1

Chen, S., & Michael, D. (October, 2005). Proof of learning: Assessment in Serious Games. *Gamasutra.com.* 1

Clark, R. E. (2005). Multimedia learning in e-course. In R. E. Mayer (Ed.), *The Cambridge handbook of multimedia learning* (pp. 589–616). New York: Cambridge University Press. 1

Clark, R., Nguyen, F., & Sweller, J. (2006). Efficiency in learning: Evidence-based guidelines to manage cognitive load. San Francisco: Pfeiffer. 1

Cobley, P. (2001). *Narrative.* New York: Routledge. 1

Constantine, L. L. (2004). Beyond user-centered design and user experience. *Cutter IT Journal, 17*(2), 2-11. 1

Cooper. R. (2007). *Alter ego: Avatars and their creators.* London: Chris Boot. 1

Craig, R. T. (1999). Communication theory as a field. *Communication Theory, 9*(2), 119-161. 1

Crawford, C. (2002). *The art of interactive design*, San Francisco: No Starch. 1

Crawford, C. (2003). *Chris Crawford on game design.* Indianapolis: New Riders. 1

Csikszentmihalyi, M. (1975). *Beyond boredom and anxiety – experiencing flow in work and play.* San Francisco: Jossey-Bass. 1

De Aguilera, M., & Méndiz, A. (2003). Video games and education: Education in the face of a parallel school. *ACM Computers in Entertainment, 1*(1). 1

de Freitas, S., & Jarvis, S. (2007). Serious games – engaging training solutions: A research and development project for supporting training needs. *British Journal of Educational Technology, 38*(3), 523-525. 1

DeFreitas, S. (2007). *Learning in immersive worlds: A review of game based learning* (Literature Review). London: Joint Information Systems Committee. 1

Dempsey, J. V., & Johnson, R. B. (1998). The development of an ARCS gaming scale. *Journal of Instructional Psychology, 25*(4), 215-221. 1

Dodge, T., Barab, S., & Stuckey, B. (2008). Children's sense of self: Learning and meaning in the digital age. *Journal of Interactive Learning Research, 19*(2), 225-249. 1

Educational games research. http://edugamesblog.wordpress.com/ 1

Egenfeldt-Nielsen, S. (2005). *Beyond edutainment: Exploring the educational potential of computer games.* Copenhagen, Denmark: IT-University. 1

Egenfeldt-Nielsen, S., Smith, J. H., & Tosca, S. P. (2008). *Understanding video games: The essential introduction.* New York: Routledge. 1

Ellis, R. (2003). *Task-based language learning and teaching*: New York: Oxford University Press. 1

Entertainment & Leisure Software Publishers Association (ELSPA), (2006). *Unlimited learning: Computer and video games in the learning landscape.* 1-66. Retrieved from http://www.elspa.com/assets/files/u/unlimitedlearningtheroleofcomputerandvideogamesint_344.pdf. 1

Federation of American Scientists. (2006). *Harnessing the power of video games for learning.* Retrieved December 6, 2006, from http://fas.org/gamesummit/ 1

Ferdig, Rick, Ed. (2008). *Handbook of research on effective electronic gaming in education.* Hershey, PA: IGI Global. 1

Field, J. (2006). *Lifelong learning and the new educational order.* London: Routledge. 1

Frasca, G. (2001) Ephemeral games: Is it barbaric to design videogames after Auschwitz? In M. Eskelinen & R. Koskimaa (Eds.), *Cybertext yearbook 2000* (pp. 172–182). Jyväskylä, Finland: University of Jyväskylä. Retrieved August 20, 2009, from http://cybertext.hum.jyu.fi 1

Frasca, G. (2004). Video games of the oppressed: Critical thinking, education, tolerance and other trivial issues. In P. Harrington & N. Wardrip-Fruin (Eds.), *First person: New media as story, performance, and game.* Cambridge, MA: The MIT Press. 1

Fullerton, T., Swain, C., & Hoffman, S. (2004). *Game design workshop: Designing, prototyping, and playtesting games.* San Francisco: CMP Books. 1

Funk, J. B., & Buchman, D. D. (1996). Playing violent video and computer games and adolescent self-concept. *Journal of Communication, 46*(2), 19. 1

Galloway, A. R. (2006). *Gaming: Essays on algorithmic culture.* Minneapolis: University of Minnesota Press. 1

Gardner, J. E., Wissick, C. A., Schweder, W., & Canter, L. S. (2003). Enhancing interdisciplinary instruction in general and special education: Thematic units and technology. *Remedial and Special Education, 24*, 161-172. 1

Garris, R., Ahlers, R., & Driskell, J. E. (2002). Games, motivation, and learning: A research and practice model. *Simulation & Gaming, 33*(4), 441 - 467. 1

Gee, J. P. (2008). Video games and embodiment. *Games and Culture, 3*(3–4), 253–263. 1

Gee, J.P. (2001). Learning by design: Good video games as learning machines. *E-Learning, 2*(1). 1

Genette, G. (1997). *Paratexts: Thresholds of interpretation.* New York: Cambridge University Press. 1

Gentner, D. (1983). Structure mapping: A theoretical framework for analogy. *Cognitive Science, 7*, 155-170. 1

Gibson, D., Aldrich, C. & Prensky, M. (2007). *Games and simulations in online learning: Research and development frameworks.* Hershey, PA: Information Science Publishing. 1

Gibson, J. J. (1977). The theory of affordances. In R. Shaw & J. Bransford (Eds.), *Perceiving, acting, and knowing: Toward an ecological psychology* (pp. 67–82). Hillsdale, NJ: Lawrence Erlbaum. 1

Giddens, A. (1984). *The constitution of society: Outline of the theory of structuration.* Berkley, CA: University of California Press. 1

Gray, C. H. (Ed.). (1995). *The cyborg handbook.* New York: Routledge Press. 1

Gredler, M. E. (2004). Games and simulations and their relationships to learning. In D. H. Jonassen (Ed.), *Handbook of research on educational communications and technology* (2nd ed.). Mahwah, N.J.: Association for Educational Communications and Technology, Lawrence Erlbaum. 1

Green, C. S., & Bavelier, D. (2003). Action video game modifies visual selective attention. *Nature, 423*, 534- 537. 1

Green, S. & Bavelier D. (2006) The cognitive neuroscience of video games. In *Digital media: Transformations in human communication*, Messaris & Humphreys, Eds. New York: Peter Lang. 1

Gunter, G., Kenny, R., & Vick, E. (2006). A case for a formal design paradigm for serious games. *The Journal of the International Digital Media and Arts Association, 3*(1), 93–105. 1

Hatano, G., & Inagaki, K. (1986). Two courses of expertise. In H. Stevenson, H. Azuma, & K. Hakuta (Eds.), *Child development and education in Japan* (pp. 262-272). New York: W. H. Freeman and Company. 1

Hays, R. T. (2005). *The effectiveness of instructional games: A literature review and discussion.* Naval Air Warfare Center Training Systems Division (No 2005-004). http://stnet.dtie.mil/oai/ 1

Hendriksen, T.D. (2006). *Educational role-play: Moving beyond entertainment. Seeking to please or aiming for the stars.* Conference paper presented at: "On Playing Roles" Seminar, Tampere, FI. 1

Hestenes, D., Wells, M., & Swackhamer, G. (1992). Force concept inventory. *The Physics Teacher, 30*, 141-158. 1

Iuppa, N., & Borst, T. (2007). *Story and simulations for serious games: Tales from the trenches.* New York: Focal Press. 1

Jenkins, H. (2006). *Convergence culture: Where old and new media collide.* New York: NYU Press. 1

Jenkins, H., Clinton K., Purushotma, R., Robinson, A.J., & Weigel, M. (2006). *Confronting the challenges of participatory culture: Media education for the 21st century.* Chicago, IL: The MacArthur Foundation. Retrieved April 24, 2007, from http://digitallearning.macfound.org/atf/cf/{7E45C7E0-A3E0-4B89-AC9C-E807E1B0AE4E}/JENKINS_WHITE_PAPER.PDF 1

Johnson, D. W., & Johnson, R. T. (1991). *Learning together and alone: Cooperative,* 1
competitive, and individualistic learning. Englewood Cliffs, NJ: Prentice Hall.

Joint Information Systems Committee (JISC), U. K. (2007). *Game-based learning*. Retrieved 1
from http://www.jisc.ac.uk/media/documents/publications/gamingreportbp.pdf.

Jonassen, D. H. (2006). On the role of concepts in learning and instructional design. 1
Educational Technology, Research, & Development, 54(2), 177-196.

Juul, J. (2004). *Half-real: Video games between real rules and fictional worlds*. Unpublished 1
doctoral dissertation, IT University of Copenhagen, Copenhagen, Denmark.

Kafi, Y. (1995). *Minds in play: Computer game design as a context for children's learning*. 1
Hillsdale, NJ: Lawrence Erlbaum Associates.

Kankaanranta, M., & Neittaanmäki, P. (Eds.). *Design and use of serious games*. Dordrecht: 1
Springer.

Kebritchi, M., & Hirumi, A. (2008). Examining the pedagogical foundations of modern 1
educational computer games. *Computers and Education, 51*, 1729–1743.

Keller, J. M. (1987). Motivational design and multimedia: Beyond the novelty effect. *Strategic* 1
Human Resource Development Review, 1(1), 188-203.

Khoo, E.T., Merritt, T., Lim Fei, V., Liu, W., Rahaman, H., Prasad, J., & Marsh, T. 2008. 1
Body music: Physical exploration of music theory. ACM SIGGRAPH Video Games Symposium, Los Angeles, USA, ACM Press.

King, M. (2008). Remapping Rhetorical Peaks: A video game for first-year writing. *Computers* 1
and Composition Online, Fall 2008. Retrieved from http://www.bgsu.edu/cconline/gaming_issue_2008/King_Rhetorical_peaks/index.html

Kirsh, D. & Maglio, P. (1994). On distinguishing epistemic from pragmatic action. *Cognitive* 1
Science, 18, 513-549.

Klemmer, S. R., Hartmann, B., and Takayama, L. (2006). How bodies matter: five themes for 1
interaction design. In DIS '06: *Proceedings of the 6th ACM conference on Designing Interactive systems*, 140-149, New York: ACM Press.

Koschmann, T. (Ed.). (1996). *CSCL: Theory and practice: An emerging paradigm*. Mahwah, 1
NJ: Lawrence Erlbaum Associates.

Lakoff, G., & Johnson, M. (1980). *Metaphors we live by*. University of Chicago Press. 1

Lanigan, R. L. (1988). *Phenomenology of communication: Merleau-Ponty's thematics in* 1
communicology and semiology. Pittsburgh: Duquesne University Press.

Laveault, P., & Corbeil, P. (1990). Assessing the impact of simulation games on learning: A 1
step-by-step approach. *Simulation/games for learning, 20*(1), 42-54.

Lee, D. & Larose, R. (2007) A socio-cognitive model of game usage. *Journal of Broadcasting* 1
and Electronic Media, 632-647.

Lepper, M. R. & Cordova, D. (1992). A desire to be taught: Instructional consequences of 1
intrinsic motivation. *Motivation and Emotion, 16*(3), 187-208.

Low, R., & Sweller, J. (2005). The modality principle in multimedia learning. In R. E. Mayer 1
(Ed.), *The Cambridge Handbook of Multimedia Learning* (pp. 147-158). New York: Cambridge University Press.

Loyens, S. M. & Gijbels, D. (2008). Understanding the effects of constructivist learning 1
environments: Introducing a multi-directional approach. *Instructional Science, 36*, 351-357.

Malone, T. W. (1981). Toward a theory of intrinsically motivating instruction. *Cognitive Science*, (4), 333-369. 1

Marsh, T. (2007). Informing design and evaluation methodologies for serious games for learning, *Learning with games 2007*, Sofia Antipolis, France. 1

Mayer, R. , Mautone, P., Prothero, W. (2002). Pictorial aids for learning by doing in a multimedia geology simulation game. *Journal of Educational Psychology, 94*(1), 171-185. 1

Mayer, R. E. (2001). *Multimedia learning.* Cambridge, UK: Cambridge University Press. 1

Mayer, R. E. (2005). Cognitive theory of multimedia learning. In R. E. Mayer (Ed.), *The Cambridge handbook of multimedia learning* (pp. 31-48). New York: Cambridge University Press. 1

Mayer, R. E. (2005). Introduction to multimedia learning. In R. E. Mayer (Ed.), *The Cambridge handbook of multimedia learning* (pp. 1–16). New York: Cambridge University Press. 1

Mayo, M. J. (2009). Video games: A route to large-scale stem education? *Science*, 323(5910) ,79-82. 1

McAllister, K. S. (2004). *Game work: Language, power, and computer game culture.* Tuscaloosa, AL: University of Alabama Press. 1

Mead, G. H. (1934). *Mind, self, and society.* Chicago University Press. 1

Mezirow, J. (1991). *Transformative dimensions of adult learning.* San Francisco: Jossey-Bass. 1

Mitchell, E. (1985). The dynamics of family interaction around home video games. Special Issue: Personal computers and the family. *Marriage and Family Review 8*(1-2), 121)-135. 1

Moeller, R. M., & White, K. (2008). Enter the game factor: Putting theory into practice in the design of Peer Factor. *Computers and Composition Online*, Fall 2008. Retrieved from http://www.bgsu.edu/cconline/gaming_issue_2008/Moeller_White_Enter_the_game/index.html 1

Mookerjee, A., & Kharma, M. (1977). *The tantric way.* London: Thames and Hudson. 1

Moulthrop, S. (2005). After the last generation: Rethinking scholarship in the days of serious play. *Proceedings of the 6th Digital Arts & Culture Conference.* Copenhagen, Denmark: IT University of Copenhagen. 1

Mulligan, K., & Smith, B. (1986). A Husserlian theory of indexicality. *Grazer Philosophische Studien, 28*, 133-163. 1

Murphy, P. K., & Alexander, P. A. (2000). A motivated exploration of motivation terminology. *Contemporary Educational Psychology, 25*, 3-53. 1

Myers, D. (2003). *The nature of computer games: Play as semiosis.* New York: Peter Lang. 1

Nardi, B., & Harris, J. (2006). Strangers and friends: collaborative play in *World of Warcraft*, 2006 20th Anniversary *Conference on Computer Supported Cooperative Work* (pp. 149-158). New York: ACM. 1

Newmann, F. M. (2007). Improving achievement for all students: The meaning of staff-shared understanding and commitment. In W. D. Hawley & D. L. Rollie (Eds.), *The keys to effective schools: Education reform as continuous improvement* (2nd ed., pp. 33-49). Thousand Oaks, CA: Corwin Press. 1

Norman, D. (1995). *Things that make us smart: Defending human attributes in the age of the machine*. Reading, MA: Addison Wesley. 1

Nousiainen, T. (2008). Children's involvement in the design of game-based learning environments. *Jyväskylä Studies in Computing*, No. 95. Jyväskylä, Finland: University of Jyväskylä. 1

Papert, S. (1993). *The children's machine: Rethinking school in the age of the computer*. New York: BasicBooks. 1

Pease, D. E. (1995). Author. In F. Lentricchia & T. McLaughlin (Eds.), *Critical terms for literary study*. University of Chicago Press. 1

Perron, B. (2009). *Video game theory reader 2*. New York: Routledge. 1

Piaget, J. (1977). Science of education and the psychology of the child. In H. E. Gruber, J. J. Vonèche, and J. Jacques (Eds.), *The essential Piaget* (pp. 695-725). New York: Basic Books, Inc. 1

Pintrich, P. R., Smith, D., Garcia, T., & McKeachie, W. (1993). Predictive validity and reliability of the Motivated Strategies for Learning Questionnaire (MSLQ). *Educational Psychological Measurement, 53*, 801-813. 1

Propp, V. (1st Ed. Transl. by Scott, L.; 2nd Ed. Revised & Edited by Wagner, L.A.). (1977). *Morphology of the folk tale*. Austin: University of Texas. 1

Randel, J., Morris, B., Wetzel, C., & Whitehill, B. (1992). The effectiveness of games for educational purposes: A review of recent research. *Simulation and Gaming, 23*(3), 261–276. 1

Raybourn, E. M. (2005). Adaptive thinking & leadership training for cultural awareness and communication competence. *Interactive Technology & Smart Education, 2*, 127-130. 1

Reese, D. D. (2007). First steps and beyond: Serious games as preparation for future learning. *Journal of Educational Media and Hypermedia, 16*(3), 283-300. 1

Reese, D. D. (2009). Structure mapping theory as a formalism for instructional game design and assessment. In D. Gentner, K. Holyoak, & B. Kokinov (Eds.), *Proceedings of the 2nd International Analogy Conference* (pp. 394-403). Sofia, Bulgaria: New Bulgarian University Press. 1

Rice, J. (2007). Assessing higher order thinking in video games. *Journal of Technology and Teacher Education, 15*(1) ,87-100. 1

Rieber, L. P. (1996). Seriously considering play: Designing interactive learning environments based on the blending of microworlds, simulations, and games. *Educational Technology Research and Development, 44*(2), 43-58. 1

Rieber, L. P., Smith, L., & Noah, D. (1998). The value of serious play. *Educational Technology, 38*(6), 29-37. 1

Ritterfeld, U., Cody, M., & Vordered, P. (in press). *Serious games: Mechanisms and effects*. New York: Routledge Press. 1

Robison, A. J. (2008). The design is the game: Writing games, teaching writing. *Computers and Composition, 25*(3), 359-370. 1

Rodriguez, H. (2006). The playful and the serious: An approximation to Huizinga's *Homo Ludens*. *Game Studies—The International Journal of Game Studies, 6* (1). Retrieved August 20, 2009, from http://gamestudies.org/0601/articles/rodriges 1

Rotman, A. (translator). (2008). *Divine stories, Divyavadana part 1*. Boston: Wisdom Publications. 1

Ruesch, J., & Bateson, G. (1951). *Communication: The social matrix of psychiatry.* New York: W. W. Norton & Co., Inc. 1

Ryan, M. L. (2001). *Narrative as virtual reality*. Baltimore: The Johns Hopkins University Press 1

Salen, K. (2007) *Game ecologies*. The John D. and Catherine T. MacArthur Foundation series on digital media and learning. (167-198) Cambridge, MA: MIT Press. 1

Satwicz, T., & Stevens, R. (2008). Playing with representations: How do kids make use of quantitative representations in video games? *International Journal of Computers for Mathematical Learning, 13*, 179–206. 1

Sawyer, B. (2002). Serious Games: Improving public policy through game-based learning and simulation. *Foresight and Governance Project, Woodrow Wilson International Center for Scholars*. Retrieved December 5, 2006, from http://wwics.si.edu/subsites/game/Serious2.pdf 1

Scardamalia, M., Bereiter, C., & Lamon, M. (1994). The CSILE project: Trying to bring the classroom into world 3. In K. McGilly (Ed.), *Classroom lessons: Integrating cognitive theory and classroom practice*, 201-228. Cambridge, MA: MIT Press. 1

Schell, J. (2008). *The art of game design: A book of lenses*. New York: Elsevier. 1

Scholes, R., Phelan, J., & Kellogg, R. (2006). *The nature of narrative.* New York: Oxford University Press. 1

Schwaber, K. (2004). *Agile project management with scrum.* Redmond, WA: Microsoft. 1

Schwartz, D. L., & Martin, T. (2004). Inventing to prepare for future learning: The hidden efficiency of encouraging original student production in statistics instruction. *Cognition and Instruction, 22*(2), 129-184. 1

Selfe, C. L., & Hawisher, G. E. (Eds.). (2007). *Gaming lives in the twenty-first century: Literate connections*. New York: Palgrave Macmillan. 1

Sell, R.D. (2000). *Literature as communication.* Amsterdam and Philadelphia: John Benjamins Publishing. 1

Shaffer, D. (2006). Epistemic frames for epistemic games. *Computers & Education, 46*(3), 223-234. 1

Shaffer, D.W., Squire, K.A., Halverson, R. & Gee, J.P. (2005). Video games and the future of learning. *Phi Delta Kappan, 87*: 104-111 1

Shelton, B. & Wiley, D. (2007). *The design and use of computer simulation games in education.* Rotterdam, Netherlands: Sense Publishers. 1

Sheridan, D. M., & Hart-Davidson, W. (2008). Just for fun: Writing and literacy learning as forms of play. *Computers and Composition, 25*(3), 323-340. 1

Smith, P. L., & Ragan, T. J. (2005). *Instructional design* (3rd ed.). Hoboken, NJ: John Wiley & Sons. 1

Squire, K. D, & Jan, M. (2007). Mad city mystery: Developing scientific argumentation skills with a place-based augmented reality game on handheld computers. *Journal of Science Education and Technology, 16*, 5-29. 1

Steinkuehler, C. (2006). Virtual worlds, learning, & the new pop cosmopolitanism. *Teachers College Record*. Retrieved July 12, 2009, from http://www.tcrecord.org ID Number: 12843. 1

Steinkuehler, C. A. (2004). Learning in massively multiplayer online games. In Y. B. Kafai, W. A. Sandoval, N. Enyedy, A. S. Nixon, & F. Herrera (Eds.), *Proceedings of the Sixth International Conference of the Learning Sciences* (pp. 521–528). Mahwah, NJ: Erlbaum. 1

Stephenson, N. (1995). *The diamond age: Or, a young lady's illustrated primer*. New York: Bantam Spectra. 1

Stubblefield, W. A. (2007). *Hacking sense: Understanding design and use as situated sensemaking*. Sandia National Laboratories. 1

Suchman, L. A. (1987). *Plans and situated actions* [Electronic Version]. Retrieved 3/2/2007. 1

Sutton-Smith, B. (1997). *The ambiguity of play*. Cambridge, MA: Harvard University Press. 1

Sweller, J. (2008). Instructional implications of David Geary's evolutionary educational psychology. *Educational Psychologist, 43*, 214–216. 1

Thomas, M., & Penz, F. (Eds.). (2003). *Architectures of illusion: From motion pictures to navigable interactive environments*. Bristol, UK: Intellect Books. 1

Tomasello, M., & Whiten, A. (1999). *The cultural origins of human cognition*. Cambridge, MA: Harvard University Press 1

Van Deventer, S., & White, J. (2002). Expert behavior in children's videogame play. *Simulation & Gaming, 33*(1). 1

Van Eck, R. (2006). The effect of contextual pedagogical advisement and competition on middle-school students' attitude toward mathematics and mathematics instruction using a computer-based simulation game. *Journal of Mathematics and Science Teaching, 25(2)*, 165-195. 1

Van Eck, R. (2007). Building intelligent learning games. In D. Gibson, C. Aldrich, & M. Prensky (Eds.) *Games and simulations in online learning research & development frameworks*. Hershey, PA: Idea Group. 1

Van Eck, R., & Dempsey, J. (2002). The effect of competition and contextualized advisement on the transfer of mathematics skills in a computer-based instructional simulation game. *Educational Technology, Research and Development, 50*, 23–41. 1

Vansteenkiste, M., Lens, W., & Deci, E. L. (2006). Intrinsic versus extrinsic goal contents in self-determination theory: Another look at the quality of academic motivation. *Educational Psychologist, 41(1)*, 19-31. 1

Vogel, J. J., Vogel, D. S., Cannon-Bowers, J., Bowers, C. A., Muse, K., & Wright, M. (2006). Computer games and interactive simulations for learning: A meta-analysis. *Journal of Educational Computing Research, 34*, 229–243. 1

Vogler, C. (1999). *The writer's journey: Mythic structure for storytellers and screenwriters*. London: Pan Books. 1

Wardrip-Fruin, N. and Monfort, N. (2003). *The new media reader*. The MIT Press. 1

Wark, M. (2007). *Gamer theory*. Cambridge, MA: Harvard University Press. 1

Wilden, A. (1987). *The rules are no game: The strategy of communication*. New York: Routledge. 1

Wood, D. (Ed.). (1991). *On Paul Ricœur, narrative and interpretation*. London: Routledge. 1

Woods, S. (2004). Loading the dice: The challenge of serious videogames. *Game Studies—The International Journal of Game Studies, 4*(1). Retrieved August 20, 2009, from http://www.gamestudies.org/0401/woods/ 1

Wright, W. (2004). *Sculpting possibility space.* Keynote presented at the Accelerating Change 2004: Physical Space, Virtual Space, and Interface conference. Retrieved June 16, 2006, from http://cdn.itconversations.com/ITC.AC2004-WillWright-2004.11.07.mp3 1

Zimmerman, B. J. (2008). Investigating self-regulation and motivation: Historical background, methodological development, and future prospects. *American Educational Research Journal*, *45*, 166-183. 1

Zyda, M. (2005). From Visual Stimulation to Virtual Reality to Games. *IEEE Computer, 38*(9), 25-32. 1

Compilation of References

Aarseth, E. (1997). *Cybertext: Perspectives on ergodic literature*. Baltimore: John Hopkins University Press.

Aarseth, E. (2004). Genre trouble: Narrativism and the art of simulation. In Wardrip-Fruin, N., & Harrigan, P. (Eds.), *First person: New media as story, performance and game* (pp. 45–55). Cambridge, MA: The MIT Press.

Aarseth, E. (2004). Quest games as post-narrative discourse. In Ryan, M.-L. (Ed.), *Narrative across media: The languages of storytelling* (pp. 361–376). Lincoln, NE: University of Nebraska Press.

Abbott, P. (2008). *The Cambridge introduction to narrative* (2nd ed.). New York: Cambridge University Press.

Abt, C. (2002). *Serious games*. Lanham, MD: University Press of America.

Adcock, A. B., & Van Eck, R. (2005). Reliability and factor structure of the Attitude Toward Tutoring Agent Scale (ATTAS). *Journal of Interactive Learning Research, 16*(2), 195–212.

Advergaming. (2009, August 23). Wikipedia, The Free Encyclopedia. Retrieved August 23, 2009, from http://en.wikipedia.org/w/index.php?title=Advergaming&oldid=309656941

Agosto, D. (2004). Girls and gaming: A summary of the research with implications for practice. *Teacher Librarian, 31*(3), 8–14.

Agosto, D. (2008). Evaluating materials. *Girls tech.* New Brunswick, NJ: Rutgers University. Retrieved from http://girlstech.douglass.rutgers.edu/gt1b.html

Alvermann, D., Hagood, M., Heron-Hruby, A., Hughes, P., Williams, K., & Yoon, J. (2007). Telling themselves who they are: What one out-of-school time study revealed about underachieving readers. *Reading Psychology, 28*, 31–50. doi:10.1080/02702710601115455

American Association of University Women. (2000). *Tech-savvy: Educating girls in the new computer age.* Washington, DC: American Association of University Women.

American Psychiatric Association (APA). (1994). *Diagnostic and statistical manual of mental disorders* (4th ed.). Washington, DC: APA.

Amory, A., Naicker, K., Vincent, J., & Adams, C. (1999). The use of computer games as an educational tool: identification of appropriate game types and game elements. *British Journal of Educational Technology, 30*, 311–321. doi:10.1111/1467-8535.00121

Anand, S. M., & Ross, P. G. (1987). A computer-based strategy for personalizing verbal problems in teaching mathematics. *Educational Communication and Technology Journal, 35*, 151–162.

Anderson, A. R., & Moore, O. K. (1960). Autotelic folk-models. *The Sociological Quarterly, 1*, 203–216. doi:10.1111/j.1533-8525.1960.tb01474.x

Anderson, B. (in press). MMOGs in support of learning: Current trends and future uses. In Van Eck, R. (Ed.), *Gaming & cognition: Theories and practice from the learning sciences.* Hershey, PA: IGI Global.

Copyright © 2010, IGI Global, distributing in print or electronic forms without written permission of IGI Global is prohibited.

Anderson, C. A. (2004). An update on the effects of playing violent video games. *Journal of Adolescence, 27*, 113–122. doi:10.1016/j.adolescence.2003.10.009

Anderson, C. A., & Dill, K. E. (2000). Video games and aggressive thoughts, feelings, and behavior in the laboratory and in life. *Journal of Personality and Social Psychology, 78*(4), 772–790. doi:10.1037/0022-3514.78.4.772

Ang, C. S., Zaphiris, P., & Mahmood, S. (2006). A model of cognitive loads in massively multiplayer online role playing games. *Interacting with Computers, 19*, 167–179. doi:10.1016/j.intcom.2006.08.006

Anton, C. (2003). Playing with Bateson: Denotation, logical types, and analog and digital communication. *American Journal of Semiotics, 19*(1–4), 127–152.

Apperley, T. H. (2006). Genre and game studies: Toward a critical approach to video game genres. *Simulation & Gaming, 37*(1), 6–23. doi:10.1177/1046878105282278

Applebee, A. N., Adler, M., & Flihan, S. (2007). Interdisciplinary curricula in middle and high school classrooms: Case studies of approaches to curriculum and instruction. *American Educational Research Journal, 44*(4), 1002–1039. doi:10.3102/0002831207308219

Arbuckle, J. L. (2005). *Amos user's guide version 6.0.* Chicago, IL: Smallwaters Corporation.

Aristoteles. (1967). *Runousoppi* [*Poetics*]. Helsinki: Otava.

Armstrong, S., & Warlick, D. (2004). The new literacy. *TechLearning, 25*(2), 24–31.

Arnseth, H. C. (2006). Learning to play or playing to learn—A critical account of the models of communication informing educational research on computer gameplay. *Game Studies—The International Journal of Game Studies, 6*(1). Retrieved August 20, 2009, from http://gamestudies.org/0601/articles/arnseth

Ascaron. (2009). *Sacred 2: Fallen Angel.* [Console game]. USA: Ascaraon.

Association of College and Research Libraries. (2007, Sep.). Gaming, information literacy, and the college student. *C&RL News,* 483–483.

Astleitner, H., & Hufnagl, M. (2003). The effects of situation-outcome-expectancies and of ARCS-strategies on self-regulated learning with web-lectures. *Journal of Educational Multimedia and Hypermedia, 12*(4), 361–376.

Astleitner, H., & Wiesner, C. (2004). An integrated model of multimedia learning and motivation. *Journal of Educational Multimedia and Hypermedia, 13*, 3–21.

Atkins, B. (2003). *More than a game: The computer game as fictional form.* Manchester, UK: Manchester University Press.

Austin, J. L. (1962). *How to do things with words.* Oxford, UK: Oxford University Press.

AWE Productions. (2005). *Agatha Christie: And Then There Were None* [Console game]. USA: AWE Productions.

Äyrämö, S.-M., & Koskimaa, R. (in press). Narrative definitions for game design: A concept-oriented study of nine computer game design books. In Van Eck, R. (Ed.), *Interdisciplinary models and tools for serious games: Emerging concepts and future directions.* Hershey, PA: IGI Global.

Baker, C. (2008). Peter Molyneux: My next game a 'significant scientific achievement. Interview with Peter Molyneux. *Wired.* Retrieved July 20, 2009, from http://www.wired.com/gamelife/2008/05/molyneux-my-nex/

Bakhtin, M. M. (1986). *Speech genres and other late essays* (Emerson, C., & Holquist, M., Trans.). Austin, TX: University of Texas Press.

Bandura, A. (1977). Self-efficacy: Toward a unifying theory of behavioural change. *Psychological Review, 84*, 191–215. doi:10.1037/0033-295X.84.2.191

Bandura, A. (1986). *Social foundations of thought and action: A social cognitive theory.* Englewood Cliffs, NJ: Prentice Hall.

Bandura, A. (1993). Perceived self-efficacy in cognitive development and functioning. *Educational Psychologist, 28*, 117–148. doi:10.1207/s15326985ep2802_3

Bandura, A. (1997). *Self-efficacy: The exercise of control*. New York: Plenum.

Bandura, A. (2002). Social cognitive theory of mass communication. In Bryant, J., & Zillman, D. (Eds.), *Media effects: Advances in theory and research* (2nd ed., pp. 121–154). London: Lawrence Erlbaum.

Barab, S. A., Thomas, M., Dodge, T., Carteaux, R., & Tuzun, H. (2005). Making learning fun: Quest Atlantis, a game without guns. *Educational Technology Research and Development, 53*(1), 86–107. doi:10.1007/BF02504859

Barab, S., & Jackson, C. (2006). From Plato's republic to Quest Atlantis: The role of the philosopher–king. *THEN Journal*. Retrieved January 15, 2009, from http://thenjournal.org/feature/78/

Barab, S., Ingram-Goble, A., & Warren, S. (2008). Conceptual play spaces. In Ferdig, R. (Ed.), *Handbook of research on effective electronic gaming in education* (pp. 1–20). Hershey, PA: IGI Global Publications.

Barab, S., Thomas, M., Dodge, T., Carteaux, R., & Tuzun, H. (2005). Making learning fun: Quest Atlantis, a game without guns. *Educational Technology Research and Development, 53*(1), 86–107. .doi:10.1007/BF02504859

Barlett, C. P., Vowels, C. L., Shanteau, J., Crow, J., & Miller, T. (2009). The effect of violent and non-violent computer games on cognitive performance. *Computers in Human Behavior, 25*, 96–102. doi:10.1016/j.chb.2008.07.008

Barthes, R. (1977). *Image—Music—Text*. New York: Hill and Wang.

Bartle, R. (2003). *Designing Virtual Worlds*. New Riders Games. Retrieved from http://www.amazon.ca/exec/obidos/redirect?tag=citeulike09-20&path=ASIN/0131018167

Barton, P. E. (2009). *One-third of a nation: Rising dropout rates and declining opportunities*. Princeton, NJ: Educational Testing Service.

Bateman, C. (Ed.). (2007). *Game writing: Narrative skills for videogames*. Boston, MA: Charles River Media.

Bateman, C., & Boon, R. (2005). *21st century game design*. Hingham, MA: Charles River Media.

Bateson, G. (1968). Information and codification. In Ruesch, J., & Bateson, G. (Eds.), *Communication: The social matrix of psychiatry*. New York: W. W. Norton & Company.

Bateson, G. (1972). *Steps to an ecology of mind*. New York: Ballentine Books.

Beavis, C., & Charles, C. (2007). Would the "real" girl gamer please stand up? Gender, LAN cafes, and the reformulation of the "girl" gamer. *Gender and Education, 19*(6), 691–705. doi:10.1080/09540250701650615

Beck, J. C., & Wade, M. (2006). *The kids are alright: How the gamer generation is changing the workplace*. Boston, MA: Harvard Business School Press.

Belfiore, E. (1992). Aristotle on tragic and comic mimesis. *Bryn Mawr Classical Review, 4*(01). Retrieved January 2009, from http://hegel.lib.ncsu.edu/stacks/serials/bmcr/bmcr-v4n01-belfiore-aristotle

Bell, P. (1997). *Using argument representations to make thinking visible for individuals and groups* (pp. 10–19). University of Toronto.

Bell, P. (2000). Scientific arguments as learning artifacts: designing for learning from the web with KIE. *International Journal of Science Education, 22*(8), 797–817. doi:10.1080/095006900412284

Bergeron, B. (2006). *Developing serious games*. Hingham, MA: Charles River Media.

Bergin, D. A., Ford, M. E., & Hess, R. D. (1993). Patterns of motivation and social behaviour associated with microcomputer use of young children. *Journal of Educational Psychology, 85*, 437–445. doi:10.1037/0022-0663.85.3.437

Bernstein, R. J. (1985). From hermeneutics to praxis. In Hollinger, R. (Ed.), *Hermeneutics and praxis* (pp. 272–296). Notre Dame, Indiana: University of Notre Dame Press.

Bertozzi, E. (2008). "You play like a girl!" Cross-gender competition and the uneven playing field. *Convergence*, *14*(4), 473–487.

Bettelheim, B. (1991). *The uses of enchantment: The meaning and importance of fairy tales*. London: Penguin Books.

Bhaskar, R., & Simon, H. A. (1977). Problem solving in semantically rich domains: An example from engineering thermodynamics. *Cognitive Science*, *1*, 193–215.

Biddle, S. J. H., Fox, K. R., Boutcher, S. H., & Faulkner, G. (2000). The way forward for physical activity and the promotion of psychological well-being. In Biddle, S. J. H., Fox, K. R., & Boutcher, S. H. (Eds.), *Physical activity and psychological well-being* (pp. 145–168). London: Routledge.

Bioshock. (2007). [Console game]. USA: 2K.

Bird, K. D. (1975). Simultaneous contrast testing procedures for multivariate experiments. *Multivariate Behavioral Research*, *10*, 343–352. doi:10.1207/s15327906mbr1003_7

Bird, K. D., & Hadzi-Pavlovic, D. (1983). Simultaneous test procedures and the choice of a test statistic in MANOVA. *Psychological Bulletin*, *93*, 167–178. doi:10.1037/0033-2909.93.1.167

Blackmon, S. (2007). Racing toward representation: An understanding of racial representation in video games. In Selfe, C. L., & Hawisher, G. E. (Eds.), *Gaming lives in the twenty-first century* (pp. 203–215). New York: Palgrave Macmillan.

Blizzard Entertainment. (2004). *World of Warcraft* [computer game]. Irvine, CA: Blizzard Entertainment.

Blumberg, F. C. (1998). Developmental differences at play: Children's selective attention and performance in video games. *Journal of Applied Developmental Psychology*, *19*(4), 615–624. doi:10.1016/S0193-3973(99)80058-6

Blumberg, F. C. (2000). The effects of children's goals for learning on video game performance. *Journal of Applied Developmental Psychology*, *21*(6), 641–653. doi:10.1016/S0193-3973(00)00058-7

Blumenfeld, P. C. (1992). Classroom learning and motivation: Clarifying and expanding goal theory. *Journal of Educational Psychology*, *84*, 272–281. doi:10.1037/0022-0663.84.3.272

Boekaerts, M., de Koning, E., & Vedder, P. (2006). Goal-directed behaviour and contextual factors in the classroom: An innovative approach to the study of multiple goals. *Educational Psychologist*, *41*(1), 33–51. doi:10.1207/s15326985ep4101_5

Bogost, I. (2007). *Persuasive games: The expressive power of videogames*. Cambridge, MA: MIT Press.

Bohannon, J. (2008). CLIMATE CHANGE: The big thaw reaches Mongolia's pristine north. *Science*, *319*(5863), 567–568. doi:10.1126/science.319.5863.567

Bohner, G., Erb, H. P., & Siebler, F. (2008). Information processing approaches to persuasion: Integrating assumptions from the dual- and single-processing perspectives. In Crano, W. D., & Prislin, R. (Eds.), *Attitudes and attitude change*. New York: Psychology Press.

Bollen, K. A. (1989). *Structural equations with latent variables*. New York: John Wiley.

Boon, R. (2007). Writing for games. In Bateman, C. (Ed.), *Game writing: narrative skills for videogames* (pp. 43–70). Boston, MA: Charles River Media.

Borchert, B. L., Hokanson, G., Slator, B., & Vender, B. (in press). Principles and signatures in serious games for science education. In R. Van Eck (Ed.), *Gaming & cognition: Theories and practice from the learning sciences*. Hershey, PA: IGI Global.

Borofsky, R. (1994). *Assessing cultural anthropology*. New York: McGraw-Hill.

Bottino, R. M., & Ott, M. (2006). Mind games, reasoning skills, and the primary school curriculum. *Learning, Media and Technology*, *31*(4), 359–375. doi:10.1080/17439880601022981

Bousquet, M. (2008). *How the university works: Higher education and the low-wage nation*. New York: New York University Press.

Boyer, E. L. (1997). *Scholarship reconsidered: Priorities of the professoriate*. San Francisco: Jossey-Bass.

Bransford, J. D., Brown, A. L., & Cocking, R. R. (Eds.). (2000). *How people learn: Brain, mind, experience, and school committee on developments of science of learning.* Washington, DC: National Academies.

Bransford, J., Vye, N., Stevens, R., Kuhl, P., Schwartz, D., & Bell, P. (2006). Learning theories and education: Toward a decade of synergy. In Alexander, P., & Winne, P. (Eds.), *Handbook of Educational Psychology* (2nd ed., pp. 209–244). Erlbaum.

Braverman, J. (2008). Testimonials versus informational persuasive messages: The moderating effect of delivery mode and personal involvement. *Communication Research, 35*(5), 666–694. doi:10.1177/0093650208321785

BreakAway. (n.d.). *Pulse: Virtual Clinical Learning Lab for Health Care Training.* [Video game]. USA: BreakAway. *Ltd.*

Bricker, L., & Bell, P. (2008). *Conceptualizations of argumentation from science studies and the learning sciences and their implications for the practices of science education* (Vol. 9). Retrieved from http://dx.doi.org/10.1002/sce.2027.

Bridgeland, J., Dilulio, J., Jr., & Morison, K. B. (2006). The Silent Epidemic. Washington, DC: Civic Enterprises, LLC.

Briñol, P., & Petty, R. E. (2006). Fundamental processes leading to attitude change: Implications for cancer prevention communications. *The Journal of Communication, 56*, 81–104. doi:10.1111/j.1460-2466.2006.00284.x

Brookfield, S. D. (2000). The concept of critically reflective practice. In Wilson, A. L., & Hayes, E. R. (Eds.), *Handbook of adult and continuing education* (pp. 33–50). San Francisco: Jossey-Bass.

Brookfield, S. D. (2005). *The power of critical theory for adult learning and teaching.* New York: McGraw-Hill.

Brosnan, M. (1998). The impact of psychological gender, gender-related perceptions, significant others, and the introduction of technology upon computer anxiety in students. *Journal of Educational Computing Research, 18*, 63–78. doi:10.2190/LVHH-EPGB-AE7J-WEV8

Broussard, S. R., La Lopa, J. M., & Ross-Davis, A. (2007). Synergistic knowledge development in interdisciplinary teams. *Journal of Natural Resources and Life Sciences Education, 36*, 129–133.

Brown, P., & Levinson, S. C. (1987). *Universals in language usage: Politeness phenomena.* Cambridge, UK: Cambridge University Press.

Bruner, J. (1986). *Actual minds, possible worlds.* Cambridge, MA: Harvard University Press.

Bruner, J. (1990). *Acts of meaning.* Cambridge, MA: Harvard University Press.

Bruner, J. (1996). *The culture of education.* Cambridge, MA & London: Harvard University Press.

Bruner, J. (2004). Life as narrative. *Journal of Social Research, 3*(71), 691–710. Retrieved January 2009, from http://www.plataforma.uchile.cl/fb/cursos_area/cognit/unidad2/tema2/doc/bruner_2004_lifeasnarrative.pdf

Bruning, R. H., Schraw, G. J., Norby, M. M., & Ronning, R. R. (2004). *Cognitive Psychology and Instruction* (4th ed.). Upper Saddle River, NJ: Merrill.

Bryson, C., & Hand, L. (2007). The role of engagement in inspiring teaching and learning. *Innovations in Education and Teaching International, 44*(4), 349–362. doi:10.1080/14703290701602748

Burgos, D., Fernández-Manjón, B., & Richards, G. (2008). Special issue: Electronic games and personalised elearning processes [Editorial]. *Computers in Human Behavior, 24*, 2475–2476. doi:10.1016/j.chb.2008.03.008

Burke, S., & Jin, P. (1996). Predicting performance from a triathlon event. *Journal of Sport Behavior, 19*, 272–287.

Bushman, B. J., & Anderson, C. A. (2002). Violent video games and hostile expectations: A test of the general aggression model. *Personality and Social Psychology Bulletin, 28*(12), 1679–1686. doi:10.1177/014616702237649

Byrne, B. M. (1989). *A primer of LISREL–Basic applications and programming for confirmatrory factor analytic models*. New York: Springer-Verlag.

Calleja, G. (2007). Digital game involvement: A conceptual model. *Games and Culture, 2*(3), 236–260. doi:10.1177/1555412007306206

Cameron, D. (2000). *Good to talk? Living and working in a communication culture*. London, UK: Sage.

Campbell, J. (1949). *The hero with a thousand faces*. Princeton, NJ: Princeton University Press.

Capra, F. (1996). *The web of life: A new scientific understanding of living systems*. New York: Doubleday.

Carbonaro, M., Cutumisu, M., Duff, H., Gillis, S., Onuczko, C., Siegel, J., & Waugh, K. (2008). Interactive story authoring: A viable form of creative expression for the classroom. *Computers & Education, 51*, 687–707. doi:10.1016/j.compedu.2007.07.007

Carr, D. (2005). Context, gaming pleasures, and gendered preferences. *Simulation & Gaming, 36*(4), 464–482. doi:10.1177/1046878105282160

Cassell, J., & Jenkins, H. (Eds.). (1998). *From Barbie to Mortal Kombat: Gender and computer games*. Cambridge, MA: The MIT Press.

Cassell, J., & Ryokai, K. (2001). Making space for voice: Technologies to support children's fantasy and storytelling. *Personal and Ubiquitous Computing, 5*(3), 169–190. doi:10.1007/PL00000018

Castranova, E. (2005). *Synthetic worlds, the business and culture of online games*. Chicago, London: University of Chicago Press.

Cavazza, M., & Pizzi, P. (2006). Narratology for interactive storytelling: A critical introduction. In S. Göbel, R. Malkewitz, & I. Iurgel (Eds.), *TIDSE 2006, LNCS 4326* (pp. 72-83). Berlin Heidelberg: Springer-Verlag. Retrieved April 2, 2009, from http://www-scm.tees.ac.uk/users/f.charles/publications/conferences/2006/Cavazza_Pizzi_TIDSE06.pdf

Chandler, R. (2007). *Game writing handbook*. Boston, MA: Charles River Media.

Charmaz, K. (2006). *Constructing grounded theory: A practical guide through qualitative analysis*. Thousand Oaks, CA: Sage Publications.

Charness, G., Fréchette, G. R., & Qin, C. (2007). Endogenous transfers in the Prisoner's Dilemma game: An experimental test of cooperation and coordination. *Games and Economic Behavior, 60*, 287–306. doi:10.1016/j.geb.2006.10.010

Charsky, D., & Mims, C. (2008). Integrating commercial office-the-shelf video games into school curriculums. *TechTrends, 52*(5), 38–44. doi:10.1007/s11528-008-0195-0

Chatman, S. (1980). *Story and discourse*. Ithaca, NY: Cornell University Press.

Chou, C., & Tsai, M. (2007). Gender differences in Taiwan high school students' computer game playing. *Computers in Human Behavior, 23*, 812–824. doi:10.1016/j.chb.2004.11.011

Christensen, D. M., Cootey, J. L., & Moeller, R. M. (2007). Playing in genre fields: A play theory perspective on genre. In *SIGDOC '07: Proceedings of the 25th ACM International Conference on Design of Communication* (pp. 1–8). New York: Association for Computing Machinery.

Ciavarro, C., Dobson, M., & Goodman, D. (2008). Implicit learning as a design strategy for learning games: *Alert Hockey. Computers in Human Behavior, 24*, 2862–2872. doi:10.1016/j.chb.2008.04.011

Civilization [computer software]. (n.d.). Novato, CA: 2K Games.

Clark, R. C. (2005). Multimedia learning in e-courses. In Mayer, R. E. (Ed.), *The Cambridge Handbook of Multimedia Learning* (pp. 589–616). New York: Cambridge University Press.

Clark, R. C., & Mayer, R. (2008). *E-learning and the science of instruction: Proven guidelines for consumers and designers of multimedia learning* (2nd ed.). San Francisco, CA: John Wiley.

Clayman, S., & Maynard, D. (1995). Ethnomethodology and conversation analysis. In ten Have, P., & Psathas, G. (Eds.), *Situated order: Studies in the social organization of talk and embodied activities* (pp. 1–30). Washington, DC: University Press of America.

Cleary, P. J. (1986). L.I.V.: R.I.P.?: Comments on Myrtek and Foerster's "The law of initial value: A rare exception." *Biological Psychology, 22*, 279–284. doi:10.1016/0301-0511(86)90031-1

Cobb, S., & Fraser, D. S. (2005). Multimedia learning in virtual reality. In Mayer, R. E. (Ed.), *The Cambridge Handbook of Multimedia Learning* (pp. 525–547). New York: Cambridge University Press.

Cobley, P. (2001). *Narrative*. London, New York: Routledge.

Cole, M., & Engeström, Y. (1993). A cultural-historical approach to distributed cognition. In Salomon, G. (Ed.), *Distributed cognitions: Psychological and educational considerations* (pp. 1–46). Cambridge, UK: Cambridge University Press.

Coleman, D. W. (2002). On foot in SIM City: Using SIM COPTER as the basis for an ESL writing assignment. *Simulation & Gaming, 33*, 217–230. doi:10.1177/1046878102332010

Conati, C., & VanLehn, K. (2000). Toward computer-based support of meta-cognitive skills: A computational framework to coach self-explanation. *International Journal of Artificial Intelligence in Education, 11*(4), 389–415.

Conrad, A. M., & Munro, D. (2008). Relationships between computer self-efficacy, technology, attitudes and anxiety: Development of the *Computer Technology Use Scale* (CTUS). *Journal of Educational Computing Research, 39*(1), 51–73. doi:10.2190/EC.39.1.d

Consalvo, M. (2003, February). *It's a queer world after all: Studying The Sims and sexuality*. Gay & Lesbian Alliance Against Defamation. Retrieved March 29, 2009, from http://www.glaad.org/documents/csms/The_Sims.pdf

Consortium for School Networking. (2008). *Measuring 21st century skills*. Washington, DC: Consortium for School Networking.

Cook, T. D., & Campbell, D. T. (1979). *Quasi-experimentation: Design & analysis issues for field setting*. Boston: Houghton Mifflin.

Cooper, J., & Weaver, K. (2003). *Gender and computers: Understanding the digital divide*. Mahwah, NJ: Erlbaum.

Cordova, D. L., & Lepper, M, R. (1996). Intrinsic motivation and the process of learning: Beneficial effects of contextualization, personalization, and choice. *Journal of Educational Psychology, 88*(4), 715–730. doi:10.1037/0022-0663.88.4.715

Cowan, N. (2005). *Working memory capacity*. New York: Psychology Press. doi:10.4324/9780203342398

Craig, R. T. (1989). Communication as a practical discipline. In B. Dervin, L. Grosberg, B. J. O'Keefe, & E. Wartella (Eds.), Rethinking communication: Vol. 1 paradigm issues (pp. 97–122). Newberry Park, CA: Sage.

Craig, R. T. (1999). Communication theory as a field. *Communication Theory, 9*, 119–161.

Craig, R. T. (2001). Dewey and Gadamer on practical reflection: Toward a methodology for the practical disciplines. In Perry, D. K. (Ed.), *American pragmatism and communication research* (pp. 131–148). Mahwah, NJ: Lawrence Erlbaum Associates.

Craig, R. T., & Tracy, K. (1995). Grounded practical theory: The case of the intellectual discussion. *Communication Theory, 5*(3), 248–272. doi:10.1111/j.1468-2885.1995.tb00108.x

Cranton, P., & King, K. (2003). Transformative learning as a professional development goal. *New Directions for Adult and Continuing Education, 98*, 31–38. doi:10.1002/ace.97

Crawford, C. (1984). *The art of computer game design*. Berkeley, CA: McGraw-Hill.

Crawford, C. (2003). *Chris Crawford on game design*. Boston, MA: New Riders.

Crawford, C. (2005). *Chris Crawford on interactive storytelling*. Berkeley, CA: New Riders Games.

Crawford, C. (in press). Interactivity, process, algorithm. In Van Eck, R. (Ed.), *Interdisciplinary models and tools for serious games: Emerging concepts and future directions*. Hershey, PA: IGI Global.

Creswell, J. W. (2007). *Quality inquiry and research design: Choosing among five approaches* (2nd ed.). Thousand Oaks, CA: Sage.

Creswell, J. W. (2008). *Educational research: Planning, conducting, and evaluating quantitative and qualitative research* (3rd ed.). Upper Saddle River, NJ: Pearson Education.

Croninger, R. G., & Lee, V. E. (2001). Social capital and dropping out of high school. Benefits to at-risk student of teachers' support and guidance. *Teachers College Record, 103*(4), 548–581. doi:10.1111/0161-4681.00127

Csikszentmihalyi, M. (1990). *Flow: The psychology of optimal experience*. New York: Harper and Row.

Culler, J. (1994). *Ferdinand de Saussure* [*Saussure*]. Helsinki: Tutkijaliitto.

Cunliffe, A. L. (2004). On becoming a critically reflexive practitioner. *Journal of Management Education, 28*(4), 407–426. doi:10.1177/1052562904264440

De Aguilera, M., & Méndiz, A. (2003). Video games and education: Education in the face of a parallel school. *ACM Computers in Entertainment, 1*(1).

de Freitas, S., & Jarvis, S. (2007). Serious games–engaging training solutions: A research and development project for supporting training needs. *British Journal of Educational Technology, 38*(3), 523–525. doi:10.1111/j.1467-8535.2007.00716.x

de Freitas, S., & Oliver, M. (2006). How can exploratory learning with games and simulations within the curriculum be most effectively evaluated? *Computers & Education, 46*(3), 249–264. doi:10.1016/j.compedu.2005.11.007

de Jong, T. (2006). Computer simulations: Technological advances in inquiry learning. *Science, 312*(5773), 532–533. doi:10.1126/science.1127750

de Jong, T., van Joolingen, W. R., Ehmke, T., Savelsbergh, E. R., Lazonder, A. W., & Manlove, S. A. (2003). *Co-Lab - collaborative laboratories for Europe*. Paper presented at the Tenth Biennial Conference of the European Association for Research in Learning and Instruction, Padova, Italy.

de Jong-Meyer, R. (2004). Systematic motivational analysis as part of a self-help technique aimed at personal goal attainment. In Cox, W. M., & Klingcr, E. (Eds.), *Handbook of motivational counseling: Concepts, approaches, and assessment* (pp. 259–281). New York: Wiley.

Debord, G. (2006). *Report on the construction of situations. Situationist International Anthology* (Knabb, K., Trans.). Berkeley, CA: Bureau of Public Secrets.

Deci, E. L., Koestner, R., & Ryan, R. M. (1999). A meta-analytic review of experiments examining the effects of extrinsic rewards on intrinsic motivation. *Psychological Bulletin, 25*, 627–668. doi:10.1037/0033-2909.125.6.627

Deetz, S. A. (1994). Future of the discipline: The challenges, the research, and the social contribution. In Deetz, S. A. (Ed.), *Communication yearbook, 17* (pp. 565–600). Thousand Oaks, CA: Sage.

DeKanter, N. (2005). Gaming redefines interactivity for learning. *TechTrends, 49*(3), 26–31. doi:10.1007/BF02763644

Deleuze, G. (1992). Postscript on the societies of control. *October, 59*, 3–7.

Dembo, M. H. (2004). Don't lose sight of the students. *Principal Leadership, 4*, 37–42.

Dempsey, J. V., & Johnson, R. B. (1998). The development of an *ARCS Gaming Scale. Journal of Instructional Psychology, 25*(4), 215–221.

Dempsey, J. V., & Van Eck, R. (2003). Modality and placement of pedagogical adviser in individual interactive learning. *British Journal of Educational Technology, 34*(5), 585–600. doi:10.1046/j.0007-1013.2003.00352.x

Dempsey, J. V., Haynes, L. L., Lucassen, B. A., & Casey, M. S. (2002). Forty simple computer games and what they could mean to educators. *Simulation & Gaming, 33*, 157–168. doi:10.1177/1046878102332003

DeShon, R. P., & Gillespie, J. Z. (2005). A motivated action theory account of goal orientation. *The Journal of Applied Psychology, 90*(6), 1096–1127. doi:10.1037/0021-9010.90.6.1096

Deubel, P. (2006, Jan.). Game on. *T.H.E. Journal*, 30–41.

DeVellis, R. F. (2003). *Scale development: Theory and applications* (2nd ed.). Thousand Oaks, CA: Sage.

Dewey, J. (1929). *Experience and nature* (2nd ed.). La-Salle, IL: Open Court.

Dewey, J. (1938). *Experience & education*. New York: Collier Macmillan.

Di Blasio, P., & Milani, L. (2008). Computer-mediated communication and persuasion: Peripheral vs. central route to opinion shift. *Computers in Human Behavior, 24*(3), 798–815. doi:10.1016/j.chb.2007.02.011

Dick, W., Carey, L., & Carey, J. O. (2005). *The systematic design of instruction* (6th ed.). Boston: Pearson.

Dickey, M. (2006). Girl gamers: The controversy of girl games and the relevance of female-oriented game design for instructional design. *British Journal of Educational Technology, 37*(5), 785–793. doi:10.1111/j.1467-8535.2006.00561.x

Dickey, M. D. (2006). Game design narrative for learning: Appropriating adventure game design narrative devices and techniques for the design of interactive learning environments. *Educational Technology Research & Development, 54*(3), 245–263. Retrieved April 2, 2009, from http://www.springerlink.com/content/h3gn553h68002q47/fulltext.pdf

Dill, K. E., Brown, B. P., & Collins, M. A. (2008). Effects of exposure to sex-stereotyped video game characters on tolerance of sexual harassment. *Journal of Experimental Social Psychology, 44*, 1402–1408. doi:10.1016/j.jesp.2008.06.002

Dillenbourg, P., Baker, M., Blayne, A., & O'Malley, C. (1996). The evolution of research on collaborative learning. In Spada, H., & Reimann, P. (Eds.), *Learning in humans and machine: Towards an interdisciplinary learning science* (pp. 189–211). Oxford: Elsevier.

Dillon, A., & Jobst, J. (2005). Multimedia learning with hypermedia. In Mayer, R. E. (Ed.), *The Cambridge Handbook of Multimedia Learning* (pp. 569–588). New York: Cambridge University Press.

Dimitriadis, G., & Kamberelis, G. (2006). *Theory for education*. New York: Taylor & Francis.

Dipietro, M., Ferdig, R. E., Boyer, F., & Black, E. W. (2007). Towards a framework for understanding electronic educational gaming. *Journal of Educational Multimedia and Hypermedia, 16*(3), 225–248.

Disessa, A. (2000). *Changing minds: Computers, learning, and literacy*. Cambridge, MA: The MIT Press. Retrieved from http://www.amazon.ca/exec/obidos/redirect?tag=citeulike09-20&path=ASIN/0262041804

Dodge, T., Barab, S., & Stuckey, B. (2008). Children's sense of self: Learning and meaning in the digital age. *Journal of Interactive Learning Research, 19*(2), 225–249.

Doise, W., & Mugny, G. (1984). *The social development of the intellect, international series in experimental social psychology* (*Vol. 10*). Pergamon Press.

Dovey, J., & Kennedy, H. W. (Eds.). (2006). *Game cultures*. Maidenhead, UK: Open University Press.

DreamWorks Interactive. (1999). *Medal of Honor* [Computer game]. Redwood City, CA: Electronic Arts.

Driscoll, M. P. (2005). *Psychology of learning for instruction* (3rd ed.). Boston: Pearson.

Ducheneaut, N., & Yee, N. Nickell, e., & Moore, R. J. (2006). Alone together?: Exploring the social dynamics of massively multiplayer online games. In R. Grinter, T. Rodden, P. Aoki, E. Cutrell, R. Jeffries, & G. Olson, (Eds.), *Proceedings of the SIGCHI Conference on Human Factors in Computing Systems* (pp. 407-416). New York: ACM.

Duffy, T. M., & Cunningham, D. J. (1996). Constructivism: Implications for the design and delivery of instruction. In Jonassen, D. H. (Ed.), *Handbook of research for educational communications and technology* (pp. 170–198). New York: Macmillan.

Dynamix. (1993). *The Incredible Machine*. [PC game]. USA: Dynamix.

Easterwood, L., & Wesson, L. (2009). Gamers are readers. *School Library Journal, 55*(4), 24–25.

Egenfeldt-Nielsen, S. (2004). Understanding the educational potential of commercial computer games through activity and narratives. *Game Research*. Retrieved September 2, 2008, from http://game-research.com/index.php/articles/understanding-the-educational-potential-of-commercial-computer-games-through-activity-and-narratives/

Egenfeldt-Nielsen, S. (2005). *Beyond edutainment: Exploring the educational potential of computer games*. IT-University Copenhagen.

Eisenberg, E. M. (1984). Ambiguity as strategy in organizational communication. *Communication Monographs, 51*, 227–242. doi:10.1080/03637758409390197

Eisenberger, R., & Cameron, J. (1996). Detrimental effects of reward: Reality or myth? *The American Psychologist, 51*, 1153–1166. doi:10.1037/0003-066X.51.11.1153

Eisenstein, E. L. (1983). *The printing revolution in early modern Europe*. Cambridge, UK: Cambridge University Press.

Elliot, A. J., & McGregor, H. (2001). A 2 x 2 achievement goal framework. *Journal of Personality and Social Psychology, 80*, 501–519. doi:10.1037/0022-3514.80.3.501

Ellis, G. (2008). Commentary on an evolutionarily informed education science by David C. Geary. *Educational Psychologist, 43*, 206–213. doi:10.1080/00461520802392216

Elsmore, T. (1994). Synwork1: A pc-based tool for assessment of performance in a simulated work environment. *Behavior Research Methods, Instruments, & Computers, 26*, 421–426.

Engeström, Y. (1987). *Learning by expanding: An activity–theoretical approach to developmental research*. Helsinki, Finland: Orienta-Konsultit.

English Haggadah with instructional guide. (n.d.). Retrieved July 20, 2009, from http://www.chabad.org/holidays/passover/pesach_cdo/aid/1737/jewish/Maggid.htm

Entertainment Arts Games. (2000). *American McGee's Alice* [PC Game]. Redwood City, California: EA Games.

Entertainment Arts. (2008). *Spore* [PC game]. USA: EA Games.

Entertainment Software Association. (2008). *Game player data*. Washington, DC: Entertainment Software Association. Retrieved from http://www.theesa.com/facts/gameplayer.asp

Entertainment, V. I. S. (2002). *State of Emergency* [PlayStation 2]. London: Rockstar Games.

Erndl, K. M. (2004). Sakta. In Mittal, S., & Thursby, G. R. (Eds.), *The Hindu world* (pp. 140–161). New York: Routledge.

Eskelinen, M. (2001). The gaming situation. *Game Studies, The International Journal of Computer Game Research, 1*(1). Retrieved March 2007 from http://www.gamestudies.org/0101/eskelinen/

Eskelinen, M. (2009). *Travels in cybertextuality: The challenge of ergodic literature and ludology to literary theory*. Doctoral dissertation thesis, University of Jyväskylä, Jyväskylä, Finland.

Fairhurst, G. T., & Sarr, R. A. (1996). *The art of framing: Managing the language of leadership*. San Francisco, CA: Jossey-Bass.

Federation of American Scientists. (2006). *Harnessing the power of video games for learning*. Retrieved December 6, 2006, from http://fas.org/gamesummit/

Fernández-Vara, C., Grigsby, N., Glinert, E., Tan, P., & Jenkins, H. (2009). Between theory and practice: The GAMBIT experience. In Perron, B., & Wolf, M. (Eds.), *Video game theory reader 2*. New York: Routledge.

Festinger, L. (1957). *A theory of cognitive dissonance*. Stanford: Stanford University Press.

Field, J. (2006). *Lifelong learning and the new educational order*. London: Routledge.

Flanagan, M. (2003). *SIMple & personal: Domestic space & the Sims*. Paper presented at the 2003 Melbourne Digital Arts & Culture Conference. Retrieved March 29, 2009, from http://hypertext.rmit.edu.au/dac/papers/Flanagan.pdf

Flavell, J. H. (1985). *Cognitive development* (2nd ed.). Englewood Cliff, NJ: Prentice Hall.

Fleischer, S. O., Wright, S. A., & Barnes, M. L. (2007). Dungeons, dragons, and discretion: A gateway to gaming, technology, and literacy. In Selfe, C. L., & Hawisher, G. E. (Eds.), *Gaming lives in the twenty-first century* (pp. 143–160). New York: Palgrave Macmillan.

Flood, G. (1996). *An introduction to Hinduism*. Cambridge, UK: Cambridge University Press.

Fludernik, M. (1996). *Towards a "natural" narratology*. London: Routledge.

Folkins, C. H., & Sime, W. E. (1981). Physical fitness training and mental health. *The American Psychologist, 36*, 373–389. doi:10.1037/0003-066X.36.4.373

Foreman, J., Gee, P., Herz, J., Hinrichs, R., Prensky, M., & Sawyer, B. (2004). Game based learning: How to delight and instruct in the 21st century. *EDUCAUSE Review, 39*(5), 50–66.

Forssell, K. (2008). Girls, games, and getting interested in technology. In K. McFerrin, et al. (Eds.), *Proceedings of Society for Information Technology and Teacher Education International Conference 2008* (pp. 991-996). Chesapeake, VA: American Association of Computer Education.

Foster, A. (2008). Games and motivation to learn science: Personal identity, applicability, relevance and meaningfulness. *Journal of Interactive Learning Research, 19*(4), 597–614.

Fransella, F. (1995). *George Kelly*. London: SAGE Publications.

Frasca, G. (2001) Ephemeral games: Is it barbaric to design videogames after Auschwitz? In M. Eskelinen & R. Koskimaa (Eds.), *Cybertext yearbook 2000* (pp. 172–182). Jyväskylä, Finland: University of Jyväskylä. Retrieved August 20, 2009, from http://cybertext.hum.jyu.fi

Frasca, G. (2003). Simulation versus narrative: Introduction to ludology. In Wolf, M. J. P., & Perron, B. (Eds.), *The video game theory reader*. New York: Routledge.

Frasca, G. (2004). Video games of the oppressed: critical thinking, education, tolerance and other trivial issues. In Harrington, P., & Wardrip-Fruin, N. (Eds.), *First person: New media as story, performance, and game*. Cambridge, MA: The MIT Press.

Freedman, A. (1996). *ReACTivating genre: ReGENERating discourse theory, research and pedagogy*. Keynote address presented at the European Writing Conferences, Barcelona, Spain.

Freire, P. (1994). *Pedagogy of hope*. New York: Continuum.

Freire, P. (2000). *Pedagogy of the oppressed*. New York: Continuum.

Frensch, P. A., & Funke, J. (1995). *Complex problem solving: The European perspective*. Mahwah, NJ: Lawrence Erlbaum Associates.

Frensch, P. A., & Funke, J. (1995). Definitions, traditions, and a general framework for understanding complex problem solving. In Frensch, P. A., & Funke, J. (Eds.), *Complex problem solving: The European perspective* (pp. 3–25). Hillsdale, NJ: Erlbaum.

Fromme, J. (2003). Computer games as a part of children's culture. *Game Studies, 3*(1). Retrieved from http://www.gamestudies.org/0301/fromme/

Fullan, M. (2004). Core concepts. *Learning to lead change: Building system capacity*. Toronto, Canada: Change Forces. Retrieved July 16, 2009, from http://www.michaelfullan.ca/Articles_04/CoreConcepts.pdf

Funk, J. B., & Buchman, D. D. (1996). Playing violent video and computer games and adolescent self-concept. *The Journal of Communication*, *46*(2), 19. doi:10.1111/j.1460-2466.1996.tb01472.x

Funk, J. B., Flores, G., Buchman, D. D., & Germann, J. N. (1999). Rating electronic games: Violence is in the eye of the beholder. *Youth & Society*, *30*(3), 283–312. doi:10.1177/0044118X99030003002

Furner, J. (1995). *Planningfor interdisciplinary instruction: A literature review.* Paper presented at the Annual Meeting on Effective Classroom Teaching, Tuscaloosa, AL.

Gadamer, H. G. (1979). The problem of historical consciousness. In Rabinow, P., & Sullivan, W. M. (Eds.), *Interpretive social science: A reader* (pp. 103–162). Berkeley, CA: University of California Press.

Gadamer, H.-G. (1986). *The relevance of beauty.* Cambridge, UK: Cambridge University Press.

Gagné, R. M., Wager, W. W., Golas, K. C., & Keller, J. M. (2005). *Principles of instructional design* (5th ed.). Belmont, CA: Wadsworth/Thomson Learning.

Galloway, A. R. (2004). *Protocol: How control exists after decentralization.* Cambridge, MA: MIT Press.

Galloway, A. R. (2006). *Gaming: Essays on algorithmic culture.* Minneapolis, MN: University of Minnesota Press.

Galloway, A. R., & Thacker, E. (2007). *The exploit: A theory of networks.* Minneapolis: University of Minnesota Press.

Gao, T., & Lehman, J. D. (2003). The effects of different levels of interaction on the achievement and motivation perceptions of college students in a web-based learning environment. *Journal of Interactive Learning Research*, *14*(4), 367–386.

Gardner, H. (1999). *The disciplined mind: What all students should understand.* New York: Simon & Schuster.

Gardner, J. E., Wissick, C. A., Schweder, W., & Canter, L. S. (2003). Enhancing interdisciplinary instruction in general and special education: Thematic units and technology. *Remedial and Special Education*, *24*, 161–172. doi:10.1177/07419325030240030501

Garfinkel, H. (1967). *Studies in Ethnomethodology.* Malden, MA: Blackwell Publishing.

Garner, R., Alexander, P. A., Gillingham, M. G., Kulikowich, J. M., & Brown, R. (1991). Interest and learning form text. *American Educational Research Journal*, *28*, 643–659.

Garner, R., Gillingham, M. G., & White, C. S. (1989). Effects of seductive details on macroprocessing and microprocessing in adults and children. *Cognition and Instruction*, *6*(1), 41–57. doi:10.1207/s1532690xci0601_2

Garrelts, N. (Ed.). (2006). *The meaning and culture of Grand Theft Auto.* Jefferson, NC: McFarland.

Garrelts, N. C. (2003). *The official strategy guide for video game studies: A grammar and rhetoric of video games.* Unpublished doctoral dissertation, Michigan State University, East Lansing, MI.

Garris, R., Ahlers, R., & Driskell, J. E. (2002). Games, motivation, and learning: A research and practice model. *Simulation & Gaming*, *33*(4), 441–467. doi:10.1177/1046878102238607

Gaydos, M., & Squire, K. (in press). Citizen Science: Designing a game for the 21st century. In Van Eck, R. (Ed.), *Interdisciplinary models and tools for serious games: Emerging concepts and future directions.* Hershey, PA: IGI Global.

Geary, D. (2002). Principles of evolutionary educational psychology. *Learning and Individual Differences*, *12*, 317–345. doi:10.1016/S1041-6080(02)00046-8

Geary, D. (2008). An evolutionarily informed education science. *Educational Psychologist*, *43*, 179–195. doi:10.1080/00461520802392133

Geary, D. (2008). Whither evolutionary educational psychology? *Educational Psychologist*, *43*, 217–226. doi:10.1080/00461520802392240

Gee, J. (2004). *Situated Language and Learning: A Critique of Traditional Schooling*. London: Routledge.

Gee, J. (2005). *Why video games are good for your soul: Pleasure and learning*. Melbourne, Australia: Common Ground Publishing.

Gee, J. (2007). *What video games have to teach us about learning and literacy* (2nd ed.). Palgrave, UK: Macmillan.

Gee, J. P. (2001). Learning by design: Good video games as learning machines. *E-learning, 2*(1).

Gee, J. P. (2007). Games and learning: Issues, perils and potentials. In Gee, J. P. (Ed.), *Good video games and good learning: Collected essays on video games, learning and literacy* (pp. 129–174). New York: Palgrave/Macmillan.

Gee, J. P. (2007). Learning and Games. In Salen, K. (Ed.), *The Ecology of games: Connecting youth, games, and learning* (pp. 21–40). Cambridge: MIT Press.

Gee, J. P. (2008). Video games and embodiment. *Games and Culture, 3*(3–4), 253–263. doi:10.1177/1555412008317309

Geisler, C., Bazerman, C., Doheny-Farina, S., Gurak, L., Haas, C., & Johnson-Eilola, J. (2001). IText: Future directions for research on the relationship between information technology and writing. *Journal of Business and Technical Communication, 15*(3), 269–308. doi:10.1177/105065190101500302

Genette, G. (1980). *Narrative discourse. An essay in method*. Ithaca, NY: Cornell University Press.

Gergen, K. (1991). *The saturated self*. New York: Basic Books.

Gergen, K. (1999). Beyond the self-society antimony. *Journal of Constructivist Psychology, 12*, 173–178. doi:10.1080/107205399266172

Gibson, J. (1977). The theory of affordances. In Shaw, R., & Bransford, J. (Eds.), *Perceiving, acting, and knowing*. Hillsdale, NJ: Lawrence Erlbaum Associates.

Gibson, J. (1979). *The ecological approach to visual perception*. New Jersey, USA: Lawrence Erlbaum Associates.

Giddens, A. (1979). *Central problems in social theory: Action, structure and contradiction in social analysis*. London, UK: Macmillan.

Giddens, A. (1984). *The constitution of society: Outline of the theory of structuration*. Cambridge, MA: Polity Press.

Giddens, A. (1991). *Modernity and self identity: Self & society in the late modern age*. Stanford, CA: Stanford University Press.

Giordano, A. (1997). Narco News Publishes "The medium is the middleman: For a revolution against media." Retrieved July 15, 2009, from http://www.narconews.com/themedium1.html

Giroux, H. (1983). *Theory and resistance in education: A pedagogy for the opposition*. South Hadley, MA: Bergin and Garvey Publishers.

Glaser, B., & Strauss, A. (1967). *Discovery of grounded theory: Strategies for qualitative research*. Piscataway, NJ: Transaction Publishers.

Glassner, A. (2004). *Interactive storytelling: Techniques for 21st century fiction*. Natick, MA: A.K. Perers.

Goffman, E. (1974). *Frame analysis: An essay on the organization of experience*. Cambridge, MA: Harvard University Press.

Good, T. L., & Brophy, J. E. (2000). *Teachers expectations: Looking in classrooms* (8th ed.). New York: Longman.

Goodwin, C. (2000). Action and embodiment with situated human interaction. *Journal of Pragmatics, 32*, 1489–1522. doi:10.1016/S0378-2166(99)00096-X

Goody, J. (1986). *The logic of writing and the organization of society*. Cambridge, UK: Cambridge University Press.

Graetz, K. A. (1995). Experimental gaming made simple: A review of social dilemmas. *Contemporary Psychology: A Journal of Reviews, 40*, 309–310.

Graner Ray, S. (2004). *Gender inclusive game design: Expanding the market.* Hingham, UK: Charles River Media.

Green, C. S., & Bavelier, D. (2003). Action video game modifies visual selective attention. *Nature, 423*, 534–537. doi:10.1038/nature01647

Greene, B. A., Miller, R. B., Crowson, H. M., Duke, B. L., & Akey, C. L. (2004). Relations among student perceptions of classroom structures, perceived ability, achievement goals, and cognitive engagement and achievement in high school language arts. *Contemporary Educational Psychology, 29*, 462–482. doi:10.1016/j.cedpsych.2004.01.006

Greenfield, P. M. (1994). Video games as cultural artifacts. *Journal of Applied Developmental Psychology, 15*, 3–12. doi:10.1016/0193-3973(94)90003-5

Greenfield, P., & Lave, J. (1982). Cognitive aspects of informal education. In D.A. Wagner and H. W. Stevenson (Eds.) Cultural perspectives on child development (pp. 181-207). San Franscisco: W.H. Freemen and Company.

Gregersen, A., & Grodal, T. (2009). Embodiment and interface. In Perron, B., & Wolf, M. J. P. (Eds.), *The video game theory reader* (pp. 65–83). New York: Routledge.

Grice, H. P. (1975). Logic in conversation. In P. Cole & J. Morgan (Eds.), Syntax and semantics: Vol. 3 speech acts (pp. 41–58). New York: Academic Press.

Grodal, T. (2000). Video games and the pleasure of control. In Zillman, D., & Vorderer, P. (Eds.), *Media entertainment: The psychology of its appeal* (pp. 197–213). London: Erlbaum.

Gros, B. (2003, July). The impact of digital games in education. *First Monday.* Retrieved from http://www.firstmonday.dk/issues/issue8_7/xyzgros/

Guberman, S. R., & Saxe, G. B. (2000). Mathematical problems and goals in children's play of an educational game. *Mind, Culture, and Activity, 7*(3), 201–216. doi:10.1207/S15327884MCA0703_08

Gunter, G., Kenny, R., & Vick, E. (2006). *A case for a formal design paradigm for serious games.* Paper presented at the 2006 International Digital Media Association Conference (iDMAa and IMS) Annual Conference, Oxford, OH.

Habgood, M. P. J., Ainsworth, S. E., & Benford, S. (2005). Endogenous fantasy and learning in digital games. *Simulation & Gaming, 36*(4), 483–498. doi:10.1177/1046878105282276

Hackbarth, S. (2001). Changes in primary students' computer literacy as a function of classroom use and gender. *TechTrends, 45*(4), 19–27. doi:10.1007/BF02784821

Hahne, A. K., Benndorf, R., Frey, P., & Herzig, S. (2005). Attitude towards computer-based learning: Determinants as revealed by a controlled interventional study. *Medical Education, 39*, 935–943. doi:10.1111/j.1365-2929.2005.02249.x

Halverson, R. (2005). What can K-12 school leaders learn from video games and gaming? *Innovate, 1*(6). Retrieved from http://www.innovateonline.info

Hämäläinen, R., Oksanen, K., & Häkkinen, P. (2008). Designing and analysing collaboration in a scripted game for vocational education. *Computers in Human Behavior, 24*, 2496–2506. doi:10.1016/j.chb.2008.03.010

Hanks, W. F. (1996). *Language and communicative practices.* Boulder, CO: Westview Press.

Hannafin, M. J., & Land, S. M. (1997). The foundations and assumptions of technology-enhanced, student-centered learning environments. *Instructional Science, 25*, 167–202. doi:10.1023/A:1002997414652

Harel, I., & Papert, S. (1990). Software design as a learning environment. *Interactive Learning Environments, 1*(1), 1–32. doi:10.1080/1049482900010102

Hargittai, E., & Shafer, S. (2006). Differences in actual and perceived online skills: The role of gender. *Social Science Quarterly, 87*(2), 432–448. doi:10.1111/j.1540-6237.2006.00389.x

Harrison, K., & Bond, B. (2007). Gaming magazines and the drive for muscularity in preadolescent boys: a longitudinal examination. *Body Image*, *4*(3), 269–277. doi:10.1016/j.bodyim.2007.03.003

Hartmann, T., & Klimmt, C. (2006). Gender and computer games: Exploring females' dislikes. *Journal of Computer-Mediated Communication*, *11*(4). Retrieved from http://jcmc.indiana.edu/vol11/issue4/hartmann.html. doi:10.1111/j.1083-6101.2006.00301.x

Hartmann, T., & Klimmt, C. (2006). The influence of personality factors on computer game choice. In Vorderer, P., & Bryant, J. (Eds.), *Playing video games: Motives, responses, and consequences* (pp. 115–132). New York: Routledge.

Hassan, I. (1992). Pluralism in postmodern perspective. In Jencks, C. (Ed.), *The post-modern reader*. London: Academy Editions.

Havelock, E. A. (1986). *The muse learns to write*. New Haven, CT: Yale.

Hayduk, L. A., & Glaser, D. N. (2000). Jiving the four-step, waltzing around factor analysis, and other serious fun. *Structural Equation Modeling*, *7*(1), 1–35. doi:10.1207/S15328007SEM0701_01

Hayes, E. (2005). Women, video gaming & learning: Beyond stereotypes. *TechTrends*, *49*(5), 23–28. doi:10.1007/BF02763686

Hayles, N. K. (2004). Metaphoric networks in lexia to perplexia. In Wardrip-Fruin, N., & Harrigan, P. (Eds.), *First person: New media as story, performance, and game*. Cambridge, London: MIT Press.

Hays, R. T. (2005). *The effectiveness of instructional games: A literature review and discussion.* Naval Air Warfare Center Training Systems Division (No 2005-004). Retrieved from http://stnet.dtie.mil/oai/

Heeter, C. (2008). Play styles and learning. In Ferding, R. (Ed.), *Handbook of research on effective electronic gaming in education* (pp. 826–846). Hershey, PA: IGI Global.

Heeter, C., Edigio, R., Mishra, P., Winn, B., & Winn, J. (2009). Alien games: Do girls prefer games designed by girls? *Games and Culture*, *4*(1), 74–100. doi:10.1177/1555412008325481

Hegarty, M. (1991). Knowledge and processes in mechanical problem solving. In Sternberg, R. J., & Frensch, P. A. (Eds.), *Complex problem solving: Principles and mechanisms* (pp. 253–185). Hillsdale, NJ: Erlbaum.

Helmrich, E., & Neiburger, E. (2007). Video games as a service: Three years later. *VOYA*, *30*(2), 113–115.

Heritage, J. (1987). Ethnomethodology. In Giddens, A., & Turner, J. (Eds.), *Social theory today* (pp. 224–272). Cambridge, UK: Tolety, Inc.

Herman, D. (2003). Stories as a toll for thinking. In Herman, D. (Ed.), *Narrative theory and the cognitive sciences*. Stanford, CA: CSLI Publications.

Herman, D. (2004). Toward a transmedial narratology. In Ryan, M.-L. (Ed.), *Narrative across media: The languages of storytelling* (pp. 47–75). Lincoln: University of Nebraska Press.

Hickey, D. T. (1997). Motivation and contemporary socio-constructivist instructional perspectives. *Educational Psychologist*, *32*(3), 175–193. doi:10.1207/s15326985ep3203_3

Hidi, S. (1990). Interest and its contribution as a mental resource for learning. *Review of Educational Research*, *60*, 549–571.

Hidi, S., & Renninger, K. N. (2006). The four model of interest development. *Educational Psychologist*, *41*(2), 111–127. doi:10.1207/s15326985ep4102_4

Hill, J. O., & Peters, J. C. (1998). Environmental contributions to the obesity epidemic. *Science*, *280*, 1371–1374. doi:10.1126/science.280.5368.1371

Holland, W., Jenkins, H., & Squire, K. (2003). Theory by design. In Perron, B., & Wolf, M. (Eds.), *Video game theory*. New York: Routledge.

Holmes, D. S. (1987). The influence of meditation versus rest on physiological arousal: A second examination. In West, M. A. (Ed.), *The psychology of meditation* (pp. 81–103). Oxford: Clarendon Press.

Holt, C. L., Lee, C., & Wright, K. (2008). A spiritually based approach to breast cancer awareness: Cognitive response analysis of communication effectiveness. *Health Communication*, *23*(1), 13–22. doi:10.1080/10410230701626919

Holyoak, K. J., & Thagard, P. (1997). The analogical mind. *The American Psychologist*, *52*(1), 35–44. doi:10.1037/0003-066X.52.1.35

Hooper, G., Fitzpatrick, G., & Weal, M. J. (2008). Does it matter who is holding the PDA in a mobile learning experience? In *JADÍS International Conference of e-Learning,* April 2008, Algarve, Portugal.

Hopkins, T. J. (1971). *The Hindu religious tradition.* Belmont: Wadsworth Publishing Company.

Horwitz, P., & Christie, M. A. (2000). Computer-based manipulatives for teaching scientific reasoning: An example. In Jacobson, M. J., & Kozma, R. B. (Eds.), *Learning the sciences of the 21st century: Research, design, and implementing advanced technology learning environments* (pp. 163–191). Mahwah, NJ: Lawrence Erlbaum Associates.

Houdé, O., & Tzourio-Mazoyer, N. (2003). Neural foundations of logical and mathematical cognition. *Nature Reviews. Neuroscience*, *4*, 507–514. doi:10.1038/nrn1117

Huitema, B. E. (1980). *The analysis of covariance and alternatives.* New York: Wiley.

Huizinga, J. (1953). *Homo ludens, a study of the play-element in culture.* Boston: Beacon Press.

Hung, W. (2006). *Application of 3C3R PBL problem design model: A 9-step design process.* Paper presented at the annual meeting of the American Educational Research Association, April 7 – 11, San Francisco.

Hung, W. (2006). The 3C3R model: A conceptual framework for designing problems in PBL. *Interdisciplinary Journal of Problem-based Learning*, *1*(1), 55–77.

Hutchins, E. (1995). *Cognition in the wild.* Cambridge, MA: MIT Press.

International Game Development Association. (2008). *2008–2009 casual games white paper.* Mt. Royal, NJ: International Game Development Association. Retrieved from http://www.igda.org/casual/IGDA_Casual_Games_White_Paper_2008.pdf

Iuppa, N., & Borst, T. (2007). *Story and simulations for serious games: Tales from the trenches.* Oxford, UK: Elsevier.

Jansz, J. (2005). The emotional appeal of violent video games for adolescent males. *Communication Theory*, *15*, 219–241. doi:10.1111/j.1468-2885.2005.tb00334.x

Jansz, J., Van Zoonen, L., & Vosmeer, M. (2006). *Videogames as technologies of gender: analyzing Final Fantasy forums.* Paper presented at the International Communications Association conference, Dresden, June.

Järvinen, A. (2009). Understanding video games as emotional experiences. In Perron, B., & Wolf, M. J. P. (Eds.), *The video game theory reader 2* (pp. 85–108). New York: Routledge.

Jefferson, G. (1984). Transcript notation. In Heritage, J. (Ed.), *Structures of social interaction.* New York: Cambridge University Press.

Jenkins, H. (2004). Game design as narrative architecture. In Wardrip-Fruin, N., & Harrigan, P. (Eds.), *First person: New media as story, performance and game* (pp. 118–130). Cambridge, MA: The MIT Press.

Jenkins, H. (2004). The cultural logic of media convergence. *International Journal of Cultural Studies*, *7*(1), 33–43. doi:10.1177/1367877904040603

Jenkins, H. (2006). *Convergence culture: Where old and new media collide.* New York: University of New York Press.

Jennings, J. R. (1987). Editorial policy on analyses of variance with repeated measures. *Psychophysiology*, *24*, 474–475. doi:10.1111/j.1469-8986.1987.tb00320.x

Jin, P. (1992). Toward a reconceptualization of the law of initial value. *Psychological Bulletin*, *111*(1), 176–184. doi:10.1037/0033-2909.111.1.176

John, T. (2009, July 13). Ridiculous life lessons from new girl games. *Wired*. Retrieved from http://www.wired.com/gamelife/2009/07/games-for-tweens/

Johnson, W. L., Vilhjalmson, H., & Marsella, S. (2005). Serious games for language learning: How much game, how much AI? In C. K. Looi, G. McCalla, B. Bredeweg & J. Breuker (Eds.), Artificial intelligence in education (pp. 306-313). Amsterdam: IOS Press.

Jonassen, D. H. (1997). Instructional design models for well-structured and ill-structured problem solving learning outcomes. *ETR&D*, *45*(1), 65–94. doi:10.1007/BF02299613

Jonassen, D. H. (1999). Designing constructivist learning environments. In C.M. Reigeluth (Ed.), Instructional design theories and model, Vol. 2: A new paradigm of instructional technology (pp. 215–239). Mahwah, NJ: Lawrence Erlbaum Associates.

Jonassen, D. H. (2000). Toward a design theory of problem solving. *ETR&D*, *48*(4), 63–85. doi:10.1007/BF02300500

Jonassen, D. H. (2002). Integration of problem solving into instructional design. In R. A. Reiser & J. V. Dempsey (Eds.), Trends and issues in instructional design & technology 107-120). Upper Saddle River, NJ: Merrill Prentice Hall.

Jonassen, D. H. (2003). Designing research-based instruction for story problems. *Educational Psychology Review*, *15*(3), 267–296. doi:10.1023/A:1024648217919

Jonassen, D. H., & Hung, W. (2006). Learning to troubleshoot: A new theory based design architecture. *Educational Psychology Review*, *18*(1), 77–114. doi:10.1007/s10648-006-9001-8

Jonassen, D. H., & Hung, W. (2008). All problems are not equal: Implications for PBL. *Interdisciplinary Journal of Problem-Based Learning*, *2*(2), 6–28.

Jones, C. (2007). Enterprise education: The frustration of a pure contest. *Education + Training*, *48*, 596–604. doi:10.1108/00400910710834030

Jones, S. (2003). *Let the games begin: Gaming technology and entertainment among college students*. Washington, DC: Pew Internet & American Life Project.

Jones, S. E. (2008). *The meaning of video games*. New York: Routledge.

Jordan, B., & Henderson, A. (1995). Interaction analysis: Foundations and practice. *Journal of the Learning Sciences*, *4*(1), 39–103. doi:10.1207/s15327809jls0401_2

Jöreskog, K. G. (1993). Testing structural equation models. In Bollen, K. A., & Long, J. S. (Eds.), *Testing structural equation models* (pp. 294–316). Newbury Park, CA: Sage.

Jöreskog, K. G., & Sörbom, D. (1993). *LISREL 8: Structural equation modeling with the SIMPLIS command language*. Chicago: Scientific Software International.

Joseph, D., & Kinzie, M. (2005, October). *Boys' and girls' game play preferences: Survey results*. Paper presented at the annual meeting of the Serious Games Summit, Washington, DC.

Juul, J. (2001). Games telling stories? A brief note on games and narratives. *Game Studies, The International Journal of Computer Game Research*, *1*(1). Retrieved June 2007, from http://www.gamestudies.org/0101/juul-gts/

Juul, J. (2005). *Half-real: Video games between real rules and fictional worlds*. Cambridge, MA: MIT Press.

Juul, J. (2009). The fear of failing? The many meanings of difficulty in video games. In Perron, B., & Wolf, M. J. P. (Eds.), *The video game theory reader 2* (pp. 237–252). New York: Routledge.

Kafai, Y. (1996). Video game design by girls and boys: Variability and consistency of gender differences. In Cassell, J., & Henkins, H. (Eds.), *From Barbie to Mortal Kombat: Gender and computer games* (pp. 90–114). Cambridge, MA: MIT.

Kahne, J., Middaugh, E., & Evans, C. (2008). *The civic potential of video games*. Boston: MacArthur Foundation.

Kaiser Family Foundation. (2005). *Generation M: Media in the lives of eight to eighteen year olds*. Menlo Park, CA: Kaiser Family Foundation.

Kankaanranta, M., & Neittaanmäki, P. (Eds.). (2008). *Design and use of serious games*. Dordrecht: Springer.

Kaptelinin, V., & Nardi, B. (2006). *Acting with technology: Activity theory and interaction design*. Cambridge, MA: MIT Press.

Karakus, T., Inal, Y., & Cagiltay, K. (2008). A descriptive study of Turkish high school students' game-playing characteristics and their considerations concerning the effects of games. *Computers in Human Behavior*, *24*, 2520–2529. doi:10.1016/j.chb.2008.03.011

Kay, M. (1997). On playing in the group. *Group Analysis*, *30*, 173–186. doi:10.1177/0533316497302003

Kebritchi, M. (2008). *Effects of a computer game on mathematics achievement and class motivation: An experimental study*. Doctoral dissertation, University of Central Florida, Orlando.

Kebritchi, M., & Hirumi, A. (2008). Examining the pedagogical foundations of modern educational computer games. *Computers & Education*, *51*, 1729–1743. doi:10.1016/j.compedu.2008.05.004

Keller, J. M. (1987). Motivational design and multimedia: Beyond the novelty effect. *Strategic Human Resource Development Review*, *1*(1), 188–203.

Keller, J. M. (1987). Strategies for stimulating the motivation to learn. *Performance and Instruction*, *26*(8), 1–7. doi:10.1002/pfi.4160260802

Keller, J. M., & Suzuki, K. (2004). Learner motivation and e-learning design: A multinationally validated process. *Journal of Educational Media*, *29*(3), 229–239.

Kelly, D. (2008). Adaptive versus learner control in a multiple intelligence learning environment. *Journal of Educational Multimedia and Hypermedia*, *17*(3), 307–336.

Kelman, H. C. (1958). Compliance, identification and internalization: Three processes of attitude change. *The Journal of Conflict Resolution*, *2*, 51–60. doi:10.1177/002200275800200106

Kelman, H. C., & Hovland, C. I. (1953). Reinstatement of the communicator in delayed measurement of opinion change. *Journal of Abnormal and Social Psychology*, *48*(3), 327–335. doi:10.1037/h0061861

Kenney, B. (2008, January). The power of place. *School Library Journal*, *54*(1), 11.

Kerman, J. (2004, June 24). That old labyrinth song. *The New York Review of Books*, *LI*(11).

Ketelhut, D. J. (2007). The impact of student self-efficacy on scientific inquiry skills: An exploratory investigation in river city, a multi-user virtual environment. *Journal of Science Education and Technology*, *16*, 99–111. doi:10.1007/s10956-006-9038-y

Kiili, K. (2005). Digital game-based learning: Towards an experiential gaming model. *The Internet and Higher Education*, *8*(1), 13–24. doi:10.1016/j.iheduc.2004.12.001

Kiili, K. (2007). Foundation for problem-based gaming. *British Journal of Educational Technology*, *38*(3), 394–404. doi:10.1111/j.1467-8535.2007.00704.x

Killingley, D. (2004). Kama. In Mittal, S., & Thursby, G. R. (Eds.), *The Hindu world* (pp. 264–287). New York: Routledge.

Kim, Y., & Baylor, A., & PALS Group. (2006). Pedagogical agents as learning companions: The role of agent competency and type of interaction. *Educational Technology Research and Development*, *54*(3), 223–243. doi:10.1007/s11423-006-8805-z

King, G., & Krzywinska, T. (2002). Introduction: Cinema/videogames/interfaces. In King, G., & Krzywinska, T. (Eds.), *ScreenPlay: Cinema/videogames/interfaces* (pp. 1–32). London: Wallflower Press.

Kirova, A. (2006). A game-playing approach to interviewing children about loneliness: Negotiating meaning, distributing power, and establishing trust. *The Alberta Journal of Educational Research*, *52*(3), 127–147.

Kirriemuir, J., & McFarlane, A. (2004). Literature review in games and learning. *FutureLab*. Retrieved February 2,

2007 from http://www.futurelab.org.uk/download/pdfs/research/lit_reviews/Games_Review1.pdf

Kisiel, T. (1985). The happening of tradition: The hermeneutics of Gadamer and Heidegger. In Hollinger, R. (Ed.), *Hermeneutics and praxis* (pp. 3–31). Notre Dame, IN: University of Notre Dame Press.

Klassen, R. M. (2007). Using predictions to learn about the self-efficacy of early adolescents. *Contemporary Educational Psychology, 32*, 173–187. doi:10.1016/j.cedpsych.2006.10.001

Kloetzel, J., & Hiltebeitel, A. (2004). Kala. In Mittal, S., & Thursby, G. R. (Eds.), *The Hindu world* (pp. 553–586). New York: Routledge.

Klug, G. C., & Schell, J. (2006). Why people play: An industry perspective. In Vorderer, P., & Bryant, J. (Eds.), *Playing video games: Motives, responses, and consequences* (pp. 91–100). New York: Routledge.

Kolb, A. Y., & Kolb, D. A. (2009). The learning way: Meta-cognitive aspects of experiential learning. *Simulation & Gaming, 40*(3), 297–327. doi:10.1177/1046878108325713

Kolb, A., & Kolb, D. (2005). Learning styles and learning spaces. *Academy of Management Learning & Education, 4*(2), 193–212.

Kolic-Vehovec, S., Roncevic, B., & Bajsanski, I. (2008). Motivational components of self-regulated learning and reading strategy use in university students: The role of goal orientation patterns. *Learning and Individual Differences, 18*, 108–113. doi:10.1016/j.lindif.2007.07.005

Kolodner, J. L. (1997). Educational implications of analogy: A view from case-based reasoning. *The American Psychologist, 52*(1), 57–66. doi:10.1037/0003-066X.52.1.57

Kolsto, S. D. (2001). *Scientific literacy for citizenship: Tools for dealing with the science dimension of controversial socioscientific issue* (Vol. 8). Retrieved from http://dx.doi.org/10.1002/sce.101.

Koschmann, T., Stahl, G., & Zemel, A. (2005). The video analyst's manifesto (or the Implications of Garfinkel's policies for studying practice within design-based research. In Derry, S., & Pea, R. (Eds.), *Video research in the learning sciences*. Mahwah, NJ: Lawrence Erlbaum Associates.

Koskimaa, R. (2000). *Digital literature: From text to hypertext and beyond*. Jyväskylä, Finland: University of Jyväskylä.

Koster, R. (2005). *A theory of fun for game design*. Scottsdale, AZ: Paraglyph Press.

Krapp, A. (2002). Structural and dynamic aspects of interest development: Theoretical considerations from an ontogenetic perspective. *Learning and Instruction, 12*, 383–409. doi:10.1016/S0959-4752(01)00011-1

Krawczyk, M., & Novak, J. (2006). *Game development essentials: Game story and character development*. Albany, NY: Thomson Delmar Learning.

Krotoski, A. (2004). *Chicks and joysticks: An exploration of women and gaming*. London: Entertainment and Leisure Software Publishers. Retrieved from http://www.futurelab.org.uk/resources/documents/lit_reviews/Games_Review.pdf

Kuhn, D. (2005). *Education for thinking*. Cambridge, MA: Harvard University Press.

Lainema, T. (2009). Perspective making: Constructivism as a meaning making structure for simulation gaming. *Simulation & Gaming, 40*, 48–67. doi:10.1177/1046878107308074

Lanigan, R. L. (1988). *Phenomenology of communication: Merleau-Ponty's thematics in communicology and semiology*. Pittsburgh: Duquesne University Press.

Lanigan, R. L. (1994). Capta versus data: Method and evidence in communicology. *Human Studies, 17*, 109–130. doi:10.1007/BF01322769

Lanigan, R. L. (2000). The self in semiotic phenomenology: Consciousness as the conjunction of perception and expression in the science of communicology. *American Journal of Semiotics, 15–16*, 91–111.

Larkin, J. H., & Simon, H. A. (1987). Why a diagram is (sometimes) worth ten thousand words. *Cognitive Science, 11*, 65–99. doi:10.1016/S0364-0213(87)80026-5

Lather, P. (1998). Critical pedagogy and its complicities: A praxis of stuck places. *Educational Theory, 48*(4), 487–498. doi:10.1111/j.1741-5446.1998.00487.x

Lave, J., & Wenger, E. (1991). *Situated learning: Legitimate peripheral participation.* Cambridge, UK: Cambridge University Press.

Lavie, N. (2005). Distracted and confused?: Selective attention under load. *Trends in Cognitive Sciences, 9*(2), 75–82. doi:10.1016/j.tics.2004.12.004

Lee, F. K., Sheldon, K. M., & Turban, D. B. (2003). Personality and the goal-striving process: The influence of achievement foal patterns, goal level, and mental focus on performance and enjoyment. *The Journal of Applied Psychology, 88*(2), 256–265. doi:10.1037/0021-9010.88.2.256

Lee, J., & Hoadley, C. (2007). Leveraging identity to make learning fun: Possible selves and experiential learning in massively multiplayer online games (MMOGs). *Innovate, 36*(6). Retrieved from http://www.innovateonline.info/index.php?view=article&ide=348&action=article

Lee, J., & Young, C. (2008). Middle level educators and online social gaming. In K. McFerrin, et al. (Eds.), *Proceedings of Society for Information Technology and Teacher Education International Conference 2008* (pp. 1726–1732). Chesapeake, VA: American Association of Computer Education.

Lee, V. E., Croninger, R. G., & Smith, J. B. (1997). Coursetaking, equity, and mathematics learning: Testing the constrained curriculum hypothesis in U.S. secondary schools. *Educational Evaluation and Policy Analysis, 19*, 99–122.

Lee, Y. B., & Lehman, J. D. (1993). Instructional cueing in hypermedia: A study with active and passive learners. *Journal of Educational Multimedia and Hypermedia, 2*(10), 25–37.

Lemmens, J. S., & Bushman, B. J. (2006). The appeal of violent video games to lower education aggressive adolescent boys from two countries. *Cyberpsychology & Behavior, 9*, 639–941. doi:10.1089/cpb.2006.9.638

Lemos, M. S. (1999). Students' goals and self-regulation in the classroom. *International Journal of Educational Research, 31*, 471–485. doi:10.1016/S0883-0355(99)00016-6

Lenhart, A., Kahne, J., Middaugh, E., Macgill, A. R., Evans, C., & Vitak, J. (2008). Teens' gaming experiences are diverse and include significant social interaction and civic engagement. *Pew Internet and American Life Project.* Retrieved January 15, 2009, from http://www.pewInternet.org/pdfs/PIP_Teens_Games_and_Civics_Report_FINAL.pdf

Leontiev, A. (1978). *Activity, consciousness, and personality* (Hall, M. J., Trans.). Englewood Cliffs, NJ: Prentice Hall.

Lepper, M. R., & Cordova, D. (1992). A desire to be taught: Instructional consequences of intrinsic motivation. *Motivation and Emotion, 16*(3), 187–208. doi:10.1007/BF00991651

Lepper, M. R., & Hodell, M. (1989). Intrinsic motivation in the classroom. In Ames, C., & Ames, R. (Eds.), *Research on motivation in education* (*Vol. 3*, pp. 73–105). New York: Academic Press.

Lepper, M. R., & Malone, T. W. (1987). Intrinsic motivation and instructional effectiveness in computer-based education. In Snow, R. E., & Farr, M. J. (Eds.), *Aptitude, learning, and instruction: III. Conative and affective process analyses* (pp. 255–296). Hillsdale, NJ: Erlbaum.

Lepper, M. R., Sethi, A. S., Dialdin, D., & Drake, M. (1996). Intrinsic and extrinsic motivation: Developmental trends and issues. In Luthar, S., Burack, J., Cichetti, D., & Weisz, J. (Eds.), *Developmental psychopathology: Perspectives on risk and disorder* (pp. 23–50). Cambridge, UK: Cambridge University Press.

Levine, J. (2006). Gaming and libraries. *Library Technology Reports, 42*(5).

Lewin, K. (1946). Action research and minority problems. *The Journal of Social Issues*, *2*, 34–46.

Lewin, K. (1951). Problems of research in social psychology. In Cartwright, D. (Ed.), *Field theory in social science: Selected theoretical papers* (pp. 155–169). New York: Harper & Brothers Publishers.

Lewis, M., Weber, R., & Bowman, N. D. (2008). "They may be pixels, but they're my pixels:" Developing a metric of character attachment in role-playing video games. *Cyberpsychology & Behavior*, *11*(4), 515–518. doi:10.1089/cpb.2007.0137

Lewis, M., Weber, R., & Bowman, N. D. (2008). They may be pixels, but they're my pixels: Developing a metric of character attachment in role-playing video games. *Cyberpsychology & Behavior*, *11*(4), 515–518. doi:10.1089/cpb.2007.0137

Leys, S. (1997). *The analects of Confucius*. New York: W. W. Norton.

Liedtka, J. M. (1998). Strategic thinking: Can it be taught. *Long Range Planning*, *31*(1), 120–129. doi:10.1016/S0024-6301(97)00098-8

Lim, C. P. (2008). Global citizenship education, school curriculum and games: Learning Mathematics, English and Science as a global citizen. *Computers & Education*, *51*, 1073–1093. doi:10.1016/j.compedu.2007.10.005

Lim, S., & Lee, J. R. (2007). Effects of coplaying on arousal and emotional responses in videogame play. Presentation at the annual International Communication Association conference, San Francisco.

Linn, M. C., & Burbules, N. C. (1991). Construction of knowledge and group learning. In Tobin, K. G. (Ed.), *The practice of constructivism in science education* (pp. 91–119). Washington, DC: AAAS Press.

Locke, E. A., & Latham, G. P. (2002). Building a practically useful theory of goal setting and task motivation: A 35-year odyssey. *The American Psychologist*, *57*(9), 705–717. doi:10.1037/0003-066X.57.9.705

Locke, J. (1968). The educational writings of John Locke: A critical Ed. with introduction and notes by James L. Axtell. London: Cambridge University Press.

Lodewyk, K. R., Winne, P. H., & Jamieson-Noel, D. L. (2009). Implications of task structure on self-regulating learning and achievement. *Educational Psychology*, *29*(1), 1–25. doi:10.1080/01443410802447023

Loertscher, D. (2000). *Taxonomies of the school library media program*. San Jose, CA: Hi Willow.

Logan, R. K. (1986). *The alphabet effect*. New York: Morrow.

Lord, F. M. (1967). A paradox in the interpretation of group comparison. *Psychological Bulletin*, *68*, 304–305. doi:10.1037/h0025105

Lord, F. M. (1969). Statistical adjustments when comparing preexisting groups. *Psychological Bulletin*, *72*, 336–337. doi:10.1037/h0028108

Lord, F. M. (1975). Lord's paradox. In Anderson, S. B., & Murphy, R. T. (Eds.), *Encyclopaedia of educational evaluation* (pp. 232–236). San Francisco, CA: Jossey-Bass.

Los Angeles Public Library. (2008). *Mission statement*. Los Angeles: Los Angeles Public Library. Retrieved from http://www.lapl.org/about/mission.html

Low, R., & Sweller, J. (2005). The modality principle in multimedia learning. In Mayer, R. E. (Ed.), *The Cambridge handbook of multimedia learning* (pp. 147–158). New York: Cambridge University Press.

Lowrie, T. (2005). Problem solving in technology rich contexts: Mathematics sense making in out-of-school environments. *The Journal of Mathematical Behavior*, *24*, 275–286. doi:10.1016/j.jmathb.2005.09.008

Loyens, S. M. M., Rikers, R. M. J. P., & Schmidt, H. G. (2007). The impact of students' conceptions of constructivist assumptions on academic achievement and dropout. *Studies in Higher Education*, *32*, 581–602. doi:10.1080/03075070701573765

Loyens, S. M., & Gijbels, D. (2008). Understanding the effects of constructivist learning environments: Introducing a multi-directional approach. *Instructional Science*, *36*, 351–357. doi:10.1007/s11251-008-9059-4

Lucas, K., & Sherry, J. (2004). Sex differences in video game play: A communication-based explanation. *Communication Research, 31*(5), 499–523. doi:10.1177/0093650204267930

Luyten, H., & Lens, W. (1981). The effect of earlier experience and reward contingencies on intrinsic motivation. *Motivation and Emotion, 5*, 25–36. doi:10.1007/BF00993659

Macgill, A. (2007). *Parent and teen Internet use*. Washington, DC: Pew Internet & American Life Project.

Malliet, S. (2006). An exploration of adolescents' perceptions of videogame realism. *Learning, Media and Technology, 31*(4), 377–394. doi:10.1080/17439880601021983

Malliet, S. (2007). *The challenge of video games to media effect theory.* Catholic University of Leuven, Leuven.

Malone, T. W. (1981). What makes computer games fun? *Byte, 6*(12), 258–277.

Malone, T. W. (1983). Guidelines for designing educational computer games. *Childhood Education, 59*(4), 241–247.

Malone, T. W., & Lepper, M. R. (1987). Making learning fun: A taxonomy of intrinsic motivations for learning. In Snow, R. E., & Farr, M. J. (Eds.), *Aptitude, learning and instruction: III. Conative and affective process analyses* (pp. 255–286). Hillsdale, NJ: Erlbaum.

Mandler, J. M. (1984). *Stories, scripts, and scenes: Aspects of schema theory.* Hillsdale, NJ: Lawrence Erlbaum Associates.

Martens, R. (2006). What about motivation? *PsycCRITIQUES, 51*(52), 11. doi:10.1037/a0005828

Maxwell, S. E., & Bray, J. H. (1986). Robustness of the quasi *F* statistic to violations of sphericity. *Psychological Bulletin, 5*, 149–165.

Maxwell, T. S. (1998). *The gods of Asia.* Delhi: Oxford University Press.

Mayer, R. E. (2005). Cognitive theory of multimedia learning. In Mayer, R. E. (Ed.), *The Cambridge Handbook of Multimedia Learning* (pp. 31–48). New York: Cambridge University Press.

Mayer, R. E. (2005). Introduction to multimedia learning. In Mayer, R. E. (Ed.), *The Cambridge handbook of multimedia learning* (pp. 1–16). New York: Cambridge University Press.

Mayer, R., Mautone, P., & Prothero, W. (2002). Pictorial aids for learning by doing in a multimedia geology simulation game. *Journal of Educational Psychology, 94*(1), 171–185. doi:10.1037/0022-0663.94.1.171

Mayo, M. (2009). Want to truly scale a learning program? Try gaming. *Kauffman Thoughtbook 2009*, Retrieved January 14, 2009, from http://blog.oheassociates.com/files/0/6/3/8/4/157742148360/Mayo_Thought_Book_9.pdf

McAllister, K. S. (2004). *Game work: Language, power, and computer game culture.* Tuscaloosa, AL: University of Alabama Press.

McCann, S. (2008, November 15). Gaming basics: Not just for boys anymore. *Library Journal.*

McCarthy, D., Curran, S., & Byron, S. (2005). *The complete guide to game development, art & design.* Cambridge, UK: Alastair Campbell.

McClurg, P., & Chaillé, C. (1987). Computer games: Environments for developing spatial cognition? *Journal of Educational Computing Research, 3*(1), 95–111.

McGrenere, J., & Ho, W. (2000). Affordances: Clarifying and evolving a concept. In *Proceedings of the annual meeting of the Graphics Interface 2000 conference* (pp. 179-186). Retrieved February 12, 2008 from http://www.graphicsinterface.org/proceedings/2000/177/

McGuire, W. J. (1985). Attitudes and attitude change. In Gardner, L., & Aronson, E. (Eds.), *Handbook of social psychology* (*Vol. 2*). New York: Random House.

McLaren, P. (1997). *Revolutionary multiculturalism: Pedagogies of dissent for the new millennium.* Boulder, CO: Westview Press Mountain Goat Software. (1998). *A visual introduction to Scrum.* Retrieved August 14, 2009, from www.mountaingoatsoftware.com/scrum-figures

McLeod, J. (1997). *Narrative and psychotherapy*. London: SAGE Publications.

Mead, G. H. (1934). *Mind, self, and society*. Chicago: Chicago University Press.

Means, T. B., Jonassen, D. H., & Dwyer, R. M. (1997). Enhancing relevance: embedded ARCS strategies vs. purpose. *Educational Technology Research and Development*, *45*(1), 5–18. doi:10.1007/BF02299610

MECC. (2004). *Math munchers* [PC CD-ROM]. San Francisco: The Learning Company.

Meeks, W. (Ed.). (1989). *The new revised standard version bible*. New York: HarperCollins Publishers.

Meredith, W. (1993). Measurement invariance, factor analysis and factorial invariance. *Psychometrika*, *58*(4), 525–543. doi:10.1007/BF02294825

Mezirow, J. (1990). Fostering critical reflection in adulthood. San Fancisco: Jossey-Bass.

Mezirow, J. (1991). *Transformative dimensions of adult learning*. San Francisco: Jossey-Bass.

Mezirow, J. (1997). Transformative learning: Theory to practice. In Cranton, P. (Ed.), *New directions for adult and continuing education: No. 74* (pp. 5–12). San Francisco: Jossey-Bass.

Mezirow, J. (1998). On critical reflection. *Adult Education Quarterly*, *48*(3), 185–198. doi:10.1177/074171369804800305

Mezirow, J. (2000). *Learning as transformation: Critical perspectives on a theory in progress*. San Francisco: Jossey-Bass.

Michael, D., & Chen, S. (2006). *Serious games: Games that educate, train, and inform*. Boston: Thomson Course Technology.

Midgley, C., Kaplan, A., & Middleton, M. (2001). Performance-approach goals: Good for what, for whom, under what circumstances, and at what cost? *Journal of Educational Psychology*, *93*(1), 77–86. doi:10.1037/0022-0663.93.1.77

Midgley, C., Maehr, M., Hicks, L., Roeser, R., Urdan, T., & Anderman, E. (1997). *Patterns of adaptive learning survey (PALS)*. Ann Arbor, MI: University of Michigan.

Mid-Hudson Library System. (2005). *Sample Public Library Mission Statements*. Retrieved from http://midhudson.org/department/member_information/missions.htm

Midway Games. (2004). *Mortal Kombat* [PC game]. USA: Midway Games.

Miller, C. R. (1984). Genre as social action. *The Quarterly Journal of Speech*, *70*, 151–167. doi:10.1080/00335638409383686

Miller, J. (1976). *Toward a new psychology of women*. Boston: Beacon Press.

Miller, J. D. (1998). The measurement of civic scientific literacy. *Public Understanding of Science (Bristol, England)*, *7*(3), 203–223. doi:10.1088/0963-6625/7/3/001

Miller, M. D., & Rainer, R. K. (1995). Assessing and improving the dimensionality of the computer anxiety scale. *Educational and Psychological Measurement*, *55*(4), 652–657. doi:10.1177/0013164495055004013

Milton Bradley. (1943). *Battleship* [Board game]. USA: Milton Bradley.

Mintzberg, H. (1994). *The rise and fall of strategic planning*. New York: The Free Press.

Mitgutsch, K. (2009). Passionate digital play-based learning: (Re)learning in computer games like *Shadow of the Colossus*. *Eludamos*, *3*(1), 9–22.

Mittal, S., & Thursby, G. R. (Eds.). (2004). *The Hindu world*. New York, London: Routledge Press.

Moran, D. (2000). *Introduction to phenomenology*. London, New York: Routledge.

Moreno, R. (2005). Multimedia learning with animated pedagogical agents. In Mayer, R. E. (Ed.), *The Cambridge Handbook of Multimedia Learning* (pp. 507–523). New York: Cambridge University Press.

Moreno, R., & Mayer, R. (2000). Engaging students in active learning: The case for personalised multimedia messages. *Journal of Educational Psychology, 92*(4), 724–733. doi:10.1037/0022-0663.92.4.724

Moreno, R., Mayer, R. E., Spires, H. A., & Lester, J. C. (2001). The case for social agency in computer-based multimedia learning: Do students learn more deeply when they interact with animated pedagogical agents? *Cognition and Instruction, 19*, 177–214. doi:10.1207/S1532690XCI1902_02

Moreno-Ger, P., & Burgos, D., Martinez-Ortiz, Sierra, J. S., & Fernández-Manjón, B. (2008). Educational game design for online education. *Computers in Human Behavior, 24*, 2530–2540. doi:10.1016/j.chb.2008.03.012

Mosler, H. J., & Martens, T. (2008). Designing environmental campaigns by using agent-based simulations: Strategies for changing environmental attitudes. *Journal of Environmental Management, 88*(4), 805–816. doi:10.1016/j.jenvman.2007.04.013

Moulthrop, S. (2005). After the last generation: Rethinking scholarship in the days of serious play. *Proceedings of the 6th Digital Arts & Culture Conference*. Copenhagen: IT University of Copenhagen.

mtvU. (2006). *Darfur Is Dying* [Online game]. Retrieved March 29, 2009, from http://www.darfurisdying.com

Muller, H. (2002). *Navigating the dilemmas of collegiate classroom discussion*. (Doctoral dissertation, University of Colorado at Boulder, 2002). Retrieved May 3, 2009, from Dissertations & Theses: A & I database. (Publication No. AAT 3057795).

Murphy, P. K., & Alexander, P. A. (2000). A motivated exploration of motivation terminology. *Contemporary Educational Psychology, 25*, 3–53. doi:10.1006/ceps.1999.1019

Murray, J. H. (1997). *Hamlet on the holodeck: The future of narrative in cyberspace*. Cambridge, MA: The MIT Press.

Myers, B. (2008). Minds at play. *American Libraries, 39*(5), 54–57.

Myers, D. (2003). *The nature of computer games: Play as semiosis*. New York: Peter Lang.

Myrtek, M., & Foerster, F. (1986). Rejoinder to Cleary's Comments on Myrtek and Foerster's 'The law of initial value: A rare exception.' *Biological Psychology, 22*, 285–287. doi:10.1016/0301-0511(86)90032-3

Myrtek, M., & Foerster, F. (1986). The law of initial value: A rare exception. *Biological Psychology, 22*, 227–237. doi:10.1016/0301-0511(86)90028-1

National Center for Women and Information Technology and the Girl Scouts of the USA. (2007). *Guide to promising practices in informal information technology education for girls*. Boulder, CO: National Center for Women and Information Technology.

National Institute on Media and the Family. (2001). *11th annual mediawise video game report card*. Minneapolis, MN: National Institute on Media and the Family. Retrieved from http://mediafamily.org/research/report_vgrc_2006.shtml

Naval Air Systems Command of USA. (2003). Bottom Gun. [computer game]. Patuxent River, MD: The Naval Air Systems Command (NAVAIR) of USA.

NCES. (2004). *The condition of education 2004, indicator 31: Remedial coursetaking. U.S. Department of Education*. Washington, DC: National Center for Education Statistics.

Neiburger, E. (2007). *Gamers...in the library?!*Chicago: American Library Association.

Neiburger, E., & Gullett, M. (2007, Winter). Out of the basement: The social side of gaming. *Young Adult Library Services, 5*(2), 34–38.

Neilsen Company. (2007). *The state of the console*. Chicago: Neilsen.

Newell, A., & Simon, H. A. (1972). *Human problem solving*. Englewood Cliffs, NJ: Prentice-Hall.

Newmann, F. M. (2007). Improving achievement for all students: The meaning of staff-shared understanding and commitment. In Hawley, W. D., & Rollie, D. L.

(Eds.), *The keys to effective schools: Education reform as continuous improvement* (2nd ed., pp. 33–49). Thousand Oaks, CA: Corwin Press.

Newmann, F. M., Bryk, A. S., & Nagaoka, J. K. (2001). *Authentic intellectual work and standardized tests: Conflict or coexistence?* Chicago: Consortium on Chicago School Research.

Newsgaming.com. (2003). *September 12th* [Online game]. Montevideo, Uruguay: Newsgaming.com. Retrieved March 29, 2009, from http://newsgaming.com/newsgames.htm

Newsgaming.com. (n.d.). *Homepage*. Uruguay: Newsgaming.com. Retrieved March 29, 2009, from http://newsgaming.com

Nicholson, S. (2007). *The role of gaming in libraries: Taking the pulse*. Retrieved from http://boardgameswithscott.com/pulse2007.pdf

Nicholson, S. (2008). Reframing gaming. *American Libraries, 39*(7), 50–51.

Nielsen, J. (1994). Heuristic evaluation. In Nielsen, J., & Mack, R. L. (Eds.), *Usability inspection methods*. New York: John Wiley & Sons.

Nintendo. (1985). *Super Mario Brothers*. [Console game]. Japan: Nintendo

Norman, D. A. (1988). *The design of everyday things*. New York: Doubleday.

Nousiainen, T. (2008). *Children□s involvement in the design of game-based learning environments. Jyväskylä Studies in Computing, 95*. Jyväskylä, Finland: University of Jyväskylä.

Now, C. (2001). *Fair play: Violence, gender and race in video games*. Oakland, CA: Children Now.

O'Hair, M. J., McLaughlin, H. J., & Reitzug, U. C. (2000). *Foundations of democratic education*. Orlando, FL: Harcourt, Inc.

OECD. (2004). *Problem solving for tomorrow's world: First measures of cross-curricular competencies from PISA 2003*. Organization for Economic Co-Operation and Development.

Oliver, M., & Pelletier, C. (2005). The things we learned on Liberty Island: designing games to help people become competent game players. In *DiGRA 2005: presentation at the Digital Games Research Association's 2nd International Conference, Changing Views: Worlds in Play*, Vancouver, British Columbia, Canada, June 16-20.

Olson, C. K. (2004). Media violence research and youth violence data: Why do they conflict? *Academic Psychiatry, 28*(2), 144–149. doi:10.1176/appi.ap.28.2.144

Olson, C., Kutner, L., Warner, D., Almerigi, J., Baer, L., Nicholi, A. II, & Beresin, E. (2007). Factors correlated with violent video game use by adolescent boys and girls. *The Journal of Adolescent Health, 41*(1), 77–83. doi:10.1016/j.jadohealth.2007.01.001

Orenstein, P. (1994). *School-girls*. New York: Doubleday.

Ossimitz, G. (2000). *Teaching system dynamics and systems thinking in Austria and Germany*. A paper presented at the system dynamics 2000 conference in Bergen, Norway, August 2000. Retrieved February 27, 2004, http://www.uni-klu.ac.at/~gossimit/pap/ossimitz_teaching.pdf

Oyen, A.-S., & Bebko, J. M. (1996). The effects of computer games and lesson contexts on children's mnemonic strategies. *Journal of Experimental Child Psychology, 62*(2), 173–189. doi:10.1006/jecp.1996.0027

Packer, M., & Greco-Brooks, D. (1999). School as a site for the production of persons. *Journal of Constructivist Psychology, 12*, 133–151. doi:10.1080/107205399266154

Pajitnov, A. (1984) *Tetris* [computer game]. Published by Spectrum HoloByte in 1986.

Pajitnov, A., & Gerasimov, V. (1984). *Tetris*. Moscow: The Dorodnicyn Computing Centre of the Academy of Science of the USSR.

Palaigeorgiou, G. E., Siozos, P. D., Konstantakis, N. I., & Tsoukalas, I. A. (2005). A computer attitude scale for computer science freshmen and its educational implications. *Journal of Computer Assisted Learning, 21*, 330–342. doi:10.1111/j.1365-2729.2005.00137.x

Pannese, L., & Carlesi, M. (2007). Games and learning come together to maximise effectiveness: The challenge of bridging the gap. *British Journal of Educational Technology, 38*(3), 438–454. doi:10.1111/j.1467-8535.2007.00708.x

Paras, B., & Bizzocchi, J. (2005). *Game, motivation and effective learning: An integrated model for educational game design.* Paper presented at the DiGRA 2005 Conference: Changing Views—Worlds in Play.

Paris, S. G., & Paris, A. H. (2001). Classroom applications of research on self-regulated learning. *Educational Psychologist, 36*, 89–101. doi:10.1207/S15326985EP3602_4

Parker, L. E., & Lepper, M. R. (1992). The effects fantasy contexts on children's learning and motivation: Making learning more fun. *Journal of Personality and Social Psychology, 62*, 625–633. doi:10.1037/0022-3514.62.4.625

Pearce, W. B. (2007). *Making social worlds: A communication perspective.* Malden, MA: Blackwell.

Penman, R. (2000). *Reconstructing communicating: Looking to a future.* Mahwah, NJ: Lawrence Erlbaum Associates.

Perotti, V. J., & Pray, T. F. (2002). Integrating visualization into the modeling of business simulations. *Simulation & Gaming, 33*(4), 409–424. doi:10.1177/1046878102238605

Peters, C. S., & Malesky, L. A. (2008). Problematic usage among highly-engaged players of massively multiplayer online role playing games. *Cyberpsychology & Behavior, 11*(4), 481–484. doi:10.1089/cpb.2007.0140

Petty, R. E., & Briñol, P. (2008). Persuasion: From single to multiple to metacognitive processes. *Perspectives on Psychological Science, 3*(2), 137–147. doi:10.1111/j.1745-6916.2008.00071.x

Petty, R. E., & Cacioppo, J. T. (1986). *Communication and persuasion: Central and peripheral routes to attitude change.* New York: Springer-Verlag.

Petty, R. E., & Cacioppo, J. T. (1986). The elaboration likelihood model of persuasion. In Berkowitz, L. (Ed.), *Advances in experimental social psychology* (*Vol. 19*, pp. 123–205). New York: Academic.

Petty, R. E., Briñol, P., & Priester, J. R. (2008). Mass media attitude change: Implication of the elaboration likelihood model of persuasion. In *Media effects: Advances in theory and research.* New York: Taylor & Francis.

Petty, R. E., Gleicher, F., & Jarvis, W. B. (1993). Persuasion theory and AIDS prevention. In Pryor, J. B., & Reeder, G. (Eds.), *The social psychology of HIV infection* (pp. 155–182). Hillsdale, NJ: Lawrence Erlbaum Associates.

Petty, R. E., Priester, J. R., & Wegener, D. T. (1994). Cognitive processes in attitude change. In Wyer, R. S., & Srull, T. K. (Eds.), *Handbook of social cognition* (2nd ed., *Vol. 2*). Hillsdale, NJ: Lawrence Erlbaum Associates.

Pew Internet & American Life Project. (2008). *Teens, video games and civics.* Washington, DC: Pew Internet & American Life Project. Retrieved from http://pewinternet.org/~/media//Files/Reports/2008/PIP_Teens_Games_and_Civics_Report_FINAL.pdf.

Piaget, J. (1977). *The essential Piaget.* New York: Basic Books.

Pinckard, J. (October 31, 2007). *Casual games worth $2.25B — But where are they going?* Gigaom. Retrieved August 3, 2009, from http://gigaom.com/2007/10/31/casual-games-worth-225b-but-where-are-they-going/

Pinkola Estés, C. (1992). *Women who run with the wolves.* London: Rider.

Pintrich, P. (2000). The role of goal orientation in self-regulated learning. In Boekaerts, M., Pintrich, P. R., & Zeidner, M. (Eds.), *Handbook of self-regulation* (pp. 451–502). Mawah, NJ: Lawrence Erlbaum. doi:10.1016/B978-012109890-2/50043-3

Pintrich, P. R., Smith, D., Garcia, T., & McKeachie, W. (1993). Predictive validity and reliability of the Motivated Strategies for Learning Questionnaire (MSLQ). *Educational and Psychological Measurement, 53*, 801–813. doi:10.1177/0013164493053003024

Polkinghorne, D. E. (1988). *Narrative knowing and human sciences*. Albany, NY: State University of New York Press.

Pratto, F., Pearson, A. R., Lee, I., & Saguy, T. (2008). Power dynamics in an experimental game. *Social Justice Journal*, *21*, 377–407. doi:10.1007/s11211-008-0075-y

Prensky, M. (2001). *Digital game-based learning*. Saint Paul, MN: Paragon House.

Prensky, M. (2001). *Digital natives, digital immigrants*. MCB University Press. Retrieved January 14, 2009, from %20Digital%20Natives,%20Digital%20Immigrants%20-%20Part1.pdf

Prensky, M. (2006). *Don't bother me mom – I'm learning!* St. Paul, MN: Paragon House.

Price, C. B. (2008). Unreal PowerPoint: Immersing PowerPoint presentations in a virtual computer game engine world. *Computers in Human Behavior*, *24*, 2486–2495. doi:10.1016/j.chb.2008.03.009

Pruitt, D. G., & Kimmel, M. L. (1977). Twenty years of experimental gaming: Critique, synthesis, and suggestions for the future. *Annual Review of Psychology*, *28*, 363–392. doi:10.1146/annurev.ps.28.020177.002051

Quaisser-Pohl, C., Geiser, C., & Lehmann, W. (2006). The relationship between computer-game preference, gender, and mental-rotation ability. *Personality and Individual Differences*, *40*, 609–619. doi:10.1016/j.paid.2005.07.015

Rainie, L., & Anderson, J. (2008). *The future of the Internet III*. Washington, DC: Pew Internet & American Life Project. Retrieved from http://www.pewinternet.org/~/media//Files/Reports/2008/PIP_FutureInternet3.pdf

Rakoczy, H. (2008). Pretence as individual and collective intentionality. *Mind & Language*, *23*(5), 499–517. doi:10.1111/j.1468-0017.2008.00357.x

Randel, J., Morris, B., Wetzel, C., & Whitehill, B. (1992). The effectiveness of games for educational purposes: A review of recent research. *Simulation & Gaming*, *23*(3), 261–276. doi:10.1177/1046878192233001

Rao, V. N. (2004). Purana. In Mittal, S., & Thursby, G. R. (Eds.), *The Hindu world* (pp. 97–118). New York: Routledge.

Raybourn, E. M. (2007). Applying simulation experience design methods to creating serious game-based adaptive training systems. *Interacting with Computers*, *19*, 206–214. doi:10.1016/j.intcom.2006.08.001

Reese, D. D. (2007). First steps and beyond: Serious games as preparation for future learning. *Journal of Educational Multimedia and Hypermedia*, *16*, 283–300.

Ricœur, P. (1991). Life in quest of narrative. In Wood, D. (Ed.), *On Paul Ricœur, narrative and interpretation*. London: Routledge.

Rieber, L. P. (2005). Multimedia learning in games, simulations, and microworlds. In Mayer, R. E. (Ed.), *The Cambridge Handbook of Multimedia Learning* (pp. 549–567). New York: Cambridge University Press.

Rimmon-Kenan, S. (1991). *Narrative fiction: Contemporary poetics*. London, New York: Routledge.

Rimmon-Kenan, S. (2006). Concepts of narrative. In M. Hyvärinen, A. Korhonen, & J. Mykkänen (Eds.), *The travelling concept of narrative: Studies across disciplines in the humanities and social sciences 1*. Helsinki: Helsinki Collegium for Advanced Studies. 10–19. Retrieved April 2, 2009, from http://www.helsinki.fi/collegium/e-series/volumes/volume_1/001_03_rimmon_kenan.pdf

Ritchie, D. (1986). Shannon and Weaver: Unravelling the paradox of information. *Communication Research*, *13*(2), 278–298. doi:10.1177/009365086013002007

Rockstar Games. (2006). *Bully* [Console game]. New York, NY: Rockstar Games.

Rodriguez, H. (2006). The playful and the serious: An approximation to Huizinga's *homo ludens*. *Game Studies—The International Journal of Game Studies*, *6*(1). Retrieved August 20, 2009, from http://gamestudies.org/0601/articles/rodriges

Roeser, R. W., Midgley, C., & Urdan, T. (1996). Perceptions of the school psychological environment and early adolescents' self-appraisals and academic engagement:

The mediating role of goals and belonging. *Journal of Educational Psychology, 88*, 408–422. doi:10.1037/0022-0663.88.3.408

Rollings, A., & Morris, D. (2003). *Game architecture and design*. Indianapolis, IN: New Riders.

Rosas, R., Nussbaum, M., Cumsille, P., Marianov, V., Correa, M., & Flores, P. (2003). Beyond Nintendo: Design and assessment of educational video games for first and second grade students. *Computers & Education, 40*(1), 71–94. doi:10.1016/S0360-1315(02)00099-4

Rosen, L., & Weil, M. (2001). *Are computer, video and arcade games affecting children's behavior? An empirical study.* Carlsbad, CA: Technostress. Retrieved from http://www.technostress.com/ADHDVideoGames3.htm

Rosenblatt, L. M. (1978). *The reader, the text, the poem: The transactional theory of the literary work.* Carbondale, IL: Southern Illinois University Press.

Roth, W. (2009). Emergence of analogies in collaboratively conducted computer simulations. In Zheng, R. (Ed.), *Cognitive effects of multimedia learning* (pp. 340–361). Hershey, PA: IGI Global.

Rouse, R. (2005). *Game design theory & practice.* Plano, TX: Wordware Publishing.

Roy, D. D. (2008). Assessing validity of web-based computer adaptive training modules. *Journal of the Indian Academy of Applied Psychology, 34*(1), 127–136.

Rubin, D. B. (1974). Estimating causal effects of treatments in randomized and nonrandomized studies. *Journal of Educational Psychology, 66*, 688–701. doi:10.1037/h0037350

Rubin, D. B. (1977). Assignment to treatment group on the basis of a covariate. *Journal of Educational Statistics, 2*, 1–26. doi:10.2307/1164933

Rucker, D. D., & Petty, R. E. (2006). Increasing the effectiveness of communications to consumers: Recommendations based on elaboration likelihood and attitude certainty perspectives. *Journal of Public Policy & Marketing, 25*(1), 39–52. doi:10.1509/jppm.25.1.39

Ryan, M.-L. (2003). Transmedial narratology and concepts of narrative. In *2nd International Colloquium on Narratology beyond Literary Criticism*, University of Hamburg, 20–22 November 2003. Retrieved April 2, 2009, from http://www.narrport.uni-hamburg.de/index2.php?option=com_content&do_pdf=1&id=110

Ryan, M.-L. (2004). Introduction. In Ryan, M.-L. (Ed.), *Narrative across media: the languages of storytelling* (pp. 1–40). Lincoln, NE: University of Nebraska Press.

Ryan, M.-L. (2005). Narrative. In Herman, D., Jahn, M., & Ryan, M.-L. (Eds.), *Routledge encyclopedia of narrative theory* (pp. 344–348). London, NY: Routledge.

Ryan, M.-L. (2005). Media and narrative. In Herman, D., Jahn, M., & Ryan, M.-L. (Eds.), *Routledge encyclopedia of narrative theory* (pp. 288–292). London, NY: Routledge.

Ryan, M.-L. (Ed.). (2004). *Narrative across media: The languages of storytelling.* Lincoln, NE: University of Nebraska Press.

Ryan, R. M., & Deci, E. L. (2000). Intrinsic and extrinsic motivations: Classic definitions and new directions. *Contemporary Educational Psychology, 25*, 54–67. doi:10.1006/ceps.1999.1020

Sandoval, W. A., & Millwood, K. A. (2005). The quality of students' use of evidence in written scientific explanations. *Cognition and Instruction, 23*(1), 23–55. doi:10.1207/s1532690xci2301_2

Satwicz, T., & Stevens, R. (2008). Playing with representations: How do kids make use of quantitative representations in video games? *International Journal of Computers for Mathematical Learning, 13*, 179–206. doi:10.1007/s10758-008-9138-2

Saussure, F. d. (1983). *Course in general linguistics.* London: Duckworth.

Sawyer, B., & Smith, P. (2008). *Serious games taxonomy.* Retrieved from the Serious Games Initiative Web site: http://www.dmill.com/presentations/serious-games-taxonomy-2008.pdf

Schafer, J. L., & Kang, J. (2008). Average causal effects from nonrandomized studies: A practical guide and simulated example. *Psychological Methods, 13*(4), 279–313. doi:10.1037/a0014268

Schaumburg, H. (2001). Fostering girls' computer literacy through laptop learning: Can mobile computers help to level out the gender difference? In *Building on the Future. Proceedings of the National Educational Computer Conference,* June 25–27, 2001, Chicago.

Schechner, R. (2006). Performed imaginaries. In Katyal, A. (Ed.), *Sacred to profane*. New York: Seagull Books.

Schott, G., & Horrell, K. (2000). Girl games and their relationship with the gaming culture. *Convergence, 6*(4), 36–53.

Schryer, C. F. (1994). The lab vs. the clinic: Sites of competing genres. In Freedman, A., & Medway, P. (Eds.), *Genre and the new rhetoric* (pp. 105–124). London: Taylor & Francis.

Schunk, D. H. (1989). Self-efficacy and cognitive skill learning. In C. Ames & R. Ames (Eds.), Research in motivation in education. Vol. 3: Goals and cognitions (pp. 13-44). San Diego, CA: Academic Press.

Schunk, D. H. (1991). Self-efficacy and academic motivation. *Educational Psychologist, 26*, 207–231. doi:10.1207/s15326985ep2603&4_2

Schwaber, K. (2004). *Agile project management with Scrum*. Redmond, WA: Microsoft.

Schwartz, B. (2000). Self-determination: The tyranny of freedom. *The American Psychologist, 55*, 79–88. doi:10.1037/0003-066X.55.1.79

Schwartz, D. L., & Hartman, K. (2007). It is not television anymore: Designing digital video for learning and assessment. In R. G. R., S. Derry, R. Pea & B. Barron (Eds.), Video research in the learning sciences. Mahwah: Erlbaum.

Searle, J. R. (1969). *Speech acts: An essay in the philosophy of language*. London: Cambridge University Press.

Seattle Public Library. (2008). *About the library: Mission statement*. Seattle: Seattle Public Library. Retrieved from http://www.spl.org/default.asp?pageID=about_mission

Selfe, C. L., & Hawisher, G. E. (Eds.). (2007). *Gaming lives in the twenty-first century: Literate connections*. New York: Palgrave Macmillan. doi:10.1057/9780230601765

Senge, P. (1994). *The fifth discipline: The art and practice of the learning organization*. New York: Doubleday.

Sengers, P. (2004). Schizophrenia and narrative in artificial agents. In Wardrip-Fruin, N., & Harrigan, P. (Eds.), *First person: New media as story, performance and game* (pp. 95–116). Cambridge, MA: The MIT Press.

Shadish, W., Cook, T., & Campbell, D. (2002). *Experimental and quasi-experimental designs for generilized causal inference*. Boston: Houghton Mifflin.

Shaffer, D. W. (2006). Epistemic frames for epistemic games. *Computers & Education, 46*(3), 223–234. doi:10.1016/j.compedu.2005.11.003

Shaffer, D. W. (2006). *How computer games help children learn*. New York: Palgrave Macmillan. doi:10.1057/9780230601994

Shaffer, D., Squire, K., Halverson, R., & Gee, J. (2005). Video games and the future of learning. *Phi Delta Kappan, 87*(2), 111, 104.

Shannon, C. (1949). *The mathematical theory of communication*. Urbana: The University of Illinois Press.

Sharritt, M. J. (2008). Forms of learning in collaborative game play. *Research and Practice in Technology Enhanced Learning, 3*(2), 97–138. doi:10.1142/S1793206808000471

Sharritt, M. J., & Suthers, D. D. (2009). Video game representations as cues for collaboration and learning. *International Journal of Gaming and Computer-Mediated Simulations, 1*(3), 28–52.

Sheff, D. (1993). *Game over: How Nintendo zapped an American industry, captured your dollars, and enslaved your children*. New York: Random House.

Sheldon, L. (2004). *Character development and storytelling for games.* Boston, MA: Thomson Course Technology.

Shelton, B., & Wiley, D. (2007). *The design and use of simulation computer games in education.* Rotterdam: Sense Publishers.

Sherlock, L. M. (2007). When social networking meets online games: The activity system of grouping in World of Warcraft. In *SIGDOC '07: Proceedings of the 25th ACM International Conference on Design of Communication* (pp. 14-20). New York: Association for Computing Machinery.

Sherlock, L. M. (2009). Genre, activity, and collaborative work and play in World of Warcraft: Places and problems of open systems in online gaming. *Journal of Business and Technical Communication, 23*(3), 263–293. doi:10.1177/1050651909333150

Sherwood Cass R-VIII School District. (2008). *Library media center mission statement.* Sherwood, MO: Sherwood Cass R-VIII School District. Retrieved from http://sherwood.k12.mo.us/high%20school/libraryweb/mission_statement.htm

Shores, M. L., & Shannon, D. M. (2007). The effects of self-regulation, motivation, anxiety, and attributions on mathematics achievement for fifth and sixth grade students. *School Science and Mathematics, 107,* 225.

Sierra On-Line. (1995). *Phantasmagoria* [PC game]. USA: Sierra On-Line.

Simpson, E. (2005). Evolution in the classroom: what teachers need to know about the video game generation. *TechTrends, 49*(5), 17–22. doi:10.1007/BF02763685

Slater, M. D., & Rouner, D. (2002). Entertainment-education and elaboration likelihood: Understanding the processing of narrative persuasion. *Communication Theory, 12*(2), 173–191.

Slavin, R. (1990). An introduction to cooperative learning. In *Cooperative learning: Theory research and practice* (2nd ed., pp. 1–46). Boston: Allyn and Bacon.

Small, R. V., & Gluck, M. (1994). The relationship of motivational conditions to effective instructional attributes: A magnitude scaling approach. *Educational Technology, 34*(8), 33–40.

Smith, B. (2006). The (computer) games people play: An overview of popular game content. In Vorderer, P., & Bryant, J. (Eds.), *Playing video games: Motives, responses, and consequences* (pp. 43–56). New York: Routledge.

Smith, P. L., & Ragan, T. J. (2005). *Instructional design* (3rd ed.). San Francisco: Jossey-Bass Education.

Sodaplay. (2007). *Sodaconstructor.* [Online game]. Retrieved from http://sodaplay.com.

Song, S. H., & Keller, J. M. (2001). Effectiveness of motivationally adaptive computer-assisted instruction on the dynamic aspects of motivation. *Educational Technology Research and Development, 49,* 5–22. doi:10.1007/BF02504925

Souvignier, E., & Mokhlesgerami, J. (2006). Using self-regulation as a framework for implementing strategy instruction to foster reading comprehension. *Learning and Instruction, 16,* 57–71. doi:10.1016/j.learninstruc.2005.12.006

Spencer-Oatey, H. (2007). e-learning initiatives in China: Pedagogy, policy and culture. Hong Kong: Hong Kong University Press.

Spering, M., Wagener, D., & Funke, J. (2005). Brief report: The role of emotions in complex problem-solving. *Cognition and Emotion, 19*(8), 1252–1261. doi:10.1080/02699930500304886

Spinuzzi, C. (2003). *Tracing genres through organizations: A sociocultural approach to information design.* Cambridge, MA: MIT Press.

Spinuzzi, C. (2008). *Network: Theorizing knowledge work in telecommunications.* New York: Cambridge University Press. doi:10.1017/CBO9780511509605

Spinuzzi, C., & Zachry, M. (2000). Genre ecologies: An open-system approach to understanding and constructing documentation. *Journal of Computer Documentation, 24*, 169–181. doi:10.1145/344599.344646

Squire, K. (2003). Video games in education. *International Journal of Intelligent Simulations and Gaming, 2*(1), 49–62.

Squire, K. (2005). Changing the game: What happens when video games enter the classroom? *Innovate, 1*(6).

Squire, K. (2006). From content to context: Videogames as designed experience. *Educational Researcher, 35*(8), 19–29. doi:10.3102/0013189X035008019

Squire, K. (2007). Games, learning, and society: Building a field. *Educational Technology Magazine, 47*(5), 51–55.

Squire, K. (2008). Critical education in an interactive age. In Silberman-Keller, D., Bekerman, Z., Giroux, H., & Burbules, N. (Eds.), *Mirror images: Popular culture and education* (pp. 105–124). New York: Peter Lang Publishing.

Squire, K. D., & Jan, M. (2007). *Mad City Mystery*: Developing scientific argumentation skills with a place-based augmented reality game on handheld computers. *Journal of Science Education and Technology, 16*, 5–29. doi:10.1007/s10956-006-9037-z

Squire, K., & Jenkins, H. (2003). Harnessing the power of games in education. *Insight (American Society of Ophthalmic Registered Nurses), 3*, 5–33.

Squire, K., & Steinkuehler, C. (2005, April). Meet the gamers. *Library Journal, 130*(7), 38–41.

Squire, K., Barnett, M., Grant, J. M., & Higginbotham, T. (2004). *Electromagnetism supercharged!: Learning physics with digital simulation games.* Paper presented at the 6th International Conference on Learning Sciences, Santa Monica, CA.

Starbuck, W. H., & Kobrow, E. (1966). The effects of advisors on business game teams. *The American Behavioral Scientist, 10*(3), 28–30. doi:10.1177/000276426601000305

Steedman, P. (1991). On the relations between seeing, interpreting and knowing. In Steirer, F. (Ed.), *Research and reflexivity* (pp. 53–63). London, UK: Sage.

Steinkuehler, C. (2006). Virtual worlds, learning, & the new pop cosmopolitanism. *Teachers College Record.* Retrieved July 12, 2009, from http://www.tcrecord.org ID Number: 12843.

Steinkuehler, C. (2007). Massively multiplayer online gaming as a constellation of literacy practices. *E-learning, 4*, 297–318. doi:10.2304/elea.2007.4.3.297

Steinkuehler, C. A. (2004). Learning in massively multiplayer online games. In Y. B. Kafai, W. A. Sandoval, N. Enyedy, A. S. Nixon, & F. Herrera (Eds.), *Proceedings of the Sixth International Conference of the Learning Sciences* (pp. 521–528). Mahwah, NJ: Erlbaum.

Steinkuehler, C. A. (2006). Massively multiplayer online video gaming as participation in a discourse. *Mind, Culture, and Activity, 13*(1), 38–52. doi:10.1207/s15327884mca1301_4

Steinkuehler, C., & Duncan, S. (2008). Scientific habits of mind in virtual worlds. *Journal of Science Education and Technology, 17*(6), 530–543. .doi:10.1007/s10956-008-9120-8

Stenning, K., & Oberlander, J. (1995). A cognitive theory of graphical and linguistic reasoning: Logic and implementation. *Cognitive Science, 19*(1), 97–140.

Sterman, J. D. (2002). All models are wrong: Reflections on becoming a systems scientist. *System Dynamics Review, 18*(4), 501–531. doi:10.1002/sdr.261

Stevens, R., Satwicz, T., & McCarthy, L. (2008). In-game, in-room, in-world: Reconnecting video game play to the rest of kids' Lives. In Salen, K. (Ed.), *The ecology of games: Connecting youth, games, and learning. The John D., & Catherine T. MacArthur Foundation Series on Digital Media and Learning.* Cambridge, MA: MIT Press.

Stockton, F. R. (1886). *The lady, or the tiger?* New York: Charles Scribner's Sons Publisher.

Stokes, B. (2005). Video games have changed: Time to consider 'Serious Games'. *Developmental Education Journal.* Retrieved December 5, 2006, from http://www.netaid.org/documents/DEJ_article-Games_and_Development_Education-June05.pdf

Strawn, G. (2007). *Change: the constant of modern times.* Keynote presentation for the Instructional Technology Conference, April 2 – 4, Middle Tennessee State University, Murfreesboro, TN.

Streitmatter, J. (1998). Single-sex classes: Female physics students state their case. *School Science and Mathematics, 98*(7), 369–375.

Sugrue, B. (1995). A theory-based framework for assessing domain-specific problem-solving ability. *Educational Measurement: Issues and Practice, 14*(3), 32–35. doi:10.1111/j.1745-3992.1995.tb00865.x

Sun, D., Ma, N., Bao, M., Chen, X., & Zhang, D. (2008). Computer games: A double-edged sword? *Cyberpsychology & Behavior, 11*(5), 545–548. doi:10.1089/cpb.2007.0145

Suthers, D. D. (2001). Towards a systematic study of representational guidance for collaborative learning discourse. *Journal of Universal Computer Science, 7*(3), 254–277.

Suthers, D. D., & Hundhausen, C. (2003). An empirical study of the effects of representational guidance on collaborative learning. *Journal of the Learning Sciences, 12*(2), 183–218. doi:10.1207/S15327809JLS1202_2

Sweller, J. (1988). Cognitive load during problem solving: Effects on learning. *Cognitive Science, 12*(1), 257–285.

Sweller, J., & Chandler, P. (1994). Why some material is difficult to learn. *Cognition and Instruction, 12*(3), 185–233. doi:10.1207/s1532690xci1203_1

Szczurek, M. (1982). *Meta-analysis of simulation games effectiveness for cognitive learning.* Doctoral dissertation, Indiana University.

Tabachnick, B. G., & Fidell, L. S. (2001). *Using multivariate statistics* (4th ed.). Boston: Allyn & Bacon.

Tahiroglu, A. Y., Celik, G., Uzel, M., Ozcan, N., & Avci, A. (2008). Internet use among Turkish adolescents. *Cyberpsychology & Behavior, 11*(5), 537–543. doi:10.1089/cpb.2007.0165

Taylor, A. (2000). Physical activity, anxiety, and stress. In Biddle, S. J. H., Fox, K. R., & Boutcher, S. H. (Eds.), *Physical activity and psychological well-being* (pp. 10–45). London: Routledge.

Taylor, C. (1989). *Sources of the self.* Cambridge, MA: Harvard University Press.

Taylor, T. (2003, May). Multiple pleasures: Women and online gaming. *Convergence, 9*, 21–46.

Tejeiro, S. R. A., & Morán, B. R. M. (2002). Measuring problem video game playing in adolescents. *Addiction (Abingdon, England), 97*, 1601–1606. doi:10.1046/j.1360-0443.2002.00218.x

Thomas, P., & Macredie, R. (1994). Games and the design of human-computer interfaces. *Educational and Training Technology International, 31*(2), 134–142.

Thompson, B. (2004). *Exploratory and confirmatory factor analysis: Understanding concepts and applications.* Washington, DC: American Psychological Association. doi:10.1037/10694-000

Thompson, N., & McGill, T. J. (2008). Multimedia and cognition: Examining the effect of applying cognitive principles to the design of instructional materials. *Journal of Educational Computing Research, 39*(2), 143–159. doi:10.2190/EC.39.2.c

Towers of Hanoi. (2002). In *Wikipedia, the free encyclopedia.* Retrieved July 13, 2009 from http://en.wikipedia.org/wiki/Tower_of_Hanoi

Tracy, K. (2002). *Everyday talk: Building and reflecting identities.* New York: Guilford Press.

Transana. (2008). *Jefferson transcript notation.* Retrieved January 9, 2008 from http://www.transana.org/support/OnlineHelp/Team1/transcriptnotation1.html

Trilobyte. (1992). *The 7th Guest.* [PC game]. USA: Trilobyte.

Turner, J. C., & Patrick, H. (2008). How does motivation develop and why does it change? Reframing motivation research. *Educational Psychologist, 43*(3), 119–131. doi:10.1080/00461520802178441

US Army (2002). America's Army. [computer game]. U.S. Army (PC). http://www.americasarmy.com/

Valve. (2008). *Left 4 Dead.* [Console game]. USA: Valve.

Van Eck, R. (2006). Digital game-based learning: It's not just the digital natives who are restless. *EDUCAUSE Review, 41*(2).

Van Eck, R. (2006). The effect of contextual pedagogical advisement and competition on middle-school students' attitude toward mathematics and mathematics instruction using a computer-based simulation game. *Journal of Computers in Mathematics and Science Teaching, 25*(2), 165–195.

Van Eck, R. (2006). Using games to promote girls' positive attitudes toward technology. *Innovate, 2*(3). Retrieved from http://innovateonline.info/index.php?view=article&id=209&action=article.

Van Eck, R. (2006). The effect of contextual pedagogical advisement and competition on middle-school students' attitude toward mathematics and mathematics instruction using a computer-based simulation game. *Journal of Mathematics and Science Teaching, 25*(2), 165–195.

Van Eck, R. (2006b, March/April). Digital game-based learning: It's not just the digital natives who are restless.... *EDUCAUSE Review, 41*(2).

Van Eck, R. (2007). Six ideas in search of a discipline. In Shelton, B., & Wiley, D. (Eds.), *The educational design and use of computer simulation games.* Boston, MA: Sense.

Van Eck, R. (2008). COTS in the Classroom: A teachers guide to integrating commercial off-the-shelf (COTS) games. In Ferdig, R. (Ed.), *Handbook of research on effective electronic gaming in education.* Hershey, PA: Idea Group.

Van Eck, R. (September, 2006). Building intelligent learning games. In D. Gibson, C. Aldrich, & M. Prensky (Eds.), Games and simulations in online learning: Research & development frameworks. Hershey, PA: Idea Group.

Van Eck, R., & Dempsey, J. (2002). The effect of competition and contextualized advisement on the transfer of mathematics skills in a computer-based instructional simulation game. *Educational Technology Research and Development, 50*(3), 23–41. doi:10.1007/BF02505023

Van Eck, R., Hung, W., Bowman, F., & Love, S. (2009). 21st century game design: a model and prototype for promoting scientific problem solving. In *Proceedings of the International Association of Science and Technology for Development's annual Computers and Advanced Technology in Education conference*, November 22 -24, St. Thomas, US Virgin Islands.

Van Haneghan, J. P., & Hickey, D. (1993). *Higher order analyses of children's beliefs about mathematics.* Poster session presented at the biennial meeting of the Society for Research in Child Development. New Orleans, LA.

van Joolingen, W. R., & de Jong, T. (2003). *SimQuest*, authoring educational simulations. In Murray, T., Blessing, S., & Ainsworth, S. (Eds.), *Authoring tools for advanced technology learning environments: Toward cost-effective adaptive, interactive, and intelligent educational software* (pp. 1–31). Dordrecht: Kluwer.

Van Merriënboer, J. (1997). *Training complex cognitive skills: A four-component instructional design model for technical training.* Englewood Cliffs, NJ: Educational Technology Publications.

Vansteenkiste, M., Lens, W., & Deci, E. L. (2006). Intrinsic versus extrinsic goal contents in self-determination theory: Another look at the quality of academic motivation. *Educational Psychologist, 41*(1), 19–31. doi:10.1207/s15326985ep4101_4

Vasey, M. W., & Thayer, J. F. (1987). The continuing problem of false positives in repeated measures ANOVA in psychophysiology: A multivariate solution. *Psychophysiology, 34*, 479–486. doi:10.1111/j.1469-8986.1987.tb00324.x

Video game genres. (2009, August 26). Wikipedia, The Free Encyclopedia. Retrieved August 26, 2009, from http://en.wikipedia.org/w/index.php?title=Video_game_genres&oldid=310139217

Vinacke, W. E. (1969). Variables in experimental games: Toward a field theory. *Psychological Bulletin*, *71*, 293–318. doi:10.1037/h0026972

Visser, J., & Keller, J. M. (1990). The clinical use of motivational messages: An inquiry into the validity of the Arcs model of motivational design. *Instructional Science*, *19*(6), 467–500. doi:10.1007/BF00119391

Vitanza, V. J. (1987). Critical sub/versions of the history of philosophical rhetoric. *Rhetoric Review*, *6*(1), 41–66.

Vogel, J. S., Vogel, D. S., Cannon-Bowers, J., Bowers, C. A., Muse, K., & Wright, M. (2006). Computer gaming and interactive simulations for learning: A meta-analysis. *Journal of Educational Computing Research*, *34*(3), 229–243. doi:10.2190/FLHV-K4WA-WPVQ-H0YM

Vogler, C. (1999). *The writer's journey: Mythic structure for storytellers and screenwriters.* London: Pan Books.

Voorhees, R. A. (2001). Competency-based learning models: A necessary future. *New Directions for Institutional Research,* 110.

Voss, J. F., & Post, T. A. (1988). On the solving of ill-structured problems. In Chi, M. T. H., Glaser, R., & Farr, M. J. (Eds.), *The nature of expertise*. Hillsdale, NJ: Lawrence Erlbaum.

Vuorela, V. (2007). Pelintekijän käsikirja. [Game-Maker□s Handbook.] Helsinki: BTJ Finland Oy.

Vygotsky, L. (1978). *Mind in society: The development of higher psychological processes.* Cambridge, MA: Harvard University Press.

Vygotsky, L. (1979). Consciousness as a problem in the psychology of behavior. *Social Psychology*, *17*(4), 3–35.

Vygotsky, L. (1981). The genesis of higher mental functioning. In Wertsch, J. V. (Ed.), *The Concept of Activity in Soviet Psychology* (pp. 144–188). Armonk, NY: Sharpe.

Vygotsky, L. S. (1962). *Thought and language*. Cambridge, MA: MIT Press. doi:10.1037/11193-000

Vygotsky, L., & Luria, A. (1994). Tool and symbol in child development. In van der Veer, R., & Valsiner, J. (Eds.), *The Vygotsky reader* (pp. 99–174). Oxford, UK: Oxford University Press.

Vygotsy, L. (1978). *Mind in society: The development of higher psychological processes.* Cambridge, MA: Harvard University Press.

Wagner, M. (2006, July 29–30). *Computer games and the three dimensions of reading literacy.* Paper presented at the Sandbox Symposium, Boston.

Wainer, H. (1991). Adjusting for differential base rates: Lord's Paradox again. *Psychological Bulletin*, *109*, 147–151. doi:10.1037/0033-2909.109.1.147

Walkerdine, V. (1997). *Children, gender, video games.* New York: Palgrave, MacMillan.

Walsh, R. (2007). *The world of shamanism*. Woodbury: Lewellyn Publications

Wang, T. (2008). Web-based quiz-game-like formative assessment: Development and evaluation. *Computers & Education*, *51*, 1247–1263. doi:10.1016/j.compedu.2007.11.011

Wang, Y., Wu, M., & Wang, H. (2009). Investigating the determinants and age and gender differences in the acceptance of mobile learning. The entity from which ERIC acquires the content, including journal, organization, and conference names, or by means of online submission from the author. *British Journal of Educational Technology*, *40*(1), 92–118. doi:10.1111/j.1467-8535.2007.00809.x

Wardrip-Fruin, N., & Harrigan, P. (Eds.). (2004). *First person: New media as story, performance, and game.* Cambridge: MIT Press.

Wark, M. (2007). *Gamer theory.* Cambridge, MA: Harvard University Press.

Watzlawick, P., Bavelas, J. B., & Jackson, D. D. (1967). *Pragmatics of human communication: A study of interactional patterns, pathologies, and paradoxes.* New York: W. W. Norton & Company.

Weaver, W. (1949). Recent contributions to the mathematical theory of communication. In C. Shannon and W. Weaver, The mathematical theory of communication (pp. 95–117). Urbana, IL: The University of Illinois Press.

Wei, R. (2007). Effects of playing violent videogames on Chinese adolescents' pro-violence attitudes, attitudes toward others, and aggressive behavior. *Cyberpsychology & Behavior, 10*, 371–382. doi:10.1089/cpb.2006.9942

Weick, K. (1979). *The social psychology of organizing.* Reading, MA: Addison-Wesley.

Weick, K. (1995). *Sensemaking in organizations.* Thousand Oaks, CA: Sage.

Weisberg, H. I. (1979). Statistical adjustment and uncontrolled studies. *Psychological Bulletin, 86*, 1149–1164. doi:10.1037/0033-2909.86.5.1149

Westwood Studios. (2008). *Command & Conquer: Red Alert 2* [computer game]. Las Vegas: Westwood Studios.

Weymouth High School. (2008). *Library/media center.* Weymouth, MA: Weymouth High School. Retrieved from http://www.weymouth.ma.us/schools/commercial/library.asp?id=305.

White, B., Frederiksen, J., Frederiksen, T., Eslinger, E., Loper, S., & Collins, A. (2002). *Inquiry Island: Affordances of a multi-agent environment for scientific inquiry and reflective learning.* Paper presented at the Proceedings of the Fifth International Conference of the Learning Sciences (ICLS), Mahwah, NJ: Erlbaum.

Wiener, D. J. (1999). Rehearsal for growth: Applying improvisational theatre games to relationship therapy. In Weiner, D. J. (Ed.), *Beyond talk therapy: Using movement and expressive techniques in clinical practice* (pp. 165–180). Washington, DC: American Psychological Association. doi:10.1037/10326-008

Wiley, J., & Jensen, M. (2006). When three heads are better than two. *Proceedings of the Annual Conference of the Cognitive Science Society.* Retrieved April 18, 2007 from http://litd.psch.uic.edu/personal/jwiley/Wiley_Jensen_06.pdf

Willingham, W. W., Pollack, J. M., & Lewis, C. (2002). Grades and test scores: Accounting for observed differences. *Journal of Educational Measurement, 39*(1), 1–37. doi:10.1111/j.1745-3984.2002.tb01133.x

Wilson, B. (2002). A study of factors promoting success in computer science including gender differences. *Computer Science Education, 12*, 141–164. doi:10.1076/csed.12.1.141.8211

Winn, B. (2008). The design, play, and experience framework. In Ferding, R. (Ed.), *Handbook of Research on Effective Electronic Gaming in Education* (pp. 1010–1024). Hershey, PA: IGI Global.

Wolf, M. J. P. (2001). Genre and the video game. In Wolf, M. J. P. (Ed.), *The medium of the video game* (pp. 113–134). Austin, TX: University of Texas Press.

Wolf, M. J. P. (2002). *The medium of the video game.* Austin, TX: University of Texas Press.

Wolf, M. J. P. (2006, December). Emerging world of anime and manga. *Mechademia, 1*, 78–85.

Wu, H. K., & Huang, Y. L. (2007). Ninth grade student engagement in teacher-centered and student-centered technology-enhanced learning environments. *Science Education, 91*, 727–749. doi:10.1002/sce.20216

Wysocki, A. F. (2003). The multiple media of texts: How onscreen and paper texts incorporate words, images, and other media. In Bazerman, C., & Prior, P. (Eds.), *What writing does and how it does it: An introduction to analysis of text and textual practices* (pp. 123–163). Mahwah, NJ: Lawrence Erlbaum and Associates.

Yee, N. (2006). The demographics, motivations, and derived experiences of users of massively multi-user online graphical environments. *Presence (Cambridge, Mass.), 15*(3), 309–329. doi:10.1162/pres.15.3.309

Zappen, J. P. (2005). Digital rhetoric: Toward an integrated theory. *Technical Communication Quarterly, 14*(3), 319–325. doi:10.1207/s15427625tcq1403_10

Zhong, C., Loewenstein, J., & Murnighan, J. K. (2007). Speaking the same language: The cooperative effects of labeling in the prisoner's dilemma.

The Journal of Conflict Resolution, *51*(3), 431–456. doi:10.1177/0022002707300834

Zimmerman, B. (2001). Theories of self-regulated learning and academic achievement: An overview and analysis. In Zimmerman, B. J., & Schunk, D. H. (Eds.), *Self-regulated learning and academic achievement: Theoretical perspectives* (2nd ed., pp. 1–37). Mahwah, NJ: Lawrence Erlbaum.

Zimmerman, B. J. (2008). Investigating self-regulation and motivation: Historical background, methodological development, and future prospects. *American Educational Research Journal*, *45*, 166–183. doi:10.3102/0002831207312909

Zizzo, D. J., & Tan, J. (2007). Perceived harmony, similarity and cooperation in 2 × 2 games: An experimental study. *Journal of Economic Psychology*, *28*, 365–386. doi:10.1016/j.joep.2006.06.008

Zweig, D., & Webster, J. (2004). Validation of multidimensional measure of goal orientation. *Canadian Journal of Behavioural Science*, *36*(3), 232–243. doi:10.1037/h0087233

Zyda, M. (2005). From visual simulation to virtual reality to games. *IEEE Computer*, *38*(9), 25–32.

About the Contributors

Richard Van Eck is Associate Professor and Graduate Director of the Instructional Design & Technology program at the University of North Dakota (idt.und.edu). He has an M.A. in Creative Writing from the University of North Dakota and a Ph.D. in instructional design and development from the University of South Alabama. He was the Media Arts and Communication director at Cochise College, an assistant professor and member of the Institute for Intelligent Systems at the University of Memphis, and served on the board of directors for the North American Simulation and Gaming Association from 2006–2009. He has published and presented extensively in the field of digital game-based learning and has created six original games for learning. He is currently conducting research on visual accommodation and EEG during videogame play, and developing a game on scientific problem for middle school students. In addition to his work in serious games, he has also published and presented on intelligent tutoring systems, pedagogical agents, authoring tools, and gender and technology. He currently lives in North Dakota with his wife Sandra, their two dogs and three cats.

* * *

Sanna-Mari Äyrämö is a PhD candidate and researcher in the Department of Art and Culture Studies, University of Jyväskylä, Finland. Her main research interests concern serious game design, narrative game design and the multidisciplinary field of narrative theories. In her current research, she focuses on the question of how to utilize narrative to support learning in computer games.

Bryan G. Behrenshausen is an instructor of communication studies at Millersville University of Pennsylvania, USA. He earned his M.A. in Communication from The University of Maine, and writes about the performativity of video gaming in algorithmic culture. His previous work has appeared in *Games and Culture* and Sage's *Encyclopedia of Play in Today's Society.*

Chris Crawford earned a Master of Science degree in Physics from the University of Missouri in 1975. He has published fifteen computer games and five books. He created the first periodical on game design, the Journal of Computer Game Design, in 1987. He founded and served as Chairman of the Computer Game Developers' Conference, now known as the Game Developers' Conference. Crawford has given hundreds of lectures at conferences and universities around the world, and published dozens of magazine articles and academic papers. He served as computer system designer and observer for the 1999 and 2002 NASA Leonid MAC airborne missions. He is now completing work on interactive storytelling technology. He lives in southern Oregon with his wife, 3 dogs, 7 cats, 2 ducks, and 3 burros.

Copyright © 2010, IGI Global, distributing in print or electronic forms without written permission of IGI Global is prohibited.

Lesley Farmer, Professor at California State University Long Beach, coordinates the Librarianship program. Dr. Farmer has worked as a library media teacher in K-12 school settings as well as in public, special and academic libraries. She serves as International Association for School Librarianship VP Association Relations, edits the IFLA School Libraries and Resource Centers Section newsletter, chaired the Educators of Library Media Specialists Section of AASL, and chaired the Education Section of Special Libraries Association. Dr. Farmer is a frequent presenter and writer for the profession. Her latest books include Teen Girls and Technology (Teachers College Press/ALA, 2008) and Your School Library: Check It Out! (Libraries Unlimited, 2009).

Larry Friedlander has been a professor of English Literature and Theater at Stanford University since 1965, with a specialty in Shakespeare and performance. Friedlander is an internationally known contributor to interactive arts and technology projects. His work during the past two decades has included collaboration with Apple Computer, Mitsubishi Electric, MIT Media Lab, Oxford University, the Musee d'Orsay, the National Museum of Scotland, and the San Francisco Exploratorium. His "interactive Shakespeare" projects set the tone for much of later experimentation with digital narrative forms. His work with Apple involved development of innovative designs for the Globe Theater Museum in London. Larry is also a former Founder and Co-director of the Stanford Learning Lab and of the Wallenberg Global Learning Network. Funded by industry consortia, these groups did research in innovative use of technologies for teaching and learning.

Matt Gaydos is a second year learning science student at the University of Wisconsin - Madison. He received a B.S. in Psychology from Pennsylvania State University. His research interests include cognitive science approaches to game studies, especially involving knowledge, expertise, learning, and perception.

Woei Hung is currently an associate professor in the Instructional Design and Technology Program at the University of North Dakota. He received his Ph.D. in Information Science and Learning Technology from University of Missouri-Columbia. Before coming to UND, he was an assistant professor and program coordinator in the Educational Technology Program at the University of Arizona South. His research areas include problem-based learning, problem solving, types and difficulty levels of problems, systems thinking and modeling, and concept mapping and formation. He received the 2006 Junior Faculty Mentee Award from the Interdisciplinary Journal of Problem-Based Learning for his 3C3R PBL Problem Design Model paper and 2007 Outstanding Publication Award from AERA (American Educational Research Association) Division I for his co-authored paper "Learning to troubleshoot: A new theory based design architecture." He is also currently the chair of the AERA Problem-based Learning SIG.

Putai Jin works at the University of New South Wales. His research interest is in educational psychology for learning and teaching.

Jasmina Kallay. After completing her M.A. in Screenwriting, Jasmina began researching screenwriting in interactive media narrative formats at University College Dublin, with primary focus on computer games, and is expected to complete her PhD in 2010. Jasmina has regularly presented her research findings at international conferences and in peer reviewed journals. As Teaching Fellow at UCD, Jasmina lectures in Digital Media theory, Screenwriting and Film History and Theory. Jasmina is also a visiting lecturer at the National Film School (IADT) and the Huston School of Film and Digital Media. As a freelance screenwriting consultant and editor Jasmina is involved with screenwriters and production/broadcasting companies in Ireland and the UK.

Raine Koskimaa works as a Professor of Digital Culture at the University of Jyväskylä, Finland. He teaches and conducts research especially in the fields of digital textuality, programmable media, and game studies. He has published widely around the issues of digital culture, digital literature, hyper and cybertextuality, game studies, reader-response studies, media use, and narratology. He is the co-editor of the *Cybertext Yearbook* Series (http://cybertext.hum.jyu.fi/), and serves in the Review Board for *Gamestudies*.

Renae Low is a Senior Lecturer at the University of New South Wales. Her research interest is in educational psychology for learning and teaching.

Steven Malliet, Ph.D., is Assistant Professor at the Department of Communication Studies, University of Antwerp (UA), and Senior Researcher at the Media and Design Academy, University College of Limburg (KHLim). His main research interests are the socio-psychological processes associated with digital game play, including the investigation of digital identification and realism, as well as the social effects of electronic game play. He has published internationally on the history of electronic games, on the observed realism of digital game play, and on game analysis. He teaches courses on new media and ICT, general media theory, and web development/usability.

Hans Martens is Ph.D. Student and Teaching Assistant at the Department of Communication Studies, University of Antwerp. He received his master's degree in Social Sciences from the Catholic University of Leuven and his master's degree in Film Studies and Visual Culture from the University of Antwerp. His main research interests are media literacy education, persuasive communication and informal learning. Hans Martens is also actively involved in the Belgian and European media educational field.

Nora Murphy is originally from the Midwest, and graduated from the University of Wisconsin-Madison with a degree in Italian Language and Literature. She immediately headed west to begin teaching and never turned back. Prior to working in the library, she taught Language Arts and Social Studies to seventh graders, which she found to be a particularly delightful challenge. She has been working as a Teacher Librarian in South Los Angeles for the past four years, where she focuses heavily on tapping into students' personal and recreational interests to engage them in academic learning. Murphy is an obsessive reader of Young Adult literature and has recently had the good fortune to begin reviewing books for School Library Journal. Her research on gaming has resulted in a weekly Game Night in her library where middle school boys and girls mingle with apparent confidence and camaraderie. Much to her students' surprise (and to her own slight embarrassment), Murphy will occasionally join in for a round of Rock Band or Guitar Hero.

Matthew Sharritt, Ph.D. is President and co-founder of *Situated Research, LLC*, located in Naperville, Illinois (www.situatedresearch.com), which specializes in advanced user experience research and usability testing within software and video games. Dr. Sharritt is a graduate of the interdisciplinary Communication and Information Sciences doctoral program (2008) and the Computer Science masters program (2003) at the University of Hawai'i, where he served as a teaching assistant. Prior, he was webmaster at Time Warner Telecom while earning his B.S. at Marquette University in Computer Engineering (2001). Sharritt's research examines ways of maximizing flow and the self-efficacy of the user experience through the design of cutting-edge video games that engage current generations on a level of which they are capable. This research has supported the idea that learning can be fun while teaching concepts that can be explored and tested through play. In his spare time, Dr. Sharritt enjoys gaming, cooking, and photography.

Lee Sherlock is a PhD student in Rhetoric & Writing at Michigan State University, where he also holds an MA in Digital Rhetoric & Professional Writing and a graduate certificate in Serious Game Design through the Department of Telecommunication, Information Studies, and Media. His current interests include the roles of genre and activity systems in digital gaming; the design and assessment of serious games; race, class, gender, and sexuality in relation to gaming; and the use of games in writing courses. He has recently published work in the *Journal of Business and Technical Communication* and *The Legend of Zelda and Philosophy.*

Kurt Squire is an associate professor at the university of Wisconsin-Madison, and associate director for educational research and development at the Wisconsin Institutes for Discovery. He is the author of over 50 scholarly books and articles, and a former games journalist, having co-founded joystick101.org. Squire is also a former Montessori teacher.

Leslie Ann Williams is a research associate professor in the Department of Educational Leadership and Policy Studies and Associate Director for Research at the K20 Center for Educational and Community Renewal at the University of Oklahoma. Dr. Williams has published numerous research articles and scholarly chapters on educational reform, learning community development, professional development, building leadership capacity to sustain systemic school improvement, and the integration of technology in teaching and learning processes to improve student achievement. She has been a Co-PI for over $27 million in grants supporting K12 school improvement in Oklahoma. Dr. Williams has been an educator for nearly 20 years, serving as a 6th-12th grade mathematics teacher, middle school principal, district mathematics curriculum director, and university professor. She received her Bachelors Degree in secondary mathematics education from Oklahoma State University, and her Masters and Ph.D. from the University of Oklahoma in the Educational Administration, Curriculum and Supervision program.

Scott Neal Wilson leads a digital game-based learning (DGBL) team at the University of Oklahoma's K20 Center. Dr. Wilson's background as middle school and/or high school science teacher, teamed with his interest in technology and its role in transforming education has provided a research interest in DGBL/serious games, technology integration, professional development (specifically technology integration PD), and management of constructivist classrooms. He has served the roles of district technology director, an instructional technology team lead, and a project manager of a wide variety of programs and projects. Dr. Wilson serves as an Associate Director for Innovative Technology Partnership at the K20 Center and is actively engaged in publishing, presenting, and authoring grants. He has B.S. in Natural Science Education from Southwestern Oklahoma State University, MLIS in Library and Information Studies from the University of Oklahoma, and a PhD in Instructional Leadership and Academic Curriculum from the University of Oklahoma.

Thomas J. Yannuzzi, PhD is an Assistant Professor of Communication Arts and Sciences at Penn State University Brandywine. He earned his B.A. in Communication and Rhetorical Theory from California State University, Fullerton; his M.A. from Temple University; and his Ph.D. in Education, Culture and Society from the University of Pennsylvania. His current research interests include enhancing critical self-reflection in professional and management education.

Index

Copyright © 2010, IGI Global, distributing in print or electronic forms without written permission of IGI Global is prohibited.

D

E

F

G

H

I

J

L

M

N

O

P

Q

R